RE ™

Special Edition

Using

IntranetWare™

Craig Zacker

Mickey Applebaum
Suzanne Miles
Jill McKee
Roger Kresge
Bill Lawrence

Special Edition Using IntranetWare

Copyright© 1997 by Que® Corporation.

Library of Congress Catalog No.: 97-67043

ISBN: 0-7897-1156-7

99 98 97   6 5 4 3 2 1

Interpretation of the printing code: the rightmost double-digit number is the year of the book's printing; the rightmost single-digit number, the number of the book's printing. For example, a printing code of 97-1 shows that the first printing of the book occurred in 1997.

Screen reproductions in this book were created using Collage Plus from Inner Media, Inc., Hollis, NH.

Contents at a Glance

Table of Contents

13 Using the Workstation Utilities 309

VIII | Implementing the IntranetWare Services

Credits

PRESIDENT
Roland Elgey

SENIOR VICE PRESIDENT/PUBLISHING
Don Fowley

PUBLISHER
Stacy Hiquet

PUBLISHING MANAGER
Fred Slone

GENERAL MANAGER
Joe Muldoon

EDITORIAL SERVICES DIRECTOR
Elizabeth Keaffaber

MANAGING EDITOR
Caroline Roop

ACQUISITIONS DIRECTOR
Cheryl D. Willoughby

ACQUISITIONS EDITORS
Christopher Booher
Jeff Riley

PRODUCT DIRECTORS
Rebecca Campbell
Erik Dafforn
Chris Nelson
Stephen Potts

PRODUCTION EDITOR
Thomas Cirtin

EDITORS
Kelli M. Brooks
Sherri Fugit
Kate Givens
Patricia Kinyon
Mike LaBonne
Tom Lamoureux
Maureen McDaniel

STRATEGIC MARKETING MANAGER
Barry Pruett

WEBMASTER
Thomas H. Bennett

PRODUCT MARKETING MANAGER
Kristine R. Ankney

ASSISTANT PRODUCT MARKETING MANAGER/DESIGN
Christy M. Miller

ASSISTANT PRODUCT MARKETING MANAGER/SALES
Karen Hagen

TECHNICAL EDITORS
Matt McLaughlin
Sundar Rajan
Dennis Teague

MEDIA DEVELOPMENT SPECIALIST
Brandon Penticuff

TECHNICAL SUPPORT SPECIALIST
Nadeem Muhammed

ACQUISITIONS COORDINATOR
Carmen Krikorian

SOFTWARE RELATIONS COORDINATOR
Susan D. Gallagher

EDITORIAL ASSISTANT
Andrea Duvall

BOOK DESIGNER
Ruth Harvey

COVER DESIGNER
Dan Armstrong

PRODUCTION TEAM
Bryan Flores
Jessica Ford
Anjy Perry
Nicole Russeler

INDEXER
Greg Pearson

Composed in *Century Old Style* and *ITC Franklin Gothic* by Que Corporation.

About the Authors

Lead Author

Craig Zacker has been employed as a network administrator, a technical writer and editor, a Webmaster, a technical support engineer and supervisor, a courseware developer, and a freelance network consultant. He now spends most of his time tinkering with computers and writing about them. His previous credits for Que include *Special Edition Using NetWare 4.1, Platinum Edition Using Windows 95, Windows NT 4.0 Workstation Advanced Technical Reference,* and *Upgrading and Repairing Networks,* among others. He can be reached at **craigz@tiac.net**.

Contributing Authors

Mickey Applebaum has been working with computer systems of one kind or another for almost 20 years. He has been specifically working with Novell's NetWare and network design and development for 13 years, starting with Novell's NetWare 4.57 product and moving through all versions of NetWare, including the latest releases of NetWare 3.12 and IntranetWare. Mickey has been providing technical support on the Internet for NetWare Users International at its NUINet Web site (**http://www.novell.com/nui/forums**) for the past year, and had been a Novell NetWire SysOp on CompuServe for six years prior to that. He is also known to have, and vocally express, many opinions on the "best" way to design file servers, networks, and other systems that go into the overall network integration. Mickey currently works as an independent network systems consultant in Salt Lake City, Utah.

Suzanne Miles is a graduate of Smith College with an A.B. degree in liberal arts. She is a CNE, ECNE, and Master CNE. Suzanne works as a network administrator and is a SYSOP for Novell on its Support Connection. She is a frequent contributor to trade magazines. Suzanne has two sons and is very involved in their various activities.

Jill McKee is a graduate of Penn State University with an associate degree in computer science. She started working with NetWare in 1990 as a network administrator and, shortly thereafter, completed her CNE. In 1994, Jill became a CNI and has continued to actively teach NetWare classes and perform NetWare integration in the field. As an ongoing effort to stay current, Jill is also a Microsoft MCT and currently working on completing the Microsoft MCSE program.

Roger Kresge is a Novell CNI and Master CNE and has been working with NetWare since 1987. He has written articles for various trade publications, and is very active in UseNet newsgroups dedicated to NetWare topics. Now working on his second career after more than 15 years as a radio and TV announcer, Roger designs, installs, and supports customer networks as a consulting engineer with Inacom Information Systems in Lancaster, Pennsylvania. Roger majored in electrical engineering at Bucknell University. In his spare time, he plays softball and enjoys science fiction books.

Bill Lawrence started using NetWare in 1983 when the software was called ShareNet and was delivered on five low-density disks. He manages LAN and PC computing for a major western utility with a network encompassing over 15,000 workstations. Bill is the author of Que's *Using Novell NetWare 4,* which covers NetWare 3.x, *Special Edition Using NetWare 3.12,* and *Special Edition Using NetWare 4.1.* He writes and speaks extensively about networking issues.

We'd Like to Hear from You!

As part of our continuing effort to produce books of the highest possible quality, Que would like to hear your comments. To stay competitive, we *really* want you to let us know what you like or dislike most about this book or other Que products.

Please send your comments, ideas, and suggestions for improvement to:

The Expert User Team

E-mail: **euteam@que.mcp.com**

CompuServe: **72410,2077**

Fax: (317) 581-4663

Our mailing address is:

Expert User Team
Que Corporation
201 West 103rd Street
Indianapolis, IN 46290-1097

You can also visit our team's home page on the World Wide Web at:

http://www.mcp.com/que/developer_expert

Thank you in advance. Your comments will help us to continue publishing the best books available in today's market.

Thank You,

The Expert User Team

Introduction

Despite the inroads made by its competition, NetWare is still the most widely used network operating system in the world, and it continues to add to its user base by selling very well. However, its market share has undeniably dropped in recent years, and Novell is determined to hold on to its place in the networking industry. The release of IntranetWare represents a turning point in the history of the product, an opening of the NetWare environment to the application services that are becoming so prevalent in the drive towards the use of the intranet for corporate file and document distribution.

At the core of IntranetWare is the NetWare operating system itself, updated to version 4.11 and incorporating all of the patches that were released for the previous version. The long awaited new clients for the Windows platforms are also included, as well as for the Macintosh OS, providing a unified appearance and feature set, as well as improved performance.

The *intranet* part of IntranetWare is reflected in the additional products included in the package. Intranets thrive on the TCP/IP protocols, and although NetWare does not yet run natively on IP, the protocols are well-integrated into the operating system. The next release of IntranetWare (due in early 1998) will address this shortcoming by supporting TCP/IP as a complete replacement for IPX, without the need for the NetWare/IP product.

IntranetWare also includes a collection of TCP/IP-based applications that enable you to develop, host, and administer intranet services on your NetWare network. With Novell Web Server, you can host multiple Web sites on a single server, publishing documents and applications for intranet or Internet clients. Web Server 3.0, a free upgrade from the 2.51 version included in the IntranetWare box, includes development tools that enable you to develop Web-based applications using the popular Perl scripting language or Novell's own NetBasic. For your clients, IntranetWare also includes a licensed version of the Netscape Navigator Web browser.

Also included with IntranetWare is the NetWare Internet Access Server (NIAS), which adds the capabilities of Novell's Multi-protocol Router 3.1 product. You can use a NetWare server to connect your network to remote sites or to the Internet using a WAN link based on dial-up, ISDN, frame relay, or other technologies.

Once you have built your intranet or connected to the Internet, your clients can access the network's TCP/IP services using an operating system TCP/IP stack, the NetWare/IP client, or Novell's IPX/IP Gateway. This gateway converts standard NetWare IPX traffic to IP, allowing NetWare clients to access TCP/IP services without the need for a TCP/IP stack on the workstation.

Since the release of NetWare 4.10, Novell made a minor but crucial name change to one of its products. NetWare Directory Services became Novell Directory Services, and this change signaled the expansion of NDS into the role of an enterprise-wide directory service. IntranetWare's Web server and FTP server both rely on NDS for authentication and administration services, and Novell's recent Windows NT products enable you to manage NT clients and domains by assimilating them into the NDS database.

NDS was originally included in the NetWare 4.0 release in 1993. Over the years, it has been refined and debugged to the point at which it is rock solid, and the most widely deployed directory service in the world. Compared to the relatively simple bindery services used by NetWare 3.x, NDS represented a fundamental change in networking philosophy when it was first released. Many administrators avoided NDS by sticking with NetWare 3.12 or running NetWare 4.x in bindery emulation mode.

Four years, however, is time enough to assimilate the new technology, and NDS is essential if you plan to take full advantage of IntranetWare's capabilities. This book is intended for networking professionals who are looking to NetWare as more than a file and print services platform. IntranetWare provides the tools to develop cutting-edge intranet application and services, and deploy them on a network of virtually any size.

This book also assumes a certain degree of expertise from the reader. Administering a network is not something that can be done by following lists of instructions. It is important to understand how the IntranetWare products do what they do—not just how to operate them. As you read this book, you will see that it assumes that you know how to use a Windows application and that you have some familiarity with NetWare and its utilities, or the experience needed to work some things out for yourself.

This book is divided into nine parts that enable you to locate particular topics of interest quickly and easily:

- Part I, "Installing NetWare 4.11"

    NetWare is the focal point of the IntranetWare product. In the chapters in Part I, you are introduced to the components that make up IntranetWare, and the various procedures by which you can install and upgrade the operating system.

- Part II, "Using Novell Directory Services"

    NDS binds all of the IntranetWare elements together by providing them with configuration and authentication services. Understanding the concepts on which NDS is based is crucial to the creation of an enterprise network using IntranetWare. The chapters in Part II introduce Novell Directory Services and cover the procedures involved in designing and managing an NDS database, as well as the new innovations that enable you to create objects that represent applications and Windows NT systems.

- Part III, "Managing the Network"

    NetWare includes a large array of utilities that you use to administer and control its various systems. The chapters in Part III cover both the workstation and server utilities, as well as the many operational statistics and configuration parameters that you can use to fine-tune your network's performance.

- Part IV, "Securing the Network"

    NetWare has two distinct access control systems: one for the NDS database and one for the NetWare file system. The chapters in Part IV examine the procedures for managing the two systems and the applications used to administer them.

- Part V, "Implementing Network Services"

    NetWare's traditional strengths are storage and printing services, and the chapters in Part V cover the mechanisms that provide these services. NetWare's file system supports several different media in addition to hard drives, including CD-ROM drives, optical disks, and tape drives.

- Part VI, "Connecting Client Workstations"

    The IntranetWare product includes new client software packages for the Windows 3.1, Windows 95, Windows NT, and Macintosh operating systems. The chapters in Part VI cover the installation of these clients and the procedures by which users can access network resources.

- Part VII, "Upgrading NetWare Communication"

    One of the primary strengths of IntranetWare is the addition of TCP/IP services with which you can build a corporate intranet or host Internet sites. The chapters in Part VII cover the implementation of the TCP/IP protocols on your NetWare network clients and servers.

- Part VIII, "Implementing the IntranetWare Services"

    IntranetWare also includes Novell Web Server and an FTP service that allow both local and remote network clients access to whatever information you care to publish. In the chapters in Part VIII, you learn how to deploy these services.

- Part IX, "Appendixes"

    NetWare has a large number of configuration parameters that you can use with the SET command to control the performance of your network. Appendix A, "NetWare SET Commands," lists these parameters along with the possible values and the defaults for each one. Appendix B, "Login Script Commands and Variables," contains listings of the commands that you can use in NetWare client login scripts to customize the workstation environment for your users.

In file and print services, NetWare has no peer among network operating systems, and the IntranetWare release makes Novell a top competitor in the application server market. In NDS, however, Novell has what the competition lacks: a fully developed, enterprise-class directory service that can be used to link the disparate elements of an heterogeneous network.

Far from being down and out, Novell is still a major player in the networking business, and IntranetWare is only the first step in what promises to be an exciting future.

Installing NetWare 4.11

Introducing IntranetWare

The release of NetWare 4.10 brought an increased measure of stability to the latest generation of NetWare, which had been plagued by three somewhat shaky releases and slow market acceptance. After three years, however, the complexities of NetWare Directory Services (NDS), now dubbed Novell Directory Services, are not nearly as daunting as they first appeared to be, and NetWare 3.12—which is no longer being developed—is beginning to show its age.

NetWare 3.12's obsolescence is especially evident in light of the increased competition from Windows NT in the network operating system market. Many networks are running both NetWare and Windows NT servers, and the administrative difficulties that arise from the need to maintain separate directories for each operating system are compounded by the individual binderies required for each NetWare 3.12 server.

Novell Directory Services is Novell's solution to the problem of individual binderies, and even the most die-hard NetWare 2.x and 3.x "believers" should have had sufficient time to familiarize themselves with its workings by now. In an effort to counter the rising popularity of Windows NT, Novell has supplemented its NetWare 4.11 release by combining the operating system with a collection of additional products and services designed to

New developments in NetWare 4.11

NetWare 4.11 includes many enhancements to the core operating system, and many new utilities that simplify the process of installing, upgrading, and maintaining your network.

New NetWare clients

IntranetWare includes new clients for Windows 3.1, Windows 95, Windows NT, and the Macintosh OS. Developed simultaneously, the clients provide a common feature set and a uniform appearance across many of NetWare's supported platforms.

TCP/IP integration

IntranetWare provides network administrators with several alternative methods for integrating the TCP/IP protocols into a NetWare network.

Intranet and Internet services

The IntranetWare package now includes both FTP and World Wide Web servers, providing a complete platform for the development and hosting of internal and external TCP/IP-based services.

address the networking industry's hunger for Internet and intranet connectivity and development tools, and calling it IntranetWare.

Novell has also beefed up NetWare's already fine security system and submitted it for certification for the (class C2) Trusted Network Interpretation [NCSC-TG-005] of the Trusted Computer System Evaluation Criteria [DoD5200.28-STD].

NetWare 4.11 is available as a stand-alone product, but IntranetWare—which includes NetWare 4.11 and a good deal more—is being offered at the same price. Most buyers, when asked whether they want something free with their purchase, will certainly say yes, but Novell has done more than bundle some extra utilities with NetWare. Instead, it has delivered a suite of networking products that extend the functionality and significance of NDS to the point at which it is the most likely candidate to be the industry standard, multipurpose, cross-platform, enterprise directory service.

This chapter introduces you to many of the IntranetWare products and services that are covered at length in this book. ▨

Network Operating System Development Cycles

The software industry has recently witnessed a growing tendency toward increasingly rapid product release cycles, as evinced by the competition between Internet/intranet software developers at Netscape and Microsoft. Often new betas follow closely on the heels of the previous releases, and version Y may be announced before version X is actually available.

This is usually not a practical approach to the development of network operating systems (NOS), for several reasons. A NOS is, by definition, a far more complex piece of software than a Web browser—or even a Web server. It is also much more of a mission-critical part of the network infrastructure. A "buggy" release that results in excessive downtime costs companies money, and frequently, network administrators their jobs.

NOS releases are therefore less frequent, particularly in NetWare's case (see Table 1.1), and usually less daring than those of other software products. If NetWare 4.0 was a milestone in NOS development, then the 4.11 release is another step along what is now a firmly established path. By itself, the 4.11 release of NetWare is a refinement of the existing product, rather than a radical innovation.

Table 1.1 NetWare Release Dates

Version	Release Date
3.12	September 1993
4.00	April 1993
4.01	July 1993
4.02	September 1994

Version	Release Date
4.10	January 1995
4.11	October 1996

What's New in NetWare 4.11?

In the 4.11 release, the basic NetWare structure remains the same, but many of the tasks traditionally associated with NetWare configuration and maintenance have been virtually eliminated. Intrepid NetWare 3.x administrators may recall the installation procedures for that product with a certain wistful nostalgia, for the need to manually load DSK and LAN drivers, bind LAN drivers to protocols, and then generate STARTUP.NCF and AUTOEXEC.NCF files is gone.

NetWare 4.11 offers two automated installation procedures—simple and custom—both of which identify a wide range of storage and network interface hardware devices, and load the proper drivers for each. The custom installation offers greater flexibility in the server boot method, the creation of NetWare volumes, and the design of the NDS tree.

Novell has also integrated support for multiple processors, previously available separately as NetWare SMP (Symmetric Multiprocessing), into the main NetWare product. The hardware is detected by the installation program, and the appropriate modules added to the STARTUP.NCF file. The installation files for the SFT III server mirroring product are also included in NetWare 4.11, with the installation procedure available as an option of the main installation program. The SFT III product still requires the purchase of a separate license, however, as well as the Mirrored Server Link (MSL) boards used to connect the two servers.

Both the simple and custom installations allow for the manual selection of drivers if you are using hardware that is not supported by the auto-detection facilities. Although the NetWare installation procedures have been refined considerably, the underlying architecture has not changed. The installation program is predominantly a shell that creates entries in the standard NetWare boot files: STARTUP.NCF and AUTOEXEC.NCF. This is a good thing because any changes to the NOS configuration that are required can be made, as always, simply by editing these files.

Upgrading NetWare

NetWare 4.11 introduces two new utilities that facilitate the operating system upgrade process. Migrating NetWare 2.x and 3.1x bindery information into an NDS database is easier and more flexible than previous versions of NetWare 4.x. NetWare 4.11 includes DS Migrate, a GUI NDS modeling application that enables network administrators to import the data from all of their bindery servers at the same time, and then model it into an NDS tree of their own design. Launched from NetWare Administrator, DS Migrate works in tandem with the NetWare File Migration utility (another GUI add-on) that moves the volume data from one server to another while leaving the trustee information intact.

These new additions provide a greater degree of automation for the upgrade process, using drag-and-drop and wizard technology to simplify what at one time was an onerous task. For backward compatibility, the NetWare package still includes the venerable DOS-based MIGRATE.EXE utility, which is still required for upgrading NetWare 2.x servers.

Patching IntranetWare

One of the most agreeable aspects of a new NetWare release is the incorporation of all of the previously released patch files into the core product. Novell's method for updating NetWare has always been to punctuate its infrequent major product revisions with numerous patch releases in the form of self-extracting archives containing replacement NLMs and other files.

Often, the same NLMs are updated several times, and standard archive names, such as LIBITx.EXE and SMSUPx.EXE, are incremented by replacing the x with a numeral. This has always been a problem because many different downloads may be required to bring NetWare up to the latest revision. Supporting NetWare can be a chore because it is often necessary to ascertain exactly what modules are running on the server before a problem can be diagnosed.

Frequently, Novell's NetWare patches are designed to address compatibility problems with third-party products. It is not uncommon for a patch that fixes one problem to cause another. Network administrators can find themselves juggling NLMs, and upgrading and downgrading certain modules to determine the perfect combination for a particular environment. Novell's policy of removing older revisions from its online services as soon as new ones are released further complicates this process.

Thus, a new NetWare revision always means that, for a period of time at least, the entire operating system is available in one place. In the case of NetWare 4.11, however, this period of time was exceedingly short. Less than a month after the product's release, Novell released the first patches for NetWare 4.11 and IntranetWare.

These first patches were released in a new way, however, that is clearly based on the service pack model used by Microsoft for its Windows NT updates. Novell's Support Pack #1 contains patches and updates for all of the IntranetWare products in a single file that can be downloaded. What's more, instead of manually replacing modules on the server, the entire Support Pack is installed as an additional product, using the INSTALL.NLM program on the server.

The concept of bundling patches into a relatively small number of releases makes it easier for network support personnel to keep their servers current and to know exactly what modules are installed. Whether this will be the method used for all future updates remains to be seen, but it is unquestionably a step in the right direction.

CLIB.NLM

The CLIB.NLM module has long been a focal point of NetWare incompatibility problems, as it is a runtime module used by many third-party NLMs to access native NetWare functions. Developing and patching this module has been a balancing act for Novell (throughout the history of NetWare 3.x and 4.x) among the requirements of all of the companies creating software for the NetWare environment.

In NetWare 4.11, the functions of the single CLIB.NLM module (along with those of MATHLIB.NLM and MATHLIBC.NLM) have been split among six separate NLMs, as follows:

- **FPSM.NLM**—Provides NLMs with support for floating point calculations
- **THREADS.NLM**—The NetWare standard NLM threads package
- **REQUESTR.NLM**—The standard Requester package
- **NLMLIB.NLM**—A library of functions providing basic runtime support for NLM programs, including POSIX-mandated functionality
- **NIT.NLM**—A library of NetWare interface tools required by some older NLM programs; included for backward compatibility
- **CLIB.NLM**—The standard C runtime library containing ANSI-mandated functions

As with the single CLIB.NLM module of previous NetWare versions, each of the six modules is loaded automatically when its functions are required by any other NLM. According to Novell, this new arrangement utilizes far less memory than the old, and the segregation of the functions into separate modules should make the process of developing updates easier.

N O T E   The CLIB NLMs provide a switch that can be applied to any NLM that does not allow the running of low-priority processes. If you receive an error message to this effect when loading a third-party NetWare module, you can include the following switch on the LOAD line to force low-priority as well as high-priority processes to run:

```
LOAD module (CLIB_OPT)/Y
```

Replace *module* with the name of the third-party module, and be sure to include the parentheses and the underscore in the CLIB switch.

Server Enhancements

At the time of the release of NetWare 4 in 1993, the Pentium processor was still a new innovation. It was understood that low-level modifications to existing software would be necessary to fully utilize the microprocessor's capabilities. Such modifications could not be made in time for the initial release, but NetWare 4.11 has been enhanced to take advantage of both Pentium and Pentium Pro processors. In addition, support for the PCI bus has been improved, allowing for the efficient use of high-speed disk and network interface adapters.

Another long-awaited improvement is the ability to support connections to an uninterruptible power supply (UPS) through a serial port. A dedicated adapter is no longer needed to run a third-party utility that automatically shuts down the server in the event of an extended power failure.

The 4.11 release also significantly improves NetWare's abend recovery capabilities. The OS_PROTECTED domain of earlier NetWare 4 versions, in which suspect or untested NLMs could be executed without endangering the operating system's kernel memory, and the DOMAIN utility that facilitated its use, have been eliminated. A NetWare 4.11 server can now better handle the abends that can result from untested NLMs. It does so by displaying and logging more detailed information regarding the cause of the abend, and by automatically restarting the server after an abend takes place.

When an abend occurs, the error information is displayed on the screen and logged to a text file on the server's DOS partition because access to the NetWare volumes on the server has been interrupted. After a period of time determined by a SET parameter, the server is automatically restarted, and the abend information is copied to a permanent log on the server's SYS volume.

In previous NetWare versions, the abend information had to be copied from the server console by hand before the server was (manually) restarted. The new abend recovery features enable servers to recover from abends even when they are unattended, saving the details of the problem for later attention by the server administrator.

NetWare's file system has also been upgraded. A NetWare volume can now support up to 16 million directory entries—up from two million in previous versions. Volumes also mount faster in NetWare 4.11, and the widespread popularity of Windows 95 and Windows NT as network clients has led to the creation of a new name space module: LONG.NAM. This module provides support for long file names on NetWare volumes, and is applied by default to volumes created during a NetWare 4.11 installation.

NDS Enhancements

NetWare Directory Services has been renamed Novell Directory Services. The name change is an indication of how NDS has been expanded beyond its role as a repository for NetWare user account information. Many of the additional services that, with NetWare 4.11, make up the IntranetWare package use the NDS database for access control and authentication.

Access to the intranet applications and services provided by IntranetWare's Web and FTP servers is controlled using the same NDS user objects that control NetWare server access. Creating new user objects is easier, due to the improved capabilities of user templates. The user template is a separate NDS object of its own, rather than a property of standard user objects. You can assign rights and other properties to a user template object, which are passed on to new user objects created using the template. You can also write scripts that prepare the new accounts for use by creating home directory structures and copying files into them.

The tasks involved in maintaining partitions and replicas of the NDS database are now performed using the new NDS Manager utility. Launched from NetWare Administrator or as a stand-alone application, NDS Manager enables you to see all your NDS partitions and replicas in a graphical interface and perform many administrative tasks (such as running DSREPAIR or updating DS.NLM) without traveling to the server console or using an RCONSOLE session.

The NetWare Administrator application itself has also been improved. 32-bit versions are included for use with the new NetWare clients for Windows 3.1, Windows 95, and Windows NT. With it, you can modify the properties of multiple objects simultaneously and administer different NDS trees in the same session. This coincides with the clients' ability to access multiple trees. You can also rename and move tree branches, as well as drag and drop objects from one tree to another.

The capability to handle multiple objects has ramifications not only in the accomplishment of administrative chores, but in the overall design of an enterprise NDS solution. There are scenarios in which the use of multiple NDS trees is a practical organizational solution, and these improved tools allow users and network support personnel unified access to all of the NetWare resources in the enterprise.

Also, NetWare Administrator can be configured to a greater degree. You can configure the buttons on the toolbar and customize the new Internet menu to add links to your most-often-used World Wide Web sites. Clearly, the intention is to create a single interface to all of a network administrator's most commonly used tools.

NetWare and DOS: After All These Years

There is no longer any question that Windows is the business operating system of choice today, and Novell no longer emphasizes the need to build equivalent functionality into both the DOS and Windows versions of its network management utilities. The NETADMIN and PCONSOLE utilities, for example, remain part of the NetWare operating system, but they exist primarily for reasons of backward compatibility with previous NetWare versions, and for the convenience of users who have become more comfortable with them.

Most of the new capabilities built in to NetWare Administrator do not exist in NETADMIN and PCONSOLE, and their venerable C-worthy interface may seem anachronistic to a user who has been reared on Windows. However, for many (equally venerable) NetWare hands, the old navigation and selection techniques used in the DOS, menu-based NetWare utilities have become second nature, and the Windows NWADMIN program, at its best, is no speed burner.

Many simple tasks, such as modifying user rights and manipulating queued print jobs, can be more speedily performed using NETADMIN and PCONSOLE. But for the purposes of this book, the emphasis is on the Windows NetWare Administrator, as it represents the leading edge of NetWare's management capabilities.

The capability to add new object types to an NDS database is one of the primary methods by which the functionality of NDS can be expanded. NetWare Application Manager contains a snap-in module that enables you to create application objects that, in conjunction with the new NetWare clients, can deliver fully configured network application icons to the desktop. This enables administrators to deliver fully configured applications to users in a controlled and consistent manner.

Once the application object is configured, the network administrator has only to associate it with user, group, or container objects to provide users with access to that application. By running a single executable from the server's SYS:PUBLIC directory called NetWare Application Launcher (NAL.EXE), all of the applications associated with a user object are placed in a single window on the client workstation, ready for immediate use.

Print Services

The creation and management of the NDS or bindery objects needed to attach a printer to a NetWare network has long been a source of drudgery to network administrators. These tasks have been combined and simplified in NetWare 4.11. A Print Services Quick Setup option in NetWare Administrator enables you to easily create associated printer, print queue, and print server objects in a single step.

NetWare Client Upgrades

Although many users have downloaded and tested them in their public beta versions, IntranetWare and NetWare 4.11 are the first releases to include the new 32-bit NetWare clients. These clients address many of the issues that have long been a problem to network users and administrators.

Client 32 is the name that has been given to the new NetWare clients for Windows 95 and Windows 3.1. For Windows 95 users, Client 32 provides more NetWare functionality than the Microsoft Client for NetWare Networks, even with the Service for NDS added. Many additional tabs containing NetWare-specific displays and controls are added to properties dialog boxes throughout the Windows Explorer, Network Neighborhood, Printer Control Panel, and other places.

The 32-bit NetWare clients provide a high degree of fault tolerance. When a network connection is broken due to hardware failure, the client immediately reestablishes the connection as soon as service is restored. In such cases, not only is the session restored, but any files left open at the time of the disconnect are returned to their previous state. Work can, therefore, continue immediately.

The Windows 3.1 version of Client 32 also provides many features to its users, but the primary improvement over previous NetWare clients is in its memory handing. Gone are the days when DOS users must expend 60K or 70K of memory just to access NetWare resources. Client 32 utilizes less than 5K of memory, some of which can be loaded high. Also provided is a TCP/IP stack and support for NetWare/IP. No other client is needed for a Windows 3.1 workstation to communicate with NetWare, intranet, or Internet resources using the TCP/IP protocols.

NetWare DOS Requester (that is, the VLM client), however, is still part of the NetWare package. It has been upgraded to conform with C2 security standards, and also includes support for NetWare/IP and the NetWare Application Launcher.

A late addition to the IntranetWare product, the new IntranetWare Client for Windows NT is not dubbed Client 32, although it is 32-bit. Windows NT has always been a problem area for Novell as far as client development is concerned, but this new release addresses virtually all of the problems of the earlier Novell clients for NT, and completes the deployment of a common client feature set across all of the Windows platforms.

Client Installation

All of the Windows clients can be installed in a number of different ways. For single installations, a single executable accomplishes the entire process, removing any existing NetWare client, identifying the network adapter, and installing all of the required software.

At many sites, however, a client must be installed on a large number of computers. To facilitate this, all of the 32-bit NetWare clients for Windows, as well as NetWare DOS Requester, have an Automatic Client Upgrade feature. When you configure the client setup program to be run from a NetWare login script (with the proper switch), the program examines the client software that is already running on the workstation, and installs the upgrade if necessary.

In the case of Windows 95 and Windows NT, the client setup can also be integrated into the operating system installation, with all of the client configuration settings included in the installation script. With these methods, you can install the NetWare clients on dozens—or even hundreds—of workstations with little or no intervention from network support personnel.

The Windows NT and Windows 95 clients ship with 32-bit ODI drivers for some of the most popular network adapters on the market, but they can also utilize the same NDIS drivers used for a Windows network client. There are, therefore, virtually no hardware compatibility problems to be found in the use of the new clients.

Macintosh Operating System Support

IntranetWare includes a new client package for Macintosh systems that further eases the network traffic confusion caused by too many diverse protocols competing for the same bandwidth. It is no longer necessary to run the AppleTalk protocol to accommodate Mac clients. The NetWare Client for Mac OS can now use either the MacIPX or NetWare/IP protocol (or both) to connect Macintosh computers to an NDS tree (or even multiple NDS trees), using the NetWare Client Tree menu.

Macintosh client systems have access to a wide array of NetWare services. They can use files and printers with the NetWare File Access and NetWare Print Service modules, even on volumes without MAC name space and servers not running NetWare for Macintosh. They can open remote server console sessions and manage their NDS user account information, or search for other directory objects on the network.

IntranetWare Modules

In addition to NetWare 4.11 core improvements, the IntranetWare package includes other modules with which you can run intranet or Internet services and improve the performance of your network. Novell has been forced to recognize the fact that, although NetWare is still the market leader, it must coexist with other network operating systems. Users are less likely to build networks to accommodate the operating system. Instead, the operating system must be able to fit the network design.

NetWare and TCP/IP

In order to increase NetWare's interoperability, much of the IntranetWare package is devoted to providing IP services to NetWare users. Many networks have standardized on the TCP/IP protocols for their network communications. Since both Windows NT and all UNIX operating systems use TCP/IP by default, NetWare's proprietary IPX protocols are the odd man out.

IntranetWare provides two methods by which NetWare clients can access IP services. The first is an IPX/IP gateway that allows NetWare clients to access IP services even though they are not running a TCP/IP stack on their computers. This gateway software installs on a NetWare server, which is running the TCP/IP protocols in the normal manner. There is also an IPX/IP gateway client that must be installed on a Windows 3.1 or Windows 95 workstation.

The gateway client is essentially a substitute protocol that communicates exclusively with the gateway server. The client system has no IP address, and uses IPX for its communications to the gateway server. When a client application requests an IP service, such as access to an intranet Web server or even to an Internet resource, the request is sent to the gateway server, which relays it to the appropriate IP resource using TCP/IP protocols in the normal manner. When the server receives a response, it is relayed to the client—again using IPX.

Thus, the IPX/IP gateway server, while providing protocol translation services, is also functioning as a proxy server. Since the client systems do not have IP addresses, there is no danger of intrusion from the Internet, and having a single point of client access to IP services enables the administrator to monitor client activities. Access to certain Internet resources can also be restricted, and a firewall can be erected to filter out selected types of traffic.

The second way of providing NetWare clients with access to IP services is to actually make them TCP/IP clients. This involves assigning each workstation an IP address and furnishing it with a TCP/IP stack. NetWare/IP is the product that enables you to use the TCP/IP protocols for NetWare communications. With NetWare/IP, TCP/IP can completely replace the standard NetWare IPX/SPX protocols, or it can run beside them. This provides the means for a gradual migration to TCP/IP as the primary networking protocols.

To implement NetWare/IP, support must be added to both the client and the server systems. The following clients that ship with the IntranetWare package all include the software required for NetWare/IP support:

- NetWare DOS Requester (VLM)
- NetWare Client 32 for Windows
- NetWare Client 32 for Windows 95
- NetWare Client for Windows NT
- NetWare Client for Mac OS

To a client system, using TCP/IP for NetWare communications makes no difference in appearance or functionality. All resources can be accessed in the usual manner, with no change in procedures and no visible effect on the client application.

The NetWare/IP server is administered using NWIPCFG, a server console utility that enables you to start and stop the NetWare/IP service, configure the service itself, and register the NetWare server into the DNS (Domain Name System).

TCP/IP Services

At the NetWare server, NetWare/IP requires both the TCP/IP support NLM and the NWIP.NLM module that emulates IPX traffic using the TCP/IP protocols. Also required are two additional networking support services: a Domain Name System (DNS) server and the Domain SAP/RIP Service (DSS).

The DNS server performs the same function as the DNS servers used for UNIX or Internet communications. It resolves the host names assigned to particular TCP/IP systems to their equivalent IP addresses. IntranetWare includes a DNS server module, or you can use any other DNS server that you may already have running on your network.

The DSS replaces the functions provided by the Service Advertising Protocol (SAP) and the Routing Information Protocol (RIP). On an IPX network, these protocols are used by servers and routers to periodically broadcast informational packets to other systems on the network. SAP, for example, is the way that one NetWare server knows of the existence of other NetWare servers on the network. In the same way, RIP is used to exchange routing information between systems.

TCP/IP has no equivalents to the RIP or SAP protocols. This is because the TCP/IP protocols were designed for use on the Internet, and having every computer on such a large network sending broadcasts every 60 seconds would flood the network with unnecessary traffic. The excess traffic generated by RIP and SAP are, in fact, one of the main reasons that many network administrators want to eliminate IPX traffic altogether.

IntranetWare includes Domain SAP/RIP Service, which maintains the information that is normally disseminated using RIP and SAP and makes it available to all systems on the network.

In order to implement NetWare/IP, each client workstation must be assigned an IP address. Keeping track of the addresses that have been assigned and assigning new ones so that there is no duplication is one of the more disagreeable chores traditionally associated with TCP/IP networks.

IntranetWare includes a service based on the TCP/IP Dynamic Host Configuration Protocol (DHCP), however, that eliminates this problem by dynamically allocating IP addresses and other configuration parameters to clients as they are needed. A service of this type automatically keeps track of all the addresses that are used on a network, and prevents any duplicate addresses from being introduced.

NetWare NFS Services

NetWare NFS (Network File System) Services, also included in the IntranetWare package, is a name given to a collection of modules that provide an assortment of TCP/IP-related services. With NetWare NFS Services, you can connect UNIX workstations to your NetWare network in order to provide file system and print access in both directions. That is, UNIX workstations can access NetWare volumes and printers, and NetWare clients can use UNIX resources in the same way.

The usefulness of NetWare NFS Services is not limited to networks with UNIX workstations, however. If you are using IntranetWare to host corporate intranet or Internet services, the NetWare NFS Services includes both FTP and DNS service modules. One or more DNS servers, as mentioned earlier, are needed to run NetWare/IP or to host an Internet domain. With the FTP service, you can provide users, both inside and outside the corporate network, with access to files on NetWare volumes, using any standard FTP client software.

Client access to NetWare resources (including anonymous FTP access) is controlled through NDS, using NetWare Administrator in the normal manner. UNIX resources are catalogued in a database maintained on an NIS (Network Information System) server. NIS is a UNIX convention that allows information about all of the resources within a specific collection of UNIX machines (called a domain) to be stored in a central location for easy access by all.

N O T E A group of UNIX systems that all access a single NIS server is called a *domain*. The term however, must be distinguished from that used when referring to the DNS. DNS domains form a hierarchy that spans the entire Internet, but an NIS domain consists of a group of computers that all function as peers. In many cases, the DNS and NIS domain names of a particular network may be identical, even though two distinct concepts are implied.

As with DNS, IntranetWare includes an NIS server module, but any existing NIS server on your network can be used instead.

Access to NetWare resources from UNIX systems and access to UNIX resources from NetWare systems is provided by a collection of discrete modules, all of which are a part of NetWare NFS Services. Among these services are the following:

- **NFS Server**—Provides access to NetWare volumes to any NFS client (such as UNIX systems)
- **NFS Gateway**—Provides NetWare clients with access to NFS (that is, UNIX) file systems
- **NFS Lock Manager**—Synchronizes file locks between NFS and NetWare file systems, preventing multiple users from modifying the same file at the same time
- **NetWare-to-UNIX Printing**—Provides NetWare clients with access to printers running the lpr (that is, the TCP/IP printing) protocol
- **UNIX to NetWare Printing**—Provides access to NetWare printers to any system running the lpr protocol (for example, UNIX)
- **DNS Server**—Provides host name to IP address translation services for all TCP/IP systems
- **NIS Server**—Provides a centralized database of system information for access by NFS clients

■ **FTP (File Transfer Protocol) Server**—Provides FTP clients on any platform with authenticated file transfer access to NetWare volumes (using the TCP protocol)

■ **TFTP (Trivial File Transfer Protocol) Server**—Provides unauthenticated file transfer access to NetWare volumes, using the User Datagram Protocol (UDP)

■ **Error Reporting Services**—Enables Simple Network Management Protocol (SNMP) management of the NFS services

As noted earlier, a good deal of IntranetWare's functionality is devoted to TCP/IP services, and some of the modules perform functions that are utilized in several ways; for example, the same DNS server needed for NetWare/IP can be used for NFS access, whether it is based on a NetWare server, a UNIX machine, or any other platform. In the same way, the FTP service might provide internal UNIX clients with access to NetWare files, while anonymous Internet users gain access to different files using the same service.

UNICON

Most of the TCP/IP services in the IntranetWare package are managed from a single utility called UNICON, which runs on the NetWare server console. As each service is installed on a NetWare 4.11 server, it is added to the Manage Services screen, providing access to configuration and management menus for that specific service. The following services are administered using UNICON:

■ NetWare DNS Server

■ NetWare DSS Service

■ NetWare NIS Service

■ NetWare-to-UNIX and UNIX-to-NetWare Print Services

■ NetWare FTP Server

■ NetWare DHCP Server

From UNICON, you can start and stop services on a NetWare server, monitor their current activities, and access the logs kept by the individual services. You can also view and modify global server configuration parameters as well as those pertaining to specific services. Like many NetWare utilities, you can use UNICON to manage the services on other NetWare servers all over the enterprise.

You can also use UNICON to set file permissions on NetWare volumes (with NFS name space) and as an FTP client, either to test the functionality of the local service or to access files on another system. You can even edit a file on a server volume.

Multiprotocol Router

IntranetWare includes a software-based routing package that can carry IPX, TCP/IP, and AppleTalk traffic simultaneously. This enables you to utilize a standard computer for LAN or WAN routing instead of purchasing a dedicated piece of equipment. NetWare's Multiprotocol Router is also designed to be a turnkey solution for high-speed Internet access.

When connected to a dedicated Internet service provider (ISP) connection using any of the major high-speed communications protocols (ISDN, leased lines, frame relay, ATM), the router can provide Internet access to an entire network.

NetWare Web Services

Once the underlying infrastructure is in place, the modules that are obviously at the top of any intranet service enterprise are the World Wide Web server and the browsers that are used to access the information that is published. As far as their primary function goes, most Web servers are fundamentally similar. What often distinguishes one package from another at the consumer level are the additional tools included with the package.

IntranetWare includes NetWare Web Server 2.5, a collection of modules that, like many others, effectively sends HTML and graphics files to HTTP clients on request and supports the industry standard configuration and Web development features, such as the following:

- Image maps
- Forms
- Access logs
- Remote and local CGI
- Perl and NetBASIC scripts
- Java applets

This book, however, covers the 3.0 release of Novell Web Server, now available as a free download from **http://www.novell.com**. The upgraded product significantly enhances the speed at which HTTP requests are processed and adds several new features, including an integrated search engine called QuickSearch.

NetWare's Web server also takes advantage of Novell Directory Services, enabling users to browse the tree from a Web client and authenticate themselves using their NDS accounts. Other forms of access control are also available, including those based on standard IP addresses and Internet host names.

Summary

IntranetWare signifies Novell's greatest extension into the realm of intranet and Internet development to date. It provides a wealth of functionality, and contains tools that are aimed at both large and small networks—helping them to come to terms with the latest technologies.

IntranetWare has a lot going for it, due in no small part to the fundamental familiarity of the products. Novell's greatest strength is its massive installed NetWare user base. By keeping their products in step with the competition and with the industry, users who bought NetWare in the past are likely to continue to do so. ●

Upgrading to NetWare 4.11

Depending on the version of NetWare that you are running now, upgrading to NetWare 4.11 is extremely simple—or quite complex. It should be obvious that the more complex upgrades involve a transition from the bindery-based account information used by NetWare versions 3.12 and earlier to NetWare Directory Services. NetWare 4.11 includes an excellent collection of utilities that can help you to manage the transition process in an orderly fashion.

If you are not yet sure that you're ready to migrate your entire network to NDS, NetWare also enables you to gradually introduce yourself, your staff, and your users to the new technology. You can install NetWare 4.11 on just one server if you want, and manage the binderies of your other servers using the NetWare Administrator tool. When you have weaned yourself away from SYSCON, NDS may seem a little less daunting. ■

Same server upgrades

You can upgrade a NetWare 3.1x or 4.x server to version 4.11 using the INSTALL.NLM utility.

Across-the-wire upgrades

If you are building a new NetWare 4.11 server, you can migrate files and bindery data across the network from your old machines.

Using DS Migrate

NetWare 4.11 includes a powerful tool for interactively modeling bindery information into an effective NDS tree.

Migrating files across the network

The NetWare File Migrator and MIGRATE.EXE utilities are used to import files to a new NetWare 4.11 server.

Using NetSync

With NetSync, you can maintain NetWare 3.1x servers on your network along with NetWare 4.11, and manage the binderies with the NetWare Administrator utility.

Choosing an Upgrade Method

If you are upgrading from a relatively recent NetWare version, such as 4.02 or 4.1, you should probably perform the *in-place* upgrade procedure. This process uses the INSTALL.NLM utility, and consists mainly of copying new system files to your DOS partition and your SYS:SYSTEM directory, and new utility files to SYS:PUBLIC.

Upgrading from NetWare 3.x or 2.x will definitely be more of a shock. You must consider the entire issue of NetWare Directory Services, just as if you were installing your first server on a new network. In this respect, you have a number of choices. If you are upgrading an entire multi-server network to NetWare 4.11 at one time, you must learn about the various elements that will have an impact on the design of your NDS tree. (See Chapter 5, "Designing an NDS Strategy for the Enterprise," for more information on creating an effective NDS tree design.)

You can use INSTALL.NLM to perform an in-place upgrade of a NetWare 3.1x server to NetWare 4.x. The advantages of this method are that the server's partitions, volumes, directories, and files are left undisturbed, as are the components of the server's printing architecture. The server's bindery information is converted into NDS data when an upgrade is performed in this manner. You can elect to either create a new NDS tree or install the bindery data and the server object into any context of an existing tree.

> **CAUTION**
>
> Although files and directories on the server volumes are left intact during the upgrade procedure performed by INSTALL.NLM, the process does purge all deleted files from the server volumes. Be sure to salvage any deleted files that you might need before you begin the upgrade process.

If you have multiple bindery servers that you want to combine into a single NDS database, the most flexible way of creating a well-designed NDS tree is to use the DS Migrate utility included with NetWare 4.11.

Licensed from Preferred Systems, Inc., DS Migrate enables you to import the bindery contents from your existing NetWare 2.x and 3.1x servers, and model the data into an NDS tree using a GUI interface that strongly resembles the display of NetWare Administrator.

N O T E   DS Migrate is launched from the NetWare Administrator Tools menu and, therefore, requires a Windows 3.1 or Windows 95 workstation to run.

To use DS Migrate, however, you must have a NetWare 4.11 server and your old bindery servers running on the network at the same time. This is known as an *across-the-wire* upgrade. You can arrive at this environment in one of two ways:

- You can build a new NetWare 4.x server and then use DS Migrate to import the bindery data from your other servers.

- You can perform an in-place upgrade on one of your existing servers, using INSTALL.NLM or MIGRATE.EXE, and then use DS Migrate to import the bindery data from the remaining servers.

You can then migrate the contents of your old server volumes to your new server, using the NetWare File Migration utility or MIGRATE.EXE, or you can leave the volumes as they are.

If you are running NetWare 2.x servers, you must use the MIGRATE.EXE utility to upgrade your servers to NetWare 4.11 because NetWare 2.x servers cannot run INSTALL.NLM, or indeed any NLMs. MIGRATE.EXE is also the only choice when you have a server with inadequate disk space in its SYS volume or DOS partition for a NetWare 4.11 installation.

In most cases, if you are still running NetWare 2.x, then your server hardware is probably several years out-of-date. To run NetWare 4.11 effectively, you should probably purchase a new computer, in which case you can use DS Migrate to import the NetWare 2.x bindery and MIGRATE.EXE to copy the volume files to the new server.

The following sections discuss the use of the methods and utilities described here, as well as a number of other techniques that you can use to upgrade your network to NetWare 4.x according to your own design and timetable.

N O T E   The NetWare upgrade utilities examined here are primarily concerned with the problems of importing bindery data to NDS and migrating files from old servers to new ones. Apart from these particular issues, the bulk of the server upgrade procedure is identical to a new NetWare 4.11 server installation. See Chapter 3, "Installing NetWare 4.11," for coverage of the operating system installation process.

Preparing to Upgrade

You are, in some cases, gambling the productivity of your network on your ability to complete the upgrade successfully in the time allotted to you, so you should take certain preparatory steps—which will increase the odds of experiencing a smooth transition process—before attempting any NetWare upgrade procedure. Consider performing the following tasks before upgrading:

- **Check your hardware**—The hardware requirements for a NetWare 4.11 upgrade are the same as that for a new installation. Make sure that you have enough available memory as well as sufficient free disk space on both SYS: and your DOS partition.

- **Gather drivers**—Make sure that you have drivers for the disk and network adapters in your server that can be used with NetWare 4.11. You may have to obtain an updated driver from a device's manufacturer if one is not included in the IntranetWare package. In fact, it is a good idea to check a manufacturer's online services for possible upgrades or bug reports, in any case.

- **Run BINDFIX**—If you will be migrating bindery information to an NDS database, be sure that the bindery is in good shape before you do so. Consult your NetWare 3.x Manuals for information on checking and repairing the bindery with BINDFIX.

- **Run DSREPAIR**—If you are upgrading from an earlier version of NetWare 4.x (and especially 4.0x), run the DSREPAIR utility included with the operating system to detect and correct any NDS problems before beginning the upgrade process. If DSREPAIR detects any problems that it cannot repair (such as those that are logged with the prefix [PBD]), do not perform the NetWare upgrade until you have resolved them.

- **Log your users off**—Make sure that no one has access to the servers you are working on while you are performing the upgrade. You don't want files to miss being migrated because someone has them locked open. Disable logins at the server console and clear any connections that have been left open. Don't forget remote users who may be dialing in using modems.

- **Leave enough time**—Don't expect to perform a server upgrade during your users' lunch hour and have them up and running when they return (even though this may, at times, be possible). Anything can happen during processes like these, and you don't need time constraints to add to the stress. Upgrades should be performed during off hours, typically at night or during a weekend.

- **Create a NetWare boot floppy**—Novell recommends copying the following files to a floppy disk before performing the upgrade so that you can always boot the server, whatever happens later:

  - From the SYS: volume, copy the LAN drivers used by your network adapters and your AUTOEXEC.NCF file.

  - From the server's DOS partition, copy the DSK drivers used by your disk adapters, all *.BAT files, all *.NAM files, INSTALL.NLM, STARTUP.NCF, VREPAIR.NLM, and SERVER.EXE.

- **Make backups**—Be sure to back up your system completely, particularly before performing an in-place upgrade. I highly recommend making two full backups on separate tapes (three full backups won't hurt at all), and performing some test file restores from the tapes before you rely on them.

Upgrading with INSTALL.NLM

The INSTALL.NLM utility is the most often used method of upgrading from previous NetWare 4.x versions. The process follows most of the same major steps as the installation of a new NetWare 4.11 server, using information from the existing operating system to provide answers to some of the questions that arise during the procedure.

The process of using INSTALL.NLM to upgrade a NetWare 3.1x server is fundamentally the same as upgrading a NetWare 4.x server, except that NetWare Directory Services is newly installed on the machine instead of being upgraded from its previous version. The options for installing the server object into an existing NDS tree or creating a new tree are exactly the same as those in a new server installation. The only difference in the process is that all of the new objects created from the bindery data are inserted into the same context as the server.

Upgrading NDS on a Single Server

During an in-place upgrade from a previous version of NetWare 4.x, NetWare Directory Services must be upgraded because the base schema have been modified in the NetWare 4.11 release. The *schema* define the types of objects that can be created in the NDS database, and the properties that are associated with them.

In order for INSTALL.NLM to upgrade the schema, your server must be running a DS.NLM module with a version number of 4.89 or greater. If you are running NetWare 4.1 or 4.02, then your DS.NLM should be sufficiently recent. You can check the version number with the MODULES command at the file server console. Part of the listing that is displayed on the console should appear something like this:

```
DS.NLM
NetWare 4.1 Directory Services
Version 4.94 December 14, 1995
Copyright 1993-1996 Novell, Inc. All rights reserved
```

If your DS.NLM is older than version 4.89, then you must upgrade it before upgrading NetWare. To do so, use the following procedure:

1. Copy the DS.NLM file from the \PRODUCTS\NW410 directory of the NetWare 4.11 CD-ROM to the server's SYS:SYSTEM directory (after making a backup copy of the existing file).

2. From the server console prompt, type **SET DSTRACE = *.** to reload NetWare Directory Services.

 TIP If you have multiple servers that require DS.NLM upgrades, and you have a NetWare 4.11 server already installed on the network, you can use the new NDS Manager utility to upgrade all of the servers at once. See Chapter 6, "Using the NDS Manager."

Upgrading NDS on an Entire Network

If you are already running NetWare Directory Services on your network, you should upgrade all of your NetWare 4.x servers to version 4.11 within a short period if possible. Running a mixed environment of different NetWare 4 versions can cause problems because of inconsistencies between the different NDS database formats. Further, you will not realize the full benefit of the performance improvements and new features that have been added to NDS in NetWare 4.11 until all of the servers on the network that contain NDS partitions and replicas have been upgraded.

CAUTION

If, for any reason, you must continue to run NetWare 4.0x servers in the same tree as NetWare 4.1x servers, I recommend that you install the version of DS.NLM found in the \PRODUCTS\NW402 directory of the NetWare 4.11 CD-ROM to all of the NetWare 4.1x servers on the network. This version is designed to be more tolerant of the mixed environment.

If you must upgrade your servers gradually, I recommend that you upgrade all of the NetWare 4.x servers in a single partition to NetWare 4.11 at the same time if possible. None of the benefits of the NDS upgrade will be realized in a partition if it contains servers of mixed versions. I recommend also that when you upgrade NetWare 3.1x servers, you place the new server objects only into partitions that do not contain NetWare 4.x servers of mixed versions. This will ensure the proper and accurate importation of data.

Preparing Your User Data for Migration   When upgrading from NetWare 4.0x, you must examine your NDS tree for anomalous entries before upgrading. NetWare 4.0x allowed objects of different types in the same container to have the same name. NetWare 4.1x no longer allows this. If, for example, you have a server object and a printer object that are both called ACCTG in the same container, you must rename one of them before performing the upgrade.

If you are intending to combine the binderies of multiple servers into a single NDS context, make sure that your users employ the same login name on all NetWare 3.1x servers. This enables their trustee rights from the different binderies to be combined into a single NDS user object.

Conversely, make sure that different users do not use the same name on different NetWare 3.1x servers. If John Smith and John Doe both use the account name JOHN on different servers, their access rights will be combined into those of a single user object.

N O T E   The bindery migration part of the upgrade procedure causes login scripts to be carried over to the newly created NDS user objects. The scripts, however, are not modified by the process. Any script changes that are required as a result of the upgrade, such as changes in server or volume names, must be made to the scripts manually.

It is also a good idea to take the time to remove from the bindery any user accounts, groups, or printing objects that are obsolete, or that you don't want migrated.

Most of the information stored in a NetWare 3.1x bindery is migrated seamlessly to the NDS database during the upgrade process. Table 2.1 summarizes the effect of the upgrade on specific objects and properties, as well as how conflicts between duplicate objects in multiple binderies are resolved.

The one subject worthy of additional comment is the NetWare 3.1x Supervisor user. This account is not transferred to the NDS tree because NDS relies on the Admin user for universal access to the entire tree. When users have supervisor equivalence under NetWare 3.1x, their new user objects in NDS are given Supervisor object and property rights only to the objects imported from their original bindery. In other words, *NetWare 3.1x Supervisors do not become Admin equivalents over the whole tree*—only over the objects they originally supervised.

Table 2.1   Converting NetWare 3.1x Bindery Elements to NetWare 4.11

NetWare 3.1x and 2.x Element	What Happens During Upgrade?	What Happens to Duplicate Elements?
User Items		
User Name	Transferred	Duplicate names must be resolved
Password	Upgraded	Password from first upgrade is used
Login script	Transferred	Script from first upgrade is used
Trustee rights to directories and files	Transferred	Rights from all servers are combined
Security equivalences	Transferred (except for security equivalences to SUPERVISOR)	Equivalences from all servers are combined
Login restrictions	Transferred	Restrictions from first upgraded server are used
Accounting balances and settings	Transferred	Settings from first upgraded server are used
Managed users and groups	Transferred (user has SUPERVISOR object and property right to managed user or group)	Managed users and groups from all servers are combined
Group Items		
Member list	Transferred	Lists from all servers are combined
Trustee rights to directories and files	Transferred	Rights from all servers are combined
Security equivalence	Transferred (except for security equivalences to SUPERVISOR)	Equivalences from all servers are combined

continues

Table 2.1   Continued

NetWare 3.1x and 2.x Element	What Happens During Upgrade?	What Happens to Duplicate Elements?
Group Items		
Managed users and groups	Transferred (group has SUPERVISOR object and property right to managed user or group)	Managed users and groups from all servers are combined
Special User Items		
SUPERVISOR user	Not Transferred	
Workgroup manager users	Converted to users who have SUPERVISOR object and property rights to managed users and groups as well as the CREATE right to the server's container object	Managed users and groups from all servers are combined
Server Items		
System login script	Converted to login script for server's container object if container has no login script already	System login script from first upgraded server is used
Default login, time, and station	Used to create USER_TEMPLATE object for server's container object unless one exists already	Settings from first upgraded server are used
Accounting settings	Transferred	Settings from first upgraded server are used
Printing Items		
Print queues	Transferred	Duplicate names must be resolved
Print queue operators and users	Transferred	List of operators and users is combined from all servers
Print servers	Transferred	Duplicate names must be resolved
Print server operators and users	Transferred	List of operators and users is combined from all servers
Printers	Transferred	Upgraded when you use PUPGRADE NLM

NetWare 3.1x and 2.x Element	What Happens During Upgrade?	What Happens to Duplicate Elements?
Printing Items		
Print job definitions		Upgraded when you use PUPGRADE NLM
Printer definitions and forms		Upgraded when you use PUPGRADE NLM

Upgrading Servers in the Proper Order   If your course of NetWare server upgrades stretches out over a period of weeks or months, the order in which the servers are upgraded becomes important. Observe the following rules when planning your upgrade program:

- Select a partition near the bottom of the NDS tree to begin your upgrades, upgrade all of the servers in that partition, then work your way up the tree.
- Upgrade all of the servers in one partition before proceeding to the next partition.
- If you have many replicas of your partitions, the upgrade process will go faster if you remove some of them before you begin. They can be re-created after the upgrade process is completed.
- When upgrading the servers in a partition, choose a server with a read/write replica first. Run DSREPAIR and perform the NetWare upgrade. Then upgrade the other servers in the partition the same way, leaving the machine with the master replica for last.

Performing the INSTALL.NLM Upgrade Process

Once you are fully prepared to perform the upgrade, shut down your existing server, and begin the normal installation process by booting the system with the drivers needed for CD-ROM or network access (depending on the location of your NetWare 4.11 source files).

After starting the INSTALL.NLM utility from the NetWare 4.11 CD-ROM (or other medium), select the Upgrade NetWare 3.1x or 4.x option when it is presented. The installation program then performs the following procedure, each very closely resembling its counterpart in the installation process for a new NetWare server:

1. New NetWare boot files are copied to the DOS partition (or floppy disks).
2. Storage hardware is identified and disk drivers are loaded.
3. Files needed to continue the upgrade are copied to the SYS volume.
4. The NetWare license is updated.
5. The network interface hardware is identified and LAN drivers loaded.
6. NetWare Directory Services is installed or updated.
7. The AUTOEXEC.NCF file is updated.
8. The rest of the NetWare system files are copied to the SYS volume.

See Chapter 3, "Installing NetWare 4.11," for more information on the individual steps of the INSTALL.NLM procedure.

Upgrading Printer Objects

Once the operating system upgrade is completed, you must load PUPGRADE.NLM to convert NetWare 3.1x bindery-based print servers and printer configurations into their NDS counterparts. You can also convert PRINTCON and PRINTDEF databases with this utility.

Using DS Migrate

Upgrading a server in place naturally involves a certain amount of risk. Should problems arise that make it impossible to complete the upgrade, reverting to the original configuration can be a timely and complex process in itself.

The other basic upgrade method is the across-the-wire procedure, which involves building an entirely new NetWare 4.11 server (or upgrading an old one in place), then migrating the account information and the contents of the volumes from the old server to the new. The primary disadvantage of this method is the additional hardware that is required. Further, the file migration makes this a much more time-consuming procedure (depending on how much data must be migrated) than the in-place method.

The advantage of the across-the-wire method is that Novell includes a new GUI utility with NetWare 4.11, called DS Migrate, that enables you to import the bindery information from all of the NetWare 2.x and 3.1x servers on your network at one time—and model it into the NDS tree of your choice—before actually writing to the NDS database. Once your NDS tree is in place, you can use the NetWare File Migration utility, another GUI addition to NetWare 4.11, to transfer files, directories, and their associated trustee rights from your NetWare 2.x and 3.1x server volumes to your NetWare 4.11 server.

The across-the-wire upgrade differs from the in-place procedure only in that the bindery and file migrations are performed over the network. The NetWare 4.11 operating system itself is always installed on each server using INSTALL.NLM; only the bindery and volume data is actually migrated. Refer to the "Upgrading with INSTALL.NLM" section earlier in this chapter or see Chapter 3, "Installing NetWare 4.11," for more information on the server upgrade and new installation procedures.

Bindery Migration Scenarios

These new migration tools—DS Migrate and the NetWare File Migration utility—can accommodate a number of different upgrade scenarios, as shown in Figure 2.1, Figure 2.2, and Figure 2.3.

FIG. 2.1

Single server upgrade—
a NetWare 2.x or 3.1x
server is replaced by a
new NetWare 4.11
server, hardware
and all. All bindery
information is imported
into the NDS database,
and all volume data is
migrated to the new
server. The old server
is retired or used as a
workstation.

Part

I

Ch

2

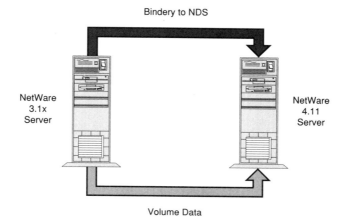

Bindery to NDS

NetWare
3.1x
Server

NetWare
4.11
Server

Volume Data

FIG. 2.2

Server consolidation—
multiple NetWare 2.x
and/or 3.1x servers are
replaced by a single
NetWare 4.11 server.
All bindery information
and volume data is
combined and migrated
to NDS and the
NetWare 4.11 server's
volumes, respectively.
The old servers are
retired or used as
workstations.

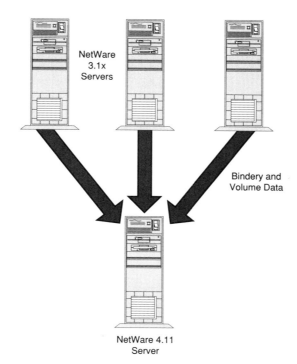

NetWare
3.1x
Servers

Bindery and
Volume Data

NetWare 4.11
Server

FIG. 2.3

Multiple server upgrade—multiple NetWare 2.x and/or 3.1x servers are upgraded to NetWare 4.11. One server is upgraded in place, bindery information for all servers is combined and migrated into the NDS database, then all of the other servers are upgraded in place. All volume data remains in its original location.

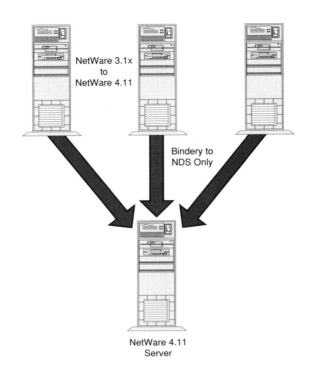

NetWare 3.1x to NetWare 4.11

Bindery to NDS Only

NetWare 4.11 Server

Importing Bindery Data with DS Migrate

DS Migrate now makes it possible to create a fully developed NDS tree during the server-upgrade process. All previous NetWare versions used INSTALL.NLM or MIGRATE.EXE to read the bindery and insert new objects into the same container as the server. For upgrading a large-scale enterprise network, this process can be very long and still require a great deal of manual tweaking afterwards. As you have seen, the upgrade of the NetWare operating system is the easiest part of the process. The problem is handling the data that builds up on a network over the years, both in the bindery and on the volumes.

With DS Migrate, the bindery data for all of your servers is assimilated into the NDS database at one time. You are also given complete design control of the tree structure before any changes are written to NDS. For a small network, DS Migrate is probably not needed. It is intended for use on larger networks in which the design of the NDS tree is crucial to the efficient operation of the network.

N O T E   DS Migrate is a subset of a product called DS Standard, manufactured by Preferred Systems, Inc. Although DS Migrate is designed only for the task of importing bindery information during the upgrade process, DS Standard can import existing NDS data, and it enables you to model your entire NDS tree into whatever structure you desire.

DS Standard must be purchased separately, and is now available from Cheyenne Software, Inc., a subsidiary of Computer Associates International, Inc. (which has purchased Preferred Systems, Inc.). ▪

DS Migrate is a Windows program that is launched from the Tools menu of the NetWare Administrator. To use DS Migrate, you therefore must have a NetWare 4.11 server already running on your network as well as a functional NDS client workstation running Windows 3.1 or Windows 95.

Migrating bindery information to an NDS database with DS Migrate is a three-step process:

- **Discovery**—DS Migrate reads the binderies of the NetWare 2.x or 3.1x servers that you have selected. All of the bindery properties are written to an interim database.

- **Modeling**—The bindery data is converted into a display that looks very much like an NDS tree, as shown in the NetWare Administrator (see Figure 2.4). This display is referred to as a *view*. Working in the view, you then model the tree into any structure that you desire. You can add, delete, or move objects, and modify any of their NDS properties, without affecting the actual NDS database in any way.

- **Configuration**—Once you have arrived at the tree design that you want to use, you log into the NDS tree and apply the view to the NDS database. All of the individual changes that are required to realize the tree structure you designed in your view are made automatically. The NDS tree propagates itself among its various replicas, just as if a series of changes were made using NetWare Administrator. The NDS tree is now ready to use.

FIG. 2.4

DS Migrate creates a display very much like that of the NetWare Administrator, but different enough to keep you from confusing the two.

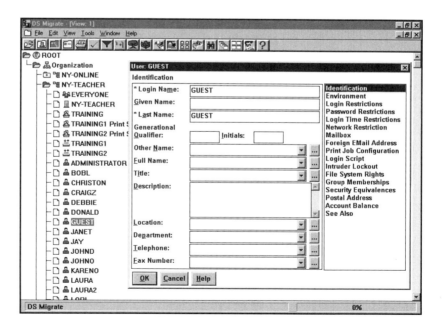

DS Migrate does an excellent job of translating bindery information into NDS data. The program combines the properties of duplicate bindery user names intelligently, and applies security equivalences and group memberships. Mail directories and their contents are also converted during the process (for NetWare 3.1x servers only).

Part

I

Ch

2

N O T E   If you are migrating data from NetWare 2.x servers, DS Migrate must create the directories
found on the source server so that their trustee assignments can be migrated. For NetWare
3.1x servers, the task of migrating file and directory trustee assignments is left to the NetWare File
Migration utility. ▓

Like INSTALL.NLM, however, DS Migrate does not migrate passwords (because this would be
insecure). You can apply new passwords during the modeling stage, either to individual objects
or globally. In fact, DS Migrate enables you to perform search and replace operations on a
number of different properties.

N O T E   The full DS Standard product enables you to perform search and replace operations on any
reference, property, or object name in the tree. ▓

DS Migrate also makes the very complicated process of remodeling the tree appear simple to
the user. After the discovery phase, all new objects are placed by default into an organizational
unit named for the server from whose bindery they came. By creating new containers and
dragging and dropping objects from one place in the tree to another, you are affecting the
complex system of trustee relationships that is the basis of NetWare security.

For example, if you move a server object to another container, then every user object with
trustee rights to the server's volumes must be updated. When you move a user object, all other
user objects with equivalent security must be modified. DS Migrate contains the tools to resolve these complex relationships at any time during the modeling process.

Matching the Model to the Network

DS Migrate is capable of modeling only the data that has been imported from the server binderies.
It does not read the contents of the NDS database into which the view will be configured. As a result,
the container, server, and volume objects that already exist in the actual NDS tree must also exist in
the modeled view, above the imported data and with precisely the same names.

Depending on which of the upgrade scenarios you are following, this process may involve creating,
renaming, or deleting objects. When you are finished, the modeled view of your NDS tree must reflect
the way that your servers and volumes will be configured on the physical network after the upgrade.

In other words, you must

- remove any objects representing NetWare 2.x or 3.1x servers that are to be retired,
- add any server objects that already exist in the NDS tree as the result of previous NetWare 4.x
  installations,
- rename any server objects (and the volume objects beneath) to the names that they will have
  after the entire upgrade process is completed.

If the modeled tree does not mirror the configuration of the actual servers and volumes its objects
represent, then DS Migrate will be unable to resolve the references to those objects during the
configuration phase.

If you are performing a complex, multi-stage NetWare 4.x upgrade, it may not be practical to manually add all of the existing NDS objects to your model. In such a case, I recommend that you obtain the full DS Standard product, which can import the NDS database as well as bindery information. That way, you can model the appearance of your entire NDS tree and modify object properties with a great deal more power and flexibility.

DS Migrate also upholds the rules for an NDS database, checking, among many other things, to see that the tree doesn't exceed the maximum allowable depth, that no fully distinguished NDS name is more than 127 characters, and that there are no more than 1,000 objects in any container.

Part
I
Ch
2

Using NetWare File Migration

The NetWare File Migration utility is another new addition to NetWare 4.11. It provides a GUI interface and wizard-based instructions that lead you through the process of migrating files and directories from NetWare 3.1x server volumes to NetWare 4.11 server volumes. In any upgrade scenario in which a new computer running NetWare 4.11 replaces an older machine running version 2.x or 3.1x, the files and directories must be migrated in cooperation with the bindery information.

N O T E The NetWare File Migration utility can only be used to migrate files and directories from NetWare 3.1x volumes. To migrate files from NetWare 2.x volumes, you must use the MIGRATE.EXE utility instead.

The File Migration utility is more than a simple disk copying program. In the NetWare file system, trustee rights are stored on the volumes with the files and directories. If the migration of the user and group information (that is, the bindery) is not coordinated with that of the files, the trustee rights will be lost, and you could be faced with an enormous amount of manual configuration before everything is right again.

The File Migration utility, like DS Migrate, is launched from the NetWare Administrator Tools menu. Launching the actual migration is quite simple. A wizard guides you through the process of specifying a source and a destination volume, then the copying begins. There are, however, a number of important factors to consider and adjustments to make before you launch the application and begin the migration process:

- Make sure that you have sufficient disk space on the destination volume to accommodate the data.
- Make sure that you have sufficient rights to all of the data that is to be migrated, on both the source and destination servers.
- You must run the File Migration utility from the same workstation that you used to run DS Migrate (so that the DS Migrate name mapping file can be used to compensate for objects' new locations that may result from the NDS tree modeling process).

- Make sure that no third-party programs are running on the source server that may lock files open. Locked files are not migrated—nor are the NetWare system files found in the SYSTEM, PUBLIC, LOGIN, and ETC directories and their NetWare-created subdirectories.

- Make sure that all name spaces utilized on the source server are also loaded on the destination server.

- Upgrade the following modules on the source server by copying the new versions from the \PRODUCTS\NW3X directory on the NetWare 4.11 CD-ROM to the SYS:SYSTEM directory on the source server:

    TSA311.NLM or TSA312.NLM (depending on the NetWare version)

    SPXS.NLM

    TLI.NLM

    CLIB.NLM

    AFTER311.NLM

    A3112.NLM

    SMDR.NLM

    STREAMS.NLM

- If the source server uses MAC name space and is running a version of MAC.NAM prior to 3.12, then you must dismount the volume containing the MAC name space, upgrade MAC.NAM with the new version found in the \PRODUCTS\NW3X directory on the NetWare 4.11 CD-ROM, and run VREPAIR on the volume before remounting it.

- Load TSA311.NLM or TSA312.NLM on the source server (depending on its NetWare version).

You can use the utility to migrate several smaller volumes into one large one if you want. When duplicate directory names are encountered during the process, the contents of the directories are combined. When file name conflicts arise, the second copy is automatically renamed with a numerical extension (.001, .002, and so on).

Using MIGRATE.EXE

Before the DS Migrate and NetWare File Migration utilities were added to NetWare, MIGRATE.EXE was the only means to import bindery information into NDS and migrate files to other server volumes. It is still your only choice if you are migrating files and directories from NetWare 2.x servers.

MIGRATE.EXE has been a part of NetWare since version 2.x. At that time, it was the operating system's sole upgrade utility because INSTALL.NLM (and indeed all NLMs) did not exist until the release of NetWare 386. MIGRATE.EXE is your only upgrade choice if any of the following is true:

- You are upgrading a NetWare 2.x server (or a LAN Manager or LAN Server) to NetWare 4.11
- You have insufficient disk space on your SYS volume for the upgrade (minimum 100M free space).
- You have insufficient disk space on the server's DOS partition for the upgrade (minimum 15M free space).

Apart from these scenarios, there is no persuasive reason to use MIGRATE.EXE instead of DS Migrate and the File Migration utility except for familiarity. If you've been using MIGRATE for years and you're used to it, then go right ahead. (You probably still run EDLIN, too.)

Part
I

Ch
2

MIGRATE.EXE is a DOS program that lacks the NetWare File Migration utility's intelligence and ease of use and has none of DS Migrate's modeling capabilities, but it does get the job done. You run MIGRATE.EXE directly from the NetWare 4.11 CD-ROM to upgrade a server in place or to migrate bindery and volume data across-the-wire.

To upgrade a server in place using MIGRATE, you must first back up your volumes (preferably twice), then run MIGRATE to copy the server's bindery information onto a workstation hard drive. You then install NetWare 4.11 as if it were a new server, restore the volumes from your backup, and use MIGRATE to apply the bindery information on the workstation drive to the NDS tree.

When upgrading across the wire, you must log in to the NetWare 4.11 server using bindery emulation (LOGIN /B), and the NetWare 4.11 server's bindery context must be set to the container where you want the new objects created from the bindery information to be created (SET BINDERY CONTEXT=).

Apart from this, the preparatory tasks you should perform before running MIGRATE are the same as those listed in the "Using NetWare File Migration" section earlier in this chapter (except for the last three, which are concerned with upgrading and loading certain NLMs).

The MIGRATE program enables you to select the bindery objects and the volumes that you want to migrate and their destinations, before the process begins, as shown in Figure 2.5. MIGRATE itself cannot migrate the elements of the network printing subsystem. Once the initial process is completed, you must run the MIGPRINT.EXE utility to migrate the printers, print queues, and print servers from a bindery into the NDS tree.

The rules by which MIGRATE imports bindery information into the NDS tree are fundamentally the same as those observed by DS Migrate and INSTALL. All of the major account properties are carried over except passwords—which, as in the other utilities, are deliberately omitted. You can add randomly generated passwords to the newly created user objects, or leave them with no passwords until the users log in for the first time.

When MIGRATE migrates files and directories, it does not have the intelligence to filter out the NetWare system files in the process. Novell recommends migrating the SYS volume to a subdirectory on the new server so that the old software can be deleted. Also, even though duplicate directories encountered during the migration are combined, files with duplicate names are not migrated. The original file is left in place, and not overwritten.

FIG. 2.5

MIGRATE lacks the Windows interface of the NetWare File Migration utility, but it is still functional and intuitive.

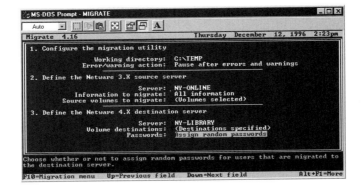

CAUTION

NetWare 2.x enabled file and directory names to be up to 14 characters in length. Files and directories on 2.x volumes that do not conform to the standard DOS 8.3 naming convention that is NetWare 4.11's default will not be migrated.

Using NetSync to Avoid Upgrading

Many network administrators find themselves running a mixed network of both NetWare 3.1x and NetWare 4.x servers. This can occur for several reasons, the most typical being economic necessity or reticence to change. If you enjoy the advantages that NetWare 4.x and the NDS database provide, such as centralized administration of user, group, and print objects, and you are stuck with NetWare 3.1x servers on your network for an extended period, then you will be glad to know that you can assimilate the binderies of NetWare 3.1x servers into your NDS tree without performing a NetWare 4 upgrade on the servers.

IntranetWare includes a feature called NetSync that enables you to administer and synchronize bindery objects for a cluster of up to twelve NetWare 3.1x servers, using Novell Directory Services. During the installation of NetSync, all of the users and groups found in the binderies of the selected 3.1x servers are imported into a single bindery context on the NetWare 4.11 server. The program then combines all of these new objects and the existing Directory Services objects in that context into a *super bindery,* which is replicated to each server in the cluster.

N O T E NetSync is intended for use when NetWare 3.1x and 4.x servers will be residing on the same network for an extended period. If you plan to upgrade your 3.1x servers within a matter of weeks, then the use of NetSync is not recommended.

Although you can manage the binderies of only twelve NetWare 3.1x servers with one NetWare 4.11 server running NetSync, you can expand the scope of the installation by using several NetWare 4.11 servers, each of which manages twelve different bindery servers.

As long as the bindery context is the same on all of the 4.11 servers, the bindery contents of all of the clustered servers will be combined in the single context and replicated to all of the clustered 3.1x servers. Novell warns, however, that this practice can require a large amount of your server memory and processing resources.

At the end of the NetSync process, the binderies on all of the servers are synchronized with the same users and groups. This enables a user of any of the bindery servers to log in to any other of the clustered servers. Access rights are not affected by the procedure. A user must still be granted the appropriate permission to access files and directories on a particular volume, but the task of creating duplicate user accounts on each bindery server is eliminated. A single object added to the bindery context of the NDS tree controls access to all of the servers in the cluster.

CAUTION

NetSync relies completely on the bindery context that is set on the NetWare 4.11 server that will be hosting the cluster. You cannot change this bindery context setting after the servers have been synchronized, or NetSync will cease to function.

From this point on, you manage the bindery users and groups with the NetWare Administrator, not with SYSCON. Any changes that you make are propagated to the binderies of each NetWare 3.1x server in the cluster. Any modifications that you make using SYSCON are not propagated, and your binderies will fall out of synchronization. You will have to synchronize them again before NetSync functions properly. Because of this, NetSync will not be suitable for your network if you have several administrators who maintain individual bindery servers using SYSCON.

NetSync consists of NLMs that run on both the NetWare 3.1x and 4.11 servers. All of the software is placed on every NetWare 4.11 server during the installation process. Issuing the LOAD NETSYNC4 command at the NetWare 4.11 server console prompt loads the module and initiates the installation process. You must first specify the names of the NetWare 3.1x servers that are to be clustered. The program then copies the required software to each of the 3.1x servers and loads the NETSYNC3.NLM and REMAPID.NLM modules there (inserting the LOAD commands into the servers' AUTOEXEC.NCF files, if desired).

The synchronization process then begins. This part of the process is subject to most of the same situations as DS Migrate when it combines the binderies of several servers, as described earlier in "Preparing Your User Data for Migration." Objects of the same name have their properties combined, with the first entry taking precedence over any others. For example, if the same user has two different passwords on two bindery servers, then the password from the first account inserted into the NDS tree will be retained. The exception to this is the Supervisor account, which is not transferred to the NDS tree for any of the clustered servers. In the same way, the Admin account is not copied to the clustered binderies even if it is located in the 4.11 server's bindery context.

N O T E   Unlike the bindery migration processes described in "Bindery Migration Scenarios" earlier in this chapter, passwords are transferred with the user accounts during synchronization. Once synchronized, passwords (and only passwords) are propagated between NetWare 3.1x and 4.11 servers in both directions. When users change their passwords with LOGIN or SETPASS, the changes are written to the NDS database and, subsequently, to all of the other bindery servers in the cluster.

Identically named objects of different types will cause conflicts during the synchronization process because they cannot be combined, and NDS will not allow objects with duplicate names in the same context in NetWare 4.11. You should examine your servers for potential conflicts of this type and resolve them before you install NetSync.

Once NetSync is operational, unloading NETSYNC4 at the NetWare 4.11 server will cause NETSYNC3 to be unloaded on each of the clustered 3.1x servers. However, the REMAPID.NLM module (which is responsible for password synchronization) must remain loaded on each 3.1x server. If it is unloaded, users will not be able to log in to the server. For this reason, I recommend that you allow the installation process to insert a LOAD REMAPID command into each server's AUTOEXEC.NCF file.

Summary

The implementation of NDS as an enterprise resource has greatly complicated the NetWare server upgrade, a task that was at one time isolated and relatively simple. Anything that involves modifying the NDS database, however, automatically raises the issues of your overall network operation and maintenance strategy. Just like the installation of a new NetWare server or the NDS tree design process, server upgrades must now be planned carefully with the big picture in mind. Failure to do so could be hazardous to your continued employment. ●

CHAPTER 3

Installing NetWare 4.11

Although elements of the IntranetWare package can be used with other versions of NetWare, usually the first step for most users is to install the NetWare 4.11 package. In Chapter 2, "Upgrading to NetWare 4.11," you learned about the various methods of upgrading your NetWare installation to version 4.11 while retaining your existing bindery information and NetWare volumes. This chapter covers the procedure of installing NetWare 4.11 onto a PC that has never been used as a NetWare server before.

People who have installed and supported NetWare servers for a long period of time have diverse emotional reactions when faced with the NetWare 4.11 installation process. Some may wax nostalgic about the way things used to be back in the NetWare 3.x days, when you had to manually load disk drivers and bind LAN drivers to protocols. Others may just be thrilled to complete the task so quickly. The bottom line, however, is that the installation of a NetWare server is simpler now than it has ever been before.

Selecting a hardware platform

Deciding on the hardware to use in the computer is half the battle of building an efficient server. Software is only as good as the hardware it's running on.

Planning a server configuration

Before you begin the installation process, you should know the server's name, the software that will run on it, and the files that will be stored on its drives.

Understanding the installation process

A NetWare server installation consists of a few basic processes that can be performed in several different ways. By knowing what is involved, you can be fully prepared when you begin the process.

If you have a computer with properly configured hardware, the installation routine should be able to lead you through every step of the process, leaving you with a server that's ready to use. Before you begin the actual installation process, however, there are several preparatory activities that, once accomplished, will all but assure you of a successful installation. These are as follows:

- **Prepare the hardware**—Before installing NetWare, make sure that all of your server's hardware is compatible and properly installed. Troubleshooting is twice as difficult when you are unsure whether the problem is caused by software or hardware.

- **Document the hardware**—Maintaining a record of the hardware in your server and its configuration not only helps you during the installation process, it will also make it easier to troubleshoot, service, or upgrade your equipment in the future.

- **Gather drivers**—A NetWare server without network and disk drivers is just a very expensive doorstop. Make sure that you have the appropriate—and most recent—NetWare drivers for your hardware before you begin the installation.

- **Choose a server configuration**—Thinking about how to best configure your server for your network is something that should be done before the installation begins. ▄

Preparing the Hardware

If you are purchasing a new PC for use as a NetWare server, the easiest way of preparing the hardware is to let someone else do it. Purchase a system from a reputable vendor that is intended for use as a server, and you should not have to be concerned with hardware resource conflicts or other compatibility problems.

Such manufacturers as Compaq and Dell offer server-ready systems at a wide range of price points, with CD-ROM drives and network adapters pre-installed. With this type of system, you should always receive drivers for all of the hardware, and find the system ready for installation, right out of the box.

Of course, the easiest path is usually also the most expensive one. You can often save some money by purchasing a PC and adapting it for use as a server yourself. If this is the case, you will probably be faced with quite a few more decisions concerning what hardware should be in the system, as well as more configuration tasks.

If you have had experience installing and configuring PC hardware for network use, then turning a PC into a network-ready server is a viable option. For the inexperienced user trying to assemble a network as inexpensively as possible, this is one area where you should not cut corners. You still need to start with quality equipment. Unlike UNIX or Windows NT, NetWare is a wholly client/server-based network operating system. If a NetWare server goes down, all of the users who rely on that server stop working. Don't gamble your business on hardware that may let you down in a pinch. Get professional help.

It is often difficult to decide what hardware a server should contain, and how much of it. Although an in-depth discussion of server hardware is beyond the scope of this chapter (and this book), the following sections offer some basic advice concerning hardware purchasing decisions for the following components:

- Memory
- Hard disk drives
- Type of expansion bus
- Keyboard, mouse, monitor, and other peripherals

How Much RAM?

The question of how much RAM is required in a NetWare server is a perennial argument among NetWare administrators. Novell advises a minimum of 20M for NetWare 4.11, but the amount required for your server depends on the amount of disk space in the server mounted as NetWare volumes, the name space modules that are installed, and especially what other software modules will be running on the server.

NetWare itself contains many optional modules that require additional amounts of memory. You must decide if your server is going to function as a print server, whether CD-ROMs are going to be mounted as NetWare volumes, and whether you are going to use utilities, such as SBACKUP, when calculating RAM.

The documentation included with IntranetWare treats its various modules as separate entities. The average NetWare 4.11 server is not likely to have all of the IntranetWare products installed on it at the same time. Therefore, the 20M mentioned earlier is for NetWare alone, and does not include the requirements for the other modules.

Apart from IntranetWare, there are hundreds of third-party software packages that run on NetWare servers, and each of these has its own memory requirements. All of these factors must be considered together when you decide how much memory to put in your server.

Expanding RAM

No matter how much memory you have in your NetWare server, you will eventually need more. It is therefore crucial that you purchase a system that allows some room for expansion. Every motherboard has its own recommended memory configurations. Purchasing a computer with the motherboard's maximum allowable amount of RAM already installed is unwise. Spend a few extra dollars on a system with a higher RAM ceiling.

Another important purchasing consideration is the distribution of RAM in your server. If your computer has four memory slots and the system comes populated with four 16M memory modules, then when it comes time to upgrade, you will have to replace some of the existing modules with larger ones. This is fine if you have another computer that needs an upgrade, but buying a system with two 32M modules is more prudent.

The biggest variable in calculating the RAM required for a NetWare server is disk space, and NetWare 4.11 modifies the equation a bit from previous versions. The rising popularity of Windows 95 and Windows NT as client operating systems is due in no small part to their capability to use long file names. Previous versions of NetWare required the use of the OS/2 name space module to support long file names on NetWare volumes. NetWare 4.11 now includes a name space module called LONG.NAM that is designed to provide long file name support for Windows clients with that capability.

What's more, NetWare now installs long file name support by default on all volumes (other than SYS) created during the installation process. An additional name space module on a NetWare volume causes two directory cache buffers to be needed for each file instead of one. This adds considerably to the memory required to mount that volume. If you will be installing other name space modules besides DOS (the default) and LONG.NAM—such as those for MAC, HPFS, or FTAM files—keep in mind that each name space requires an additional buffer for every file on the volume, whether the file actually uses it or not.

Thus, if you have only a few Macintosh systems on your network, with modest storage needs, you are probably better off creating a single volume with MAC name space where they can store their files, rather than installing MAC name space on all of your volumes.

Novell has published several different RAM calculation formulae in its product manuals over the years, but these are admitted to be very rough calculations. A rough estimate of the RAM required for a NetWare 4.11 server would be to multiply the amount of disk space in the server (in megabytes) by .008, add this number to the default 20M, and include an additional 1–4M for file caching. This does not include the memory required for NLM programs, however.

The final word on calculating memory requirements for NetWare, however, should always be "more is better." No memory goes unused by the NetWare operating system. All of the memory that is not allocated for a specific task or module goes into a file cache buffer pool. This pool is used to cache recently accessed files from the server's volumes. The more memory that is installed in the server, the greater the number of files that can be cached for future use. This increases file access times, improves client performance, and saves wear and tear on the hard drives. With memory prices as low as they are, you might consider installing some additional memory in your servers, above the required minimum.

What Disk Drives?

In today's market, there are only two choices when it comes to the type of hard drives to use in your NetWare server: EIDE and SCSI. SCSI is tried and true. It has been used for server drives for many years and has a number of architectural features that make it particularly suitable for server use. EIDE is something of a newcomer, but only when considered for server use.

IDE drives have also been around for a long time, but it is only recently that the Enhanced IDE specifications now in use have allowed for drives larger than 504M. The new standards also allow up to four devices to be installed in a system, where the limit used to be two.

As far as the hard drives themselves are concerned, EIDE and SCSI drives are very similar. Most manufacturers produce the same drives in both EIDE and SCSI versions, and examining the units themselves will demonstrate that the SCSI drive is basically the EIDE model with a few additional SCSI logic chips installed.

The difference between the two technologies is more in the way that the units are addressed than in the units themselves. Most systems today are equipped with support for EIDE drives on the motherboard. SCSI, however, requires an additional system board most of the time, called a *SCSI host adapter*. The host adapter receives the I/O requests from the operating system and sends the appropriate commands to the hard drives to fulfill them.

Ultimately, SCSI is still the preferable server hard drive type, for several reasons:

- **Expandability**—A single SCSI host adapter can accommodate up to seven devices. Dual channel adapters are also available that support up to 14 devices using a single bus slot. A computer can run as many SCSI adapters as it has available slots. IDE is limited to four devices on two channels.

- **Multitasking**—The SCSI host adapter is capable of queuing commands for each of the devices it controls. While a command is executing on one drive, the adapter can be processing commands for other drives.

- **Compatibility**—A SCSI host adapter can control any combination of hard disk, removable, CD-ROM, or tape drives, with full interoperability. SCSI is a ratified, proven, and accepted standard. There are hundreds of models of SCSI devices on the market.

When purchasing a server, take into account that the hard drives are not used in the same way as those in a standalone PC. Dozens or even hundreds of users may be accessing files on a single volume at the same time. Obviously, a hard drive has only one set of heads, and can physically read only one file at a time. That's why it is often preferable in a server to use several lower-capacity SCSI drives rather than one big one.

By using multiple SCSI drives, I/O requests for files on different drives can be processed simultaneously, instead of sequentially, as they would be if all of the files were on a single drive. Of course, this is not to say that you should buy 14 100M hard drives instead of a single 1.4G drive. However, four 1G drives would be preferable to one 4G drive.

NetWare has, throughout its history, been thought of mainly as a network file and print services platform. In such a role, disk drives are obviously of paramount importance when constructing a new server. IntranetWare has been designed to expand the role of NetWare into an application services platform, which places a greater emphasis on memory and processor performance. However, high performance disk drives are still an important part of every server.

In all but the lightest duty servers, SCSI drives are recommended over EIDE. There are now products conforming to several different SCSI drive standards available, which provide marked improvements over the original 5M/sec speed. Table 3.1 lists the various SCSI types and their basic characteristics.

Part
I

Ch
3

Table 3.1   Server Disk Drive Alternatives

Name	Data Transfer Rate	Interface Type	Max Distance	Max Devices
IDE	5 MBps	Parallel	< 1 meter	2
Extended IDE	10 MBps	Parallel	< 1 meter	2
SCSI	5 MBps	Parallel	< 10 meters	7
SCSI-2	10 MBps	Parallel	< 10 meters	7
Fast-Wide SCSI	20 MBps	Parallel	< 10 meters	7
Ultra SCSI	40 MBps	Parallel	< 3 meters	7

What Kind of Bus?

Efficient communications over a network are dependent on all of the components between the source of the signal and its destination. If any one component cannot keep up with the others, then it becomes a bottleneck, slowing down the entire system. One of the most common areas of a NetWare server in which bottlenecks occur is the *system bus*, that is, the means by which data is transferred from hard drives and other storage devices to the network interface card.

When purchasing a computer to be used as a NetWare server, there are two basic rules of thumb:

- Any system bus is preferable to ISA.
- All adapter cards should use the fastest bus available.

Despite all of the other bus types developed over the years, every PC sold still has ISA slots, and while ISA devices may be acceptable for use in workstations, a server warrants a better level of performance. All too often, users invest a great deal of money in a computer that is to be used as a NetWare server, and suffer with poor performance for want of a $200 SCSI adapter.

The Micro Channel, EISA, and VESA local buses are all satisfactory alternatives to ISA, but these have been eclipsed by PCI, which got off to a shaky start as far as NetWare servers are concerned, but is now the industry standard high-speed system bus. Most high-end systems today include PCI slots; if your computer has them, be sure to purchase both SCSI and network adapters that make use of the PCI bus.

Other Components

Because a NetWare server is wholly dedicated to its activities as a server, such components as the keyboard and the monitor are largely inconsequential. These, therefore, are areas in which you can try to save a bit of money, if possible. Most systems that are packaged as servers are intended to run either NetWare or Windows NT. A Windows NT server can also be used as a client, so often a decent quality monitor and video display adapter are included, along with a mouse.

If you can substitute a lesser quality monitor and video card for your NetWare server and avoid purchasing a mouse with the system, you can save several hundred dollars. It is unfortunate that cheap, monochrome monitors are no longer available, as they were ideal for use with NetWare servers.

Consider also where your server will be located when making these decisions. If you have a server closet or data center that houses multiple servers, you can save money, as well as space, by obtaining a switch box that enables a single monitor and keyboard to be shared among several systems.

Although these components are areas where you may safely skimp in order to save money, there are others where you definitely should go for the best quality. Frequently neglected items in the purchase of a server are the "unsexy" components, such as the case, the fans, and the power supply.

Part

I

Ch

3

CAUTION

Once again, consider the location in which the server will be housed. Remember, the server will be running 24 hours a day (you hope), and you want to be sure that it is sufficiently cooled at all times. Most server systems today come with at least two fans, plus one mounted atop each processor chip. Today's Pentium and Pentium Pro processors generate tremendous amounts of heat and require a constant stream of air to cool them. Be sure to leave adequate space around the computer's air intakes, and don't allow them to become clogged with dust.

Unless you have a climate-controlled computer center, check to see whether heat and air conditioning runs at night in the room where the server will be located. Many office buildings shut off all services at night and during weekends to save money. Depending on the local climate, this could expose your equipment to extreme levels of heat and cold.

The case and the power supply for your server both depend on the components that will be contained therein. If you plan to add internal components to the system, then be sure to get a tower case that can hold them and an adequate power supply. You can also purchase additional hard drives, tape drives, and CD-ROMs as external units, which contain their own power supplies, eliminating this problem.

Also, for a server, an uninterrupted power supply (UPS) is a must. Be sure to purchase one of sufficient voltage to support your system long enough to shut it down gracefully. Most UPS units are designed to keep a system running only for 15 to 30 minutes. This is useless during the night if no one is there to shut down the system. You should also consider using one of the software products that automatically downs the server when it receives a signal from the UPS unit during a power outage. NetWare now supports UPS connections through a standard serial port, so there is no need to install an additional card in the computer for UPS support.

Documenting the Hardware

Once you have a properly equipped server, it is important that you document everything within it. This not only facilitates the NetWare installation, but any troubleshooting efforts you may have to perform later, as well as calls made for service. The NetWare installation program does an excellent job of identifying the components in the server, but you want to be sure that everything is found and correctly identified during the procedure.

If you have purchased a system intended for use as a server, you may already have complete documentation. If you have selected the equipment yourself, you will want to gather the following information:

- The number and type of processors
- The amount and type (speed) of RAM
- The number, type, brand, and capacity of the hard drives
- The type of CD-ROM drive
- The type and brand of SCSI adapter and SCSI IDs of all connected devices
- The number and brand of network interface cards and the hardware settings for each one (IRQ, I/O port, memory address, and so on)

The main purpose of this list is to be sure that the NetWare operating system recognizes and utilizes all of the components in your server. If you have assembled the system yourself, the best course of action is to boot the system to DOS and be sure that all of the components are functional before you begin the NetWare installation. This way, you can be sure that any installation difficulties you may have are not due to hardware problems.

Gathering Drivers

A NetWare server is a brain with no body unless it has access to both hard disk drives and the network medium itself. The NetWare installation process is largely concerned with establishing these connections. In order to do so, you must have the proper drivers for your hardware. You will need drivers for your SCSI host adapters and for the network interface cards in your server. Drivers for many of the most popular SCSI and network adapters are included with the operating system, but in some cases you will have to supply drivers yourself.

If you have purchased a server package, you should have received drivers with the computer. Very often, these are provided on a CD-ROM, and you may have to run a utility on the CD that enables you to create driver disks. I recommend that you do this before beginning the NetWare installation.

If you purchased the server components yourself, check to see if drivers intended for use with NetWare 4.11 are included in the package. If not, most manufacturers have Web or FTP sites from which you can download the latest driver releases.

Finally, if you will be installing NetWare from the server's own CD-ROM drive, you will need the drivers necessary to access the CD-ROM from DOS. The IntranetWare package contains a bootable Novell DOS disk that also contains a CD-ROM runtime executable. You will need only the device driver for your CD-ROM drive, which must be run from a CONFIG.SYS file.

Choosing a Server Configuration

Once you have gathered all of the hardware and software you need, it is time to think about some of the choices that must be made during the course of the NetWare installation. Considering these matters now will help you to avoid making rash decisions during the installation that you will regret later.

During the NetWare installation process, you will have to make the following decisions:

- How large should the DOS partition be?
- What should the server's name be?
- What should the server's internal IPX number be?
- How large should the SYS volume be?
- How large should the other volumes be?
- Should volumes be mirrored or duplexed?
- Should volumes span disk drives?
- What should the name of the NDS tree be?
- How should the NDS tree be designed?

Some of these questions are relatively inconsequential, while others are crucial to the operation of your network.

Creating a DOS Partition

Your first activity, before you even begin the installation, is to create a DOS partition from which you will boot your server and load the NetWare operating system. It is possible to boot from a floppy disk, but the DOS partition is much faster and more reliable.

Create a normal primary DOS partition on the servers first hard disk drive and make it bootable, using the system files on the Novell DOS disk. Be sure to leave all of the other space on the hard drive that you intend to use for NetWare volumes unpartitioned.

Novell recommends a DOS partition of 15M, to contain all of the files needed for NetWare to load. You may want to include additional space in the DOS partition for two reasons:

- To store additional software that may be needed when the server is down or the volumes dismounted, such as the NetWare VREPAIR.NLM utility, network client software, and a text editor.

■ To allow sufficient space for the storage of a core memory dump. A core dump is an image of the computer's memory taken at the time of a catastrophic software failure, such as a server *abend* (abnormal end). Trained technical personnel can use this information to determine the cause of the problem. To store a core dump, you will need an additional amount of disk space equivalent to the amount of RAM installed in the computer.

Naming the Server

Each NetWare server on a network must have a unique name by which it is identified by other systems on the network. A server name can be up to 47 characters, but I strongly recommend that you keep it short. Your users will not appreciate having to type a long, complicated name.

Consider also that the server name is a name that you (and your company) will have to live with for a long time. As with vanity license plates, no joke remains funny for long when you see it every day.

Every NetWare server is also assigned an internal IPX number. This is an eight-character hexadecimal value that is also used to uniquely identify the server. The NetWare installation program will generate a random value for this number, which, in the custom installation, you can modify if you want. Usually, there is no reason to do so.

Designing a NetWare Volume Configuration

The decisions you make regarding the number and size of the NetWare volumes created during the installation are very important. Once your volumes are populated with data, the only way to reconfigure them will be to back them up, delete the partitions entirely, recreate new volumes, and restore the data.

NetWare always creates a default volume called SYS during the installation process. This is the volume where the NetWare system files and logs are stored. How large a SYS volume is created is up to the installer. Novell recommends at least 150M for the NetWare files, but this is reliant on several factors.

The SYS volume is traditionally used for the storage of NetWare system utilities and other software used primarily by network support staff. The exception to this is the PUBLIC directory, to which all users are allowed read-only access. PUBLIC contains all of the NetWare utilities, such as MAP and NLIST, that are regularly accessed by users. It also is the location of the NetWare Application Launcher and management utilities, such as the NetWare Administrator and the NDS Manager.

NetWare print queues always reside on the SYS volume, as subdirectories of the MAIL directory. Although this storage is temporary, printer output files can be very large. The NetWare Directory Services database also resides on SYS. Consider the NDS design for your enterprise, and leave enough room for any NDS partition or replica you will be hosting on this server.

You can also elect to place the installation files for the NetWare clients on the SYS volume for user access, as well as the NetWare documentation files. These will, of course, require additional disk storage space over the base 150M that Novell recommends. Finally, there are many third-party NetWare utilities that you may want to run from SYS.

Be aware that network software often consists of more than the files that are copied during installation. There are also log and database files to consider. Network backup software is a good case in point. If you back up workstation hard drives or other servers to a tape drive on the NetWare server, the databases created by some backup programs can grow extremely large, often to hundreds of megabytes.

CAUTION

Be sure to consider all factors when sizing the SYS volume. Don't forget that your print queues are dynamic. Running out of disk space on this volume can cause many kinds of problems with the NetWare operating system. A full SYS volume is particularly dangerous to a server containing part of the NDS tree. Lack of disk space can prevent changes from being written to the NDS database and inhibit the replica synchronization process.

Part
I

Ch

3

The creation of other volumes on a NetWare server is completely up to the installer. You can create as many volumes as you want and name them whatever you choose, although the use of the names VOL1, VOL2, and so on, is a common practice.

The number of volumes on a NetWare server is often predicated on the number of disk drives in the computer. Although you can create NetWare volumes that span multiple drives, this practice is not recommended, as the failure of one drive will cause the entire volume to be lost.

Another consideration in the creation of volumes, as discussed in the section "How Much RAM?" earlier in this chapter, is the addition of name spaces and the additional memory that they require. You may want to create volumes of a certain size and containing specific name spaces for the exclusive use of certain machines on your network.

It is always a good idea to develop a storage strategy before you create your volumes. For example, you may want to consider storing your applications on one volume, and your users' home directories on another. This type of planning can make future administration chores, such as file system rights assignment, much easier.

You might choose to mirror or duplex your volumes. Mirroring and duplexing are techniques by which data on a NetWare volume is continuously replicated for purposes of fault tolerance. NetWare is capable of taking two 1M drives, for example, and creating a single 1M mirrored volume from them. All data written to the volume is automatically written to both drives simultaneously. If one drive should fail, data can be accessed from the other with no delay.

When a partition is mirrored, both drives are attached to the same host adapter. If the adapter should fail, then disk activity is suspended for both drives. A partition is considered to be duplexed when each hard drive is connected to a different host adapter, as shown in Figure 3.1. This way, any one drive or any one host adapter can fail, and disk access will continue.

FIG. 3.1
Duplexing provides greater fault tolerance than mirroring because each disk drive is connected to its own host adapter.

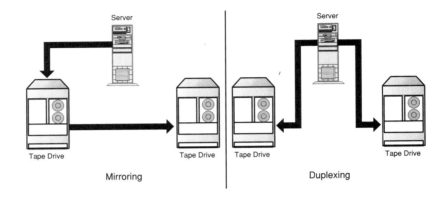

Obviously, duplexing represents a greater level of security, but both mirroring and duplexing are relatively wasteful fault tolerance mechanisms, as you are effectively cutting your storage capacity in half. If it is critical that your volumes remain accessible at all times, then it may be worthwhile for you to mirror or duplex partitions. In fact, you can mirror up to eight partitions with identical data, if you want. For most users, however, the performance of regular system backups is sufficient protection for a server's data.

With these considerations in mind, decide how many volumes you want to create on your server, what sizes they should be, and what you will name them.

Designing the NDS Tree

By far, the most complicated part of a NetWare installation is the creation of a NetWare Directory Services database. This is because the design of an NDS tree should take the entire enterprise into consideration—not just a single server. See Chapter 5, "Designing an NDS Strategy for the Enterprise," for more information on NDS design.

It is not essential, however, for there to be a comprehensive enterprise network design in place before you install a NetWare server. During the installation process, you can choose whether to create a new NDS tree or install the server as part of an existing one.

If you elect to create a new tree, be aware that one tree can always be merged into another, so this may be the safest option if you are unsure how to proceed. The new tree created by the installation program contains a single container object in which the server is located. Since, with NetWare 4.11, you can now move and rename NDS tree branches, it is easy to adapt the default tree to any design that you may subsequently develop.

Beginning the NetWare 4.11 Installation

If you have considered all of the items discussed thus far in this chapter, you should be fully equipped to install a NetWare server. In order to begin the installation, you must next decide what the source of your installation files will be. You must boot to DOS on the computer that will become your NetWare server, and do what is necessary to access the NetWare installation files.

If you are going to install NetWare from a local CD-ROM drive, you must install the device driver needed to access the CD-ROM from DOS, and run the NOVCDEX.EXE file from the Novell DOS disk to assign a drive letter to the CD-ROM. The device driver is typically run from the CONFIG.SYS file with a parameter containing a variable that is used to identify the drive. Then NOVCDEX.EXE is executed from the AUTOEXEC.BAT file, or from the DOS prompt, also with a switch containing the same drive variable name. This mounts the CD-ROM as a DOS drive letter and provides access to the NetWare CD.

N O T E A Novell DOS boot disk (which includes such essential utilities as FDISK, FORMAT, and NOVCDEX.EXE) is included with the IntranetWare package to facilitate the installation process. You could just as well use MS-DOS, substituting MSCDEX.EXE for NOVCDEX.EXE.

Part
I
Ch
3

During the installation process, you will have the opportunity to switch the CD-ROM from DOS-based access and mount it as a NetWare volume. In any case, once the NetWare installation process is completed, remove (or remark out) the commands in the CONFIG.SYS and AUTOEXEC.BAT files that mount the CD-ROM as a DOS device. You will have to do this if you want to mount the CD-ROM as a NetWare volume, but even if you don't, these drivers occupy memory that could be better used elsewhere.

The other alternative is to install NetWare from a CD-ROM mounted as a volume on another server, or from a replica of the CD-ROM files on another NetWare volume. In either case, you must install a NetWare DOS client in order to access the remote volume from the computer on which you are installing NetWare, and map a drive letter to that volume.

Once you have access to the NetWare installation files, you are ready to switch to the drive letter (or directory) representing the root of the NetWare 4.11 installation CD-ROM, and run INSTALL.EXE.

Performing a Simple Installation

The NetWare installation program enables you to perform a simple or a custom installation. The procedures are essentially the same, except that the simple option makes many of the installation decisions for you, while the custom option prompts you each step of the way.

If the decisions you made as a result of reading the section "Preparing the Hardware" earlier in this chapter, correspond exactly to the following selections, then you can run the simple installation and save yourself a bit of time.

The simple installation assumes that you want your NetWare server configured so that

- you boot the system from a DOS partition containing at least 15M of available disk space,
- an internal IPX address will be randomly selected by the installation program,

- all of the hard disk space in the computer except for the DOS partition will be used to create NetWare volumes,
- you will not be mirroring or duplexing drives,
- each disk drive will be used to create a separate NetWare volume,
- an NDS tree will be created with a single container for all of the objects created during the installation,
- and, no additional products or protocols other than IPX will be installed during the procedure.

You will be prompted for all of the other information required during the installation. Apart from automated responses to the prompts concerning the items listed earlier, the simple installation is identical to the custom installation process, covered in greater detail in the following section.

Performing a Custom Installation

The custom installation option allows you greater flexibility concerning several aspects of the installation procedure, particularly in the following areas:

- Creation of volumes
- Creation of NDS objects
- Installation of additional products

Both the simple and custom installation methods activate the program's automatic hardware detection feature by default, prompting you for driver information only when it is needed. If, for any reason, you want to disable this feature, run the INSTALL program with the /nad switch, as follows:

```
INSTALL /nad
```

You will then be prompted to provide information about the hardware in your computer.

Choosing the Product to Install

Once you run the INSTALL program, you are asked to specify the language version of NetWare to be installed. The NetWare 4.11 CD-ROM contains the entire NetWare product and documentation in the following languages:

- German
- English
- Spanish
- French
- Italian
- Portuguese

After selecting a language, you are presented with a menu offering the following options:

- NetWare Server Installation
- Client Installation
- Diskette Creations
- ReadMe Files

You can install NetWare clients, create client installation diskettes, and view the NetWare ReadMe files later in the installation process or after the installation is complete. Choose NetWare Server Installation to continue the procedure.

N O T E When installing any new software, it's a good idea to check the README files for late-breaking product developments.

The next menu enables you to choose whether to install NetWare 4.11 or NetWare 4.11 SFT III. The SFT (System Fault Tolerance) III version of NetWare allows two identical NetWare servers to be mirrored using a dedicated link. If one server crashes or fails for any reason, the other takes over instantaneously. The NetWare CD contains the files needed to install SFT III, but an additional license for the product is required, as well as the hardware used to connect the two servers.

After selecting NetWare 4.11, you are prompted for the server's name, and an IPX internal network address is generated. You can use the random value supplied, or enter one of your own. Any eight-digit hexadecimal value (except 00000000 and FFFFFFFF) is acceptable.

Copying Server Boot Files

In the next part of the installation process, the NetWare boot files are copied to the server's DOS partition. By default, the files are copied to a directory called C:\NWSERVER, although you are given the opportunity to change this, if you want.

The DOS partition contains all of the files required by the NetWare boot process, including disk (or SCSI adapter) drivers, the STARTUP.NCF file—which contains commands to be executed prior to volume mounting—and NetWare's main executable, SERVER.EXE.

N O T E Text files with an NCF extension function as executable batch files for the NetWare command processor, much like BAT files do for DOS. Any command that you can run from the NetWare server console prompt can be included in an NCF file.

Once the server boot files have been copied, you are presented with a screen offering the opportunity to change the codes for the country in which you are located, the language you want to use, and the keyboard map you want to use. If you will be running NetWare in English within the U.S. using a standard keyboard, no changes to this screen are necessary.

The installation program then prompts you to specify the naming format for the default DOS name space on your NetWare volumes. Choosing DOS Filename Format allows only

DOS-compatible characters to be used by NETX workstations. NetWare Filename Format enables the use of NetWare-compatible characters that may not be allowed by DOS.

The installation program then gives you the option of adding one of the most frequently used SET commands into the server's STARTUP.NCF file. SET is the server console command line utility that is used to configure many NetWare technical parameters. Certain SET commands can only be issued from the STARTUP.NCF file because they affect the way that drivers are loaded into memory during the server boot process.

The SET RESERVED BUFFERS BELOW 16 MEG = 200 command pre-allocates a specified amount of server memory in the area below the 16M barrier. This memory is called using a special API command by certain device drivers that are incapable of addressing the memory above 16M. For example, all ISA-based SCSI host adapters are limited to the memory below 16M. If you are using an ISA SCSI adapter, or if you are loading an ASPI (Advanced SCSI Programming Interface) driver in order to run different types of SCSI devices using the same adapter, then the SET RESERVED BUFFERS command should be included in your STARTUP.NCF file.

N O T E As mentioned in the section "What Kind of Bus?" earlier in this chapter, the use of ISA devices in a computer with more than 16M of RAM is strongly discouraged. The ISA bus was designed for use with the Intel 80286 microprocessor. The 80286 has only 24 address lines, making 16M the maximum amount of memory that it can address. There was no reason to design a bus that could address any more than that.

An ISA device can handle memory addresses of up to 0x00FFFFFF (in hexadecimal form). When it tries to address any memory above that point, instead of proceeding to the next address (0x01000000), it rolls over to 0x00000001—overwriting whatever happens to be stored there. In a NetWare server, this causes memory corruption and usually an abend. The SET RESERVED BUFFERS command ensures that enough memory is available for an ISA device driver to load below 16M, preventing it from trying to read any memory addresses above that limit.

The final activity in the DOS part of the NetWare installation process is to insert the SERVER.EXE command into the computer's AUTOEXEC.BAT file. If you agree to this procedure, your computer will automatically load NetWare whenever it is booted.

 T I P To take advantage of the new NetWare feature that enables the server to be automatically restarted after an abend, you must allow the SERVER.EXE command to be inserted into the AUTOEXEC.BAT file.

Installing NetWare SMP

Now that you've finished the DOS part of the installation process, SERVER.EXE is executed and the INSTALL.NLM module is loaded automatically. Technically, you are now running a NetWare server; but without access to the computer's disk drives and to the network medium itself, the server is useless. The bulk of the installation process is concerned with creating a procedure by which access to these resources is automatically established every time the server is booted.

Before the procedure begins that enables you to access the server resources, however, the server examines your hardware and determines whether or not you are running a computer with multiple processors. If your computer has more than one processor, NetWare will ask you if your want to install Symmetrical Multi-processing NetWare (SMP).

NetWare SMP, previously sold as a separate product, is now included as part of the NetWare 4.11 operating system. With this option, certain NetWare server tasks can be broken down into separate threads, which are executed by different processors at the same time.

N O T E NetWare SMP can handle systems with up to 32 microprocessors, and spread LAN interrupts among them—providing a general speedup to the system. If your system uses *Advanced Programmable Interrupt Controllers* (APICs), the computer will continue to function if one of the auxiliary processors should fail. Failure of the primary processor always causes the system to halt.

NetWare itself gains something of a performance boost from SMP. However, only certain third-party NLMs are capable of taking advantage of more than one processor. Applications must be developed specifically for a multiprocessing NetWare environment, and as of yet, there are few. ■

Installing NetWare SMP will cause the SMP.NLM and MPDRIVER.NLM modules to be launched from the STARTUP.NCF file, along with a *platform support module* (PSM) file specifically designed for your multiprocessor system. NetWare ships with PSMs for several multiprocessor systems. If one is not included for your system, you must obtain it from the computer's manufacturer. The program also adds the SET UPGRADE LOW PRIORITY THREADS = ON command to your AUTOEXEC.NCF file, which prevents background processes on the server from being neglected.

Installing Device Drivers

Device drivers are the software components that enable the NetWare operating system to communicate with the hard drive controllers and network interface adapters in your computer. They provide the commands that NetWare must use to accomplish specific tasks using that device and specify the hardware parameters that are used to locate the device in the system.

NetWare 4.11's hardware detection routines have been greatly improved since previous versions. If you purchase a computer containing well-known, popular hardware devices, then it is very likely that this portion of the installation process will be virtually effortless for you. The program will detect your hardware, configure and load the correct drivers for the installed devices, and add the appropriate commands to the STARTUP.NCF and AUTOEXEC.NCF files for you, so that the drivers are loaded each time you boot NetWare.

Loading Disk Drivers   IntranetWare ships with drivers for a wide array of hardware devices by many different manufacturers. NetWare disk drivers have an extension of DSK, and must be loaded from the STARTUP.NCF file if they are used to drive the adapter attached to the hard drive containing the SYS volume.

N O T E   The LOAD command is used in the STARTUP.NCF file—just as it may be used from the server command prompt or any other NCF file—to load a module into the server's memory. The LOAD command recognizes only four file name extensions:

- **NLM**—NetWare Loadable Modules
- **DSK**—NetWare Disk Drivers
- **LAN**—NetWare LAN Drivers
- **NAM**—NetWare Name Space Modules

Additional parameters may be included on a LOAD line to further define the way in which the command is to be executed.

Some of the drivers in the package are developed by Novell, and others by the device's manufacturer. If any problems should arise that you think may be driver-related, it is always best to contact the device manufacturer for help. Other users are almost certain to have had the same problem, and very often a driver update or other information is available for download over the Internet, or some other online service.

However, device drivers often fit into the "if it ain't broke, don't fix it" school of computer maintenance. Avoid the temptation to upgrade drivers simply because a new version becomes available. If you are not experiencing any problems, and the manufacturer doesn't recommend that all users perform the upgrade, then it is probably best to leave things as they are. Unless your NetWare server is intended for testing purposes, you don't want to risk the downtime that might occur as the result of a problematic device driver.

The NetWare installation program will first attempt to locate the hard disk drive adapters in your system. If your adapter is a PCI, EISA, Micro Channel, or Plug and Play ISA device, it is very likely that it will be detected automatically. If it is not, the reason may be that your adapter was detected but not positively identified, or that drivers for your adapter are not included in the IntranetWare package. In either case, you will be presented with a screen containing a list of drivers from which to choose.

If your system has a CD-ROM drive, you might have to select a CD-ROM device driver as well. This driver enables the CD-ROM drive to be used as a NetWare device. You can then mount a CD like a NetWare volume and enable your users to access it.

If you are forced to select a driver manually, you may also have to supply the hardware configuration parameters that NetWare needs to locate the adapter. This may include a combination of any of the following:

- IRQ
- I/O port
- Slot number
- Memory address
- DMA channel

This is the time when the documentation that you gathered before the installation process comes into play. If you are unsure of your adapter's hardware settings, you will have to use the "trial and error" method to discover them, open the computer and read them from the card, or abort the installation and boot to DOS so that you can run the device's configuration utility.

N O T E If you have purchased a high-end, server-ready system from a major manufacturer, you can be all but certain that the hardware will be automatically detected. Remember, however, that the primary function of the NetWare installation utility at this point is to build the appropriate entries in a STARTUP.NCF or AUTOEXEC.NCF file. No matter what problems you have, you can always modify these text files manually to try different settings or load different drivers. ▤

Loading LAN Drivers   The installation program next attempts to locate and identify the network interface cards in your computer and select appropriate drivers. This process is almost identical to that of installing disk drivers. If your network adapter is not identified, a listing of available drivers appears from which to choose. Once again, you may have to supply a driver that you have obtained from the device manufacturer and specify hardware configuration settings for the device.

Part

1

Ch

3

NetWare drivers for network interface adapters have an extension of LAN, and are nearly always loaded from the AUTOEXEC.NCF file, which is executed after the disk drivers are loaded and the server's volumes mounted.

It is not uncommon for a NetWare server to have more than one SCSI adapter and/or LAN card installed. If two identical devices are installed, their device driver must be loaded twice, with two different sets of configuration parameters, so that the two devices can be distinguished from one another. If the devices are not identical, then a separate driver is required for each one.

N O T E Many device drivers are capable of loading *re-entrantly*. This means that loading the same driver twice does not require double the memory required by a single device. Certain parts of the driver code are shared, while separate sets of hardware parameters are maintained. This is why you may see a driver listed only once in the NetWare server's MODULES listing, even though you have loaded it two or more times. ▤

The installation program provides you the opportunity to install multiple drivers for both disk and LAN adapters. As noted earlier, you can always edit the NetWare NCF files to modify settings or add LOAD lines for additional drivers. The most important tasks to be accomplished at this stage of the installation are to mount the SYS volume and gain access to the network through at least one LAN adapter. If the installation or configuration of additional disk or LAN drivers becomes too much of a problem, you can safely delay these tasks and proceed with the rest of the installation process.

Once the disk and LAN drivers for your server have been installed and configured (whether manually or automatically), a window appears displaying the selected drivers for your approval. If all of your drivers are properly displayed, choose Continue Installation.

Installing Additional Protocols   Back in the days when installing NetWare was much more of a manual process, it was necessary, once the LAN drivers were loaded, to manually bind them to the appropriate protocols, indicating what frame type was to be used for network communications. This was done using BIND, a NetWare server console command. Once the appropriate commands had been entered at the server console, the INSTALL.NLM utility copied them to the AUTOEXEC.NCF file for future execution whenever the server was booted.

N O T E   A frame type is an indicator of the way that the packets transmitted over your network are formatted. An Ethernet network can use four possible frame types for NetWare communication:

- Ethernet_802.2
- Ethernet_802.3
- Ethernet_II
- Ethernet_SNAP

Each of these four frame types uses a packet header that is very slightly different from the others. Ethernet_802.2 is the default frame type for NetWare 4.x, and Ethernet_II is traditionally used on networks running TCP/IP, as well as IPX. You can bind multiple frame types to a single LAN driver, but the most important aspect of this matter is that all of your servers and workstations utilize a common frame type, or communication between them will not be possible.

You may be surprised to know that although the NetWare 4.11 installation program has greatly simplified the process of loading drivers and binding protocols since previous versions, the ultimate result is exactly the same. LOAD and BIND command lines are automatically generated now, but they use the same syntax that they always have, and they are then added into the AUTOEXEC.NCF file, just as they have always been.

During the next phase of the installation procedure, NetWare loads its default IPX protocols automatically and presents you with a screen displaying your selected LAN drivers, indicating that they are bound to the IPX protocol. If you want to install additional protocols on your server, you must choose View/Modify Protocol Settings.

Because a great deal of the IntranetWare package is devoted to TCP/IP products and services, it is likely that you will want to install TCP/IP as an additional protocol on your server. To do this, you must be prepared with an IP address for your server and a *netmask* (often called a *subnet mask*).

N O T E   Like any computer running TCP/IP, a NetWare server must have an IP address that does not conflict with the address of any other system on the network. Depending on whether or not your network is connected to the Internet, and how the connection is made, you may need an address that has been registered with the Internet Network Information Center (InterNIC).

If TCP/IP is widely used in your organization, there should be some mechanism in place by which IP addresses are assigned to users and records maintained. Note also that unlike many other operating systems, NetWare requires the value for the subnet mask setting be expressed in hexadecimal, not decimal, format. Thus, the subnet mask expressed in decimal format as 255.255.255.0 would be FF.FF.FF.0 in hexadecimal format. ▦

Each protocol must be individually bound to at least one LAN driver in order to function. NetWare gives you complete freedom as to the combination of LAN drivers and protocols you elect to bind. If your server is connected to two networks (that is, if it has two LAN adapters installed), you can elect to bind IPX to one LAN adapter and TCP/IP to the other (for example, you can bind both protocols to both adapters, or any combination you want). As always, adjustments can be made later simply by editing the AUTOEXEC.NCF file.

When modifying protocol settings, you must first select the LAN driver whose protocol bindings you want to modify. You can then add or remove protocols from each LAN driver individually. If you are adding TCP/IP, you will be prompted for the IP address and netmask that your server will use. Once you have selected all of the protocols that you want to load and have indicated which LAN adapters they should be bound to, choose Continue Installation. The drivers you have chosen will be loaded, and the protocols bound. Following this, the appropriate commands are added to the STARTUP.NCF and AUTOEXEC.NCF files, after which the installation process continues.

Creating NetWare Volumes

Now that you have loaded your disk drivers, the NetWare server should be able to access your hard drives, and it is time to create and mount the volumes where the operating system files and your data will be stored.

Before you do this, however, consider the source of your NetWare installation files. If you are installing NetWare from a local CD-ROM, you may face a conflict at this time because the DOS drivers are still loaded. It is also entirely possible that you have just loaded a NetWare driver that will address the same device. This is certainly true if your CD-ROM drive is connected to the same host adapter as your hard disk drives.

In some cases, the presence of the NetWare CD-ROM driver in memory can cause the DOS driver to lock up the system at some future point in the installation. In the hope of preventing this, the NetWare installation program presents a screen offering you two options:

▦ Continue accessing the CD-ROM via DOS.

▦ Try to mount the CD-ROM as a NetWare volume.

If you are able to successfully mount the CD-ROM drive as a NetWare volume, then you should have no problems accessing the CD-ROM during the rest of the installation. It is possible, however, that the presence of the DOS driver in memory may hinder the creation of the NetWare volume. If this is the case, continue to access the CD-ROM using the DOS drivers and proceed with the installation.

T I P   If you should experience an unrecoverable system lockup due to a CD-ROM driver conflict during the installation, at this point you should be able to reboot the system. However, be sure to remove the commands that load the DOS CD-ROM drivers from the system's CONFIG.SYS and AUTOEXEC.BAT files first.

When NetWare finishes loading and you have access to the system console prompt, you will find that the INSTALL.NLM and CDROM.NLM modules have already been copied to the C:\NWSERVER directory on your DOS partition. You can load these modules from the C:\NWSERVER directory (with the commands LOAD C:\NWSERVER\INSTALL and LOAD C:\NWSERVER\CDROM) and continue the installation procedure by choosing Volume Options from INSTALL's Installation Options menu.

Partitioning the Disks   In order to access a hard disk drive with DOS, the procedure is to create one or more DOS partitions on the drive with the FDISK utility, and then format the partitions for the FAT file system using FORMAT.COM.

In NetWare, the process is similar, although the utilities are different. First, you create NetWare disk partitions on your hard drives, and then you create volumes within the partitions.

A single hard disk drive can only contain one NetWare partition, but it can have any number of non-NetWare partitions on it as well. For example, if you created a DOS partition on your primary hard drive for the NetWare system boot files, you will likely want to fill the rest of the drive with a NetWare partition.

You can, however, utilize a part of the available space on the drive for a NetWare partition, and create additional partitions for DOS, HPFS, NTAS, or any other file system you want. In this way, a single computer can be configured—for training or testing purposes—to run several different operating systems, each with its own disk partition.

The installation program gives you the option to create NetWare disk partitions manually or automatically. The automatic option will utilize all of the available disk space on each of the computer's hard drives for the creation of NetWare partitions.

Choose the manual method if you want to

- leave some disk space unpartitioned on any of the computer's hard drives,
- change the Hot Fix area's size on any NetWare partition,
- delete NetWare partitions that already exist on the hard drives before creating new partitions,
- mirror or duplex NetWare disk partitions.

When you choose the manual option, you are presented with a screen from which you can select Create NetWare Disk Partition. If you have more than one hard disk drive in your computer, you are then prompted to choose the drive on which you want to create a partition.

Selecting a drive produces the Disk Partition Information screen. The manual method enables you to specify the size of the NetWare partitions that you create. You can use any space that is left over on a drive to create a partition for another file system (using the appropriate utility for that file system).

When you specify a size for you NetWare partition, notice that the size of the Data Area under Hot Fix Information changes. Hot Fix Redirection is a fault tolerance feature that is automatically activated on all NetWare partitions. When the drive is partitioned, two percent of the allocated space is reserved as the Hot Fix area. When a write operation to a NetWare server volume encounters a bad block on a hard drive, the data is diverted to the Hot Fix area, rather than being lost.

In most cases, two percent of the partition is more than enough (and in the case of large capacity drives, usually too much) for the Hot Fix area. However, you can modify the value if you want, by changing the size of the Data Area (in megabytes), or by changing the percentage of the redirection area. In either case, the other value is recalculated when you make the change.

At this point, you are ready to actually create the partition. Follow the prompts and, if necessary, repeat the process to create partitions on other drives.

Mirroring and Duplexing Partitions   Mirroring and duplexing are methods of providing fault tolerance to NetWare partitions by replicating the data from one drive to other drives. Mirroring disk partitions requires that you have two hard drives of approximately the same size. A single partition is created on each drive, and then the two partitions are synchronized, so that they will remain identical replicas. Any data placed on a mirrored volume is always written to both drives. If one drive fails, then the other takes over seamlessly and immediately. Duplexing means you have each drive attached to different controllers, mirroring both drives on the same controller.

The process of mirroring or duplexing partitions begins with the creation of NetWare partitions on each hard drive, in the normal manner. Once the partitions have been created, choose Mirror and Unmirror Disk Partition Sets from the Disk Partition and Mirroring Options menu. You are presented with a display that lists the NetWare partitions on your system and shows the current mirroring status for each. At this point, all partitions should appear as Not Mirrored.

N O T E   The following four values can be shown in the mirroring status indicator:

- Mirrored
- Not Mirrored
- Out of Sync
- Remirroring

Out of Sync indicates that the partition was once mirrored or duplexed with another partition, but that the mirroring process is no longer taking place. The data on the two partitions is no longer identical. This partition cannot be accessed until it is brought back into synchronization with its partners.

Remirroring indicates that data is currently being written to, or deleted from, the partition in an effort to synchronize it with its partners. The status should shortly return to Mirrored. ■

Part

I

Ch

3

To mirror or duplex partitions, select one disk partition and press the Insert key to display the other partitions to which it can be mirrored. Select a secondary partition, and the process of mirroring the drives will begin.

N O T E The NetWare installation program does not distinguish between mirroring and duplexing. If you want duplexed partitions, then it is up to you to select drives that are connected to different host adapters.

It is important that the two partitions that you propose to mirror or duplex be nearly the same size. If they are not, NetWare will inform you of this fact, and offer to resize the larger of the two partitions. Any disk space that is removed from the larger partition in order to make it the same size as the smaller one will not be available for use with NetWare.

Once the partitions have been synchronized (which should be almost immediate because the partitions do not contain any data yet), they are displayed in the Disk Partition Mirroring Status as a mirrored pair.

Configuring Volumes   Once your NetWare partitions have been created, it is time to create volumes on them. The actual task of creating a volume is simple, but the process warrants careful consideration, because you will have to live with the decisions you make here for some time to come.

The only thing that is absolutely required is that you create a volume called SYS, where the NetWare system files are stored. Apart from this, you can create any number of volumes (up to eight per partition), of any size, and with any names you want.

When you enter the volume creation phase of the NetWare installation, a screen is displayed containing the volumes suggested by the installation program. These volumes have not yet been actually created, so you are free to modify many of the parameters.

By default, the installation program creates a single NetWare volume for each disk partition found in the computer. The partition on the first hard drive (the one with the DOS partition) is named SYS. Subsequent volumes are named VOL1, VOL2, and so on.

You can modify the following properties when creating NetWare volumes:

- Change the volume's size
- Change the volume's name (except for SYS)
- Change the volume's block size
- Turn file compression for the volume on or off
- Turn block suballocation for volume on or off
- Turn data migration for the volume on or off

When you select one of the proposed volumes, a Volume Information screen is displayed where you can modify its parameters to suit your working environment. You can also delete a volume entirely.

Sizing Volumes The most important aspect of creating NetWare volumes is deciding their sizes. There are several criteria that you should consider before deciding how large your volumes should be. Among these are the following:

- Security
- Performance
- Fault tolerance
- Name spaces

By creating individual volumes on your NetWare server, you simplify the task of administering the rights that will be assigned to your users. For example, Novell recommends that the SYS volume be devoted wholly to NetWare-related files. This way, destructive access to that volume can be restricted to network support personnel. NetWare requires a minimum of 150M for the SYS volume (with the NetWare documentation installed), but more than this will probably be required, perhaps much more. The actual NetWare system files may fill only a fraction of this amount, but as discussed in "Designing a NetWare Volume Configuration" earlier in this chapter, many other files will have to be stored on SYS as well. Take all of those factors into account before sizing your SYS volume.

Fault tolerance is another important consideration when sizing volumes. You can easily make all of the disk storage space in your server, apart from the SYS volume, into one big user volume. This will make things easier for both you and your users, but it also may cause a major problem. If you have several disk drives in your server (each with its own partition), a volume can be created that spans drives. The problem with this is that the failure of one drive will cause the entire volume to be lost.

You can protect your server against this eventuality by making frequent backups or even by mirroring or duplexing a spanned volume, but most authorities, including Novell, recommend against the practice of spanning volumes across drives.

Volume divisions are also the best way of segregating name spaces to economize on memory. Name spaces must be installed for an entire volume, and it would be very wasteful to have to install several name spaces on one huge volume, just to store a handful of MAC or UNIX files.

To change a volume's size, select the volume and—in the Disk Segment Size field—specify the size (in megabytes) that you want the volume to be. Disk space that is freed by deleting a volume or reducing it in size appears in the device list as Free Space. You can then allocate that free space to another existing volume by increasing its size, or you can create a new volume.

Part

Ch

3

CAUTION

Once a volume has been created, you can increase its size at any time by adding any free space that is available to its size using the INSTALL.NLM utility. However, the only way of reducing a volume's size is to back up its contents, destroy the volume, and recreate it, after which you can restore the files back to the new volume.

Naming Volumes   In the Volume Information screen, you can select the Volume Name field to change the name of the volume to anything that you want (except in the case of SYS, which cannot be renamed). NetWare volume names can be up to 15 characters long, and use letters, numbers, and the exclamation point (!), at sign (@), pound sign (#), dollar sign ($), percent sign (%), ampersand (&), and parentheses. Do not use spaces in volume names.

As with server names, consider the fact that you and your users may have to type these volume names frequently. Keeping the names short and avoiding the shift characters is a good idea, for convenience's sake. Many administrators who organize their server volumes according to their contents find that descriptive names, such as APPS, DATA, and MAC, are both useful and intuitive.

Changing a Volume's Block Size   The NetWare file system subdivides a volume into smaller units called blocks. The *file allocation table* (FAT) and the *directory entry table* (DET) store information about each block on every NetWare volume. This information is used to rapidly locate specific files on the server's hard drives.

The size of the blocks on a particular volume is determined by the amount of disk space allotted to that volume. As volumes increase in size, so do their block sizes. The total amount of server memory required by the FAT and the DET is based on the number of total blocks on all of the server's volumes.

Table 3.2 contains the standard NetWare block sizes, and the sizes of the volumes to which they are assigned, by default.

Table 3.2   NetWare Volume Sizes and Their Default Block Sizes

Volume Size	Block Size
0–31M	4K or 8K
32–149M	16K
150–499M	32K
500M or more	64K

Larger block sizes are therefore more efficient as far as memory is concerned, but they are less efficient when it comes to disk storage capacity. When a file is written to a NetWare volume, a sufficient number of blocks is allocated for the purpose of storing the file. After the file is written, however, there is almost always some disk space left over in the last allocated block.

For example, when storing a 17K file on a 25M NetWare volume, five 4K blocks would be required. The last block would only have 1K worth of data stored on it, however, so 3K is wasted. On a 100M volume, the same file would require only two 16K blocks, thus saving memory, but in this case 15K of the last block is wasted. As the block size increases, so does the wasted space.

N O T E Although NetWare 3.x had no solution for the problem of wasted block space, NetWare 4.x includes an optional feature that partially remedies the problem. See the next section in this chapter, "Understanding Block Suballocation," for more information.

Although NetWare uses the values in Table 3.2 as its defaults, you can change the block size for any volume to any of the values shown earlier. Selecting a different block size for your volumes may be a good idea, if you know what kind of files are to be stored on them. If, for example, you plan to dedicate a particular volume to large database files, a block size of 64K would be recommended. Likewise, if you plan to store a great many small files on a volume, a 4K block size will minimize waste.

A volume's block size can only be changed during its creation. Once the volume exists, the only way to modify the block size is to destroy it and recreate it.

Understanding Block Suballocation Block suballocation is a feature that was introduced in the NetWare 4.0 release to address the problem of the volume space wasted by the larger block sizes. When block suballocation for a volume is enabled (which it is by default), a block can be subdivided into 512-byte segments. When a file occupies only part of a block, a sufficient number of 512-byte segments within that block are allocated to the file. The rest of the segments can be used by other files that also require a fraction of a block. Thus, you may find a single block that contains the tail ends of several different files, each of which occupies only as many 512-byte segments as it needs.

The waste of space inherent in the file system is not completely eliminated by the suballocation process because there are surely parts of the 512-byte segments that go unused. But it is reduced substantially.

T I P You can prevent a specific file from being suballocated by assigning it the DS file attribute using the FLAG, FILER, or NetWare Administrator utility. Certain frequently changed files, such as databases, can benefit from not being suballocated.

Block suballocation for a volume can be disabled in the Volume Information screen, during the creation of a volume only. The only persuasive reason to disable this feature is if you plan to utilize NetWare's High Capacity Storage System (HCSS). See "Understanding Data Migration" later in this chapter for more information on this option.

Understanding File Compression NetWare 4.x also includes another feature that helps to maximize disk storage efficiency. Many users are familiar with file compression utilities that enable you to manually reduce the size of a file for transport or storage. NetWare uses this technology to compress unused files stored on server volumes, increasing the amount of space available for new files.

File compression is enabled on a volume level. If you choose not to enable compression when your volumes are created, you can enable it later, but once compression is turned on, it cannot be turned off, except by deleting and recreating the volume.

NetWare's file compression system works by examining the dates of the files on the server volumes. Files that have not been accessed in a specified period of time are compressed, and the compressed version replaces the original. If access to that file is requested at a future time, the file is decompressed on-the-fly and delivered to the user, after only a minor delay.

Once compression is enabled on a volume, files are always decompressed on demand. However, the compression process can be scheduled, so that all of the files to be compressed on a given day are processed during off hours, when server activity is low. The compression parameters are controlled by SET commands that you can issue at the file server console prompt or include in your server's AUTOEXEC.NCF file.

By default, the NetWare file compression system operates in the following manner:

1. The NetWare server begins scanning its compression-enabled volumes at midnight and ceases at 6 AM. These times can be altered using the SET COMPRESSION DAILY CHECK STARTING HOUR and the SET COMPRESSION DAILY CHECK STOP HOUR commands.

2. Any files that have not been accessed in 14 days become candidates for compression. This period can be modified using the SET DAYS UNTOUCHED BEFORE COMPRESSION command.

3. A test compression is performed on all candidate files. If a file cannot be compressed by at least 20 percent, it is left in its decompressed state. This factor can be adjusted using the SET MINIMUM COMPRESSION PERCENTAGE GAIN command.

4. Before a file is saved in its compressed state, the server checks the amount of free disk space on the volume. If less than 10 percent of the volume space is free, the compressed file is not committed and warnings are issued to the network administrator. The free space percentage can be changed with the SET DECOMPRESS PERCENT DISK SPACE FREE TO ALLOW COMMIT command. The interval between warning messages is set with the SET DECOMPRESS FREE SPACE WARNING INTERVAL command.

5. Once a compressed file is saved to the volume, it is decompressed and delivered to any user that requests it. If a user accesses the file only once in a 14-day period (the SET DAYS UNTOUCHED BEFORE COMPRESSION interval) it is left on the disk in a compressed state. If it is accessed two or more times in 14 days, it is left in an uncompressed state, whereupon the 14-day countdown begins again. This behavior can be modified with the SET CONVERT COMPRESSED TO UNCOMPRESSED OPTION.

The entire compression system can be shut down using the SET ENABLE FILE COMPRESSION command. When this is done, files are still decompressed on demand, but no compression activities are performed by the system. However, the compression system is based on each NetWare file's Date Last Accessed attribute. When the compression system is re-enabled, there may be a large number of files to be processed, resulting in an extended period of heavy server activity.

Even when the compression system is operating, you can interactively affect the compression behavior of specific files by modifying certain NetWare file attributes using the FLAG, FILER, or NetWare Administrator utilities. NetWare includes the following compression-related attributes:

- **DC (Don't Compress)**—Prevents a file from being compressed by NetWare under any circumstances.

- **IC (Immediate Compress)**—Causes a file to be compressed by NetWare as soon as possible, regardless of time settings.

- **CC (Can't Compress)**—A status flag generated by NetWare, indicating that a file was not compressed because the minimum compression percentage gain threshold was not reached. Cannot be changed by the user.

- **CO (Compressed)**—A status flag generated by NetWare, indicating that the file has been compressed. Cannot be changed by the user.

File compression is enabled on all NetWare volumes, by default. It can be disabled during the creation of a volume from the Volume Information screen. As with block suballocation, the use of file compression is recommended in most cases. If, however, you will be implementing the NetWare High Capacity Storage System or if you run a 24-hour network that cannot tolerate the additional burden of compression activities at any time, then the system should be disabled.

Understanding Data Migration *Data migration* is a NetWare feature that enables seldom-used files to be migrated from their volumes and stored on other media, instead. Typically implemented using optical disk or tape drives, a data migration system scans volumes for files that have not been accessed in a given period, much like the file compression system. However, in the case of data migration, the files are completely removed from the NetWare volume, and stored on less-expensive, higher-capacity media.

On the volumes, tiny key files are left in place of the actual files. This enables users to view the files in a directory listing, just as if they were physically located on the volume. When a user requests access to a file that has been moved, the data migration system accesses the file on the appropriate medium and copies it back to the NetWare volume, after which it can be accessed normally. To the user, the only indication that the file has been migrated is a delay while the file is accessed from a (slower) optical disk or tape.

Data migration is typically used with NetWare's High Capacity Storage System. This is a feature that enables a server's storage capacity to be greatly increased by the addition of an optical disk autochanger, or jukebox. This device contains one or more optical drives and a robot mechanism capable of inserting disks into the drives. In this way, enormous amounts of storage space are available to network users without any manual intervention (such as swapping disks in and out of a drive by hand). This type of storage is sometimes called *nearline storage*, defining a halfway point between online and offline.

N O T E   Block suballocation and file compression must be disabled if data migration is used. By default, data migration is disabled on all new NetWare volumes.

As with compression, the migration of specific files can be controlled through the use of NetWare file attributes, as follows:

Part

Ch

3

■ **DM (Don't Migrate)**—Prevents a file from being migrated under any circumstances.

■ **M (Migrated)**—A status flag set by NetWare, indicating that a file has been migrated from the volume to another storage device. Cannot be changed by the user.

To modify a volume's data migration status, change the setting in the Volume Information screen.

Saving Volumes   Once you have created all of your volumes and modified their settings, press the F10 key from the Manage NetWare Volumes screen to save the volumes to the disk partitions. NetWare will then mount the volumes, making them ready to accept data.

Copying NetWare Files

At this point, you have finally implemented the NetWare server's two most critical services: storage and communications. Now that your NetWare volumes are mounted and ready to go, it is time to begin copying the core NetWare system files to their permanent home on the SYS volume.

N O T E   Remember that the NetWare boot files are still located on the server's DOS partition. NetWare places copies of all of your disk, LAN, and protocol drivers there, as well as vital utilities, such as VREPAIR.NLM, INSTALL.NLM, and CDROM.NLM. If you should experience a problem that causes your SYS volume to be lost or damaged, you can still boot the server to DOS in order to make repairs. ■

If you are installing NetWare from a local CD-ROM drive, you are next presented with a screen displaying the path from which the NetWare system files will be copied. The path shown should be correct, but you can modify it, if necessary. The path on the CD-ROM should be as follows:

drive or volume:PRODUCTS\NW411\INSTALL\IBM\DOS\XXX\ENGLISH

If you are installing a non-English version of NetWare, the last directory on the path should reflect your chosen language.

N O T E   If you are installing NetWare from source files on a remote CD-ROM or server volume, your network connection will have been interrupted by the loading of the NetWare LAN drivers. Just as the NetWare CD-ROM driver can interfere with its DOS counterpart, your NetWare client drivers have been replaced by the server LAN module.

Service can continue with the LAN driver, but the interruption forces you to log in again to the server where the NetWare source files are located. When you are presented with a client authentication screen, the user name should already be present. When you enter your password, the file copy procedure will continue. ■

The installation program will now create the NetWare system directories on the server's SYS volume and copy the files that are needed to complete the next phase of the installation.

Installing NetWare Directory Services

When you install a NetWare 4.x server, you have two options, as far as NetWare Directory Services is concerned. You can either install your server into an existing NDS tree on the network, or you can create a new NDS tree.

After the preliminary file copies are completed, the server scans the network for existing NDS trees. If any are found, you are given the opportunity to select the tree into which the server will be installed. You can also elect to create a new tree, instead.

If no NDS trees are found, you are asked if you are installing the first NetWare 4.x server on your network. If this is the case, answer Yes, and the procedure for creating a new NDS tree begins by asking you to specify the name of the tree that you are going to create.

Apart from this step, the procedures for creating a new NDS tree and installing the server into an existing tree are very similar. In each case, you must perform the following two basic tasks:

Part

I

Ch

3

- **Set up time synchronization**—This tells the server the time, its time zone, and how to handle daylight saving time.
- **Specify the NDS context**—This tells the server where in the NDS tree's hierarchy the server object and its associated user and group objects are to be located.

The primary difference between the two scenarios is that in an installation to an existing tree, you are specifying the context in terms of NDS object names that already exist, while in a new installation, you specify object names that are to be created.

> **CAUTION**
>
> Designing an NDS tree for an enterprise network is not a task that is to be taken lightly, or improvised as you go through the process. Chapter 5, "Designing an NDS Strategy for the Enterprise," is concerned with this subject, and should be consulted before you commit yourself and your organization to any particular strategy.

Unless you are familiar with your company's plans regarding NDS, or you have designed an NDS hierarchy before beginning the NetWare installation, I recommend that you create a new NDS tree with a very simple structure. You can create a tree with a single organization containing all of the objects created by this installation. Later, this new tree can be merged into an existing NDS database, or it can be refined and enlarged to better suit your network, at a later time.

Locating Lost Trees   There are several reasons why one or more other NDS trees on your network might not be detected. Some of the possibilities are as follows:

- The server's network interface card is configured incorrectly or malfunctioning.
- An incorrect or non-functioning LAN driver has been installed.
- The wrong frame type or LAN number was specified when binding IPX to the LAN driver.
- Service Advertising Protocol (SAP) packets are being filtered on your network.

For any of the first three problems, you must diagnose and repair the problem, and then choose the Recheck for NetWare 4 Network option to begin the scanning process again. The last problem is environmental, and can be worked around. Many networks choose to filter out SAP packets, especially over WAN links, because they consume significant amounts of bandwidth.

If, for example, you are installing your server at one location and trying to connect to the NDS tree located at another site over a WAN, you can still communicate with the remote server, even without the SAPs that advertise its presence. To do this, you must specify the name of the NDS tree you are trying to locate and the IPX internal network number of a server in that tree. (The IPX internal network number is the hexadecimal number selected at random at the beginning of the NetWare installation.)

Setting Up Time Synchronization   NetWare Directory Services consists of a database that can be distributed and replicated across an entire enterprise. A single NDS tree can service a global corporation, with offices and servers scattered all over the world. The NDS database can also be partitioned and replicated.

A partitioned database is one that has been split into pieces, which are then stored in different places. The entire database, or the individual partitions, are then replicated to various servers around the enterprise, for reasons both of performance and fault tolerance.

Because changes made to the database at any location must be disseminated to all of the partitions and replicas, time synchronization is a crucial element of NDS maintenance.

NDS and Time Synchronization

Suppose a network administrator in New York changes a server's Admin password at exactly 4:00 PM EST. One minute later, at 1:01 PM PST, another administrator in Los Angeles changes the same Admin password to something else. If the clocks in the networked computers in New York and Los Angeles are not precisely synchronized, then it is entirely possible that those two password changes might arrive at the Tokyo office in the wrong order. Tokyo would think that the NY password was valid, while both U.S. offices would know otherwise.

Multiply this phenomenon by the number of objects in the NDS database, and the potential for chaos is enormous. Therefore, time signals are exchanged across the enterprise network, and every NDS event is time stamped to ensure that commands are executed in the proper order.

In most cases, setting up the NDS time synchronization parameters involves nothing more than selecting your time zone from the list presented. When you select a time zone, a screen containing time configuration parameters for your area is displayed for your approval.

The time server type refers to the time synchronization functions that your server is going to perform for the NDS tree. There are four types of time servers:

- Single reference
- Reference
- Primary
- Secondary

If you are creating a new directory tree, your server will be designated a single reference server. If you are installing the server to an existing tree, your server will be designated a secondary server. In nearly all cases, it will not be necessary to modify the time server type setting.

The screen also contains settings for the appropriate abbreviation for your time zone (such as EST for eastern standard time) and the number of hours difference between your time zone and UTC (universal time coordinated or Greenwich mean time).

The rest of the settings concern daylight saving time (DST): whether you use it in your time zone, what the appropriate abbreviation is (such as EDT, for eastern daylight time), how much DST is different from standard time in your zone, and the dates when DST begins and ends.

If all of the settings are correct, accept them and the installation proceeds.

Specifying the Server's Context   If you are installing the server into an existing NDS tree, you are next prompted to log in to that tree, using the Admin account and password. This gives you the rights to create new objects in that tree.

The next screen displays a textual representation of the NDS tree's hierarchy. Its function is to enable you to specify the context into which the server's objects are to be installed. In a new tree installation, the object names you specify in this screen are created in the new NDS tree you are creating. In an existing tree, you can specify either objects that already exist, or objects you want to add to the existing hierarchy. To learn more about NDS context and its notation, see Chapter 4, "Novell Directory Services (NDS) and NetWare Administrator."

Next to Company or Organization, specify the name of a top-level container in your tree. For the simplest possible NDS tree, stop here. A single container object is created using the name you've entered, and the server object will be placed within it.

If you want, the next three lines on this screen enable you to create Organizational Unit objects, in a hierarchical manner. The Level 1 object will be contained within the Company or Organization object you already specified. The Level 2 object will be contained within the Level 1 object, and so on. Your server will be placed in the bottom level container object.

As you specify object names, notice that the Server Context displays below the Level 3 line changes to reflect the hierarchy you are creating. You are not limited to just the four levels shown in this screen. You can edit the Server Context line directly, specifying a container object up to 25 levels deep, into which you want the server installed.

If you are creating a new tree, there will be entries at the bottom of this screen where you must enter the Administrator Name you want to use for your NDS tree and its Password.

> **CAUTION**
>
> Keep track of this NDS Administrator user and password information. This account is created with your new tree, and is the only means of accessing and modifying both the server and the tree until you create additional user objects. The password entered here also becomes the Supervisor password for bindery emulation purposes.

At this point, the new NDS database is created (or the existing one updated), and the objects related to the server placed in the context you provided.

Installing the NetWare License

The installation program next prompts you to insert your NetWare license disk into the server's floppy drive. The license file is then copied to the server and registered on the network. If another NetWare server with the same license is detected on the network, you will be bombarded with periodic warning messages until one of the servers is deactivated.

Reviewing the STARTUP.NCF and AUTOEXEC.NCF Files

At this time, all of the commands and settings that you created during the installation are written to two text files, STARTUP.NCF and AUTOEXEC.NCF, that are executed whenever the server boots.

The STARTUP.NCF file is stored on the server's DOS partition, and contains all of the commands that must be executed before access to the SYS volume is available. STARTUP.NCF consists mainly of commands that load disk drivers, and SET commands that affect the way that subsequent modules are loaded into memory.

The AUTOEXEC.NCF file contains the time zone parameters you configured earlier, specifies the server's name and internal IPX address, and loads LAN drivers and binds them to protocols, among other things.

In the case of both of these files, you are given the opportunity to make any changes or additions that you want before they are saved to disk. Any command that can be executed from the server console can be inserted into one of the NCF files for execution during the boot process.

N O T E You can also modify these files later using the INSTALL.NLM utility or any text editor. You must restart the server before any changes you make can take effect. ▪

After the NCF files are saved to disk, the remaining NetWare system files are copied to the SYS volume. A status screen displays the file names as they are copied. After copying the remaining files, the core NetWare installation is completed.

You can go on to use INSTALL.NLM to install other IntranetWare products if you want, or you can restart your server, to demonstrate that it is ready to run.

> **CAUTION**
>
> Once again, be sure to remove any DOS CD-ROM or network driver commands from your computer's CONFIG.SYS and AUTOEXEC.BAT files before restarting the server.

Summary

The installation process is one of the most successfully improved parts of NetWare 4.11. This chapter provides information on many aspects of the installation process that will be all but invisible to most users during the actual procedure. In most installations, the default values suggested at almost every stage of the procedure will be acceptable, and a new NetWare server will be created with very little difficulty. ●

Part
I

Ch
3

Using Novell Directory Services

Novell Directory Services (NDS) and NetWare Administrator

The original concept behind NetWare was to unite a collection of personal computers by connecting each of them to a central computer that provided communications and storage services for all. Users could work on the same data and share the same hardware simultaneously. When the concept grew popular, the departmental networking model was applied to every department, soon resulting in a corporate internetwork composed of many or even hundreds of servers.

Originally, NetWare required that each server be administered individually. Access to the resources controlled by a server was provided by setting permissions in a flat-file database called a bindery. A user that required access to every server in the company needed a separate account in each bindery. As networks grew larger, the bindery concept became increasingly difficult to administer.

Novell Directory Services, introduced as part of the NetWare 4.0 release, addressed the problem of multiple-user accounts by replacing the bindery with an object-oriented database that spans the entire network. Incorporating all NetWare resources and their users into a single, hierarchical database, NDS unites all of an organization's server-centric departmental networks into a single enterprise network. In this chapter, you learn about the basic principles with which an NDS database is constructed and utilized.

The result of using NDS is that users have a single account with which they can gain access to any server or other NetWare resource in the enterprise. A single account means one login instead of many, and a single point of administration for the network support staff.

N O T E NDS was introduced as NetWare Directory Services in the NetWare 4.0 release. In NetWare 4.1, the name was changed to Novell Directory Services to reflect how the database's utility had expanded beyond the realm of NetWare. The two names are interchangeable, and do not reflect a significant change in the product.

IntranetWare expands the role of the NDS database even further. TCP/IP services, such as the NetWare Web and FTP servers, use NDS accounts to control user access to specific intranet applications and resources. Developers of third-party applications can even create their own customized extensions to the NDS database, which can provide authentication and access control services for whatever resource is provided by the application.

The NetWare operating system includes the tools and utilities with which you create, access, and maintain the NDS database. Chief among these is NetWare Administrator. In NetWare 4.11, NetWare Administrator is positioned as the central administrative utility for Novell Directory Services. Many other utilities are launched from Administrator's menus, and the program functions as the front end for the NDS database itself.

Understanding NDS Architecture

Novell Directory Services is a database of the resources found on a NetWare network, the users that access the resources, and various logical groupings that are used to facilitate network administration tasks and structure the database. NDS is designed to make the components of a large enterprise computing network accessible and comprehensible to the people that use them.

The fundamental unit of the NDS database is the *object*. The entire database is composed of objects that represent physical or logical entities. Every NetWare server, for example, is represented by an object, as is every volume on that server. Every NetWare user is also represented by an object, and so are non-physical elements, such as user groups and user profiles. Other objects represent printers, print servers, and print queues.

The NDS database is therefore composed of many different types of objects. Each object type is distinguished by its own set of properties. A *property* is a field associated with an object type that is designed to hold a particular type of information suited to the needs and characteristics of the object itself.

A user object, for example, has properties designed to hold information about the identity of the user and the specific network resources to which the user has been given access, among other things. A group object, on the other hand, has some different properties, most notably a list of the user objects that belong in the group.

The data associated with the properties of a specific object are called the *values* for those properties (see Figure 4.1). Therefore, a user object will have a property in which the user's name is stored. The value for that property might be John Smith in one user object, and Jane Doe in another.

FIG. 4.1

All NDS objects are composed of properties, and each property can have a specific value.

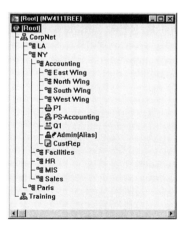

Objects	Properties	Values
DoeJ	Given Name	John
	Last Name	Doe
	Require Password	Yes

The NDS database is located on NetWare servers scattered around an enterprise network. When an application on a client computer requires access to a network resource, the NetWare client sends an access request to the NDS database using a proprietary Novell Directory Services protocol. NDS processes the request and then either grants or denies the client access to the resource.

The NDS Hierarchy

Part

II

Ch

4

The NDS database is structured much like the directory tree used by most file systems. It stems (perversely) from a root at the top of the tree (written as [Root]), and has objects arrayed in branches in a hierarchical fashion, as shown in Figure 4.2. The structure of the tree is designed by the administrator of the network. The objective is to create a tree that represents the networking infrastructure of the entire enterprise in a logical manner.

FIG. 4.2

The NDS tree hierarchy should be designed to facilitate the needs of both users and administrators.

To facilitate the creation of the structure, there are two basic types of NDS objects: *container* and *leaf*. Leaf objects are those described earlier, that is, the objects that represent the actual building blocks of the network. Container objects, not surprisingly, exist only to hold other container objects and multiple leaf objects.

Container objects are used to create the logical divisions that form the structure of the tree. The two most commonly used container objects are *organizations* and *organizational units.* Organizations can only be located at the top of the tree, and organizational units form the layers beneath.

N O T E   There is another type of container, called a *country object,* which can be created only directly from the root of the NDS tree. The country object is a holdover from the CCITT X.500 directory service standard, upon which NDS is partially based. Country objects are not often used in NDS trees because many NDS-aware applications expect to find only organization or organizational unit objects directly beneath the [Root].

When planning your tree, it is a good idea to avoid the use of country objects unless your network must interface with another directory service that requires them. You can always use organization objects to represent the countries in an international NDS tree.

A typical NDS tree design uses these container objects to represent the natural divisions of the enterprise. You can use containers to represent the various branch offices of your company, the floors of your building, or the departments in your organization. The guiding principle behind NDS tree design is to locate user objects in the vicinity of the network servers and printers that they use every day. The tree should also be designed so that both users and administrators can locate objects representing resources in remote areas of the enterprise in an intuitive manner.

N O T E   The arrangement of container objects in the design of your enterprise's NDS tree should be determined by the needs of your network users and staff who support the network. See Chapter 5, "Designing an NDS Strategy for the Enterprise," for more information on this complex and very important process.

Containers also act as logical groupings of the objects within them. Just as rights flow downstream in the NetWare file system, access rights assigned to a container object are inherited by all of the objects in the container. You can therefore use containers like the groups found in NetWare binderies, and even create container login scripts that are executed by every user object in the container during the login process.

Partitions and Replicas

Every client workstation on the enterprise network must access the same NDS database. Because the system is designed to accommodate very large networks with many thousands of users, clearly it would not be possible to have everyone access the database on one server. Copies of the database, called *replicas*, are therefore situated on NetWare servers throughout the enterprise in order to balance the load.

All NetWare 4.x servers run NDS, but this does not mean that every server has a complete replica of the entire database stored locally. Because of this, and because of the continual updates that are copied to replicas all over the network, there is always a great deal of background communication traffic going on between NDS servers.

When an enterprise network encompasses multiple locations connected by WAN links, you can split the NDS database to optimize communication between servers. In most cases, users access the resources on their local servers more frequently than those at remote locations. It, therefore, makes sense to store the part of the NDS tree that represents those resources at that location. To do this, the database is split into segments called *partitions*. Each partition is stored on a different server, and is replicated on servers at the other locations.

Thus, every user has access to the entire NDS database at all times, and the partitions and replicas provide fault tolerance to the NDS system. When an enterprise NDS database is properly partitioned and replicated, any server on the network can fail without interrupting client access.

The way that the database is partitioned, and the number and types of replicas that are used, are decisions that are, again, left to the network administrators. See Chapter 6, "Using NDS Manager," for more information on creating partitions and replicas in a logical and efficient manner.

Understanding the Directory Schema

The rules that define the object types permitted in the NDS database, and the properties associated with each type, are known as the *directory schema*. NetWare includes a default set of schema that represent the resources commonly found on all NetWare networks and the containers used to organize them in the NDS tree. However, it is possible for other applications to extend the schema to create object types of their own. The basic components of the directory schema are the following:

- Object classes
- Attribute types
- Attribute syntaxes

Every object in the NDS database is defined by one or more *object class*. The object classes are basic templates that govern the creation and use of a particular object type. Object classes define the properties (or attributes) that the final object will possess. They are chosen from a set of *attribute types,* which are based on a collection of *attribute syntaxes*. The following are some of the attributes provided by object classes:

- **Super classes**—These are the superior object classes whose attributes are inherited by other object classes. The schema have a class hierarchy of their own that is independent of the tree's object hierarchy. The process by which an object type is defined is simplified through the specification of super classes as the source of more general object attributes.

  Individual attributes that are unique to this object are then defined explicitly. For example, the Device super class contains attributes that are inherited by object classes that represent network devices, such as servers and printers. Some of the attributes in a super class are also inherited from the Top class, which is the uppermost class in the hierarchy and the super class of all other super classes.

- **Containment classes**—These restrict a particular object's location in the NDS tree. An example of a containment class is the attribute of an organization object that states that it can only be contained by the Root or by a country object.
- **Naming attributes**—These impose restrictions on the name that can be assigned to a particular object. A naming attribute is used, for example, to restrict the name of a country object to two characters.
- **Mandatory/optional properties**—These are attributes that determine whether particular properties of an object must be assigned a value when the object is created, or can be left blank. For example, the last name property of a user object is mandatory.

Attribute types dictate the nature of the data that can be supplied as a value for a particular property of an object. For example, the property of a user object that stores the user's telephone number is restricted to numerical values by an attribute type. Attribute types also indicate the length of the property's field, and whether or not it can contain multiple values. In addition, attribute types specify the attribute syntax that are to be applied to that property.

Attribute syntax defines the rules that are applied to the data when the same property is compared in multiple objects. If, for example, you search the NDS database for all users that have been registered as working in the Sales department, the property in which the departmental information is stored will be assigned an attribute syntax that causes the case of the value to be ignored. Thus, the results of the search will include users that have been registered as belonging in the Sales department, as well as those *in* sales. In the same way, an application can successfully compare telephone numbers, even when some of the values contain hyphens, and some don't (that is, 555-1234 as compared to 5551234).

Certain modules included in the IntranetWare package create their own NDS objects, and there are now many third-party products that extend the schema to create new object types for use by their applications.

To aid in this process, NetWare provides a collection of object classes, attribute types and syntax called the *base schema*, which application developers can use as templates for the creation of object types based on the general categories of objects found in the default NDS database. To the base schema, the developer adds additional super classes, which further refine the attributes of the object.

Some network backup software products, for example, extend the schema to create an object type for the job queue in which pending backup and restore procedures are stored for execution at specific times. This object functions a lot like a print queue, and very likely uses some of the same super classes as the NetWare print queue object. The application extends the schema and creates the object during the installation process, and such utilities as NetWare Administrator are able to view and manipulate the new object types by accessing a snap-in module provided by the application developer.

Once created, the new object is addressed by the backup software, using standard NDS API calls, enabling it to store application data in the NDS database itself. This data can later be used by the software in any way that it sees fit. By allowing new object types to use pre-defined elements like object classes and attribute syntax, Novell has designed NDS to facilitateAHis kind of proprietary extension, and has madcÌThe necessary programming tools publicly available.

The goal of NDS, as repeatedly stated by Novell, is to crb°4e a universal network directory that can accokmèdate all of the computing resources used by an enterprise, whether they run Novell products or not. The NDS database is sometimes referred to simply as the Directory for this reason. (The capital *D* is used to distinguish the NetWare Directory from a typical file system directory.) Its ultimate intention is for Novell Directory Services to be used as the Directory for the Internet itself.

Objects and Their Properties

The schema provides a menu of object types, with varying properties aoó@purposes, that are used to populate the NDS tree. In NetWare Administrator, each object type is represented by its own icon, and the tree diso9Ay creates a rg÷ esentative dequì[tion of the entir e network that the user can easily navigate and manipulate.

Novell Directory! %rvices is a part of nearly evaŸ   transaction uõÅt takes place on a NetWare 4.x network. The core NetWare file and print services use NDS objects to regulate and authenticate access to nerwèrk volumes ang ®rinters. In order for a user to access a particular volume on a NetWare server, for example, a relationship must be established between the user's object and the corresponding volume object in the NDS database.

The NDS tree contains more than just user and volume objects, however. Table 4.1 defines no less than thirty-two object types. Maintaining and documenting the complex matrix of relationships between all of these objects is the primary function of the NDS database. When it functions properly, it is almost invisible; when it doesn't work, NetWare grinds to a screeching halt.

Part

II

Ch

4

Table 4.1   Novell Directory Services Objects in NetWare 4.11

Object Icon	Object Name	Description
A F P	AFP Server	An AppleTalk Filing Protocol server. Create this object to document the existence of an AFP server on your network.
	Alias	An object that represents or points to another object. Create this object when you must list an object in the directory tree by a different name or in a different part of the directory tree.
DOS	Application (DOS)	An object representing a networked DOS application that is delivered to clients using NetWare Application Manager.

continues

Table 4.1 Continued

Object Icon	Object Name	Description
	Application (Windows 3.x)	An object representing a networked Windows 3.x application that is delivered to clients using NetWare Application Manager.
	Application (Windows 95)	An object representing a networked Windows 95 application that is delivered to clients using NetWare Application Manager.
	Application (Windows NT)	An object representing a networked Windows NT application that is delivered to clients using NetWare Application Manager.
	Auditing File	An object used to administer the access rights of NetWare auditing logs.
	Bindery Object	An object created as a result of an upgrade of a NetWare 2.x or 3.x server. You can't create this type of object directly, and it has no corresponding type among the NetWare 4.1 list of leaf objects.
	Bindery Queue	A queue on a NetWare 2.x or 3.x server that's referenced in the NDS directory tree.
	Communications Server	A server that provides communications features, such as shared modems and faxing.
	Computer	An object created to document the existence of a non-server computer on your network.
	Country	A container object that represents a country.
	Directory Map	An object created to reference or point to a particular directory on a network file server. NetWare-aware utilities can then reference the literal directory, using the directory map object name.
	Distribution List	A collection of objects that have Message Handling Service (MHS) mailboxes. These objects can be addressed together when sending MHS messages.
	External Entity	An object that references something that exists outside the directory tree.

Object Icon	Object Name	Description
	Group	An object that represents a group of users. By using group objects, you can grant users access to files, directories, printers, and so on, collectively rather than individually.
	License Certificate	An object that is created whenever an application is installed that can use NetWare Licensing Services for software metering.
	Licensed Product	A container used by NetWare Licensing Services to contain license certificate objects for the purpose of software metering.
	LSP Server	An object that is created when you register a License Service Provider into NDS with the NetWare Licensing Service modules loaded.
	Message Routing Group	A collection of MHS servers that exchange messages with each other.
	Messaging Server	A server that runs the MHS NLM and stores messages.
	NetWare Server	An object that represents a server running NetWare.
	Organization	A container object that represents an organization or company.
	Organizational Role	An object that represents a job responsibility that requires associated access rights to network resources. As with a group, you can grant users access to directories, files, shared printers, and so on, by associating the users with the organizational role object.
	Organizational Unit	A container object that represents a department or division of an organization or company.
	Print Queue	An object that represents a print queue, used to store print jobs that are waiting to be printed on a shared printer.
	Print Server	An object that represents a print server, which controls flow of print jobs from print queues to shared printers.
	Printer	An object that represents a shared printer.

Part

II

Ch

4

continues

Table 4.1   Continued

Object Icon	Object Name	Description
	Profile	An object that stores a login script (set of instructions automatically executed at login time) that you can assign to users.
	Template	A leaf object that is used to facilitate the creation of multiple leaf objects with similar characteristics.
	User	An object that represents a human being who logs in to, and uses, the network.
	Volume	An object that represents a disk volume installed in a NetWare file server.

Different object types have different sets of properties, depending on the object's purpose. The properties defined by the directory schema are designed to contain information that can be placed into four basic categories:

- Names
- Addresses
- Descriptions
- Memberships

Certain properties are designated (by an object class) as being mandatory. A value is required for these properties in order for the object to fulfill its basic function. All objects have a name property, which obviously is required to distinguish one object from another of the same type.

Many properties contain optional properties, though, that are frequently ignored by network administrators. Address information, for example, need not be limited to the network address that identifies specific computers on the network. You can also use the NDS database to store personal information about users, such as street addresses and phone numbers, serving almost as a human resources database, if desired.

When NDS objects represent pieces of equipment, such as servers and printers, adding values to properties describing the nature of the device and its location can often make life easier for everyone who uses the equipment. How many phone calls to the help desk could be saved if every user could tell which of the many printer objects in the tree is the color printer on the third floor?

Perhaps the most important information stored in the property fields of most objects concerns memberships, that is, a listing of each object's relationships with other objects. A user object, for example, contains properties that list the groups of which the user is a member, the files and directories to which the user has rights, and the other users with which he has a security equivalence, among other things. Conversely, a group object has a list of its members, and a volume object has a list of its trustees.

Many objects contain properties that are highly specialized, designed to hold data that is suitable only for the object's specific function. You will learn about the creation and use of the various object types throughout this book as you examine the specific networking processes with which they are concerned.

Understanding NDS Object Naming

Every object in the NDS tree must be given a name when you create it, but if you have an enormous NDS database with hundreds of servers and thousands of users in it, chances are you will have some duplication, such as two user objects called SmithJ. Fortunately, Novell Directory Services enables you to create two objects of the same name as long as the two objects are not located in the same container object.

N O T E Versions of NetWare prior to 4.11 enabled you to create objects of different types in the same container using the same name. However, NetWare 4.11 requires unique names for all objects in a given container, regardless of object type.

When there are two identically named objects in one NDS tree, there must also be a way of distinguishing them. NDS is capable of uniquely identifying any object, based on its context in the NDS tree. An object's *context* is simply its location in the tree expressed as a complete hierarchical listing of the containers that hold the object, extending all the way back to the [Root] object.

Part

II

Ch

4

Distinguished Names

Suppose that there are two User objects with the name SmithJ, one in the Accounting department, and one in Sales. To uniquely identify each of these users, you must use a complete NDS name, listing all of the containers in which the object resides. This is also known as the object's *distinguished name*, (DN). A distinguished name consists of the object name itself, followed by the name of the object's immediate container and then all of the other intermediate containers between the object and the root, in ascending order. Each object name is separated from the others by a period. Thus, the distinguished name of SmithJ in the Accounting department would be:

SmithJ.East Wing.Accounting.NY.CorpNet

This is easily differentiated from SmithJ in the Sales department, whose distinguished name would be:

SmithJ.Executive Wing.Sales.NY.CorpNet

The name of the user object alone is called a *relative distinguished name* (RDN), or a *partial name*. Objects in a distinguished name that are farther away from the [Root] object are said to be *less significant*; those closer to the [Root] are *more significant*. Thus, East Wing is the least significant container object in the distinguished name SmithJ.

TIP   It may seem odd to some users that an object's hierarchy in the NDS is expressed from least to most significant. This is the opposite of most file systems, which, for example, build a path name by specifying directories starting at the root and working their way down to a file name. It may be helpful to consider a complete NDS name as you would your street address, which is expressed in terms of your name, your house number, followed by the street name, the name of the town, the state, and ZIP Code.

The NDS Context

NetWare's NDS clients expand all object names into their full distinguished names before any communication is sent to the NetWare server. When you log in to your NDS tree by specifying your user object name and password, the client appends your current context to the object name before it is sent to the server.

Your context, which is specified in your client software (either in a NET.CFG file or a Windows Registry entry) is the full distinguished name of your user object, minus the actual leaf object name. The primary function of the context is to insulate users from the need to specify objects' long distinguished names whenever possible.

The context is also applied when users access network resources. If SmithJ wants to access a server or a printer that is located in the same container as his user object, he merely has to specify the name of the desired leaf object, and his default context is, again, automatically appended.

This is why you should make every effort, when designing your NDS tree, to locate User objects in the same container as the server and printer objects that the users access on a regular basis. The client's name context is used as the default whenever a user specifies any object name in an NDS-aware application.

Thus, SmithJ (in Accounting) would have `East Wing.Accounting.NY.CorpNet` listed in his client software as his default context. Logging in as simply SmithJ, he will never be confused with his colleague in Sales because his context is automatically sent along with his user object name.

Typeful and Typeless Names

There is another aspect of NDS notation that is included in a distinguished name. The DNs specified in the earlier examples have been *typeless* names, so called because they do not include the abbreviations for each object type. *Typeful* (or *typed*) names included an object type specification for each object listed in the name. The abbreviations used for NDS object types are as follows:

Object Type	Abbreviation
All leaf objects	CN (for *Common Name*)
Organizational unit	OU

Object Type	Abbreviation
Organization	O
Country	C

Therefore, the typeful version of the distinguished name SmithJ would be noted as follows:

```
CN=SmithJ.OU=Executive Wing.OU=Sales.OU=NY.O=CorpNet
```

Typeful distinguished names are always supplied to the NetWare server by an NDS client, but it is usually not necessary for the user to include the abbreviations when specifying the name of an object because the client uses a default typing rule to apply the abbreviations itself. In most cases, the defaults are correct.

The *default typing rule* states that, for any fully distinguished name supplied by a client, the least significant partial name will be a leaf object (causing the CN= abbreviation to be prepended to it), the most significant partial name will be an organization (O=), and all of the partial names in between will be organizational units (OU=).

The default typing rule works out very well, in most cases, but if you have country objects in your NDS tree, it may be necessary to identify them as such by adding the C= abbreviation to the country object in your distinguished names. If only one partial name out of a full DN is typed, then the default typing rule is applied only to the partial names that are typeless. This means that if you supply the following DN to an application:

```
SmithJ.Executive Wing.Sales.NY.C=US
```

the default typing rule will be applied to expand the name as follows:

```
CN=SmithJ.OU=Executive Wing.OU=Sales.OU=NY.C=US
```

The country object designation will not be modified by the application of the default types to the other names. However, the country object name will be tested to ensure that it is exactly two characters long. If it is not, the name will be rejected.

> **CAUTION**
>
> NDS clients do no checking of any kind to determine whether or not the types that they assign to particular names are correct. They will not, for example, check to see that there is indeed an OU called Sales before applying the OU= abbreviation to the name. If the types are incorrect, the name will be rejected by the server as nonexistent.

Context Qualifiers

When a name context is specified in the configuration of an NDS client, it is always appended to any partial name specified in a client application. It is up to the user to be aware of this fact, and to behave accordingly. Suppose that SmithJ wants to access a printer whose object is in another container. His computer specifies the following as his name context:

```
OU=East Wing.OU=Accounting.OU=NY.O=CorpNet
```

and he types the following as the path to the printer object:

```
laser4.North Wing
```

His client will end up sending the following DN to the server:

```
CN=laser4.OU=North Wing.OU=East Wing.OU=Accounting.OU=NY.O=CorpNet
```

This name will be rejected by the server as pointing to a nonexistent container because what SmithJ really wanted was for the `North Wing` container to replace the `East Wing` container, as follows:

```
CN=laser4.OU=North Wing.OU=Accounting.OU=NY.O=CorpNet
```

The only way to appropriately specify the name of the desired object, in this case (without typing out the entire name), is to use a context qualifier. A *context qualifier* is a means of instructing the client to append only a part of the name context to the given input.

The use of context qualifiers is never mandatory. They are just another convention designed to help users avoid typing long NDS names.

> **T I P**   Most Windows applications today enable you to use a point-and-click interface when it is necessary to supply the distinguished name of an NDS object. Once you have achieved a thorough understanding of the notation of NDS names, however, you may find it easier to type a qualified object name than to navigate the graphical interface, just as a veteran DOS user can accomplish certain tasks faster from the command line than through a GUI.

Using Trailing Periods   To use one type of context qualifier, you add one or more periods to the end of a partial name: each period represents one container that should be omitted from the context when it is added. Thus, in the example found in the preceding section, the way to correctly specify the location of the printer object would be:

```
laser4.North Wing.
```

The period after `North Wing` indicates that the first container (`East Wing`) should be left off the context when it is appended to the name. Two periods would cause both the `East Wing` and the `Accounting` containers to be omitted, resulting in the following path:

```
CN=laser4.OU=North Wing.OU=NY.O=CorpNet
```

This technique is also known as *trimmed masking*.

Using a Preceding Period   When you add a period in front of a partial name, the NDS client utilizes only the object type abbreviations from the context, replacing the names with those specified by the user. This type of context qualifier is often misunderstood because the name that you supply must account for every container level specified in the context.

For example, if a user called DoeJ had the name context in her NDS client configured as:

```
OU=Accounting.OU=NY.C=US
```

she could specify the location of an object in a different container by using the following name:

`.laser3.Sales.LA.US`

The preceding period would cause each container in her name to be given the object type abbreviation of the equivalent container in her context. Thus, the full distinguished name that the server would send to the client would be:

`CN=laser3.OU=Sales.OU=LA.C=US`

The three containers (`Sales`, `LA`, and `US`) are typed by the context qualifier, and the leaf object name is assigned the abbreviation `CN` by the default typing rule. Without the preceding period, all of the names would be typed by the default rule, and the `US` container would be mistakenly identified as an organization object instead of a country object. This is an important distinction, because even if the object name `US` is correct, the server will reject it if the object type is wrong.

This technique (which is known as *masking*) must be used carefully because the object types are applied to the name supplied by the user from right to left. This means that if DoeJ had specified only the name

`.laser3.Sales.LA`

(perhaps because both her context and the desired object had `US` as their most significant container), the `DN` sent to the server would appear as follows:

`OU=laser3.OU=Sales.C=LA`

The client does not check to see if this is a valid name (which it isn't), or even if it specifies a leaf object (which it doesn't). It is up to the server to reject this name by generating an error message to the client.

Understanding Bindery Context

The NDS context has thus far been treated solely as an element of a NetWare client configuration. However, the term context also has relevance on the NetWare server.

Although it is recommended that you use NDS clients on your NetWare 4.11 network, there are several reasons why you might use NetWare's bindery emulation feature. *Bindery emulation*, as the name implies, refers to the capability of NDS to support standard NetWare 2.x/3.x bindery logins.

You may be in a situation in which you have a large number of non-NDS client workstations, and the transition to NDS client software will take place over an extended period of time. These workstations would probably be running the NetWare Shell (NETX) on DOS or Windows 3.1 or the Microsoft Client for NetWare Networks on Windows 95 without the additional NDS support module.

You may even have clients that are running NDS-capable software, such as the NetWare DOS Requester (VLM) or one of the Client32s, but which are using bindery emulation until the machines can be reconfigured or the users trained.

N O T E   NDS-capable clients can force a bindery login by adding the /B switch to the LOGIN.EXE command (for the NetWare DOS Requester), or by marking the Bindery Connection check box in the Client32 Login dialog box.

When clients log in using bindery emulation, they (figuratively) log in to a server, not an NDS tree. However, because there is no bindery in NetWare 4.x, they are, in fact, logging in to a particular context of the NDS database as found on a NetWare server.

A bindery client cannot see the contents of the whole NDS tree. It is only capable of seeing and accessing the objects that are located in containers that have been specified as part of the bindery context.

The *bindery context*, as configured on a NetWare server, should mainly consist of the containers in which the server and print objects needed by the bindery clients are located. Unlike a workstation, which can only have a single context, a server can have up to sixteen containers specified as its bindery context. Multiple bindery contexts would typically be needed when bindery users require access to servers and printers found in various containers.

CAUTION

When setting multiple bindery contexts on a NetWare server, objects with duplicate names that are found in different contexts will conflict. Bindery users are able to access only the object found in the context listed first on the SET BINDERY CONTEXT command line. Objects with the same name located in subsequent contexts are ignored.

Setting a Server's Bindery Contexts

When you install a NetWare 4.11 server, by default it receives a master or read/write replica for the NDS partition that stores its directory tree context. It is essential that a replica containing the context used by bindery emulation clients be present on the server they use for their primary login. Because bindery emulation clients log in to a server and not a tree, they do not have access to any part of the NDS database that is not located on their login server.

During the NetWare installation process, the context in which the server object is created is set up to be that server's bindery context. You can change the bindery context and add bindery contexts by running the SET BINDERY CONTEXT command from the server console prompt or adding it to the server's STARTUP.NCF or AUTOEXEC.NCF file.

To set the server's bindery context to be Accounting.NY.CorpNet, type the following from the server console's system prompt:

```
SET BINDERY CONTEXT=.Accounting.NY.CorpNet
```

If you want to include multiple containers in the server's bindery context, specify each one in a single SET BINDERY CONTEXT command separated by semicolons (;). For example, to set the containers Accounting.NY.CorpNet, Sales.LA.CorpNet, and Paris.CorpNet as the bindery contexts of the server, enter the following command (on one line) from the server console:

```
SET BINDERY CONTEXT=Accounting.NY.CorpNet; Sales.LA.CorpNet; Paris.CorpNet
```

Remember that the server must have master or read/write replicas of the NDS partitions in which each of the specified containers are located.

Navigating the Tree

Context, to a Novell Directory Services user, is more than a static configuration parameter specified in your client software. Your context is your location at any given time in the NDS tree. This is somewhat comparable to an understanding of your default directory in DOS. When you want to run a program, you must take into account where the executable file is in relation to your current directory.

NDS, however, lacks an equivalent of the DOS PATH command. More often, you must specify a path to an object in another container using one of the notation methods covered in the "Understanding NDS Object Naming" section earlier in this chapter, or you must navigate your way through the tree to the proper context.

The following sections introduce you to the NDS—included with NetWare 4.11—that you can use to traverse the NDS tree and locate objects in other containers. As with most NetWare-related tasks, utilities are included with the operating system that enable you to use the DOS command prompt, the character-based, C-worthy interface, or a Windows GUI.

You will be called upon to use the techniques discussed in these sections many times in other chapters. These skills are basic to an understanding of NDS and to the administration of a NetWare 4.x enterprise network. Also, if you can pass along some conception of NDS to your users, they will be able to better make use of the network resources available to them without calling for help.

Using *CX*

CX is NetWare's command-line NDS navigation utility. Just as the DOS CD command works with directories, CX enables you to change your context to any other container in the tree. You can then reference any object in that container by specifying only its common name.

For example, if you wanted to use the NetWare CAPTURE command to direct your print output to a printer in another container, you would normally have to specify the full distinguished name of the printer object, as follows:

```
CAPTURE P=laser3.Sales.LA.CorpNet
```

If you used country objects in your tree—or some other construction that invalidated the default typing rule—you might even have to specify object types as well:

```
CAPTURE P=CN=laser3.OU=Sales.OU=LA.C=US
```

If, however, your current context was the same as that of the printer object, you could omit everything but the printer's common name from the command, as follows:

```
CAPTURE P=laser3
```

Because you are in the same context, you don't have to enter the complete directory name; CAPTURE assumes that the object you specified is in the same context. All NetWare 4.11 commands and utilities are designed so that you can easily use the objects in your current context.

Using CX is the best way to get a full understanding of how the NDS naming system works, and how context is used by the NetWare utilities. This is because a CX command is immediately processed by the NetWare client on your workstation, where the NDS name information you've entered is canonicalized and then sent to the NetWare server.

N O T E *Canonicalization* is the process by which an NDS name supplied by the user is expanded to a typeful, distinguished name using the workstation's current name context, the default typing rule, and any context qualifiers that may have been specified. ▨

When the server processes the canonical name sent by the client, it either allows the change of context or rejects the NDS name as invalid. The distinguished name that was sent to the server is then displayed at the workstation, either as the new context or as part of an error message. If you specify an incorrect name, therefore, you are immediately shown the results of your mistake and given the opportunity to try again. If you can use CX effectively, then the behavior of the other NDS utilities will be that much clearer.

Using *CX* to Learn Your Current Context   Running the CX command with no parameters displays your current position in the directory tree. If you're located at the root of the tree and type CX and press Enter, the command displays the following information:

```
[Root]
```

If your current context is Accounting.NY.CorpNet and you enter CX, the following context information is displayed:

```
Accounting.NY.CorpNet
```

Using *CX* to Specify a New Context   The most common use of CX is to modify your current context by specifying the name of a different container in the directory tree. If the new container can be found by moving downward from your current location in the tree, then you can just enter CX followed by the name of the container that you want as your new context. If, for example, your current context is the [Root] of the tree and you want to change it to Accounting.NY.CorpNet, then the following command is needed:

```
CX Accounting.NY.CorpNet
```

CX switches you to the context you specify and displays your new context.

The preceding example shows the new context as a typeless name because the default typing rule can be applied effectively to identify the objects. If you used country objects in your tree (or if you want to for any other reason), you can also use typeful names, causing the preceding command to look like this:

```
CX OU=Accounting.OU=NY.O=CorpNet
```

Using CX with Relative Context Specifiers   In the previous section, you changed your context from the [Root] to a different container. In effect, you supplied the full distinguished name of your desired context. In "The NDS Context" earlier in this chapter, however, you learned how the NetWare 4.11 clients append your current default context to any NDS name that you specify in an application.

The CX command is no exception to this. When you use CX to switch contexts from one container to another located farther down the same branch, you can simply specify the new container name relative to your current position in the tree.

In other words, if your current context is `Accounting.NY.CorpNet`, you can switch it to the `East Wing` container by using the following command:

```
CX East_Wing
```

This CX command works because your client software appends your current context to the command, as shown:

CX Command	**Current Context**	**Requested Context**
CX East_Wing +	Accounting.NY.CorpNet	= East_Wing.Accounting.NY.CorpNet

CAUTION

Like any DOS command-line program, CX interprets spaces as the divisions between command-line parameters. When you specify container names that have spaces in them, you must either enclose the entire NDS name in quotes, or substitute the underscore character for the spaces. Thus, CX `East_Wing` or CX `"East Wing"` will function properly, while CX `East Wing` will not.

As long as you are moving downward in the NDS tree hierarchy, the technique of specifying the new container name relative to your position is effective. If, however, you wanted to change your context to the `Sales.LA.CorpNet` container, none of the following commands would work correctly:

```
CX Sales
```

```
CX Sales.LA
```

```
CX Sales.LA.CorpNet
```

This is because, in each case, your current context would be appended to the partial name given, resulting in the following nonexistent containers:

```
Sales.Accounting.NY.CorpNet
```

```
Sales.LA.Accounting.NY.CorpNet
```

```
Sales.LA.CorpNet.Accounting.NY.CorpNet
```

You can prevent the CX command from adding your current context to your CX commands in two ways: with the use of a flag or by masking the name with a context qualifier. If you include the /R (for *root*) parameter in the command, CX treats the requested context as being relative to the [Root] of the directory tree. If you include the /R switch in the preceding examples, then CX Sales /R and CX Sales.LA /R will still result in an error because the contexts given do not exist off of the [Root], but CX Sales.LA.CorpNet /R will function properly because the full distinguished name of desired context is given.

You can get the same results as using the /R flag by masking the name with a context qualifier, as shown in "Context Qualifiers" earlier in this chapter. By preceding the specified context with a period, as in CX .Sales.LA.CorpNet, you get the same result as when you type CX Sales.LA.CorpNet /R because the object types from your current context are being applied to the name you have supplied, resulting in the following typeful name that is sent to the server:

OU=Sales.OU=LA.O=CorpNet

The CX Sales and CX Sales.LA examples will again fail, even with the preceding period, because the context qualifier causes the object types from the current context to be applied to the most significant name first. Thus, these names will be interpreted as O=Sales and OU=Sales.O=LA, respectively, neither of which are valid in this tree.

Using Periods to Move Up the Directory Tree By using the /R flag with the CX command or using a preceding period, you are in essence instructing your client software to travel up the tree all the way to the root in order to define a new context. You may, however, not want to move all the way to the top of the tree. You might just want to travel upwards a few levels on the same branch.

It is possible to move up a few levels without specifying an entire context from the root by using the other type of context qualifier: trimmed masking. This involves the use of periods to take the place of the containers immediately above the current context in the NDS hierarchy.

In its simplest form, you don't have to specify any container names at all with the trimmed masking technique. If you issue the CX command with a single period as a parameter, your context will be moved up one level in the tree. If your current context is:

East Wing.Accounting.NY.CorpNet

then the CX . command (don't forget the space) will change the context to:

Accounting.NY.CorpNet

In the same way, two periods (as in CX ..) will move your context up two levels to:

NY.CorpNet

What is actually happening here is that each period is causing the least significant name to be left out of the default context that is appended to the given NDS name. Because these commands supplied no name, the resulting canonicalized name sent to the server ends up being the context alone, minus one name for each period. Because of this, you can also use trimmed masking in combination with partial names. If, for example, your context name is

East Wing.Accounting.NY.CorpNet

then the command CX West_Wing. will be valid. This works because the current context is appended to the partial name given, minus the least significant container name, because of the period. The result is as follows:

CX Command	Adjusted Context		Requested Context
CX West_Wing +	(East_Wing.Accounting. ➡NY.CorpNet - East_Wing)	=	West_Wing.Accounting.NY.CorpNet

You can use as many trailing periods as you have levels in your NDS tree. In the previous example, it is not strictly necessary to travel all the way up to the [Root] of the tree to change the context from Accounting.NY.CorpNet to Sales.LA.CorpNet. Because both contexts are found within the CorpNet container, you can use the command CX Sales.LA. to prevent the Accounting and NY names from being appended, as follows:

CX Command	Adjusted Context		Requested Context
CX Sales.LA. +	(Accounting.NY.CorpNet ➡- Accounting.NY)	=	Sales.LA.CorpNet

Using *CX* to Display Directory Tree Information

Besides displaying your current context or switching to another context, CX can also be used to display the structure and contents of your NDS tree.

You can use the /T (for *tree*) parameter to view the tree structure of the container objects found below a given context. For example, the CX /T command displays the tree hierarchy beginning at your current default context, as shown in Figure 4.3.

FIG. 4.3
The /T switch causes the CX command to display a character-based representation of the NDS tree beneath the current context.

You can also display the tree structure starting with another context by specifying that context in the command. To see the directory structure of the entire NY container, issue the CX .NY.CorpNet /T command.

N O T E   Note that the same rules for specifying partial NDS names (the name of the user object alone) also apply when using CX with the /T parameter. Preceding and trailing periods, as well as the /R parameter, can all be used in combination with /T. ▪

By default, the /T parameter causes CX to display only container objects. To display both container and leaf objects, you must use the /A parameter along with /T. You also can combine the /T and /R parameters. To view the structure of the entire tree, starting with the root and including all objects, issue the CX /T/R/A command to produce a display like that shown in Figure 4.4.

FIG. 4.4
By using the CX /T/ R/A command, you can display the entire contents of your NDS tree in a hierarchical fashion.

To display a simple (non-hierarchical) list of the container objects in your immediate context, use the CX /CONT command. To view the container objects in another context, add the context name to your CX command before the /CONT parameter, as follows:

```
CX .Sales.LA.corpNet /CONT
```

Table 4.2 summarizes the options available for use with the CX command.

Table 4.2 CX Command Options

Option	Action
CX	Displays your current context.
CX context name	Switches you to the context you specify and adds your current context to the context you specify.
CX .context name	Switches you to the context you specify relative to the root of the directory tree.
CX context name	Switches you to the specified context, adding your current context minus its least significant name to the context you specify.
CX /R	Interprets the context you specify relative to the root of the directory tree; if you don't specify a context, the root context is used.
CX /T	Displays the directory tree starting with your current context or the context that you specify.
CX /CONT	Displays the container objects immediately below your current context or the context that you specify.
CX /T/A	Displays both container and leaf objects in your current context or in the context that you specify.

Option	Action
CX options /C	Displays the results of the given CX command in a continuously scrolling fashion.

 TIP You send a display of your entire directory tree to a file or a printer by redirecting the command as CX /T/A/R/C > DIRTREE.TXT or CX /T/A/R/C > LPT1.

Browsing the Tree with NETADMIN and PCONSOLE

Although the primary purpose of CX is to change a user's context, other NetWare utilities incorporate a context-changing mechanism into their interfaces. Such DOS utilities as NETADMIN and PCONSOLE, though menu-based, are not graphical, yet their primary function is to manipulate the properties of NDS objects.

It is therefore important for users to be able to change their current context within the utility in order to locate the required objects. NETADMIN and PCONSOLE are both utilities that are based on the C-worthy interface, an ASCII-based, mouseless, menu-driven standard since the early days of NetWare.

DOS, obviously, has been largely left behind in today's workplace, and Novell is now focusing its development efforts on NetWare Administrator and other Windows-based utilities. Programs like PCONSOLE and NETADMIN are still part of the NetWare package, but they no longer have the same capabilities as their Windows counterparts.

Using NETADMIN   NETADMIN, first introduced in the NetWare 4.0 release, started out as the DOS equivalent of NetWare Administrator. It can be used to create and delete most types of NDS objects and manage their properties. As the functionality of NDS and the NetWare Administrator utility was improved, however, it became impractical to implement all of the improvements into NETADMIN.

Although it is still a usable tool for standard NDS management tasks, NETADMIN lacks several of NetWare Administrator's important new features. For example, although the version of NETADMIN included in NetWare 4.11 can move and rename subtrees, it cannot manipulate multiple objects simultaneously or address two NDS trees at once, nor does it have the drag-and-drop capabilities that are native to a Windows-based program.

NETADMIN is also incapable of creating or manipulating the new object types created by extensions to the directory schema, such as the application objects created for use with the NetWare Application Launcher program.

Using PCONSOLE   PCONSOLE existed long before NetWare 4.0 was released. PCONSOLE has always been the control center for NetWare's printing architecture. When NDS was introduced, PCONSOLE was given a dual role. It can now function as a print maintenance utility in either bindery or NDS mode. The F4 key switches the menu structure between the two modes, enabling you to manage both NDS and bindery printers using the same program.

Part
II

Ch
4

Although NetWare Administrator has the same print object management capabilities as PCONSOLE, it also simplifies the process of creating print objects with its Print Services Quick Setup feature. The NetWare Distributed Print Services product, which is scheduled for release in version 2 of IntranetWare, eliminates the separate NDS objects devoted to printing and is also managed from NetWare Administrator.

Changing Context in the C-Worthy Interface The nature of NetWare's menu-based DOS utilities makes it impossible for them to display a graphical representation of the NDS tree. As with the DOS utilities that require navigation of the file system, such as FILER, you must change to the context (or directory) containing the items that you want to manage before you can manipulate their properties.

Both NETADMIN and PCONSOLE (in NDS mode) display your current context at the top of the screen at all times, and have a Change Context selection on their main options menus (see Figure 4.5). Selecting Manage Objects in NETADMIN or one of the print objects menu items in PCONSOLE displays a listing only of the objects found in the current context.

FIG. 4.5

Both the NETADMIN and PCONSOLE utilities display your current NDS context and enable you to change your current context.

To manage objects in another context, you must first select Change Context from the NETADMIN or PCONSOLE menu. When you do this, both utilities pop up an Enter Context box into which you can manually supply a new context, using any of the notation techniques covered in the "Using CX" section earlier in this chapter. All of the typing rules and context qualifiers that are used with CX are valid here, as they are from any NetWare prompt that requires the specification of an NDS name.

When you press Enter after specifying a context, the name you have entered is immediately canonicalized and sent to the server. If the object name is incorrect or does not exist, an error message is generated, and you are returned to the Enter Context prompt.

In this sense, therefore, these menu-based utilities function just as CX does on the command line. However, instead of typing in a new context, you can also elect to browse the NDS tree by pressing the Insert key at the Enter Context prompt.

N O T E   The technique used to browse the NDS tree in NETADMIN and PCONSOLE is very much like that used to browse the file system in other NetWare DOS-based utilities, such as FILER. See Chapter 13, "Using the Workstation Utilities," for more information on using the C-worthy interface.

Pressing the Insert key displays—in an Object, Class window—all of the container objects in your current context. The object name and its class are listed along with two objects representing the current context and its parent, as shown in Figure 4.6.

FIG. 4.6

You move about the NDS tree in NETADMIN and PCONSOLE by selecting an object from the display of your current context.

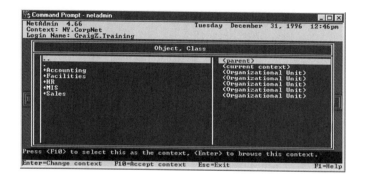

CAUTION

The navigational displays in NETADMIN and PCONSOLE are somewhat anomalous in that they use the standard DOS notation metaphor of one period (.) to represent the current context and two periods (..) to represent its parent, that is, the next highest level in the tree. Do not mistake these entries for references to the context qualifiers that call for the placement of periods either preceding or following an NDS name.

From the Object, Class display, you navigate the NDS tree by selecting one of the listed container objects to move downwards in the tree, or the (parent) object to move upwards. As you move about the tree, the display at the top of the screen changes to reflect your current context. Pressing the F10 key accepts the context shown, and returns you to the main menu where you can choose to modify the objects found in that context.

Obviously, the view of the NDS tree that is provided by the C-worthy interface is not as comprehensive or intuitive as that of a graphical utility that can show the actual tree structure of the database. A user that is relatively unfamiliar with the design and structure of the tree would probably be better served by using the NetWare Administrator utility. However, NETADMIN and PCONSOLE are not without their usefulness.

Many long-time NetWare users are very accustomed to the eccentricities of the C-worthy interface, and can manipulate the DOS utilities with remarkable speed. The responsiveness of such programs as PCONSOLE and NETADMIN is also generally faster than that of

Windows-based utilities, such as NetWare Administrator, if only because of their smaller size. For everyday maintenance activities, such as assigning trustee rights, managing print queues, and creating user objects, the DOS-based utilities remain a viable option.

Using NetWare Administrator

By virtue of its capability to display the entire contents of an NDS tree (or even of multiple trees) at the same time, NetWare Administrator lessens the importance of the context when it comes to maintaining the tree. Unlike NETADMIN or PCONSOLE, NetWare Administrator does not limit you to managing only the objects in your current context. You can highlight any object in the tree display at any time and access the Details dialog box to display and modify its properties.

Setting the NDS Browser Context   Strictly speaking, when you are using NetWare Administrator, your context is represented by the container object at the top of the tree display in the active window. This context is displayed in the title bar of that active window, which you can modify by selecting the Set Context option from the View menu.

The Set Context dialog box, as shown in Figure 4.7, enables you to specify a different context and even a different NDS tree, again using the standard NDS notation techniques. Buttons are also provided that enable you to select a tree from a listing of those found on the network and to browse the current tree for a new context.

FIG. 4.7
The Set Context dialog box enables you to specify both the tree and the container that you want to appear as the top level of the active browser window.

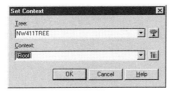

When you click the Browse Context button on the toolbar, you are presented with a Select Object dialog box, as shown in Figure 4.8. This is the standard browser dialog box that is used in NetWare Administrator whenever you are required to select an NDS object. The browser dialog boxes presented in various circumstances differ only in the object types that are listed and the context that is initially displayed.

In this case, the Select Object dialog box lists only the container objects and server volumes in your current context.

N O T E   The display of server volumes, in the case of the Change Context button on the Select Object dialog box, is provided presumably as a navigational aid to remind the user what volumes are located in each container. Selecting a volume object as your context is, of course, not possible and results in an error message. ▓

FIG. 4.8

NetWare Administrator's Select Object dialog box is shown whenever the user is called upon to specify the name of a particular NDS object.

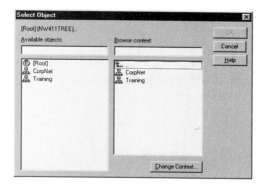

When the Select Object dialog box is displayed for other purposes, the available options may change. For example, when you select a user object on the tree and modify its properties in order to grant that user a new security equivalence, you will be presented with a Select Object dialog box that differs in two ways:

- It lists all of the object types to which the user can be made equivalent, not just containers.

- It begins by displaying the objects in the context where that user object is found, not the objects in your (the administrator's) current context.

Apart from the objects that are displayed and the starting point, however, the process of navigating the tree in the Select Object dialog box is always the same.

Using the Select Object Dialog Box   In the upper-left corner of the Select Object dialog box, the current context is displayed, which changes as you navigate the tree. The dialog box is split into two panes, labeled Available Objects and Browse Context.

When you are using the dialog box to select a new context for the main window display, these panes may be confusing because they both display the container objects found in the current context. When the Select Object dialog box is used for other purposes, these panes are more easily distinguished because the left side will usually contain both the container and leaf objects in the current context, while the right pane lists only containers.

In any case, you use the right pane to navigate the tree and the left pane to select the desired object. As with the NETADMIN context selector, the right pane of the Select Object dialog box uses two periods plus an arrow to designate the parent container of the current context, enabling you to move upwards in the tree. To move downwards, you select the name of one of the container objects shown in the left pane.

Another way in which confusion can arise when you are selecting a container object using the Select Object dialog box is that you do not want to navigate to the desired container in the right pane. The object of the exercise is to display the container that you want to select in the left pane. Therefore, you must actually navigate to the parent of the desired container in the right pane.

Part

II

Ch

4

In other words, if your current context is CorpNet and you want to change your context to Accounting.NY.CorpNet, it may seem natural to navigate all the way to the Accounting container in the right pane, as shown in Figure 4.9.

FIG. 4.9

Although it may seem to be correct, you cannot set a new context in the Select Object dialog box while displaying the contents of the desired container object.

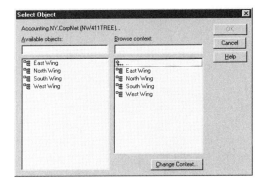

When you navigate to the desired context via the right pane, the context indicator in the dialog box says Accounting.NY.CorpNet, and it appears as though everything is going right. However, you then notice that the OK button is grayed out and that there is no way to actually save your changed context.

The reason the OK button is unavailable is that you have not actually selected an object in the left pane. When you attempt to do this, however, you see that the left pane lists only the objects that are contained in the Accounting.NY.CorpNet context.

In order to actually select the desired container, you must move upwards in the tree to the NY.CorpNet context so that the Accounting container is displayed in the left pane, as shown in Figure 4.10. You can then select the Accounting container in the left pane, which activates the OK button.

FIG. 4.10

In order to set your context to Accounting.NY. CorpNet, you must browse to the NY.CorpNet container and then select Accounting.

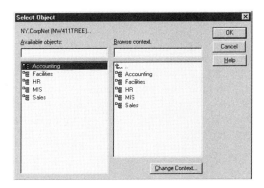

Once you select OK, the desired context is placed into the Set Context dialog box. Press OK in the Set Context dialog box, and your active NDS browser window is modified so that the new context appears at the root of the display.

 TIP You can change the context of your active browser window in NetWare Administrator to the next highest container by pressing the Backspace key or choosing View, Go Up a Level.

Summary

This chapter introduces several important concepts that are crucial to understanding Novell Directory Services and the role that it plays in the operation of a NetWare network. You must understand how NDS objects are named and their various notation conventions in order to efficiently administer them. In later chapters, as you learn to work with the NDS database and the tools used to manage it, you will apply these concepts again and again. ●

Part
II

Ch
4

Designing an NDS Strategy for the Enterprise

Now that you've learned something about the capabilities provided by Novell Directory Services, it is time to begin thinking about how you can put its power to work for your network. Designing an effective NDS tree for an enterprise network can be a deceptively difficult task. There are many different factors to consider, each of which will affect your design decisions to some degree.

Like many things, tree design is a matter of making compromises. You must balance the need for organizational integrity with the technical limitations of the product. You must balance ease of use against ease of maintenance, and performance against fault tolerance. An NDS tree is a constantly evolving entity, yet it often must have a rigid foundation that is permanent and immutable.

This chapter is not intended to scare you, or to intimidate you into thinking that NDS is incomprehensible. On the contrary, the intention behind it is to familiarize you with the process of designing a tree, provide a few basic guidelines, and warn you about the possible consequences of thoughtless actions. ■

Why a well-designed NDS tree is important

The decisions that you make when designing your NDS tree affect its future efficiency and usability for users and administrators alike.

Applying organizational paradigms to Novell Directory Services

In order to find objects easily, your NDS tree should be structured in a way that reflects the organization of your network or your company.

Building a balanced tree

A properly balanced NDS tree distributes objects evenly throughout its containers and forms a symmetrical structure that is easily expanded.

NDS performance considerations

The design of your NDS tree can have a profound effect on its performance. A well-structured tree provides faster logins and minimizes the network traffic created by NDS operations.

Sizing Up the Tree

The philosophy behind Novell Directory Services is to provide users with access to resources all over the enterprise, using a single login. NDS was designed to accommodate extremely large networks. Novell defines a "small" network as one with five or six servers and approximately 500 NDS objects in its tree. A large network, in comparison, could consist of hundreds of servers and many thousands of objects, spread around the world. Whether or not a single Directory can service such a vast collection of resources is solely dependent on the scheme by which it is organized.

Obviously, if you are running a single-server network with a handful of users, your design choices are limited. NDS, in that case, can be a convenient repository for information about your users, and provide you with a graphical interface with which to maintain the server. NDS on a single-server network, however, will perform roughly the same function as the NetWare 3.x bindery. In a case like this, a single container object is usually all that is called for, with all of the tree's objects within it.

A simple, single-branched NDS tree requires little effort to design. In fact, the NetWare installation program creates a tree just like this, as its default. As networks grow larger, however, NDS tree design becomes necessarily more complex, and it is important, if not crucial, to recognize that the task is not one to be taken lightly.

Every user on the network is impacted by the performance of the NDS database, including (most likely) the person who signs your paychecks. A tree that is designed haphazardly, organized clumsily, or improvised thoughtlessly will inconvenience everyone involved, in several different ways—first, when the network performs poorly, second, when you must take the time to reorganize the tree, and third, when everyone has to become familiar with the new arrangement.

An Evolving Design

This is not to say that an NDS tree is etched in stone. Quite the opposite is true. An effective tree design mutates constantly, reflecting changes in personnel, in technology, and in your organization itself. One always hopes that a network will grow, but in today's economy, that may not be the case, and you may find yourself condensing your tree.

Fortunately, the tools included in NetWare 4.11 make it easier than ever to modify your tree to suit the needs of your enterprise. NDS objects can now be renamed and moved, and even whole tree branches dragged and dropped to new locations. As you become more comfortable with NDS and its capabilities, you will be led almost instinctively to change design elements in ways that will make the NDS database easier to use or maintain.

You may also be forced to make major adjustments to compensate for sweeping changes in your network. Your firm might merge with another company, or open a new branch office, or move to a new location—all changes that can have a major effect on an NDS tree design.

In most cases, these design changes can be accommodated by NetWare, as well. You can merge one NDS tree into another, or create new branches at the highest level, but all of these tasks are infinitely easier if you have a good design.

Creating a Hybrid NDS Design

What is an NDS design? What is it based on? How can a design created for my network as it stands today account for an unpredictable future? These are questions that might run through your head as you sit in front of a blank sheet of paper, trying to design your NDS tree.

To begin with, the most useful bit of advice that you may ever receive regarding NDS database design is this: An efficient NDS tree should not be based on any single organizational framework that already exists in your enterprise. A NetWare Directory Services database should be a unique construction, based on its own set of requirements, limitations, and peculiarities. An effective NDS design will incorporate all of the following elements:

- A flowchart of your company's management organization
- A map of your office, building, or campus
- A network diagram

A good NDS design should not be composed of only one of these elements, but should be all of them at once—and more. For NDS to operate at its best, you should take organizational elements from all of the sources in the preceding list, and combine them to create a structure that is intuitive to its users, convenient for those who maintain it, and well-suited to the physical limitations of your network.

An efficient NDS tree design is therefore a hybrid of the bureaucratic, the geographic, and the logistic, combined into a whole that is greater than the sum of its parts.

Part
II

Ch
5

Getting Started

The process of designing an NDS tree is not necessarily one that begins seated before a blank sheet of paper. If you are intimately familiar with NDS and the tools used to maintain it, you might certainly be able to design a tree this way. However, the best way to learn about what works well, as far as Novell Directory Services is concerned, is to experiment. Whether or not you are able to do this depends on your situation, and that of your network.

If you are building a new network, installing NetWare 4 servers, and creating an infrastructure from scratch, you will very likely be able to arrange some time to experiment with NDS design elements before the network goes live. By doing this, you can familiarize yourself with such tools as NetWare Administrator, as well as the tasks involved in actually creating and locating objects on the tree. Unfortunately, you will be lacking the one thing necessary to make this a realistic scenario: traffic.

Until you have the opportunity to see how a particular NDS design functions under a full load of users doing real work, you will never know if it is completely suitable for use on your network. Some of the most important factors affecting your tree design will be finding out the way that certain arrangements simply perform better than others.

Novell Directory Services is a far more complex system than the NetWare 3.x bindery. It has superior capabilities, and as a result, it requires more processing time and more network traffic overhead. The flexibility of NDS also provides the network administrator with different methods of performing the same tasks. Learning which methods provide the best performance is often a trial-and-error process, because no two networks are ever exactly alike.

If you are upgrading a bindery-based NetWare network to NetWare 4 and NDS, you may want to consider a gradual migration. Some sites elect not to make use of NDS during their initial NetWare 4 rollout. Clients can log in using bindery emulation at first, giving the network support personnel time to come up-to-speed on the new features of the operating system. One department or workgroup at a time can then be converted to full NDS logins. A gradual rollout allows administrators to see the effects of their tree design decisions in a real-world environment, without jeopardizing the productivity of the entire enterprise.

N O T E   If you are upgrading bindery data to NDS, the DSMIGRATE utility included with NetWare 4.11 is an excellent tool for experimenting with various tree designs using your actual bindery data. Because nothing is actually written to NDS until after the design is completed, you can try any organizational principles you like, in complete safety. DSMIGRATE is launched from the Tools menu of NetWare Administrator. █

Ultimately, though, the time will come when you have to look at some of the basic tree design guidelines available here, and in other places, and just try something. The more you learn about how NDS works on your network, the better your tree will become.

Using Multiple Trees

One of the founding principles of Novell Directory Services was that there should be one database that encompasses all of the resources of a given enterprise. However, from the beginning, it was possible for multiple NDS trees to coexist on a single physical network. This was assumed to be necessary for situations where several discrete companies shared a single network cabling infrastructure, as in a prewired office building.

It soon became apparent, however, that new products are not always used in the exact way that their developers planned. Many cases began to develop in which a single enterprise had two or more NDS trees. Sometimes done by design, sometimes by mistake, very often multiple NDS trees were the result of a tendency toward renegade experimentalism that is often found in people who tinker with networks for a living.

Originally, it was possible to log in to only one NDS tree at a time. To access a server on another tree, you had to perform a bindery emulation attachment to that server alone. Now, however, the new NetWare Client32s for Windows 3.1, Windows 95, and Windows NT that are included with IntranetWare enable you to log in to, browse, and access resources on multiple NDS trees simultaneously. What's more, the new versions of NetWare Administrator enable you to manage multiple trees at once—even dragging and dropping objects from one tree to another (see Figure 5.1).

FIG. 5.1
NetWare Administrator can now display windows that open on different NDS trees.

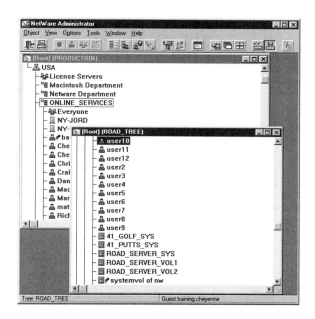

In other words, it could be said that the use of multiple trees on your enterprise network is now a valid design option. Depending on your company's business, you might want to create an R&D tree that is separate from the Production tree. Technical staff could then experiment freely, without affecting the rest of the company's network resources.

Another possibility would be to create separate but similarly designed trees at different locations, rather than maintaining a single, partitioned tree using WAN links. Many of the activities that can make NDS performance sluggish are related to partitions that must be maintained and replicated over slow wide-area connections.

Many enterprises maintain connections to their remote offices for the purposes of sending e-mail and providing access to central databases. Unless it is necessary for large numbers of users to have continuous access to NetWare resources at other sites, a single tree encompassing many remote locations may be wasteful and impractical.

Part
II

Ch
5

Naming Conventions

One of your main objectives in designing an NDS tree should be to enable users to locate objects easily. As you saw in Chapter 4, "Novell Directory Services (NDS) and NetWare Administrator," fully qualified NDS names can sometimes be quite long. Using and remembering them is all the more difficult when the objects themselves have obtuse and illogical names. Object names should, therefore, be somewhat descriptive of the objects they represent.

Many times, advice on the naming of NDS objects warns users to keep the names short as contexts sometimes have to be typed by users. To some extent, this is a valid point. But the GUI NDS clients that are now used on many workstations make name length less of an issue. Don't use cryptic acronyms and awkward abbreviations for device names just because they're short.

N O T E   Although GUI clients allow you more latitude, as far as name length is concerned, don't go overboard, either. Object names can be up to 64 characters in length, but that doesn't mean that you have to use all 64. Highly descriptive names, such as ACCOUNTING_SERVER_IN_THE_ CORNER_BY_THE_WINDOW, will most certainly not be appreciated by your users.

The most useful attribute that you can apply to object names is consistency. It is strongly recommended that, as part of your NDS tree design, you create a naming standards document that defines specific rules concerning how objects should be named.

For example, just deciding on a common format for user names can be a boon. If, when John Doe is hired, he suggests the user name JOHNNYD, how many times do you think he will have to tell people that his user name is not JOHN, or JOHNDOE, or JOHND? The simple practice of deciding that all user objects should be named with the first initial and then the first seven letters of the user's surname will save time and effort all over the enterprise, every day.

The same sort of intelligent decision should be applied to other object types also, such as servers and printers. The names that you assign to shared resources are most useful if they somehow identify what the object is, where it is, or who uses it.

For example, giving your printer objects names like PRINTER1 and PRINTER2 is less helpful than naming them MKTG-COLR, ACCT-WIDE, or other such descriptive designations. Even a new user will be able to determine that these names refer to the color printer in the Marketing department, and the wide-bed printer in Accounting.

N O T E   When it comes to servers, avoid the common practice of naming your machines after cartoon characters, TV shows, and the like. Not only are these names useless, telling you nothing about the system they represent, but they convey an unprofessional air that doesn't reflect well on you.

Another practice that can make your object names more usable is to avoid unusual characters, such as underscores (_) and tildes (~). Not only are these annoying to type, but they are difficult to say, as well. At least half of the time, you have to explain what character you are talking about.

As far as container objects are concerned, don't be afraid to incorporate your company's vernacular into your naming conventions. Every business develops its own jargon, whether it be acronyms, abbreviations, or nicknames. If QA is understood by everyone to refer to the Quality Assurance department, there is no reason to use anything else. The only exceptions to this would be names that are impermanent or derogatory in nature. You wouldn't want to name a workgroup's container object after its supervisor, for example, or call the legal department's container SHARKS.

NOTE Another consideration when naming objects is the prospect of merging NDS trees at a later date. With NetWare's DSMERGE utility, you can combine two NDS trees into one structure, but you will be unable to combine them if the NDS trees themselves or top level organization (or country) objects have duplicate names.

It is possible to rename objects before merging the trees, but this causes a disruption to your users' habits that is part of the reason for merging the trees in the first place. If you know that you will be merging trees at a future time, make sure that tree names and top-level object names are unique.

Naming conventions are particularly important when you have an NDS tree that is maintained by a number of different people. Everyone with the rights to modify the tree should be familiar with the design decisions that went into its creation. You should maintain a standards document containing a list of NDS design rules for your network, and make it available to all of your administrators. This document should include information like the following:

- Object naming standards
- Instructions regarding when, where, and how new branches should be created
- Where particular objects should be placed in relation to other related objects
- What detailed information should be included with each type of object

When the rules are in place from the very beginning, the tasks involved in maintaining the tree will go that much more smoothly.

NOTE Like all aspects of your network, don't forget to update the documentation on your NDS tree after making changes. Keep electronic copies handy, but don't forget to print copies for your disaster recovery procedures notebook.

Using Country Objects

Novell recommends that, in nearly all cases, a single organization object be created to contain all of the other objects directly off of the root of the NDS tree. This gives you the ability to specify global properties that will be applied to all of the objects later added to the tree.

The primary exception to the single organization object rule is when you elect to use country objects at the top level of your tree. The country object is exceptional in several ways. It can only be created directly off of the root, and its name can only be two characters long.

Obviously, the country object is intended for use in NDS trees that span international boundaries. Certain types of systems utilize a standardized set of country codes to locate users around the world. The X.500 standard created by the Consultative Committee for International Telegraphy and Telephony (CCITT), for example, contains two-letter country codes that are used to create e-mail directory names on global systems.

The NDS country object exists to provide compatibility with these X.500 systems. Its use, however, is not required. If your enterprise consists of networks in various countries connected by wide-area links, you do not have to use country objects unless you must maintain compatibility with one of the systems that use country codes.

In fact, the use of country objects is not recommended, unless absolutely necessary. There are certain applications that expect to find an organization object as the top-level container of a full NDS context name. When such an application is given a name with a country object at the highest level, it may function improperly. In cases like this, it will usually be necessary to supply a fully qualified typeful name. By explicitly indicating that the top-level container is a country name, the application should function properly.

Designing Around WAN Links

As mentioned earlier in "Creating a Hybrid NDS Design," the design of your tree will be influenced by the other organizational models used in your enterprise. At the very top of the tree, however, your primary consideration should be the communications capabilities of your network.

If your enterprise network uses WAN links to connect to other sites at speeds that are slower than your internal network, you must create a separate container unit for each site as high as possible in the NDS tree. Thus, if you are designing a tree for a company with three locations, you would typically begin your tree design by creating a single organization object at the top of the tree and then three organizational unit objects representing the three offices below that, as shown in Figure 5.2.

FIG. 5.2

The first rule of NDS tree design is to reflect your network's WAN links as high as possible in the tree hierarchy.

You want to create an NDS database that is distributed around the network in such a way that network users and their local resources are represented by objects in an NDS partition that is found on a server at their location. When users log in to the tree in order to access the servers in their own office, you don't want them to have to use the WAN link in order to do so. This would slow down the entire login process dramatically, and create needless traffic over the WAN connection.

To prevent logins across a WAN link, you would divide your NDS tree into partitions. Essentially, you are splitting the database into several pieces, and storing them on servers at your different locations. In the previous example, the three organizational units representing the company's three offices would each be a separate partition, stored at the office it represents.

When a user logs in to the tree, therefore, his own user object and his office's network resources are found in the local partition, and no WAN communication is necessary to perform the login. The user, however, is still able to access resources at the other locations, because this is still one NDS tree and one database.

WAN communications are obviously necessary to maintain the integrity of the NDS database when it is partitioned at separate sites, and these communications are usually the primary cause of slow NDS performance. The practice of partitioning the tree so that logins are at local servers minimizes the delays encountered by users as much as possible. For more information on creating NetWare Directory Services partitions and replicas, see Chapter 6, "Using NDS Manager."

Designing Around Partitions

WAN links are not the only reason to partition an NDS database. Even if you have a large network in a single location, it would be impractical to have all of your users accessing a single server for NDS communications. NDS is designed to support networks with thousands of users, and just as you would spread the user accounts across multiple NetWare server binderies in version 3.x, you want to divide the NDS into logical partitions and store them on various servers, in order to balance network traffic.

As with the WAN connections discussed earlier in "Designing Around WAN Links," the NDS tree design must reflect the boundaries between the partitions, but on a network at a single location, communications all run at the same speed (presumably), and the organization of the tree and the partitions is more arbitrary.

When you are considering how to partition your tree, network communications generally hold more weight than other organizational principles. You may want to consider creating a partition on each of the network segments that comprise your enterprise's internetwork, whether or not these segments reflect the company's departmental or geographical divisions.

Although the effects might not be as obvious as when you compare WAN links to local network connections, there are definite benefits to keeping network communications on a single segment whenever possible, rather than routing between networks.

Building the Tree

Once you have accounted for the restrictions imposed by your network's communications capabilities, you are free to complete the NDS tree design in the way that will best suit the people who use it. An NDS database must perform well in two distinct ways: Users must be

Part
II

Ch
5

able to access the network's resources, and network support personnel must be able to maintain the tree. Toward this end, you must decide what organizational principles make a tree design usable, convenient, and efficient for both your tree's users and those who maintain it.

For users of the tree:

- Access to frequently used network resources should be convenient.
- NDS objects should precisely identify network resources and indicate their physical location.
- Remote resources should be easy to locate in the tree.

For those who maintain the tree:

- Specific objects should be easily locatable in the NDS hierarchy.
- Users with similar access requirements should be placed in the same container whenever possible.
- Users should be placed in the same container as their most commonly used resources.
- Objects should be evenly distributed within containers.

To satisfy these requirements, examine the way that your users work together, and consider the organizational methods described in the following sections when designing your tree.

Geographical Divisions

To a certain extent, geographical divisions are a required element of NDS tree design, as you read earlier in this chapter (see "Designing Around WAN Links"). An enterprise network that is spread out over multiple sites will naturally be divided at the top of the NDS tree to reflect those sites. However, it is possible to continue to use geographic location as the basis of the tree's design at the lower levels.

A geographically designed tree consists of organizational units that correspond to the rooms, wings, floors, or buildings in which users and equipment are located. This is an arrangement that often lends itself particularly well to the creation of an NDS hierarchy. Organizational units representing floors contain objects representing wings or rooms in which the leaf objects are distributed, as shown in Figure 5.3

In many ways, the geographical method produces a logical and effective tree design. Tree navigation is not a problem; anyone who knows the physical layout of the office should be able to locate any object. Because people who work in the same area frequently require access to the same network resources, placing their user objects in the same container enables network administrators to assign access rights to the container object, rather than to multiple user objects.

FIG. 5.3
An NDS tree modeled along geographical guidelines can be an effective design.

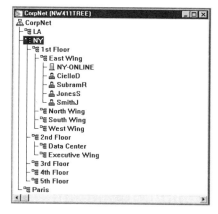

CAUTION

Whenever possible, assign access rights to multiple users through container objects, rather than creating group objects. Because group objects can consist of users from anywhere in the tree, the logic used to process their trustee assignments is much more complicated and time-consuming than that of container objects.

It also makes sense to place the objects that represent the resources needed by these users in the same container. This can introduce a problem, however, depending on how the enterprise or even the network itself is physically laid out. There may be a single server associated with a group of users whose object should logically be placed in the same container as the user objects. Very often, however, the server is located in a different place, such as a data center or server closet. The same can be true of printers in some cases.

For example, suppose you have customer service representatives occupying the east and south wings of the fourth floor. The customer service supervisors are located in the west wing of the fourth floor, and the VP of customer service is on the eighth floor in the executive wing. All of these users require access to the customer service database, located on one server in the basement data center.

If you are intent on maintaining the geographical design, this type of network layout will result in a tree with all of the servers in a single container, all of the VPs in another, and all of the workers in a third. This presents a number of organizational problems.

Locating all of the server objects in one container may or may not be a bad thing. When a user has to access files on a server belonging to another department, having all of the server objects in one place makes it very easy to find the files. However, it also can make it more inconvenient for users to access their own home servers. There are two possible solutions to dilemmas like these:

Part

II

Ch

5

- Break the geographical model, and locate objects in containers that don't necessarily reflect their physical locations.
- Retain the geographical model, and create alias objects in other containers, as needed.

Both of these techniques are more than just solutions to these particular problems. Consider them instead as tools that can be used to remedy all kinds of difficulties that can crop up in your tree design.

When it comes to actually creating and maintaining an NDS database, it is very likely that no one organizational model is going to provide the perfect solution to all of your design problems. Therefore, don't let your design be constrained by a particular model just because it looks good on paper.

Users don't particularly care where a server is physically located; they just want convenient access to its volumes. If you decide to place your server objects in the same containers as their users, that is fine, as long as you decide on one way of doing things and stick to it. Consistency of design is far more important than geographical accuracy.

The use of aliases is another good way of ensuring the proximity of server objects and user objects in your tree. Alias objects are simply reflections of other objects, created in order to enable one object to be in two places on the tree at once. If you locate all of your server objects in a single container representing your data center, you can make them readily available to their users by creating aliases in other containers throughout the tree.

An alias object would also be a good choice for the problem of the VP in the previous example. Because the VP is effectively isolated from the rest of the customer service department, the most efficient choice is to create an alias of the VP's user object, placing it in one of the customer service containers.

The geographical model can also be the source of additional work for the people maintaining the tree. One of the problems caused by this type of design is that adherence to the physical locations of people and equipment often causes tree modifications to be necessary, even when there is no change being made to users' resource requirements or access rights.

In other words, if the entire accounting department is moved from the west wing of the third floor to the north wing of the sixth floor, you will have to alter the tree to reflect the change, even though their computing environment is unaffected. This is a simple example, probably requiring only the renaming of a few container objects, but keeping up with all of the individual comings and goings of a large enterprise can be difficult.

Departmental Divisions

One way to avoid some of the tree maintenance tasks imposed by the geographical model is to take advantage of the divisions that have already been created to organize the management of your company or organization. A tree of this type would have a series of high-level organizational unit objects representing the company's basic departments, as shown in Figure 5.4.

FIG. 5.4
An NDS tree divided along departmental divisions can also be an effective design.

As with the geographical model, the departmental arrangement would naturally group users with their commonly used resources, and allow access rights to be applied effectively using container objects instead of individual users or group objects. A departmental tree arrangement would also be easy to navigate, and would require updates when users changed departments, but not when they moved to a new physical location.

N O T E NetWare Directory Services necessarily requires more regular maintenance than the NetWare 3.x bindery. Depending on the model by which the NDS tree is designed, this can require regular access to information not normally provided to network support personnel, such as departmental transfer notifications, relocation requests, and employees' personal information.

A departmental model would also eliminate the problems of the isolated VP and the remote server. A single container object representing the customer service department would contain the users, the supervisors, the VP, and the server.

The departmental model, however, would have to be violated almost immediately, in the case of a WAN-connected NDS tree. It is very likely that all of the sites that form an enterprise will have duplicate departments. The object representing each office may therefore have a container for the local sales department, marketing department, and so on.

It is possible to have objects of the same name in a single tree, as long as they are not located in the same container, but this could make locating a particular object difficult, if you did not know which office it was in.

Other Divisions

There are, of course, other organizational models that can be used to fashion an NDS tree design. Whether these are effective or not is highly dependent on the nature of the network and the enterprise that it serves.

Part
II
Ch
5

Some network administrators design their trees according to the wiring scheme of the network itself. They create containers representing network segments and insert objects representing the equipment that operates on those segments.

Such a physical tree scheme could work, but it is subject to two immediate problems that are good examples of things to avoid in any tree design. The first is the fact that although network administration personnel might be intimately familiar with the way that the company network is segmented, the average user almost certainly will not be. To them, the container object names will be meaningless, and navigation around the tree may be difficult.

The second problem of a tree design based on the physical wiring is related to the fact that user objects in an NDS tree represent people, not computers or desks. If an office is wired with a network connection to each desk that remains unchanged no matter who sits there, then it will be necessary at times to relocate user objects when people are moved around the office. This can cause changes in the tree that are largely unpredictable to anyone who is not familiar both with users' movements and with the network wiring diagram.

There are other types of organizational models that may be logical ways to organize personnel records or corporate organizational charts, but which would fail as NDS tree designs. Avoid creating containers based on artificial divisions that have nothing to do with the users' work habits or network requirements, such as alphabetical name listings or job titles. Placing users in the same container because their names begin with the same letter or because they are both vice presidents may seem to be organized, but the resulting trees will not perform well.

Constructing the Tree

Once you have decided on the model that you will use to design your tree, you can set about fashioning the hierarchy. Novell advocates the creation of what it calls a "balanced" tree: a structure that forms the basic shape of a cone, as shown in Figure 5.5.

FIG. 5.5

A balanced NDS tree design contains levels of containers that form a cone shape.

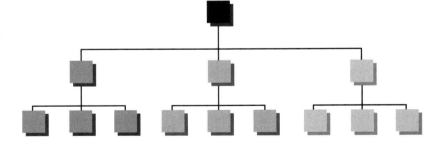

Having too many containers at the top level, or too many layers of containers, can cause a tree to perform badly, both in its usability and its speed. If the top level of your tree contains many objects, perhaps because your company has many sites or many departments, the tree will appear flat. To remedy this, add another layer of containers that logically group the sites into states or countries, for example.

Having too many vertical levels also makes the tree difficult to navigate, and lengthens the time needed to process rights that are inherited from upper-level containers. Once again, you should not feel that you have to duplicate your chosen organizational model to the point at which the NDS tree performs badly. Don't feel obliged to create dozens of container objects with only five or six users each, just because your company has created its workgroup assignments that way.

Once you have established the basic principles that you will use to construct your tree, you will find that the process of building it becomes rather easy. The final step is to document your decisions so that everyone who will perform maintenance tasks on the NDS database is aware of the design principles and naming conventions you have chosen.

Summary

Creating an effective NDS tree design can be a difficult task, particularly for a large enterprise network. If you stick to a few basic rules, however, you should be able to create a tree that functions adequately on your first attempt:

- Partition your tree at the top level according to wide area network connections.
- Place user objects in the same container as the objects they regularly use.
- Create a balanced, cone-shaped tree.
- Decide on an organizational structure and naming conventions for your tree and stick to them.
- Arrange your tree so that container objects can be used to assign trustee rights, rather than group objects.

Once you become accustomed to the way that NetWare Directory Services performs, you will probably think of ways to improve your design. You can later introduce your changes gradually, so as not to create too much disruption of service at one time. ●

Part

II

Ch

5

Using NDS Manager

In Chapter 5, "Designing an NDS Strategy for the Enterprise," you learned the basic concepts needed to create an effective NDS tree structure. However, one of the most important attributes of the NDS database on a multi-server network is its capability to be partitioned, that is, split into several pieces that are stored on different NetWare servers.

NDS partitions can also be replicated, so that multiple copies of each partition are scattered throughout the network. Creating an effective pattern of NDS partitions and replicas for your enterprise network is just as important as the tree design itself, for reasons of performance as well as fault tolerance. ■

How to plan the layout of partitions and replicas for your network

The distribution of partitions and replicas depends on the layout of your network.

How the partitioning of the NDS database affects your network

Splitting the NDS tree into partitions raises several important network maintenance and performance issues that you must understand to maintain a healthy database.

How to create partitions and replicas with the NDS maintenance utilities

NetWare 4.11 includes a new NDS Manager utility for Windows that enables you to create and maintain partitions and replicas all over your network from a workstation.

Understanding NDS Database Distribution

When you design an NDS tree, you are largely concerned with the creation of a logical structure that makes it easy for users and administrators to locate specific objects. The tree design itself does not directly affect NDS performance because all of the objects are stored as records in the database. The tree hierarchy exists only as properties of the objects.

If you have only one NetWare server on your network, obviously the entire NDS database is located on that one server. The NDS database is always stored on the server where you created the NDS tree during the NetWare installation process. If you proceed to add more servers to your network, the database is still stored on that original server's SYS volume.

On a small network with relatively few users, the negative effects of this arrangement may not be immediately apparent. However, on a network with many users, storing the NDS database on one server means that every user must access that server while logging in to the NDS tree, no matter how many other servers there are on the network. This can result in severe traffic problems that only increase as the network grows.

Suppose, for example, your enterprise network consists of three segments, with each segment having its own server and 50 workstations. Logic dictates that you arrange things so that the users on each segment store their data on the local server. Most of the network traffic is therefore isolated to the individual segments. If the NDS database is stored entirely on one server, then NDS traffic from all 150 workstations must be regularly sent to the segment on which that one server is located, as shown in Figure 6.1.

FIG. 6.1
A single NDS server is the focus of network traffic from all over the enterprise.

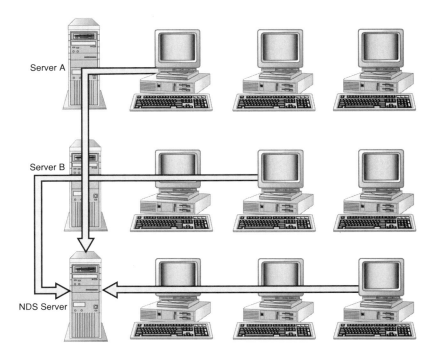

Server A

Server B

NDS Server

This concentration of traffic can denigrate the performance of every computer on the segment containing the NDS server. Worse than this, however, is the fact that this arrangement makes that one server a single point of failure for the entire NetWare network. If the NDS server goes down or is unavailable for any reason, then users cannot log in to the network at all.

Partitioning the Tree

As a solution to the traffic problem, you can split the NDS database into *partitions*, and store each partition on a different server. For the three-segment network described in the previous section, the clear solution is to create a partition for each of the network segments. Each partition should contain the objects representing the users and the server found on that segment, as shown in Figure 6.2. This way, the traffic generated by each workstation's NDS requests remains on the local network.

FIG. 6.2
Splitting the NDS database into three partitions balances the traffic across the three network segments.

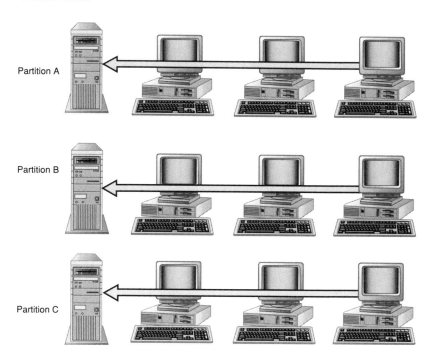

Partition A

Partition B

Partition C

Part
II
Ch
6

This arrangement makes NDS into a *distributed* database because discrete portions of the whole, located where they can do the most good, work together by communicating among themselves. To users, the NDS tree is a single entity because clients, servers, and the NWNET library cooperate. When a user whose object is in one partition requests access to a server in another partition, the communications between the two partitions are wholly transparent to the user.

You are not, of course, limited to three partitions, nor must each partition be stored on a different server. When one of your name servers is down, for example, you may end up with the master replicas of two partitions on the same server. By distributing the database around the enterprise, Novell Directory Services can support networks of almost unlimited size and complexity. You can place data where it is most likely to be needed, and expand the NDS tree as your network grows.

Replicating the Tree

Partitioning the directory database enables you to balance the traffic load generated by NDS functions and provides scalability for your network, but it does not resolve the problem fault tolerance. If a server containing an NDS partition goes down, then all of the resources represented by objects in that partition are cut off from the network.

Another problem that results from the partitioning of the database is caused by WAN links. Network segments that are connected by relatively slow wide-area links are a natural choice for partitioning. You can store the NDS objects for a remote office in a partition located on a server in that office.

The problem arises, however, when real-time communication between the partitions is needed. In the case of a network with many partitions at remote locations, simply displaying the full NDS tree in the NetWare Administrator utility could be an agonizingly slow process because of all the traffic traversing the slow WAN links at the same time.

Both of these problems are resolved by the capability to create replicas for each partition. A *replica* is an exact duplicate of a partition stored on another server. Whenever changes are made to the partition, those changes are applied to all of the partition's replicas. A partition can have multiple replicas, but each one must be stored on a different server. All of the replicas of a given partition are known collectively as a *replica ring* or a *replica list*.

There are four types of replicas:

- **Master replica**—The primary copy of the partition. Only the master replica can be used for partition management tasks, during which time all of the other replicas are locked.

- **Read/write replica**—Sometimes called a *secondary* replica, a read/write replica is a copy of a partition, the objects of which can be modified by NDS utilities, and used by clients for both authentication and login requests.

- **Read-only replica**—A protected copy of a partition that can be used for authentication purposes, but not login requests. A read-only replica can be updated only through the NDS synchronization process.

- **Subordinate reference replica**—When a partition is stored on a server, special replicas of its subordinate partitions are automatically created when those partitions are not replicating the same server.

  Subordinate reference replicas cannot be modified by users, and do not contain network resources in the traditional sense. Their function is to provide references to the locations of subordinate partitions, thus helping to bind the tree together. Adding a read/write or read-only replica of a subordinate partition to a server causes the subordinate reference replica to be deleted.

Read-only replicas are used much less often than read/write replicas because of their limited usefulness, but they do cut down on the amount of network traffic needed for the replica synchronization process.

Every NDS partition should have at least one replica, so that the failure of any one server cannot cripple the network. It is also sensible to create at least one replica of each partition at a remote location, if possible, so that a site-specific disaster, such as a fire or theft, cannot cause part of the tree to be lost.

It is also possible for each remote office represented in the NDS tree to have replicas of every partition, providing users at that location with local access to all of the objects in the entire tree. A NetWare client always accesses an NDS object from the nearest replica that can be located, making the proximity of replicas to their users an important aspect of NDS design. However, there is a tendency among some administrators using NDS for the first time to create too many replicas. It is not necessary for every NetWare server to have replicas of all of the NDS tree partitions, nor must every remote office necessarily have local replicas of the entire tree, if clients do not use them regularly.

The result of this practice can be excessive delays as NDS synchronizes the data on all of these replicas, as well as high network traffic levels, that are only compounded by slow WAN links. The recommended practice is to first create sufficient replicas for fault tolerance purposes, and then monitor the effect that they have on the NDS synchronization process, and on network performance in general.

Database Partitioning and Tree Design

The decisions regarding how you should partition and replicate your tree should be an integral part of the tree design process. You create a partition by selecting a container object from the tree. That container becomes the *partition root object*, and all of the other objects and subtrees in that container are permanently stored in that partition.

The partition root object contains information about the replicas of that partition that exist on the network, as well as the synchronization status of those replicas. A partition can be created from any container object in the tree.

A partition whose root object is higher up in the tree (that is, closer to the [Root] object) than that of another partition is said to be *superior*. The partition root object that is farther from the [Root] object is said to be *subordinate*. The most superior partition in any NDS tree is the one that contains the [Root] object itself, which is known as the *[Root] partition*.

N O T E   Do not confuse a partition root object with the [Root] of the NDS tree. Every partition has a root object (which is actually a Country, Organization, or Organizational Unit object), but there is only one [Root] in the tree. ▪

The first rule to observe when creating partitions is the same as that for creating your tree design: Use WAN boundaries as your highest level divisions. No user should have to traverse a WAN link in order to log in to the NDS tree. The users, servers, and other objects representing the network resources in each remote office should have their own partition.

Part

II

Ch

6

The number and location of the replicas of a remote office partition depend on the number of servers at the remote location, and the needs of the users. In a case where the users' computing activities are largely restricted to local resources, it can be a good idea to locate all of the necessary fault tolerance replicas on servers at the same remote site.

If, however, users regularly access services at other sites, such as when branch offices all access databases stored at the main office, it can be beneficial to create a replica of the partition containing the database servers at each branch site.

As you move downward through the tree, you should create partitions based on the number of objects in your subtrees, the proximity of users to the resources that they must access regularly, and your plans for expanding the network. Partitions that are too large (over 1,000 objects) slow down the replica synchronization process, while having many small partitions can be difficult to manage.

Fortunately, once you get beyond the boundaries imposed by WAN links, the partitioning of your network can be a trial and error process. Creating new partitions and combining existing ones is an easy process if you observe a few basic rules (see "Managing Partitions and Replicas" later in this chapter). You can then gauge the performance of NDS on your network and make adjustments, if necessary.

Walking the Tree

The NDS tree always appears as a unified entity to users, no matter how it is partitioned, but there are extensive activities behind the scenes that make this possible. Every NetWare server on which a partition replica is stored functions as a *name server,* that is, a representative of the entire NDS tree.

A name server can process NDS requests from any client, but a request may be for access to an object that is not stored in that particular name server. There is, therefore, an algorithm by which each name server can search the other name servers on the network for a replica containing the desired object. This process is called *walking the tree.*

When a name server fails to find a requested object in its replicas, it begins the search process with the partition immediately superior to it in the tree hierarchy. Every partition root object contains a list of references to the partitions that are immediately superior and subordinate to it. A client request for a specific object specifies the full distinguished name of that object. If the name server does not recognize the name of the desired object or any of its containers, it knows that it at least can supply the name of a partition that is closer to the [Root] object.

Obviously, any object in the tree can be found by beginning a search from the [Root], but that is also the least efficient method. The purpose of walking the tree is to move upward in the tree hierarchy only as far as is necessary to locate a name server that contains the desired object in one if its replicas. Eventually, as the request is passed upward to the name servers in superior partitions, one of the containers in the name of the requested object is found, and the distinguished name is then used to trace the path downward to the object itself.

Suppose, for example, that name server B (see Figure 6.3) receives a request for access to a print queue called Q3.Marketing.NY.CorpNet. Server B contains only the Sales partition, and knows nothing about the Marketing partition, or the NY or CorpNet containers. Server B therefore passes the request to Server A, the name server of the partition immediately superior to it. Server A searches its own partition and discovers that it does not contain the Marketing object either, but it does contain the NY object.

Because of this, Server A knows that the request does not have to travel any higher in the tree because the Marketing object must be located in one of the partitions subordinate to the NY partition. Server A then passes the request to Server C, which does contain the Marketing partition. Here, the Marketing container is found, and subsequently, the Q3 object.

FIG. 6.3
Walking the tree is the process by which partitions are systematically searched for a requested object.

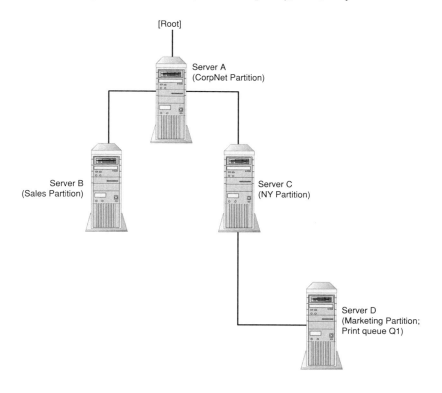

By walking the tree, the request for a particular object takes a more direct route to its destination than a full search from the [Root]. On a large network, a full search could involve extensive delays as the request traverses multiple WAN links unnecessarily because the desired object is actually stored at the local site.

Understanding NDS Synchronization

Distributing the NDS database around the enterprise provides many benefits, but it also causes many problems. Chief among these is the need to propagate changes that are made to NDS objects to other name servers. If, for example, a user calls a network administrator and requests access to a particular server volume, the administrator might use the NetWare Administrator utility to make the user a trustee of that server, and expect the job to be done.

For the administrator, the job is done, but not for NDS. It may be the case that the administrator's changes were applied to the master replica of the partition containing the server object, while the user's workstation is accessing that server object from a read/write replica of that same partition. To address this problem, NDS performs a periodic process in which the replicas of a partition are compared, and any changes that have been made are propagated throughout the replica ring. This process is called *synchronization*.

Clearly, the process of updating all of a partition's replicas with the changes made by administrators is not one that can be deferred until a nightly update procedure. However, neither are the changes made in real time. NDS is said to be a *loosely synchronized* database because it is possible for two replicas of the same partition to supply different information for certain periods of time.

NDS is designed to accommodate many more read operations than writes. Every partition on the network undergoes a periodic synchronization of all of its replicas (called a *convergence*), but a significant amount of network traffic overhead is saved by not performing these operations continuously.

A fully synchronized NDS tree is one in which all of the replicas of every partition are exact duplicates. There may be periods during the update process when replicas are out of synch, but these are kept as brief as possible. When an administrator makes a change to a partition, the synchronization process is scheduled to begin ten seconds later. Each replica is updated in turn, which is one of the reasons why too many replicas can slow down NDS operations.

When a partition has several read/write replicas, changes can be made to different replicas by different users. This means that all of the changes made on each replica must be propagated to all of the other replicas, which complicates the process considerably.

Understanding Time Synchronization

The distributed nature of the NDS database and the unavoidable convergence delays caused by the synchronization process present another significant problem. It is entirely possible for two network administrators to modify the properties of the same NDS object in two different replicas. Depending on the type of changes the administrators make, the order in which those modifications are applied to the object can be crucial. The same is true of sequential changes made to a single object in one replica. The modifications must be propagated to the other replicas in the proper order for the replicas to be identical.

To ensure that NDS events are processed in sequence, each modification receives a *time stamp* that uniquely identifies the event, and the time that it occurred. The process by which each of a partition's replicas is synchronized is governed by the time stamps affixed to the changes found in each replica. In other words, as changes are propagated to replicas around the network, the changes are applied in the order indicated by their time stamps. If a user deletes an object from the master replica at 9:54:05 and another user makes changes to the same object in another replica at 9:54:08, then the object will be gone when all of the replicas are synchronized and the second user's changes discarded.

In order for the time stamps to be functional, however, each name server on the network must keep the exact same time. This task is complicated by two factors: the fact that servers can be located in different time zones with different daylight saving time habits, and the notorious inaccuracy of the hardware clocks in computers.

NetWare includes a program called TIMESYNC.NLM that synchronizes the time on all of the servers that run it. Each server maintains a UTC (universal time coordinated, also known as Greenwich mean time) time setting that is periodically checked against the other servers on the network using SAP (Service Advertising Protocol) communications.

▶ **See** "Service Advertising Protocol (SAP)," **p. 243**

Server Time Settings   When you install a NetWare 4.x server onto your network, you supply the information needed to initiate the time synchronization process. First, you specify the time zone in which the server is located, the number of hours difference between local time and UTC time, and the daylight saving time settings for the local area. The installation program uses this information to create several SET commands in the server's AUTOEXEC.NCF file, as in the following example, which is used in the eastern United States time zone:

```
SET TIME ZONE = EST5EDT
SET DAYLIGHT SAVINGS TIME OFFSET = 1
SET START OF DAYLIGHT SAVINGS TIME = (APRIL SUNDAY FIRST  2:00:00 AM)
SET END OF DAYLIGHT SAVINGS TIME = (OCTOBER SUNDAY LAST  2:00:00 AM)
SET DEFAULT TIME SERVER TYPE = REFERENCE
```

The first SET command supplies the abbreviations used for the local time zones, and specifies the five hour difference between the eastern U.S. and UTC time. This value is always expressed in terms of how many hours must be added to the local time to make it equivalent to UTC time. Continental European sites, for example, would specify negative numbers.

The daylight saving time commands specify the one hour difference between standard and daylight time, and provide the formula with which the beginning and end of DST are calculated.

The final command specifies how the server should interact with the other servers on the network when synchronizing time. NetWare defines four different types of time servers. Creating an efficient time synchronization strategy for your network by selecting the correct time server type for each of your servers is an important aspect of the NetWare installation process. The four time server types are as follows:

- **Secondary**—A secondary time server periodically requests a time signal from a primary or reference server and adjusts itself to the time provided.
- **Primary**—A primary time server participates in a process by which the average time of all of the primary and reference servers on the network is computed, and adjusts its clock accordingly.

Part II
Ch 6

- **Reference**—A reference time server is understood to be connected to an external device that provides an accurate time setting. It participates in the computation of the average server time, but unlike a primary server, it never adjusts its clock.

- **Single reference**—A single reference time server is used on a network where there is only one time server. It does not require any communication with other time servers.

On a medium- or large-size network, most of the servers should be secondary time servers. When a secondary server receives a time signal from a primary or reference server, it adjusts its clock to compensate for 100 percent of the time discrepancy. A computer's clock usually generates a hardware interrupt approximately every 55 milliseconds, or 18.18 times per second. TIMESYNC.NLM adjusts the clock's time by modifying the frequency of these interrupts to match the time signal.

A primary time server participates in the determination of the correct time for the network, which a secondary time server does not. When a primary server determines that an adjustment to its clock is needed, it compensates for only 50 percent of the discrepancy, instead of the secondary server's 100 percent. The primary server does this to prevent a condition known as *oscillation*, in which two time servers each attempt to correct themselves by the same amount at the same time, resulting in the same discrepancy.

A reference time server functions identically to a primary server, except that it never adjusts its clock. Because its time is assumed to be correct, due to the use of an external radio clock or modem as a time reference, its participation in the calculation of the average server time will eventually bring the other primary servers into synch with it.

It is not essential that you have a reference server on your network because for the purposes of NDS, it is not even essential that the network time be correct. The only thing that matters is that the time is synchronized. If you have more than one reference server, however, it is crucial that both utilize an external time signal that is absolutely accurate. If you have two reference servers with a time discrepancy between them, your network time can never be synchronized because the reference servers do not adjust themselves.

N O T E   Reference servers typically use a radio clock or a modem to acquire time signals from an atomic clock, such as that housed at the U.S. Naval Observatory. You can purchase third-party software and hardware products that enable a NetWare server to function as a reference server using these signals.

A single reference server, unlike the other three types, requires no communication with other time servers at all. This makes it usable on a single server network where there is no need for synchronization.

Planning Network Time Synchronization   The downside to the time synchronization process, not surprisingly, is network traffic. If you have a network with 100 servers, you can make them all primary time servers, but the amount of bandwidth devoted to time-related SAP communications can be significant. On the other hand, creating 99 secondary servers and one primary or reference server would not be advisable either because the failure of the primary server would leave the secondary servers without a time signal to which they can synchronize.

You should therefore have several primary time servers on a large network, for fault tolerance purposes, and make all of your other NetWare servers secondary time servers. As far as reference time servers are concerned, NDS does not require any at all. The primary purpose of time synchronization in NetWare is to ensure that all servers keep the same time; whether or not the time is actually correct is irrelevant.

Some client/server applications, however, may require that the network time be exactly correct, in order to work together with other systems or keep accurate transaction records. In these cases, a reference server is required because PC clocks themselves are often extremely inaccurate.

> **CAUTION**
>
> Manually correcting the time on your network is more than a matter of using the `SET TIME` command on the server console, as it was in NetWare 3.x. Resetting the time on a secondary time server is obviously useless because its time is derived from another source. Resetting the time on a primary server is also ineffective because its time reflects an average of all of the primary and reference servers. The time should instead be reset on a reference server, and you must be sure to unload TIMESYNC.NLM before modifying the time on the server clock. Otherwise, the discrepancy between the server clock's time and the network time will cause errors until synchronization is once again achieved.

Configuring a customized time synchronization strategy can be as easy as specifying the appropriate type of time server during the server installation process. You can also change the time server type by modifying the `SET DEFAULT TIME SERVER TYPE` command in the AUTOEXEC.NCF file.

The values for the other time-related `SET` commands are stored in a text file called TIMESYNC.CFG in the server's SYS:SYSTEM directory. You modify this file directly to permanently change time configuration parameters, as simply executing the equivalent `SET` commands affects only the current session.

NetWare considers the default time synchronization configuration to consist of one single reference time server, with all of the other servers as secondary servers. This can be a problem because of fault tolerance. If you elect to use multiple primary or reference servers, you can use the TIMESYNC.CFG file to exercise greater control over which primary or reference servers are used by each secondary server as a time source.

This technique can eliminate the use of SAP communications for time synchronization purposes entirely, thus reducing the broadcast traffic on your network. However, you must configure the TIMESYNC.CFG settings for every server, after determining which time source is the best for each secondary server.

The TIMESYNC.CFG commands used to customize the time synchronization communications properties are as follows:

```
Type = timeservertype
Service Advertising = OFF
```

```
Configured Sources = ON
Time Source = server1
Time Source = server2
Time Source = server3
```

The `Time Source` parameters should specify the names of the servers to be contacted for time signals, in order of preference.

Managing Partitions and Replicas

The new Windows clients that ship with IntranetWare include a new GUI utility called NDS Manager. This application provides a complete set of tools for creating NDS partitions and replicas, as well as diagnosing and repairing problems in the NDS database. NDS Manager can run as a stand-alone application, or it can be launched from the Tools menu of NetWare Administrator.

 T I P   To run NDS Manager from Tools menu of the NetWare Administrator, you must either modify the NWADMN3X.INI file (for Windows 3.1) to include the following section:

```
[Snapin Object DLLs WIN3X]
NDSMGR = NMSNAP16.DLL
```

or modify the Windows 95 Registry by selecting the Snapin Object DLLs *WIN95* key in HKEY_CURRENT_USER\Software\NetWare\Parameters\NetWare Administrator and creating a new string value called NDSMGR with NMSNAP32.DLL as the value data.

In previous versions of NetWare, you used a C-worthy utility called Partition Manager (PARTMGR.EXE) from the DOS prompt to create partitions and replicas. Partition Manager is still included with NetWare, but NDS Manager includes functionality that its DOS counterpart lacks, such as the following:

- The capability to repair the NDS database from a workstation. In previous versions of NetWare, you had to run the DSREPAIR program from the server console prompt or an RCONSOLE session to repair the tree.
- The capability to print partition and replica information.
- The capability to update the version of Novell Directory Services running on your network servers by replacing the DS.NLM module.
- The capability to check the current synchronization status of a partition's replicas.

You can still run DSREPAIR.NLM at the server, however, as well as DSMERGE, which enables you to combine two NDS trees into one, and DSTRACE, with which you can monitor NDS communications activities.

Creating Partitions

When you run NDS Manager, you can display your NDS tree's partitions and replicas in two different ways: the Tree view and the Partitions and Servers view. The Tree view (see Figure

6.4) provides an expandable display of the containers and servers in your NDS tree on the left side of the screen. Selecting a container that is the root object of a partition displays a list of the partition's replicas on the right, and the servers where they are located. Selecting a server displays all of the replicas stored on that server.

FIG. 6.4

NDS Manager's tree view enables you to browse the NDS tree and display the partition replicas.

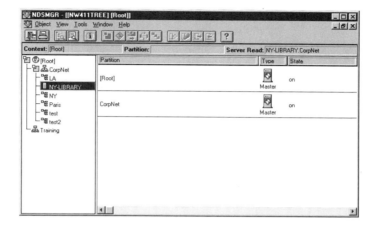

As with the NetWare Administrator program, you set a context in NDS Manager in order to work with only a portion of the NDS tree at a time. This way, it is possible to delegate the NDS maintenance activities among several administrators. However, as with the development of the conventions by which your tree is designed, you should establish policies to be observed by all administrators governing the use of NDS Manager and the creation of partitions and replicas.

N O T E The capability to set a context in NDS Manager also enables you to work on multiple NDS trees from any workstation on the network. ▦

You use the Tree view to create a new partition by selecting a container object from the tree and selecting Create Partition from the Object menu. As with most Windows utilities, you can also use the button bar, a pop-up context menu, or a hotkey to perform nearly all functions.

You can also use the Partition Manager utility to create a new partition in roughly the same way, by selecting a container object using the standard keystrokes of the NetWare C-worthy utilities, as shown in Figure 6.5.

Creating Replicas

Although you can only create new partitions from NDS Manager's Tree display, you can perform most other functions from either view. The Partitions and Servers view splits the screen into two lists (see Figure 6.6). The top half displays the containers that are partition root objects. When you select a partition, the servers on which its replicas are stored are shown on the right.

Part

II

Ch

6

FIG. 6.5

To create a partition using PARTMGR, select a container object from the NDS Object, Class display.

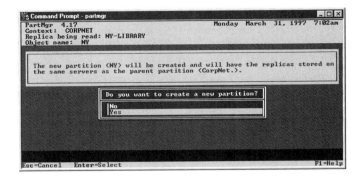

FIG. 6.6

The Partitions and Servers view enables you to see the replicas associated with a container object or a server.

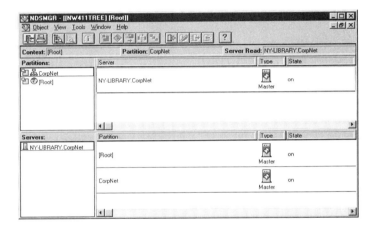

The bottom of the screen displays a list of the servers on which partitions and replicas are stored. Selecting a server name displays all of the replicas on that server. These displays are, therefore, simply different ways of looking at the same information. Which one you use depends on whether you are concerned with the distribution of a partition's replicas, or the condition of a particular server.

You can create a new replica by selecting any partition in either view, choosing Add Replica from the Object menu, and browsing for a server name. You can choose whether to create a read/write or read-only replica, but only one replica of any partition can be created on a single server.

Manipulating Partitions and Replicas

NDS Manager also enables you to manipulate partitions and replicas in other ways by selecting the desired item from one of the view screens and choosing from the following functions:

■ **Merge Partition**—Merging a partition is essentially the process by which a separate partition is deleted. Because the NDS data cannot actually be erased, it is merged into the parent partition, that is, the next highest partition in the tree.

- **Move Partition**—Moving a partition is the same as moving a branch of the NDS tree to another context. All of the container and leaf objects in the partition are moved to the new location. However, you cannot move a partition in this way if it has subordinate partitions in the subtree. An option is provided that lets you create an alias of the partition root object in the old location, using the same object name. This way, any references to that object remain valid.

- **Delete Replica**—Replicas can be deleted at will, with the exception of the master replica, which must remain intact.

- **Change Replica Type**—With two exceptions, you can change any replica to another type (master, read/write, or read-only). You cannot directly change a master replica to another type, but you can change a read/write or read-only replica to the master replica. The old master is then reduced to a read/write replica. Subordinate reference replicas cannot be changed in this way. To place a replica on a server that currently contains a subordinate reference replica, use the Add Replica command.

You can also perform these functions (with the exception of Move Partition) using the Partition Manager utility.

Controlling NDS Management Operations

The acts of creating, deleting, or manipulating partitions and replicas using NDS Manager may seem momentary, but the application actually begins processes that can take a long time, depending on the size and configuration of your NDS tree. The most important rule to observe when you are working with partitions and replicas is to be patient, and wait until an entire operation is completed and all of the replicas synchronized before performing the next task.

The operations that are particularly complex and time-consuming are the creation and merging of partitions. These involve large numbers of changes that must be synchronized among all of the replicas involved. Before performing these operations, be sure that the NDS database is fully synchronized, and that all of the servers involved are operational and available.

You can quickly determine the synchronization status of your partitions by selecting the Check Synchronization command from NDS Manager's Object menu. This command scans the NDS tree for ongoing synchronization activities, and displays a dialog box like that shown in Figure 6.7.

Part

II

Ch

6

FIG. 6.7
The Check Synchronization command enables you to quickly ascertain the status of your network's NDS synchronization activities from a workstation, as well as display information about each partition.

To monitor the current operations involved in the synchronization process in real time, you can activate the DSTRACE screen at the server console prompt with the synchronization option by issuing the following two commands:

```
SET DSTRACE = ON
SET DSTRACE = +SYNC
```

These commands cause a Directory Services screen to be added to the server console. On this screen, look for messages indicating that each partition has been successfully synchronized, like the following:

```
(97/03/17 04:45:43)
SYNC: Start sync of partition <[Root]> state:[0] type:[0]
SYNC: SkulkPartition for <[Root]> succeeded
SYNC: End sync of partition <[Root]> All processed = YES.
```

CAUTION

Although you can safely leave the DSTRACE screen activated on your server, it is not recommended that you leave the +SYNC option activated for long periods of time, as it uses a significant amount of CPU resources to update the console display. You disable the option by issuing the SET DSTRACE = -SYNC command at the server console prompt.

Another issue that is important to the maintenance of a healthy and efficient NDS database is the hardware capabilities of your servers. You have read in this chapter about the effect of NDS on your network's communications traffic, but the many background processes performed by the directory also take their toll on servers' processor, cache, and disk I/O resources.

It is therefore recommended that your server hardware be up to the tasks required of it. Sufficient memory, fast processors, and efficient disk drives all contribute to the speed and efficiency of partition management and replica synchronization activities. In a distributed environment, your NDS performance can only be as good as your weakest server. One under-powered computer can drag down the NDS performance of many fast machines.

Upgrading and Repairing NDS

Although the Partition Manager utility enables you to perform basic NDS functions, such as the creation of partitions and replicas, NDS Manager has many additional capabilities. Such operations as directory service updates and repairs formerly had to be performed from individual server consoles or RCONSOLE sessions. These functions can now be performed for any server on the network from a workstation running NDS Manager.

Installing NDS Upgrades

Another important element of the NDS infrastructure is the DS.NLM module that controls the revision of the NDS software on each name server. You can view the NDS version used by each of your partitions with NDS Manager by selecting a container object and choosing the appropriate commands from the Object menu to display a dialog box like that shown in Figure 6.8.

FIG. 6.8

The NDS version displayed for each partition in the tree depends on the DS.NLM module running on the servers where the partition's replicas are stored.

Novell periodically releases upgrades to the DS.NLM file, and it is important to make sure that if you install an updated version, you install it to all of the name servers on your network. To do this, however, you do not have to install the module to each server individually. You can use NDS Manager's NDS Version Update feature, which enables you to propagate DS.NLM from one server to any number of others.

When you select a server in either the Tree or Partitions and Servers view, the NDS Version/ Update command is activated in NDS Manager's Object menu. In the NDS Version Update dialog box (see Figure 6.9), you can see the DS.NLM version of the selected server and a list of all the other servers on the network. You can select any or all of the servers as targets for an upgrade, or have the program scan for all servers with older versions and automatically upgrade them.

FIG. 6.9

The NDS Version Upgrade feature enables you to deploy a new DS.NLM module to all of the servers on your network in one step.

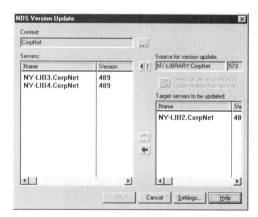

Part

II

Ch

6

Repairing the NDS Database

In addition to its other functions, NDS Manager includes database repair features that had previously been available only in the DSREPAIR program, which runs on the server console. To repair the entire NDS database with DSREPAIR, you must run the program on each server that contains replicas, either by traveling to the server console or opening a separate RCONSOLE session. With NDS Manager, you can initiate repair procedures on any partition and all of its replicas from the same workstation.

To perform repairs with NDS Manager, you select a partition in either one of the two standard views and open the Partition Continuity window from the Object menu (see Figure 6.10). Each row in this window represents a server on which one or more replicas of the selected partition is stored, and displays that server's view of the replicas stored throughout the enterprise.

FIG. 6.10

From the Partition Continuity window, select the replica that you want to repair.

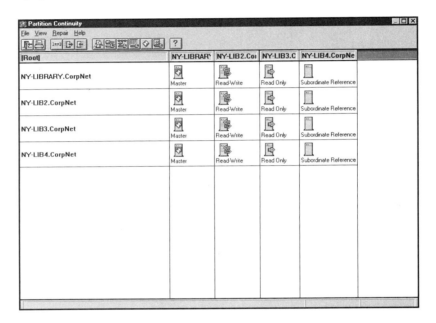

Under normal conditions, the display in the Partition Continuity window may seem redundant because each row contains icons representing the same replicas. However, when problems occur, it is valuable to have the list of replicas as it is maintained by each name server. Database damage could cause a server to lose track of one of the partition's replicas, and this display lets you see whether or not each server is aware of all of the replicas.

Each of the partition's replicas is represented by an icon that indicates the type of replica (master, read/write, read-only, or subordinate reference). When you open the Partition Continuity window, the replicas of the chosen partition are scanned by NDS Manager, and if a synchronization error is detected in any of the replicas, its icon is changed to include an exclamation point in a yellow triangle, as shown in Figure 6.11.

To perform a repair operation, you select a replica from the grid and choose one of the options on the Repair menu. NDS Manager then launches the appropriate DSREPAIR option on the correct server and displays the results of the process when it is completed. The same options (and many others) are available in the DSREPAIR.NLM program itself, which you can run from the server console. The Repair options in the Partition Continuity are as follows:

FIG. 6.11
When NDS Manager detects a synchronization error in a replica, it modifies its icon to inform the user.

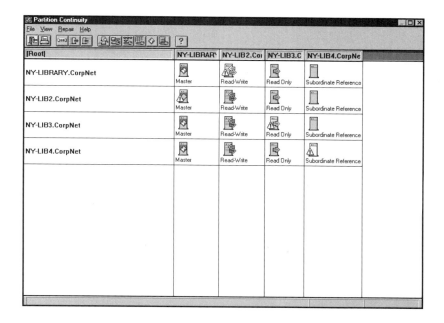

- **Verify Remote Server IDs**—Every replica contains unique ID numbers for the NDS objects in the partition, as well as a list of remote server IDs and the ID number of the local server as found in the other servers' databases. This function verifies that the server name and the corresponding IDs on all of the servers are valid, repairing any IDs that are found to be incorrect. An incorrect ID can prevent NDS communications between servers from taking place.

- **Repair Replica**—This function checks the remote ID information on all of the other servers in the replica ring, but can only change the ID on the selected replica. You should perform the Repair Local Database process before running this procedure.

- **Repair Network Addresses**—This operation checks to see that all network servers are broadcasting the correct network and node addresses by comparing the addresses in the SAP tables of each server with those stored in the servers' NDS objects.

- **Repair Local Database**—This function repairs inconsistencies in the NDS database files stored on the local server. The program makes repairs to a copy of the files, and prompts for permission before the repairs are written to the actual database files. This repair may fail to completely resolve all problems in the NDS tree. However, once access to the database is restored, you can address any further problems by deleting and recreating a replica containing damaged objects, or by requesting updates from the master replica (using the Receive Updates command in the Repair menu).

- **Assign New Master**—This function enables you to convert a read/write or read-only replica into the master replica, in cases where the master has been lost or irreparably damaged. The function is for use in cases of database damage only. It should not be used to convert replicas in situations where the Replica/Change Type command, found in the main NDS Manager screen, can be used instead.

Part II
Ch 6

■ **Remove Server**—If the NDS database is damaged to the point at which servers are attempting to synchronize with a server that no longer contains a replica of this partition, this function removes the server from the replica ring. Do not use this function when you remove a server containing a replica from the network; simply delete the server object itself instead, and the replica ring will eventually be updated. When you select this function, NDS Manager will first attempt to perform a Delete Replica operation. Only if the replica cannot be deleted due to corruption will the Remove Server process proceed.

■ **Repair Volume Objects**—This function checks to see that the volumes mounted on the server correspond with the volume objects in the NDS tree, and that they are properly associated. Unassociated volumes are repaired by searching for the appropriate volume object in the tree. If no volume corresponding to a volume object exists, NDS Manager will create one.

CAUTION

Using NDS Manager's database repair functions or DSREPAIR to perform routine NDS partition and replica maintenance operations can cause severe damage to the database. Such options as Assign New Master and Remove Server should be used only when the database is damaged and when there is no alternative solution available.

The Repair Local Database function is the most complete form of database repair provided by NDS Manager. To do its work, the NDS files must be locked during the procedure, preventing client access to NDS objects. It is therefore recommended that that this process be performed only during periods of minimum network use.

It is for this reason that NDS Manager includes the more moderate repair functions listed earlier in this section. You can verify Remote Server IDs and Repair Network Addresses without the files being locked or service interrupted. In some cases, these procedures can resolve mild corruption issues without the need for a more drastic procedure.

Summary

Partitioning and replication is an important aspect of NetWare administration on any network with two servers or more. As Novell Directory Services becomes an increasingly important repository for enterprise network information, maintaining the health and efficiency of the database likewise becomes a more important task for network administrators. NDS Manager greatly simplifies the various activities involved in this task, forming a GUI partner to the NetWare Administrator. ●

CHAPTER 7

Creating and Managing NDS Objects

In previous chapters, you learned about the basic operational concepts of Novell Directory Services, and about the process of creating an effective and efficient NDS design. In this chapter you learn how to realize your design by actually creating many of the container and leaf objects that make up your NDS tree.

Creating NDS objects and managing their properties are two of the primary tasks of the NetWare administrator. After you have created the structure of your NDS tree and populated it with User objects, you will find that such tasks as managing object rights, adding new User objects, and modifying your tree design will have you working with your NDS management skills on a regular basis.

Creating container objects to form the structure of your Novell Directory Services directory tree

Your NDS tree design is a crucial part of setting up an efficient NetWare 4.1 network.

Creating User objects

Each user on your network must have an individual account, which appears as a leaf object in the NDS tree.

Managing user properties, account restrictions, passwords, and security equivalencies

To secure your network properly, you must carefully assess what resources your users must access, and to what degree.

Creating groups, user templates, and organizational roles

Other types of NDS objects exist to simplify the job of the network administrator by creating generic user attributes that you can assign to any leaf object.

Creating alias objects

An Alias object is a duplicate of a leaf object that can reside in a different context.

Before You Begin

Before you can create objects in the NDS database, you must have the appropriate rights. If you log into the NDS tree as the default Admin user, you automatically have rights to create objects anywhere in the NDS tree. However, if you are working on an existing NDS database, you may have to request appropriate rights from the administrator.

> **CAUTION**
>
> Unlike the Supervisor user in the NetWare bindery, it is possible to modify the rights of the Admin user to limit its access because large networks may distribute administration tasks among support personnel at different locations. It is possible to have an NDS tree in which no one user object has full administrative access to the entire structure. Be careful when modifying the properties of the Admin object, so that you do not leave all or part of your tree without administrative access.

NDS object and property rights are assigned through a security system that is similar to, but wholly independent from, NetWare file system security. In other words, you may have the rights to access a particular server volume, but not to modify the properties of the volume object, and vice versa.

NDS security issues are a complex subject, as is NetWare file system security. These subjects are covered fully in Chapter 14, "Understanding NDS Object and Property Rights," and Chapter 15, "Understanding Directory and File Rights."

This chapter assumes that you already have the appropriate rights to create and modify NDS database objects, and that you understand the ramifications of the directory and file rights that you assign as properties of the objects you will create.

Creating Objects

Whether you elect to use NetWare Administrator in Windows, or the NETADMIN program in DOS, the actual act of creating a new NDS object is very simple. It is the task of managing the many different properties of each object type that complicates the process.

Depending on the size of your network, building your tree structure and populating it with leaf objects can be a simple job or a monumental one. Part of the skill in creating NDS objects lies in knowing the techniques that will make the creation process easier, and simplify your later administrative tasks, as well.

For example, it may not seem to be too much of a problem to assign certain trustee rights to each User object as you create it, but when you repeatedly have to go back later and modify the same rights for each user, the job suddenly becomes much more onerous. If you understand NDS objects and the capabilities of the various utilities before you begin, you can avoid mistakes like this before they happen, and save you and your colleagues work in the process.

Creating Objects with NetWare Administrator

Because of its capability to graphically display the entire tree, NetWare Administrator is the preferred tool for building the structure of the NDS database. The graphical display also enables you to create objects anywhere in the tree without having to explicitly change your context to the container in which the object is to be located.

NetWare Administrator uses the directory schema to enforce the creation of objects only in tree locations that are appropriate to that object type. For example, if your context is set at the [Root] of the NDS tree and you attempt to create an object, NetWare Administrator will allow you to create only Country, Organization, or alias objects.

If you are building a new NDS database, you already have a rudimentary tree as a result of the NetWare installation process. This basic tree consists of one organization object and possibly a number of organizational unit objects. Alternatively, you may be adding new branches to an existing tree.

In either case, you create the NDS database structure that you desire by adding container objects to the tree first, and then populating them with users and other leaf objects.

N O T E   Although the directory tree structure for a very small network may be very simple and require no additional containers beyond those created during the installation process, the design of a large tree is critical to the efficient operation of the NDS database and the NetWare network.

There are many factors affecting the tree design that you should consider before you begin to create container objects. You should read Chapter 5, "Designing an NDS Strategy for the Enterprise," make some basic NDS design decisions, and possibly sketch out a Directory tree structure on paper before you actually create a working database. ▪

Creating Container Objects   Like most Windows applications, NetWare Administrator provides several ways of accomplishing the same task. To create a new container object, highlight the context into which the object is to be placed, and either choose Object, Create; click the Create a New Object button on the toolbar; or right-click the context and choose Create from the pop-up menu. The New Object dialog box is displayed, as shown in Figure 7.1.

FIG. 7.1

The New Object dialog box enables you to create any object type that is capable of being stored in the current context.

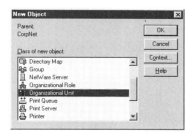

Part

II

Ch

7

N O T E   If the object type that you want to create is not listed in the New Object dialog box, it is
because the directory schema does not allow that type of object to be created in your
current context. For example, you cannot create a Country object in any context but the [Root],
or an Organization object that is subordinate to an Organizational Unit.

Select the type of object that you would like to create from the list of icons provided. In this
case, you will choose either a Country, Organization, or Organizational Unit object, because
the current context is [Root], and those are the only object types that can be created there.
A Create *object* dialog box then appears, as shown in Figure 7.2.

FIG. 7.2

In the Create object
dialog box, you specify
the name of the new
object and how you
would like to proceed
after the object is
created.

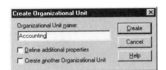

In the Create dialog box, specify the name for the container you are creating. As part of the
tree design process, you should have decided on the naming conventions that you will use for
your NDS objects. Names can be up to 64 characters in length, must be unique in that context,
and can contain nearly all standard characters, including spaces.

Although object names will be displayed using the upper- or lowercase letters you specify in
the dialog box, they will be treated as case-insensitive in all subsequent operations. Thus, the
names NY, Ny, and ny are considered to be duplicates.

CAUTION

If your NDS tree is to be used to support bindery emulation users, you should modify your object naming
conventions to support bindery naming standards. Bindery names can be no more than 47 characters in
length (longer names will be cut off), and cannot use the / \ , : * ? characters. You should also avoid
duplicate object names, even in different contexts, as only one will be accessible to bindery users.

Having specified the object name, you are provided with two check boxes that you can use to
indicate how you would like to proceed once the new object is created. If you mark the Create
Another object box, a new Create dialog box is presented immediately after you have clicked
OK to create the new object. You can then specify the name for another object of the same
type, in the same context.

If you select Define Additional Properties, you will be taken immediately to the Details dialog box for your new object, where you can continue the process of configuring the properties of that object.

When you are creating the structure of your NDS tree, it is probably a good idea to create all of the container objects first, and then continue by creating user objects and assigning their properties.

Creating User Objects   User objects are the most commonly found leaves on your Directory tree. Large networks can have NDS trees with thousands of user objects, distributed in containers throughout the enterprise. Sometimes, users are created automatically, such as when they are imported from other databases, or when bindery-based NetWare servers are upgraded to NetWare 4.11. You can read about these upgrade procedures in Chapter 2, "Upgrading to NetWare 4.11."

When performed manually, the process of creating user objects is similar to that of creating containers, but you must also consider the needs of your users and the method that you will use to assign values to the user object properties.

To create a single user object, you must highlight the container object into which the user is to be located. As before, you can display the New Object dialog box, either by choosing Object, Create, clicking the Create a New Object button on the toolbar, or right-clicking the context and choosing Create from the pop-up menu. Select User from the object listing provided, and you are ready to continue.

N O T E   The procedure for creating other types of leaf objects is exactly the same as that for creating a User object. As you learn about other leaf object types later in this chapter, you can create them by selecting the appropriate object name from the New Object dialog box. ◼

NetWare Administrator provides a shortcut for creating user objects in the form of a Create User Object button on the toolbar, that simplifies the process and brings you directly to the Create User dialog box shown in Figure 7.3.

FIG. 7.3
The Create User dialog box enables you to specify the name, home directory, and template to be used when creating a new user object.

TIP Once again, the first function of the Create dialog box is to specify a name for the object. If you observe no other naming standards in your NDS database, you should have one for the names of your user objects. When you employ a standard form to create each user's object (as well as login) name, you save both your support staff and your users the need to waste time remembering other users' object names.

Typically, User object names are constructed using all or part of the user's surname, plus one or more initials, such as JSMITH or SMITHJ. Frequently, surnames are cut off at six or seven characters, especially when home directories are automatically created because they are restricted to the DOS 8.3 naming scheme.

Avoid the use of first names or nicknames, such as JOHNS or JOHNNYS, as these are prone to duplication and obfuscation. Your naming scheme should also include a contingency for the situation where the formula results in two users with the same object name. You can resolve a dilemma like this in any way you want, as long as you do it the same way in every case.

Although you can choose to place the user's surname first in the object name, you need not do so for purposes of alphabetization, because you are required to enter a value in the Last Name field of the Create User dialog box. Last Name is the only other property that is required for the creation of a user; it enables you to search the NDS database for the names of particular users, no matter how their object names are constructed.

At the bottom of the Create User dialog box are the same two check boxes that you saw when creating containers, enabling you to Define Additional Properties or to Create Another User immediately after the object is created.

Two other check boxes are also provided. Check the Use Template box if you want to create your new object with the property values that have previously been assigned to a user Template object. See the section entitled, "Creating Users with Templates," for more information about this process.

Creating Home Directories   When you check the Create Home Directory box in the Create User dialog box, you must specify the location on a NetWare server volume where the new user is to have a directory created for his or her own personal use.

Home directories for NetWare users are typically created under a single subdirectory (such as USERS). You can select this subdirectory by clicking the browser button in the Create User dialog box. By default, the home directory will have the same name as the User object, although you can change it if you want.

When home directories are created, users are automatically given full trustee rights (except Supervisor) to their own directory. They can then allow other users to access their files as needed. Some network administrators assign all users Write and Create rights to the USERS directory, giving them access to all of the home directories. They are denied Erase rights, however. This way, the home directories can be used as a file-oriented "mailbox," of sorts. Thus, when SmithJ wants to give a certain file to DoeJ, he can simply copy the file to her home directory. Once it is there, only DoeJ can erase the file.

T I P Network users have a tendency to fill all of the disk space provided to them with remarkable speed. When creating home directories for your users, it is a good idea to establish volume usage limitations so that your drives don't run out of space too quickly. It is also a good idea not to place your users' home directories on a server's SYS volume, as disk space shortages there can cause severe problems for NDS and other systems.

Once you have specified values for all of the required User properties, you can click the OK button to create the new User object, and proceed to the next operation.

Creating Users with Templates Generally, when you are managing a large number of users, avoid assigning trustee rights, security equivalences, and other such properties directly to individual user objects. NetWare provides many different techniques by which multiple User objects can inherit their property values from a common source, thus lessening the amount of object maintenance required.

Most techniques for managing users are examined in the "Managing Object Properties" section later in this chapter. One of these techniques—the use of templates—is only effective during the actual creation of a User object, so it must be examined here.

The Directory schema in NetWare 4.11 includes an object type called a Template, that is used to store a default user configuration. You create a Template object by selecting Template from the NetWare Administrator's New Object dialog box, just as you would any other object. The Details dialog box for a Template object looks very much like that of a User object (see Figure 7.4). You assign values to the properties that you want to be applied to new User objects as you create them.

FIG. 7.4
The Template object is used to assign default property values to new User objects as they are created.

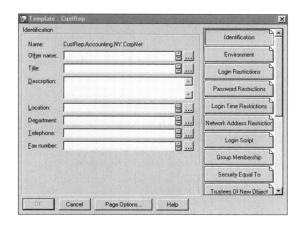

N O T E Previous versions of NetWare 4.x enabled you to create an object called USER_TEMPLATE from a User object, which could then later be applied during the creation of other User objects. NetWare 4.11, however, is the first NetWare version in which the Template appears as an object class of its own, named, created, and managed as an independent NDS object in its own right. ▪

Part
II

Ch
7

You can create as many Template objects as you like. Typically, you would create Templates to accommodate the needs of various types of users in your enterprise. If, for example, you have a standard set of directories or applications to which all users need access, you can assign the appropriate rights to the Template object. In the future, whenever you create a new User object and specify that template, those rights will be copied to the User object. It is important to understand two issues about Template objects:

- Templates can be used only during the creation of a new User object. You cannot assign a Template to an object that already exists, although you can achieve the same result using an Organizational Role. (See "Using Organizational Roles" later in this chapter.)

- Templates are accessed only during the creation of User objects. Modifying the template will not change the properties of User objects that have already been created.

Because of these restrictions placed on Templates, they should only be used to assign permanent property values to User objects. Once assigned using a Template, property values can only be changed by modifying each User object individually.

As mentioned earlier, to apply a Template to a new User object, you specify the name of the Template object in the Create User dialog box, or browse to the object using the standard Select Object dialog box. As the new object is created, the property values assigned to the Template are copied to the new User.

After the User object is created, the Template is never accessed again by that user. You can safely change the properties of the Template, or delete it entirely, without affecting the User objects created with it.

Creating Objects with NETADMIN

You can create Container and User objects in the DOS environment with the NETADMIN utility, but its capabilities are no longer the same as those of NetWare Administrator. Originally, NETADMIN and NetWare Administrator were created with the same feature set, but while the Windows-based NetWare Administrator utility has been improved, NETADMIN remains unchanged from the NetWare 4.1 release. The differences in the two programs' capabilities will be more pronounced in the "Managing Object Properties" section later in this chapter. However, during the object creation process, it is important to note that NETADMIN does not support the NetWare 4.11 Template object.

To create an object in NETADMIN, you must first change your current context to the container in which you will create the new object. Once you are in the proper context, select Manage Objects from the NETADMIN Options menu and press the Insert key to pop up the Select an Object Class menu. The Create Object menus that appear for container and User objects are similar in functionality to those of NetWare Administrator (see Figure 7.5).

▶ **See** "Browsing the Tree with NETADMIN and PCONSOLE," **p. 101**

FIG. 7.5

Creating a Container object with NETADMIN requires nothing more than the container's name.

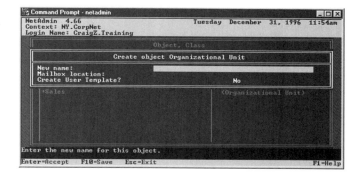

The object naming conventions and the required properties are the same in NETADMIN as they are in NetWare Administrator. Once you have specified the required values, the F10 key creates the object and returns you to the listing of all of the objects in your current context. In previous NetWare versions, user templates could be created as part of the container object creation process by exercising the Create User Template option shown in Figure 7.5.

The Create Object User menu displayed by NETADMIN sets the Copy User Template option to Yes by default (see Figure 7.6). Because NetWare 4.11 Template objects are not supported in NETADMIN, there is no means of specifying the Template object name. Instead, NETADMIN searches the current context for an object called USER_TEMPLATE. Failing to find the object, parent contexts are searched up to the [Root].

FIG. 7.6

The pop-up menu displayed during the creation of a new User object in NETADMIN supports only the NetWare 4.1 style of user template.

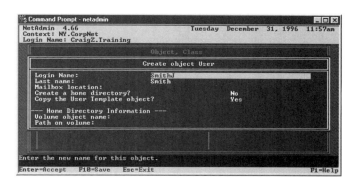

Oddly enough, NetWare 4.11 Template objects do appear in NETADMIN's object listings, but the program is incapable of displaying or modifying their properties. If you intend to take advantage of NetWare 4.11's new Template objects, be sure to create your new user with NetWare Administrator, instead of NETADMIN.

T I P

If you create a Template object with NetWare Administrator and name it USER_TEMPLATE, it will be recognized as a valid template by the NETADMIN utility. However, you will still be limited to the use of only one template in a particular container.

Part

II

Ch

7

Managing Object Properties

Once you have created your User objects and the containers in which they reside, you must configure the properties of the objects, in order to invest your users with the rights they need to accomplish their work. You can specify object properties as you create the objects, or you can build your NDS tree structure first, and consider the properties afterwards.

Generally, the latter option is preferable, because there are many ways to assign the required property values to your users without modifying the User objects directly, such as inheritance from containers. Unlike the creation of objects, the management of object property values is an ongoing maintenance task, one which you must consider in terms of future convenience as well as the immediate task at hand.

User Object Properties

As discussed in Chapter 4, "Novell Directory Services (NDS) and NetWare Administrator," the properties of a User object can be said to fall into the following four general categories:

- Names
- Addresses
- Memberships
- Descriptions

Name and address properties can contain information that is specific to the user, such as the User object name, the user's own name, and other identification information such as the network address of the user's computer, the user's telephone and fax numbers, and other contact data. Other properties can describe the user's access restrictions, job title, office location, or mailing address.

Most crucial to the functionality of the User object are the membership properties, some of which account for the resources to which the user has been granted access, in terms of trustee rights and security equivalences.

When you double-click a User object in NetWare Administrator (or select Details from the Object menu or the User object's pop-up menu), the User Details dialog box is displayed, as shown in Figure 7.7. This dialog box has no less than 18 pages, accessed using the buttons that run down the right side of the display. The following sections describe the properties found on each page, and how they can be used by the network administrator to control users' network access.

 T I P You can navigate through the property pages of the User Details dialog box by using the Ctrl+PageUp and Ctrl+PageDown keys, or by right-clicking the dialog box and selecting a page from the pop-up menu provided. You can also control which buttons are displayed in the dialog box, and their order, by clicking the Page Options button on any property page.

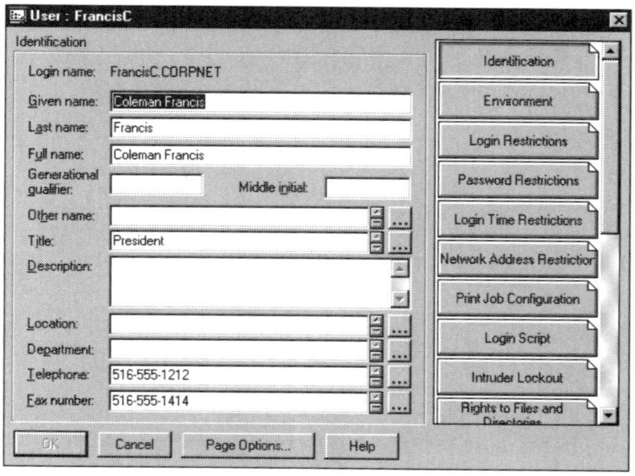

FIG. 7.7
The User Details dialog
box is the repository
for all of the property
values assigned to an
individual User object.

Identification The Identification page, as the name implies, contains properties that can store personal information about users and their function in the enterprise. Except for the last name, all of these fields are optional.

If desired, NDS can function as a complete database of users' contact and job description information. NetWare Administrator is capable of searching for users based on these user identification fields and many other object properties, making it a useful communications tool for users and administrators.

Obviously, most of the Identification information will be unique to each user, making this a rather maintenance-intensive page. Many of the properties are also designed to contain information that may not be readily available to network support personnel in the average enterprise, such as postal address information.

Because of the maintenance needed and information required, the Identification page is not often used to its fullest. However, it can be a helpful storage space for information that is important to network support personnel, such as users' phone numbers and locations. With the appropriate rights, users can search the database for specific information using the NLIST utility as well as NetWare Administrator.

Environment The Environment page contains properties that list the default preferences of the user. Most of these properties have values that are automatically generated during client installation or use.

The user's preferred language is listed, which is used when running a program that calls the NWLANGUAGE environment variable. If, for example, you have installed the NetWare online documentation in multiple languages, this property is used to determine which language is displayed by default.

You can add values to the language property, which will function as alternates should the desired resource not be available in the preferred language.

The Network Address field identifies the workstation that the user has logged in from by displaying an address for each of the protocols that it is using to connect to the NDS tree. For IPX connections, the workstation's Media Access Control (MAC) address (which is hard coded into the computer's network interface adapter) is displayed. For TCP/IP connections, the IP address is shown.

The network address is an automatically generated, multi-valued field. If a user is logged in from two workstations, then the address information for both machines is shown.

NOTE The Network Address field does not retain a history of the user's network access. Only the addresses of currently connected workstations are displayed.

The Default Server property is accessed whenever a user specifies the name of a network resource (such as a volume or a printer) without indicating the server with which the resource is associated. The default server can be changed at any time. If no server name is specified, then the default will be the same as that of the user who created the object.

The Home Directory property automatically displays the location of the user's home directory, if one was created during the creation of the user. You can modify this field to specify another directory, but you must create the directory and grant the user the appropriate rights manually.

 TIP If you make changes to any of an object's property pages, the white tab in the upper-right corner of the page's access button will turn black. Changes are not applied until you click the OK button to close the dialog box.

Login Restrictions The Login Restrictions page enables you to apply general controls to a User object, in order to limit the user's network access. You can completely disable the account without affecting any other settings (which is useful if the account is to be reactivated later).

You can specify an exact date and time for the user's account to expire, and you can control whether the account can be used to log in from multiple workstations simultaneously.

Password Restrictions Password enforcement is the most basic of network security measures, and the Password Restrictions screen enables the network administrator to set the rules by which users maintain their passwords, according to the level of security required for the network.

The first check box on this screen controls whether users can change their passwords at all. Some high-security sites provide the passwords for their users; this option can ensure that users' passwords are not changed except by a network administrator.

 TIP Assigning passwords to users may at first seem to be more secure than allowing users to make up their own. However, users are more likely to write down an assigned password in an obvious place, defeating the purpose of the exercise. It is often more effective to educate users on secure password procedures and impose rules, such as requiring frequent password changes and minimum password lengths.

If the Allow User to Change Password box is enabled, then the other properties on the screen control the nature of the passwords supplied by the user, and the frequency of password changes. From this page, you can control the following options:

- **Require a Password**—Determines whether users must have passwords at all
- **Minimum Password Length**—Determines how long users' passwords must be
- **Force Periodic Password Changes**—Determines whether users must change their passwords regularly
- **Days Between Forced Changes**— Determines the interval between required password changes
- **Date Password Expires**—Specifies a date and time when the current password expires
- **Require Unique Passwords**—Determines whether any of a user's last eight passwords can be reused
- **Limit Grace Logins**—Determines whether users are allowed to log in with an expired password
- **Grace Logins Allowed**—Specifies the number of times users can log in with an expired password
- **Remaining Grace Logins**—Determines the number of grace logins that a user has left before the account is locked out if the user's password isn't changed

You can also change the user's password from this dialog box, provided that you can specify the old password. Users with Supervisor rights to the object can change the password at any time without specifying the old password. This prevents users from being permanently locked out of their accounts should they forget their passwords.

N O T E Unlike the other properties in the Details dialog box, password changes are applied as soon as you click the OK button, and cannot be undone.

Login Time Restrictions Using the grid shown in Figure 7.8, you can restrict the time that a user is allowed to log in to the network. You can use this option for security purposes, to prevent unauthorized network access during specified hours, or simply to prevent users from remaining logged in while network maintenance operations, such as backups, are performed.

Network Address Restrictions The Network Address Restrictions page enables you to specify the workstations from which a particular User object can log in. When this feature is enabled, any attempts to log in to the network from a computer not matching one of the specified addresses will be denied.

The level of security provided by address restrictions depends on the protocol and network type used by the workstation. For example, IPX workstations will have their MAC addresses listed on this page. On Ethernet and token-ring networks, this is very secure, because the MAC address is hard-coded into every network interface adapter.

Part
II

Ch

7

FIG. 7.8
The Login Time Restrictions grid enables you to limit users' network access for certain times of day.

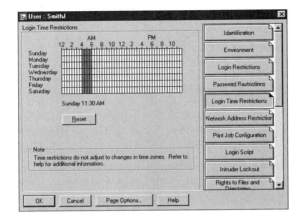

Conversely, TCP/IP connections are referenced by their IP addresses, which can easily be changed in the workstation client software configuration. If an intruder is able to find out an authorized user's IP address, this feature provides little security.

Print Job Configuration   The Print Job Configuration page enables you to create multiple pre-defined sets of printing parameters, consisting of the print options that would normally be specified on CAPTURE or NPRINT command lines.

When printing from Windows applications, values for these options are set in the Windows Printer Setup or Properties (depending on your Windows version). It is only necessary to create print job configurations on the print job configuration page if you will be printing from DOS-based applications that provide no internal printer control, like NPRINT, or if you want to avoid specifying values for these options in a CAPTURE command.

Login Script   Novell Directory Services provides three different types of login scripts, any or all of which can be executed when a user logs in to the network. The Login Script page in the User Properties dialog box is for the creation of the user login script.

The user login script is executed after the container and profile scripts. Instead of, or in addition to, a user login script, you can also specify the Profile object that contains the script to be executed after the container script and before the user script.

If you do not create a user login script, then the default login script is executed, instead. This is a script, hard-coded into the LOGIN utility, that executes several basic commands, such as mapping drives to SYS and the user's home directory, and making SYS:PUBLIC a search drive. You can prevent the execution of the default login script by including the NO_DEFAULT command in the container or profile script.

N O T E Login script commands are the same for all three scripts. Most network administrators favor the use of container or profile scripts, but if there are commands you want to execute that are uniquely intended for this user (and which cannot be programmed generically using variables or some other means), you would type them into this page. For more information on creating and debugging login scripts, see Chapter 19, "Accessing Network Resources." ▇

Intruder Lockout The Intruder Lockout page displays the status of a User object when it has been locked out by NetWare's intruder detection feature. Intruder detection is an option that is enabled and configured in the property pages of a container object. It is designed to prevent unauthorized users from penetrating password security through repeated login attempts.

When you enable intruder detection, you specify the number of incorrect login attempts that can be performed before the account is locked. You also specify the amount of time that the account remains locked before anyone can log in again.

The Account Locked property on the Intruder Lockout page indicates when an intruder has been detected, displays the number of failed login attempts and the time that the account is scheduled to be reset. This information is also added to the system log. An administrator can unlock the account at any time after an intrusion by unchecking the Account Locked box on this page.

Rights to Files and Directories Arguably the most important and most commonly used of the property pages, the Rights to Files and Directories page enables an administrator to grant a user access rights to specific NetWare volumes, directories, and files. By clicking the Find button, as shown in Figure 7.9, the NetWare Administrator searches for the volumes, directories, and files to which the users have already been granted rights. These are displayed in the Files and Directories field.

FIG. 7.9
The Rights to Files and Directories screen enables you to control the user's access to the NetWare file system.

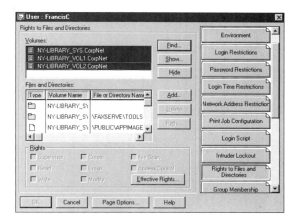

Part
II

Ch
7

N O T E   Although you can set and modify rights on the Rights to Files and Directories page, trustee rights to files and directories are stored in the NetWare file system, not in the NDS database. That is why the user's current rights are not immediately visible, but are displayed only after you use the Find button to implement a search for trustee rights.

If you highlight one of the entries in the Files and Directories list, the Rights box displays the NetWare rights that have been explicitly granted to the user for that directory or file. Clicking the Effective Rights button displays the user's overall rights to that resource, taking into account inherited rights, security equivalences, explicitly granted rights, and inherited rights filters.

To grant a user's new rights, you click the Add button, and browse to the desired resource in a standard Select Object dialog box. Once the object is added to the list, you use the check boxes to indicate what rights the user should have. For more information on NetWare file system access rights, see Chapter 15, "Understanding Directory and File Rights."

As with many of the other User object properties, granting file and directory access rights to individual user objects can be time-consuming and inefficient. Later in this chapter, you will learn other, more efficient methods of assigning rights to your users.

Group Membership   The Group Membership property page lists the groups of which this user is a member. Group objects are one of the methods that you can use to assign property values to many users at the same time. All of the properties defined in the group object are automatically inherited by all of the members of the group. See "Using Group Objects," later in this chapter, for more information.

Security Equal To   A security equivalence is the easiest way to grant one user the same rights as another user. You can browse to any NDS tree object and add it to the list on that page, and the user will automatically be granted all of that object's rights and privileges. See "Using Security Equivalences," later in this chapter, for more information on the problems inherent in this method of rights assignment.

Postal Address   The Postal Address page is a repository for the user's mailing address information, including a mailing label facsimile that is included to comply with the X.500 e-mail standard.

All of the properties on this page are optional. If you fill in the address fields on the top of the page, you can click the Copy to Label button to copy the data to the mailing label format.

Account Balance   NetWare includes an accounting feature that enables you to track a user's connect time and disk read/writes for internal billing purposes. On this page, you can specify the user's balance, which is decremented as the user accesses the network. The value of the user's balance is determined by the rates and scales that you configure for the accounting feature.

You can also specify a Low Balance Limit on this page. When the user's balance falls below the limit established here, network access is cut off.

See Also   This is a completely free-form, undefined, optional property, that can be used for any special purpose by the network administrator.

Applications   The NetWare Application Launcher (NAL) is a new feature of NetWare 4.11. It extends the Directory schema to enable the creation of Application objects in the NDS database. An application object includes the path to a networked application, along with a set of customized environmental controls that facilitate its use.

Once the application object has been created, users can be granted access to the application by adding a reference to the object to the user's Applications property page. Then, running the NetWare NAL.EXE program from a server's PUBLIC directory causes all of the users' applications to appear as icons in a window on their desktops.

You can grant the user rights to the application by clicking the Add button, and browsing to the desired Application object. Once the object is added to the list in the Applications page, you can indicate whether the application's icon is to appear in the NAL window, and whether the application should be automatically launched when NAL.EXE is executed. For more information on launching applications with NAL, see Chapter 8, "Networking Applications with NDS."

Launcher Configuration   Because the NetWare Application Launcher can be used to restrict users' network access only to designated application resources, this Launcher Configuration page is provided to control the behavior of the NAL.EXE program when it is executed by this particular user.

NetWare Registry Editor   The NetWare Registry Editor enables you to edit the entries that have been stored for this user in the Novell Network Registry, a database of preference settings for all users who access a common application like NetWare Administrator. With the registry database, users can configure a NetWare application to use specific display and configuration options. Because the settings are stored on the network, the options are always applied, even when the user runs the application from a different workstation.

Assigning Property Values

Some User object properties will have values that are necessarily unique for each User object, such as name and address. Other properties, particularly those that fall into the membership category, such as trustee rights and security equivalences, will have values that are the same for many different users who perform the same job function. What's more, these trustee and security properties are more likely to change than will a user's basic identification information.

In the interest of efficiency, both in the initial configuration of User objects, and in their future maintenance, network administrators usually try to avoid modifying individual object properties as much as possible. In fact, on many networks, there will be no trustee rights, security equivalences, login scripts, or other such properties assigned to individual User objects at all. Instead, all of the required values are inherited from other objects.

The techniques for assigning trustee rights and other properties by groups are as old as NetWare itself. Even when using the bindery, if you have to grant 20 users the right to access a given server, it makes far more sense to create a group with 20 members and assign the rights to the group itself, than to assign the rights to 20 individual users.

The decision to group users logically is all the more sensible when, some time later, you have to assign the same 20 users rights to another server. One step replaces 20, and the network administrator gets to go home on time.

Although the NetWare bindery enables you to create user groups for assigning trustee and other rights, Novell Directory Services greatly expands this facility, providing many other ways to assign property values to many users at once.

You have already learned about one of the NDS methods for automatically configuring property values in the "Creating Users with Templates" section earlier in this chapter. A Template object is unusual in that it only functions during the creation of User objects, but its basic purpose is to provide a single set of property values that are imposed on multiple user objects.

The other ways in which network administrators can assign property values to multiple users without manipulating the individual User objects are as follows:

- Inherited container properties
- Security equivalences
- Inherited group properties
- Inherited organizational role properties
- Profile login scripts
- Alias objects
- Multiple object modifications

The following sections describe each of the techniques of assigning properties to multiple users, and how you can use them to manage your NDS database more efficiently.

Container Object Properties

The most commonly used and most efficient method of assigning property values is to configure a container object such as an Organization or Organizational Unit. All of the values assigned to a container are automatically inherited by all of the objects in that container. This includes other container objects and their contents. Thus, as in the NetWare file system, property values flow down the NDS hierarchy from the container of their origin to the bottom of the tree.

The general practice in NDS database design is to place User objects in the same container as the servers and printers that they access on a regular basis because values flow down the NDS hierarchy. The container inheritance model is very efficient because all of the objects involved are almost always located in the same NDS database partition. In addition, users with the same network resource needs are naturally grouped together, making it easy to configure their access.

For example, if you place all of the users in the Accounting department in one Organizational Unit container, along with their servers and printers, you can probably apply a single network access configuration to all users in the department. To do so, you modify the property pages of the Organizational Unit object.

You can assign appropriate rights to the required directories on the department servers, create a login script to map network drives to the same drive letters for all of the users in the Accounting group, and perhaps configure a more rigid intruder detection regimen (to protect the accounting data).

All of the users in the Accounting department will then have the same attributes. If, in the future, it becomes necessary to change the user configuration, you have only to modify the properties of the single Container object again.

The Details dialog box for Organization and Organizational Unit objects contains the following property pages:

- Identification
- Postal Address
- Print Job Configuration
- Rights to Files and Directories
- See Also
- Login Script
- Applications
- Launcher Configuration
- Printer Forms
- Print Devices
- Print Layout
- Intruder Detection

Except for the last four pages in the list, the properties associated with a container object are fundamentally the same as those found in a user Details dialog box. See "User Object Properties" earlier in this chapter for information on these properties. The following sections examine the property pages that are unique to a container's Details dialog box.

N O T E Unlike a User object, double-clicking a container object in NetWare Administrator expands or contracts the tree branch, rather than displaying the Details dialog box. To modify the properties of a container object, you must highlight the object name and select Details from the Object menu, press the Enter key, or right-click the object and select Details from the pop-up menu.

Printer Forms   Printer Forms are definitions of paper sizes that you can create and assign to print jobs. If you have a printer that accommodates different sizes of paper, you can use form definitions to minimize the number of paper changes required to print your jobs.

For example, if you have different forms for letter- and legal-size paper, you can configure the print server to service all of the print jobs in the queue that use one form, before requiring that you switch the paper in the printer. No matter what the order of the jobs in the queue, all those requiring a particular form will be serviced first.

Print Devices   The Print Devices page enables you to create a list of the printers found in the container. Each printer definition is created from an imported PDF file (a selection of which is included with NetWare) that specifies the printer's capabilities and the control sequences needed to activate each feature.

Defining printers on the Print Devices page is not necessary when users are printing from Windows applications, or from DOS-based applications that supply their own printer drivers. This page enables an application with no internal printer command functions, such as NPRINT, to fully utilize the capabilities of your network printer.

Print Layout   The Print Layout page displays a graphical representation of the printer, print server, and print queue objects found in the current container, and the relationships among them, as shown in Figure 7.10.

FIG. 7.10

The Print Layout page of a container's Details dialog box displays the relationships among the print objects in the current container.

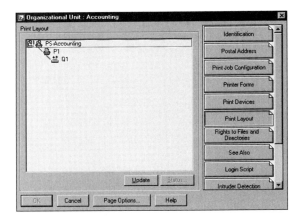

If you have a large number of printer objects in one container, it can be difficult to determine which objects are associated with which. This page enables you to see the relationships easily. You can also highlight an object and click the Status button to ascertain its current condition.

N O T E   The status screen for a print queue object does not display the jobs currently in the queue. To see and manipulate queued print jobs, you must open the Details dialog box (from the Object menu or the pop-up menu) for the print queue object itself. ■

Intruder Detection   NetWare's Intruder Detection feature enables the network administrator to specify how many failed login attempts a user is allowed within a given period of time. Depending on the level of security you require, you can prevent unauthorized users from trying to penetrate network passwords through repeated login attempts.

When you enable intruder detection, you set the number of incorrect login attempts that a user is allowed and the time period in which those attempts must occur for the behavior to be considered an intrusion, as shown in Figure 7.11.

FIG. 7.11

On the Intruder Detection property page, you can increase network security by limiting users' login attempts.

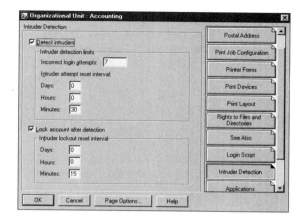

You can then specify whether an account is to be locked once an intrusion is detected, and the time period that the account will remain locked. Once an intruder has been detected and an account locked, no access to the account is allowed until the lockout reset interval has expired, or an administrator unlocks the account.

N O T E You can monitor a user's intruder lockout status, and manually unlock a disabled account, only from the Intruder Lockout property page, in the User object's Details dialog box. See the "Intruder Lockout" section earlier in this chapter for more information.

Using Security Equivalences

Security equivalences are one of the most commonly used methods of propagating object property values. By making Object B an equivalent to Object A, B automatically receives all the same property values held by A. The relationship travels in one direction only, however. Object A does not receive B's property values.

An object can be the holder of multiple security equivalences. In this instance, the property values of all of the equivalent objects are combined.

Security equivalence relationships are not limited to like objects. Technically, a User object becomes the security equivalent of its container. The same is true when a user is made a member of a group. The User object becomes the security equivalent of the Group object.

Network administrators can also explicitly define security equivalences, using the Security Equal To property page found in the Details dialog box of many objects. For example, the easiest way to grant users full object and file system rights is to make them an equivalent of the Admin object.

Of course, this only holds true if the properties of the Admin object remain unchanged from when it was created. This is the fundamental problem with using security equivalences to define property values for your objects. The rights of the inheritors change whenever the rights of the equivalent object are modified.

Part

II

Ch

7

In other words, if you have a department full of users with the same requirements, you can configure one of the User objects with the required properties, and then make all of the other users equivalent to the first one. However, if the source object should change, due to the user being transferred or terminated, then all of the equivalents change as well.

N O T E It is very easy to create a complex matrix of security equivalences that is difficult to keep track of and maintain. There is no graphical tool that displays object equivalences. The only way to know what objects another object is equivalent to is to look at the Security Equal To property page.

Security equivalences are frequently used by the NDS database internally, but it is recommended that you refrain from establishing your own security equivalences between objects. ▪

Using Group Objects

As mentioned earlier, groups have been a fundamental NetWare tool from its inception. However, because most NDS trees are designed with User objects in the same containers as their most commonly used servers and printers, inherited container rights are more prevalent on NetWare 4.11 networks.

Groups objects still remain a viable alternative to manipulating individual user properties. Even though they are leaf objects, Groups function just like containers, as far as inherited rights are concerned. When you assign properties to the Group object, they are inherited by all members of the group.

The properties available to Group objects are relatively limited. The Group Details dialog box contains only five pages:

- Identification
- Members
- Rights to Files and Directories
- See Also
- Applications

Four of the five pages are identical to their counterparts in a container object. The fifth, Members, contains a listing of the objects that have been made part of the group. When a User object is made a member of a group, the Security Equal To page of the User object's Details dialog box lists the Group object as an equivalent.

Interestingly, it is the security equivalence property that causes values to be inherited by the group members, not the membership in the group itself.

The primary advantage of using Group objects to provide property values to users is also the primary drawback. Group memberships are completely independent of the NDS tree hierarchy. You can add User objects from any container in the tree to a group.

Unfortunately, this very quality makes the processing of group relationships far more difficult than that of container/leaf relationships. If you have a large tree, and particularly one that is divided into partitions, and most especially if your partitions are located at different sites connected by WAN links, the processing of Group object properties will be far slower than that of inherited container values.

You should, therefore, not consider groups to be the functional equivalent of a container, as far as inherited property values are concerned. Use groups only when you must provide certain values to users that are spread out over the enterprise.

Using Organizational Roles

An Organizational Role object is designed to be an alternative to the creation of security equivalences between User objects. In the example given earlier, making one user the equivalent of another was not recommended because the equivalent User object may be modified or deleted.

Organizational Role objects address the dynamic nature inherent in user equivalences by defining an object that represents a particular job, rather than the person performing that job. This way the properties of the job remain intact, even if the personnel changes.

Organizational Role objects have a limited set of properties. They are used primarily to define the file system and NDS object rights needed to perform a particular job.

The object's Details dialog box contains only four pages:

- Identification
- Postal Address
- Rights to Files and Directories
- See Also

The users that fill an organizational role are called its occupants. You select the users that are to occupy the role in the Occupant property on the Identification page. The other properties function just like their equivalents in a User Details dialog box.

Using Profile Objects

Profile objects enable you to create a single login script that can be executed by multiple users that are not in the same container. In the same way that User objects can inherit property values from container or group objects, they can get their login scripts from either containers or Profile objects.

The Profile object's Details dialog box has four pages:

- Identification
- Rights to Files and Directories
- See Also
- Login Script

Part
II
Ch
7

The commands used for a profile login script are exactly the same as those for container and user scripts. When a user logs in, the profile script is executed after the container login script and before the user script, if both exist.

To associate a profile login script with a User object, you must first create the script in the Profile object's Details dialog box. Then you open the Details dialog box of the User object and specify the name of the Profile object in the proper field on the Login Script page.

 Even though Profile objects can be associated with any User object in the NDS tree, it is best if the User object is located on the same server as the profile login script. Accessing Profile objects on another server can slow down the login process, especially if the other server is connected by a WAN link.

Using Aliases

Alias objects are one of the most powerful tools for managing NDS properties and their values. An Alias object is simply a copy of another NDS object that is located in a different place on the tree. Users can access an alias just as if they were accessing the actual resource.

For example, if you have a printer that is accessed by users in many different containers, you can create an alias of the Printer object in each container. This way, users can access the printer just as though the object is in their own container.

Aliases can be an important element in your NDS tree design. If you opt to model your tree on the geographical layout of your network, creating a single container to represent your data center or server closet can make it difficult for users to access server volumes.

However, with Alias objects, accessing objects in other containers becomes a viable alternative. You can locate all of your server and volume objects in one container, and then create aliases for the volume objects in the various containers with users that need access to them.

Not only can you use aliases to bring network resources to your users, you can also bring your users to the resources by creating aliases of User objects. If network support personnel routinely travel to different departments of your enterprise that are organized into different containers in your tree, it can be very convenient for them if an alias to the Admin object is placed in each container. This way, the support person can log in from any workstation, and find Admin in the current context.

You can use this same technique to give managers and supervisors access to resources in different containers. Create aliases in all of the required containers so that they can log in from anywhere they happen to be, and you can very likely get away with not having to explain contexts and containers to the users.

N O T E   Alias objects are linked to the source objects they are created from. When you use an alias, NDS communication is needed to verify operations against the property values of the original object. As with any NetWare communication process, crossing WAN links can slow the procedure. Keeping alias relationships on the local network is one of the reasons why it is important to properly replicate your NDS partitions.

You can create aliases of both container and leaf objects. If you move a container object to another location on the tree, you are given the option to leave an alias of the container in its place. This way, any other objects that reference the container in its old location can continue to do so.

Creating an Alias Object   To create an alias, you simply create a new object in the usual way, selecting Alias from the New Object list, and specify the object that you want to be aliased. When you create an alias in a different container from the original, you can give it the same name as its source, or use another name to indicate that the object is an alias. In any case, the object in the NetWare Administrator is shown with a different icon, to indicate its status.

Managing Alias Properties   When you access an Alias object's Details dialog box, you are actually accessing the properties of the original object. In NDS terminology, accessing the properties of an alias' original object is known as *dereferencing*. As far as the Details dialog box is concerned, you have no choice but to dereference, because those properties don't exist in the Alias object.

The only properties that are native to the Alias object itself are its name and an access control list containing the object's own trustees. When you view the trustees of an Alias object, you have a choice of whether you will view them as dereferenced or non-dereferenced. You control this behavior with NetWare Administrator by selecting either Get Alias Trustees or Get Aliased Object Trustees from the Options menu.

N O T E   In the NETADMIN utility, you choose whether to display the properties of the Aliased object or the alias itself in the Manage According to Search Pattern window. If you answer Yes to the Show Alias Class question, you will see the non-dereferenced properties of the Alias object. Answering No (the default) displays the properties of the aliased object.

Suppose, for example, you create an alias of the Admin User object, and call it Admin(Alias). If you have the Get Alias Trustees option activated (which is the default), highlighting the Alias object and selecting Trustees of this Object from the Object menu will display the Trustees of Alias Admin(Alias) dialog box shown in Figure 7.12. This non-dereferenced dialog box shows the trustees of the Alias object itself, not those of the Admin object.

Part
II

Ch
7

FIG. 7.12

An Alias object possesses an access control list containing trustees of its own, independent from those of the aliased object.

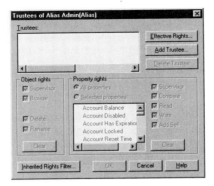

If you choose Options, Get Aliased Object Trustees, and create the same Admin (Alias) object, a different dialog box is displayed called Trustees of the Aliased Object of Admin(Alias), as shown in Figure 7.13. These are, in fact the dereferenced trustees of the Admin object itself.

FIG. 7.13

You can also manipulate the access control list of the aliased object by accessing the dereferenced properties of the alias.

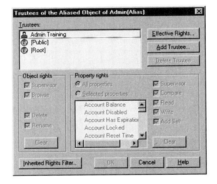

In order to move, rename, or delete an Alias object, you must have trustee rights to the Alias object itself, not to the Aliased object. The move, rename, and delete functions of NetWare Administrator automatically turn dereferencing off, so that it is the Alias object that is manipulated. To move, rename, or delete the original object, you must address the object itself. You cannot perform these functions from the alias.

Understanding Alias Behavior   It is important to realize that an Alias object is an exact duplicate of the original, that has been placed in another context. None of the properties of the original object are changed. An Alias object inherits the original object's password, and runs the login script of the original object's parent container. When the original object is deleted, then its aliases are deleted as well.

Even though an alias might physically reside in Container B, it does not inherit property values from that container object. Instead, it continues to inherit the property values from the original object's parent container, A. If Container A's properties change, than so do those inherited by the Aliased object. When the Aliased object changes, so do its aliases.

This behavior can cause problems, however. Because an Alias object inherits property values only from the original object's container, it fails to inherit the rights to the local printers and print queues from the Alias object's own container. Thus, if a user travels to a remote location and logs in using an alias in the local context, his alias will not have rights to the local printers, under normal circumstances.

To address this problem, you must explicitly grant the original User object rights to those Printer and Print Queue objects. You can do this by creating an Organizational Role object in the container where the alias resides, and making the User object an occupant of the role.

Because the Organizational Role resides in the container at the remote location, it inherits from its container object the property values that give it rights to the local printers.

Alias objects are also subject to the same restrictions as the originals. For example, an alias of an Organization object can only be created off of the [Root] or in a Country container, just as if you were creating an actual Organization object.

> **CAUTION**
>
> Aliases are most useful when used to replicate leaf objects. Be careful when creating aliases of container objects, because it is possible to create an alias loop. For example, creating an alias of an organizational unit object in that object's own parent container can cause an NDS utility like NetWare Administrator to be caught in an endless loop of references that can ultimately monopolize your system resources and crash the program, or even terminate the server.

Modifying Multiple Objects

The version of NetWare Administrator that ships with NetWare 4.11 includes a new feature that may alter NDS object maintenance practices of some network administrators. For the first time, it is possible to directly modify the property values of multiple user objects simultaneously, without using a mechanism like a container or a group from which the users inherit values.

To modify multiple objects, you select as many User objects in the NDS tree as you want, using the standard Windows keyboard and mouse combinations, such as Shift+click to select a range of objects and Ctrl+click to select multiple objects that are not adjacent.

After highlighting the objects to be modified, select Details on Multiple Users from the Object menu. A standard Details dialog box appears, in which you can make any changes that you would make to a single User object. When you click OK, your changes are applied to each of the selected objects in turn.

Although this technique is not likely to replace the others already covered in this chapter, particularly on large NDS trees, it does provide a useful alternative to the creation of additional container or Group objects.

Part

II

Ch

7

Moving and Renaming Objects

NetWare Administrator and the NETADMIN utility enable you to move leaf objects from one container to another and to rename any object in the tree, except for the [Root].

To move an object in NetWare Administrator, you must highlight the object, and choose Object, Move. This displays the Move dialog box shown in Figure 7.14. Enter the full distinguished name of the container object into which the object is to be moved, or click the browse icon to display a standard Select Object dialog box.

N O T E Windows users may intuitively try to dra-g-and-drop objects in order to move them. This will not work, however, as the drag-and-drop mechanism is already used to create trustee rights between objects. You can drag and drop objects between two tree browser windows, but only when the windows are displaying different NDS trees.

FIG. 7.14
You can move leaf objects from any container to any other using NetWare Administrator's Move dialog box.

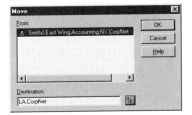

N O T E Container objects can only be moved when they represent partitions of the NDS database. These moves can be accomplished with the NDS Manager utility.

You can rename any container or leaf object in the tree by highlighting it and selecting Rename from the Object menu. This displays the Rename dialog box shown in Figure 7.15.

FIG. 7.15
You can rename any object in the NDS tree (except the [Root]) using NetWare Administrator.

When you rename an object, you are given two options that can provide backwards compatibility to your users. If you mark the Save Old Name check box, the original name of the object is saved as an additional value of the Name property. This way, it is possible to search for the old name and still find the object.

Even greater functionality is provided when you mark the check box that automatically creates an alias of the renamed object and gives it the original name. All references to the old name in applications and operating systems will then continue to function normally.

Searching the NDS Database

Novell Directory Services is designed to accommodate networks of virtually unlimited size. As a result, NDS trees can easily consist of thousands or even tens of thousands of objects. To locate specific objects, NetWare provides the means to search for objects by name, by object class, and by the values of specific properties.

You can search for NDS objects in the Windows environment with NetWare Administrator, and in DOS with the menu-based NETADMIN program and the NLIST command-line utility.

N O T E NETADMIN provides the same search functionality as NetWare Administrator. For information on using the NLIST utility to search for NDS objects from the DOS command line, see Chapter 13, "Using the Workstation Utilities."

When you select Search from NetWare Administrator's Object menu, the dialog box shown in Figure 7.16 is displayed. To perform a search, you first specify the context in which you want to search. The default is the container object that is highlighted when you activate the search function. Mark the Search Entire Subtree box if you want to continue to search downwards through the tree.

FIG. 7.16

NetWare Administrator's Search feature enables you to perform complex searches for objects and their properties.

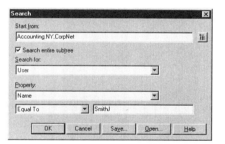

In the Search For field, you specify the type of object for which you are searching. Choose Unknown if you want to search all object types. Then, select the property that you want to use for your search. The properties displayed in the drop-down list vary depending on the object class you have chosen.

Once you have selected a property, choose an operator for the value that you will specify next. You can search for objects with values that are equal to the one you specify for the selected property, values that are not equal, or objects in which the selected property is either present or not present. Finally, in the last field, enter the value for which you want to search, and click OK.

For example, to perform a simple search of the whole tree for SmithJ's User object, you would set the context to [Root], select User in the Search For field, Name in the Property field, Equal To as the operator, and SmithJ as the value.

Part

II

Ch

7

T I P You can use the asterisk as a wild card when specifying alphanumeric property values. For example, you can search for all users whose names start with the letter S by searching for S*. You cannot however, use the question mark to represent a single character, as you can in DOS.

When you click OK, the search is performed, and the results are displayed in a new window, as shown in Figure 7.17. you can then view and modify the found object properties in the usual manner.

FIG. 7.17
Search results are displayed in a new browser window in NetWare Administrator.

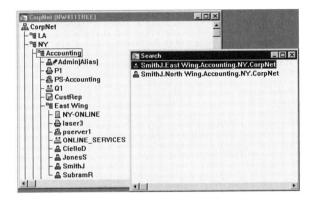

You can also create much more complex searches by the options you select as search criteria. You can build lists of users by their addresses or phone numbers or other information, or determine which users possess rights to certain resources.

Once you have set the parameters for a search, you can click the Save button to create a quick search template, which is a file with an extension of SCH. Whenever you want to perform the same search again, you can simply open the file and begin the search.

Summary

In this chapter, you learned how to build your NDS tree by creating objects and managing many of their properties. Many of a network administrator's NDS maintenance tasks revolve around the assignment of rights, both to the NetWare file system and the NDS database. These tasks are crucial to the operation and security of your network, and each has a separate chapter devoted to it. For more information, see Chapter 15, "Understanding Directory and File Rights," and Chapter 14, "Understanding NDS Object and Property Rights." ●

CHAPTER 8

Networking Applications with NDS

Since its inception, NetWare has provided users access to common hardware resources, such as hard drives and printers. However, although the network operating system can provide the means to store data on a network drive, it was never able to exercise any influence over what data was stored and how it was used. These decisions were left up to the network administrator.

Over the years, administrators developed different methods for using hard drive space. Some use it solely for data files, such as spreadsheets and databases, so that they can be accessed by multiple users. Others install applications on network drives, so that programs as well as data can be shared. Finally, at some sites, even the workstation operating environment or system is installed on a server's drives, eliminating the need for local workstation storage entirely.

In all of these scenarios, however, someone has to install users' applications at each client workstation, and fashion an environment that provides the user with the appropriate rights to access the networked files. NetWare 4.11 finally addresses this problem, by including tools that

How to install the NAL snap-in modules

Before you can create application objects, you must extend the NDS schema and apply the DLL files that enable NetWare Administrator to view and manage the new object types.

How to package your applications as NDS objects

You can create new object types in the NDS database that represent applications, including the environmental parameters needed to make them run.

How to deliver applications to clients using the NetWare Application Launcher (NAL) utility

NAL eliminates the need to perform individual program installations on each client workstation.

enable the network administrator to use Novell Directory Services to control access to applications themselves, and not just the files of which they are comprised.

NetWare Application Launcher is a new feature of NetWare 4.11 that enables you to package your networked applications as NDS objects and deliver them directly to your users' desktops as program icons. However, although the result shown to the user is a standard Windows icon, application objects carry with them many more properties than a simple shortcut to a program's executable file.

Application objects provide clients with access to programs without the need to perform many of the configuration tasks for each user that are usually associated with the process, such as the following:

- Running an installation program at the workstation
- Modifying icon properties (command-line switches, the working directory, and so on)
- Mapping a drive to the volume where the application is stored
- Creating search drives to locate additional files
- Capturing print output for delivery to a network printer
- Distributing technical information to users (how to operate the program, who to call for assistance, and so on)

Preparing the Application

Obviously, before you can create an NDS object that references an application on a server drive, the application must be there. The first step of preparing to use the NetWare Application Launcher services is to install the application from your workstation to a server volume, in the manner recommended by the manufacturer.

Installing the program for network access may not be as easy as it looks, however. While the application is installing, you must learn about it, to see what will be needed to run it from a network drive. The point of using NetWare Application Launcher is to try to avoid performing individual workstation installations. To do so, you may have to duplicate the actions of the application's installation program.

Some applications have a network installation option that makes preparing it to run from the server relatively easy. An option of this type will typically install all of the needed files to the network drive, rather than the local workstation. Applications without such an option may copy some files to directories on your local drive, even when you specify a network directory as the target of the installation.

 T I P Windows programs are particularly susceptible to using files on the local drive, as DLL files are often copied to the \WINDOWS\SYSTEM directory without the user being informed. One method for tracking this activity is to clear the archive bits from all of the files on your workstation before you begin the installation. (You can do this by issuing the ATTRIB -A *.* /S command at the drive root, from the

DOS prompt.) Then, you can be sure that any files having an archive bit after the installation were either added or modified. (You can find out what files have the archive attribute set with a `DIR *.*` `/S/AA ¦ MORE` command at the C:\ (root) DOS prompt.)

The other issue to take note of during the installation is modifications that are made to INI files or to the Windows 95 or Windows NT registry. These can be more difficult to spot. The archive bit trick can tell you what files have changed (including the USER.DAT and SYSTEM.DAT files that comprise the Windows registry), but it cannot tell you exactly what the changes were.

Sometimes you can locate the changes by examining the registry or the INI files themselves. Try searching for the application's name (and variations including abbreviations), its manufacturer's name, and the name of the directory to which you installed it. You can also sometimes find this information in the product documentation.

Another method would be to export the entire registry contents to a file before the installation, then export it again to a different file afterwards. By comparing the two export files, you could locate the changes that have been made during the installation process.

After all this, you may end up with some applications that you simply cannot run without going through the installation process at the workstation. If you cannot create an effective application object to run the program, you should certainly be able to create an object that launches the application's installation program. If you add the proper instructions to the object's properties, you can configure the object so that users can perform the entire installation themselves.

Extending the Directory Schema

Application objects are not a standard component of the Novell Directory Services database. They are actually a perfect example of NDS's extendibility. In Chapter 4, "Novell Directory Services (NDS) and NetWare Administrator," you learned how the objects in the NDS database and the properties that they possess are dictated by the Directory *schema*. Further, you learned that the schema can be extended to add new object types to the database, or new properties to existing objects.

In this case, the Directory schema are extended by the installation of one of the following new NetWare clients:

- IntranetWare Client32 for Windows 3.1
- IntranetWare Client32 for Windows 95
- IntranetWare Client for Windows NT

An extension to the Directory schema is realized in two phases: first, the NDS database itself is modified to add the new objects and their properties. Second, a Windows dynamic-link library (called a *snap-in module)* is installed on the server's SYS: volume and configured for use by NetWare Administrator.

Using Snap-In Modules

Different libraries are installed depending on the workstation operating system that you use to access NetWare Administrator. Table 8.1 lists the names of the libraries and other ancillary files needed for each client operating system, and the directory to which each is installed on the server, by default.

Table 8.1   Snap-In Modules Required for NetWare Application Launcher

Operating System	Library Name	Installation Directory
Windows 3.1	APPSNP3X.DLL	SYS:PUBLIC
	APPRES3X.DLL	SYS:PUBLIC\NLS\ENGLISH
	APPSNAP.HLP	SYS:PUBLIC\NLS\ENGLISH
Windows 95	APPSNP95.DLL	SYS:PUBLIC\WIN95
	APPRES32.DLL	SYS:PUBLIC\WIN95\NLS\ENGLISH
	APPSNAP.HLP	SYS:PUBLIC\WIN95\NLS\ENGLISH
Windows NT	APPSNPNT.DLL	SYS:PUBLIC\WINNT
	APPRES32.DLL	SYS:PUBLIC\WINNT\NLS\ENGLISH
	APPSNAP.HLP	SYS:PUBLIC\WINNT\NLS\ENGLISH

Whichever operating system you use, the Directory schema are extended to enable you to create objects of a new type representing Windows applications. This part of the extension of the NDS schema that adds new objects and their properties is performed on the NDS database itself. The snap-in modules then enable you to view and manage the application objects in NetWare Administrator. Without the modules, the new objects appear in the NDS tree with a question mark icon and the designation Unknown Object.

N O T E   You must use NetWare Administrator to create and manage application objects. The DOS-based NETADMIN utility lacks the capability to address the NDS objects created with extensions to the Directory schema. Application objects appear in the NETADMIN program screens by name, but attempts to view their properties result in an error message.

Although, in the case of NetWare Application Launcher, the schema are extended by a NetWare program, NDS is designed so that it is possible for third-party software developers to extend the schema for their own uses, as well. Some NetWare utilities, for example, extend the schema to create queue objects, much like print queues, that their applications use to store pending jobs that have been created by users, such as system backups and fax transmissions.

NetWare Administrator can access and utilize multiple snap-in modules at the same time, so that new object types created by many different programs can all be visible and manageable.

Manually Installing the NetWare Application Launcher Snap-In Module

When you launch NetWare Administrator, the locations of the snap-in modules needed to view schema extensions are read from the NWADM3X.INI file (for a Windows 3.1 workstation), or from the Windows Registry (for a Windows 95 or Windows NT workstation). If you run NetWare Administrator from a server that does not have the snap-in modules installed, you will have to install them yourself.

To install the snap-in modules, copy the files required for your operating system (as shown in Table 8.1) to the new server. You can place the files in the designated directories or in any directory to which you have access, keeping in mind the following requirements:

- If you place the DLL file in the same directory as the executable for NetWare Administrator, no further actions are necessary. You can run Administrator, which will examine the schema on the server. If the schema have not yet been extended, you are asked if you want to modify them, after which you should be able to see the new objects in the NDS tree.

- If you place the snap-in modules in another location, you must modify the configuration of NetWare Administrator so that they can be found (as explained in the following sections).

Modifying the NWADM3X.INI File   If you are running NetWare Administrator in Windows 3.1, you should find a file called NWADM3X.INI in the WINDOWS directory on your workstation. Open this file in a text editor and locate (or create) a section called:

```
[Snapin Objects DLLs WIN3X]
```

Under that section heading, create an entry that assigns a name to the snap-in object and points to the location of the DLL file that you copied to the server. For example:

```
SNAPIN1=\\NY-LIBRARY\SYS\PUBLIC\APPSNP3X.DLL
```

The name that you assign the object (that is, SNAPIN1 in this example) is not important. It is used only to differentiate the multiple snap-in libraries that may be listed here.

N O T E   Note that the path to the DLL file on the server is given as a UNC (Universal Naming Convention) name. This is the default naming system used by Windows. It consists of the server, volume, directory, and file name, in that order, separated by backslashes and beginning with a double backslash.

Modifying the Windows Registry   If you are running NetWare Administrator on Windows 95 or Windows NT, the configuration data is stored in the operating system's registry. To modify the registry, you must run the Windows Registry Editor, REGEDIT.EXE. (Windows NT includes a 32-bit version of the registry editor, called REGEDT32.EXE.)

In the Registry Editor, locate the following key:

```
HKEY_CURRENT_USER
        \Software
                \NetWare
                        \Parameters
                                \NetWare Administrator
                                        \Snapin Object DLLs WIN95 (or WINNT)
```

Modify the APPSNP95.DLL or APPSNPNT.DLL Value Name, and insert the path to the directory where you have placed the snap-in modules in the Value Data field.

Creating Application Objects

Once your Directory schema have been extended, you can create application objects for the supported operating systems just as you would any other NDS objects. Once you have created the object, you configure its properties. The properties of an application object provide many ways to create a fully serviceable environment in which the application will run.

If you configure an application object correctly, you can use NetWare Application Launcher to deliver fully functional program icons to your users' desktops. You can avoid having to run the installation program for the workstation by using the object's properties to duplicate almost any action that is typically performed during an installation routine, including file copies, INI file modifications, and registry updates.

Finally, you create a list of trustees for the application object. These are the users who are to be granted access to the application. Once the object is properly configured, you can give new users access to the application simply by making them trustees of the object.

To create a new application object, you open NetWare Administrator, and select the container object in which you want to locate the application. When you choose Object, Create (or press the Insert key or click the Create a New Object button on the toolbar or right-click the container and choose Create from the pop-up menu), you see the New Object dialog box shown in Figure 8.1. Select Application and click OK.

TIP NetWare Application Launcher was first released as part of the Client32 for Windows 95 package. This was version 1.0 of the software. Client32 for Windows 3.1 shipped with NAL version 1.02, and NetWare Client for Windows NT with version 1.1. In the 1.0x versions, the Directory schema are extended to enable the creation of four different application objects, for the DOS, Windows 3.1, Windows 95, and Windows NT operating systems.

In NAL version 1.1, the four different application objects were consolidated into one single application object type that contains a property which lists the operating systems for which the application is intended. NAL version 1.1 can manage and delete the objects created with earlier versions of the software, but it is recommended that you use the Windows NT client to extend your Directory's schema whenever possible. This way, your application objects are created with the latest version of the software.

FIG. 8.1

Extending the Directory schema adds additional object types to the New Object dialog box.

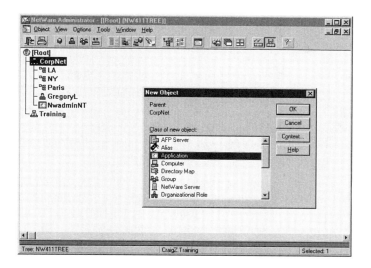

After you select the application object type, the Create Application dialog box appears, as shown in Figure 8.2. You are prompted to enter the name of the new application object, as well as the most fundamental property of the object, the executable file that actually launches the application. Enter the path to the executable, or browse to it in the normal manner.

FIG. 8.2

In the Create Application dialog box, you enter values for the only two properties that are required in an application object: the object name and the location of the application executable.

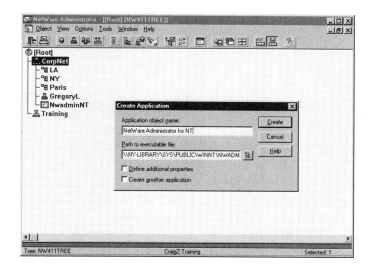

The Create Application dialog box also has the same two additional options that you find when creating most other objects. One check box enables you to immediately create another object of the same type, and another enables you to define additional properties for the object, once it is created.

Configuring Application Objects

The process of configuring an application object is more comprehensive than that of most other objects. Unlike Users and other leaf object types, application objects will rarely inherit property values from other objects, such as containers and groups. The properties of the object itself will nearly always have to be configured to accommodate the needs of the application.

Remember that the overall purpose of creating application objects in the first place is to reduce the amount of individual support that network administrators have to provide for each user workstation. To accomplish this goal, you must consider the needs of the user as well as the needs of the application.

Application objects are equipped with properties that are designed to hold information for users that will hopefully prevent them from having to call for help. Anytime that you spend providing users with customized help and instructions online will almost certainly be rewarded with fewer support calls and increased user productivity.

The following application object properties need to be configured:

- Identification
- Environment
- Drive mappings
- Printer ports
- Description
- Fault tolerance
- Scripts
- Contacts
- Associations
- Administrator notes

The following sections cover each of the screens in an application object's Details dialog box, and the properties that you use to create an environment in which the program can run effectively.

Identification   The Identification screen (see Figure 8.3) contains the basic information that will be used to create the program icon that NetWare Application Launcher delivers to your users. The Application Icon Title field is the label that will accompany the program icon in the launcher window. By default, this is the same as the application object name, but it need not be. You can use any name that you want to identify the application to your users.

Although the icon found in the program executable is used by default, you can use any icon that you want for your application. Just browse to any ICO, EXE, or DLL file and scan it for alternative icons.

FIG. 8.3
The Identification screen contains the basic information used to create an icon on users' desktops.

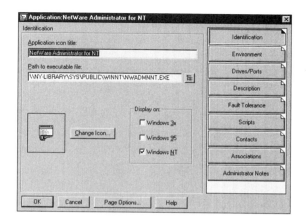

The Display On box controls which operating systems users must run in order to display this application object in the launcher window. This is important if your application runs only on certain operating systems, or if you have different versions of the application for different platforms.

Only version 1.1 of NetWare Application Launcher includes platform selection capability. Previous NAL versions had separate object types for each of the three Windows platforms. If you have an application that could run in all three environments, you would have to create three separate objects, one of each type, to accommodate all of them.

A good example of this treatment for separate platforms is the NAL client application itself. The product includes separate executables for each of the three Windows operating systems. Normally, you would have to create three different objects in such a case.

However, NAL also includes a *wrapper* executable called NAL.EXE. Users can execute this program from any Windows platform. The NAL.EXE program detects the platform being used and launches the appropriate executable for that operating system. Thus, you could theoretically create one application object for NAL.EXE, rather than three separate objects for the platform-specific executables.

Of course, creating an application object for the application launcher itself is absurd, but the example illustrates the different ways in which applications can be designed to accommodate various operating systems.

The final field on this screen contains the path to the application's executable file itself. This property should already have a value, assigned when you created the object. It is best to use a UNC path name to the executable. It is possible to use a drive letter that has been mapped to a network drive, but only if all of your users will be using the same drive mappings.

N O T E   Some applications require a drive letter and cannot run from an absolute network path
name. When needed, you can specify a drive letter on the command line, and configure the
application object to create the appropriate drive mapping before the executable is launched. You can
then release the drive mapping when the user exits the application. See "Drives/Ports," later in this
chapter.

If you do map the application to a drive letter and then change the drive mappings that you
assign to your users at a later time, the object properties will have to be changed also. An absolute path like a UNC name makes more sense and leaves one less item to debug when you are
testing the functionality of your objects.

N O T E   Do not include command line parameters in the executable file field. The environment
screen (covered in the next section) provides a place for these, instead.

Environment   The Environment screen contains the other basic properties that are typically
found in the configuration of a Windows icon. In the field provided, you can specify any command line parameters that are to be included when the application is executed. The use and
syntax of these parameters is determined wholly by the application itself.

The Working Directory field (see Figure 8.4) indicates the default directory that the application will use to locate files. Depending on the application, this might be used to specify a directory where additional program files are located, or it may reflect the location of the default data
directory to be used by the application. Again, this field is treated no differently than if you
were altering the properties of a normal Windows program icon or shortcut.

FIG. 8.4
The Environment screen
contains many of the
same properties that
are found in a typical
windows icon.

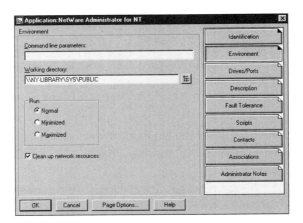

You can also specify whether the application is to be maximized or minimized when it is
launched, or whether it should simply run in its default size. You will later have the opportunity
to specify that certain applications should be launched immediately when a user runs the

application launcher program. You can configure a particular program to run automatically, in a minimized state, whenever a user logs in.

The final option on this screen, the Clean Up Network Resources check box, is the first option that extends the power of the application launcher beyond that of a typical program. You will find further examples of NAL's extensibility as you configure the properties on the other screens in this dialog box. You can create environmental controls, such as drive mappings and printer port captures, specifically for this application.

Marking the Clean Up Network Resources check box means that any of the configuration parameters that are set when this application object is launched will be reset to their original state when the application is closed.

The potential value of this feature must be contemplated to be fully appreciated. Rather than using a login script to create a permanent connection to a server for each user just so that he or she can run a single application, you can use an application object to create the server connection. Users are then connected to the server only when they are actually running the application. An arrangement like this could enable you to use a 50-user license for that server, rather than a 100-user license, not to mention the savings in administration time and network traffic.

Drives/Ports   The Drives/Ports panel enables you to create drive mappings and printer port captures specifically for use with the application you are setting up. When users activate an icon in the NAL window, the mappings and captures are created before the application file is executed.

You can therefore reference the drive letters and printer ports in the application's command line and working directory fields, if needed, because they will exist when those fields are read by the client operating system.

Configuring the environment for individual applications saves on having to create login scripts that provide the required mappings and captures for all of a user's applications. User logins proceed more quickly, and network resources are not accessed until they are needed.

Creating Drive Mappings   You can create any kind of drive mapping from the Create Drive Mappings panel that you would from a login script. The Option field (see Figure 8.5) enables you to select whether you want to create a regular drive mapping (by selecting Drive) or a search drive. If you select S1, a search drive is created (or inserted if the drive letter selected already exists). S16 maps the drive and places it last in the search path.

The drive field enables you to select the drive letter to be mapped, or use the first available drive letter on the user's workstation (by selecting Next). You enter (or browse to) the volume or directory for the mapping in the Path field.

Mark the Root check box to make the directory you select the root of the chosen drive letter. This prevents users from seeing the directories above that which has been mapped to the drive letter.

FIG. 8.5

The Drive/Ports panel enables you to map drives and capture ports specifically for use with this application.

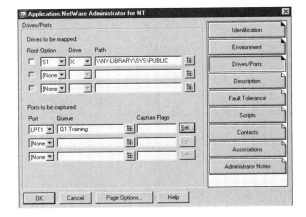

CAUTION

It is important to consider the existing workstation environment when configuring drive mappings. Although you can dynamically set and release a drive mapping with NAL, the drive mapping must be available before the application is launched.

An existing workstation drive letter will not be remapped by the launch of an application object. If a user has already mapped drive H: to a particular volume, a mapping for drive H: to a different volume for an application object will be ignored, possibly affecting the performance of the application.

You must be aware of users' existing mappings when using the drive mapping feature. In many cases, you can avoid users' own mappings by assigning drive letters in the latter part of the alphabet (without conflicting with search drives, which are assigned to Z: and work backward, by default). Users typically have only a few search drives, so selecting drive S: or T: can usually be a pretty safe bet.

It is also important to avoid drive mapping conflicts between application objects. You can map the same drive letter to two different directories in two different application objects. When you check the Clean Up Network Resources check box in the Environment screen, all of the mappings that are created before the application is launched are erased when it is closed. Problems will arise, however, if a user attempts to run both applications at the same time. The drive mappings of the application that is launched first will be retained until that application is terminated.

N O T E   Drive mappings and port captures created by application objects are only erased if NetWare Application Launcher is running when the application is closed. If you shut down the launcher while your applications are still running, the environment created by the application objects will remain intact after the applications have been closed. ▪

If you are going to be committed to the use of NetWare Application Launcher for your users, it is usually best to take complete control of the user environment, so that conflicts do not arise as the result of users' own workstation configuration efforts. In fact, you can use NAL in place of the Windows shell, restricting users only to the applications and configurations that you allow them.

Capturing Printer Ports   As with drive mappings, you can define printer port captures that are applied before an application is loaded and removed once the program has been terminated. You may, for example, have a graphics application on your network that prints to a color printer. Because the cost of a color printer's operation is much higher than that of a black-and-white printer, you might want to restrict access to it. By creating an application object that captures a port to the queue serviced by the color printer, you can control access to the application and the printer at the same time.

To capture print output, you select the LPT number in the Port field, and enter (or browse to) the name of the desired print queue object. Selecting a port activates the Set button, which enables you to turn three of the standard NetWare port capture parameters on or off. By default, all port captures use the NetWare client settings that have been configured in the printer driver. However, if you activate any of the Override Workstation Setting check boxes in the Set Capture Flags dialog box (see Figure 8.6), you can change the settings for the Notify, Banner, and Form Feed parameters for this port capture only.

FIG. 8.6

The Set Capture Flags dialog box enables you to override the default printer port capture settings.

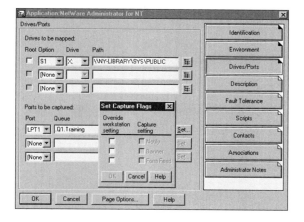

As you manipulate the port capture settings, notice how the appropriate switches are added to the Capture Flags field back in the Drives/Ports screen.

N O T E   Port settings are like drive mappings in that they must be free before they can be assigned by the application object. ◼

Description   The Description property is simply a blank field in which you can enter any information or instructions intended for the users of the application, up to approximately 4K in size. When users view the Properties of one of the icons in the NAL window, the Description information is displayed in the default screen of the dialog box.

Fault Tolerance   The Fault Tolerance panel contains two new options that have been added to version 1.1 of NetWare Application Launcher: fault tolerance and load balancing. These features enable NAL to accommodate an almost unlimited number of users, and provide users with access to their applications, even when their primary server is unavailable.

Both fault tolerance and load balancing are methods by which users can automatically access alternative application objects. When you have a large number of users who must access a single application—more users than can be handled by a single server—the normal solution is to install the application on several servers. You then create multiple NDS objects for the same application in various locations.

The problem with having multiple copies of the application is that you must grant your users rights to only one of the applications, essentially splitting them into groups, each of which is serviced by one of the application objects. If the rights are not carefully assigned, then one server could be servicing many more users than another. What's more, if a server goes down, then all of its users' icons become non-functional, even though other servers could conceivably take up the slack.

You can balance the number of users accessing the same application on different servers by installing your application on each server and creating an application object for each copy. Then in the Fault Tolerance panel of one of the objects, you activate the Enable Load Balancing check box, and add the objects representing the other copies of the same application to the list, as shown in Figure 8.7.

FIG. 8.7
Fault tolerance and load balancing provide users with access to alternative objects representing the same application on different servers.

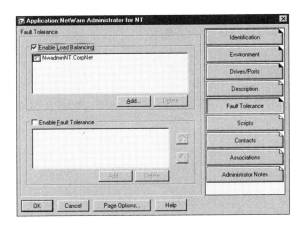

As your users access the application, they will automatically be distributed among the various objects listed. Load balancing is generally used when you have duplicate resources that perform equally well. That is, you would not want to balance your users among applications installed on servers at different physical sites. This would cause the application to perform better for some users than for others who would end up accessing the application across slower WAN links.

You could, however, effectively list objects at different sites in the fault tolerance list, on the same screen. Fault tolerance functions a lot like load balancing, except that users are not given access to the alternative objects listed unless the application that they were assigned to use is unavailable.

Thus, if you have one copy of a particular application at each of your company's three offices, the application object at each site could list the other two as alternates. If the server at one office should go down, then users attempting to launch that application will immediately be diverted to the other objects in the fault tolerance list (in order of appearance). Their access may be slower because they are accessing a remote server, but any productivity is better than none.

You can use both load balancing and fault tolerance at the same time, to provide your users with continuous application access, even in conditions of high traffic or server malfunction.

Scripts   In "Preparing the Application" earlier in this chapter, you read about how you often must familiarize yourself with the behavior of your applications before you can effectively create objects to represent them. In many cases, your object must duplicate the effect of an installation program on each workstation that launches it. You've seen, in previous sections, how you can perform standard procedures, such as custom drive mappings and port captures, but a system like NAL could not possibly provide a sufficient array of features to accommodate any application.

Instead, you can create opening and closing scripts that are associated with a particular object. The scripts use the same basic language and syntax as NetWare login scripts, because NAL makes calls to the same interface that processes workstation login scripts in a GUI environment.

Scripts are executed after the application environment is applied, and before it is removed, respectively. With scripts, you can program changes to the INI or registry files on your users' workstations, copy files, and set other environmental attributes that might be needed to run your application.

The effects of scripts are not automatically negated when the application is closed, as other application environment settings are. That is why you can create both pre- and post-execution scripts. If necessary, you can use a post-execution script to clean up the effects of the pre-execution commands.

Although application scripts are similar in function and capabilities to login scripts, there are some differences. Unlike login scripts, application scripts do not execute visibly. There is no provision for a window that displays results as the script's commands are executing, nor can scripts play sounds or prompt for user input. This alone explains why some of the following login script commands cannot be used in application scripts:

- CLS
- DISPLAY
- EXIT *filename*
- FDISPLAY
- FIRE PHASERS
- INCLUDE
- LASTLOGINTIME
- MACHINE=
- NO_DEFAULT
- NOSWAP
- PAUSE
- PCCOMPATIBLE
- SCRIPT_SERVER
- SET
- SET_TIME
- SWAP
- WRITE

However, all of the documented identifier variables that work in login scripts are also functional in application scripts. This means that your scripts can pull environmental information from the NetWare client, the NDS database, and the NetWare operating system itself, by using variables, such as %FULL_NAME, %FILE_SERVER, and %LOGIN_NAME.

▷ **See** "Login Scripts," **p. 455**

You can also use application scripts to run other programs before or along with your application because application scripts contain a facility that login scripts lack. Normally, to execute a program from a script, you precede it with the number sign (#), causing the processing of the script to pause until the external program relinquishes control. You can use this technique to apply the changes normally made by an application's installation program to INI files or the registry of the client workstation. For example, including the following command in a pre-execution script will launch the Windows 95 Registry Editor and apply the changes found in a file called REGSET.REG:

```
#REGEDIT /S REGSET.REG
```

If necessary, you can then program the post-execution script to undo whatever changes you have made.

However, you can also execute an external program from an application script by preceding it with the *at* symbol (@), which causes the external program to be launched as the script processing continues. The external program remains active on the workstation until it is closed by some other means. You can use this feature to load programs that are needed or used with the application.

The use of pre- and post-execution scripts depends solely on the needs of the application. Many of today's software products are network-aware, and require little special treatment to be adapted for use as an application object. Others may be designed solely for use on stand-alone PCs, and may cause you great difficulty, even to the point at which it is not worth the effort to try and replicate the effects of the installation program.

In cases in which the application is not network-aware, you can always place disk images or installation files on a network directory, and then create an application object that references the installation program for the application. You can then include, in the application object, the instructions needed for users to perform the installation themselves.

You can take this technique even further, by using application objects to perform workstation upgrades, as well. Application objects can be used to install network clients, operating system upgrades, or any other software update that is packaged as an executable file.

Contacts   The Contacts screen is designed to hold a list of NDS objects representing the users that should be contacted to obtain help for this particular application, including the names of network support personnel. Like the Description panel, the use of this property is optional.

Associations   The Associations screen is where you store the list of the User, Group, or container objects that are to be allowed access to this application. When you add a User object to this list (see Figure 8.8), the application's icon appears in the user's NAL window. Users can also inherit an association from a parent container or a group of which they are a member.

FIG. 8.8
The Associations panel in the application object Details dialog box lists the objects that have been made trustees of the application.

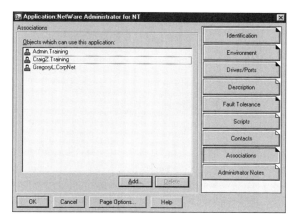

Creating an association in this manner makes the user, container, or group object a trustee of the application object. Interestingly, you can establish the same relationship from the trustee object's Details dialog box. A user object contains application properties, which you can configure in the screen shown in Figure 8.9.

FIG. 8.9
The Details dialog box of a User object contains an Applications panel that enables you to automatically launch an application when NAL.EXE is executed.

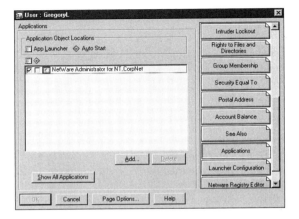

As you can see, in the Details dialog box of a User object you can configure whether a chosen application object is to appear in the launcher window, execute automatically when NAL is launched, or both. You can also click the Show All Applications button, which presents a listing of all the applications to which the User object is associated. This is much like an effective rights display, in that all of the objects to which the user has inherited rights from containers and groups are listed (see Figure 8.10).

FIG. 8.10
The Application Objects dialog box displays all of the applications to which a user has explicit or inherited rights.

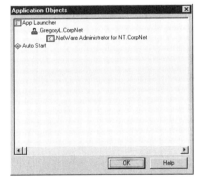

N O T E It is extremely important for the network administrator to be aware that associating a User object with an application object in the Application Objects dialog box simply makes the application's icon appear when the user runs NAL. It does not give the user trustee rights to manipulate the application object itself. More importantly, it does not give the user the rights to access the files needed by the application to run. ▨

You must grant users rights to the NetWare file system independently of their application object rights. When you cause a new icon to appear in a user's NAL window, the icon will not function unless the user also has at least read and file scan rights to the directory containing the application files. The file rights that are needed to run an application can vary widely. You may have to grant additional rights to certain files or directories, for the application to function properly.

Administrator Notes

This is another informational screen, that is intended to hold the network administrators' notes about the deployment of the application and the configuration of the object. It is always a good idea to document any system that might have to be supported by other people, and this panel provides approximately 30K of space for such documentation where it is not likely to be lost.

The information in this field is not visible to normal users; it can only be viewed in NetWare Administrator by those who have Supervisor rights to the object.

Using NetWare Application Launcher

When you run the installation program that extends your Directory schema, the NetWare Application launcher client files are copied to your server's PUBLIC directory. There are three executables provided for the NAL client, one each for the 16- and 32-bit Windows platforms supported by NAL (that is, Windows 3.1, Windows 95, and Windows NT), plus a wrapper executable called NAL.EXE.

When the wrapper program is executed, it ascertains which operating system is running on the workstation, and launches the appropriate executable, NALW31.EXE (for Windows 3.1 clients) or NALWIN32.EXE (for Windows 95 and NT clients). You can, therefore, configure all of your client workstations to execute NAL.EXE, and the appropriate version of the launcher will always be loaded, even if the user logs in from different computers.

N O T E NAL versions before 1.1 included a fourth executable, NALW95.EXE, which was used exclusively by Windows 95 workstations. In version 1.1, the NALW32.EXE program supports both Windows 95 and Windows NT. When NAL.EXE is executed on a Windows 95 workstation, NALW32.EXE is copied to the Client32 directory (usually C:\NOVELL\CLIENT32), along with NALBMP32.DLL, NALRES32.DLL and NAL.HLP, which are placed in C:\NOVELL\CLIENT32\NLS\ENGLISH. █

Loading NAL.EXE

Depending on the needs and expertise of your users, there are several strategies with which you can enforce the use of NetWare Application Launcher. For example, you can place an icon or shortcut to NAL.EXE in a workstation's Startup group, so that it loads with Windows.

If you want to restrict your users to the applications that you designate for them, you can also use NAL as a replacement for the Windows shell. On a Windows 3.1 or Windows 95 workstation, you can replace PROGMAN.EXE or EXPLORER.EXE as the shell by changing the SHELL= line in the SYSTEM.INI file to point to NAL.EXE.

When you replace the shell, NetWare Application Launcher runs in place of the Windows 3.1 Program Manager or the Windows 95 Explorer shell. Users can access only the applications that you make available in the NAL window. If you allow users the right to close NAL, they are left with an empty desktop, and no means to run any applications at all.

N O T E   When you replace the Windows shell with NAL, you should copy the NAL program files to the workstation, rather than running them from the network drive. You should also be sure to include the directory in which you place the files in the local PATH statement, so that NAL can always find the files that it needs to operate.

You can also run NAL as your shell on a Windows NT 4.0 workstation, although, this involves an additional measure of risk for the administrator. If any problem arises on a Windows 3.1 or 95 workstation while shelling to NAL.EXE, you can always boot the workstation to a DOS prompt and manually edit the SYSTEM.INI file, to return to the original shell.

You can't boot to DOS with Windows NT, which is not based on a DOS kernel. To change the program used as the shell, you must modify the Windows NT registry, using the REGEDT32.EXE program to access the following key:

```
HKEY_LOCAL_MACHINE
        Software
                Microsoft
                        WindowsNT
                                CurrentVersion
                                        WinLogon
                                                Shell
```

The value of the Shell key is EXPLORER.EXE by default, and you must change it to NAL.EXE, again in a directory on the local drive. As with Windows 95 and 3.1, the NAL files should be on the local drive, in a directory on the workstation's path (which you change in the System Control Panel).

Once you have booted Windows NT with NetWare Application Launcher as the shell, you must again edit the registry in order to change the shell back, should problems arise. However, you will only be able to edit the registry if you create an application object for REGEDT32.EXE, or if you have configured the workstation to enable remote registry editing.

CAUTION

Novell does not officially endorse the use of NAL as the Windows NT shell, although it has been done successfully. In most cases, however, this would not be a practical arrangement. Windows NT is often positioned as an operating system for users with greater than average computing needs. It also requires a higher-end computer (with more memory and a faster processor) to operate efficiently. This usually results in users with a level of computing expertise that does not warrant the restrictions imposed by replacing the NT shell with the NAL shell. It makes little sense to give users a more powerful computer, and then restrict their access to its resources.

Configuring NAL

In the "Associations" section earlier in this chapter, you learned that you can assign application objects to users through the Details dialog box of either the Application or the User object. There is also a panel in User and container objects that enables you to configure the way that the application launcher will appear and operate on users' desktops.

When you first access the Launcher Configuration screen in a user object's Details dialog box, all of the options are grayed out, as the object is configured to use the launcher settings of the parent container, by default. Organization and Organizational Unit objects both have the same panel in their Details dialog boxes, enabling you to configure properties that are inherited by the users in the container, just as other NDS and file system rights are inherited.

N O T E   A user's launcher configuration properties can be inherited only from container objects, such as Organizations and Organizational Units. They cannot be inherited from Group objects.

As with the other types of rights, it is generally recommended that you configure individual workstation objects only in exceptional cases. Configuring the settings in your container objects is far less time-consuming than modifying User objects.

When you click the Use Current Settings radio button in the dialog box, the options are activated (as shown in Figure 8.11), and you can configure the properties, as follows:

- Exit the launcher
- Log in/log out
- Refresh icons
- View folders
- Create personal folders
- Save window size
- Enable timed refresh
- Inherit container applications
- E-mail attribute

Settings that are changed do not take effect until NAL.EXE is closed and relaunched. The following sections examine the various properties, and their effect on the launcher window.

Exit the Launcher   The exit option controls whether or not the user is permitted to exit the application launcher, once it is launched. If your users load the launcher from their windows Startup group, they may not know how to reload the launcher, should they close it by mistake. If you disable this setting, the File/Exit command is grayed out, and other means of closing the launcher window are disabled.

If you are using NAL as the Windows shell, then exiting the launcher shuts down Windows, as well. You should always leave this option enabled, in this case, so that users can perform a controlled Windows shutdown.

FIG. 8.11
The Launcher Configura-
tion dialog box enables
you to control how
NetWare Application
Launcher appears to a
user.

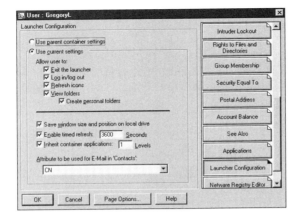

Log In/Log Out   The Log In/Log Out option enables users to log in and out of the network
from within the launcher (by choosing File, Login). This function simply calls the appropriate
NetWare client login program from the workstation (LOGINW31.EXE, LOGINW95.EXE, or
LOGINWNT.EXE). Be sure that the program is available to the launcher, either in the current
directory, or in another directory that is in the workstation's PATH.

Refresh Icons   The refresh option controls whether users can manually refresh the icons in
the launcher window (using the View/Refresh option). If you assign users' rights to a new
application object, this option enables users to display the icon in the launch window without
closing and restarting it.

View Folders   The View Folders option splits the user's NAL window into two panes, as
shown in Figure 8.12. The right pane contains the application icons, and the left pane contains a
tree display of the objects to which the user has been granted rights. Application objects that
have been explicitly associated with a User object are listed in a folder named for the user.
Objects inherited from containers are stored in a folder named for the container object.

FIG. 8.12
The View Folders option
displays a user's appli-
cation objects in a tree
display modeled after
the NDS database.

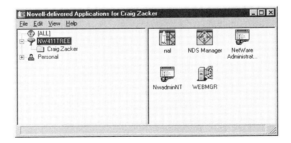

Users who are not familiar with the layout of the NDS tree may be more confused by this display than aided by it. In many cases, users will not care where the application object is stored in
the tree, or how rights to the object have been granted to them. In these cases, it may be best
to disable this feature.

Create Personal Folders   You can also give your users the right to create folders of their own in the NAL window. Personal NAL folders are logical groupings of application objects that users can customize to their own tastes. These folders are stored in the NetWare Registration Database on the server, so they appear even when a user logs in to the network from different workstations.

You manage your personal folders using the commands in the application launcher's File menu. You can create, rename, and delete folders, all of which appear in the NAL tree display under the Personal label. Once folders have been created, a user can drag and drop icons into them to form application groups that suit their own needs, as shown in Figure 8.13.

FIG. 8.13
Personal folders are logical groupings of application icons created and managed by the user.

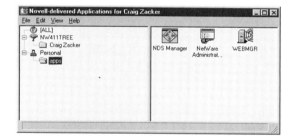

Users can only manage the contents of personal folders. Icons that are dragged from container or user object branches of the tree display are copied, not moved. The originals always remain intact, unless the application object itself is moved in the NDS tree by the network administrator.

Save Window Size   The Save Window Size feature enables users to place the NAL window on the desktop and adjust its size. The settings that the user selects are then saved to the NetWare Registration Database. The next time the user runs NAL, the window will appear in the same place on the screen and be the same size. The default value for this option is on.

Enable Timed Refresh   Timed refresh allows a user's NAL display to be automatically updated to reflect new icons at regular intervals. When this option is disabled, users must manually choose View, Refresh to see new application icons that have been recently associated assigned to them (assuming that they have been granted the right to refresh the screen manually).

When you enable timed refresh, the default interval is 3,600 seconds, or 60 minutes. It is recommended that you do not set this value too low, because the continual refreshes of many different users can add significantly to your network traffic levels.

Inherit Container Applications   By default, users inherit assignments to application objects only from their immediate parent container. The Inherit Container Applications option enables you to modify this property to increase the number of levels from which application assignments are inherited. For example, users located in the Accounting.NY.CorpNet context will normally be granted access only to the applications that have been associated with their User objects, and with the Accounting container object. If you increase the value for this property to 2, then the users will have access to the applications associated with both the Accounting and NY containers, as well as their own User objects.

E-Mail Attribute   The E-mail attribute field enables you to select the property of the User objects in your tree that stores the users' e-mail address. This e-mail address then appears in the Contacts screen of an NAL icon's Properties dialog box when the user selects the name of one of the contacts listed there. If you have a MAPI-compatible e-mail application installed, then the user can send an e-mail directly to the chosen contact.

Using the NAL Client

The client portion of NetWare Application Launcher presents an extremely simple display to the user. By default, launching NAL.EXE causes a standard window to appear (see Figure 8.14), labeled Novell-delivered Applications for that particular user. The window contains icons that look like any other Windows icons, which the user double-clicks to launch the application, in the usual manner.

N O T E   If you have granted your users the right to see folders, then the NAL window also contains a tree display, as shown in "View Folders" earlier in this chapter. ▣

FIG. 8.14
The NAL window provides a simple interface in which the most novice users can easily locate their applications.

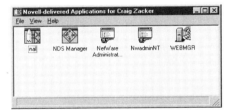

To display additional information, select an icon and choose File, Properties (or right-click the icon and select Properties from the pop-up menu). This displays a properties dialog box for the application that contains six panels, displaying much of the information that you configured into the object during the creation process (see Figure 8.15).

As you can see, the Properties dialog box is the user's most convenient source of information about the application. This is why it is recommended that you take the time when creating your application objects to enter the description and contact information that can be so useful here. The more you allow users to easily help themselves, the less often they must call for assistance.

FIG. 8.15

The Properties dialog box for an icon contains most of the application object's configuration information.

Summary

NetWare Application Launcher is a significant addition to the capabilities of Novell Directory Services and a harbinger of the future of large-scale directory services, in general. By representing all types of network resources—human, hardware, and software—as objects, it becomes easy to define the relationships between them and to control their access. Future plans for NDS involve the assimilation of networks running other operating systems and even Internet resources into a single directory. The prospects for the improvement of networking systems are virtually unlimited. ●

Using NDS as a Global Directory Services Solution

Directory Services are organizational tools that enable administrators to view the essential elements of a computer network as objects. The objects represent not only the hardware and software elements of a network, such as computers and printers, but people as well, and even intangible concepts, such as the jobs that people do and the departments and user groups with which they are associated.

Directory services function by the establishment of rules that govern the relationships between different types of objects. These rules define the function of each object and the ways that it can interact with other objects.

Of course, these concepts are hardly new to people who are familiar with NetWare and the Novell Directory Services database. NetWare users have, for several years, had the capability to create objects that represent their NetWare servers, their printers, and the users that access them, along with a wide selection of other object types.

Novell Workstation Manager for Windows NT

By adding the capability to create NDS objects that represent Windows NT systems, the Novell Workstation Manager for Windows NT product eliminates the need for NetWare clients to maintain separate user accounts on Windows NT workstations and servers.

Installing the Workstation Manager components

Workstation Manager consists of an enhanced IntranetWare Client for Windows NT and additional modules that extend the schema of the NDS database.

Lightweight Directory Access Protocol (LDAP) services for Novell Directory Services (NDS)

LDAP enables information stored in the NDS database to be published on intranet or Internet services.

Accessing the NDS database using an LDAP client

Microsoft's Internet Explorer contains a rudimentary LDAP client feature that enables users to search for users in the NDS database.

However, while NDS is a powerful tool for NetWare network administrators, its usefulness in the enterprise network has always been hampered by its incompatibility with other network types. It has been difficult for the highly competitive manufacturers of networking products to face up to the fact that the concept of the one-vendor shop is all but dead. Consumers want to use the best product for the task at hand, and they want all of the available products to be able to work together.

Although other manufacturers are currently developing directory service products, Novell Directory Services is already deployed at a great many more locations than any competing standard. Novell has also begun to make significant inroads towards the expansion of NDS to function beyond the limits of the NetWare network. In this chapter, you learn about the products and concepts that have recently been announced, and which begin to position NDS as a universal directory service. ■

Searching for a Higher Standard

As networking technology progresses, particularly in the area of Internet and intranet development, it becomes increasingly clear that the formulation of universal standards for data communication is essential to the advancement of the industry. Small workgroup networks assembled to perform specialized tasks are now being connected to other networks that may of different types. In order for these different network models to communicate with each other, they must have a common language at every level of the communications hierarchy.

The efforts expended in the development of these common languages seem to have proceeded from the bottom of the basic OSI networking model, that is, the physical manifestation of the network, and slowly worked their way towards the top, which is the application's network interface. The industry-wide acceptance of certain low-level network types, such as Ethernet, has given way to the adoption of a standard set of transport protocols: TCP/IP. Work is now progressing on standards that can be applied to the upper reaches of the networking model, and the development of the protocols needed to implement global directory services is part of this effort.

This phenomenon is being manifested on networks of nearly any size. Smaller networks may want nothing more than an administrative interface that provides unified network access control and eliminates the need to manually configure individual computers. Large private networks are creating intranet services on which clients use a universal interface on any computing platform to access information resources that span the entire enterprise.

Finally, the Internet itself is growing at a tremendous rate, and is sorely in need of a global, distributed directory that can provide users with access to information about people, documents, and other resources, located all over the world.

Work is proceeding on all of these levels, and as the pieces begin to fall into place, the potential value of these directory services to computer networks of every size becomes increasingly apparent.

Managing Windows NT Systems with NDS

When Windows NT first made its appearance in 1993, NetWare had an overwhelming percentage of the network operating system market. Over the course of several years, Windows NT has gradually eroded that market share. However, in a great many cases, it has done so not by replacing NetWare entirely, but by operating alongside it on the same network, using a simple domain-based organizational paradigm left over from Microsoft's LanManager product.

Many administrators have come to realize that there is a place for both network operating systems on their enterprise networks, but there has a been a problem from the beginning that complicates the task of maintaining both systems. Microsoft has been promising a directory service for Windows NT since 1993, and the talk of the upcoming "Cairo" release is getting to be as old as the city itself. In the interim, Windows NT uses a system of domains, which are collections of Windows network workstations that have been granted access to particular Windows NT servers.

The use of domains enables a network administrator to create accounts for many users on a single machine. However, whether domains are used or not, a user must log in to a Windows NT machine before access even to the computer's local resources is granted. This means that a combined NetWare/Windows NT network has always had two completely separate access control systems that must be maintained, with a separate account for every user on each network.

Novell has now addressed this multiple user account problem, and greatly enhanced the usefulness of Novell Directory Services, by releasing a version of their IntranetWare Client for Windows NT that includes a new product called Workstation Manager for Windows NT.

Workstation Manager allows for the creation of a new object type in the NDS database that represents a computer running Windows NT. This object, called an NT Client Configuration, is then associated with the User objects of the people who must access that workstation. When the user performs an NDS login, a Dynamic Local User account is automatically created in the Windows NT Security Access Manager (or SAM) by the NetWare client software. The user is then logged in to the Windows NT machine, and work proceeds normally.

The Windows NT client working in conjunction with the NDS database enables all of a user's login information—for both the NetWare and Windows networks—to be stored in the NDS database. This eliminates the need for Windows NT domains and the manual creation of separate user accounts for each network.

Workstation Manager does not allow NDS to completely take over the administration of the Windows NT network. It is still necessary to create shares in the normal manner, and assign access permissions to users and groups, but you can configure group memberships as part of the NT Client Configuration object. This configuration provides a newly created user account with ready-made access to existing Windows network shares.

Installing Workstation Manager for Windows NT

Workstation Manager consists of two parts:

■ Snap-in modules that extend the NDS schema and enable users to create and manage NT Client Configuration objects, using NetWare Administrator

■ A revised version of the NWGINA module (the module used for logging in to a network) for the IntranetWare Client for Windows NT that dynamically creates the accounts in the NT Security Access Manager

Extending the Schema   In Chapter 4, "Novell Directory Services (NDS) and NetWare Administrator," you learned about the Directory schema that control the types of objects that you can create in the NDS database, their properties, and their relationships to other object types. In this respect, the installation of Workstation Manager is no different from that of NetWare Application Launcher. The schema of the NDS database itself are extended to allow the creation of a new object type, and two new DLLs are entered into the Windows NT Registry, causing them to be loaded when NetWare Administrator for Windows NT is launched.

These DLLs cause the new object to be recognized as valid by NetWare Administrator. If these DLLs are not available, then any NT Client Configuration objects in the NDS tree are not recognized. They appear in the NDS browser with a question mark icon, and they cannot be created or managed. This failure can occur if

■ the NWSMGR32.DLL and NWSMGRR.DLL files are deleted from the SYS:PUBLIC\WINNT directory,

■ you run NetWare Administrator from a Windows NT workstation that has not had its Registry modified by Workstation Manager installation sequence,

■ you run NetWare Administrator from a Windows 3.1 or Windows 95 workstation,

■ you run NetWare Administrator from a Windows NT workstation using a different Windows NT user account than that with which you installed Workstation Manager.

The extension of the schema is performed when you run the ADMSETUP.EXE program that ships as part of the client package. This is the utility that copies the Windows NT versions of the NetWare GUI utilities to the server of your choice. In the latest version of the client, NetWare Administrator and NetWare Application Launcher, which have always been part of the client, are joined by a third option: that for Workstation Manager, as shown in Figure 9.1.

You must run the ADMSETUP.EXE program and install Workstation Manager option on every Windows NT workstation that you will use to create and manage NT Client Configuration objects in the NDS tree.

Replacing NWGINA   The second part of Workstation Manager software consists of an updated version of the NWGINA module, which is installed when you run the IntranetWare Client for Windows NT SETUPNW.EXE program. NWGINA is the NetWare Graphical Identification and Authentication Interface, a long and awkward acronym for the login dialog box that appears when you boot the Windows NT system with Novell's latest client installed. NWGINA replaces the Windows NT GINA during the client installation.

FIG. 9.1

The latest version of the ADMSETUP.EXE program includes the option to install Workstation Manager.

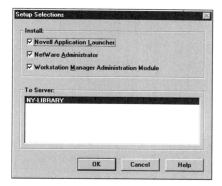

Workstation Manager ships as part of a new version of the full Novell client package, the primary difference of which is an updated NWGINA module that runs on the Windows NT system with local Administrator equivalence. This provides the module with the rights to create new user accounts on the Windows NT machine.

Once the Workstation Manager components are installed, the NDS connection is always authenticated and established first during the IntranetWare client login sequence, using the NDS User object specified in the client configuration. Once the standard NetWare login process is completed, Workstation Manager proceeds as follows:

1. The NWGINA module reads the properties of the user's NDS object and detects its association to a particular NT Client Configuration object.

2. NWGINA reads the properties of the NT Client Configuration object from the NDS database, which contains the account that is to be used to log in to the Windows NT system.

3. NWGINA searches the Windows NT system's Security Access Manager (SAM) to see if the desired account already exists.

4. If the account exists, then the login proceeds on the Windows NT machine using this account. If no such account exists, then NWGINA creates a new account on the Windows NT machine using the information contained in the NT Client Configuration object, and the NT logon sequence proceeds.

The account on the NT system can be created using the name and password of the associated NDS User object, or another name and password defined as properties of the Configuration object.

The installation and activation of the new NWGINA module is a completely separate process from that of extending the schema. Assuming that ADMSETUP.EXE has already been executed, you might think that simply running the SETUPNW.EXE program in the usual manner completes the job. After all, you are able to create and manage the new Client Configuration objects, and you have copied the new client files to the workstation with SETUPNW.EXE.

You will find, however, that even though you can complete all of the necessary configuration tasks, no new Windows NT users will be created until you complete two additional steps:

1. Run the SETUPNW.EXE program with the /W switch, specifying the name of the NDS tree (or trees) into which you will log in, in the form SETUPNW.EXE /W:ndstree. You can specify additional trees on the command line, separated by commas.

2. Apply the Registry changes in the WORKMAN.REG file (found in the I386 directory of the client installation files) by double-clicking the file name or its icon in the Windows NT Explorer program.

Once you have completed these two steps (and restarted the system), the Windows NT login parameters will be read from the NDS database, rather than from the configuration on the local machine.

Creating Windows NT Client Configuration Objects

Once Workstation Manager's snap-in modules are installed using ADMSETUP.EXE, you can see, when you run NetWare Administrator, that a new object type is available: the NT Client Configuration. You create a Client Configuration just as you would any other NDS object. Instead of representing a computer user, the Client Configuration represents the Windows NT computer itself. For more information on creating NDS objects with NetWare Administrator, see Chapter 7, "Creating and Managing NDS Objects."

The Client Configuration object is configured and associated with the objects representing the users who require access to that particular machine. Additional properties of the NDS object enable the network administrator to exercise full control over the process of logging on to the Windows NT machine, without ever having to perform any user account management tasks at the Windows NT machine itself. Those Client Configuration object properties are found in the following panels of the object's Details dialog box in NetWare Administrator:

- Identification
- Login tabs
- Login scripts
- Profile and policy
- Welcome screen
- Dynamic local user
- Client upgrade
- Associations

The following sections describe the properties of the NT Client Configuration object, which you can configure in its Details dialog box, and how you can use them to control the environment of the Windows NT workstation.

Identification   The Identification panel displays the distinguished name of the NT Client Configuration object and provides a description field, which is purely for the convenience of the administrator. It has no function other than as a place to store notes on the object.

There is also a check box that is used to enable a Windows NT workstation login when the network is unavailable. This is an important option, because if left unchecked, the user cannot log in to the Windows NT system without successfully completing an NDS login first. Except in cases where a high degree of system security is required, this box should be left checked.

Login Tabs   The Novell client's login dialog box contains several tabbed panels, whose appearance you can suppress, if you do not want users to be able to modify the login dialog box settings. The Login Tabs page enables the network administrator to select which of the following panels are accessible by the user during the login process:

- **IntranetWare**—Enables the user to specify whether to perform an NDS or bindery login, as well as the default user name and context
- **Windows NT**—Enables the user to specify the user name and password for the Windows NT logon
- **Login Scripts**—Controls what NetWare scripts run during the login process and whether script results are displayed to the user
- **Variables**—Enables the user to specify values for variables used during login script processing

For more information on the IntranetWare Client for Windows NT login dialog box, see Chapter 22, "Using Windows NT with NetWare."

Login Scripts   The Login Scripts page provides the same control over script processing as in the Novell client's configuration dialog box and the login dialog box. The difference, of course, is that with NDS you can configure these options from any remote Windows NT workstation running NetWare Administrator.

From this panel (see Figure 9.2), you control whether NetWare login scripts should be processed at all, and how their results should be displayed on the workstation during the login process. You can also specify the use of alternate login and profile scripts, and furnish values for the variables that you use in login script routines.

FIG. 9.2
The Login Scripts panel enables the remote configuration of the Windows NT client with the same parameters found in the NetWare client configuration dialog box.

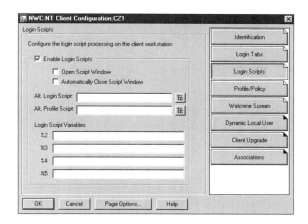

Part

II

Ch

9

Profile/Policy   User profiles are collections of Windows NT Registry settings that enable multiple users to maintain their own individual desktop configurations. A user can create icons, specify wallpaper, and configure the Start menu to his or her own liking. The settings are then stored in a profile for that user that is accessed the next time the user logs in.

When you store the profiles on a network drive (also known as roaming profiles), then a user can log in from any machine on the network and work with the same desktop configuration. In the Profile/Policy panel (see Figure 9.3), you specify whether you want to enable support for roaming profiles, and the location of the profiles on the network.

FIG. 9.3

With user profiles and system policies, Windows NT workstation configuration settings can follow a user to any computer on the network.

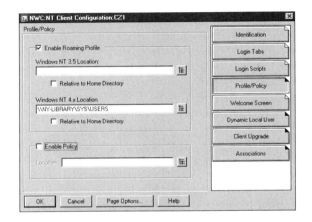

Because the format of the policy files in Windows NT 4.0 differs from that in version 3.51, fields for each version are provided. When you mark the Relative to Home Directory check box, you enable support for the profiles of multiple users on the same machine. Without multiple user profile support, the administrator can enforce the use of a specific profile for all users of this machine by entering the path to a single profile.

N O T E   Path names to user profiles and system policies must be expressed using the standard Universal Naming Convention (UNC) notation (\\server\volume\directory\file). ▨

To specify a profile for each user, append a subdirectory name to the path you specify in this field that is equivalent to the user's login name. For example, you can specify the path \\SERVER\SYS\USERS in the field, and then create subdirectories that are named for your users, in which you store their profiles. When the user SMITHJ logs in to the machine represented by this particular object, his profile is accessed from the \\SERVER\SYS\USERS\SMITHJ directory.

N O T E   If users are to be allowed to change their profiles, then they must have the appropriate rights to the directories where they are stored. If you grant the users only READ rights to their profile directory, then you force them to begin with the same profile every time they log in. ▨

System policies are another method of storing and applying Registry settings, except that these are configured by the network administrator. Usually, policies are used to limit users' access to certain parts of the operating system. By default, the Novell client looks for a policy file called NTCONFIG.POL in the *SERVER*\SYS\PUBLIC\WINNT directory. You can, however, specify the location of an alternate policy file by filling the Enable Policy check box and entering a path name in the field provided.

Welcome Screen   You can specify the name of a bitmap file to be displayed in place of the default NetWare logo, whenever the Windows NT workstation is started, along with a text message. Note that the graphic file supplied with the Novell client itself instructs the user to press Ctrl+Alt+Del in order to log in. If you replace the graphic file, be sure that all of your users are aware of the login procedure.

Dynamic Local User   The Dynamic Local User panel (see Figure 9.4) controls the core functionality of Workstation Manager, that is, whether or not a user account is created on the Windows NT machine during the login process. If you disable this feature, then a Windows NT logon is attempted using the account name found in the Windows NT screen of the Novell client's login dialog box. Failing this, no login to the Windows NT system will occur, and an error message is generated.

FIG. 9.4

The Dynamic Local User panel defines the parameters used to create user accounts on the Windows NT workstation.

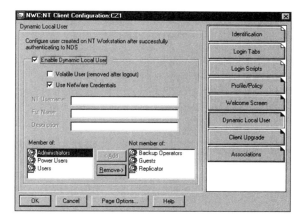

If you do enable the dynamic local user feature, the NWGINA module, after logging in to the NDS tree, reads the information entered in this panel to determine what user account should be used to log in to Windows NT. You are given the option of using the same credentials as the NDS User object, or you can specify an Windows NT user name of your own choosing.

The client first checks to see if an account using the specified name already exists on the Windows NT machine. If a valid userid exists, that account is used to perform the login. If an account does not exist, one is created by the NWGINA module, a random password is selected, and the Windows NT login proceeds.

You can control whether or not the newly created user accounts are deleted from the Windows NT machine when the users log out, by marking the Volatile User check box. Otherwise, any accounts created by NWGINA remain in the system's Security Access Manager.

You can also specify the names of Windows NT groups to which the newly created users should belong. This feature enables you to automatically provide your dynamically created Windows NT users with the rights they need to access remote resources on the Windows network.

Client Upgrade   The Client Upgrade panel enables you to take advantage of the Novell client's Automatic Client Upgrade feature, in conjunction with Workstation Manager. In order to upgrade the NetWare client software on a Windows NT machine, an account with Administrator equivalence must be used when logging on. Normally, the accounts created by Workstation Manager do not possess this equivalence, and the upgrade cannot be performed.

When you check the Enable Automatic Client Upgrade box, you are using NDS to signal the workstation that a client software upgrade should be performed. To prevent such an upgrade from occurring more than once, NWGINA, after a successful NDS login, compares the time stamp of the NT Client Configuration object with its own logs to ascertain if the object's configuration has changed since the last login.

If the time stamps match, the client assumes that the software upgrade has already taken place during a previous login, and proceeds with the normal dynamic local user logon sequence. When the time stamps do not match, NWGINA creates a special user account on the workstation, one with Administrator privileges. After the logon, the login script that you specify in the Client Upgrade panel is executed instead of the normal script, or any others you have specified in the Login Scripts panel.

This client upgrade script is one that you create especially to perform the client software upgrade, containing a command that executes SETUPNW.EXE with the appropriate switches (usually both /ACU, which activates the Automatic Client Upgrade feature, and /U=UNATTEND.TXT, in which UNATTEND.TXT is a properly formatted installation script file). See Chapter 22, "Using Windows NT with NetWare," for more information of the use of the Automatic Client Upgrade feature, and the creation of installation scripts.

After the client software upgrade has been completed, the workstation must be rebooted, and the normal login procedure is observed. This time, the object time stamps should match (unless you have modified the NT Client Configuration object in the interim), and a normal dynamic local user logon to the Windows NT system is performed.

Once again, the Client Upgrade panel replicates a function that can also be performed at the client workstation itself, but Workstation Manager enables the administrator to configure the entire process remotely, and to easily perform upgrades on multiple systems.

Associations   The Associations panel (see Figure 9.5) is simply a list of the NDS objects representing the users that will access the Windows NT workstation. You can add individual User, container, or Group objects to this list, to associate multiple users with one Client Configuration.

FIG. 9.5

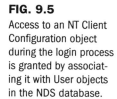

Access to an NT Client Configuration object during the login process is granted by associating it with User objects in the NDS database.

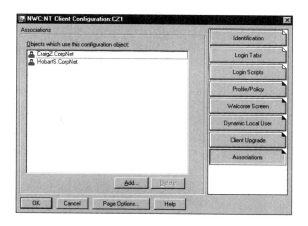

The installation of Workstation Manager also adds a Client Configuration panel to the Details dialog box of a User object. Here, you can also associate a user with a Client Configuration by browsing the tree and selecting the desired object.

Using LDAP with Novell Directory Services

You've seen so far in this chapter how Novell is seeking to expand the facility of Novell Directory Services to encompass other enterprise computing platforms besides NetWare. Workstation Manager for Windows NT addresses a specific shortcoming of NDS that has affected its usefulness for several years. Other developments in the area of directory services are being explored, however, that are much more universal in their scope.

Introducing LDAP

LDAP, the Lightweight Directory Access Protocol, is an emerging standard that is in the process of being implemented by nearly all of the major players in the field of networking and directory services. LDAP is a protocol that runs over a standard TCP session, and allows for communications between directory services and their clients.

LDAP was designed at the University of Michigan to be a lighter alternative to the Directory Access Protocol (DAP) used by the X.500 directory service standard. X.500 is a global, distributed directory service that is based on the OSI networking protocol standards.

Best known for the seven-layer reference model that is often used to illustrate network communications processes, the OSI standards also define a collection of protocols that fully conform to layers of the reference model (something that the more commonly used protocol suites, such as TCP/IP and IPX/SPX, do not do). The OSI protocols have been in development for many years, and continue to show no indications of a practical, commercial deployment in the foreseeable future.

DAP requires an OSI protocol stack to operate, thus making it an impractical choice for use on the average business network. LDAP, on the other hand, operates using the standard TCP/IP protocol stack, thus enabling clients running on traditional business platforms to access X.500 directories.

X.500, while a powerful directory service, is itself no simple piece of software, making it equally impractical for use by small and medium sized networks. Many different network vendors have their own directory services in various stages of development, and most have committed to the use of LDAP for communications with their clients.

Understanding the LDAP Directory Services Model

The LDAP version 2 standard, which is currently published as RFC (Request for Comments)-1777 by the Internet Engineering Task Force (IETF), defines a model for a directory service that is derived from X.500, and is similar to that used for Novell Directory Services in several ways. The LDAP service is based on individual *entries*, which are composed of *attributes* and *values*. Each attribute has a type, which is a generic identifier for the kind of information it provides.

For example, an entry representing a person has a *common name* attribute in which the person's full name is stored. This attribute type is abbreviated cn, and typically noted as cn=John Smith. Although the common name attribute is also found in the NDS database, LDAP defines many other attributes with different type names. These are defined in RFC-1778, "The String Representation of Standard Attribute Syntaxes."

N O T E The standards documents upon which LDAP is based are accessible by anonymous FTP at **ftp://ds.internic.net/rfc**. Two other sites containing extensive information on LDAP can be found at the University of Michigan (**http://www.umich.edu/~rsug/ldap**) and Critical Angle (**http://www.critical-angle.com/ldapworld/Welcome.html**). ▨

Each entry is located somewhere in the directory service's hierarchy, a tree-like structure that groups entries according to some standard organizational principle. Many directory services (such as X.500) are organized according to country abbreviations and, beneath that, cities, states, or institutions, such as schools and corporations.

As with NDS, an entry is uniquely identified by a *distinguished name*, that defines its place in the hierarchy. An LDAP distinguished name includes object types, and is separated by commas (unlike NDS, which uses periods). Thus, a typical distinguished name for a person in LDAP notation can take the following form:

cn=John Smith, o=ABC Corporation, c=US

N O T E It must be noted that, although it must have an understanding of the directory services structure in order to function, the LDAP standard does not define the directory service itself. LDAP is strictly a protocol that is used for communications between a directory service and its clients. Originally devised for use with X.500, LDAP can be used with many other directory services, including NDS. ▨

As it is adapted for use with other services, version 2 of the LDAP standard has demonstrated certain shortcomings that are being addressed by version 3 of the protocol, currently under development. Security and access control issues are chief among these shortcomings, as are the capabilities needed to enable LDAP to be used for communications between directories, and not just between directories and their clients.

Developing Directory Services

Such directory services as X.500, which are designed to provide a global information source, are usually developed from the top down, meaning that the first priority is the creation of a hierarchy that can make the location of specific data feasible. For example, a worldwide telephone directory that is organized as one huge alphabetical list would be very difficult to use.

X.500 can, in fact, be described as a global telephone directory with delusions of grandeur. At this time, it is the hierarchy of countries, locations, organizations, and other categories that is most important, because this is what makes the entire project possible on a global scale. It is the organizational hierarchy that allows the database to be distributed among many hundreds of sites, and that makes it possible to browse and search the directory efficiently.

The information that is stored in most global directory services is primarily listings of people and contact information. You can download LDAP clients that enable you to browse and search through various directories to locate people and discover their e-mail addresses and other information.

Microsoft and Netscape have both released e-mail modules that have LDAP capabilities, and this will certainly be the first exposure that average Internet users will get to a global directory. By interfacing with one of several commercial directory services, people will be able to look up that old friend from high school or a contact in another company and retrieve an e-mail address in seconds.

Novell Directory Services, on the other hand, was developed from the bottom up. Originally designed as a replacement for the NetWare bindery, the primary emphasis was on the information stored in each entry, and how it was used in the NetWare environment. The creation of an organizational hierarchy came later, and was left largely up to the individual network administrator.

As global directory services continue to develop, their usefulness will no doubt expand beyond their *white pages* orientation, to include entries that represent documents and applications, as well as people. The hierarchy is largely in place, and work is commencing on the content.

At the same time, NDS is developing also, but in the opposite direction as global directory services. With the addition of the capabilities provided by NetWare Application Launcher and Workstation Manager, as well as third party products that can extend the directory schema, the comparatively rich content of NDS entries can now be distributed beyond the boundaries of the enterprise network through the use of LDAP.

Part
II

Ch
9

Introducing Novell LDAP Services for NDS

Novell's LDAP Services for NDS enables you to publish the contents of your NetWare network's NDS database to an intranet or the Internet. Users with an LDAP client can access the information in NDS and use it for any application that a developer might produce. What's more, an LDAP client can also operate interactively with NDS, updating information in the database, which is then distributed and replicated throughout the enterprise using the standard NDS communication mechanisms.

LDAP and directory services are both in a state where their potential overshadows their reality. Microsoft and Netscape have both begun to integrate LDAP client services into their Web browsers, and Netscape has recently released a directory server product that relies on LDAP. None of the major software manufacturers, however, have a directory service as fully developed and widely deployed as NDS is today.

By adding the LDAP service to your NetWare servers, you can use the tools included with the IntranetWare package to begin developing applications today that utilize the information on your network's users, applications, and other resources that are stored in the NDS database.

Running the LDAP Services for NDS

The LDAP Services for NDS were not available at the time of the original IntranetWare release. They are currently available as a free download from Novell's Web site at **http://www.novell.com/corp/esd/softform.html**.

Novell does not include an LDAP client with their product. You can perform simple LDAP searches using Microsoft Internet Explorer 3.01 or Netscape Communicator, but other LDAP clients are freely available on the Internet that provide more complete, bi-directional access to your NDS database via LDAP.

Installing the LDAP Services

Expanding the LDAP Services self-extracting archive creates two disk image directories. You install the LDAP services by running the SETUP.EXE program in the DISK1 directory from any Windows 95 or Windows NT 4.0 workstation. The hardware requirements for the product are minimal. The LDAP services require less than 1M of storage space on your SYS: volume, and 1M of RAM, plus 80K for each connected client. You must also be running TCP/IP on your server, and on all LDAP client workstations.

The installation is a very simple one. The SETUP.EXE program copies the LDAP Services NLM to the server you select, extends the Directory schema, and installs the snap-in module (LDAPSNAP.DLL) that enables NetWare Administrator to view and manage the new LDAP Server and Group objects that are added to the NDS database. You must run the SETUP program at every workstation that you will use to manage the LDAP objects.

N O T E You must have Supervisor object rights to the root of the NDS tree in order to install the LDAP Services for NDS.

Once the software has been installed, you need only launch the LDAP Services NLM at the server console, using the LOAD NLDAP command. A new screen appears on the server console, which displays the ongoing activities of the LDAP service.

You can configure the types of information displayed on the LDAP Service screen by modifying the properties of the LDAP Server object in the NDS database. However, the default configuration parameters should be sufficient for the service to be immediately operational.

Searching the NDS Database with the Internet Explorer Address Book

The Internet Mail and News module of Microsoft's Internet Explorer 3.01 product contains a rudimentary LDAP client in its Address Book application. Although nowhere near as comprehensive as SWIX, you can configure Address Book to search your NDS database for users' names, and display their e-mail addresses.

By default, Address book is pre-configured to access one of several commercial LDAP servers that provide white pages service. To add your NetWare server to the configuration, you launch the Internet Mail application, open Address Book, and choose File, Directory Services.

N O T E If there is no Directory Services item on the File menu of your Address Book, then you must download an update to the Internet Mail and News modules from Microsoft's Web site at **http://www.microsoft.com**.

Click the Add button, and enter the host name or IP address of your NetWare server in the Directory Service field of the Properties dialog box, as shown in Figure 9.6. You must also change the default Authentication Type because, by default, Address Book binds to the LDAP Service anonymously, which prevents it from scanning the objects in the tree. Instead, select the Password option and supply a user name, using the LDAP format explained in "Understanding the LDAP Directory Services Model," earlier in this chapter.

The same restrictions apply to the use of passwords as when you configured the SWIX client. You must either enter a user name that does not require a password, or reconfigure the LDAP Group object in the NDS database to allow the use of passwords.

In the Advanced screen, notice that the Search Base is set to a default value of c=US. If you do not use Country objects in your NDS database, no US object will be found, causing an error. Blank out this field in order to scan your entire NDS tree, or enter the name of the container object from which you want all searches to begin.

FIG. 9.6

The Internet Mail module of Microsoft's Internet Explorer 3.01 can be configured to look up e-mail addresses in your NDS database.

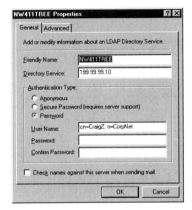

Once Address Book is configured properly, you should be able to click the find button and search for a name in your NDS database using only LDAP. If you have assigned e-mail addresses to your User objects, they will be displayed with the found objects.

Configuring the LDAP Services

When you install the Novell LDAP Services, the schema of your NDS database are extended to add two new object types: the LDAP Server and the LDAP Group. You can install the LDAP Services onto multiple NetWare servers, if needed, to provide access to users at multiple sites, or balance the traffic load.

Whenever you change the configuration of one or both of the LDAP objects, the service must be restarted before the changes will take effect. NetWare Administrator will inform you of this fact, and automatically restart the service, as long as no LDAP clients are connected to the server. If there are active clients, you must see to it that they are disconnected, and then manually unload and reload the NLDAP.NLM module at the server console prompt.

Configuring the LDAP Server Object   Each installation of the LDAP Services is represented by an LDAP Server object, that contains a few basic configuration panels, as follows:

- General
- Log File Options
- Screen Options

The following sections cover the screens found in the LDAP object's Details dialog box.

General The General screen displays the name of the NetWare server running the LDAP Services and the LDAP Group to which the server belongs. You also can set several parameters in this screen that control the basic functions of the LDAP service, as follows:

Parameter	Default	Min. Value	Max. Value
Search Entry Limit	500 entries	0	2,147,483,647
Search Time Limit	3600 secs.	1	2,147,483,647
Bind Limit	0 binds	0	4,294,967,295
Idle Timeout	900 secs.	0	4,294,967,295
TCP Port	389	0	65,535
UDP Port	389	0	65,535

The Search Entry Limit indicates the maximum number of entries that are returned as the result of any search. The Search Time Limit is the amount of time that the server will devote to delivering data to a client. For both of these settings, the transaction is interrupted when the specified value is reached.

The Bind Limit is the number of clients that are allowed to connect to the LDAP service at any one time. A value of zero indicates that the number of users is unlimited. Because each LDAP connection requires 80K of server memory, you may want to impose a limit if you are concerned about your server's memory situation.

The Idle Timeout indicates the length of time (in seconds) that an LDAP connection is maintained with no activity. Again, a value of zero indicates that there is no limit imposed.

The TCP and UDP Ports are the numbers that identify the process at the server to which incoming network traffic using the Transport Control Protocol and User Datagram Protocol is delivered. The value of 389 is the standard port for LDAP communications and should generally not be changed, as all LDAP clients would have to be changed as well.

Log File Options In the Log File Options panel (see Figure 9.7), you indicate the information that you want captured to the LDAP Services log, which is a standard ASCII text file, as well as the location and maximum size of the log file. Selecting all of the information is a good way of learning about the LDAP communication process, but the logs generated as a result can be enormous. Once you are satisfied with the performance of the service, you can modify the parameters so that only error messages from All Options are logged.

FIG. 9.7

The LDAP server can capture an enormous amount of information to its log file.

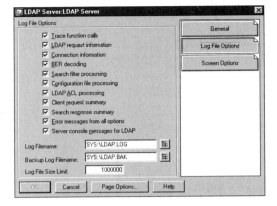

Screen Options   The Screen Options are the same as those for the log options, controlling what information is displayed on the LDAP Server screen on the server console. It is recommended that you display less information on the screen than you capture to the log, as even a single transaction can generate several pages worth of information when all of the options are selected.

Configuring the LDAP Group Object   LDAP Server objects are automatically made members of an LDAP Group—represented by a different NDS object—that contains a larger array of configuration parameters, all of which are applied to all of the servers in the group. The parameters to be configured include the following:

- General
- Server list
- Access control
- Attribute map
- Class map

The following sections cover the screens found in the LDAP Group object's Details dialog box.

General   You can restrict LDAP users' access to a part of the NDS tree by specifying the name of a top level object as a suffix. Only entries specified with the selected object in their distinguished name are visible to LDAP clients.

The Referral attribute enables you to specify the name of an alternate LDAP server that you want to process any requests that cannot be handled by the current server group, for any reason. Enter the name of another server in the form LDAP://*hostname* or LDAP://*ipaddress*.

When you check the Enable NDS User Binds box, you permit the use of unencrypted passwords when binding to an LDAP server. The Novell LDAP Service does not support the use of encrypted passwords. Use of this option will allow your NDS passwords to be transmitted over the network as clear text when using LDAP, opening up a potential security breach.

As an alternative, you can specify a proxy user name that should be used when users bind to the server anonymously. Instead of receiving only the rights granted to the [Public] object, anonymous users receive the rights granted to the NDS object you specify (which should also not require a password). This enables you to grant users additional rights through an LDAP client that they would not possess when running a normal NDS utility, such as NetWare Administrator. The rights granted to the proxy user, however, should also be governed by the lack of security inherent in the LDAP client connection.

Server List   The Server List is simply a listing of the LDAP Server objects that are included as part of the current LDAP group. By default, in a single server installation, the LDAP server is automatically made a member of the LDAP group.

Access Control   As you have seen, the standard NDS access control mechanisms still apply when users access the directory using an LDAP client. However, the LDAP standard enables you to implement a second layer of access control, to be used in place of, or along with, NDS security.

LDAP security takes the form of one or more access control lists, that you use to specify what rights certain users have to certain attributes. When you click the Add button on the Access Control panel, you see a dialog box like that shown in Figure 9.8.

FIG. 9.8

LDAP's access control lists provide a second level of security to LDAP clients.

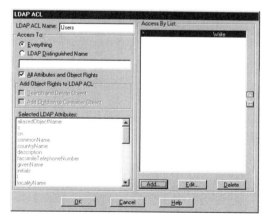

To create an access control list, you must specify a name for the list, and then designate what objects or attributes should be accessed, and who should be given that access.

When you select the Everything button, access is granted to all of the objects in the directory. Alternatively, you can specify the LDAP Distinguished Name of a container or leaf object to which rights are to be granted.

Next, you designate whether or not users should be granted all object and attribute rights to the selected objects. If you clear the All Attributes and Object Rights check box, then the options below that box are enabled. You can designate whether users have the rights to search for and delete the selected objects, and add new container or leaf objects to a selected container. You can also select the specific attributes to which users are granted rights.

Note that the object and attribute rights that you select here are still subject to the specific rights designations that you create in the list of users who are to receive access. For example, you can select the Add Children to Container Object option, but unless your users are granted the Write right, they will not be able to actually create new objects.

You must next select the users who are to be granted the object and attribute rights you have selected. Click the Add button in the Access By List box to display the dialog box shown in Figure 9.9.

FIG. 9.9

You can elect to grant object and attribute rights to all users or to specific ones.

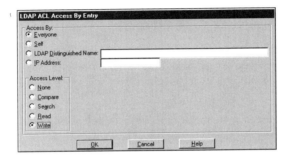

Here, you can choose whether the selected object and attribute rights are to be granted to everyone, to a specific user by name, or to a specific system by IP address. You can also choose Self, which enables every user to access the selected attributes of their own user object only.

In addition, you must specify the level of access that is to be granted to the users you have selected. You can create multiple Access By lists, providing various degrees of access to different clients. The access levels are as follows:

- **None**—Prevents all access to the selected object attributes
- **Compare**—Enables clients to specify attribute values that are compared to the corresponding values of specific objects
- **Search**—Enables clients to locate objects that contain specific attribute values (includes the Compare right)
- **Read**—Enables clients to read the values of the selected object attributes (includes the Search and Compare rights)
- **Write**—Enables clients to modify the values of the selected object attributes (includes the Read, Search, and Compare rights)

Once you have completed all of the procedures above, click the OK button to create the access control list. You can create as many access control lists as are needed, to control the rights of different object attributes.

Attribute Map   Both NDS and an LDAP-compliant directory services consist of objects (or entries) that are composed of properties (or attributes). Although some NDS properties store the same information as certain LDAP attributes, many others do not, and even those performing the same function may be known by different names.

In order to make LDAP function with NDS, there must be a table that lists LDAP attributes and their equivalent NDS properties. The Attribute Map screen contains just such a table (see Figure 9.10). In many cases, the configured default values will be sufficient for use with a given application, but you can modify the table to map attributes to whatever properties you want.

Part
II

Ch
9

FIG. 9.10
NDS operates with LDAP by mapping specific attributes to NDS properties.

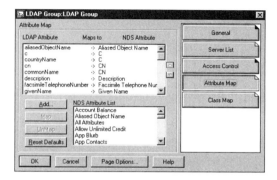

To change an existing mapping, you make a selection from the list and choose a different NDS property to be mapped to the given LDAP attribute. To add a new mapping, click the Add button, type the name of the new LDAP attribute, select an NDS property from the list, and click the Map button.

Class Map   The Class Map panel performs the same function as the Attribute Map, but at a higher level. LDAP classes are the equivalent to object types in NDS. Most of the NDS container object types have directly equivalent LDAP classes, but the NDS User object, for example, is mapped to an LDAP class called newPilotPerson, by default.

Because LDAP is designed to be usable with different directory services, it has no predetermined schema standard. When you attempt to create new NDS objects using the SWIX client, the process fails because the client sends information to the Novell service about two specific LDAP object classes that do not exist on the default Class Map.

Overcoming this object class mismatch is a matter of consulting the LDAP service log to find the names of the offending classes, and then creating mappings for them in the Class Map screen. For example, in order to create new User objects using SWIX, you must add class mappings that equate the NDS User object with two LDAP classes: pilotObject and quipuObject. Adding new mappings, or modifying the existing ones, is accomplished using the same procedures as in the preceding section, on the Attribute Map screen.

Summary

Even though there is certainly further development to be done before any directory service, including NDS, is capable of doing everything that is expected of it, Novell's solution undoubtedly has more real world capabilities available for use today than that of any other manufacturer. They have all but resolved one of the major shortcomings of NDS by enabling the assimilation of Windows NT accounts into the directory. LDAP is a technology that demonstrates more potential than actual usefulness at this time, but the outlook for the future of enterprise directory services is highly positive. ●

PART III

Managing the Network

CHAPTER 10

Understanding NetWare Communication

The OSI reference model

The OSI model stratifies network communications into seven discrete layers, as a tool to promote the comprehension of the various processes involved.

Basic network types

IntranetWare is compatible with several different physical and low-level protocol specifications that are ratified and maintained by independent standards bodies.

NetWare protocols

NetWare utilizes several of its own proprietary protocols to perform its primary transport functions.

The client connection process

When a client workstation connects to a NetWare server, a complex exchange of signals takes place before the user is granted access to network resources.

While opening a file that is stored on a network drive may not seem that much more complicated than one on a local drive, there are actually a great many communications processes that occur on a network that are not immediately evident to the average user. The process of building a LAN involves the selection of many different products that determine how these communications are conducted. When you choose NetWare as your network operating system, you are in effect making a good many of these communications decisions at one time.

As with many aspects of modern computing, learning all that there is to know about network communications can be a life's work. However, a high-level view of the processes that contribute to the operation of your NetWare network will help you to understand what can be done to maximize its efficiency and how to troubleshoot any communications problems that may occur. ■

Introducing the OSI Reference Model

In 1977, a gathering of representatives from over 100 countries, including the American National Standards Institute (ANSI) from the U.S., became the International Organization for Standardization. Formed as a vendor-independent body to create technological standards for the international community, ISO is best known for its part in the development of a document that is formally called "The Basic Reference Model for Open Systems Interconnection." Colloquially, this document is known as the *OSI reference model*.

NOTE   Many people find it curious that the International Organization for Standardization is often referreffto by the designation ISO. In fact, ISO is not an acronym or abbreviation. It is derived from the Greek word *isos*, meaning *equal*. The group's creators thought that this was a particularly meaningful short name for an organization devoted to the development of standards that were to be observed by widely disparate bodies. It is also a valid term in English, French, and Russian, the official languages of the organization. If an actual acronym was used, it would necessarily be different in each language.

The reference model actually began as two separate documents, one developed by the ISO, and the other by the CCITT (which translates from the French as the International Telegraph and Telephone Consultative Committee). The two documents were combined and released as ISO 7498, in 1983. The CCITT was renamed the Telecommunications Standardization Sector of the International Telecommunications Union (ITU-T0) in 1992, and the same reference model document was published by them as the X.200 standard.

The OSI reference model was designed to be part of a project that would involve the development of a family of networking protocols that would be independent of any one manufacturer. The model splits the network communication process into seven layers, ranging from the actual physical network medium at the bottom to the application interface at the top, as shown in Figure 10.1.

It was thought that this stratification would allow for the simultaneous development of protocols at each of the layers. By carefully defining the responsibilities of the protocol operating at each layer, seven development groups could work independently, and develop a usable set of protocols in a relatively short period of time.

Although the OSI protocols have been developed, they have never become available in a commercially viable form. In addition, much of the development of the protocols used in the NetWare operating system occurred before the reference model was published. For this reason, NetWare's communications protocols do not conform exactly to the divisions of the OSI model, nor do the TCP/IP protocols or those of the other networking products that dominate the market.

Despite this fact, however, the OSI reference model has persisted, both as a teaching aid and as part of the everyday networking vocabulary for computer professionals worldwide. Even though the NetWare layers do not correspond exactly to those of the model, the concepts of protocol layering and data encapsulation are crucial to an understanding of the network communication process, and the OSI model is one of the best ways of illustrating these concepts.

FIG. 10.1
The OSI reference model.

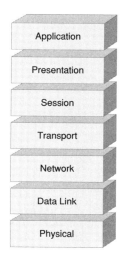

Networking Layers

The OSI reference model splits the network communications process into the following seven layers:

- **Application**—The Application layer is the interface between the actual application running on a system and any network resources that it may need to function.

- **Presentation**—The Presentation layer is responsible for performing any syntax translations that are needed to enable different systems to communicate.

- **Session**—The Session layer controls the nature of the dialog between the two communicating computers, and provides a checkpointing capability that an application can use to roll back transactions in the event of a communications problem.

- **Transport**—The Transport layer can perform many of the same functions as the Network layer. Its function is to bring the data transmission's quality of service up to the requirements of the application by performing whatever functions have not been furnished at the Network layer.

- **Network**—The Network layer is responsible for the routing of data from its source to its ultimate destination, with it often passing through several intermediate computers in the process. The Network layer can also provide other end-to-end services, such as error detection, error correction, and flow control.

- **Data Link**—The Data Link layer controls access to the network medium, enabling multiple computers to share the same cable. It is also responsible for splitting a transmission into discrete packets, and provides the addressing information that identifies the packets' source and destination systems. The Data Link layer can also provide error checking and other functions.

■ **Physical**—The Physical layer is the actual medium used to convey signals between computers, as well as the code that enables binary data to be transmitted using electrical or optical impulses, or some other form of energy.

The Protocol Stack

These seven layers represent the sum total of the communication processes that are involved between two systems on a computer network. These communications are realized using different protocols at different layers of the model. A *protocol* is a set of rules shared by two entities, governing the way in which they communicate. As you learn about how computers communicate on a NetWare network, you will examine the protocols that are used at the different layers.

The combination of protocols used on a particular system is often referred to as a *stack*. A network transmission begins at the top of the protocol stack with a request for a network resource that is made at the Application layer, and travels downwards through the layers until it reaches the network medium. In the process, the various protocols in the stack apply their own control data to the request in the form of packet headers (and sometimes a footer). Each successive header is affixed to the beginning of the existing packet, forming a frame around the original request, as shown in Figure 10.2.

FIG. 10.2
A request for access to a network resource is surrounded by several frames as it is passed down the networking stack.

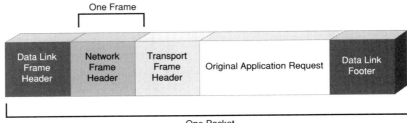

When the packet leaves the system at which it originated, it travels over the network cable to its destination, where it travels up the protocol stack. The individual protocol headers are read and then stripped away, and the request ultimately reaches its destination. These two computers are known as *end systems*, because they represent the source and the destination of the transmission.

Packets can also traverse several network segments on the way to their destination. The systems that the packets pass through on their journey are known as *intermediate systems*. Packets only travel as high as the Network layer in intermediate systems because they are there only for the purpose of being routed to other network segments (see Figure 10.3).

The following sections describe the basic NetWare functions that are performed at the various layers of the OSI model, along with the protocols that can be used. Some layers, such as the Physical and Data Link, describe various protocols from which you can choose when you build a network. The protocols higher up in the stack are part of the core operating system itself, and are automatically installed as part of the standard NetWare installation.

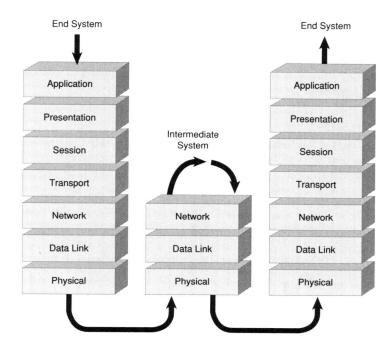

FIG. 10.3
Packets may pass through several intermediate systems on the way to their destination.

The Physical Layer

The Physical layer of the OSI model is the only part of the system that you can actually see. As you probably know, all of computing is based on binary code, and networking is ultimately the transmission of that code from one computer to another. The Physical layer is simply the medium that is used to convey that transmission.

The Network Medium

In the vast majority of cases, and particularly on NetWare networks, the medium is a copper cable that forms a single electrical circuit from one device to another. The binary code is transmitted over the cable by varying the electrical current in a controlled manner that represents the zeroes and ones. This is called a *baseband* network, because the cable only carries a single signal. The opposite of this, in which the cable carries many signals at once, is called a *broadband* network. For example, the telephone is a baseband service, while cable TV is broadband because it carries many channels on a single cable.

Networks, however, can also run over many other kinds of media besides copper. Fiber-optic cable uses light impulses to transmit a signal. Fiber can span much greater distances than copper, but also costs a great deal more to install and maintain. Other networks might use microwaves, radio waves, lasers, or other media to satisfy the physical requirements of the installation.

The most important factor to consider about the Physical layer of the network is that it is concerned only with transmitting signals on the network medium. It has no conception of what the signal contains, where it is going, or why. Every network interface has a transceiver that translates data from the computer into the appropriate signals, sends them on their way, and performs the opposite function for incoming signals.

LAN Hardware

The Physical layer, obviously, includes all of the hardware that is used to connect the computers on your network. This includes the network interface adapters in your computers, the cables that connect them, and all of the other connectors, hubs, transceivers, and other equipment used in the process.

As you will see, the selection of the hardware used at the Physical layer of the networking model is intimately related to the protocols that operate at the Data Link layer. In most cases you will select a Data Link protocol, such as Ethernet or token ring, and this decision will leave you with a few hardware alternatives from which to choose.

Strictly speaking, though, the Physical layer defines the nature of the hardware that is used in the network, but not the way that it is installed. Factors like cable lengths, proximity of cables to sources of electrical interference, and the wiring of hubs and repeaters are part of the Data Link protocol specification. Thus, the way in which the network hardware is manufactured is a Physical layer consideration, but the way in which it is installed is not.

In its early days, NetWare networks were often wired using coaxial cable for ARCnet or Ethernet installations. Today, however, most business LANs use telephone-type cable installations with *unshielded twisted pair* (UTP) or *shielded twisted pair* (STP) cable to connect the computers. In fact, although you can assemble a small network yourself using pre-packaged cables, the wiring for most new LAN installations is typically installed at the same time as the telephone cables.

Signaling Types

Once the medium is in place, the most fundamental protocol on the network is the code used to signal binary information from one machine to another. For example, on a copper cable network, variations in electrical voltage are used to represent zeroes and ones. The actual voltage used is not relevant, just its pole. A positive voltage represents the value zero, and a negative represents the value one. By shifting the voltage between positive and negative voltages, a stream of values can be transmitted over the cable. This is called polar signaling, and it is illustrated in Figure 10.4.

The problem with polar signaling is that when you attempt to transmit two or more zeroes or ones consecutively, you do so by making no change in the voltage. The receiving system must accurately gauge the incoming signal to determine if an extended period of positive voltage represents one zero, or two, or ten. Because of the speed at which the code is transmitted on a computer network, this is impractical.

FIG. 10.4

Polar signaling is the simplest method of transmitting binary code, but it lacks a timing signal.

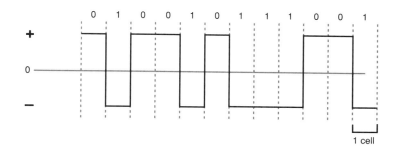

As a result, the coding mechanisms that are actually used on LANs include a timing signal, that is, a method of determining when each individually transmitted bit begins and ends. Some types of coding systems for broadband networks use an external time signal, a regular clock pulse that both the sending and receiving systems can use to accurately time the coding intervals. On a baseband network, which transmits only a single signal, though, this is impossible.

Instead, computer LANs (which are nearly always baseband networks) integrate the time signal into the transmission. Ethernet networks use a signaling scheme called *Manchester coding* to transmit binary data. In Manchester coding, no matter what the value of the bit being transmitted, there is a voltage transition at a regular interval. This interval defines the duration of a *cell*, that is, the period of time during which a single bit of data is transmitted. The transition occurs at the midpoint of each cell, and functions as the timing signal. This integration of the timing function into a coding system is called *biphase signaling*, because the time interval that represents each bit is split in two by the timing signal.

In Manchester coding, the value of each bit is represented by the direction of the voltage transition that is used as the timing signal for each cell. When the timing signal goes from a positive to a negative value, this represents a zero. When it goes from negative to positive, this represents a one, as shown in Figure 10.5. Thus, any voltage transitions other than those that occur at the midpoint of the cell are ignored. They exist only to prepare the signal for the proper transition at the midpoint.

FIG. 10.5

Manchester coding is used by all Ethernet networks.

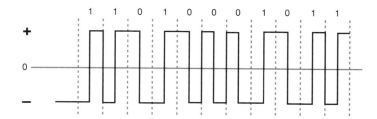

Another variation on this signaling method, called *Differential Manchester*, is used on token-ring networks. This system also uses a midpoint transition in each cell for timing purposes, but the actual value of the bit being transmitted is determined solely by the presence or absence of another voltage transition at the beginning of the cell, as shown in Figure 10.6. The direction of the transition is not relevant; only its existence is important. When a voltage transition is present at the beginning of a cell, the bit value is said to be zero. When this transition is absent, the bit value is one.

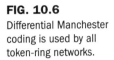

FIG. 10.6

Differential Manchester coding is used by all token-ring networks.

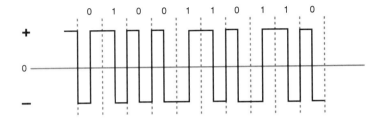

Other types of networks may use different signaling schemes, but all of them have some means of transmitting a time signal along with the data.

The Data Link Layer

As you have seen, the signaling type determines how strings of ones and zeroes can be transmitted over a network medium, but the Physical layer does not address several other crucial aspects of network communications. At the Data Link layer of the OSI model, a protocol is implemented that takes other systems on the network into account, for the first time.

The Data Link layer is not concerned with the delivery of data to its ultimate destination. In fact, Data Link protocols are not aware of any systems on the network other than their immediate neighbors. Their job is to transmit data to the next station on the network, and receive any data that is transmitted to them. If the incoming data is intended for that system, then it is delivered to the system proper. Otherwise, the unneeded data is discarded.

NetWare does not specify the use of a particular Data Link layer protocol as part of the operating system. You must select the protocol that you want to use on your network, and purchase the appropriate hardware to support it. NetWare includes drivers for many different hardware products, to support the protocol that they provide. Although there have been several other Data Link protocols used with NetWare over the years, the market has now been reduced to the point at which nearly all business LANs use either Ethernet or token ring.

These are colloquial names for two standards developed by the Institute of Electrical and Electronics Engineers (IEEE). Ethernet is the term that is most often used when referring to the 802.3 standard, and token ring refers to 802.5. You will learn the basic concepts that differentiate these two network types in the following sections.

Hardware Configuration Standards

A Data Link protocol is realized by a combination of software and hardware. The network interface adapters that you install in your computers, in combination with a software driver provided by either the hardware manufacturer or Novell, perform all of the tasks that are associated with the Data Link layer of the OSI model.

The selection of a protocol also imposes restrictions on the installation of the network medium. The IEEE 802.3 standard, for example, defines three possible types of cable that can be used on an Ethernet network: *Thick Ethernet* and *Thin Ethernet* (also called *Thicknet* and *Thinnet,* respectively), which use coaxial cable, and *10BaseT,* which uses unshielded twisted pair telephone cable.

10BaseT Ethernet is, by far, the most popular network type being used today. Token ring has its advantages, but maintains a distant second place in popularity, largely due to its greater expense.

The specification documents for Ethernet and token ring also describe in detail how the cable should be installed. There are a great many rules that must be observed concerning cable lengths, topologies, the number of network segments that can be interconnected, the proximity to other services, and so on. Suffice it to say that installing the cable for a LAN of more than 10 or 12 workstations is usually not a do-it-yourself project.

It is important to note that Data Link protocols like Ethernet and token ring, despite their long history of use with NetWare, are not limited to use with any one operating system or computing platform. You can find UNIX and Windows NT networks that run Ethernet, even at the same time as NetWare. The protocol is concerned with transmitting data over a network medium in a controlled and stable manner. Except for specific pieces of data, the contents of the packets are irrelevant, just as postal workers are unconcerned with anything but the address on an envelope.

Part
III

Ch
10

Packet Switching

LANs are baseband networks, and this means that only one signal can be transmitted over the network medium at any one time. However, a computer network can have dozens or even hundreds of computer systems, all of which are connected with the same cable and are therefore vying for the use of the same bandwidth.

N O T E Actually, there are ways to transmit multiple signals over a baseband network simultaneously. The process is called multiplexing, and involves the division of the signal's frequency, or amplitude, or phase among several discrete signals. These methods are not used in typical LAN communications, however, although they are being explored as possible ways of increasing the speed of WAN links.

A Data Link layer protocol addresses this problem by dividing the data that is to be transmitted over the network into *packets*. Packets are chunks of data of a specified size that are transmitted over the network, and then reassembled at the destination. Each system on the network, therefore, takes control of the medium long enough to send a single packet at a time. If you were to examine the signals that are passing through the network cable at any one time, you would see a stream of packets generated by different systems and traveling to different destinations.

For this reason, LANs are called *packet switched networks*, because they continually share the network bandwidth with other systems. By contrast, the telephone system uses a *circuit switched network*. When you place a call, a circuit is established between the two stations that remains open for the entire duration of the session. The telephone signals travel along the same path through the network during the entire call. On a packet switched network, individual packets may take different routes to the same destination, and even arrive in a different order. Sufficient information is provided for the receiving system to assemble the packets back into the correct order.

Packet Headers

As data is passed to the Data Link layer from the Network layer above it, it is packaged into packets of the appropriate size, often called frames. To each frame is affixed a header that contains the information needed to get the frame to its destination. This is, essentially, the address on the envelope.

Among other things, the frame header contains the network and node addresses of the computer sending the packet and the computer that is destined to receive it. The node address (often called the MAC address) is hard coded into all Ethernet and token-ring network interface adapters by their manufacturers. Each manufacturer registers a prefix for its adapters and sees to it that every device has a unique address.

Ethernet and Frame Type Selection

When you have an Ethernet network, you must, during the NetWare installation process, select a frame type for your network communication. Reading about the IEEE standards in this chapter may add to your confusion regarding this selection. You are asked to choose among four Ethernet frame types:

- Ethernet_802.2
- Ethernet_802.3
- Ethernet_II
- Ethernet_SNAP

These options actually define marginal differences in the layout of the header that is applied to each frame.

802.3, as you have read, is the primary document that defines the standard known as Ethernet, including a particular layout for its frame header. However, a document called IEEE 802.2 defines another frame containing Logical Link Control information. This frame is, in fact, carried within the 802.3 frame as part of its payload.

Selecting the Ethernet_802.2 frame type, therefore, actually implies the use of the 802.3 packet, within which the 802.2 frame is carried. Ethernet_802.2 is the default frame type for NetWare 4.11. It can be used with the IPX and OSI protocols, and is required for the use of such features as NetWare's NCP Packet Signature feature.

Ethernet_802.3 frames, however, can be used only with the IPX protocols. The reason for this is that the Ethernet_802.2 frame header contains a field that is used to specify which Network-layer protocol is being carried in the packet. Ethernet_802.3 frames lack this field and can therefore be used to carry only one protocol.

Ethernet_II refers to a different standard document that was developed before the IEEE standards. This is the standard that is correctly referred to as Ethernet, but it defines a frame that differs from the 802.3 frame only in the use of a single field. Ethernet_II is typically used when you intend to run the TCP/IP protocols on your network, and also supports AppleTalk Phase 1.

Ethernet_SNAP (Sub-Network Address Protocol) is another variant that defines a secondary frame that is carried within the 802.3 frame. It can be used with the IPX, TCP/IP, and Appletalk Phase 2 protocols.

Thus, the actual differences between the four frame types are extremely minimal. Apart from the question of whether or not you expect to use particular protocols or certain NetWare features on your network, the most important factor in selecting a frame type for your network is to be sure that all of your servers and workstations have at least one frame type in common.

Error Checking

The Data Link protocol also performs a service that NetWare counts on to ensure the accurate transmission of data. Before transmitting each packet, the chip set on the network adapter in the source system computes a CRC (cyclic redundancy check) value for the packet's contents and stores it in a field of the packet frame. This value is transmitted to the destination along with the rest of the packet.

Upon receipt, the destination system performs the same computation, and compares the resulting value to the one delivered with the packet. If the two values match, then the packet is presumed to have been transmitted accurately. If they do not match, then an *alignment error* is declared, the packet is discarded, and procedures for retransmission are initiated.

Even though the Data Link protocol is not part of the operating system, NetWare relies on this error-checking mechanism. Additional error checking is performed higher up in the networking stack, but that is a check for transmission accuracy only between the two end systems. The Data Link layer's bit-level error checking involves the intermediate systems involved in the transmission as well.

Media Access Control

Perhaps the most important function of the Data Link layer is *media access control*, or MAC. A LAN consists of many different systems, all vying for the use of the same network bandwidth. If multiple systems attempt to transmit data at the same time, packet collisions result, and the data is corrupted.

Media access control, therefore, is a system that enables each computer on the network to obtain access to its share of the available bandwidth in an orderly manner. The two most popular Data Link protocols, Ethernet and token ring, use entirely different media access control algorithms. More than anything else, these MAC algorithms are what define the fundamental differences between these two protocols.

Carrier Sense Multiple Access with Collision Detection   Ethernet uses a media access control mechanism with the unwieldy name of Carrier Sense Multiple Access with Collision Detection, or CSMA/CD. When a system is ready to transmit data over the network, it first monitors the medium for traffic in progress. After a set period of time passes with no traffic, the network adapter in the system transmits.

Of course, it is entirely possible that another system might have been listening at the same time, and could transmit its own packet at the same moment. The more computers that you have on a network segment, the greater the likelihood that this will occur. When two or more packets are transmitted by different systems at the same time, a *collision* is said to occur. This is also sometimes referred to as a *signal quality error*, or SQE.

Collisions are expected on an Ethernet network. That is why there is a mechanism to deal with them. When a system detects that its transmission has collided with that of another system, it transmits a *jam pattern*. This is a random sequence of 32 to 48 bits that is designed to alert all of the other systems on the network that a collision has occurred. Usually, both of the systems involved in the collision will detect its presence.

After transmitting the jam pattern, both systems randomly select a delay interval before they begin to attempt retransmitting. This process is called *backing off*. Usually, retransmissions should proceed without the same two systems again colliding. However, if additional collisions should occur, the selection of a delay interval is modified using a process called *truncated binary exponential backoff*. This process increases the range of delay intervals from which one is chosen, making subsequent collisions less likely.

Collisions usually occur during the brief interval after a system has begun to transmit and before 64 bytes have been sent. A collision that occurs after the entire packet has left the network adapter is called a *late collision*. Late collisions are not expected, and are a definite indication of a potentially serious problem. In most cases, late collisions occur because of improper cable installations—such as network segments that are too long or contain too many workstations, or possibly a hardware defect in a network cable or interface.

Even though collisions are an expected occurrence on Ethernet networks, they still cause delays. Since more systems on a network result in more collisions, Ethernet networks are particularly susceptible to performance degradation under heavy traffic.

Token Passing   Token-ring networks use a media access control mechanism that does not allow collisions to occur under normal circumstances. Rather than each computer determining when it should begin to transmit, this system uses a specialized packet called a token that is circulated around the network from station to station.

Only one token is permitted on the network at any time, and a computer is only allowed to transmit data when it is in possession of the token. When a station is ready to transmit data, it must wait until the token is passed to it by the preceding workstation in the ring. Then, it appends its data to the token, changes a flag in the token from *free* to *busy,* and transmits.

N O T E   Most token passing systems now include a feature called *early token release*, which enables a system to pass the token immediately after it transmits a packet. In this way, the next system on the ring can receive a free token and transmit sooner, with minimal danger of a packet collision.

The packet is then transmitted in turn to each computer in the ring. Eventually, the packet traverses the entire ring, including the destination computer, and arrives back at its source. The original transmitting system then examines the packet that it has received back, and runs a CRC check to determine if it was transmitted successfully.

Because it does not result in collisions, token passing does not cause an increase in performance degradation as traffic increases. As a result, Token-ring networks are thought to perform better under heavy traffic conditions.

The Network Layer

As you move upwards through the protocol stack, you find that protocols become progressively less involved with the nuts and bolts of network communications. The Network layer is not involved with signaling types or media access, but it is the first layer of the OSI model to be concerned with the end-to-end transmission of data across the network.

Network communications often must travel through several network segments to reach their destination. This means that the packets must travel through one or more routers in the process. A router is an intermediate system that is connected to two or more networks, and enables traffic to enter through one interface and exit from another.

Complex internetworks can be organized so that there are several possible routes that a packet can take in order to reach its destination. Network layer protocols are involved in the routing process, and the selection of the best possible route to a certain destination. In contrast, Data Link layer protocols are completely ignorant of these concepts.

This is why the header affixed to a Network layer protocol also carries the network addresses of the source and destination systems. The destination system specified at the Network layer is absolute. It represents the actual end system for which the data is intended. However, the network address specified in a Data Link protocol header may be that of an intermediate system, because a protocol operating at that layer cannot be aware of systems found on remote network segments.

The Network layer is also the first place where the NetWare operating system actually supplies the protocol that is used for network communications. The Internetwork Packet Exchange protocol, or IPX, is the default protocol used by NetWare at the Network layer.

Unlike the Data Link layer protocols, IPX was not designed by an independent standards body. Instead, it is a proprietary protocol designed by Novell specifically for use with NetWare.

N O T E   As you might guess by the similarity of their initials, IPX performs many of the same functions as the Internet Protocol (IP). Both provide a connectionless carrier service for many other protocols operating at higher layers. Although IPX is still the default Network layer protocol used by NetWare, it is also possible to use TCP/IP instead of, or in addition to, NetWare's own proprietary protocols.

The increased emphasis on TCP/IP in the IntranetWare release is evidence of Novell's commitment to what has now become the industry standard networking protocol suite. For more information on TCP/IP, see Chapter 24, "Understanding TCP/IP."

IPX is a crucial part of the NetWare protocol stack, because it is used as the carrier for many of the other protocols operating at higher levels. IPX is a *connectionless* protocol, meaning that it transmits packets to other systems on the network without guaranteeing their arrival.

A *connection-oriented* protocol transmits interrogatory packets to the destination system and awaits a response before any actual data is transmitted. It also includes some means by which the destination system acknowledges the receipt of the arriving packets. This provides added reliability, but at the price of much more control data that must be transmitted over the network. A connectionless protocol may be described as *unreliable*, in a technical sense, but this does not mean that its packets are less likely to reach their destination.

An efficient protocol stack is designed so that the quality of service that is required from the protocols is spread out over several layers, without redundancy. Earlier in this chapter, in "Error Checking," you read that NetWare relies on the bit-level error checking performed by other protocols at the Data Link layer. NetWare could well institute its own error checking mechanism in its own protocols, but that would be redundant, and inefficient.

In the same way, the IPX provides connectionless delivery service to several different protocols operating at higher layers. When it is necessary, a protocol operating at the Transport layer may provide additional services that guarantee packet delivery, or perform other functions. This is the equivalent of sending only your most important letters by Special Delivery, rather than needlessly spending the money to send all of your mail that way.

The IPX header, besides specifying the network addresses of the source and destination systems, also includes a reference to the process on the destination machine for which the packet is intended. These processes are referred to as *sockets*. Several standard socket numbers are reserved for use by internal NetWare functions, such as the following:

Socket Number	Description
0451h	NetWare Core Protocol
0452h	Service Advertising Protocol
0453h	Routing Information Protocol
0455h	Novell NetBIOS

Socket Number	Description
0456h	Diagnostic Packet
9000h	NetWare Link Services Protocol (NLSP)
9004h	IPXWAN Protocol

Other sockets with values from 4000h to 7FFFh can be assigned by various server processes.

The IPX header also includes a packet type code that specifies the upper-layer protocol that is being carried within the IPX frame. The possible values are as follows:

Code	Description
0	Unknown Packet Type
1	Routing Information Packet (RIP)
4	Packet Exchange Packet
5	Sequenced Packet Exchange (SPX)
17	NetWare Core Protocol

Part III

Ch 10

The Upper Layers

When you reach the Transport layer, you begin to see protocols that have been designed to satisfy the specific needs of NetWare clients and servers. Up until this point, you've learned about protocols that were designed to perform general services. Transport layer protocols, on the other hand, are more involved with the contents of the envelope, rather than just the address and its delivery.

Various network communications tasks require different levels of service, and NetWare provides a number of specialized protocols that operate at the Transport layer and above, to satisfy specific needs. This is in keeping with the theory already mentioned, that efficient network communication should provide only the quality of service needed, and no more.

It is also true that, as you examine the protocols that operate at the upper layers of the networking stack, the distinctions between the layers become increasingly nebulous. Some of the protocols that are carried within IPX packets operate strictly within the bounds of the Transport layer, while others include functions that rightfully belong in the Session layer or above. The following sections describe the upper-layer protocols that are part of NetWare's proprietary networking stack, all of which are transmitted as the payload of IPX packets.

Sequenced Packet Exchange (SPX)

NetWare's native protocols are often referred to as IPX/SPX, representing a combination of Network and Transport layer protocols that together provide an extremely reliable data transmission, much like the TCP/IP combination. SPX is a connection-oriented protocol that provides reliable delivery of packets, as well as error correction, flow control, and packet sequencing services.

Despite its frequent comparison with TCP, the truth is that SPX is not a heavily used protocol on a typical NetWare network. It is used primarily for the transmission of print job data, RCONSOLE sessions, and other tasks—such as network backups, which require guaranteed delivery and do not have other means of verifying the accuracy of the transmitted data.

Connection Establishment   Before a connection-oriented protocol begins transmitting data, it establishes a connection with the destination system. The SPX protocol does this by sending packets that contain only control instructions. The various types of control packets are defined by the connection control byte that is included as part of the 12-byte header that SPX adds to every packet. This byte can have the following values:

Value	Description
20h	Attention
80h	System packet
40h	Acknowledgment required
10h	End of message

If it is ready to receive data, the destination returns a response to the sender. This establishes a virtual connection between the two systems that will remain in effect for the entire duration of the transmission. Each system identifies the connection with an ID number, so that the packets that make up this particular transmission sequence can be identified. Once all of the data has been successfully transferred, control packets are again exchanged, in order to break down the connection.

The connection created during an SPX transmission should not be confused with the client/server connection that begins when a user logs in to a NetWare network. An SPX connection usually exists only for a relatively short period of time during which a particular task is being performed. There can, however, be extended delays during the transmission of data, during which specialized packets are transmitted at regular intervals to keep the connection alive.

Packet Acknowledgment   The SPX header contains fields that perform several other important tasks that add to the quality of service provided by the protocol. One of these is the acknowledgment number that is returned by the receiving system to the sender.

Each packet sent during a particular SPX transmission is assigned a sequence number. This number uniquely identifies each transmitted packet. The receiving system acknowledges that a packet has been received successfully by returning a control packet to the sender that specifies the sequence number of the next packet that it expects to receive.

N O T E   The sequence number assigned to each packet also performs another function. When packets travel to a system on another network segment, they often can take one of several possible routes to the destination. Changing conditions on the network can even cause packets within the same SPX transmission sequence to take different routes, possibly arriving at the destination system out of order. When this occurs, the sequence number is used to reassemble the packets into a properly ordered sequence. ▪

If, for example, one hundred packets have been transmitted, but the destination system finds that the last packet is corrupted, it will return a response with an acknowledgment number of 99, and the sender will retransmit the lost packet.

A protocol in which packet transmissions are acknowledged by responses from the destination is said to be a *reliable* protocol. Most connection-oriented protocols are also reliable, but these are actually two separate concepts.

The addition of connection-oriented, reliable service to a protocol results in a great deal of additional data that must be transported across the network. There are more control bytes in each packet, because of the size of the SPX header, and there are more packets, because of the control responses and acknowledgments that must be transmitted back to the sender. This is why protocols like SPX are used only when necessary.

Configuring SPX Parameters   As an added measure of reliability, the sending system also re-transmits packets automatically, if it does not receive an acknowledgment within a specified period of time. You can reset this time-out period, and several other operational parameters for the SPX protocol using a server console utility called SPXCONFG.NLM.

You can run SPXCONFG as a menu-based utility, or specify settings from the command line. Table 10.1 lists the SPXCONFG settings, their defaults, their possible values, and the abbreviations used on the command line.

Table 10.1   SPXCONFG Settings and Parameters

Setting	Default	Range	Abbreviation
SPX watchdog abort time-out— The period that must elapse without the receipt of a packet before a system declares an SPX connection to be invalid	540	540–5400 ticks	A=
SPX watchdog verify time-out— The period that must elapse without the receipt of a packet before a system requests the transmission of a keep-alive packet	108	10–255 ticks	V=
SPX ack wait time-out— The period that a system waits to receive an acknowledgment before retransmitting a packet	54	10–3240 ticks	W=

continues

Table 10.1 Continued

Setting	Default	Range	Abbreviation
SPX default retry count— The number of times that a packet will be re-sent without acknowledgment	10	1–255	R=
Maximum concurrent SPX sessions— The number of SPX sessions that can be opened by an application	1000	100–2000	S=
Maximum open IPX sockets— The number of sockets that can be opened by an application	1200	60–65520	I=

Flow Control   Another function of the SPX header is to control the rate at which data is transmitted to the destination system. If data is transmitted too quickly, then the destination system can be overwhelmed, and forced to discard packets.

Flow control is provided by the inclusion of an allocation number in the response packets returned to the sending system by the recipient. This number specifies the number of packet receive buffers that are available at the destination. The sender modifies its rate of transmission based on the fluctuations of the allocation number in the acknowledgments it receives from the destination.

Flow control is a particularly important feature in light of the fact that one of the most common uses of the SPX protocol is to send data from print servers to printers or port drivers. Different types of printers accept data at vastly different rates, and it is important that print job data not be lost due to an overflow situation.

Packet Exchange Protocol (PXP)

The Packet Exchange Protocol is also a connection-oriented, Transport layer protocol, but it is designed for use only with transmissions that consist of a single request and reply. This is because the protocol lacks a mechanism to prevent the transmission of duplicate requests.

Some types of data transmissions, such as sending a print job to a printer or posting a payment to a financial database, can cause deleterious effects if the transmission is sent more than once. If a job is sent to a printer and no reply is received, then sending the job again might result in a second printout.

Other data transmissions, such as a request that a block be read from a file, can be repeated with no ill effect to the application, other than a slight waste of bandwidth. A transaction of this type, which can be repeated without negatively affecting the performance of the application, is called an *idempotent* transaction.

The PXP header is small when compared to that of an SPX packet. It consists only of a four-byte transaction number that is used to associate a request with its reply. PXP is not as reliable as SPX, but it is more reliable than the service provided by IPX alone, and it significantly reduces the amount of control traffic produced by a transaction.

Service Advertising Protocol (SAP)

The Service Advertising Protocol is used by NetWare file servers, print servers, gateway servers, and multiprotocol routers to periodically broadcast their availability to other systems on the network. This information is stored in the NDS database, where it can be accessed by any other workstation or server.

For example, when you issue the NLIST SERVER command from a workstation, you receive a listing of all of the servers on your network. This listing is made possible by the fact that each server issues its own SAP packets, approximately every 60 seconds (by default). When you bring a NetWare server down, it broadcasts a SAP packet indicating that it will no longer be available for use.

SAP packets are also used by servers to request specific information from other servers. A good example of this is the copy protection mechanism that prevents the same NetWare license from being used on multiple servers on the same network. For this purpose, there are separate SAP packet header formats for requests and replies.

All SAP packets contain a packet type field in their header that contains one of the following values:

Value	Description
1h	Standard server request
2h	Standard server reply
3h	Get nearest server request
4h	Get nearest server reply

Standard server requests and replies are used for the periodic SAP broadcasts generated by all servers. Get nearest server requests and replies are for the specific purpose of locating the closest possible server to a specific system.

SAP requests contain only one other field that identifies the type of server. SAP reply packets, however, include a series of fields that provide information about the server, as follows:

- **Service type**—A code indicating the function of the transmitting server (for example, file server, job server, print server, archive server, remote bridge server, etc.)
- **Server name**—The full name of the transmitting server
- **Network address**—The address of the network segment on which the transmitting server is located
- **Node address**—The MAC address of the network interface adapter in the transmitting server

Part III
Ch
10

■ **Socket number**—Used to identify the process associated with the server name and type

■ **Number of hops**—The number of intermediate network segments between the transmitting and receiving servers

A SAP packet can contain up to seven server entries, each of which is composed of these six fields.

NetWare has long been criticized for the amount of network traffic that is generated by SAP and RIP (Routing Information Protocol) packets. Continual broadcasts of what is usually redundant information by every NetWare server on a network can, in some cases, be excessive. The introduction of Novell Directory Services, however, has greatly reduced this traffic.

On a bindery-based NetWare network, each server is required to maintain a list of all of the network services identified by periodic SAP broadcasts. The services are identified by socket numbers, which are used in IPX headers in lieu of the service name. Each server can support a list of up to 65,000 sockets.

On a network that uses NDS, the list of services is stored in the directory services database, rather than in each server. Service information is disseminated throughout the network using the normal NDS upgrade procedures, rather than through broadcasts. In addition, NetWare clients request service information with NDS queries. Responses are then returned using unicast transmissions, rather than broadcasts.

Routing Information Protocol (RIP)

The Routing Information Protocol is similar to SAP, in that it is used to disseminate information to systems all over the network. RIP, however, as the name implies, deals with the information needed for systems to make network routing decisions.

Although the term router has come to refer to a specialized piece of hardware, any NetWare server with two or more network interface adapters installed functions as a router. A router, therefore, can be directly aware of the systems located on two network segments. If, however, it must transmit data to a system located on a third segment, it must have a way of knowing how to reach that segment.

This knowledge comes from a *routing information table* that is maintained in each router, which contains data obtained from the RIP packets that are broadcast by every router on the network. Each router shares the information about the networks to which it is attached with the other routers, giving each one an overall picture of the entire network. RIP packets can contain up to 50 network entries, each of which is comprised of several information fields.

With this information, a server or workstation can determine the most efficient route to another system located anywhere on the network. Efficiency is gauged by the number of hops and ticks needed to reach the destination, both of which are included in each network entry found in a RIP packet.

A *hop* refers to a network segment that must be traversed in order to reach the destination. If a packet must pass through two routers or other intermediate systems in order to reach its destination, it is said to be two hops away.

A *tick* is a unit of time, equivalent to approximately 1/18 of a second, that is used to measure how long it takes a packet to reach a destination on another network segment.

When there are two or more possible routes to a destination, the one requiring the fewest number of ticks is selected. If the number of ticks is the same, then the route requiring the fewest hops is used. The regular RIP broadcasts also inform other routers when a system is down and a route is no longer available. This enables an alternate route to be used, if available, rather than sending packets on a dead-end journey.

N O T E As with SAP, RIP broadcasts can be responsible for creating a large amount of network traffic. Novell has introduced an alternative to RIP for the communications that must take place between routers, called the NetWare Link Services Protocol. For more information, see Chapter 29, "Migrating to NetWare Link Services Protocol (NLSP)." ▣

Part
III

Ch
10

NetWare Core Protocol (NCP)

The NetWare Core Protocol is the most often used of the upper-layer protocols because it is responsible for all of the file system transfers on a NetWare network. It is also the most difficult protocol to categorize. Although basically operating at the Transport layer, its capabilities extend beyond this at times to the Session, Presentation, and Application layers.

NCP is used for two of the most common network tasks: connection control and service requests. *Connection control* is the process of establishing a connection to a NetWare server. Unlike an SPX connection, NCP is used to create the type of user connection that you see listed in the Connection Information screen of the MONITOR utility. An NCP connection stays open for the entire duration of a user's network session.

Service requests are generated whenever a NetWare client accesses a network resource. An NCP request is used whenever an application opens a file on a NetWare volume, or prints a file to a NetWare queue.

Because of this flexibility of purpose, NCP transmissions can include a widely varying array of services. Some tasks, such as writing a file to a NetWare drive, require an acknowledgment for every packet transmitted, and NCP can in this case function as a fully reliable, connection-oriented protocol. In other cases, a lesser degree of service is required, and the protocol's quality of service is modified accordingly.

To accommodate its various uses, NCP uses different headers for requests and replies. A code is included in each that identifies the function of the packet. The codes for the Request Type field are as follows:

Type	Function	Description
1111	Create a service connection	Used to begin the process of establishing a connection with a NetWare server
2222	Server request	Used to request access to a file or other resource on a NetWare server
5555	Connection destroy	Used to terminate an NCP connection with a NetWare server
7777	Burst mode transmission	Used to initiate an NCP Burst Mode transfer

The codes for the Reply Type field are the following:

Type	Function	Description
3333	Server reply	Indicates that the packet contains a reply to a 2222 request
7777	Burst mode protocol packet	Indicates that the initialization of a burst mode transfer has been completed successfully
9999	Positive acknowledge	Used to indicate that a previously received request is currently being processed, thus preventing the connection from timing out; can also be used to indicate the existence of a problem satisfying a request

NetWare Core Packet Burst Protocol (NCPB)

Unlike SPX, which is used relatively infrequently, the NetWare Core Protocol is used for all NetWare file system transfers, and is therefore responsible for the transmission of large amounts of data. This data must be transmitted reliably, but the additional network traffic caused by the acknowledgments generated for every packet proved to be untenable for high volume transfers.

To address this problem, Novell developed a variation on NCP that can transmit multiple data packets with only a single acknowledgment, called the NetWare Core Packet Burst Protocol, or NCPB, or *burst mode*. Burst mode transmissions use a modified *sliding window* technique to transfer a series of packets before an acknowledgment is required.

A sliding window transmission is one in which the size of the window can be varied to accommodate the reception capabilities of the destination system, using a *transmission rate control algorithm*. If packets are being dropped at the destination because the transmission rate is too fast, the sending system will first attempt to adjust the *interpacket gap*, that is, the amount of lag time between packets. This gives the receiving system more time to assimilate each packet.

If necessary, the sender may also reduce the size of the window itself, sending fewer packets for each acknowledgment. NetWare clients can configure the initial size of the packet burst read and write windows by modifying their NET.CFG or Control Panel settings. By default, the PBURST READ WINDOW SIZE is 24 packets for Client32 for Windows 95, and 16 for the NetWare DOS Requester. The PBURST WRITE WINDOW SIZE values are 10 packets for both clients. You can also disable packet burst transmissions entirely, although this can have an adverse effect on file system performance.

When packets are lost during an NCPB transmission, the receiving system is able to return a list of the packets that are missing to the sender, enabling it to retransmit only the packets that are needed, rather than rolling back the entire transmission to the point at which the first error occurred.

A related feature of NCP that also increases the efficiency of file system transfers is the *large Internet packet*, or LIP. At one time, NetWare routers could transfer packets no larger than 576 bytes, despite the capability of Ethernet and token-ring adapters as well as most routers to generate much larger packets. A larger packet, arriving at the first router it encountered, would be broken down into smaller packets and reassembled by the destination system. LIP now enables the router itself to determine the maximum size for an NCP packet, which is larger than 576 bytes in most cases, reducing control traffic still further.

Part III

Ch 10

Summary

NetWare's use of proprietary protocols, such as IPX, has become a point of serious contention among network administrators recently. The industry is clearly moving towards the use of open standards, such as the TCP/IP protocols. Novell's release of IntranetWare clearly indicates that they are committed to the use of TCP/IP with NetWare, particularly for intranet and Internet services. However, many networks remain committed to NetWare for their core IPX file and print services, and with good reason: NetWare substantially outperforms the IP-based counterparts in other operating systems when it comes to these crucial services, and is likely to remain in use for some time to come. ●

Monitoring NetWare Performance

One of the most important jobs of the network administrator is to be aware of the ongoing condition of the network and anticipate problem areas before they cause a service outage. There are, of course, any number of things that can go wrong, and although no one can keep continuous tabs on them all, NetWare provides tools that enable you to track your network's activity on several fronts.

You can categorize network processes in several different ways, each of which can be a logical approach to your systems maintenance activities. You've learned about the OSI reference model that divides network communications into seven layers. These layers proceed from physical concerns (that is, the network medium itself) to the application layer (the way your applications interact with your operating system and the network).

Another valid approach to system maintenance is to break the network down into three categories: server processes, workstation processes, and communications processes. These methods are not carved in stone, nor is it strictly necessary to approach the problem this way at all. The categorization process is simply a means of comprehending an extremely complex system by breaking it into individual segments.

The NetWare tools that you learn about in this chapter are capable of providing you with an enormous amount of statistical data, and in order to comprehend even a part of it, you must understand what subsystem is being discussed, and how it relates to the overall performance of the network. ▨

Using the NetWare Performance Monitoring Tools

To know absolutely everything about the performance of your network requires more tools than are included in the IntranetWare package, but those that are provided can furnish a wealth of information, if you take the time to learn about them.

Performance monitoring is done primarily from the NetWare server console, or an RCONSOLE session, with utilities that run as NLMs. By far, the most comprehensive NetWare utility of this type is MONITOR.NLM. MONITOR displays hundreds of real-time statistics about various aspects of your NetWare network, including the following:

- Current user connections
- Open file information
- Server disk activity
- Currently loaded software modules
- Server memory utilization
- Server processor utilization
- LAN/WAN communication activity

Another program, called SERVMAN.NLM, enables you to configure your server by assigning SET parameter values, and displays information on communications and the storage system configuration.

Except for SERVMAN, these utilities are primarily dedicated to the display of information, and not to interactive configuration. There are exceptions to this, however. From MONITOR, you can disconnect active clients, configure server parameters, and lock the server console.

The server utilities all take the form of NLMs, executable programs that you launch on the server console using the LOAD command. Their interface is menu-based, and they operate much like that of the NetWare C-worthy utilities that run on DOS workstations, such as NETADMIN and FILER.

▶ **See** "Using the NetWare Text Menu Utilities," **p. 310**

Be aware that as with any other NLM, the NetWare performance monitoring utilities require a certain amount of server memory to operate. The memory requirement for each program increases as you open more display windows on each screen. If your server is short on available memory, it is recommended that you close these utilities when they are not in use.

Monitoring Server Processes

Unlike other network operating systems, such as UNIX and Windows NT in which every computer can function as both a server and a client, NetWare segregates these functions completely. Client computers only can communicate with servers, and not with each other. As a result, the efficient operation of the NetWare server is crucial to the operation of the network.

The MONITOR program is the primary indicator of a server's status, providing information that enables you to gauge when it is operating beyond its capacity. Although MONITOR provides an enormous amount of information, it is only necessary to keep track of a few major parameters on a regular basis. The other statistics are useful for troubleshooting purposes, and for obtaining a more detailed picture of NetWare processes.

N O T E It is a good idea to check the current operational statistics for your server before you install a new piece of hardware or software. By noting the differences between your baseline figures and those taken after the installation, you can assess the effect of the new product on your system. ▪

Essential NetWare Statistics

Such utilities as MONITOR provide a wealth of information about NetWare, almost an embarrassment of riches. The sheer number of statistics and the technical terms used to describe them can be daunting, even to an experienced NetWare administrator. However, NetWare generally does an extremely good job of regulating itself, and servers have been known to run for years without administrative intervention.

Most of NetWare's operational statistics are used for troubleshooting purposes. When something goes wrong, MONITOR can provide an extremely detailed view of the server's current status. For routine maintenance purposes, however, there are only a few statistics that you should monitor regularly.

The Cache Buffers percentage in MONITOR's Resource Utilization screen is the most important statistic to watch. Indicating the amount of free memory available on the server, you should check this parameter both before and after you load new software on the server. Take note also whether the percentage drops gradually over a period of days or weeks. This could indicate that an NLM is failing to release memory as it is loaded and unloaded on a regular basis.

The processor utilization percentage on MONITOR's General Information screen is another important statistic. The utilization of the server's processor fluctuates constantly as various instructions are executed, but if the value regularly approaches 100 percent, this could indicate that an NLM is monopolizing the processor or that your server traffic is too heavy.

You should also be aware of the statistics concerning the packet collisions on your network. Ethernet networks, which comprise the vast majority of business LANs, should experience a certain number of collisions under normal conditions. When you compare the Total Packets Sent and Received on MONITOR's LAN/WAN Information screen with the Send OK Single and Multiple Collision Count figures, the number of collisions should be well below one percent of the total packets. Higher figures could indicate a hardware problem in the network infrastructure or a problem with a LAN driver.

Using MONITOR

When you load the MONITOR program on the server, the first screen that appears displays a window containing general information about the server, and a menu providing access to all of the program's other screens. At first, an abbreviated General Information window appears. You can switch to the expanded version of the display by pressing the Tab key (see Figure 11.1).

FIG. 11.1
MONITOR's main screen displays general server information and the main menu.

At the top of the screen, basic information about MONITOR is displayed, including the version number, the server name, the directory tree name, and the version of NetWare running on the server. The following information appears in MONITOR's General Information box, which is the top half of the MONITOR display:

- **Server Up Time**—Shows the total elapsed time in days, hours, minutes, and seconds since the server was last started.

- **Active Processors**—Displays the number of processors installed in the server that are currently being used by NetWare. The use of multiple processors requires the installation of NetWare SMP during the standard server installation process.

- **Utilization**—The percentage of time that the server's processor was busy during the last second. This number is a gauge of how busy the file server is from a processing standpoint. On multiprocessor servers, this figure represents an average of the utilization for all processors.

- **Original Cache Buffers**—The amount of memory devoted to the cache buffer pool when the server was first started. When you boot a server, all of the memory that is not used by the loading of modules and the mounting of volumes is made available for caching. As other processes require additional memory, it is allocated from the cache buffer pool.

- **Total Cache Buffers**—Displays the current number of available cache buffers.

- **Dirty Cache Buffers**—Shows the number of cache buffers containing file information that has been changed and that are waiting to be written to disk. When the server is not being used, this value should be zero. A continuously high number of dirty cache buffers may indicate the existence of a bottleneck in your server's I/O system.

- **Current Disk Requests**—Indicates the number of disk read and write requests that are waiting to be processed. This number is a gauge of the server's disk I/O (input/output) backlog.

- **Packet Receive Buffers**—Shows the number of memory buffers that are allocated to receive incoming packets from workstations.

- **Directory Cache Buffers**—Shows the number of memory buffers devoted to the caching of the server volumes' directory entries.

- **Maximum Service Processes**—Shows the maximum number of NetWare service processes that may be allocated. A service process, also called a task handler, manages a particular task that is being performed on a server by a workstation, such as copying a file to or from a server volume or executing a server-based application file.

- **Current Service Processes**—Shows the number of service processes that are currently allocated. This is a good gauge of how busy the server is and how many concurrent requests the server is handling at any one time. When the current service processes approaches the maximum, server performance will degrade unless you increase the maximum (using the SET MAXIMUM SERVICE PROCESSES command). You must have sufficient memory in the server to support the allotted number of processes.

- **Maximum Licensed Connections**—Indicates the number of user logins and workstation attachments allowed on the server by your NetWare license. This count includes only users and external devices (such as print servers) that are logged in to the server.

- **Current Licensed Connections**—Indicates the number of user logins and workstation attachments now in use.

- **Open Files**—Indicates how many files are currently being accessed by all client and server processes.

The bottom half of the display is MONITOR's main menu. The menu options are as follows:

- Connection Information
- Disk Information
- LAN/WAN Information
- System Module Information
- Lock File Server Console
- File Open/Lock Activity
- Cache Utilization
- Processor Utilization
- Resource Utilization
- Memory Utilization
- Scheduling Information
- Multiprocessor Information
- Server Parameters

Part
III

Ch
11

From the Lock File Server Console screen, you can specify the password that is used to block all access to the server console. This feature locks all of the console screens—not just MONITOR. To unlock the console, you must supply the password given or the Admin user password. You also can lock the console with the Admin password automatically by launching monitor with the command LOAD MONITOR L.

The Server Parameters screen duplicates part of the SERVMAN.NLM utility's function. It enables you to modify the values for a large number of highly specific parameters that affect the performance of the server. The most important rule of thumb regarding these parameters is that you never should modify their values without exploring the full ramifications of your actions. Many of these settings affect the most fundamental NetWare functions, and can severely degrade your server performance if handled incorrectly.

With a few exceptions, including the two screens just mentioned and the Connection Information screens, from which you can disconnect users from the server, the screens accessed from MONITOR's main menu are purely informational. The statistics found on these screens are examined in the subsequent sections of this chapter.

Viewing Memory Statistics

Memory is the single most crucial commodity to a NetWare server. Each driver and NLM that you load on the server consumes memory, as does each additional pop-up window that is displayed by a server utility, such as MONITOR. Memory is also an essential element of the server disk storage subsystem. The more disk space that you have mounted as NetWare volumes, the more server memory is required.

Memory never is wasted in a NetWare server. All of the memory that is not utilized to load modules and mount volumes during the server boot process goes into a file cache buffer pool that is used to speed up disk access by holding the most recently accessed files in memory. The larger the cache buffer pool, the more files that can be cached, and the better server disk performance gets.

Information on how memory is being used on a server can be found on two of MONITOR's screens: Resource Utilization and Memory Utilization.

Resource Utilization   NetWare can allocate memory for dozens of different tasks, and MONITOR's Resource Utilization screen enables you to keep track of precisely how much memory is being used for each type of task. No other part of MONITOR provides a more detailed look at the inner workings and structures of NetWare 4.11, and no other part is as obscure. When you choose Resource Utilization from MONITOR's main menu, a two-part memory screen similar to the one shown in Figure 11.2 appears.

The top part of the screen lists six server memory usage statistics (five specific memory areas or *pools* and the total server memory). This screen provides a clear look at the five basic areas into which NetWare divides the memory installed in the server. For each item, the number of bytes allocated and the percentage of the total installed memory are shown. These areas are illustrated in Figure 11.3.

FIG. 11.2

MONITOR's Resource Utilization screen displays statistics concerning the distribution of memory among the server processes.

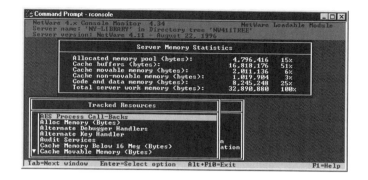

FIG. 11.3

Memory in a NetWare server is allocated into five distinct pools.

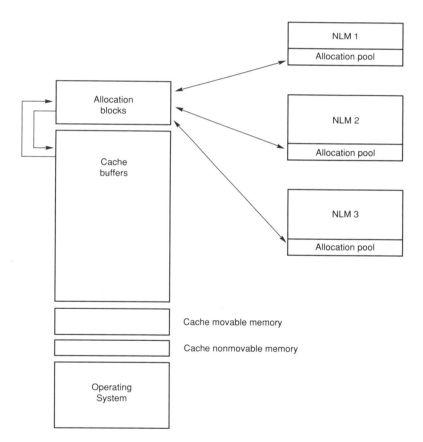

The function of each of the memory pools is shown in the following list:

■ **Allocated Memory Pool**—Memory organized into 4K allocation blocks for use by NLMs. From this area, each NLM is given its own allocation pool. When the allocated memory pool must be increased in size, additional memory blocks are created from the cache buffers pool. When the memory is no longer needed, it's returned to the cache buffers area.

- **Cache Buffers**—Stores all memory not needed by the other four memory areas. This memory is allocated to the other pools as needed, and also used to cache files that have been accessed by server users and processes.

- **Cache Movable Memory**—Stores various informational tables maintained by NetWare, including the directory entry table, the file allocation table (FAT), and the table of connected users.

- **Cache Non-Movable Memory**—A small memory area that stores miscellaneous memory tables and the cache memory used during the file compression and decompression processes.

- **Code and Data Memory**—3M–4M of memory required for the NetWare operating system itself, apart from all of the modules that are loaded on the server.

The main indicator in the Server Memory Statistics window that you should check on a regular basis is the cache buffers percentage. Opinions vary concerning the figure that should be considered the danger zone, but if your cache buffers percentage drops below 40 percent, you definitely should install additional memory in the near future. Alternatively, you can unload some unneeded modules on the server (such as MONITOR itself) to free up memory for essential processes.

Tracked Resources   The bottom half of the Resource Utilization screen displays a list of the server's tracked resources. These resources are various operating system functions—such as record locking, print job queuing, and router and server tracking—that can be called by server modules.

When you select a particular resource, you see a list of the modules that are using this resource in the Resource Tags window. When you select a module, a window opens that displays the amount of memory being used to execute the selected function for the selected module. You can therefore determine the exact modules that are utilizing memory from a particular pool.

System Module Information   MONITOR's System Module Information screen displays essentially the same information as the Resource Utilization screen, but organizes it in a different way. Instead of allowing you to choose a resource tag and see what modules are using that resource, this screen enables you to choose a module and displays a list of the resource tags that the module is currently using.

When you select one of the listed modules, you see the by-now-familiar Server Memory Statistics window at the top of the MONITOR screen, and a window listing all of the module's resource tags (elements that use operating system resources, such as memory and service processes) appears. When you select a particular resource tag, more detailed information about the resources used by this tag appears, as shown in Figure 11.4.

FIG. 11.4
MONITOR enables
you to view the exact
memory resources
that are being used
by a particular software
module running on
the server.

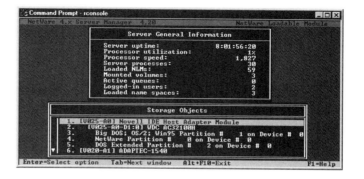

Memory Utilization MONITOR's Memory Utilization option enables you to display information and statistics about the server memory used by specific modules. You can select the name of an NLM or driver running on your server and see the total amount of memory that it is using. From this screen, you also can manually trigger the performance of what is normally an automatic NetWare function, known as *garbage collection*, for the selected module. Garbage collection is a process that collects unused fragments of memory and returns them to the server's pool of available memory blocks where they can be reused.

When you select the Memory Utilization option from MONITOR's main menu, two windows are displayed (see Figure 11.5). The top window shows the memory statistics for the server's pool of memory allocation blocks, which is the area that supplies memory to NLMs. This pool is divided into 4K cache pages. The first statistic shown, 4K Cache Pages, displays the total number of pages in the pool.

The Cache Page Blocks figure indicates the number of blocks into which the allocated memory pool has been divided. NetWare makes memory available to NLMs in units known as blocks, which are sized in 4K, 16K, or 256K units so that small, medium, and large amounts of memory can be located and supplied quickly. The Percent In Use and Percent Free statistics show how much of the allocated memory pool is in use and how much still remains available. The next four statistics in the top window indicate how much of the pool is in use and how much is available, measured in both bytes and blocks.

N O T E Do not confuse the memory blocks described here with the block size that you specify when creating a NetWare volume. The size of a memory block is automatically determined by the operating system based on the total amount of memory being allocated.

T I P Pressing the Tab key expands the Allocated Memory window to its full size, allowing you to see all of the statistics.

FIG. 11.5

The Memory Utilization screen in MONITOR displays the total memory used by specific software modules.

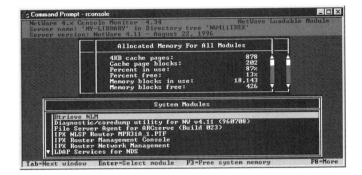

At the bottom of the memory utilization screen is a list of the software modules that are currently loaded on the server. By selecting a module from the list, you can view the amount of memory that it is using. The same eight statistics just described for the overall server memory situation are then displayed for the selected module only.

N O T E   While you are viewing a particular module's memory usage statistics, you can perform a garbage collection for that module by pressing the F3 key. If any free memory pages are found, they are returned to the cache buffer pool, from which they can be reallocated. You also can free up memory for all of the currently loaded modules by pressing F3 when the Allocated Memory or All Modules screen is displayed.

It is not necessary for you to manually perform memory maintenance activities, such as garbage collection, on a regular basis. Under normal conditions, NetWare automatically frees up all available memory every 15 minutes. However, this feature makes it easy to determine the exact amount of memory that is actually being used by any module loaded on the server.

Viewing Processor Utilization Statistics

MONITOR'S Processor Utilization option enables you to gauge the amount of processor time that is used by the various NLMs and other tasks running on your server. When you choose Processor Utilization from MONITOR's main menu, a list of the server's processes and interrupts is displayed. Selecting an item from the list displays its real-time processor utilization statistics. You also can mark multiple processes with the F5 key to view their statistics together on one screen, or view the statistics for all processes by pressing F3.

When you select a process, an interrupt, or a group of processes and interrupts, a window appears that displays three columns of information about the selected items (see Figure 11.6). The Time column shows the amount of time (in approximate units of millionths of a second) that the server processor spent executing the instructions generated by that process during the last second. The Count column shows the number of times the process ran during the last second, and the Load column shows the percentage of the processor's time that that particular process occupied.

FIG. 11.6

MONITOR's Processor Utilization screen enables you to see which server modules require the most processing time.

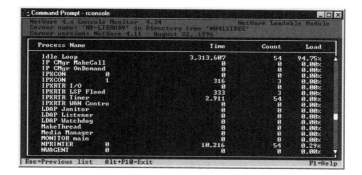

When you view the processor utilization statistics for all processes and interrupts at the same time, you get a good feel for the server tasks that consume the most server processor time. Ideally, all processes should use processor time in balanced proportions, but if your server seems to be running slowly and consistently shows high processor utilization, you can use MONITOR's processor utilization statistics to look for the NLM processes that are consuming an inordinate amount of the processor's time. Thanks to the efficiency of today's microprocessors, the biggest processor consumer is usually the process labeled Idle Loop, which shows the time the processor spent doing nothing.

At the bottom of the display you see the total number of sample time units for the last second. When you view processor utilization statistics, some server processing time is required to collect and display the statistics. This overhead, shown at the bottom of the list, is labeled Histogram Overhead Time.

CAUTION

More than any other MONITOR screen, the display of the processor utilization statistics for all of the current processes utilizes a significant amount of server resources. It strongly is advised that you do not leave this screen active for long periods of time, as degradation of other processes can result.

If you encounter a situation in which a server is experiencing a general slowdown, processor utilization is one of several statistics that you should examine. Most of the modules and applications that run on NetWare servers do not require a large amount of processor time. This is because client/server programs, by definition, utilize the client system's processor for most of the individual user's calculations.

Another reason for low processor overhead under NetWare is that many of the server's processes are involved with disk I/O, and storage devices naturally run slower than microprocessors. A disk access request that is computed using a few nanoseconds (that is, billionths of a second) of processor time can take many milliseconds (thousandths of a second) to be satisfied by the server's disk subsystem. In many instances, the processor sits idle until the disk processes that it has ordered have been completed, and the next process can begin.

Part

III

Ch

11

Therefore, if you see a server process that is consistently monopolizing the processor's time, to the detriment of other subsystems, this is often a sign that the module is misbehaving in some way. If possible, you should examine the offending process to see what it is currently doing. It may be trying to address a non-responsive device, or it may be hung, that is, caught in a processing loop from which it can't escape.

Unloading and restarting the module may resolve the problem, if this is possible, or you simply may be running an application that needs further debugging by its developers. Programs that are particularly ill-behaved may prevent you from doing anything to remedy the problem, except restarting the server.

Viewing and Setting Scheduling Information   MONITOR's Scheduling Information screen looks a lot like the Processor Utilization option when you view statistics for all of the running processes. The difference is that Scheduling Information enables you to do more than merely observe. From this screen, you can adjust the priority of each server process. Thus, if a particular NLM is monopolizing the system processor, you can reduce the CPU time that is being allotted to that process, allowing other NLMs to run more efficiently.

When you display the Scheduling Information screen (see Figure 11.7), a list of all of the server's running processes appears with the relative processor usage for each displayed at two-second intervals. The significance of the information shown in the Time, Count, and Load columns is exactly the same as in the Processor Utilization screen. The Sch Delay column displays the current processing priority for each process. By default, all processes have a delay of zero, meaning that all processes receive the same priority.

FIG. 11.7

MONITOR's Scheduling Information screen enables you to adjust the priority of the processes running on the server.

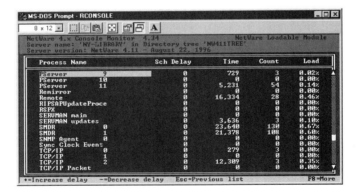

To give a process less priority, highlight it and press the plus (+) key on the server's numeric keypad. The schedule delay setting for this process (as listed in the Sch Delay column) increases by increments of 1 each time you press the plus key. Each multiple of two reduces the CPU time allotted to the process by one half. To increase the priority of a process that you have previously delayed, highlight the process and press the minus (–) key on the numeric keypad.

There is seldom a good reason to delay a process. If you have an NLM that regularly monopolizes processor time, you are better off using a different product or waiting for an upgraded version of the module than trying to adjust processor priority. If, however, you must run a poorly behaved NLM, you can try to limit its processor time by assigning it a schedule delay.

 TIP To apply automatically a schedule delay to a process when you boot the server, you use the SCHDELAY.NLM utility. This is a server console command-line program that you use by specifying the process and the desired delay on the program's LOAD line. For example, to impose a schedule delay on the REMOTE.NLM process, you would use a command, such as LOAD SCHDELAY REMOTE 2. You can force schedule delays whenever you boot the server by including SCHDELAY commands in the AUTOEXEC.NCF file.

Viewing Multiprocessor Information   The standard IntranetWare package now includes the NetWare SMP product that enables the use of symmetric multiprocessing on NetWare servers. When you view the statistics on MONITOR's Processor Utilization and Scheduling Information screens, you see values that apply only to the server's main processor. To view statistics on the operation of multiple processors, you must access the Multiprocessor Information screen from MONITOR's main menu.

This screen only is available if you have installed the NetWare SMP option during the operating system installation. The top of the Multiprocessor Information screen displays the following information:

- **Total Processors**—Displays the number of processors found in the computer, including any that are not activated for use with NetWare.
- **Active Processors**—Displays the number of processors that actively are being used by NetWare.
- **Combined Lock Assertions**—Indicates how many times program threads have tried to acquire locks during the last interval. Very high values (50,000+) can indicate the existence of a problem in a multiprocessing application.
- **Combined Lock Collisions**—Indicates the number of times that threads have tried to acquire locks on resources that already are locked.
- **Maximum Lock Wait**—Displays the largest number of collisions that occurred for a single lock.
- **Combined Utilization**—The average utilization percentage for all of the active processors in the server. This is the same value shown as the Utilization figure in MONITOR's General Information window.

The use of multiple processors in NetWare further complicates an already complex relationship between server subsystems. Only applications that have been specifically designed to take advantage of multiple processors will realize any increase in speed or efficiency. What's more, the performance levels of many common server processes are bound by factors other than processor speed, such as disk I/O.

The fact that NetWare is not a processor-bound network operating system is demonstrated by the high processor utilization figure that is devoted to the Idle Loop in many servers. This indicates that the processor is more than efficient enough to handle its required tasks. In fact,

Part
III
Ch
11

the processor usually spends more time waiting for other systems to catch up than it does actually performing calculations.

A multiprocessor-aware application splits its processes into separate routines called threads that can be executed by different processors at the same time. Obviously, these threads must be designed so that one is not directly dependent on another's output, or one processor might have to wait for another to complete an instruction before it can proceed with its own task.

The other major concern that multiprocessing imposes on application developers is that two threads cannot address the same SMP memory resources at the same time. This is the same situation that could arise if two users were to attempt to edit the same network file simultaneously. The changes applied by the first user could be overwritten and lost when the second user saves the file.

NetWare prevents conflicts in SMP processing by using the file locks. When one user is editing a file, other users are prevented from writing changes to that same file. A similar type of mechanism is used in NetWare SMP, called *mutual exclusion locks*, or *mutexes*. A resource that is being accessed by one thread is effectively locked, preventing another thread running on another processor from accessing it.

A *lock assertion* is when a process takes control of a resource. An attempt by another process to access a locked resource is called a *lock collision*, and is something that the application developer tries to prevent. Thus, the Combined Lock Assertions and Combined Lock Collisions statistics on the Multiprocessor Information screen can be a good indicator of how well an application has been adapted for use with multiple processors.

The bottom window of the Multiprocessor Information screen contains a menu with three items:

- Information by Processor
- MUTEX Information
- Thread Information

Information by Processor The Information by Processor screen displays basic status information for each of the active processors in the server. This includes the utilization percentage, the number of interrupts, and the current state of each processor. The values for the possible processor states are as follows:

- **Running**—Indicates that the processor is activated and functioning
- **Idle**—Indicates that the processor is activated but not currently working
- **Faulted**—Indicates that the processor has failed, possibly due to a hardware problem
- **Dispatching**—A transitory state that should appear only briefly, if at all
- **Assigned**—Like dispatching, a transitory state that, if displayed for an extended period of time, can indicate the existence of a hardware problem with the processor.

Each processor in the server is numbered, beginning with device 0. This is the default processor, the one that is used by all modules that are not capable of addressing multiple processors.

It is important to make sure that the utilization for processor 0 is as nearly the same as that of the other processors as possible.

There is a SET command that is used to specify how processor 0 should be used in an SMP environment. By default, processor 0 is shared by the native NetWare kernel (that executes all processes that do not support multiprocessing) and the SMP NetWare kernel (that divides all multithreaded processes among the available processors). If this sharing forces the utilization of processor 0 to a point that is much higher than the other processors, you can dedicate it solely to the native NetWare kernel with the command: SET SMP NETWARE KERNEL MODE=DEDICATED. For more information on using SET commands to configure NetWare SMP, see Appendix A, "NetWare SET Commands."

MUTEX Information   The MUTEX Information window displays a table of the *mutexes* (mutual exclusion locks) created by the multithreaded applications running on the server. The following information is displayed for each mutex:

- **Count**—Displays the number of lock assertions this mutex received during the current update interval.

- **Fails**—Displays the number of lock assertions for this mutex that failed during the current update interval, that is, the number of times that a thread attempted to access a data structure that already was in use.

- **Wait**—Displays the number of threads that waited to acquire this mutex during the current update interval.

- **M Wait (Mutex Wait)**—Displays the largest number of times that one thread failed to acquire this mutex during the current update interval.

- **Lock Type**—Indicates the type of mutex. Possible values include spin, sleep, and barrier. A spin lock enters a processing loop until the desired data structure is freed. A sleep lock does no processing while waiting for access. A barrier lock waits for other specified threads to reach a certain point before it begins processing.

When the lock statistics in the main Multiprocessor Information window are excessively high, you can use the MUTEX Information display to determine which exact threads are at fault.

Thread Information   The Thread Information window displays a list of the threads currently running on the server, and the following information for each one:

- **Processor**—Indicates which processor the thread is running on.

- **State**—Displays the current operational status of the thread. Possible values include Running, Migrating (moving sleeping threads between single-processing and multiprocessing environments), and Semaphore (coordinating processing activities to prevent data corruption), but only Halted is cause for concern. The halted state indicates that the thread has failed, possibly due to a flaw in the application.

- **Utilization**—Displays the percentage of the processor's utilization that is devoted to this thread.

The Thread Information screen can help you determine whether or not processor 0 is being overwhelmed by SMP threads, by demonstrating how much of the processor's attention is devoted to each process.

Viewing Disk Information

To view information about the disk drives installed in the server, choose Disk Information from MONITOR's main menu. There, you see a list of the currently active drives. Select the disk you want to view and a two-part screen appears (see Figure 11.8).

FIG. 11.8

Viewing disk informa-tion with MONITOR enables you to see statistics for each of the disk drives installed in the server.

The top part of the screen shows 10 items of information about the selected disk:

- **Driver**—Displays the name of the *host adapter module* (HAM) driver that controls access to the disk drive.

- **Disk Size**—Indicates the capacity of the selected disk drive in megabytes.

- **Partitions**—Shows the number of partitions that exist on the disk (including both NetWare and non-NetWare partitions).

- **Mirror Status**—Indicates whether the drive is mirrored or duplexed (or neither), so that all information written to it is duplicated on another disk. The possible values for this setting are Mirrored, Not mirrored, or Remirroring (indicating that a mirrored pair is in the process of being created or updated). For more information about disk mirroring and duplexing, see Chapter 3, "Installing NetWare 4.11."

- **Hot Fix Status**—Displays the status of NetWare's Hot Fix feature. Hot Fix checks each disk block as data is written to it. If the information written to a block can't be read, then the block is marked as bad, and the data is rewritten to a free disk block in a special Hot Fix redirection area of the disk, reserved during the volume creation process. The Hot Fix Status setting should be Normal. If it shows Not-hot-fixed, check the disk for excessive bad blocks or some other failure.

- **Partition blocks**—Shows the total number of blocks in the NetWare partition on the disk.

- **Data blocks**—Indicates the number of blocks available for general use by server users.

- **Redirection blocks**—Displays the number of blocks reserved for use by the Hot Fix feature. This pool of blocks is used to replace blocks that fail the read-after-write test.
- **Redirected blocks**—Shows the number of blocks already used from the pool of redirection blocks.
- **Reserved blocks**—Lists the number of blocks used to store operating system information, such as the redirection table.

The Drive Status window at the bottom of the disk information screen lists several items of information about the selected server disk. To list the volume segments on the disk, choose (select for list) next to Volume Segments On Drive. The screen shows the number of megabytes for each segment and the name of the volume that the segment belongs to. Because a NetWare volume can span across multiple disk drives, this figure may not represent the total size of the volume.

The Read After Write Verify option enables you to choose one of three methods that NetWare can use to verify the information that is written to the selected disk drive. The three options are: Software Level Verify, Hardware Level Verify, and Disable Verify. During the installation of the disk drive, NetWare tries to choose the setting that is best suited to the disk drive type, based on its reliability.

When you select software-level verification, NetWare writes information to disk from its cache memory and then rereads the information from the disk and verifies that it matches the original. Hardware Level Verify instructs the disk controller to perform the read-after-write verification. This method is faster, but may not detect write errors resulting from disk controller failure. You should use Disable Verify only when you have total confidence that the disk and the controller have an internal verification method other than the standard controller verification that is completely fail-safe (in other words, never).

For maximum disk integrity, set the Read After Write Verify setting to Software Level Verify, although disk write performance may be slightly diminished.

The Drive Light Status option lets you flash the hard disk drive light for the selected disk drive. This method is a useful way to identify the actual disk with which you're working. This option displays the setting Normal by default, which means that the drive light isn't flashing, except to reflect real disk activity.

Alternatively, you can select the Flash Light setting, which causes the disk activity light to flash at a regular interval. To stop the flashing, select the Return to Normal setting. Many types of disks are incompatible with the flash feature. If this is true for the disk you selected, you see Not Supported next to the Drive Light Status option.

The Drive Operating Status option displays the current condition of the selected disk drive. The normal setting for an operating drive is Active. From this screen, you can change the status to Inactive, in order to disconnect the drive for service or replacement. Before deactivating a drive, use the DISMOUNT command to deactivate any volumes that are stored there.

Changing the drive status to inactive should only be used when the disk drive in question is *hot swap capable,* or installed in a housing or array that is separate from the actual server.

Part III
Ch 11

Never try to work with a drive (or any other component) that is internal to the server while the system is running, unless it has been specifically designed for that kind of treatment.

Two final options appear in the Drive Status window if you have disk drives with removable media. The Removable Drive Mount Status option has two possible settings—Mounted and Dismounted. Mounted indicates that the disk is now mounted and operational, and Dismounted means that the disk isn't in use and is ready for removal. The Removable Drive Lock Status also has two possible settings—Locked and Unlocked. When the drive is locked, the media can't be removed. When the drive is unlocked, the media can be removed and changed.

Viewing Drive Information with SERVMAN   NetWare's SERVMAN utility can be used to display more extensive information about the disk drive hardware that is installed in the server. As with MONITOR, SERVMAN is an NLM that when loaded at the server console, provides a menu of information and configuration screens from which to choose.

When you select Storage Information from SERVMAN's main menu, you see a screen like that shown in Figure 11.9. A numbered list of Storage Objects displays each of the host adapter modules (HAMs) running on the server, the disk drives being addressed by those modules, and the partitions found on each drive.

FIG. 11.9

SERVMAN's Storage Information screen displays extensive information about the storage hardware installed in the server.

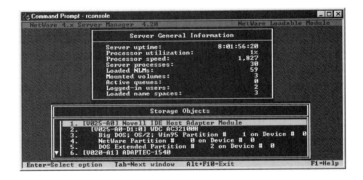

Selecting an item from the Storage Objects list displays a screen containing information about that item. When you select the screen for a host adapter module, a window appears that displays the hardware settings for the device that is being addressed by the HAM. The information displayed depends on the adapter being addressed and the bus type of the computer but can include such standard items as I/O ports, memory addresses, interrupts, and the number of devices connected to the host adapter.

Beneath each host adapter module in the Storage Objects list is an indented entry for each of the disk drives connected to that adapter. The Device Information screen for each drive displays its device type, its capacity (in megabytes), and drive hardware information, such as the number of heads, cylinders, sectors per track, the sector size, and the size of the blocks stored on the disk.

The Storage Objects list also contains an entry for each partition found on each disk drive. There can be only one NetWare partition on a drive, but this screen displays non-NetWare partitions as well. The information displayed for a DOS or other type of partition is minimal, consisting of the partition type, its size, and its location on the disk. When you select a NetWare partition, however, you see a screen displaying size, mirroring, and Hot Fix information for the partition, not unlike that shown in MONITOR's Disk Information screen.

SERVMAN's main menu also contains a Volume Information item that displays a statistics screen for each of the volumes on the server, as shown in Figure 11.10. This screen provides an excellent insight into the workings of the NetWare file system, and the features that help to increase both its speed and efficiency.

FIG. 11.10

The SERVMAN Volume Information screen displays statistics about the file system features in use on each volume.

The statistics shown include the following:

- **File System Name**—Lists the file system used to create the selected volume.

- **Loaded Name Spaces**—Lists the name spaces currently installed on the selected volume. Possible values are DOS (the default), MAC, LONG (for Windows 95 and NT long file names), OS2, NFS, and FTAM. Any or all of these name spaces can be installed on a single volume, to the detriment of disk storage capacity and I/O efficiency.

- **Read Only**—Indicates whether the volume is found on a read-only device, such as a CD-ROM drive.

- **Compression**—Indicates whether NetWare's file compression system is active for this volume. This feature causes files to be compressed when stored on a NetWare volume to save disk space and then decompressed on-the-fly as the files are requested by users. Compression is turned on by default when a volume is created.

- **Suballocation**—Indicates whether NetWare's block suballocation feature is activated for this volume. This saves disk space by storing several small file fragments in a single disk block, rather than devoting an entire block to each one. The feature is activated by default when a new volume is created.

- **Suballocation Unit Size**—Block suballocation divides each disk block into smaller units of equal size in order to allocate them to different file fragments. The suballocation unit size is 512 bytes.

- **Migration**—Indicates whether NetWare's automatic file migration feature is active for this volume. This feature causes files that have gone unused for long periods of time to be copied to another (less expensive) storage medium, such as an optical disk drive, until the files are requested by a user. The files are replaced by a small key that points to the alternative device. When a user requests access to a migrated file, it is automatically returned to its original location.

- **Migrated Files**—Displays the number of files that have been migrated to alternative Media.

- **Block Size**—Displays the size of the blocks into which the volume is divided. Possible values are 4, 8, 16, 32, or 64 kilobytes. The default block size is chosen during the installation of the volume, but may be specified by the installer instead. Volumes that will be used to store large files can benefit from the use of larger blocks.

- **Sectors per Block**—Indicates the number of disk drive sectors that comprise each block.

- **Total Blocks**—Displays the number of blocks on the volume.

- **Free Blocks**—Displays the number of blocks currently not being used.

- **FAT Blocks**—Displays the number of blocks being used to store the volume's file allocation table (FAT). This table contains the block location of each file stored on the volume, and must be consulted whenever a file is accessed.

- **Freeable Limbo Blocks**—Displays the number of blocks containing files that have been deleted from the volume, which can be freed by the administrator through the use of the PURGE utility.

- **Non-Freeable Limbo Blocks**—Displays the number of blocks occupied by deleted files that cannot be purged.

- **Directory Size (Blocks)**—Displays the number of blocks on the volume that are devoted to the storage of directory entries. Directory entries are always stored in 4K blocks, no matter what block size is chosen for the volume. Each block holds 32 directory entries.

- **Directory Entries**—Displays the number of 128-byte directory entries allocated to the storage of information about the files and directories on the volume. The default DOS name space requires one directory entry for each file and directory stored on the volume. Each additional name space requires one extra directory entry for every file. Additional directory entries are dynamically created if the number of files on the volume causes the allocated supply to be exhausted.

- **Used Directory Entries**—Displays the number of directory entries currently being used by the data stored on the volume.

- **Extended Directory Space**—Indicates the amount of disk space devoted to the storage of the additional directory information needed by some name spaces for listings of long file names and additional attributes. This information is stored in a separate system file that is divided into 128-byte segments called *extants*. When a directory entry requires additional space beyond its 128 bytes in the directory entry table, one or more extants are allocated for its use. The first extant for a particular entry is located by a numerical reference stored in the original directory entry.

Viewing File Status Information   You can use MONITOR to view the status of any file stored on a server volume. When you choose File Open/Lock Activity from MONITOR's main menu, you are presented with a list of the server's volumes. From here, you can navigate down the file system tree to any file on the volume.

When you select a file, two windows appear, containing information about the file's current status and the users who are currently accessing it (see Figure 11.11). The window at the top of the screen displays the following seven items:

- **Use Count**—Displays the number of users or connections that currently have the selected file open, locked, or logged.
- **Open Count**—Displays the number of connections that have the file open.
- **Open for Read**—Displays the number of connections that have the file open in read-only mode.
- **Open for Write**—Displays the number of connections that have the file open for writing.
- **Deny Read**—Displays the number of connections that have opened the file in a mode that denies other connections the capability to read the file.
- **Deny Write**—Displays the number of connections that have opened the file in a mode that denies other connections the capability to write to the file.
- **Open Status**—Shows whether the file is locked.

FIG. 11.11

MONITOR's File Open/ Lock Activity screen enables you to see who is accessing any particular file on a volume.

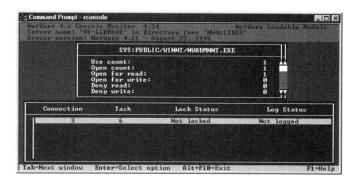

The window at the bottom of the screen lists the connections that have the file open and whether or not they have the file locked. The Connection column shows the number of each connection that is accessing the file. The Task column is a number defined by the NLM. The Lock Status column indicates whether or not the file is locked. There are three possible lock types: Exclusive (the file is locked so no other user can read or write to it), Sharable (other users can read the file), and TTS Holding Lock (the record lock has been released by the application, but the Transaction Tracking System is holding the record lock until the transaction is completely written to disk).

The Log Status column shows whether the file is logged for future locks. Some applications require that multiple files be locked before a transaction can occur. In these cases, a lock is logged or reserved first while the other files that need to be locked are being logged.

Viewing Cache Utilization Information   NetWare's disk and memory subsystems work together to provide users with efficient file system access. You learned earlier in this chapter that all server memory not used for other purposes becomes part of a cache buffer pool for the server's disk volumes. Files that are cached in memory can be furnished to users far more quickly than those that must be read from a disk drive.

The Cache Utilization screen in MONITOR enables you to see how effectively the cache is being used by NetWare (see Figure 11.12). There are virtually no problems indicated by the statistics on this screen that can't be resolved by installing more memory in the NetWare server. No other single hardware upgrade will have a more palpable effect on the performance of your server.

FIG. 11.12

MONITOR's Cache Utilization screen displays information about the memory that is used to cache the files stored on NetWare volumes.

The following list describes each item found on the Cache Utilization screen:

- **Short Term Cache Hits**—Shows the percentage of the disk read requests made within the last second that were satisfied from data found in the cache. A cache hit means the disk read request could be satisfied without actually having to read the disk drive because the information requested is already stored in memory.

- **Short Term Cache Dirty Hits**—Shows the percentage of disk write requests within the last second that were made to a block that was already dirty. A dirty block is a cached block containing changed information that is being held in memory while waiting to be written to disk. When data is written to a dirty block, two (or more) disk write requests can be satisfied by writing the cached block to disk only once, thus saving time and disk wear.

- **Long Term Cache Hits**—Shows the percentage of disk reads that have been satisfied with data from the cache since the server was last started. A figure over 80 percent, and ideally, closer to 90 percent, indicates that the disk cache is operating smoothly. If the value is significantly lower, your server could greatly benefit from the installation of additional memory.

- **Long Term Dirty Cache Hits**—Shows the percentage of disk writes made to a dirty cache block since the server was last started.

- **LRU Sitting Time**—Indicates how long ago the least recently used (LRU) cache block actually was used (in days, hours, minutes, and seconds). This figure tells you how rapidly the information in your server's disk cache is turning over. NetWare leaves information in disk cache for as long a period as possible. When new information needs to be cached, the LRU cache blocks are used.

- **Allocate Block Count**—Shows how many disk cache block requests were made since the server was last started.

- **Allocated from AVAIL**—Displays the number of cache blocks that have been allocated from memory that was not being used for any other purpose since the server was last started.

- **Allocated from LRU**—Displays the number of cache blocks that have been allocated from memory that has already been used for caching since the server was last started. When NetWare tries to cache files and finds that no free cache memory blocks are available, it locates the least recently used memory blocks in the cache, performs any disk writes that have been cached in those blocks, and then clears them for storage of the new files.

- **Allocate Wait**—Displays the number of times since the server was last started that a request for a cache block was delayed because no cache blocks were available and the LRU algorithm had to be run. If this number is high or increases steadily, it is an indication that more memory is needed in the server.

- **Allocate Still Waiting**—Indicates the number of cache block requests that are currently waiting to be satisfied. Ideally, this number should remain at or near zero. If the number is steadily increasing, then the server does not have enough memory available for disk caching.

- **Too Many Dirty Blocks**—Indicates the number of times since the server was last started that a write request was delayed because there were already too many writes waiting to be performed. A high value for this statistic can indicate a memory shortage, or a slowdown in the I/O subsystem.

- **Cache ReCheckBlock Count**—Shows the number of times since the server was last started that a request for a cache block had to be repeated because the requested cache block already was in use. If this count is high or steadily increasing, it indicates that not enough cache blocks are available to satisfy all requests, and that more memory should be installed in the server.

Part
III

Ch
11

Monitoring Network Communications

Apart from information on the server's purely internal processes, NetWare utilities, such as MONITOR, can also be used to display information on network communications. Although these network communications utilities do not replace more sophisticated tools, such as protocol analyzers and network cable testers, their statistics can sometimes point out the existence of a problem before it becomes severe enough to cause a service outage.

Displaying Connection Information

The most fundamental network communications elements are the server's user connections themselves. When you select Connection Information from MONITOR's Available Options menu, a list of the current user connections appears. This list displays the connection number assigned by the server and the login name for each user. From this list, you can either display information about a specific connection or disconnect a user from the server.

To remove a connection, highlight the connection and press Delete, or mark multiple connections with the F5 key and press Delete. After confirming that you want to clear the selected connections, NetWare removes them. To view more information about a connection, highlight the connection and press Enter. You see the information screen shown in Figure 11.13.

FIG. 11.13
MONITOR's Connection Information screen displays information about the user's activities.

When you press the Tab key to display the upper windows of the Connection Information screen in its entirety, the following statistics about the selected connection are shown:

- **Status**—Indicates the current condition of the connection. The possible settings are as follows:

Setting	Description
Normal	The connection is logged in and operating normally.
Authenticated	A Directory Services connection has been established, but no access to server resources has been granted.

Setting	Description
Waiting on a Lock	The connection is waiting for another workstation to release a lock on a resource.
Waiting on a Semaphore	The connection is waiting for the semaphore controlling a resource to be released.
Not-Logged-In	The workstation client has attached to the server, but the user hasn't logged in.

- **Network Address**—Displays three numbers, separated by colons: the physical network number, the node address of the network adapter in the user's workstation, and the socket number assigned to the connection. Socket numbers are used to accommodate separate processes or programs on the same workstation. Each program uses a separate socket number and communicates individually with the server.

- **Connection Time**—Shows how long the user has been logged in to the server.

- **Requests**—Displays the number of requests made by the connected client to the server since the last login.

- **Kilobytes Read**—Displays the number of kilobytes read from server drives during the course of the connection.

- **Kilobytes Written**—Displays the number of kilobytes written to server drives during the course of the connection.

- **Semaphores**—Displays the number of semaphores that the connection has in use. Certain programs use semaphores to control access to a particular resource, such as a shared data file or program.

- **Logical Record Locks**—Displays the number of logical record locks in use by the client.

- **Supervisor Equivalent**—Indicates whether the user has supervisor-equivalent status. This is true when the user has the SUPERVISOR directory tree right to the server object.

- **Console Operator**—Indicates whether or not the user is a console operator.

Part
III

Ch
11

The bottom half of the Connection Information screen lists the files that the workstation currently has open. You can view the record locks in use in a particular file by highlighting the file and pressing Enter. A window opens and, under the headings Start and End, the beginning and ending locations (or *offsets*) of the locked record are displayed. Under the heading Record Lock Status is the record lock type and whether the file is logged. Possible record lock types are as follows:

Lock Type	Description
Locked Exclusive	The record is locked so that no other user can read it or write to it.
Locked Shareable	Other stations can read the record but cannot write to it.
Locked	The record has been logged for a lock, which will be completed when other files or records are available for locking.

continues

continued

Lock Type	Description
TTS Holding Lock	The record lock has been released by the application, but the Transaction Tracking System is holding it until the transaction has been completely written.

The Record Lock Status column also can show whether the record is logged for future locks. Some applications require that multiple records be locked before a transaction can occur. In these cases, a lock is logged or reserved first while other records are checked. After all records are logged and ready to lock, the locks are imposed.

Viewing LAN/WAN Information

MONITOR's LAN/WAN Information screen enables you to choose one of the network adapter drivers installed in the server and view a large number of performance statistics for the connected adapter. When you select LAN/WAN Information, a list of available LAN drivers is displayed. You should see at least one entry for each network interface adapter installed in the computer.

If you have identical adapters installed, you may see the same driver listed twice, with different hardware settings. You also may see listings for multiple frame types running on the same network (if you are using Ethernet adapters). When you select a driver name, a screen like that shown in Figure 11.14 appears.

FIG. 11.14
MONITOR displays a vast number of statistics for each LAN adapter installed in a NetWare server.

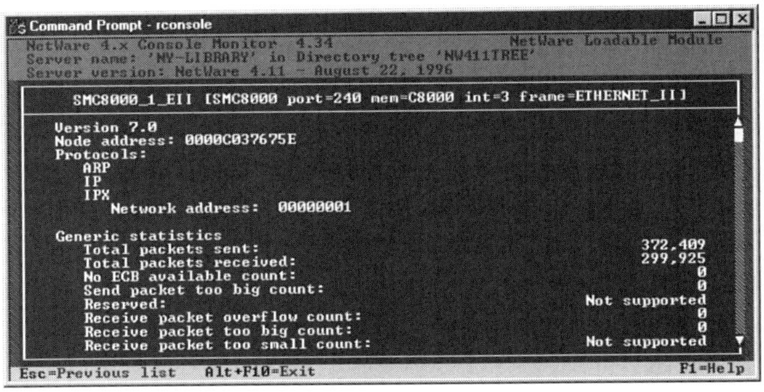

At the top of the screen is the version number of the adapter driver running on the server, and node address of the adapter itself. Ethernet and token-ring adapters both have unique node addresses hard coded into the device, while the node addresses on other network types may be assigned by the administrator.

Also listed are the protocols running over the selected adapter, and the address of the network to which the adapter is attached. Beneath are two sets of statistics. The first is a group of generic statistics that are usually available for any network adapter. The second is a collection of custom statistics that will differ according to the network type and the capabilities of the adapter itself.

You may find that some of the generic statistics are not supported by the adapters in your server, but in almost all cases, the crucial entries are displayed. All of the displayed statistics accumulate until the server is restarted. Some of the most important statistics are as follows:

- **Total Packets Sent**—Displays the number of packets transmitted by the server over the selected adapter. The size of a data packet depends on the type of network (such as Ethernet or token ring).

- **Total Packets Received**—Displays the number of packets received by the server over the selected adapter.

- **No ECB (Event Control Block) Available Count**—Displays the number of packets sent to the server which could not be processed because no packet receive buffers are available. A large or steadily incrementing number may indicate the maximum number of packet receive buffers has been reached. You can raise the maximum with the SET MAXIMUM PACKET RECEIVE BUFFERS command.

- **Send Packet Too Big Count**—Displays the number of packets transmitted by the server that were too big for the network to carry. This value normally should be very low or zero.

- **Receive Packet Overflow Count**—Indicates the number of times that incoming packets had to be discarded because the network adapter's receive buffers were full. This value should remain very low or zero.

- **Receive Packet Too Big Count**—Displays the number of packets received by the server that were too big for its receive buffers.

- **Send Packet Retry Count**—Displays the number of times that a packet could not be successfully transmitted by the server due to a hardware failure.

- **Checksum Errors**—Displays the number of received packets for which the checksum value in the packet did not match the value computed at the server upon receipt. A high number indicates that data is being corrupted during transmission, usually due to a hardware problem in one of the network interfaces or in the network medium itself.

- **Hardware Receive Mismatch Count**—Displays the number of received packets for which the packet length specified in the packet header did not match the length of the packet actually received. A high value for this statistic is another indicator of packet corruption due to a hardware problem.

- **Total Send OK Byte Count Low**—Displays the total number of bytes successfully transmitted.

- **Total Send OK Byte Count High**—Displays the upper 32 bits of the Total Send OK Byte Count. When the Total Send OK Byte Count Low figure reaches 4G, it restarts at zero and Total Send OK Byte Count High is incremented to one.

- **Total Receive OK Byte Count Low**—Displays the total number of bytes successfully received.

Part

III

Ch

11

- **Total Receive OK Byte Count High**—Displays the upper 32 bits of the Total Receive OK Byte Count. When the Total Receive OK Byte Count Low figure reaches 4G, it restarts at zero and Total Receive OK Byte Count High is incremented to one.

- **Send OK Single Collision Count**—Displays the number of frames involved in a single collision that were successfully transmitted.

- **Send OK Multiple Collision Count**—Displays the number of frames involved in multiple collisions that were successfully transmitted.

- **Send OK But Deferred**—Displays the number of frames whose transmission was successful but delayed because the network medium was busy.

- **Send Abort From Late Collision**—Displays the number of transmitted frames that experienced a collision after 512 bits were transmitted. On an Ethernet network, a certain number of normal collisions are expected, but late collisions are indicative of a hardware problem in the network infrastructure that should be addressed immediately.

- **Send Abort From Excess Collisions**—Displays the number of frames whose transmissions were aborted as a result of too many collisions.

- **Send Abort From Carrier Sense**—Displays the number of transmissions that failed due to loss of carrier sense, usually indicating the existence of a hardware problem.

- **Send Abort From Excessive Deferral**—Displays the number of transmissions that failed due to excessive deferrals, possibly indicating the existence of a hardware problem or an excessive traffic condition.

Summary

A NetWare network is a highly complex system, and as you learn more about it, you realize how much more there is to learn. However, you don't need to know everything about the operating system in order to keep a NetWare server running well. Making occasional checks of a few key statistics, as shown in this chapter, often can be sufficient to ensure that your server remains in operation. ●

Using the Server Console Utilities

Although many users may see NetWare simply as a means of sharing hard drives and printers, it is in fact a fully functional operating system in its own right, with a user interface that supports a wide array of internal commands and its own proprietary executables: NetWare Loadable Modules (NLMs).

Although typical network users do not have reason to access the NetWare server console, it can provide network administrators with a wealth of information about network processes and status. It is also the primary interface for the configuration of NetWare's many functions, features, and variables.

Several of the most commonly used server console utilities provide real-time statistics for the server's ongoing processes. In Chapter 11, "Monitoring NetWare Performance," you learn how to use programs like MONITOR, IPXCON, and TCPCON to gauge your network's efficiency and identify problem areas. ■

Introducing the NetWare Server Console

When you install NetWare 4.11, you create a DOS boot partition on your server computer, where the primary NetWare operating system files are stored. Among these files is SERVER.EXE, which is the NetWare main executable. When you run SERVER.EXE from the DOS prompt, you load the NetWare operating system on top of DOS.

Once loaded, SERVER.EXE completely takes over as the computer's operating system. DOS can be removed from memory, if desired, and NetWare provides all services needed to execute server functions.

In the early stages of the installation process, before any drivers have been loaded, NetWare consists of nothing but its internal command processor. This is manifested as the server console, which is shown as a largely empty screen, displaying only the name that you have assigned the server, a colon, and a flashing cursor, like the following:

```
NY-LIBRARY:
```

This is the *server console prompt*, otherwise known as the colon prompt or by other colloquial names, including (believe it or not) "snake eyes." The colon prompt is the indicator that the server console is ready to accept a command, just as a drive letter prompt is traditionally used for the same purpose in DOS. While a command is running, the prompt may scroll off of the console screen as the results of the command are displayed, but once the process is finished, the colon prompt reappears, indicating that the server is ready for another command.

 The server console prompt has a command history feature that enables you to scroll back through all of the commands that you have previously entered. As with the DOSKEY utility, you press the up and down cursor keys to move backward and forward through the list of commands. Once the desired command is displayed at the prompt, you can use the left and right cursor keys to move through the command line and modify it, if necessary. Then, you press Enter to execute the command.

As in DOS, there are many different commands that you can run from the server console prompt. Some of them are internal commands, meaning that the functionality to execute the task is included as part of the SERVER.EXE file. Other commands require external program files that must be loaded into memory.

At the point just after SERVER.EXE is loaded, the NetWare operating system is running, but it is entirely useless. It is a head without a body, because it has none of the drivers loaded that enable it to store data on hard disk drives and communicate with the network. The rest of the NetWare installation process consists of executing various server console commands and loading the drivers and programs that provide these essential services.

Using NetWare Command Files (NCFs)

As the NetWare startup process progresses, the drivers for the hardware installed in your computer are loaded and configured from the server console prompt. Other NetWare commands are also executed to configure the server according to your specifications.

You can start up NetWare manually—if you have the knowledge and the inclination to execute the required commands—from the colon prompt. All that the NetWare startup program does is execute the required commands for you in the proper order and using the proper syntax.

At the end of the process, there may be twenty or more individual commands required to bring your server to the point at which it is fully operational and ready to accept user connections. These commands have to be executed every time the server is started. To facilitate this process, NetWare enables you to create the equivalent of DOS batch files, that is, executable ASCII text files containing all of the required commands, which are loaded in sequence whenever you run the file. In NetWare, these are called NetWare Command Files, and must have an extension of NCF.

Just as DOS has its AUTOEXEC.BAT file, which is executed whenever the operating system loads, NetWare has an AUTOEXEC.NCF file in the SYS:SYSTEM directory that contains the commands that were configured during the installation process. A second file, called STARTUP.NCF, is created on the server's DOS partition and stored with SERVER.EXE. The STARTUP.NCF file contains the commands (such as disk drivers) that must be executed before the operating system can access the SYS volume (where the main NetWare program files are located).

Both AUTOEXEC.NCF and STARTUP.NCF are executed automatically during the server boot process, thus preventing you from having to execute all of those console commands manually.

Even though they are nothing but ASCII text, NCF files are also manually executable at the NetWare server console prompt. Just by typing AUTOEXEC at the colon prompt, the NCF file is loaded, and each of its commands executed.

Although there may be no reason for you to manually execute AUTOEXEC.NCF, you can create your own NCF files for any purpose you want. Whenever you have two or more server commands that you must regularly execute in sequence, you can simply type them into a text file and save it with an NCF extension. Then, you have only to type the file name at the colon prompt to execute those commands.

Part
III

Ch
12

N O T E Several of the IntranetWare modules, such as INETCFG.NLM and the Novell Web Server, create NCF files during their installation, which are executed from the AUTOEXEC.NCF file. Unlike DOS batch files, when one NCF is launched from another, control is returned to the original NCF file after the processing of the second NCF is completed.

Using External NetWare Programs

Although NetWare has many internal commands that are executed from the colon prompt, its versatility is derived from its capability to run external programs. Most external NetWare programs take the form of NetWare Loadable Modules, or NLMs. An NLM is a program that has been specifically written to run on the NetWare operating system.

IntranetWare includes many different NLMs, some of which are part of the NetWare 4.11 operating system itself, and others that are included with the other software products in the package. In addition, there are hundreds of third-party programs that have been written as NLMs, providing many different services to NetWare users and administrators.

Unlike the executables for other operating systems, you do not run an NLM simply by typing its name at the colon prompt. Instead, you have to use NetWare's LOAD command. LOAD is an internal command whose only purpose is to execute external NetWare program files. Thus, to execute the NetWare INSTALL utility, which is found in a file called INSTALL.NLM, you would type the following at the colon prompt:

LOAD INSTALL

In many cases, there will be additional parameters on the LOAD line, depending on the program's function. Not surprisingly, you use the UNLOAD command to remove from memory any module that you have previously loaded.

N O T E Many of NetWare's NLMs have an Exit option that you can use to unload the program from memory. Because a program may consist of several NLMs, it is always preferable to use the Exit function when available, rather than the UNLOAD command. ▨

Although most of the external programs that run on NetWare have NLM extensions, there are several other file extensions that are also recognized by LOAD as valid program files. These extensions are as follows:

- ▨ **HAM**—Host Adapter Modules are part of the NetWare Peripheral Architecture (NWPA), a modular interface for the connection of multiple device types to a single host adapter. A HAM driver addresses a particular host adapter installed in the server.
- ▨ **CDM**—Custom Device Modules are the other half of the NWPA system. Working with a HAM driver, CDMs address specific devices connected to a host adapter, such as disk drives or tape drives.
- ▨ **DSK**—Drivers used to initialize host adapters for hard disk and other mass storage systems installed in the server.
- ▨ **LAN**—Drivers used to initialize the network interface adapters installed in the server.
- ▨ **NAM**—Drivers used to initialize NetWare name spaces, that is, the capability to store different file systems on NetWare volumes.

When you look in your server's STARTUP.NCF and AUTOEXEC.NCF files, you see many different LOAD commands, which execute most or all of these file types.

Navigating the Server Console

NetWare is a multitasking operating system, so it is possible to run many different NLMs at the same time. In many cases, loading an NLM file will cause an additional screen (or screens) to be created on the server console, after which the colon prompt returns.

The new screens remain active as long as the programs remain loaded, and you can switch back and forth between the different console screens at will. A heavily loaded server may have ten or more different screens to choose from on the server console.

Depending on the program, the screens displayed can be purely informational, or they can be interactive, enabling you to control the functions of the program and navigate through the program's own menus.

When there are multiple screens on the server console, you can cycle through them, in order, by pressing the Alt+Esc key combination. As you hold the Alt key down, the name of each screen is shown in the top-left corner of the display.

When you press Ctrl+Esc, a numbered listing of the available screens is shown. You can select one of the screens (by number) to display it immediately.

NetWare 4.11 also includes a built-in server screen saver, which displays a snakelike pattern on the server console after 10 minutes of keyboard inactivity. The screen saver is also a gauge of the server's processing activity. The busier the server, the faster the snake moves, and the longer its tail becomes.

Logging Console Messages with CONLOG

Many NetWare console commands display information of various types right on the console screen. This information remains on the screen until new commands cause it to scroll off. Some commands even display several pages worth of information at one time.

TIP You can clear the server console screen at any time by using the CLS or OFF command.

Unfortunately, once information scrolls off the screen, there is no way to scroll down again to redisplay. This is why NetWare includes a utility called CONLOG.NLM. During the NetWare 4.11 installation process, the command to load CONLOG.NLM is placed in the server's AUTOEXEC.NCF file. When loaded, CONLOG captures all of the information that is displayed on the server console screen to a file called CONSOLE.LOG, which is stored in the SYS:ETC directory.

NOTE CONLOG only captures the information displayed on the system console screen itself. The information on the additional screens spawned by other NLMs (such as MONITOR) is not logged.

Keeping a log of the activity at the server console is a great idea, especially if your server is managed by multiple administrators and you aren't always sure what changes were made by whom. However, the log file can grow to be enormous if you aren't careful. You can load CONLOG with the following parameters to control the log file:

CONLOG Parameter	Purpose
FILE=directory/filename	Specifies the name and location of the log file if you don't want to use the default of SYS:ETC\CONSOLE.LOG.

Part
III

Ch
12

continues

continued

CONLOG Parameter	Purpose
SAVE=directory/filename	Specifies name of the backup file. CONLOG saves the log to the backup file when the log reaches its maximum allowed size or when the server is restarted.
MAXIMUM=number of Kbytes	Specifies the maximum allowed size of the log in kilobytes.
ENTIRE=YES	Specifies that CONLOG capture the existing system console screen when CONLOG is loaded.
HELP	Displays help information concerning the preceding parameters.

If you want to use CONLOG, limit the growth of the log file to 1M, maintain a backup file and capture the console screen at load time, place this command in your server's AUTOEXEC.NCF file:

```
LOAD CONLOG SAVE=SYS:ETC\CONBACK.LOG MAXIMUM=1000 ENTIRE=YES
```

Using RCONSOLE

At many network sites, NetWare servers are not immediately accessible to the people who have to use them. For reasons of security (against intrusion, theft, or damage), servers are often kept in a locked closet or data center, making it difficult to gain access to the console.

Although it is usually not necessary to access the server console on a daily basis, and indeed some servers are left running for months or years without intervention, it is important that access be possible, in case of problems.

Because servers are not always easily accessible, NetWare includes a utility called RCONSOLE, that enables a network administrator to access the server console from a remote workstation, either over a LAN connection, or by dialing in with a modem. When you use RCONSOLE to access the server, you can perform exactly the same tasks that you would if you were sitting at the actual server console.

N O T E   When you use RCONSOLE to access the NetWare server console, you are essentially conveying the keystrokes of your workstation to the actual console. Because both the remote and local keyboards remain active, it is possible for the keystrokes of an RCONSOLE user to conflict with those of a person working at the actual console. Two users cannot perform different tasks at the same console at the same time. ▨

RCONSOLE is a client/server utility. It requires the loading of certain NLMs at the server, and the executing of a DOS program at a workstation. The following sections describe how to configure these components for both LAN and modem connections.

Preparing the Server for Use with RCONSOLE

In order for the NetWare server to respond to connection requests from the RCONSOLE client, you must load several NLMs at the server console. The first NLM is REMOTE.NLM, which you execute by typing LOAD REMOTE at the server console prompt. NetWare then prompts you to choose a password that users must supply from the workstation to begin an RCONSOLE session. If you specify no password and simply press Enter, then the Admin user password is used.

T I P   You can also specify the RCONSOLE password as part of the LOAD command line. This is particularly useful when loading REMOTE.NLM automatically, such as from the AUTOEXEC.NCF file. If you want to use the password *turkey*, for example, you can type LOAD REMOTE turkey and press Enter.

Configuring the Server for LAN RCONSOLE Connections   The other NLMs that you must load depends on whether you plan to use RCONSOLE to connect to the server through the network or via a modem connection. For network access, you must load the RSPX.NLM module. Load it by typing LOAD RSPX at the console prompt and pressing Enter.

N O T E   By default, the RSPX.NLM module uses NetWare's packet signature option to communicate with workstations. A packet signature is an optional identification that a server or workstation can embed in a data packet to guarantee the identity of the packet's sender, and prevent the server from responding to forged packets. The version of RCONSOLE supplied with NetWare 3.x doesn't support packet signatures. If you want users running RCONSOLE from a NetWare 3.x server to be able to connect to your NetWare 4.11 server, you must turn off RSPX's packet-signature checking by adding the SIGNATURES OFF parameter to its LOAD line. So to load RSPX with packet signature checking disabled, type LOAD RSPX SIGNATURES OFF. ▨

Configuring the Server for Modem RCONSOLE Connections   If you plan to use RCONSOLE to connect to the server by modem, you must load three NLMs, in addition to REMOTE. The commands you enter at the server console prompt are as follows:

```
LOAD AIO

LOAD AIOCOMX

LOAD RS232
```

After RS232.NLM loads, you are prompted to specify the number of the COM port on the server to which the modem is attached (1 or 2), and the baud rate at which the modems will communicate (2,400, 4,800, 9,600, 19,200, or 38,400). You can also include the COM port and baud rate as parameters on the RS232 load line, as follows:

```
LOAD RS232 2 9600
```

N O T E   NetWare's AIOCOMX.NLM module tests for the presence of a 16550 buffered UART chip on your computer's COM ports. If it fails to locate one, the module will not allow communications at over 2,400 bps. If your PC's serial ports do not have 16550 UART chips, you can buy an internal modem with the chip on-board, or install a serial port card with buffered UARTs. ▨

Part

III

Ch

12

There are two optional parameters that you can add to the RS232.NLM command line. If you add the C parameter, RCONSOLE's call-back feature is enabled. (You read about configuring a list of call-back numbers in the following section.) If you add the parameter N, you're specifying that connections will be made by using a *null-modem cable*.

In addition, after you load RS232.NLM, a special console command, MODEM, becomes available. When you type MODEM and press Enter, NetWare prompts you to enter an AT command string that is to be sent to the server's modem. When you type the command string and press Enter, the result of the command appears on-screen. You can also type the command string as a parameter on the MODEM command line itself, as in MODEM ATF, which would reset the modem to its factory defaults.

You use MODEM to send any special AT command strings that might be needed to the modem. If you have several separate AT commands to send to the modem, you can create an ASCII file containing the commands and run it from the MODEM command line by preceding the file name with the *at* (@) sign, as in:

```
MODEM @SYS:SYSTEM\MODEMCMD.TXT
```

Unless you are using nonstandard modems, no special AT programming should be necessary to establish an RCONSOLE connection.

N O T E   If you want to configure the server to accept RCONSOLE connections over both LAN and modem connections, you can load all of the NLMs discussed in this section, as long as REMOTE is loaded first.

Automating the Server's RCONSOLE Configuration   You may want the RCONSOLE NLMs to load whenever you boot the server so that you can use RCONSOLE without any special preparation. You can automate the loading of the files by adding the appropriate commands to the server's AUTOEXEC.NCF file. You can modify the AUTOEXEC.NCF file at the server by using INSTALL.NLM or EDIT.NLM, or by using any text editor at a workstation.

To configure the server to respond to RCONSOLE, for example, your AUTOEXEC.NCF file would contain statements such as the following:

```
LOAD REMOTE TURKEY
LOAD RSPX
LOAD AIO
LOAD AIOCOMX
LOAD RS232 2 9600
```

One problem associated with loading the RCONSOLE elements in the AUTOEXEC.NCF file is that including your password on the REMOTE command line in clear text is a significant breach of security. However, NetWare 4.11 provides a way to keep the password private. To do so, you must manually load REMOTE.NLM, specifying your password. Then, type REMOTE ENCRYPT at the colon prompt, and enter the password to be encrypted when you are prompted to do so.

The command returns an encryption key for the password you have entered. From this point on, you can specify this encryption key on the REMOTE command line, along with the -E switch (used when requiring the password to be encrypted), as follows:

```
LOAD REMOTE -E 66745ACF4856E3
```

This protects the password in the command file that loads the NLMs, and enables you to specify your password normally, when entering an RCONSOLE session.

> **CAUTION**
>
> When loading REMOTE.NLM from any NCF file, but especially from AUTOEXEC.NCF, you must be sure to specify a password on the LOAD line. If you do not, processing of the NCF file will cease while waiting for user input. If there is no one present at the server to enter a password, the file will not execute completely, and your server may not be fully operational.

Connecting with RCONSOLE from a Workstation

Once the server is ready to respond to workstation requests for RCONSOLE connections, you are ready to run the client program at a workstation. The workstation must be running DOS, or a GUI operating system capable of running a DOS session, such as Windows 3.1, Windows 95, or Windows NT. The PC must also be either a NetWare client or be equipped with a modem.

Activating RCONSOLE from a Network Client   The RCONSOLE.EXE utility is stored on the server in the SYS:PUBLIC directory, with other ancillary files found in SYS:PUBLIC. To begin a network RCONSOLE session, you must log in to the network, execute RCONSOLE.EXE, and then select SPX from the Connection Type menu. (SPX is the *sequenced packet exchange* protocol, a proprietary NetWare protocol that operates at the Transport layer of the OSI protocol stack.)

You are then presented with a listing of the servers on your network that have been configured for remote console access via SPX. Select the desired server, and you will be prompted to enter the password that you specified when you loaded REMOTE.NLM on the server. When the password authentication process is completed, the connection is established and the current contents of the server console are displayed at the workstation.

> **N O T E**   RCONSOLE does not use Novell Directory Services; it accesses the server directly. Therefore, the account that you use to log in to the network, and the rights that it possesses, are irrelevant (as long as you have access to the RCONSOLE utility itself).

Activating RCONSOLE over a Modem Connection   To connect to a server by modem, you must have access to the RCONSOLE files. If you are connected to a NetWare network, you can access RCONSOLE.EXE from the SYS:PUBLIC directory of any NetWare 4.x server. To configure RCONSOLE for use on a stand-alone PC, you must transfer the following files from the SYS:PUBLIC directory of a NetWare 4.11 server to a directory on the workstation:

Part
III

Ch
12

In SYS:PUBLIC	In SYS:PUBLIC\NLS\ENGLISH
RCONSOLE.EXE	RCONSOLE.HEP
IBM_RUN.OVL	RCONSOLE.MSG
IBM_AIO.OVL	TEXTUTIL.HEP
TEXTUTIL.IDX	TEXTUTIL.MSG

To connect to the server using a modem, run the RCONSOLE program from the workstation, and choose Connection Type, Asynchronous. The first time you run the program, select Configuration from the Asynchronous Options menu. The Current Modem Configuration screen appears, as shown in Figure 12.1.

FIG. 12.1

The first time you run RCONSOLE in asynchronous mode, you must configure the program to use your modem.

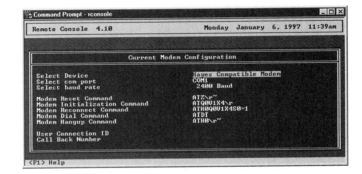

In the configuration screen, you select whether you are using a modem or a null modem cable. You also select your modem's COMM port and the speed at which you will connect to the server. Select the same speed that you configured the server's modem to use.

At the asynchronous configuration screen, you can also specify the AT command strings to be sent to the modem during five specific connection events: reset, initialization, reconnect, dial, and hang-up. The default command strings should work correctly with all modems using the standard Hayes AT command set sold in the U.S. today, using tone dialing. (For pulse dialing, change the modem dial command to ATDP.)

RCONSOLE also prompts you to enter a User Connection ID. This ID number is displayed on the NetWare server when you access it using RCONSOLE. Enter the ID of your choice.

Finally, you're prompted to enter a call-back number. This is an optional feature that enables you to dial the number of the server modem, after which the server hangs up and calls you back at a predetermined number. This not only allows the bulk of the phone charges to be incurred by the telephone line at the server end, it also adds security by virtue of the fact that the server can only dial from a preconfigured list of phone numbers.

Obviously, there would be no additional security if you could simply enter a number and have the server call it back. Instead, the value you enter into the Call Back Number field is a reference to a callback number file that you have previously created on the server.

To use the callback feature, you create an ASCII file consisting of all the callback phone numbers that you will need for the server, one to a line. Name the file CALLBACK.LST and save it in the server's SYS:SYSTEM directory. Then, in RCONSOLE's modem configuration screen, you specify the line number containing the phone number that the server is to call back.

After you have entered your configuration settings, press Esc to save them and return to RCONSOLE's main menu. Select Connect to Remote Location, and a list of servers and phone numbers appears. (This list is blank if you're using RCONSOLE for the first time.) Press Insert to add an entry to the list, and enter the name of the server you want to call and the phone number of its modem.

You are now ready to dial in to a server, by selecting its entry from the list, and pressing Enter. RCONSOLE activates your modem and dials the server you specified. After you connect to the server, enter the REMOTE password, and the server's console screen appears.

Using RCONSOLE

When you access a remote server using RCONSOLE, you can enter commands at the console prompt and use the server console just as you would from the server console itself—with a few exceptions. From the actual server console, you press Ctrl+Esc or Alt+Esc to navigate among the various console screens. These keystrokes can't be used in RCONSOLE. Instead, use the following keystrokes to navigate the RCONSOLE interface:

Keystroke	Function
Alt+F1	Display the RCONSOLE menu
Alt+F2	End the current RCONSOLE session
Alt+F3	Cycle forward through the server console screens
Alt+F4	Cycle backward through the server console screens
Alt+F5	Display the network address of the workstation

Using RCONSOLE Menu Options

Pressing Alt+F1 while using RCONSOLE displays a menu (see Figure 12.2) with the following options:

Part
III

Ch
12

FIG. 12.2

Pressing Alt+F1 displays RCONSOLE's Available Options menu.

- **Select A Screen To View**—Displays a list of the currently available server console screens, enabling you to choose one.
- **Directory Scan**—Enables you to display a list of the files in any directory on the server's volumes or on its DOS partition. When you choose Directory Scan, you enter a directory specification (such as SYS:SYSTEM or C:\DOS). You can also include file name wild cards (such as C:\DOS*.EXE). References to the C: drive always refer to the server's drive, not the workstation's.
- **Transfer Files To Server**—Enables you to copy files from the workstation to the server (only). You enter a source directory and file spec on your workstation and a target directory on the server. NetWare then copies the files you have designated.

  Transfer Files To Server offers no benefit over the more traditional COPY or NCOPY commands if you're using RCONSOLE over a network connection. However, if you're connected by modem, this is the only way to transfer files to the server from within RCONSOLE.
- **Invoke Operating System Shell**—Enables you to shell out to the workstation's DOS prompt temporarily while the RCONSOLE connection is maintained.
- **End Remote Session With Server**—Terminates the connection with the remote server and returns you to RCONSOLE's opening screen.
- **Resume Remote Session With Server (ESC)**—Closes the RCONSOLE menu and returns you to the server console screen.
- **Workstation Address**—Displays the workstation's network address.
- **Configure Keystroke Buffering**—Offers four options for sending your keystrokes to the server when entering commands via RCONSOLE. As an RCONSOLE user, you may be sharing your server access with other RCONSOLE users or with someone actually typing at the server keyboard. When you choose Configure Keystroke Buffering, you can select one of the following four options:

Option	Description
No keystroke buffering (normal mode)	The keys you press are sent to the server as soon as you type them. This is RCONSOLE's normal mode of operation.
Keystroke delay (send when keyboard is idle)	When you choose this option, your keystrokes are held for a specified number of milliseconds or until the server keyboard is idle (whichever comes first). When you choose this option, you're prompted for the number of milliseconds (from 0 to 50,000) for which your keystrokes should be buffered.

| Manual keystroke send (ALT+F8 to send) | Causes your keystrokes to be held until you manually send them by pressing Alt+F8. |
| On demand buffering (ALT+F9 to enter a buffered command) | Use when you want to invoke keystroke buffering only when needed. Your normal keystrokes aren't buffered, but when you press Alt+F9, a box opens and prompts you to enter the text you want to send to the server. When you press Enter, the text is sent. |

Displaying Server Information with Console Commands

One common use of the server console is to display server status and configuration information. In addition to the commands discussed in this chapter, NetWare also offers NLMs called MONITOR, IPXCON, and TCPCON that display more detailed information about ongoing processes. You learn about these additional programs in Chapter 11, "Monitoring NetWare Performance."

NAME

The NAME console command displays the most basic item of information about the server: its name. Typing NAME at the server console prompt displays the following information:

```
This is server NY-LIBRARY
```

As with all console commands that display information on the console screen itself (that is, without spawning a screen of their own), the results of the NAME command remain on the screen until it scrolls off to make room for information displayed by other commands.

CONFIG

The CONFIG command displays a summary of the server's configuration data, including the following:

- Server name
- IPX internal network address
- Installed network adapters
- LAN driver dates and version
- Network adapter hardware settings
- Network adapter node addresses
- Network adapter frame types

Part
III

Ch
12

- Network adapter board names
- Network addresses
- LAN protocols
- NDS tree name
- Server bindery context

The following example shows typical information for a server named NY-LIBRARY that has one token-ring card installed:

```
File server name: NY-LIRARY
IPX internal network number: 2BEA5A7C
     Node address: 000000000001
     Frame type: VIRTUAL_LAN
     LAN protocol: IPX network 2BEA5A7C
Server Up Time:  49 Minutes 55 Seconds
Novell IBM Token-Ring (PTF)
     Version 3.24    July 26, 1994
     Hardware setting: Slot 3, I/O ports A20h to A23h, Memory D8000h to DBFFFh
       and CC000 to <MS>   CDFFFh, Interrupt 2h
     Node address: 0000F6900CB8
     Frame type: Token-Ring
     Board name: TOKEN1
     LAN Protocol: IPX network 00000045

Tree Name: NW411TREE
Bindery Context(s):
     CorpNet
```

MODULES

The MODULES console command displays a list of all the NLMs, LAN drivers, disk drivers, and name space modules that are currently loaded on the server. Also included is the version, date, and copyright information for each module. This is an invaluable tool for troubleshooting server problems of all types.

Many NLMs and drivers that run on your server may require the services of other modules in order to run properly. In most cases, these other modules will be *spawned* (that is, loaded automatically). As a result, you may find that the MODULES listing for your server contains a great many more entries than you can account for with your LOAD commands. Abends or other server malfunctions are as likely to be caused by version conflicts between these support modules as they are by the NLMs you have loaded explicitly.

MEMORY

Use the MEMORY command to display the amount of RAM installed in the server. When you type MEMORY, a message similar to the following appears on the server console:

```
Total server memory:  16,000 Kilobytes
```

TRACK

Use the TRACK console command to display the information received from servers and other network devices that advertise their availability. Servers, gateways, and routers advertise their availability by broadcasting their names and network addresses to other servers at regular intervals (usually once a minute). These broadcasts notify all devices on the network about which servers are up or down and which routers can be used to move information from one physical network to another. Broadcasts that advertise server availability are part of NetWare's Routing Information Protocol/Service Advertising Protocol (RIP/SAP) or NetWare's IPX router, which uses NetWare Link Services Protocol (NLSP), Novell's link state routing protocol for IPX networks.

To turn on the TRACK display, type TRACK ON at the colon prompt. The following is a typical NetWare TRACK display:

```
RIP Tracking Screen
IN    [00099001:000000000001]  11:00:04 am    PS1                1
IN    [00099001:000000000001]  11:00:05 am    NW411TREE 1_____    0
IN    [00099001:000000000001]  11:00:08 am    NY-LIBRARY        1
OUT   [00099001:FFFFFFFFFFFF]  11:00:08 am    PS1                1  NY-LIBRARY 1
         MRKTING       1   WWFC1_____   1   WWFC1_____   1
OUT   [00000001:FFFFFFFFFFFF]  11:00:08 am    PS1                1   NY-LIBRARY
1
         MRKTING       1   WWFC1_____   1   WWFC1_____   1
OUT   [00000002:FFFFFFFFFFFF]  11:00:08 am    PS1                1  NY-LIBRARY        1
         MRKTING       1   WWFC1_____   1   WWFC1_____   1
OUT   [00099001:FFFFFFFFFFFF]  11:00:38 am    00000002  1/2     00000001  1/2
OUT   [00000001:FFFFFFFFFFFF]  11:00:38 am    00000002  1/2     00099001  1/2
OUT   [00000002:FFFFFFFFFFFF]  11:00:38 am    00000001  1/2     00099001  1/2
IN    [00000001:00008D000008]  11:00:54 am    Get Nearest Server
OUT   [00000001:00008D000008]  11:00:54 am    Give Nearest Server NW411TREE
1_____
IN    [00000001:00008D000008]  11:00:54 am    Route Request
OUT   [00000001:00008D000008]  11:00:54 am    00099001  1/2
<Use ALT-ESC or CTRL-ESC to switch screens, or any other key to pause>
```

Each line of the display begins with IN or OUT. Lines beginning with OUT display a broadcast made by the server you're viewing. Lines beginning with IN record a broadcast made by another device and received by your server.

After IN or OUT, there are two numbers in brackets, separated by a colon. The first is the number of the physical network where the broadcast originated. The second number is a code that denotes the type of broadcast sent or received. The two most common types of broadcasts are designated by 000000000001 (which indicates that the broadcast is a server advertising that it's up and available) and FFFFFFFFFFFF (which means that the broadcast is meant for all devices on the network).

The broadcast time is next, followed by information about the broadcasting device. The following example shows a broadcast with only the server name:

```
[00099001:000000000001]  11:00:08 am    NY-LIBRARY                1
```

This broadcast is an advertisement that the server is up.

Part
III

Ch
12

Directory trees also advertise availability. If you watch the TRACK display closely, you can see the directory tree or trees on your network advertising their availability just as file servers do.

The following is an example of another type of message. Notice that the message ends with Get Nearest Server:

```
IN    [00000001:00008D000008] 11:00:54 am   Get Nearest Server
```

This message indicates that a workstation just loaded a NetWare client and is broadcasting a request to attach to a server. The server responds with the following broadcast:

```
OUT   [00000001:00008D000008] 11:00:54 am   Give Nearest Server NW411TREE1
```

This broadcast indicates that a server or directory tree is available to permit the workstation to attach and is sending a reply to the Get Nearest Server broadcast.

The message Route Request indicates that the server received a request to provide route information about its internal *router*. A NetWare server functions as a router when it has two network adapters inside, each connected to a separate network.

A device sends a route request broadcast when it needs to send information to another device on a different network. A route request broadcast looks like the following example:

```
IN    [00000001:00008D000008] 11:00:54 am   Route Request
```

The display shows two numbers in brackets: the network address where the broadcast originated and the node address of the device sending the request. Here, the request was received from node 00008D000008 on network 00000001.

The server responds with a broadcast similar to the following:

```
OUT   [00000001:00008D000008] 11:00:54 am   00099001   1/2
```

Notice that the broadcast line ends with the information 00099001 1/2. The number 00099001 is the network address for which routing information was requested. The last item, 1/2, shows the number of *hops* and the number of *ticks* required to reach this network. A hop is a router that must be crossed. A tick is a time interval of approximately 1/18 of a second. When the device that sent the route request receives the responses from all routers, it analyzes the hop counts and the number of ticks included in each response to discover the shortest and fastest route to the destination network.

Periodically, a server that functions as a router will send broadcasts that display the hop count and routing information for all of the networks to which the server can provide routing. These broadcasts look like the following:

```
OUT   [00000001:FFFFFFFFFFFF] 11:00:38 am   00000002   1/2      00099001   1/2
```

Each network is listed with the hop count and number of ticks required to reach that network. Remember that the first number inside the brackets (00000001) shows the address of the network from which the broadcast is being sent, and the FFFFFFFFFFFF indicates that the broadcast is meant for all devices on this network. You can tell that this broadcast is advising all devices on network 00000001 that the server can provide routes to networks 00000002 and

`00099001`. In both cases, the hop count is 1, and the number of ticks required to route to the network is 2.

A routing server also periodically broadcasts a list of the servers for which it can provide routes. This broadcast looks like the following:

```
OUT   [00000002:FFFFFFFFFFFF] 11:00:08 am   PS1    1   NY-LIBRARY    1
NW411TREE_____   1
```

The server broadcast is announcing that it can provide routes to servers PS1, NY-LIBRARY, and NW411TREE. Listed after each server is the hop count required to reach this server.

On a busy network with many servers, workstations, and routers, the TRACK ON display shows a constant cascade of information, and you may not be able to read fast enough to view the information you want to see. Fortunately, you can press a key to pause the display, but you may find that pausing the screen at the precise moment desired is a stimulating test of eye-hand coordination.

Note also that the TRACK display is a separate screen, and not a part of the standard server console display. Its information is not stored by CONLOG. To turn off the display, switch to the system console prompt and type TRACK OFF.

DISPLAY SERVERS

The DISPLAY SERVERS command lists all of the known network servers on the console monitor. DISPLAY SERVERS shows all server devices, not just file servers. Print servers, database servers, communication servers, and any other devices that advertise their availability using SAP broadcasts are displayed. Directory trees also are displayed. Beside each server you see a number that lists the hop count or the number of network routers that must be crossed to reach the server.

Part
III

Ch
12

DISPLAY NETWORKS

The DISPLAY NETWORKS command is similar to DISPLAY SERVERS. DISPLAY NETWORKS lists the currently available physical networks on the console monitor. Network numbers are shown in hexadecimal format. As in the TRACK screen, DISPLAY NETWORKS shows the hop count and number of ticks required to reach each network.

TIME

The TIME command displays the current server date and time. TIME also shows the server's current daylight savings time status and whether the server time is synchronized to the network time used by NDS. You configured time synchronization when you installed the server.

VERSION

The VERSION console command displays the version, revision level, and licensing information relevant to the version of NetWare now running on the server. The display appears as follows:

```
Novell NetWare 4.11 December 22, 1996
 Copyright 1983-1996 Novell Inc.
All Rights Reserved.
Patent Pending - Novell Inc.


OEM Identification:  1
Maximum Number of License Connections:  100
Installed Licenses:
Serial Number   Connections   License Type   Version   Expiration
60002340        100           WEB/CONN       4.11      NONE
```

SPEED

The SPEED command displays NetWare's calculation of the server's processing speed. To see your server's speed rating, type SPEED and press Enter. The results can indicate that your server PC may not be set to its maximum operating speed. The approximate speed calculations for various Intel processors are shown in the following table:

Processor	Clock Speed	Rating with *SPEED* Command
80386	33MHz	320
80486	25MHz	600
80486	33MHz	900
80486	50MHz	1200
80486	66MHz	1800
Pentium	66MHz	3600
Pentium	90MHz	4800
Pentium	100MHz	5400
Pentium	120MHz	6500
Pentium	133MHz	7200
Pentium	166MHz	9000
Pentium Pro	200MHz	10800

The speed rating is computed by evaluating three factors:

- The CPU type (for example, 80486, Pentium, Pentium Pro)
- The CPU clock speed
- The number of memory wait states (0, 1, 2, and so on)

If the speed rating shown by your server is significantly lower than these numbers, make sure that your server's processor is configured to operate at its maximum speed.

PROTOCOL

The PROTOCOL console command displays the list of NetWare 4.1 registered communication protocols and frame types in use on the server. The display appears as follows:

```
The following protocols are registered:
  Protocol: IPX  Frame type: VIRTUAL_LAN  Protocol ID: 0
  Protocol: IPX  Frame type: ETHERNET_802.3  Protocol ID: 0
  Protocol: IPX  Frame type: ETHERNET_802.2  Protocol ID: E0
  Protocol: ARP  Frame type: ETHERNET_II  Protocol ID: 806
  Protocol: IP  Frame type: ETHERNET_II  Protocol ID: 800
  Protocol: IPX  Frame type: ETHERNET_II  Protocol ID: 8137
  Protocol: IP_HDR_UNCOMP  Frame type: PPP  Protocol ID: 2F
  Protocol: IP_HDR_COMP  Frame type: PPP  Protocol ID: 2D
  Protocol: IP  Frame type: PPP  Protocol ID: 21
  Protocol: IPX  Frame type: PPP  Protocol ID: 2B
```

N O T E The Protocol ID number is a unique hexadecimal number assigned to each protocol that is used in packet headers to identify the data being transmitted.

You can use the command with the REGISTER parameter to install new protocols that become available after you purchase NetWare 4.11.

Part III
Ch 12

Controlling Access to the Server

Two console commands control whether new users can log in to or attach to the server. A third command enables you to remove the connection of an existing user.

DISABLE LOGIN

The DISABLE LOGIN console command prevents new users from logging in to or attaching to the server. Currently connected users are not disturbed.

ENABLE LOGIN

The ENABLE LOGIN command reverses the effect of DISABLE LOGIN. When you first start a server, logging in is enabled by default, so you need to use ENABLE LOGIN only if you've previously used DISABLE LOGIN.

CLEAR STATION

The CLEAR STATION command disconnects a user from the server with no warning. To clear a user, you must first know the connection number for this user. You can learn a user's connection number with the NLIST /A /B command or by using the MONITOR utility. When you know the connection number of the user you want to clear, type CLEAR STATION, followed by the connection number. If, for example, you want to remove the user on connection 7, type **CLEAR STATION 7** and press Enter.

Sending Messages to Users

At times you may need to send a message to some or all of the users connected to the server. Two commands enable you to send messages from the server console: BROADCAST and SEND. Each command sends a message that is displayed in a pop-up window on a Windows, OS/2, or Macintosh workstation, or on the top line of the screen display in DOS.

BROADCAST

To use BROADCAST in its simplest form, type BROADCAST followed by the message (up to 55 characters long) that you want to send. To notify all users that the SERV1 server is going down in five minutes, for example, type the following and press Enter:

BROADCAST SERV1 GOING DOWN IN 5 MIN, PLS LOG OUT NOW

NetWare sends the following message to every user connected to the server:

SERV1 GOING DOWN IN 5 MIN, PLS LOG OUT NOW

You can also send messages to individual users by including their login names or connection numbers on the BROADCAST command line, mixing login names with connection numbers, if desired. You can broadcast a message to four individual users with the following command:

BROADCAST "OUR MEETING IS AT 2" to SMITHFD, ADAMSJF, 5, 13

The simple form of the login name is used, not the fully qualified Novell Directory Services name.

Users can prevent receipt of BROADCAST messages at their workstations by using the SEND /A=N command. See Chapter 13, "Using the Workstation Utilities," for more information about the workstation SEND command.

SEND

The SEND command is used exactly like BROADCAST. The only difference is that messages sent with SEND are treated as regular-priority messages, similar to messages you receive from another user's workstation, while messages sent with BROADCAST are treated as high-priority alerts from the server console. Users can prevent the receipt of SEND messages by using the SEND /A=C command, but BROADCAST messages require the SEND /A=N command (A=C stands for *accept=console*; A=N stands for *accept=none*).

Controlling the Server

The following commands enable you to start and stop the NetWare server, as well as control the server console's behavior.

SERVER.EXE

SERVER.EXE is NetWare's main executable file. You run it from the DOS prompt to load NetWare into memory, execute the STARTUP.NCF and AUTOEXEC.NCF files, and mount the SYS: volume.

You may find, at times, that there are commands in your server's NCF files that you do not want to execute. A new module loaded from STARTUP.NCF might crash your system, or you might occasionally require full console access when you normally run SECURE CONSOLE from the AUTOEXEC.NCF file. In these cases, you can run SERVER.EXE with any of the following parameters, to control its operation:

Parameter	Description
-sfilename	Enables you to load NetWare with an alternate STARTUP.NCF file. Replace *filename* with the (path and) name of the NCF file to be executed.
-ns	Prevents the STARTUP.NCF file from being executed during the NetWare boot process (ns must be lowercase).
-na	Prevents the AUTOEXEC.NCF file from being executed during the NetWare boot process (na must be lowercase).

Part
III

Ch
12

DOWN

When you need to stop a NetWare server, it is important that you shut it down in the proper manner. NetWare uses server memory to cache file writes for as long as several seconds, which means that a file that hasn't yet been written to disk may remain in server memory. Turning off the server at the wrong moment can corrupt or destroy these files. Shutting down the server properly flushes the memory buffers to disk first, and then stops the server.

The DOWN command is the correct way to stop a NetWare server. Before stopping the server, the DOWN command completes any file writes stored in memory and clears all connections. It also provides a warning when users have server files open, enabling you to abort the process before their work is interrupted.

Once the server is shut down, a message is sent to all attached users stating that their server connection has been terminated. You can then safely turn off the server PC, or use the EXIT command to return to the DOS prompt.

EXIT

After you DOWN the server, you can use the EXIT command to return to the DOS prompt of the server PC.

If you have executed the REMOVE DOS command before running EXIT, then DOS is no longer in memory, and the server reboots rather than exiting to the DOS prompt.

RESTART SERVER

If you used the DOWN command to stop the server but didn't type EXIT to return to the DOS prompt, you can restart the server by typing RESTART SERVER.

REMOVE DOS

The REMOVE DOS command frees a small amount of memory (12K for Novell DOS 7) for NetWare's use by removing the DOS support that was used to boot the NetWare operating system. Once DOS is removed from memory, you can no longer access files on the server's DOS partition. This means that you cannot load NLMs from the server's C: drive, log abend information, or create a core dump on the DOS partition. It also disables NetWare 4.11's Auto Restart after Abend functionality.

In addition, issuing the EXIT command after DOS is removed causes the server to reboot. Many network administrators create a convenient NCF file that executes the commands needed to initiate a server reboot. The file should contain the following commands:

```
REMOVE DOS
DOWN
EXIT
```

N O T E With NetWare 4.11, you can achieve the same result as the batch file shown without removing DOS by creating an NCF file containing the commands DOWN and RESTART SERVER.

SECURE CONSOLE

The capability to load NLM files from the server's DOS partition, from its floppy disk drives, or from any directory on a server volume opens up some disturbing security risks. A user with access to the server console can load any NLM, possibly crashing the server or damaging its files. NLMs automatically have supervisory access to all the server's resources, so you must use caution to prevent unauthorized NLMs from being executed on your server.

The SECURE CONSOLE command prevents NLMs from being loaded from a DOS drive or from any server directory other than SYS:SYSTEM. The SEARCH command, which enables you to designate directories on the server from which NLMs can be loaded without path names, is disabled.

Because some aspects of NetWare security (such as account and password expirations) are triggered by time and date changes, the capability to change the date and time may represent a security risk. SECURE CONSOLE prevents users from changing the server time at the console with the SET TIME command, requiring instead that all time changes be made by NetWare's time synchronization system.

To ensure the security of your server console, you can place the SECURE CONSOLE command in the server's AUTOEXEC.NCF file. However, once activated, the only way to negate the effect of SECURE CONSOLE is to down and restart the server. If it became necessary to start the server with an unsecured console, you would have to start NetWare without running the AUTOEXEC.NCF file (using the SERVER -na command).

NOTE The use of the SECURE CONSOLE command does not conflict with the functionality of RCONSOLE. ▨

SEARCH

The SEARCH command tells the LOAD command where to look for NLM files. By default, when you supply only a file name on a LOAD command line, LOAD searches the SYS:SYSTEM directory for the file and fails if it is not found there. With SEARCH, you can create other search paths, which LOAD will scan after it has failed to find a file in SYS:SYSTEM.

To view the current list of search directories on your server, type SEARCH without any parameters. You see a message similar to the following:

```
Search 1: [Server Path] SYS:SYSTEM\
```

To add another search directory, you use the ADD parameter. To add the directory named \NWSERVER, which is on the server's C drive, for example, type **SEARCH ADD C:\NWSERVER** and press Enter. NetWare adds C:\NWSERVER as the second NLM search path. You can do the same with directories on NetWare volumes or other DOS drives.

You can also control the order in which NetWare searches the areas by specifying a number when you add a search area. Suppose that you already have two search areas—SYS:SYSTEM and C:\NWSERVER—but want to add SYS:NLM to the list, so that it is the first directory searched. From the server console, type SEARCH ADD 1 SYS:NLM, and NetWare makes SYS:NLM the first area searched. SYS:SYSTEM and C:\NWSERVER become the second and third areas, respectively.

To remove a search area, use the DEL parameter along with the number of the search path. To remove C:\NWSERVER from the search list, type SEARCH first, to display the following list:

```
Search 1: [Server Path] SYS:NLM\
Search 2: [Server Path] SYS:SYSTEM\
Search 3: [DOS Path] C:\NWSERVER\
```

The list confirms that C:\NWSERVER is search area 3. You then remove this search area from the list by typing SEARCH DEL 3.

Part
III

Ch

12

Controlling Disks

Several server console commands enable you to work with server disks. You can activate and deactivate volumes, detect new drives that have been added to the server, or resynchronize disks that are part of a mirrored pair. NetWare also lets you work with disks by using the

MONITOR and INSTALL utilities. You can learn about the MONITOR NLM in Chapter 11, "Monitoring NetWare Performance," and you can read about INSTALL in Chapter 3, "Installing NetWare 4.11."

MOUNT and DISMOUNT

Use the MOUNT and DISMOUNT commands to activate or deactivate a NetWare volume from the server console. When you use the MOUNT command to mount a NetWare volume, the volume becomes available to server users. To mount a specific volume, type MOUNT and then the volume name, such as MOUNT VOL1. You can mount all server volumes by typing MOUNT ALL.

Using the DISMOUNT command makes a volume unavailable; it takes a volume offline so that you can perform maintenance or change the volume's configuration. To dismount a volume, type DISMOUNT and the volume name, such as DISMOUNT VOL1. Obviously, you should dismount a volume only after warning the users who access this volume.

N O T E   One of the primary reasons for dismounting individual volumes is to allow the VREPAIR utility to address them, for the purpose of correcting errors on the volume or removing name spaces. ▨

VOLUMES

The VOLUMES console command shows a list of the currently mounted volumes. The VOLUMES display shows three columns of information about each mounted volume: the name, the volume's file name spaces, and the volume's *flags* (any special options, such as compression, data migration, or block suballocation).

Name space is a NetWare term that refers to the file-naming methodology used by a particular workstation operating system. Commonly implemented NetWare name spaces are DOS (the default), LONG (for the long file names used by Windows 95 and Windows NT), HPFS (for OS/2's High Performance File System), MAC (for Macintosh systems), and NFS (for Network File System used by networked UNIX workstations).

The volume flags column uses the following abbreviations to show which optional features are implemented on the volume: Cp (compression), Sa (suballocation), and Mg (data migration). You decide whether to activate these options during volume installation (see Chapter 3, "Installing NetWare 4.11").

LIST DEVICES

Use LIST DEVICES to display all of the storage devices that the server PC currently recognizes, including CD-ROM drives and hard drives that are not being used by NetWare.

ADD NAME SPACE

You use the ADD NAME SPACE console command to permit storage of non-DOS files on a server volume. Before you can use ADD NAME SPACE, you must load the matching name space module (which will have a NAM extension) for the type of non-DOS file that you plan to store.

To use ADD NAME SPACE to enable the storage of Macintosh files on the server volume named VOL1, for example, type **ADD NAME SPACE MAC to volume VOL1**. (You can optionally omit **to volume**.) You must have MAC.NAM loaded before executing this command. The NetWare volume is then configured to store the additional name space.

> **CAUTION**
>
> Volumes with additional name spaces require more memory to cache files and directory entries, and disk space to store the additional information. Do not add name spaces to a volume if it is nearly full of data, or if your server is short on memory.

ADD NAME SPACE only has to be executed once for each additional name space on a particular volume. You must, however, continue to load the appropriate NAM modules whenever the server is restarted, before mounting the volumes.

SCAN FOR NEW DEVICES

Use SCAN FOR NEW DEVICES to check for disk hardware that has been added since the server was last booted. Disk storage systems with hot swap capabilities are now available, that enable you to add and remove devices without restarting the server or the PC. The SCAN FOR NEW DEVICES command enables NetWare to seek and locate any new disk devices that you add.

MIRROR STATUS

NetWare lets you mirror disk partitions so that there are two copies of the data that the partition contains. During installation, each disk partition is assigned a number. The MIRROR STATUS command displays the status of each partition by number and shows whether or not the partition is mirrored. If a partition is mirrored, the command shows the number of the secondary mirrored partition. If a partition isn't mirrored, this condition also is indicated.

Part
III

Ch
12

REMIRROR PARTITION

The REMIRROR command resynchronizes a mirrored partition pair that has become unsynchronized, perhaps because one of the disks failed and had to be replaced. If you need to remirror partition 3, for example, type REMIRROR PARTITION 3. You must specify a proper partition number, which you can find out by using the MIRROR STATUS console command.

Because the entire contents of one partition must be written to another, remirroring is a highly I/O intensive process. Whenever possible, it should be performed during off-hours when production is low.

ABORT REMIRROR

If you don't want a remirroring operation to be completed, you can use this console command to stop the process. To abort the remirroring of partition 3, type ABORT REMIRROR 3. Use the MIRROR STATUS console command to determine the proper partition number.

Configuring the Server

NetWare 4.11 is a dynamic operating system. By using console commands, you can adjust a large number of server configuration options while the operating system is running.

RESET ROUTER

Every NetWare server maintains a router table that tracks the availability of other servers and routers. By default, NetWare updates the router table every minute. When servers or routers go down unexpectedly (without benefit of the DOWN command), the remaining servers' router tables are inaccurate until they can update themselves. The RESET ROUTER command initiates the update process on a particular server.

DISABLE TTS

You can use the DISABLE TTS command to deactivate the NetWare *Transaction Tracking System* (TTS). Database application developers use TTS to protect data files from the corruption that can result from an incomplete update transaction. In the course of developing an application that uses TTS, you may need to deactivate TTS for testing purposes.

NOTE Under normal circumstances, leave TTS enabled because NetWare uses it to protect its own security files, especially the NDS database from corruption.

ENABLE TTS

The ENABLE TTS command reverses the effect of DISABLE TTS. Use this command to reactivate TTS if you previously deactivated it.

REGISTER MEMORY

Use the REGISTER MEMORY command when you have more than 16M of RAM installed in a file server with an ISA bus. When you use the REGISTER MEMORY command, you identify the memory above 16M by including two parameters on the command line—the *location* and *amount* of memory above 16M. Enter the location as the hexadecimal number for the starting address of the memory above 16M. If, for example, the memory above 16M starts at the 16M address (as it generally does), you enter the address 1000000. This is the hexadecimal equivalent to the decimal number 16,777,216, or 16M.

In addition to the starting location, you must specify the amount of memory above 16M, which should also be a hexadecimal number. If a total of 24M is installed in the server, 8M of which is located above 16M, your amount parameter is 800000—the hexadecimal equivalent to the decimal number 8,388,608, or 8M.

Thus, to use these parameters with the REGISTER MEMORY command, type REGISTER MEMORY 1000000 800000 at the server console.

> **CAUTION**
>
> Exercise caution when you use memory above 16M with 16- and 24-bit ISA bus disk controllers, such as the NetWare-supported disk coprocessor board. These devices use direct memory access (DMA) in a way that can cause memory address conflicts when they attempt to address memory above 16M.

EDIT.NLM

NetWare includes a text editor NLM, called EDIT, that's very useful when you must create or edit ASCII files from the server console. When you type LOAD EDIT, the editor starts by prompting you to enter the name of the file you want to edit. To edit the server's AUTOEXEC .NCF file, for example, enter SYS:SYSTEM\AUTOEXEC.NCF. The file you specify is then displayed in an editor that is similar to the login script editor in NETADMIN. If you specify a file that doesn't exist, NetWare prompts you to confirm that you want to create the file.

Alternatively, you can specify the name of the file you want to create or edit on the command line. If you type LOAD EDIT SYS:SYSTEM\AUTOEXEC.NCF and press Enter, the EDIT NLM automatically retrieves and loads the AUTOEXEC.NCF file.

SET

The SET command is the most versatile and powerful server configuration tool included with NetWare. You can use the SET command to modify an extensive array of server configuration settings. Fortunately, most of these operating system parameters are set to defaults that should function well in most cases. However, as you learn about the SET commands that are available, there are many that you can use to fine-tune the server's performance to the needs of your network.

The options available with SET are so extensive that NetWare 4.11 includes a menu-based utility called the NetWare Server Manager (SERVMAN.NLM), which provides menu-assisted help for each SET option. You learn about SERVMAN in "Using the NetWare Server Manager" later in this chapter.

Viewing *SET* Parameters   When you type SET (without any parameters) and press Enter, you see a screen similar to the following, which lists thirteen categories of configuration parameters:

```
Settable configuration parameter categories
    1. Communications
    2. Memory
    3. File caching
    4. Directory caching
    5. File system
    6. Locks
    7. Transaction tracking
    8. Disk
    9. Time
    10. NCP
```

Part
III

Ch
12

```
    11. Miscellaneous
    12. Error Handling
    13. Directory Services
Which category do you want to view:
```

When you select one of the categories, a list of the configuration parameters for the category you chose, and also the current setting, appears. The screen also displays the range of possible settings for each parameter and gives a brief description of its purpose.

You use these SET options to fine-tune various aspects of the file server's operation and performance. The parameters that can be adjusted with the SET command affect many of NetWare's most fundamental operational systems. Making changes to these parameters intelligently requires, in most situations, a systems-level understanding of NetWare beyond that required to install and use the software. Changes to the default settings of most of these parameters should only be made when you are completely aware of the adjustment's possible ramifications.

Using *SET*   To begin to learn how to use SET, take the following steps to look up and change one of your server's current configuration settings. For this example, you will change the setting that controls the amount of memory the server can use to store its directory. When most or all of the directory is in memory, NetWare can locate files on its volumes much faster than if it has to scan the directory from the hard disk drives. Your first step is to use the SET command at the server console to look up the current setting. Type SET and press Enter at the colon prompt.

From the list of categories displayed, choose option 4, Directory Caching. A list of parameter settings appears, one of which is Maximum Directory Cache Buffers. Information similar to the following appears on-screen:

```
Maximum Directory Cache Buffers: 500
Limits: 20 to 20000
Description: maximum number of directory cache buffers that can be
        allocated by the system
```

The current cache buffer setting is 500 buffers. The default size for a NetWare cache buffer is 4,096 bytes (although you can use a SET command to change it). The 500 in this example means that up to 500 memory cache buffers (that is, $500 \times 4,096$ or 2,048,000 bytes or 2M of memory) can be used by the server to store the directory list.

You can use the information in the display to build a SET command that changes the value for this parameter. To increase the number of buffers that NetWare can use for directory caching, for example, use the following command:

```
SET MAXIMUM DIRECTORY CACHE BUFFERS=750
```

Notice that the parameter setting's name (MAXIMUM DIRECTORY CACHE BUFFERS) is preceded by the command SET and followed by an equal sign and the new setting you want to use (=750). You can use this method to build SET commands for any of the many SET options.

In practice, you probably don't need to increase the Maximum Directory Cache Buffers setting unless you have an unusually large number of files stored on the server. Before deciding to increase the maximum setting, you can use NetWare's MONITOR utility to look up the actual amount of memory used by directory caching.

Although the parameter adjustments made by many SET commands take effect immediately upon their execution, there are others that can only be set from the server's STARTUP.NCF file, that is, before the server boot sequence is completed. You can also place SET commands in the AUTOEXEC.NCF file, so that they are executed whenever NetWare is loaded. Appendix A, "NetWare SET Commands," contains a complete listing of all of the parameters that can be adjusted using the SET command, their possible values, and the circumstances under which they can be executed.

Using the NetWare Server Manager

The NetWare Server Manager (or SERVMAN.NLM) is a utility that can be used to view a variety of server statistics, and offers a menu-assisted alternative to using SET commands from the server console prompt.

To start the Server Manager, type LOAD SERVMAN at the server console prompt. SERVMAN's main menu appears, offering menu options at the bottom and general information about the server at the top (see Figure 12.3).

FIG. 12.3

The NetWare Server Manager's main menu enables you to view and modify server configuration information.

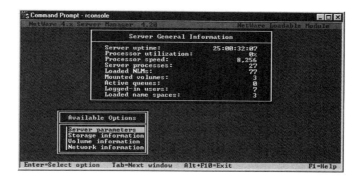

Part

III

Ch

12

Some of the statistics displayed by SERVMAN duplicate those shown by MONITOR. Server Uptime shows how long the server has been operating since its last reboot. Processor Utilization is a measure of the percentage of time that the server CPU was busy in the last second. Processor Speed is NetWare's measure of the server's CPU speed. This is the same rating shown by the SPEED command.

Server Processes are the same statistics shown in MONITOR's display (where they're labeled Service Processes). A service process is a memory buffer and task manager that manages incoming requests from workstations, as follows:

- **Loaded NLMs**—Indicates the number of NLMs that are running.
- **Mounted Volumes**—Displays the number of volumes that are mounted and available.
- **Active Queues**—Shows the number of queues being serviced by a print server.
- **Logged-In Users**—Indicates the number of users who have connections on the server.
- **Loaded Name Spaces**—Shows how many file system name spaces are in use on the server. As you recall, a *name space* is a file-naming system used by a particular workstation operation system, such as DOS or Macintosh.

Viewing and Changing *SET* Parameters   You can use Server Manager to view and change the same server options that you control using the SET commands, by choosing Server Parameters from SERVMAN's Available Options menu. You can also use the Server Parameters option to automatically update your AUTOEXEC.NCF, STARTUP.NCF, and TIMESYNC.CFG files so that your changes take effect each time you boot the server. SERVMAN also lets you copy all of your current SET command settings to a file, so that you can easily view them all in one place and save them for future reference

When you highlight Server Parameters and press Enter, the following list of 13 SET command categories appears:

Communications	Locks
Directory Caching	Memory
Directory Services	Miscellaneous
Disk	NCP
Error Handling	Time
File Caching	Transaction Tracking
File System	

When you choose one of these categories, a window opens that lists the current settings for each option in this category. When you highlight an option, the range of possible settings and a brief explanation of the option are shown in a pop-up window. You can select the current setting for a particular option and change it if you want. The options and available settings are identical to those listed in the tables of SET commands found in Appendix A.

After you finish working with a particular category, press Esc to return to the category list. Before you return to the main menu, SERVMAN displays an Update Options menu, which offers the chance to update both your AUTOEXEC.NCF and STARTUP.NCF files and your TIMESYNC.CFG file. You're offered these options only if you made changes while viewing SET command settings.

SERVMAN also provides an interesting way to document your current SET command settings. An option labeled Copy All Set Parameters to File also appears on the Update Options menu. When you choose the copy option, SERVMAN prompts you to enter the name of a file (it suggests SYS:SYSTEM\SETCMDS.CP as a default). When you enter a file name, the current settings for all the SET command options are listed in this file. The file, in ASCII format, can be viewed with any text editor or word processor.

Viewing Server Storage Information   Use the Storage Information option on SERVMAN's main menu to view information about disk controllers, disk drives, and disk partitions. When you choose this option, the Storage Objects box appears, listing objects, such as disk driver modules, hard disks, and hard disk partitions (see Figure 12.4). When you select an item, a window at the top displays information about the item.

FIG. 12.4

The NetWare Server Manager can display information about your storage devices.

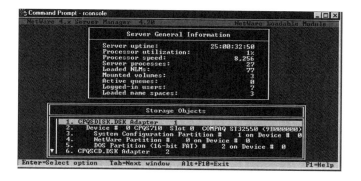

When you highlight the name of a disk driver module, the top window shows information about the host adapter that is addressed by the driver. The display includes the number of devices connected to the adapter and the adapter's I/O port, memory, interrupt, and DMA address information.

When you select a hard disk drive, the number of the host adapter to which the disk is connected is shown, as are the device type, capacity, number of heads, cylinders, sectors per track, sector size, and block size. When you select a disk partition, the partition type, size (in blocks), mirroring information, and hot fix information are displayed.

After you finish viewing information about storage devices, press Esc to return to SERVMAN's main menu.

Viewing Volume Information   SERVMAN also lets you view information about each of your server's volumes. When you choose Volume Information from SERVMAN's main menu, a list of the mounted volumes on the server appears. When you highlight a particular volume, a window opens that displays statistics about the volume. The volume's name spaces are listed, as well as the current status of optional features such as compression, data migration, and suballocation. The volume's block size, sectors per block count, and number of blocks devoted to storing directory information are also displayed.

After you finish viewing information about Volume Information, press Esc until you return to SERVMAN's main menu.

Viewing Network Information   The final option on SERVMAN's menu, Network Information, displays the server's network communication statistics (see Figure 12.5). The total number of packets sent and the total number received are listed. The Packets Waiting to Be Sent statistic shows the current number of packets waiting to be transmitted. This number should stay at or near zero if the network communication system is functioning correctly. The Unclaimed Packets statistic shows the number of packets that were received and couldn't be deciphered. Get ECB Buffers and Get ECB Requests Failed show the number of successful and unsuccessful times that a network adapter's driver requested an ECB (event control buffer) to transmit or receive server packets.

Part
III

Ch
12

FIG. 12.5

The NetWare Server Manager can display information about your server's communication system.

The Maximum Number of LANs count shows the maximum number of network adapters that can theoretically be installed in the server. The Current Number of LANs count shows the actual number of networks to which the server is connected. The Loaded Protocol Stacks count shows the number of different protocols that are active in the server.

Summary

NetWare provides a great deal of functionality at the server console, much of which should generally not be used while the server is functioning in a production environment. However, when you are testing new software, building a new server, or troubleshooting problems, it is good to have knowledge of the server console commands and their capabilities. ●

CHAPTER 13

Using the Workstation Utilities

NetWare 4.11 includes a large number of utilities that are designed for use on DOS and Windows workstations. You've learned about the specific uses of many of these programs in various chapters of this book.

The Windows operating systems have come to be dominant among NetWare workstations, and NetWare Administrator is, of course, NetWare's multipurpose Windows utility. NetWare, however, was originally designed to support DOS, and that functionality still remains part of the operating system.

In many cases, the common networking tasks that are performed by users and administrators can be accomplished very quickly with a DOS utility, and without the need to load a large Windows program. ■

How to use the NetWare C-worthy utilities

NetWare includes several menu-based utilities for the DOS environment that all share the same characteristic interface.

How to use the NetWare command-line utilities

The DOS command line can be a very powerful interface to virtually all of the features provided by NetWare's Windows and C-worthy utilities.

How to install and use the IntranetWare online manuals

The complete set of user manuals for the IntranetWare products are accessible using DynaText, a Standard General Markup Language (SGML) hypertext viewer for Windows.

Where coverage of other workstation utilities can be found in this book

Many of the NetWare workstation utilities are discussed in chapters devoted to their specific functions.

Using the NetWare Text-Menu Utilities

Before the Windows operating systems took over the desktop, Novell developed a collection of menu-based utilities for NetWare that run in the DOS environment. Despite their appearance, these utilities are not graphical; they use only the standard ASCII character set, and in particular the extended ASCII characters that provide line drawing and shading capabilities, as shown in Figure 13.1.

FIG. 13.1

The appearance of the C-worthy interface is achieved using only the ASCII character set.

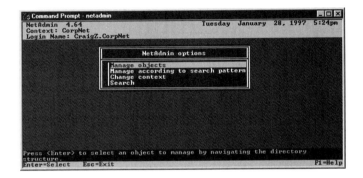

Unlike Windows-based programs, which tend to use an interface that is dictated by the operating system, the NetWare utilities were developed at a time when there was no industry standard for a DOS menu application. It was therefore left to Novell's developers to come up with a functional interface that could be used for the many different tasks that the utilities must perform. The result of Novell's development efforts was what has come to be known as the C-worthy interface.

The following sections provide general information on this interface that can be applied to any of the programs that utilize it. Nearly all of the C-worthy programs use these same techniques in various ways. You may find slight deviations from these procedures in some places, due to the different types of tasks performed by the various utilities, but once you understand the basic concepts, you should have no trouble adapting your general knowledge to the specific programs.

N O T E The C-worthy interface is also functionally similar to many of the NetWare server console utilities, such as MONITOR and SERVMAN. It is important that you be able to use the interface correctly because, on the server, there are no Windows-based alternatives. ▪

Introducing the C-Worthy Interface

C-worthy programs always contain a main menu screen that serves as a gateway to the program's various functions. Using the keyboard's cursor keys, the user navigates through layers of menus that enable a single program to perform many different tasks. Created at a time before Windows made the mouse a ubiquitous piece of personal computer equipment, C-worthy programs are wholly keyboard driven.

The standard multi-function interface used in Windows programs today is the tabbed dialog box, which is a single window that contains several screens worth of controls. This concept did not exist when the C-worthy interface was developed, and in any case, could not easily be adapted to a mouseless, text-based environment.

Instead, C-worthy programs utilize what can sometimes be a bewildering number of layered menus and pop-up windows (see Figure 13.2). You may find the function that you need buried five layers deep or more in the menu structure. Sometimes, you might recall the exact appearance of the screen that you want to use, but have some trouble locating it, until you become accustomed to the menu structure.

FIG. 13.2

C-worthy utilities can consist of many layers of menus and information screens.

Once you have gained some experience with the interface, however, you will find that these utilities provide a measure of convenience that is often welcome in the Windows world. Before NetWare 4.x, these C-worthy utilities were the only option for the network administrator.

In the hands of an experienced user, such programs as SYSCON, which was used to maintain user accounts and file system trustee rights in the NetWare bindery, can be manipulated with great speed and agility, something that tends to be lacking in NetWare Administrator.

Although the C-worthy utilities are still part of the NetWare operating system today, their development has slowed down to a virtual halt. DOS command-line utilities are still seen as a viable alternative to Windows, but character-based menu programs, to a great extent, are not. New features added to NetWare Administrator are generally not being duplicated in the C-worthy counterparts anymore.

It is not likely, however, that these utilities will be dropped from the operating system any time soon. There are still some NetWare sites that work primarily in the DOS environment, and in any case, there are still times when a DOS program's low memory and disk space requirements are welcome.

Introducing NetWare's C-Worthy Utilities

Although Novell has positioned NetWare Administrator as the primary NetWare utility for Windows and continues to add features to it, these same functions are distributed among several different C-worthy utilities. All of them are found in the SYS:PUBLIC directory of every

NetWare server and should be executable by any user due to the default READ and FILE
SCAN rights, as well as the search drive that is mapped to the PUBLIC directory for all users
in a server's context, by default. In every case, the utility is named for the program's executable file. Of course, the configuration changes that users can make to the NetWare environment with these utilities are restricted by the file system and NDS object rights available to
them.

Table 13.1 lists the C-worthy utilities installed as part of the base NetWare 4.11 product, and
describes the basic functions of each one. The specific uses of each utility are covered in the
chapters devoted to the functions that they support. Chapter references are provided, where
appropriate.

Table 13.1   C-Worthy Utilities Included with NetWare

Utility	Description	Chapter
NETADMIN	The primary Novell Directory Services utility for the DOS environment; enables you to create, manage, and delete NDS objects of all types.	7
FILER	The primary NetWare file system utility for DOS; enables you to manage file and directory attributes and trustee lists; copy, move, and rename files; and conduct salvage and purge operations.	15
PCONSOLE	Enables you to create, configure, and manage the NDS objects that comprise the NetWare printing architecture.	17
PRINTCON	Enables you to create print job templates that define the various configuration parameters that can be applied to jobs printed using CAPTURE, NPRINT, and DOS applications with no internal printer driver support. Seldom used, and not needed at all for printing in Windows.	
PRINTDEF	Enables you to create printer definitions that are used by PRINTCON when configuring print jobs. As with PRINTCON, this utility is included in NetWare primarily for reasons of backward compatibility, and is rarely used today.	

Utility	Description	Chapter
RCONSOLE	Enables you to access the NetWare server console from a workstation, using a network or modem connection.	12
NETUSER	Enables users to manage user drive mappings, printer port captures, search drives, server attachments, messaging status, and NDS context, using a menu interface.	
COLORPAL	Enables you to change the default screen colors used to display the C-worthy utilities.	

Using the NetWare Command-Line Utilities

Although some users feel more comfortable using menu-based programs, NetWare 4.11 also includes a large number of command-line utilities for the DOS environment that provide quick and easy access to nearly all administrative functions. Although a command-line program is, by its very nature, less intuitive than a menu-based application, the NetWare utilities are generally easy to use, and include help files that provide a quick reference resource for switches and syntax.

 TIP All of the NetWare command-line utilities include help files that contain syntax information and a list of parameters. You can access these screens by running the program with the / ? switch, as in NLIST /?.

As the Windows operating systems grew to dominate the desktop PC environment, users became acclimated to the delays incurred as large applications load into memory. When a network administrator is presented with one of the many small NetWare tasks that must be performed every day, such as working with the contents of a print queue or granting file system rights, command-line utilities provide a quick alternative to loading NetWare Administrator.

Part
III

Ch
13

Utilities that Display Information

NetWare 4.11 includes utilities that can display detailed information about the files and directories on your server volumes, and about the objects in your NDS database. In addition, the capability to list particular elements according to their attributes and recurse subdirectories and subtrees enables you to effectively search the file system or the NDS tree for specific items.

Using *NDIR*

Every user should be familiar with the DOS DIR command, and the information that it displays, such as file size, and the date and time that the file was last modified. You use various switches with DIR to control how the file and directory information is displayed.

The NetWare file system, however, maintains much more information about each file and directory that it stores, and the NDIR program is the NetWare counterpart to DIR, providing the same functionality, but expanded to accommodate the additional NetWare attributes. NDIR is an extremely flexible file and directory listing command that enables you to selectively display information about the NetWare file system, based on almost any of the dates, attributes, or other types of information stored with each file and directory.

The syntax for using NDIR is as follows:

NDIR *directory\filename /options*

Notice that with NDIR you specify a directory and file name, followed by a list of options. A forward slash (/) separates the directory and file specification from the option parameters.

By default, NDIR lists the following information about files:

- File name
- File size
- Date last updated
- Owner name

For directories, NDIR lists the following:

- Directory name
- Inherited rights filters
- Your effective rights to the directory
- Creation date and time
- Owner name

In addition, the total number of files and subdirectories listed is shown, as well as the total size of the files, in both compressed and non-compressed form.

If you type NDIR with no parameters, you see the list of files and subdirectories in your current directory. NDIR's file and subdirectory list is similar to the following:

```
Files           Size    Last Update      Owner
-----------     ------  ---------------  ------------
BACKOUT.TTS     16,384   4-23-93  9:24a  [Supervisor]
TTS$LOG.ERR      2,382  12-23-96  9:23a  [Supervisor]
VOL$LOG.ERR      2,124  12-23-96  9:23a  [Supervisor]
MRKTING/SYS:*.*
Directories     Filter      Rights      Created        Owner
------------    ----------  ----------  -------------  ------------
DELETED.SAV     [--------]  [SRWCEMFA]  11-27-96 1:44p  [Supervisor]
ETC             [SRWCEMFA]  [SRWCEMFA]  11-27-96 1:50p  [Supervisor]
```

```
LOGIN      [SRWCEMFA]   [SRWCEMFA]   11-27-96 1:44p   [Supervisor]
MAIL       [--------]   [SRWCEMFA]   11-27-96 1:44p   [Supervisor]
NET411     [SRWCEMFA]   [SRWCEMFA]   11-28-96 2:35p   Admin.WWFC
PUBLIC     [SRWCEMFA]   [SRWCEMFA]   11-27-96 1:44p   [Supervisor]
QUEUES     [S-------]   [SRWCEMFA]   11-28-96 5:30p   MRKTING.B_POWDER.WWF
SYSTEM     [--------]   [SRWCEMFA]   11-27-96 1:44p   [Supervisor]
23,405  bytes (65,536  bytes in 8 blocks allocated)
3  Files
8  Directories
```

NDIR goes far beyond this simple directory listing, however. In NetWare 3.x, the functionality of NDIR was spread out among several utilities, including CHKVOL, CHKDIR, and LISTDIR. NetWare 4.x consolidates all of these functions into one program by using an extremely long list of possible parameters.

Although the length of the parameter list may seem intimidating, most of the options are actually quite intuitive. It also is not necessary to pore over the list and commit the parameters to memory. The program's help files provide a ready reference, and most users rely on a few standard commands that provide the information they need. Table 13.2 lists the options and parameters that you can use with NDIR.

Table 13.2   NDIR's Options and Parameters

Parameter	Option Name	Purpose
Formatting Options		
C	CONTINUOUS	Display entire NDIR listing without page breaks
DA	DATES	Format NDIR output to display dates
D	DETAIL	Display detailed file or directory information one entry at a time
R	RIGHTS	Format NDIR output to display rights and attribute information
COMP	COMPRESSION	Display compression statistics
L	LONG NAMES	Display Windows NT & Windows 95 long file names
MAC	MACINTOSH	Display Macintosh names
Listing Options		
FO	FILES ONLY	Display files only
DO	DIRECTORIES ONLY	Display directories only
S	SUBDIRECTORIES	List contents of current directory and all of its subdirectories

continues

Part III

Ch 13

Table 13.2 Continued

Parameter	Option Name	Purpose
Listing Options		
attribute	ATTRIBUTES	List files and directories with this attribute turned on (replace *attribute* with a NetWare attribute abbreviation)
AC	ACCESS DATE	List files that match access date
CR	CREATION DATE	List files and directories that match creation date
UP	UPDATE DATE	List files and directories that match update or modification date
AR	ARCHIVE DATE	List files and directories that match archive date
SI	SIZE	List files that match size
OW	OWNER	List files and directories that match owner
FI	Find	Locate files in local and network search drives
Sorting Options		
SORT	SORT	Display list in sorted order
SORT UN	UNSORTED	Display list in unsorted order
REV SORT	REVERSE SORT	Sort in descending rather than ascending order
Comparison Parameters		
= or EQ	EQUALS	Check for equality
NOT	NOT EQUAL	Check for inequality
LE	LESS THAN	Check for a lower value
GR	GREATER THAN	Check for a higher value
AFT	AFTER	Check for a later date
BEF	BEFORE	Check for an earlier date
Volume Options		
VOL	VOLUME	Show volume information
Space Restriction Options		
SPA	SPACE	Show size restriction information

Using *NLIST*

NLIST is a utility that you can use to list the objects in your Novell Directory Services database, and display various categories of information about them. You can also use NLIST to search for specific objects in the NDS tree, based on their names, their object type, or the values of specific properties.

To build a basic list of objects of a particular class, type NLIST followed by the name of the object class you want to view. For example, to list all the User objects in your current Directory tree context, type NLIST USER. To list all print servers, use the NLIST "PRINT SERVER" command. Notice that when the name of the object type includes a space, you must enclose the name in quotation marks when you use that name in an NLIST command.

> **N O T E** Always use the singular name of the object class you're listing. If you mistakenly use the plural name of an object in an NLIST command, such as NLIST USERS or NLIST "PRINT SERVERS", the command returns an error message. ▉

If you want to list information for all object classes, replace the object class in the NLIST command with an asterisk. To list all objects in your current directory context, type NLIST *, which displays a list similar to the following:

```
Current context: CorpNet
Partial Name                                           Object Class
-----------------------------------------------------------------------
Users                                                  Group
NY-LIBRARY                                             NetWare Server
HR                                                     Organizational Role
NY                                                     Organizational Unit
Q1                                                     Print Queue
PS-CorpNet                                             Print Server
P1                                                     Printer
Admins                                                 Profile
Admin                                                  User
FrancisC                                               User
HobartS                                                User
GregoryL                                               User
KinneyS                                                User
NY-LIBRARY_SYS                                         Volume
NY-LIBRARY_VOL1                                        Volume
user                                                   Template
A total of 16 objects was found in this context.

A total of 16 objects was found.
```

Notice that the objects are grouped alphabetically according to object class.

You can specify that NLIST show only particular objects by specifying all or part of an object name in the NLIST command. To list only the user object SMITHJ, for example, type NLIST USER=SMITHJ. You can also use the asterisk (*) as a wild card in your object names, which is especially useful if you have instituted an object naming scheme on your network. For example, you might be able to list the names of all of the server objects in your company's New York office with the command NLIST SERVER=NY*.

Part

III

Ch

13

Building Advanced Lists   Using NLIST merely to list your NDS objects is of little value; you can do that more elegantly with NWADMIN or NETADMIN. With additional parameters, however, you can build lists that are much more useful.

The parameters that you can use with NLIST are summarized in Table 13.3. The following sections discuss these parameters in more detail.

Table 13.3   The *NLIST* Parameters

NLIST Parameter	Description	Use
/A	Active	Displays only the users who are logged in
/B=server	Bindery	Displays objects on a pre-NetWare 4.1 server; if no server is entered, current default server is used
/C	Continuous	Displays the results of the command without pausing when the screen is filled
/CO "context"	Context	Displays objects in the specified directory tree context
/D	Detail	Shows all property values for the listed objects
/N	Name only	Displays only object names
/R	Root	Starts the search for objects from the root of the Directory tree
/S	Search All	Lists all objects in the current context and all contexts below it
/TREE	Tree	Displays names of the directory trees on your network
/VER	Version	Displays version information
/?	Help	Displays help information

Listing Active Objects   The /A parameter causes NLIST to display only the NDS objects that are active. For example, to display a list of only the User objects that are currently logged in to the network, you would use the command NLIST USER /A.

Listing Bindery Objects   The /B parameter makes NLIST capable of listing information about servers running NetWare 2.x and 3.x. (B stands for *bindery*, the name of the security files used by NetWare 2.x and 3.x servers.) To use NLIST to display a list of the users on a NetWare 3.12 server named SERVER1, type NLIST USER /B=SERVER1.

Listing Objects in Other Contexts   By default, NLIST lists only the objects found in your current Directory tree context. You can change this behavior in several ways, however. To search a context other than the current default, use the /CO switch, and specify a valid NDS context name, enclosed in quotation marks, as follows:

```
NLIST USER /CO "ACCOUNTING.NY.CORPNET"
```

To extend the search of the specified context to include all of its subtrees, you use the /S parameter, as in NLIST USER /S or NLIST USER /CO "ACCOUNTING.NY.CORPNET" /S. You can also begin the search at the root of the tree by including the /R parameter. Thus, to search for all of the User objects in the entire NDS tree, use the following command:

```
NLIST USER /R /S
```

> **N O T E**   You must have at least the READ object right to a container in order to display its objects
> using NLIST. ▓

Displaying Name Information Only   When you use NLIST to display objects, the program provides a selection of information about the objects you list, by default. The information displayed depends on the object type. To specify that NLIST show only the object names and no additional information, use the /N (for *name*) parameter. To see a list of user names in your current context, and only the object names, type NLIST USER /N.

Displaying Property Values   The /D parameter displays all the property values associated with each object listed. If you want to see all the information for the user SMITHJ, for example, issue the following command:

```
NLIST USER=SMITHJ /D
```

The amount of information displayed for each user is extensive. The user's home directory, last login time, login script, and a complete list of the User object's trustees and their rights, are displayed.

Combining Parameters   You can combine NLIST's parameters to achieve powerful results. For example, if you want to list all users who are now logged in to your network, type the following:

```
NLIST USER /A /S /R
```

The NLIST command searches the entire directory tree and lists only the users who are now logged in. When you use two or more parameters together—as with the /A, /S, and /R parameters in this case—you must place a space between them.

> **T I P**   If a printed copy of NLIST results would be more beneficial, add >LPT1: to the NLIST command to
> route the output to a printer port. (Specify any active port in place of the LPT1: designation.)

Listing Your Network's Directory Trees   NLIST includes a special parameter, /TREE, which you can use to list the names of all of the directory trees on your network. To display the names of your network's directory trees, type NLIST /TREE.

Listing Objects by Property Value   NLIST's most compelling benefit is its capability to list objects based on the values of their object properties. In Chapter 7, "Creating and Managing NDS Objects," you learned about the properties that are an integral part of every NDS object, and their possible values. You use two NLIST parameters, SHOW and WHERE, to build NLIST displays based on the values of specific properties.

Showing Property Values   The SHOW parameter determines which property values are displayed in an NLIST listing. To list all users in your directory tree context and display each user's most recent login time, for example, issue the command NLIST USER SHOW "LOGIN TIME".

Notice that the property name is enclosed in quotation marks because it consists of more than one word, and that it is located after the parameter SHOW. The preceding NLIST command displays a list similar to the following:

```
User: FRANKLBJ
Login Time: 3:44:03pm 12-31-97
User: PATTERJL
Login Time: 8:28:50am 12-26-97
User: SMITHFD
Login Time: 7:44:17pm 12-31-97
User: JONESEJ
Login Time: 6:44:37am 12-31-97
```

To display more than one property value, list each property name in a separate set of quotation marks after the SHOW parameter, separating each with a comma and a space. To list each active user's login time and network address, for example, type the following and press Enter:

```
NLIST USER SHOW "LOGIN TIME", "NETWORK ADDRESS" /A
```

You learned in the preceding section that the /A parameter limits NLIST's listing to only the users who are now logged in. You see a resulting list similar to the following:

```
User: Admin
Login Time: 3:45:04pm 12-31-96
IPX/SPX Network Address
Network: 2
Node: 6010A
Socket: 4003
User: PATTERJL
Login Time: 3:55:04pm 12-31-96
IPX/SPX Network Address
Network: 1
Node: 8D000008
Socket: 4003
```

Using *WHERE* to List Objects Conditionally   You use the SHOW parameter to indicate which property values should be displayed; the WHERE parameter is used to determine which objects NLIST will display, based on the values of specific properties. For example, if you're looking for a list of inactive users that have not logged in to the network since 01/01/97, you can use the WHERE command to check for users who have a value in the LOGIN TIME property that is less than 01/01/97. The command to do this appears as follows:

```
NLIST USER WHERE "LOGIN TIME" LT 01/01/97
```

Notice that the parameter WHERE is followed by the property name, in quotation marks, the LT (for *less than*) parameter, and the date. You can use any of the following parameters to compare property values to literal values in your NLIST commands:

Parameter	Description
= or EQ	Equal to
LT	Less than
LE	Less than or equal to
GT	Greater than
GE	Greater than or equal to
NE	Not equal to
EXISTS	Property exists (has a value)
NEXISTS	Property doesn't exist (doesn't have a value)

Properties that consist of single items of information are good candidates for WHERE searches using NLIST commands. Examples are the user properties LOGIN TIME and SURNAME, and also properties that consist of lists of similar values, such as the MEMBER property for a group or the USER property for a print queue.

Properties that contain irregularly formatted values, such as the LOGIN SCRIPT property, are not good examples for the WHERE parameter, except for EXISTS and NEXISTS searches. If you are unsure about the kind of information that a particular property stores, you can use NLIST with the SHOW option to display the values now assigned to this property. When you know the format of the property value, you can build a WHERE clause to compare it to a literal value.

You also can use the asterisk as a wild card when you build NLIST WHERE clauses. To list all print queues with names that start with LASER, for example, type NLIST QUEUE WHERE NAME = LASER*.

Combining the *NLIST* Parameters You can combine NLIST's WHERE, SHOW, /A, /B, /C, /CO, /D, /N, /R, and /S parameters to create listings of network objects and property values that show precisely the information you need, but you must observe a few basic rules as you do so. Always list the slashed parameters (/A, /B, /C, /CO, /D, /N, /R, and /S) at the end of the command, and separate each slash parameter from the next one with a space. If your NLIST command uses a WHERE clause and a SHOW option, place the WHERE clause first, but both should be placed after any object type specification.

The general syntax for the NLIST command is as follows:

```
NLIST <object type> [WHERE <property name> EQ¦LT¦LE¦GT¦GE¦NE¦EXISTS¦NEXISTS
➥<value>] [SHOW <property name(s)>] <options>
```

The combinations that you can build with NLIST are limited only by the object and property types available and your creativity.

Part
III

Ch
13

Using *NVER*

The NVER utility displays information about the configuration of your workstation's network adapter, the LAN drivers and communications protocols being used, your NetWare client, and the servers to which you are currently attached. A typical NVER display (on a Windows 95 workstation running Novell's Client32) appears as follows:

```
DOS:     V7.00

NetBIOS protocol specification:  Version -2.0

LAN driver:  ELNK3 Ethernet Adapter ETHERNET_II Version 4.00
             IRQ 0, Port 0

IPX API version:      3.32
SPX API version:      3.32

VLM: Version 32.00 Revision A  using Extended Memory

Attached file servers:

Server name:  NY-LIBRARY
Novell NetWare 4.11 (August 22, 1996)
```

> **CAUTION**
>
> Do not use the NVER command on Windows NT workstations running the IntranetWare Client for Windows NT. Executing the NVER.EXE program causes the DOS command window to hang.

Using *NPATH*

The NPATH utility is used to display the sequence of search paths that your workstation is configured to use when locating files. With NPATH, you can determine the directory from which a particular file is being accessed. Running NPATH with no parameters produces a display of your current search paths, like the following:

```
Based on the following workstation information:
     Current working directory: C:\
     Utility load directory: Z: = CN=NY-LIBRARY_SYS: \PUBLIC
     NWLANGUAGE=English
     PATH=C:\UTIL;C:\WINDOWS;C:\WINDOWS\COMMAND;Z:\PUBLIC

The search sequence for message and help files is:
     C:\
     Z: = CN=NY-LIBRARY_SYS: \PUBLIC\NLS\ENGLISH
     Z: = CN=NY-LIBRARY_SYS: \PUBLIC
     C:\UTIL
     C:\WINDOWS
     C:\WINDOWS\COMMAND
     Z: = CN=NY-LIBRARY_SYS: \PUBLIC
     Z: = CN=NY-LIBRARY_SYS: \PUBLIC\NLS\ENGLISH
```

Many NetWare programs require access to other files besides their executables, such as overlays and message files, in order to run. If you have servers on your network with different versions of the same NetWare utilities, your search path configuration could conceivably result in the use of an incorrect message file, or some other version conflict that results in an error message.

The error message will usually specify the name of the file that is incorrect or missing. When you specify the name of the program that you are trying to run, and the offending file name, in an NPATH command, the display shows the directories where each of the files being loaded into memory is located. For example, the command NPATH FILER FILER.MSG results in the following display:

```
The specified utility FILER.EXE is executing from:
        F: = CN=NY-LIBRARY_SYS: \PUBLIC
The specified file FILER.MSG is located at:
        F: = CN=NY-LIBRARY_SYS: \PUBLIC\NLS\ENGLISH
```

For greater detail, add the /D switch to produce the following:

```
The specified utility FILER.EXE is executing from:
        F: = CN=NY-LIBRARY_SYS: \PUBLIC

The specified file FILER.MSG is located at:
        F: = CN=NY-LIBRARY_SYS: \PUBLIC\NLS\ENGLISH
                Language: English (English)
                Version: 4.17
                Date: 8-25-94
                Time: 7:51:00 am
```

Adding the /A switch will list the locations and version numbers of all copies of the specified files found on your search paths.

Using *WHOAMI*

WHOAMI is a simple utility that displays basic information about the identity of the user that is currently logged in at your workstation. For an NDS user, the display appears as follows:

```
Current tree:  NW411TREE

User ID:     SMITHJ
Server:      NY-LIBRARY  NetWare 4.11
Connection: 4 (Directory Services)
```

WHOAMI also includes a number of parameters that are applicable to bindery users only. These are as follows:

Option	Description
/G	Displays that groups of which the user is a member
/O	Identifies the supervisor of the object

continues

Part

III

Ch

13

continued

Option	Description
/R	Displays the user's effective rights
/S	Displays the user's security equivalences
/W	Displays the user's workgroup manager
/ALL	Displays all of the information provided by the previous options

For NDS users, the information equivalent to that generated by these WHOAMI parameters can be displayed using the NLIST utility.

Managing NetWare from the Command Line

The command-line utilities that you have seen thus far in this chapter are designed to display information in specific ways. There is an entirely different class of command-line utility that is used to modify NetWare properties. Coverage of these utilities has been integrated into other chapters of this book, so that they can be discussed alongside the concepts governing the various NetWare features.

The RIGHTS utility is used to create and display file system trustees and manage their rights from the DOS command line.

▶ **See** "Controlling File System Access with *RIGHTS*," **p. 361**

With the FLAG utility, you can modify the attributes of NetWare files and directories. NetWare also includes its own utilities for copying network files and renaming directories. Although NCOPY and RENDIR are functionally similar to the DOS XCOPY and RENAME functions, their internal operation takes advantage of the network environment to provide increased efficiency. You learn how to use FLAG and NCOPY in Chapter 16, "Managing Network Files and Directories."

The CX utility is used to change your default context on the NDS tree.

▶ **See** "Using *CX*," **p. 95**

PSC enables you to control network printers and print servers from the command line, as demonstrated in Chapter 17, "Implementing Network Printing."

Summary

As you have seen, NetWare provides several ways to accomplish the same tasks, depending on the circumstances and on the computing environment that you prefer to use. While NetWare Administrator is clearly positioned as the flagship utility for the operating system, there are many occasions when other alternatives might be preferable. ●

PART IV

Securing the Network

CHAPTER 14

Understanding NDS Object and Property Rights

The Novell Directory Services (NDS) database is a repository for information that is crucial to the operation of your network. It contains the data that defines the network's users, describes what resources are available to them, and controls their access. To ensure the uninterrupted operation of the network, NetWare provides a security system that is designed to control user access to the NDS database itself, as it is important that the information in the database is not damaged or lost.

In the same way that NetWare provides access control for its file system, which enables you to regulate the files and directories that users can browse, read, and modify, the NDS database is protected by a security system that protects its contents.

The differences between NDS rights and other NetWare security systems

Novell Directory Services has its own system of object and property rights, separate from all other NetWare systems.

Using object rights to limit access to the directory tree

You can control the parts of the NDS tree to which users have access, as well as the degree of access they are allowed.

How property rights control users' access to individual objects

By manipulating property rights, you can enable users to view some of an object's properties while others remain hidden.

Configuring users' object and property rights

Use NetWare Administrator or the NETADMIN utility to control the object and property rights assigned to users.

Object and property rights are stored in an NDS object's *access control list*. This list is an attribute of every NDS object, and contains the following information:

- The names of the object's trustees
- The properties to which the trustees have access
- The rights that each trustee possesses for each property

N O T E   The most important aspect to understand about NetWare's system of NDS object and property rights is that it is wholly independent from the rights that you grant users to files and directories. Even though many of the same terms are used to refer to each, understand that you can have the rights to access the files on a NetWare volume, and still not have rights to the volume object or its properties.

Understanding Object Rights

The primary function of object rights is to control who has the ability to view and access different parts of the directory tree. When you give a user rights to an object, you make that user a *trustee* of the object.

As in the NetWare file system, you can grant several different object rights that control the degree of access to the object. The five available object rights are shown in Table 14.1.

Table 14.1   Novell Directory Services Object Rights

Object Right	Description
SUPERVISOR	Gives users full control over an object including the browse, create, delete, and rename rights, and the ability to grant other users additional rights
BROWSE	Enables users to view an object's listing in the directory tree
CREATE	Enables users to create a new object in the directory tree
DELETE	Enables users to remove an object from the directory tree
RENAME	Enables users to change an object's name

Any user that does not have the BROWSE right to a particular object cannot see that object in the Directory display of any NetWare utility. If the object is a leaf, then it is merely invisible. If the object is a container, then users without the BROWSE right cannot see the container object, or any of the objects contained within it.

The other object rights enable users to RENAME or DELETE existing objects, or CREATE new ones. If you assign a user the CREATE right to a container object, then that user can create any number of objects within that container.

Granting the SUPERVISOR right as part of an object trustee assignment provides the user with all of the possible object rights, plus rights to all of the properties that make up the object.

Assigning Object Rights with NetWare Administrator

NDS maintenance tasks often involve managing a particular user's rights to other objects. In order to see a list of all the objects to which a given user has rights, you must scan the access control lists of the other objects to find those that have the user as a trustee.

Fortunately, NetWare Administrator can do this for you. If you want to see the objects to which user SmithJ has rights, you select SmithJ's user object and choose Rights to Other Objects from the Object menu (or from its pop-up menu after right-clicking the object). The Search Context dialog box shown in Figure 14.1 then appears.

FIG. 14.1

The Search Context dialog box enables you to control how much of the directory tree is searched for object trustee rights.

In the Search Context dialog box, you set the context at which the search for trustee rights is to begin. By default, the user object's current context is displayed, but you can browse to any container in the tree, and search from there. If you mark the Search Entire Subtree box, then the search begins at the specified container and travels downward to the bottom of the tree.

In a small tree, there is no reason not to search from the [Root]. However, on a very large network, particularly one with multiple NDS partitions and WAN links, a search of the entire NDS database can take quite a long time, so setting the context lower down in the tree than [Root] is recommended.

Using the Rights to Other Objects Dialog Box   Once the scan of object access control lists is complete, the objects to which the user has explicit rights are listed in a Rights to Other Objects dialog box, as shown in Figure 14.2. Use the Rights to Other Objects dialog box to assign additional object and property rights to the user, and modify or delete existing rights.

N O T E   The Rights to Other Objects dialog box displays only the objects to which the user has been given explicit object and property rights. Rights that are inherited from other objects are not shown in the Assigned Objects list. To include inherited rights, you must view the objects' effective rights. See "Understanding Effective Rights" later in this chapter for more information. ▪

Part

IV

Ch

14

FIG. 14.2

The Rights to Other Objects dialog box is NetWare Administrator's primary tool for creating, modifying, and deleting object rights.

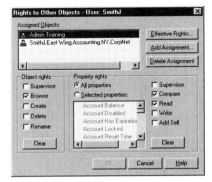

To see the object rights that the user has to a particular object, select the desired entry in the Assigned Objects listing. The check boxes in the Object Rights area are then activated, displaying the currently active rights. You can mark or clear the check boxes to change the rights as needed, or click the Clear button to revoke all rights to the object.

You can also use the Add Assignment and Delete Assignment buttons to modify the contents of the Assigned Objects list.

Using the Trustees Dialog Box The rights relationships between NDS objects can be difficult to comprehend at times. This is due in part to the fact that NetWare Administrator enables you to approach these object relationships from both directions, that is, from the point of view of the object being granted rights or the object to which rights have been granted. When you highlight an object and select Trustees of This Object from the Object menu (or from the pop-up menu), you see a Trustees dialog box (as shown in Figure 14.3) that is quite similar to the Rights to Other Objects dialog box, except that it lists all of the objects that have explicit rights to the highlighted object.

N O T E No scan of the NDS tree is needed when displaying the Trustees dialog box, because each object stores its own list of the objects that have been granted rights to it. ▪

FIG. 14.3

The Trustees dialog box lists all of the objects that have been assigned rights to the selected object.

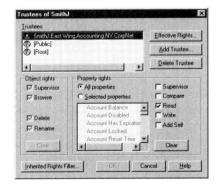

Although you would typically select a User object and display its Rights to Other Objects dialog box to assign the user rights to other objects like servers and printers, you would be more likely to use the Trustee dialog box by selecting a server or printer object itself. The trustees that you add to a server or print object's dialog box are as likely to be container objects as users, because the trustee rights that you assign to a container object are automatically inherited by the objects in the container. This saves the administrator from having to assign rights to each object in the container individually.

The Trustees dialog box contains a listing of the object's current trustees, which you can modify with the Add Trustee and Delete Trustee buttons. As with the Rights to Other Objects dialog box, you select a trustee and manage its object rights with the check boxes provided.

N O T E When you view the trustees of a container object, the check box for the CREATE object right is shown in the dialog box. The Trustee dialog box for a leaf object has no CREATE check box because a `leaf` object, by definition, is the end of a tree branch. ▦

Assigning Object Rights with NETADMIN

The DOS-based NETADMIN utility does not provide the same flexibility as NetWare Administrator. It can display only the trustees of a particular object; you cannot select an object and display all of the objects to which it has been granted rights. To modify the rights of an object's trustees, you select Manage Objects from NETADMIN's main menu, choose an object, and select View or Edit the Trustees of this Object.

When you then select Trustees, a Property, Rights, Trustee screen appears like that shown in Figure 14.4. In this screen, object and property rights are combined in one display. To add a new trustee and grant it object rights, you press Insert, specify (or browse for) an object name, and select [Object Rights] from the Properties screen.

FIG. 14.4
NETADMIN displays all of an object's trustees—with their object and property rights—in a single listing.

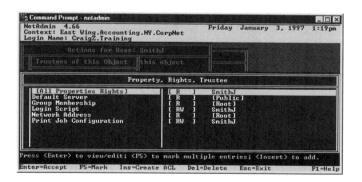

Once the object has been added to the trustee list, you can modify its object rights by selecting the object and adding or deleting rights from the Entry Rights Allowed box, using the standard C-worthy interface metaphor. (Insert key to display additional rights. Enter to select, or F5 to select multiple rights. Select any rights to delete, and press the Delete key.)

▶ **See** "Using the NetWare Text-Menu Utilities," **p. 310**

Part
IV

Ch
14

Understanding Property Rights

Object rights enable users to see NDS objects' places in the tree, and enable users to create, delete, and rename the objects themselves, but they do not allow users to access the properties of the objects of which they are trustees. Property rights must be assigned independently from object rights, in most cases. In the same way, a user can have rights to an object's properties, but not to the object itself.

The exception to this access rule is that the SUPERVISOR object right automatically includes rights to all of the objects' properties. Otherwise, each object has its own list of properties, which varies according to the object type. You can grant a user rights to all properties, or to individual properties selected from the list of available properties options. The rights that you can assign a user to each property of an object are described in Table 14.2.

Table 14.2   Novell Directory Services Property Rights

Property Right	Description
SUPERVISOR	Gives users complete control over the value for a particular property
COMPARE	Entitles users to check a property value for equality with another value
READ	Enables users to view the value for a property
WRITE	Enables users to add, change, or erase a property value
ADD SELF	Enables users to add or remove themselves (the user object name) as a part of the property value list

When you have the SUPERVISOR right for a particular property, you have full control over the value for that property. When you have the COMPARE right, you don't see the value for this particular property, but you can check to see whether that property is equal to a particular value. For example, you can use the NetWare Administrator utility to list all users for whom the property NETWORK ADDRESS is equal to a particular network address.

With the READ property right, you can view the value for a property but cannot change it. With the WRITE property right, you can change or erase the value for a property. You can use the ADD SELF property right for properties whose values consist of a list of object names. A common example of the ADD SELF property right use is the User property for the Print Server object type. The User property stores the list of users who are allowed to use the print server. To allow users to add or delete themselves to the list of users for a particular print server, you would give them the ADD SELF property right to the Print Server's User property.

Assigning Property Rights with NetWare Administrator

To assign property rights in NetWare Administrator, you use the same Rights to Other Objects and Trustees dialog boxes as when managing object rights, as described in the "Assigning Object Rights with NetWare Administrator" section earlier in this chapter.

Whichever dialog box you elect to use, the operation of the Property Rights area is the same. As shown in Figure 14.5, you can assign rights to all of an object's properties at once, or select rights to be assigned to individual properties.

N O T E   When you give a container object certain rights to all properties, those rights are inherited by all of the objects in the container. However, individual property rights assigned to a container object are not inherited.

FIG. 14.5

You can assign rights to all of an object's properties, and different rights to specific properties.

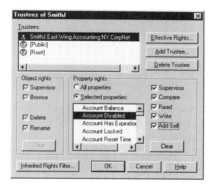

When you select an object in the Assigned Objects or Trustees box (depending on which dialog box you're using), and click the All Properties radio button, the check boxes representing the five property rights are activated.

If you click the Selected Properties radio button, you must scroll through the list of properties presented and make a selection before the rights check boxes are activated. You can use the standard Windows Ctrl+click and Shift+click combinations to select multiple objects from the list.

N O T E   The properties listed for an object vary according to the object type. Every field in the object's Details dialog box should be represented, although the property names may vary for reasons of length.

You can also assign certain rights to all properties, and then assign different rights to selected ones. For example, you can assign the READ right to all properties, and then click Selected Properties and choose the Telephone property. Initially, the rights check boxes are grayed out, but as soon as you mark one of the boxes, a check mark appears in front of the property name, and all of the check boxes are activated (see Figure 14.6).

Part
IV

Ch
14

FIG. 14.6

Rights assigned to individual properties, as indicated by a check mark, override the rights assigned to all properties.

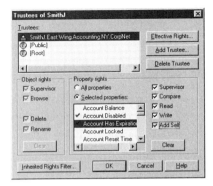

For example, the check mark indicates that individual rights have been defined for the Account Disabled property. Whatever rights you assigned to all properties no longer apply to Account Disabled because individual property rights always override rights granted to all properties.

This means that you can also use individual property rights to revoke rights that have been granted to all properties. You can, for example, grant READ rights to all properties, and then select the Account Balance property, from which you want to revoke the READ write.

To revoke a right, you click one of the rights check boxes to activate that property's individual rights, and then click the same check box again. This leaves the rights check boxes activated, but empty. As long as the check mark remains next to the Account Balance property, its individual rights override the All Properties rights (thus revoking the READ privileges), even though no rights are assigned.

To remove the individual rights from a selected property, and return to it all of the rights assigned to all properties, click the Clear button. The check mark next to the property is removed, and the rights check boxes are once again grayed out.

Assigning Property Rights with NETADMIN

You assign property rights in NetWare Administrator using the same basic procedure as for object rights, as described in the "Assigning Object Rights with NETADMIN" section earlier in this chapter. Once you have selected an object to be added as a trustee, you are presented with a Properties list, as shown in Figure 14.7.

You can select either individual properties or [All Properties Rights] from the list (using the F5 key to mark multiple properties), after which the trustee is added to the Property, Rights, Trustee listing along with the chosen properties. You can then modify the actual rights to each property by pressing Enter and manipulating the rights list in the usual manner.

FIG. 14.7

The Properties list in NETADMIN displays all of the properties possessed by the selected object, as well as an entry representing all of the properties.

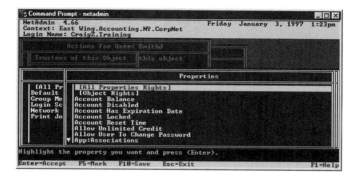

In NETADMIN, each individual property for each trustee is listed separately in the Property, Rights, Trustee window. To assign certain rights to all properties, and different rights to specific properties, you add the same trustee to the list as many times as is necessary, once to define the rights to all properties, and then once for each individual property that you want to manage. You can add the same trustee to the list as many times as there are different properties for that object.

Understanding Rights Inheritance

As with other NetWare maintenance tasks, such as assigning object property values and file system trustee rights, you can create trustees of NDS objects and properties individually by assigning rights to individual user objects. This, however, can be an extremely tedious and time consuming process, and in most cases unnecessary.

Like file system trustee rights, object and property rights flow downward through the NDS tree. Any rights that you grant to a container object are automatically inherited by all of the objects within that container. This is most easily demonstrated by the fact that the Admin user created during the NetWare installation is given SUPERVISOR object rights to the NDS tree's [Root] object. As a result, Admin has full rights over the entire tree, as all containers stem from the [Root].

N O T E Although NetWare file and directory rights and NDS object and property rights are considered to be two separate systems, there are connections between the two. For example, the Admin user has full rights to all files and directories on NetWare volumes. This is not because separate file system rights have been granted to the Admin object. It is, instead, the result of Admin's inheritance of SUPERVISOR object rights to the NetWare server objects in the tree. Granting any user the SUPERVISOR object right to a server gives them supervisor rights to the files and directories on that server. ▨

Part

IV

Ch

14

Unlike the Supervisor user in bindery-based versions of NetWare, the Admin user has no inherent qualities that differentiate it from other User objects, except for the rights that it has been granted. The Supervisor account in NetWare 3.x cannot be deleted, nor its rights removed. The Admin user need not exist at all, and its rights can be limited or removed entirely.

> **CAUTION**
>
> Before limiting the rights of the Admin user, be sure that some other user object has been granted the rights that you intend to remove. In NetWare 4.x, it is possible to "orphan" parts of your tree by leaving them without a Supervisor. Once the Supervisor rights to an object are removed from all other objects, there is no way to get them back.

Using the [Public] Object

Another example of object rights that are configured during the NetWare installation is demonstrated by the ability of any user to see all of the objects in the NDS tree. This is not a natural capability of the User object. It is possible for users to view the tree only because the BROWSE object right has been granted to them. In fact, every object in the tree is automatically granted the right to browse every other object.

Novell Directory Services contains a special entity that is used to grant this BROWSE object right. It is called [Public], and although it is not displayed as part of the tree, it shows up in NetWare Administrator's trustee lists with the same globe icon as the [Root] (see Figure 14.8).

FIG. 14.8
Object and property rights assigned to [Public] are inherited by all NDS objects and by clients connected to the network.

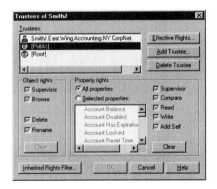

Any rights granted to [Public] are automatically inherited by all of the objects in the NDS tree. What's more, these rights are also available to NDS clients that have connected to the network, but have not yet logged in to the NDS tree. It is the BROWSE rights to [Root] that have been granted to [Public] that allow you to use the NetWare CX utility to change your context, even before you've logged in.

N O T E Like the LOGIN.EXE program itself, CX.EXE is located in the LOGIN directory on the SYS: volume of every NetWare server. All files in the SYS:LOGIN directory are available to users before they actually log in to the network. ▪

Using Inherited Rights Filters

If you wanted to prevent users from being able to browse the NDS tree, there are two possible methods that you could use. First, you could simply revoke the [Public] object's right to BROWSE the [Root]. This would prevent all of the objects in the tree from inheriting the BROWSE right, and leave them unable to see other NDS objects. Blocking the [Public] object's BROWSE right is a good global solution, but lacks specificity.

The second method is to use an inherited rights filter to prevent rights from being passed down the tree. If you imagine object and property rights as flowing down the NDS tree like the tributaries of a river, an inherited rights filter functions as a dam, blocking the flow of specific rights at selected locations.

Suppose, for example, that your enterprise has undertaken a secret research project, and you want to prevent your competitors from learning anything about it. You could create a container for all of your research team's leaf objects, and then apply an inherited rights filter to the container object to prevent all object and property rights from being inherited.

You can select the exact object and property rights that you want to filter, but in this case, you want to filter all of them. The result is that none of the other users can see the objects in the protected container, because [Public]'s trustee rights to the [Root] are being blocked at the container.

With the inherited rights filter in place, you can still grant selected users explicit object and property rights to the protected container, or to the objects in the container, enabling them to view and access the objects in the normal way. Inherited rights filters block only the rights that flow down the tree, not those that are explicitly granted to an object.

Creating Inherited Rights Filters with NetWare Administrator   In NetWare Administrator, you can assign object and property rights using either the Rights to Other Objects dialog box or the Trustees dialog box. However, you can only create inherited rights masks in the Trustees dialog box.

When you select an object in the NDS tree, and choose Trustees of this Object from the Object menu (or from the pop-up menu, after right-clicking the object), the Trustees dialog box has an Inherited Rights Filter button, which displays the dialog box shown in Figure 14.9.

By default, all of the check boxes in the Inherited Rights Filter dialog box are filled, indicating that no filters are in place, and that all inherited rights are being applied to the object.

Part

IV

Ch

14

FIG. 14.9

You can configure the inherited rights filters for both object and property rights in one NetWare Administrator dialog box.

To enable a filter, you clear the check box of one of the object or property rights, thus preventing that right from being inherited by the selected object. The object and property rights selectors function exactly like those that you use to assign rights. You can apply filters to individual properties as well as to all properties, using the same techniques as described in the "Assigning Property Rights with NetWare Administrator" section earlier in this chapter.

Creating Inherited Rights Filters with NETADMIN   To apply inherited rights filters in NETADMIN, you select an object, then choose the View or Edit Trustees of this Object option. In the Trustees of this Object menu, you select Inherited Rights Filters, and by default an empty list appears.

When you press the Insert key, the same Properties list appears as when you are assigning rights. After selecting [Object Rights], [All Properties Rights], or individual property rights, the items you have chosen are added to the Inherited Rights Filters listing, as shown in Figure 14.10.

FIG. 14.10

Inherited rights filters are applied using NETADMIN in much the same way as object and property rights are assigned.

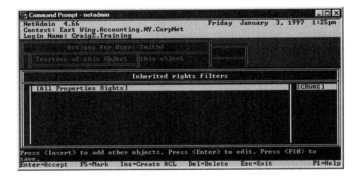

Items that are newly added to the Inherited Rights Filters list are shown with the letters [CRWAS], indicating that all five property rights can be inherited by the object. Press Enter, and the Property Rights Allowed list appears. Then, press Insert to transfer rights to the Rights Disallowed list, which enables the filters.

Understanding Effective Rights

As you have seen, the object and property rights held by a particular object can be configured in several different ways. Rights can be explicitly granted, inherited from container objects, and blocked by inherited rights filters, all at the same time. Other factors, such as security equivalences and group memberships, can also affect an object's rights.

Sometimes the rights granted by different methods are redundant. Sometimes rights applied by one method override those from another; at other times the rights are combined. The cumulative effects of all of these different factors result in the object's *effective rights*. The effective rights are the net result of the following influences:

- The rights directly granted to the object.
- The rights received through security equivalence or group membership. (If an object has security equivalence to another object, it has the same Directory tree rights as that object. If an object is a member of a group and the group has Directory tree rights, the object automatically has the same rights.)
- The rights that the object receives via [PUBLIC].
- Rights inherited from container objects. Inherited rights apply only if there are no rights directly granted to the object and no rights acquired through security equivalence.
- Inherited rights that are blocked by inherited rights filters.

Use the following two rules to determine your effective rights:

- *If an object has directly granted rights or rights acquired through security equivalence or group membership,* combine the directly granted rights, the rights gained through security equivalence and group membership, and the rights granted to [PUBLIC]. Inherited rights and rights blocked by inherited rights filters don't have any effect.
- *If an object has no directly granted rights and no rights granted through security equivalence,* combine the rights granted to [PUBLIC] and the rights inherited from higher container objects. Then subtract any rights blocked by inherited rights filters.

You can also view an object's effective rights in both NetWare Administrator and NETADMIN. In NetWare Administrator, both the Rights to Other Objects and Trustees dialog boxes have an effective rights button. Once you make a selection from the Assigned Objects or Trustees box, you can display its effective rights, which are shown in a dialog box like that in Figure 14.11.

FIG. 14.11
The Effective Rights dialog box shows the cumulative results of all rights management techniques.

Part
IV

Ch
14

In the Effective Rights dialog box, the effective object rights and rights to all properties are shown by default. Click Selected Properties to activate the properties list, which you can use to view the effective rights of individual properties.

In NETADMIN, you choose Effective Rights from the Trustees of this Object menu and specify a trustee name, producing an effective rights listing like that shown in Figure 14.12.

FIG. 14.12
NETADMIN can display the effective rights only for the trustees of an object.

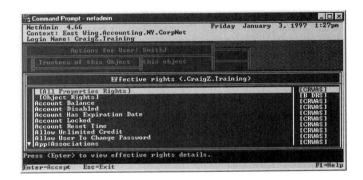

It is extremely important to understand the principle of effective rights to the NDS tree. As with the NetWare file system, rights can be applied and denied in so many ways that it is very difficult to keep track of them. The effective rights displays of NETADMIN and NetWare Administrator are the only places where the overall effects of all possible influences can be seen in one place.

Using Object Rights to Secure the Novell Directory Services Tree

When you operate a small network, object and property rights often do not play a major role. Network support personnel are assigned a security equivalence to Admin, giving them full rights over the tree, and normal users receive only the BROWSE object right through [Public].

Large networks are quite a different story, however. By Novell standards, a large network has an NDS tree with many thousands of objects. The enterprise may be spread out over many different sites, each with its own network support personnel.

The information systems management infrastructure for such an enterprise network may also be large and complex. Very often, it is no longer practical or wise for a single person (or persons) to have full rights to every resource on the network. In addition, the people performing many of the routine NDS maintenance tasks may not be sufficiently senior to warrant an Admin equivalence.

This is where NDS object and property rights come in. You can use these rights to divide the NDS maintenance tasks among many different people with different levels of expertise.

Maintaining Personnel Information

As you have seen, the NDS database can be used to store many kinds of information about users. The search functions of the various NetWare utilities can make it easy for users to locate specific pieces of information, such as other users' telephone and fax numbers, mailing addresses, and so on.

In most organizations, this sort of location information would typically be maintained by Human Resources personnel. However, rarely do such people have sufficient training to be trusted with any significant NDS database access.

You can, however, use a system of property rights that will allow the human resources staff access to specific informational properties of user objects. An administrative assistant can easily be trained to input users' addresses and phone numbers, as long as there is no danger of objects being deleted, or other properties modified. In such a scenario, you can even configure the user's access so that the only properties that they can see are the ones they are allowed to modify.

There are several different ways to configure this arrangement for access by non-administrators. The end result will be to make the Human Resources personnel trustees of all new User objects that are added to the tree. The trustees should have READ, WRITE, and COMPARE rights to the specific properties that they will maintain, such as Telephone, Location, the mailing address properties, and so on. All other property rights (including the default READ right) can be filtered out, to limit the confusion that can arise from a vast list of cryptic property names.

Dividing Object Maintenance Tasks

As mentioned earlier, the Admin user is granted full SUPERVISOR object rights to the [Root] of the NDS tree. The rights are inherited by all of the objects in the tree, resulting in unlimited access. You can, however, modify the rights of the Admin user, to split the responsibility of maintaining the tree objects among several people.

For example, you may not want the average network support person to have full rights to the objects in the Accounting container, as there may well be server volumes there that contain highly sensitive financial data. If you grant another (trusted) user the appropriate rights to the Accounting container, you can safely revoke those same rights from the Admin user.

CAUTION

It is extremely important to be aware of the fact that, because the rights of the Admin user can be modified or revoked, it is possible to orphan part or all of the NDS database. That is, you can leave parts of the NDS tree without a supervisor. Be sure to grant another user the rights that you intend to revoke from the Admin user. Also, do not rely on security equivalence to the Admin user, if you intend to limit its rights.

Part
IV

Ch
14

If your NDS tree is split into partitions, you may want to create a separate user with SUPERVI-SOR object rights in each container object holding a partition. Different people would therefore be responsible for maintaining the objects in each partition. This is particularly helpful if the partitions are located in different offices, with separate network support staffs.

 Even if you do not intend to split the enterprise's object maintenance responsibilities, limiting the rights of the Admin user can be a prudent security move. If you grant another user SUPERVISOR object rights to [Root], then you can safely limit Admin's rights. It will then become more difficult to penetrate your security measures, because an intruder would be forced to discover the user name, as well as the password of the SUPERVISOR user.

Summary

As you can see, NetWare's system of NDS object and property rights provides an enormous degree of flexibility when it comes to securing your NDS database and delegating Directory maintenance tasks. You can provide users with all of the access they need—without giving them more than they can handle. ●

CHAPTER 15

Understanding Directory and File Rights

In Chapter 14, "Understanding NDS Object and Property Rights," you learned about the various rights that you can assign to control access to NDS objects and their properties. The NetWare file system uses a very similar system of rights to control access to the files and directories stored on NetWare volumes. These two security systems, the directory and file systems, are largely separate, although they use many of the same terms.

In order to access the files stored on NetWare volumes, users must be granted the appropriate rights. At the same time, the network administrator must see to it that users do not have rights to files they should not access, or the capability to damage the files, whether accidentally or deliberately. The NetWare file system provides the means to exercise the precise amount of access control needed to make files usable, and still keep them safe. ■

How file system rights and NDS object rights are connected

NetWare's two access control systems operate independently to a large degree, but they are still related in several important ways.

The different rights that can be assigned to files and directories

NetWare controls file system access by providing eight different rights that are combined to provide the degree of control required.

How rights are inherited

File system rights flow downstream in both the volume directory structure and the NDS database.

Using the NetWare utilities to assign file system rights

NetWare includes utilities that enable you to control file system rights from a Windows GUI, a menu-based DOS utility, or from the command line.

Comparing File System Rights and NDS Object Rights

Access control for both the NetWare file system and the NDS database is based on the creation of *trustees*, which are objects that have been assigned rights to a given resource. A user can be a trustee of an NDS object, or of a directory on a NetWare volume. In each case, a list of trustees, called an *access control list*, or *ACL*, is stored with the object being accessed. In other words, every file and directory on a NetWare volume has a list of the trustees that have been granted access to it, as does every object in the NDS database.

Each trustee in an ACL is assigned certain rights to the network resource. The file system and NDS also use many of the same names for the rights that can be granted. A user, for example, can be granted Supervisor rights to a container object in the NDS tree, meaning that the user has rights to modify the properties of the NDS objects in that container. The same user can also be assigned Supervisor rights to a NetWare directory, providing full access to the files and subdirectories that it contains.

In the first case, where a user has Supervisor rights to a container object, the user is a trustee of an NDS object: the container. In the second case, where the user has Supervisor rights to a directory, the user is a trustee of a directory, which is not an NDS object, but still possesses a Supervisor right. It is important that you learn to distinguish between these two rights systems because, in many cases, the access that they provide is used for completely different purposes.

For the most part, a NetWare administrator will not have to grant users NDS object rights on a regular basis. File system rights, however, are needed by every user on the network. The granting of rights to files and directories is one of the most common network maintenance tasks. Learning to create an efficient file system access strategy is one of the basic administrative skills that mark a good network technician.

Differentiating File System and NDS Rights

Many people are confused by NetWare's different access control systems, and this is not without cause. Veteran NetWare administrators may be very familiar with the concepts involved in assigning file and directory trustee rights to users, which have not changed since NetWare 3.x. But the file system and the NDS object rights system do intersect in several important ways. Some of these ways are obvious. For example, a user is always represented by an NDS object in both the NDS and file systems.

When you grant a user rights to a directory (clearly a file system activity), you are actually adding a User object to the directory's access control list. The same is true when you grant NDS object rights to a user; the User object is added to another object's ACL.

Another source of confusion is based on the display in NetWare 4.11's most commonly used access control utility: NetWare Administrator. In a browser window, NetWare servers and their volumes are displayed as NDS objects, which they are. However, when you expand a volume object, you are shown a display of the file system contained within (see Figure 15.1).

FIG. 15.1
The NetWare Administrator utility can display elements of both the NDS database and the NetWare file system.

It is crucial that you understand that *the files and directories within a NetWare volume are not NDS objects themselves,* even though the volume itself is an NDS object.

The volume object is the functional dividing line between the two access control systems in NetWare Administrator. It has an ACL that can contain trustees with NDS object rights, and another list of trustees with file system rights to the root directory of the volume. All of the files and directories within the volume, however, have only a single access control list, containing file system trustees.

When ACLs Collide

For the most part, objects with both file system and NDS access control lists keep the two separate. Users can have rights to access the files and directories on a volume, and not have the rights to modify the NDS volume object. Conversely, granting NDS rights to a volume object does not automatically provide access to the files and directories in the volume.

However, there are cases in which the granting of NDS object rights overlaps into the realm of file system rights. When you install NetWare on a server, objects are created in the NDS tree representing the server itself, and each of the volumes on the server. In NDS, the server object is not a container of the volume objects. Normally, you use the volume objects to access the file system; double-clicking a volume displays its directories and files.

NDS rights and file system rights are separated in the volume objects. If you grant a user the Supervisor object rights to a volume object, the user can modify the properties of the object, but cannot access the files and directories on the volume.

However, if you grant a user the same Supervisor object rights to a server object, the user gains full supervisor rights to the server's file system, as well as to the object. In the same way, if you grant a user the Write right to a server object's Object Trustees (ACL) property, the user gains full access to the file system. Because these rights are the equivalent of Supervisor access to the files, they cannot be blocked with an inherited rights filter.

N O T E Interestingly, although the Supervisor file system right cannot be blocked by an inherited
rights filter, the Supervisor object right can. Therefore, an IRF placed on a server object can
prevent users from inheriting the Supervisor object right, which in turn would prevent them from gaining
access to the file system. ▪

The Supervisor object right is how the Admin User object receives rights to the files and directories on all of the network's volumes. Admin is automatically granted the Supervisor object right to [Root]. As a result, it inherits the same right to all of the other objects in the tree, including servers. It is this inherited Supervisor object right to all of the tree's server objects that provides it with file system access. All you would have to do to revoke all of Admin's special privileges would be to remove it from the access control list of [Root].

Understanding Trustee Rights

In the NetWare file system, every file and directory has its own list of trustees. A trustee can be a user, a group of users, or any one of several other NDS objects that can be granted file system rights. Many of the objects that can be added to a file system trustee list do not actually require access to the files themselves. The objects are granted access solely for the purpose of passing along the rights to other objects through inheritance.

Each trustee can be assigned up to eight rights to a file or directory, each of which allows the trustee a different kind of access. The Supervisor right provides full access to the file or directory. It is the equivalent to the combination of the other seven rights: Read, Write, Create, Erase, Modify, File Scan, and Access Control.

Each of the eight rights can be applied to either files or directories, enabling the network administrator to fine tune users' access to suit a wide variety of situations. Table 15.1 lists the rights that you can assign to files and directories and the effect that they have on each.

Table 15.1 NetWare 4.11 Directory and File Rights

Right	Definition
READ	Enables a trustee of a file or directory to execute or read the contents of the file, or any file within that directory. The READ right is needed to execute a program file or view the contents of a data file.
WRITE	Enables a trustee of a file or directory to modify the contents of the file, or any file within that directory. Without the WRITE right, changes made to a data file in an application cannot be saved to disk. The READ right is almost always assigned along with WRITE.
CREATE	Enables a trustee of a directory to create a new file or subdirectory in the directory. CREATE must also be assigned to a file or directory in order to salvage the file, or any files in that directory, after they have been deleted.

Right	Definition
ERASE	Enables a file trustee to delete the file. When applied to a directory, enables the trustee to delete any file or remove any subdirectory from the directory.
ACCESS CONTROL	Enables a trustee of a file or directory to grant other objects rights to the file or directory, and to modify its inherited rights filter. The ACCESS CONTROL right, however, cannot be used to grant another object the SUPERVISOR right.
MODIFY	Enables a file trustee to rename the file, or change its attributes. When applied to a directory, enables the trustee to rename or change the attributes of the directory itself, as well as any files or subdirectories contained within it. MODIFY rights do not enable trustees to change the contents of files in the directory, as logical as that may sound.
FILE SCAN	Enables a trustee of a file or directory to list its name (and other attributes). When applied to a directory, enables the trustee to list the names of the files and subdirectories contained within the directory. No access, however, is granted to the contents of the files. In nearly all cases, FILE SCAN rights are granted along with any other rights, although it is not strictly necessary to be able to list files in order to operate on them in other ways.
SUPERVISOR	Provides a trustee with the equivalent of all the other rights to the file, or to the directory, with all its files and subdirectories. The SUPERVISOR right also overrides the effect of any explicit rights assignments or inherited rights filters applied to the file, or to the directory and any of the files and subdirectories contained within it.

Understanding Users' Default Rights

When you create a User object in the NDS database, the user is automatically made a trustee of two directories:

■ The SYS:PUBLIC directory, to which the user is granted READ and FILE SCAN rights, allowing access to the NetWare utilities

■ The user's home directory (if one is created), to which all rights are granted, including Supervisor.

N O T E Users are only granted full rights to their home directories when the directory is created at the same time as the User object. If you create a home directory for a user that already exists, you must manually assign the user's trustee rights. ■

Combining Rights

When you are assigning trustees rights to files and directories, the object is to provide them with the access that they need to accomplish their work, and no more. You can easily assign all of your users full rights to the entire file system, but this is likely to result in security breaches, nonfunctional applications, and lost data.

N O T E   The combination of rights to directories and files that you do assign is determined by the needs of the user and of the application. One of the first rules that a network administrator learns is to separate applications from data files. This rule is based on the concept of assigning different degrees of access to each. ■

Obviously, users must have the capability to scan, read, and write data files, such as word processing documents, spreadsheets, and databases. Beyond this, whether users should be permitted to create or delete files depends on the nature of the data.

However, it is important that the program files that make up an application be protected. They must be scanned and read by users to be operational, but there is no reason to write, modify, or delete program files, so these rights should be withheld.

Separating Applications and Data   The following scenario demonstrates only the most basic of access control techniques. The nature of today's applications, and the ways in which data is used in a business enterprise complicate the whole issue enormously. Take, for example, the fact that many applications use configuration files to store user preferences that must be located with the rest of the application files.

This is where NetWare's capability to assign rights to both files and directories comes into play. The network administrator can grant users the READ and FILE SCAN rights to the directory containing an application, and then add the WRITE right to the individual configuration files. Users inherit minimal rights to all of the files of the directory, except for the configuration files, to which they are explicitly granted additional access.

Hiding Files and Directories   The network administrator is also likely to face access control problems that are more extreme, and NetWare's file system rights can handle these as well. Certain users in an enterprise, for example, such as those in Accounting or Legal departments, must routinely work with sensitive documents that must be protected from outside access, even by the users in other departments.

In such a case, network administrators can not only prevent outsiders from reading or writing to these files, they can prevent users from even seeing that the files and directories exist, by withholding the FILE SCAN right.

You can use this filtering technique to hide any files or directories of which users need not be aware. Be advised, though, that you generally cannot revoke the FILE SCAN right from files or directories that users must access. It may seem like a good idea to allow users READ rights to program files or directories while withholding FILE SCAN, in order to prevent them from copying or otherwise manipulating the files. However, many applications will not be able to locate their ancillary files without the capability to scan the directory in which they are located.

Understanding Rights Inheritance

Rights inheritance is a crucial element of access control maintenance. Without it, network administrators would be forced to grant each individual user the appropriate rights to every individual file needed by that user. The task would be monumental, even on small networks, and agonizingly tedious.

Instead, both of NetWare's access control systems allow trustee rights to be passed down the object hierarchy. This inheritance is manifested in two ways:

- Objects that are granted trustee rights to file system directories also inherit rights to all of the files and subdirectories contained in that directory.

- Trustee rights that are assigned to NDS container objects are passed down to all of the leaf and container objects below them.

File System Inheritance

In its simplest form, the first type of rights inheritance—rights to file system directories—means that when you make a user a trustee of a directory, the rights that you assign are passed down to all of the files in that directory as well. This, in effect, establishes a default for that directory. You can then create additional trustee assignments for specific files in the directory that add or subtract certain rights to that file only.

This leads to one of the most basic rules of NetWare trustee assignments: *Trustee rights granted to a specific file override the rights granted to the file's parent directory.*

The override means that even when you create a file trustee that grants fewer rights than the parent directory's trustee assignment, the file rights take precedence, effectively blocking the inheritance of rights from the directory. The only exception to this rule is when you assign the Supervisor right. Once you grant a user the Supervisor right to a directory, the user inherits the same right to all of the files and subdirectories below, which cannot be blocked by any means.

This rights inheritance is not limited only to the files contained in a particular directory. All of the subdirectories of that directory, and the files that they contain, inherit the directory's trustee rights as well. Often, a metaphor of a river is used to describe this effect. Trustee rights are said to flow downstream from the directory to which they are assigned.

Thus, if you make a user a trustee of a volume's root directory, whatever rights you assign that user will flow down to all of the directories, subdirectories, and files below the root—in other words, the entire volume.

Novell Directory Services Inheritance

In the previous section, you saw how you can use rights inheritance in the file system to reduce the number of trustees that you have to create. You can reduce the number further because trustee rights are not inherited only within the file system, they are passed down in the Novell Directory Services tree hierarchy, as well.

NDS objects can have trustee rights to other objects, as well as to files and directories. Because file and directory rights become a property of an object, those property values flow down the branches of the NDS tree, just like any other properties.

Just as you can grant a user rights to a directory, so that the rights to the files in the directory will be inherited, you can grant file system rights to a container object, so that the leaf objects in the container will inherit those rights.

Thus, although a container object itself has no use for file system rights, it can be assigned rights to a volume's files and directories, just as though it was a User object. Then, all of the User objects in that container, as well as its child containers and their User objects, receive the same rights.

N O T E   The READ and FILE SCAN rights to the SYS:PUBLIC directory that users receive by default are granted through rights inheritance from a container object. When you install a NetWare server, the container holding the server and volume objects is granted the rights, which are then inherited by every user created in that container.

Using Security Equivalence

The inheritance of trustee rights from container objects is another area where the two access control systems in NetWare can be confusing because both use trustees in different ways. The container object may be a trustee of a directory in the file system, and the leaf objects inherit those trustee rights from the container, but the leaves are not necessarily the container object's trustees.

In actuality, the rights that User objects inherit from their containers are granted through *security equivalence*. Security equivalence is an entirely different NDS object property that is independent from the file system trustee list. An object that is the security equivalent of another object inherits all of the host's property values.

Thus, a user object, as a security equivalent, inherits its container's trustee rights to the file system, as well as any NDS object and property rights that it may possess. A user can, therefore, become a trustee of the file system and of certain NDS objects through the same security equivalence.

N O T E   Although users are automatically made security equivalents of their parent containers (and of all their ancestral containers, by proxy), the User object does not appear in the list of security equivalents displayed by any of the NetWare utilities.

Taking advantage of this inherent relationship between container and leaf objects is the most commonly used means of providing users with rights to the file system (and to NDS objects as well, for that matter). In many cases, all of the users in a particular container require the same access rights, so it only makes sense to grant those rights once, to the container, rather than making a trustee of each individual user.

This, again, creates a default configuration for all of the leaf objects in the container. If there are any exceptional cases, that is, users who require special access, individual trustee rights can still be granted to the User object. In many cases, however, network administrators find that they do not have to grant any individual user rights at all; users' needs can all be satisfied by rights inherited from other objects.

The use of security equivalence to grant file system rights is not limited to the relationship between containers and leaves. Any NDS object can be made the security equivalent of any other object, and inherit its properties, including file system rights, as a result. You can therefore configure the file system rights for one User object, and make other users its security equivalent.

CAUTION

There is an important drawback to the practice of granting rights with security equivalences, however. Security equivalence is a dynamic relationship between objects. Changing the properties of an object causes the properties of its equivalents to change in the same way.

It is not recommended that you select one user to be the recipient of a trustee assignment, and then make other users its equivalent. If that original user should change jobs, or leave the company, modifying its rights will affect all equivalent users.

CAUTION

It is particularly important to consider the nature of security equivalences when you are working with the Admin object. If you should decide to limit the rights of the Admin user for security reasons, be sure that other users possess the same rights as Admin, whether individually or in combination. In addition, make certain that those rights are granted independently, and not through security equivalence to the Admin object. Otherwise, revoking rights from Admin will limit the rights of the equivalent users as well, and you could be left with parts of your NDS tree orphaned (that is, lacking a user with Supervisor rights).

NDS provides an alternative to the practice of using equivalences, in the form of a special NDS object called an Organizational Role, which is discussed in the next section.

Using Organizational Roles

The Organizational Role (or OR) object is specifically designed for the purpose of defining the file system rights needed to perform a particular job, when the users holding that job change on a regular basis. Rather than use a security equivalence to another User object, you create an Organizational Role object, and configure it as a trustee of the files and directories needed to fill the role.

You then add one or more User objects as occupants of the role. Each occupant inherits the file system rights that you have granted to the OR object. When the personnel performing the job change, you have only to add or remove their User object names from the list of occupants.

Because the OR object serves no other purpose than to provide a specific set of rights to other objects, there is no other reason for it to be modified—as an equivalent User object might be.

Using Group Objects

Anyone who has ever administered NetWare 3.x servers should be familiar with the concept of the user group. On bindery-based servers, the group is the way to create a single set of file system trustee rights and assign them to multiple users. The default rights to the SYS:PUBLIC directory are granted, in NetWare 3.x, by making the Everyone group a trustee of that directory. All users were automatically made members of the Everyone group, by default.

NetWare 4.11 still has groups that operate in much the same way as their bindery counterparts, but they are now NDS objects, and their functionality has largely been superseded by file system rights that are inherited from container objects. There are several reasons why this is so.

One reason is that the container objects already exist for the purpose of creating the NDS tree structure, with the leaf objects forming natural memberships. Creating an additional group object to represent the users in a container would be redundant, when the users are already part of a logical group that can be used in the same way.

N O T E There is no longer an Everyone group that is automatically created during the installation of a NetWare server because is it generally more efficient to assign rights to container objects, rather than groups. However, you can manually create a group called Everyone. After you do this, all of the User objects that you create in the same container as the group Everyone will automatically become members. This is only true when the group is named Everyone, however, and only new User objects are added to the group. Existing users must be manually configured as members. ▨

Another reason for using NDS objects rather than the concept of bindery-based groups involves performance concerns that are specific to Novell Directory Services. The primary advantage realized in assigning file system rights with group objects is also its primary disadvantage. Unlike container objects that can only pass rights downwards through the NDS hierarchy, groups can have members whose User objects are located anywhere in the tree.

This is now the main reason for the continued existence of the group object. Group objects can be used to define a collection of users that is completely independent of the NDS container/leaf object structure, and grant them file system rights.

However, because group members can be located anywhere in the tree, processing the rights inherited from a group is a more complicated operation that those inherited from a container object. The inheritance of container rights is, by definition, a local phenomenon, while group rights inheritance involves access to the entire NDS tree, including remote partitions.

It is for this reason that you should only use group objects to provide file system rights to users when container objects or other alternatives are unsuitable.

Using Inherited Rights Filters

Many network administrators arrange the directory structure of their volumes to accommodate NetWare's file system rights inheritance behavior. There are times, however, when it is necessary to prevent rights from being passed down from a directory to its files or subdirectories.

N O T E Inherited rights filters can also be used in NetWare's other access control system to prevent NDS object and property rights from being passed down the Directory tree. Do not confuse object filters with file system filters.

To prevent rights from flowing downward, you create an *inherited rights filter*, which functions something like a dam, blocking selected rights from flowing downstream, as shown in Figure 15.2. Inherited rights filters, or IRFs, are not applied to specific trustees of a directory or file. They are general barriers that prevent all rights from being passed to a certain file or directory, and everything below it in the tree.

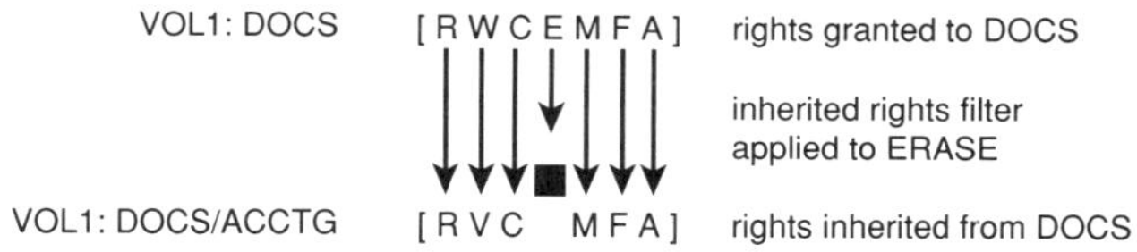

FIG. 15.2

Inherited rights filters prevent specified trustee rights from flowing down the directory tree.

VOL1: DOCS   [R W C E M F A]   rights granted to DOCS

inherited rights filter
applied to ERASE

VOL1: DOCS/ACCTG   [R V C   M F A]   rights inherited from DOCS

When you create an IRF at a specific point in a directory structure, you select which rights are to be blocked. You can, for example, have a directory to which users have full rights, and create a filter to block only the WRITE and ERASE rights to a certain file in that directory. Users will still inherit other rights from the directory, but will be prevented from changing or deleting the file.

N O T E The only file system right that you cannot block with an inherited rights filter is Supervisor. Once users are granted Supervisor rights to a particular directory, their access to all of the files and subdirectories below cannot be blocked by any means. (It is possible, however, to block the Supervisor object right with an IRF.)

As the name implies, inherited rights filters can only prevent rights to a file or directory from being inherited. They have no effect on rights that are specifically assigned to a particular element of the file system. You can, therefore, grant your users READ and FILE SCAN rights to an entire volume, and place IRFs on certain directories. The users will not be able to see that those directories even exist.

Then, for users who require access to those filtered directories, you need only make them trustees of the filtered directories, in any of the usual ways. Rights explicitly granted are not filtered, and those users will have the access that they need.

It should be noted that inherited rights filters introduce an entirely new twist on the issue of access control procedures. IRFs are the only subtractive access control mechanism; that is, they are the only means by which existing rights can actually be withdrawn, without the use of explicit trustee assignments. IRFs can make it difficult to keep track of users' effective rights to particular files and directories. For this reason, they are used less frequently than the other access control mechanisms discussed in this chapter, and many network administrators eschew them entirely.

Understanding Effective Rights

As you have seen in this chapter, there are many methods of providing your users with the access rights to the NetWare file system that they need. You are free to choose any of these methods, or all of them, to suit your needs. This, however, can result in a confusing array of mechanisms, all of which are influencing a single user's rights at the same time.

The phrase used to describe the cumulative effect of all of these access control mechanisms is *effective rights*. A user's effective rights to a particular resource are determined by evaluating the combined influences of the following factors:

- Rights inherited from container objects
- Rights obtained through security equivalences
- Rights granted by group memberships
- Rights provided by organizational role occupancies
- Rights inherited from parent directories
- Rights blocked by inherited rights filters
- Rights explicitly granted to the user

Fortunately, NetWare Administrator and FILER contain features that enable you to view an object's effective rights to a file or directory so that you do not have to keep track of all of these factors yourself. Even with this capability, though, the process can be inconvenient—particularly when administrators make use of all of the various methods of granting file system access rights.

It is recommended that you establish a regimen of access control procedures for your network that make use of only a few of these techniques, and stick to them. If you have a staff of network support personnel with different access control philosophies, you could end up with one person applying IRFs, while another uses group memberships, while yet another prefers to use organizational roles. This can result in extreme confusion. As with most aspects of network administration, prior planning and the development of a working standard are the keys to efficient maintenance.

Creating File System Trustees

As with most networking tasks, NetWare provides multiple utilities that can accomplish the same administrative tasks in various workstation environments. You can select whichever program you want, depending on your preferred operating system environment.

For the Windows graphical interface, you can use NetWare Administrator, which provides full control over both NDS object and file system access control functions. NETADMIN provides control over file system trustee rights in a menu-based DOS environment. FILER enables you to control some aspects of file system rights, and the RIGHTS utility provides DOS command-line trustee functions.

Of course, in order to assign file system rights to other users, you must possess the appropriate rights yourself. This means that you must have the SUPERVISOR or ACCESS CONTROL right to every directory or file for which you want to create trustees.

The following sections discuss the mechanics of assigning trustee rights to the NetWare file system, using NetWare Administrator, NETADMIN, FILER, and RIGHTS.

Controlling File System Access with NetWare Administrator

With NetWare Administrator, you can approach the task of creating file system trustees from two directions. You can expand a Volume object, select a file or directory, and add objects to its trustee list, or you can select an NDS object and specify the files and directories to which it should have access.

Whichever method you choose, the process consists of highlighting an item in the NDS browser and displaying its Details dialog box by selecting Details from the Object menu, by pressing the Enter key, or by right-clicking the item and selecting details from the pop-up menu.

Adding Trustees to a File or Directory   When you expand a volume object in NetWare Administrator, the files and directories displayed are not NDS objects themselves. You are actually crossing the boundary from the world of NDS object rights to that of file system rights when you expand a volume object.

The Details dialog box of a directory contains a screen called Trustees of this Directory, shown in Figure 15.3. This screen lists all of the NDS objects that have been assigned explicit trustee rights to this directory. It also displays the inherited rights filters that have been applied.

N O T E   The Details dialog box for a file contains a Trustees of this File screen with the exact same elements as that shown in Figure 15.3, as does the Trustees of the Root Directory screen in a Volume object's Details dialog box. The procedures for modifying file and root trustee rights are identical to those for directories.

FIG. 15.3

The Trustees of this Directory screen displays the NDS objects that have been granted rights to this directory.

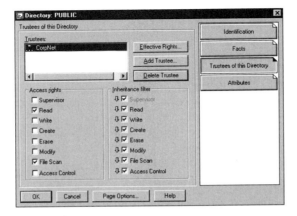

When the trustees screen is first displayed, the Access Rights check boxes are grayed out because none of the objects in the Trustees listing are selected. The Inheritance Filter check boxes are active, however, because they are applied to the directory itself, and not to particular trustees of the directory.

By default, all of the Inheritance Filter check boxes are marked, indicating that inheritance of all rights is allowed. To apply a filter, you deselect the check boxes of the rights that you want to block. This causes the icons next to those rights to change, indicating that rights to the selected directory, and any of the files or directories it contains, have been blocked.

N O T E   There is a check box for the Supervisor right in the Inheritance Filter box, but it is always grayed out, as it is not possible to block the inheritance of the Supervisor right in the NetWare file system.

When you select an object in the trustee list, the Access Rights check boxes are activated to display the rights that the object has been granted to the directory. You can change the assigned rights by marking or clearing check boxes as needed.

The Add Trustee button generates the standard dialog box with which you can select an NDS object that is to be made a trustee of the directory. A file system trustee can be a User object—or any of the NDS objects discussed in this chapter—from which users can inherit file system rights, such as:

- container objects (Country, Organization, or Organizational Unit objects),
- group objects,
- organizational role objects,
- template objects.

Once the object is added to the list, you can specify the rights it is to have by manipulating the Access Rights check boxes.

The trustees that are listed in the Details dialog box are only those that have been granted explicit rights to this directory. Objects that have inherited rights to the directory are not listed, nor are those that gain rights as a result of group membership, occupancy of occupational roles, or security equivalence.

The rights displayed for the trustees that are listed are, again, only those that have been explicitly granted to the trustee. The user (or other object) can have effective rights that differ from those displayed here, due to the influence of other inheritances and security equivalences. Click the Effective Rights button to display the accumulated rights to the directory for the highlighted trustee.

Granting File System Rights to an NDS Object   To approach the equation from the other side, you can also select an NDS object in the browser window of NetWare Administrator, display its Details dialog box in the usual manner, and select the Rights to Files and Directories dialog box, as shown in Figure 15.4. The NDS object can be that of a user, a group, or any other appropriate trustee.

> **CAUTION**
>
> File System rights are always controlled in NetWare Administrator through the Details dialog box. Do not make the mistake of activating the Rights to Other Objects, or the Trustees of this Object dialog boxes, as they are concerned only with NDS object and property rights, not file system rights.

FIG. 15.4

You can grant rights to files and directories from an NDS object's Rights to Files and Directories panel.

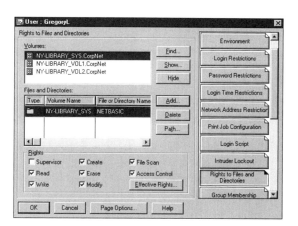

When the Rights to Files and Directories panel is first displayed, its lists of volumes, files, and directories are always empty. This is because file system trustee assignments are not stored in the NDS database. Instead, they are part of the file system itself, and to display them here, you must scan the trustee lists of the files and directories to find the NDS object whose rights you are modifying.

You have two choices when displaying the file system elements to which the object has rights. If you click the Find button, you are prompted to specify an NDS context where the file system scan is to begin. If you want the trustee search to continue down through the NDS hierarchy, click the Search Entire Subtree check box.

N O T E Depending on the size of your network and the way in which your NDS database is partitioned, the volume scan can take quite a long time if you select a context too high up in the tree. In many cases, it will only be necessary to scan the volumes in the current context, which is the default. ▨

The trustee lists of the files and directories in each volume object found in the specified context are then scanned. As a result of the scan, the volumes found are displayed at the top of the screen, and any files and directories of which the object is a trustee are listed beneath.

Alternatively, you can click the Show button to select a volume object to be scanned for trustees. This process is much quicker than scanning all of the volumes in the context, or a whole branch of the NDS tree.

Whichever method you choose, however, the result is the same. The files and directories of which the selected object is a trustee are shown in the Files and Directories list. When you select an item in the list, the object's rights to that item are shown by the Rights check boxes, which you can modify as needed.

Once again, the rights displayed here are only those that have been explicitly granted to the selected object. You can, however, click the Effective Rights button to display the accumulated effect of the explicitly granted rights, security equivalences, and all inherited and filtered rights.

N O T E Notice that you cannot modify inherited rights filters in the Effective Rights dialog box. This is because the filters are not part of a file or directory's trustee list. They are, instead, a global mechanism that affects the rights of all trustees in the same way. ▨

To grant the object rights to a file or directory that is not listed, click the Add button, and navigate to the desired element. You can do the add whether or not you have previously scanned for trustee rights using the Find or Show buttons. Once the file or directory is added to the list, you can manipulate the explicit rights and view the effective rights as needed.

▶ **See** "Using Group Objects," **p. 166**
▶ **See** "Using Organizational Roles," **p. 167**

Controlling File System Access with NETADMIN

Unlike NetWare Administrator, the NETADMIN utility can approach the task of assigning file system trustee rights only from the NDS object paradigm. You select a User or other type of object, and then display or modify its rights to specific files and directories. To select a specific file or directory and work with its trustee list or to apply an inherited rights filter, you must use the FILER utility, covered in "Controlling File System Access with FILER" later this chapter.

Once you select an NDS object, using NETADMIN's `Manage Objects` command, choose View or Edit Rights to Files and Directories from the Actions menu. The Rights to Files and/or Directories screen is then presented, as shown in Figure 15.5.

FIG. 15.5

With NETADMIN, you scan the file system for the files and directories to which your selected NDS object has trustee rights.

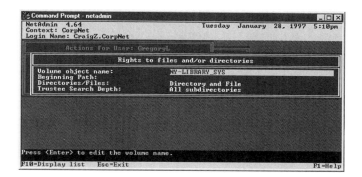

In the Rights to Files and/or Directories screen, you specify the part of the NetWare file system that you want to scan for files and directories to which the selected object has been granted rights by supplying values for the following four items:

- **Volume Object Name**—The volume that is to be scanned
- **Beginning Path**—The name of the directory where the scan is to begin
- **Directories/Files**—Whether to scan for files or directories, or both
- **Trustee Search Depth**—Whether or not the scan should be limited to the selected directory, or continue down the directory tree branch

As in all of the NetWare utilities that use the C-worthy interface, you can type a value in these fields, or press the Insert key to browse the NDS tree or a volume's directory structure.

Once you have configured your search settings, pressing the F10 key begins the scan of the path you specified. A Trustee Directory Entry screen then appears, containing a list of all of the files and/or directories of which the selected NDS object is a trustee, as shown in Figure 15.6.

The list also displays the rights currently held by the object, using the standard rights notation of initials within square brackets (that is, `[SRWCEMFA]`).

To modify the rights held by the object, select a file or a directory from the list, and press Enter to display the list of Trustee Rights Granted. You can then add or delete rights from the list, as needed.

To make the object a trustee of a new file or directory, again use the Insert key to add an item to the list of Trustee Directory Entries by entering the desired file or directory name or browsing to it, and then specify the rights to be granted to the object.

FIG. 15.6
Create trustee assignments for your selected NDS object by adding them to the Trustee Directory Entry list.

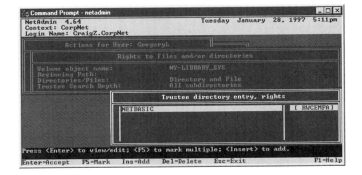

Controlling File System Access with FILER

While the NETADMIN utility controls file system rights by listing the files and directories to which a particular NDS object has been granted access, FILER enables you to select a file or directory, and specify the rights that should be granted to each of the NDS objects in its trustee list.

To work with the trustees of a file or directory, select Manage Files and Directories from FILER's main menu, and browse to the desired file or directory. When the desired element is highlighted, press the F10 key, and select View/Set Directory Information (or View/Set File Information) from the Options menu to display an information screen like that shown in Figure 15.7.

N O T E If you select Rights List from the Options menu, a list of the directory or file's trustees, and their assigned rights, is displayed. However, you cannot add or delete trustees from this screen, or modify their rights. ▓

FIG. 15.7
FILER can display an Information screen about each file and directory, which you can use to set trustee rights and apply inherited rights filters.

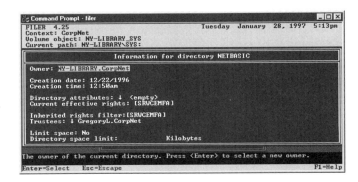

On the Information screen you can see the directory's owner, its attributes, and its date and time of creation, in addition to other data. The Current Effective Rights field displays the current rights to the directory (or file) that are held by the account that you have used to log in to the network.

From this Information screen, you can apply an inherited rights filter to the directory (or file) by highlighting the appropriate field and pressing Enter. As always, the default settings allow all rights to be inherited. You apply a filter by deleting entries from the Inherited Rights screen.

The Information screen also provides access to a list of the directory or file's trustees. When you highlight the Trustees field and press enter, the screen shown in Figure 15.8 appears. This screen is essentially the opposite of the NETADMIN screen shown in Figure 15.6. Instead of displaying a list of the files and directories to which a user has rights, this screen lists the users (or other NDS objects) that have rights to the chosen file or directory.

FIG. 15.8
FILER displays the NDS objects that have been added to a particular file or directory's trustee list.

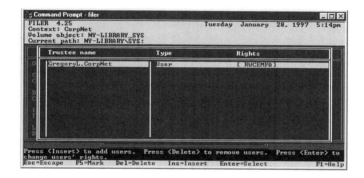

The trustee list screen operates just like its NETADMIN counterpart, and like most of NetWare's C-worthy utilities. Press the Insert key to select a new NDS object to be added as a trustee, or highlight an existing trustee and press Enter to work with its rights.

Controlling File System Access with *RIGHTS*

Despite the continued progress of the computer industry toward the use of graphical user interfaces, there are a great many common tasks that can be performed more quickly and easily from the command line. NetWare includes a command-line utility called RIGHTS, which enables you to perform nearly all of the same file system access control maintenance tasks as the other utilities covered in this chapter, such as granting and revoking trustee rights, viewing effective rights, and applying inherited rights filters.

Table 15.2 displays the parameters that can be used with the RIGHTS command.

Table 15.2   Parameters Used with the *RIGHTS* Command

Parameter	Purpose
(no parameter)	Display the current user's effective rights to the current directory
/T	Display the trustees of directory or file
/NAME=	Specify the trustee object whose rights are to be managed

continues

Table 15.2   Continued

Parameter	Purpose
/F	Modify the inherited rights filter for a directory or file
/I	View the effective rights information for a directory or file
/S	Apply a command to all subdirectories
/C	Scroll the screen displays generated by the RIGHTS command without pausing
/VER	View version information for the RIGHTS executable
/?	View Help information for the RIGHTS command

The general syntax of RIGHTS calls for you to specify the name of the directory or file whose trustee list is to be accessed, followed by the names of one or more NDS objects whose rights are to be manipulated, followed by options that control the functions of the program, as follows:

```
RIGHTS [directory/file] /NAME=[object] <options>
```

File and directory names can be specified using NetWare paths, drive letters, relative path names, or the standard DOS directory identifiers (one period and two periods). Object names can be specified using any of the standard NDS notation techniques.

Viewing Effective Rights with *RIGHTS*   RIGHTS can even perform some functions that the other utilities can't. With NetWare Administrator and NETADMIN, it is only possible to view a user's effective rights to a particular directory when the user is a trustee of that directory.

If you issue the RIGHTS command with no parameters from a DOS prompt, your current effective rights to the default directory are displayed. However, you can also display the effective rights of any user, to any directory or file, using the following syntax:

```
RIGHTS [directory] /NAME=[object] /I
```

The results of the command show the rights that have been assigned to each directory in the path, the rights that were inherited from each directory, and the trustee object's current effective rights, as follows:

```
RIGHTS F:\PUBLIC\WINNT /NAME=HOBARTS /I
Name= hobarts
Path                                                             Rights
-----------------------------------------------------------------------
NY-LIBRARY\SYS:\
Inherited Rights Filter:                                     [       ]
Inherits from above:                                         [       ]
                                                              _ _ _ _
Effective Rights =                                           [       ]
-----------------------------------------------------------------------
```

```
NY-LIBRARY\SYS:\PUBLIC
Inherited Rights Filter:                                        [SRWCEMFA]
Inherits from above:                                            [        ]
                                                                 _ _ _ _
Effective Rights =                                              [ R     F ]
-------------------------------------------------------------------------
NY-LIBRARY\SYS:\PUBLIC\WINNT
Inherited Rights Filter:                                        [SRWCEMFA]
Inherits from above:                                            [ R     F ]
HobartS                                                         [   C     ]
                                                                 _ _ _ _
Effective Rights =                                              [ R C   F ]
-------------------------------------------------------------------------
```

The preceding display shows that the user HobartS has the READ, CREATE, and FILE SCAN rights to the SYS:PUBLIC\WINNT directory. READ and FILE SCAN are inherited from the PUBLIC directory, and the CREATE right to the WINNT directory has been explicitly assigned to this user.

Viewing Trustees with *RIGHTS*   When you add the /T switch to a RIGHTS command, the trustees of the specified file or directory are displayed, along with their assigned rights, as follows:

```
RIGHTS F:\PUBLIC\WINNT /T
NY-LIBRARY\SYS:\PUBLIC\WINNT
User trustees:
     HobartS.CorpNet                                           [   C     ]
     FrancisC.CorpNet                                          [ RWCEMFA]
----------
No group trustees have been assigned.
```

Managing Trustee Rights with *RIGHTS*   To add a new trustee to a file or directory, or modify the rights of an existing trustee, you specify the file or directory name and the name of the trustee objects, separated by the rights that you want to add or subtract. For example, to grant a user the WRITE and ERASE rights to a directory, the command appears as follows:

```
RIGHTS F:\PUBLIC\WINNT +WE /NAME=HobartS
```

If the HobartS object is not already a trustee of the WINNT directory, it will be added. If it is already a trustee, the WRITE and ERASE rights are added to any other rights that have already been granted.

You can revoke certain rights by preceding the rights' initials with a minus sign instead of a plus sign, and modify the rights of multiple objects with one command, by specifying the object names, separated by commas, as follows:

```
RIGHTS F:\PUBLIC\WINNT -WE /NAME=HobartS,FrancisC
```

TIP   You can use the +ALL or -ALL switch to add or revoke the combination of all trustee rights, except Supervisor. The +ALL switch is thus the equivalent of +RWCEMFA (and easier to spell). You can also use the abbreviation N (without a plus or minus sign) to revoke all rights.

To remove an object from a file or directory's trustee list entirely, you use the REM switch, as shown:

```
RIGHTS F:\PUBLIC\WINNT REM /NAME=FrancisC
```

Controlling Inherited Rights Filters with *RIGHTS*   The /F switch is used to control inherited rights filters with the RIGHTS command. To display the current filter status of a file or directory, you simply specify the file or directory name with /F, as follows:

```
RIGHTS G:\DOC /F
NY-LIBRARY\VOL1:
Directories                                                         Rights Filter
- - - - - - - - - - - - - - - - - - - - - - - - - - - - - - - - - - - - - - - - - - - - - - - - - - - - -
DOC                                                                [SRWC MFA]
```

The rights shown in the resulting display are those that can be inherited by the directory or file. In the preceding example, a filter is in place that blocks the inheritance of the ERASE right from the DOC directory.

Modifying an IRF is much like assigning trustee rights, except that you don't specify an object name. To remove the ERASE filter from the DOC directory, you would use the following command:

```
RIGHTS G:\DOC +E /F
```

It can be confusing to think of using a plus sign to remove a filter, so it is better to think of this command syntax as adding or removing the capability to inherit rights. You use a plus sign to add the rights that you want to be inherited, and a minus sign to block those that you don't want inherited.

Summary

A good understanding of the access control measures that you can use to protect the NetWare file system are crucial to the efficient operation of a network. These are concepts that network administrators use every day, and a familiarity with the tools available for rights management tasks—as well as planning ahead—can make these regular jobs less of a chore. ●

Implementing Network Services

CHAPTER 16

Managing Network Files and Directories

In Chapter 15, "Understanding Directory and File Rights," you learned how to protect the files on your NetWare volumes by limiting users' access with file system trustee rights. Every file and directory maintains a list of trustees, that is, NDS objects that are allowed varying degrees of access to that file or directory.

There is, however, another feature of the NetWare file system that you can use to control access to files and directories on a global basis. NetWare adds a number of attributes to every file and directory stored on a volume beyond the four that are familiar to DOS users (READ, WRITE, SYSTEM, and HIDDEN). Many of the features of the NetWare file system are controlled by the status of these file attributes, enabling you to specify how a file or directory is stored, and how it can be accessed by users.

In this chapter, you learn about the NetWare file system, and how to take advantage of the powerful features that it provides. ■

Compression and block suballocation

NetWare includes features that enable its file system to store the maximum amount of data on a given volume.

Controlling NetWare file access with system attributes

By manipulating attributes, you can prevent users from accidentally deleting files or allow several users to share a single file.

Using the NetWare file system utilities

NetWare includes several utilities that are similar to their DOS counterparts, but are specifically designed to take advantage of the NetWare environment.

Reclaiming deleted files

NetWare automatically saves deleted files so that they can be salvaged for reuse.

Understanding the NetWare File System

Because NetWare is strictly a client/server network operating system, server data storage is a crucial element of its services. Unlike peer-to-peer networks, on which users can access the resources of any other computer, NetWare clients communicate only with NetWare servers. As a result, the file system used on a server must be able to accommodate a great many simultaneous users of completely different types.

It is not uncommon for a NetWare server to have hundreds of users connected to it, any or all of whom may be accessing files stored on a single disk drive. In addition, the drives themselves may have to accommodate the peculiarities of several different client operating systems, each having its own unique data storage requirements.

Partitions, Volumes, and Segments

NetWare, like any operating system, utilizes hard disk space by creating its own partitions on the drives installed in the file server. *Partitions* are physical divisions that are created on a hard disk drive to accommodate the needs of different file systems. When you create a partition, a specific portion of the drive's storage space is permanently allocated, and can't be used by any other partition.

Each drive can only have a single NetWare partition on it, but it can also have any number of partitions for other operating systems, as well. For example, you learned in Chapter 3, "Installing NetWare 4.11," that it is common practice to create a DOS partition on a NetWare server's boot drive, on which the core operating system files are stored. Creating other non-NetWare partitions on a NetWare server's drives is usually pointless because these partitions cannot be accessed while NetWare is running.

Unlike DOS, however, NetWare does not store data directly on partitions. Instead, NetWare creates logical structures on a server's drives, called *volumes*. Volumes are logical structures because they do not necessarily correspond to the physical configuration of the server's hard disk drives or partitions. You can create multiple volumes on a single partition, or you can combine several partitions into a single volume.

The number of volumes found on a server, their sizes, and their configuration is all controlled by the network administrator during the NetWare installation process. Each NetWare partition can contain up to eight volume *segments*. Each of these segments can be a complete volume unto itself, or it can be a part of a volume that is composed of up to 32 segments, stored on the same or different partitions.

Every NetWare partition maintains a volume definition table, redundant copies of which are always stored in sectors 32, 64, 96, and 128 of the partition. This volume table defines the size and location of the volume segments that are stored on that partition, as well as storing information on how the segments are combined with the segments on other partitions to form whole volumes. The volume definition tables of a server's NetWare partitions are read whenever volumes are mounted, and modified whenever you add, delete, or modify the size of a volume.

The flexibility that NetWare provides in the creation of volumes is rarely fully utilized due to the potential consequences. Although it is possible to create volumes that are composed of segments on up to 32 different drives, this practice is usually not recommended because the loss of one segment due to a drive failure causes the entire volume to be lost.

Once a NetWare volume is mounted, all of its segments are combined into a single logical unit containing the sum of the segments' disk space. Files stored on the volume can be located on any of its constituent segments, or split among two or more segments.

> **N O T E** Once created and mounted, the volume is a single entity, but is still subject to the limitations imposed by the hard drives on which it resides. If, for example, you create a volume that is composed of two segments, one on a brand new high-speed drive, and the other on a five-year-old relic, the performance of the entire volume will be degraded by the slower drive. ▪

Disk Allocation Blocks

NetWare volumes are divided into blocks, the size of which is specified by the installer when the volume is created. The installation default block size is determined by the volume size (see Chapter 3, "Installing NetWare 4.11"). All of a volume's blocks must be the same size, either 4, 8, 16, 32, or 64 kilobytes. When a file is stored on the volume, an appropriate number of blocks are allocated to suit the size of the file.

The selection of a block size for a volume should be made with the size of the files to be stored there in mind. A volume that is going to be used to store massive database files should have a larger block size because using fewer blocks greatly increases the speed at which the data can be accessed. This speed increase is a result of a combination of factors:

- **Fewer disk reads**—When a file is stored using 4K blocks, many more disk reads may be needed (depending on the size of the file) to access the file than when 64K blocks are used. A greater number of disk reads means more hardware overhead as the hard disk drive's heads access each separate block.

- **Less memory**—Fewer blocks means fewer FAT entries that must be read in order to access the same file.

- **Faster read-ahead**—NetWare includes a read-ahead cache feature that attempts to anticipate users' needs by reading sequential files into cache memory before they are actually requested. This practice is based on the fact that when a particular file is read from disk, there is a high probability that the very next file on the disk will be needed also. Larger blocks enable this process to read more data into memory faster.

Smaller files are better served by a smaller block size. In NetWare 3.x, the default block size for a NetWare volume was 4K, which is usually suitable for the average network. NetWare 4.x, however, selects a default block size based on the volume's storage capacity. With hard drives growing ever larger, volumes are increasing in size, too. Any volume of 500M or more is assigned a 64K default block size by NetWare.

One of the inherent problems of the division of a volume into blocks is the waste that is incurred by the storage of files. This is a problem also found in other file systems, such as the DOS FAT and NetWare 3.x. When a file is written to a volume, a sufficient number of blocks are allocated to store the data. Rarely, however, does the file fit exactly into the space provided.

There is nearly always a tail end of the file that is smaller than a block, but which must have an entire block allocated to it, nevertheless. When you add up the space wasted by the storage of hundreds or thousands of files, you find that a significant portion of your hard disk is being squandered.

Block Suballocation

The waste of disk space caused by allocating an entire block when only a few bytes might be needed was one of the original reasons for keeping volume block sizes small. 64K blocks would tend to waste far more space than 4K blocks. However, the NetWare 4.x file system addresses this problem by further breaking down a volume's blocks into 512-byte sections, through a process called *block suballocation.*

When a file only occupies a part of a block, the remaining space in that block is suballocated, allowing other files to use it. Thus, you may have many different files, each with a leftover tail end that is stored in a single block with other tail ends, rather than devoting another entire block to each file.

N O T E Block suballocation is an optional feature of the NetWare file system. By default, it is enabled when you create a volume, but you can disable this feature for any volume during the creation process, if needed. In most cases, however, there is no persuasive reason to do this. ▪

Suballocation works by dedicating disk blocks for use as *suballocation reserved blocks*, or SRBs. Different SRBs are created as needed for the storage of small (less than one block) files or fragments of different sizes. The maximum number of SRBs created at the time of the volume's creation is determined by dividing the volume's block size (in bytes) by 512 and subtracting 1. Thus, a volume with 64K blocks will have at most 127 of its blocks devoted to SRBs, a volume with 32K blocks will have 63 SRBs, and so on.

Suballocation reserved blocks are all the same size, but different SRBs are dedicated to the storage of different size fragments. When a file is stored on the volume, the data is written first to as many blocks as can be completely filled. Then, the size of the leftover data is scanned, and an SRB is located that is designed to store fragments of that size. Thus, there will be one SRB that contains all of the fragments between 1 and 512 bytes in size, another that contains the 513 to 1,024-byte fragments, and so on, in 512-byte increments. Fragments that are within 511 bytes of a full block are not suballocated.

When it becomes necessary because a particular SRB is full, a new SRB for fragments of a particular size is allocated. Fragments might also be split among two or more SRBs that are dedicated to smaller size fragments in order to ensure that all SRBs are utilized as efficiently as possible.

As files are modified and their sizes change, their fragments may be moved to different SRBs. This reorganization can result in empty spaces being left in SRBs, so a periodic cleanup routine is performed that optimizes the SRB chain by consolidating the fragments and eliminating the empty spaces. Any SRBs that are left unpopulated by this process are released back to the file system.

All of these suballocation and maintenance processes are completely invisible to users. No administrative intervention is required or allowed.

There is still a certain amount of waste possible in the suballocation system because SRBs allocate space in 512-byte units, parts of which can still be left empty, but block suballocation increases the overall storage efficiency of the NetWare file system enormously, and allows larger volume block sizes to be used in situations in which they would otherwise be completely impractical.

Part
V
Ch
16

N O T E When you upgrade a server from NetWare 3.x to 4.x, you can choose to enable block suballocation on the server volumes. When you do this, new files are suballocated as they are created, but the migrated 3.x files themselves are not suballocated until they are opened by a user. To maximize your server's storage capacity, therefore, it is usually recommended that you re-create your volumes with a larger block size and suballocation enabled during the server upgrade process. ■

File Allocation Tables

As with many file systems, the blocks that are used to store a file on a NetWare volume need not be contiguous. The blocks can be scattered about on different areas of the disk, and even on different volume segments. As a result, an index is needed that keeps track of which blocks are allocated to each file.

On a NetWare volume, as on a DOS partition, the file index is called the *file allocation table*, or FAT. Each volume has its own FAT, which is stored as a regular file, but is read into a special memory array that allocates an eight-byte structure to each block on the volume.

Each eight-byte structure contains two pieces of information about the block it represents:

- ■ **FAT Value**—The ordinal number of the block in the FAT chain of the file stored there
- ■ **FAT Link**—The number of the block containing the next part of the file

Each file, therefore, is stored in a non-consecutive series of blocks, and the FAT is used to number those blocks and define the order in which they should be accessed.

For example, suppose that a file is stored on four blocks: the 9th, 5th, 12th, and 8th blocks on that particular volume. When a user's application requests access to that file, the directory entry table points to block 9 as the file's starting point. When the structure for block 9 in the FAT is consulted, it contains a FATValue of 0, indicating that this block contains the beginning of that file, and a FATLink of 5, indicating that block five contains the next part.

N O T E   NetWare's file allocation tables always number the blocks in a FAT chain beginning at
zero.

Block 5 is then consulted, which has a FATValue of 1 and a FATlink of 12. The application,
therefore, traverses each of the structures in the FAT that represents a block on which the
desired file is stored, in the correct order. This series of structures is known as the *FAT chain*
for a given file because each entry provides a link to the next structure, until a listing of all of
the blocks containing that file's data is assembled, as shown in Figure 16.1.

FIG. 16.1
The file allocation table
is an index of a NetWare
volume's blocks and the
files that are stored
there.

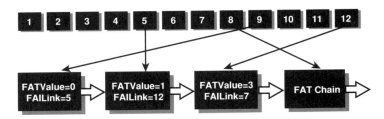

Turbo FATs   Depending on the block size chosen for the volume, a large file (that is, greater
than 64K) can consist of a great many blocks, resulting in a very long FAT chain. When such a
file is accessed frequently, NetWare creates what is known as a *turbo FAT* for that file.

Turbo FAT means that after the FAT chain is traversed to assemble the list of blocks that comprise the file, the list is stored in memory so that subsequent requests for the same file can be
satisfied much faster. If another access to the file is not requested, then the turbo FAT is deleted after a time period that defaults to 5 minutes 29.6 seconds.

N O T E   The time interval that a Turbo FAT is retained in memory can be modified using the SET
TURBO FAT RE-USE WAIT TIME command at the server console prompt. Possible
values range from 0.3 seconds to 65 minutes 54.6 seconds.

Sparse Files   The NetWare file system has another way of manipulating its FAT structures
that is used to conserve disk space that is often wasted by other file systems. Many database
applications write files that contain large amounts of blank space. This may be space that once
contained records that have since been deleted, but instead of shrinking the size of the file, the
application simply populates the space with zeroes.

Writing a file with blank space leaves a file of the same size, but with less data stored in it.
Sometimes, database files of this type can contain megabytes worth of empty space that could
be used elsewhere. NetWare will not write an empty block, and addresses this problem by
creating sparse files. A *sparse file* is a trick of the file allocation table that allows the empty
space to exist logically, without consuming physical disk space.

Sparse files are created simply by modifying the FATValue of certain FAT structures to reference blocks that do not actually exist. A particular structure in a file's FAT chain may have a
FATValue of 3. When the FATlink value is used to proceed to the next structure in the chain,

its FATValue might be 8. Even though these two structures represent only two blocks worth of actual data, four additional blocks (that is, FATValues 4 through 7) are assumed to exist logically, even though they do not exist physically.

Thus, six blocks worth of the database file are represented by two blocks of actual data. If an application attempts to access the blocks represented by FATValues 4 through 7, a string of zeroes is returned, as though the empty blocks were actually present in the database file. Meanwhile, space that would otherwise be used to store data with a null value is actually being used to store other files.

Sparse files can, therefore, make a volume seem as though it is larger than it actually is. When you are working with sparse files, you must be aware of whether or not the application that you are using is aware of them. For example, if you are backing up a volume to tape, it is preferable that the backup software copy only the actual data found in a sparse file, and not the (virtual) empty space. Otherwise, you will be filling your tape with long strings of zeroes, and wasting storage space.

In the same way, you should be aware of sparse files when you are copying data on NetWare drives. If you use the DOS COPY or XCOPY command to copy sparse files to another location on a NetWare volume, the sparse nature of the file will be lost. This is because DOS utilities are unaware of the nature of sparse files.

When a non-NetWare utility reads a sparse file into memory, the NetWare client supplies actual strings of zeroes in place of the virtual blocks. The file that is then written is no longer sparse because zeroes are occupying the disk space that was previously saved by the logical blocks of the sparse file. To copy a sparse file to another location while retaining its sparse nature, you must use the NetWare NCOPY utility with the /F (force sparse files) switch.

Directory Entry Tables

As you have seen, NetWare volumes use file allocation tables to determine where files are located on a volume, but a volume is more than a long list of files. More information is needed to create the directory structure in which the files reside.

This information is stored in the *directory entry table* (or DET), which, like the FAT, is stored as a file on each NetWare volume. However, although the FAT structures represent the volume's blocks, the DET contains an entry for each file and directory stored on the volume.

Two copies of the directory entry table are stored on every NetWare volume, each DET composed of 4K blocks, no matter what block size you have selected for the volume. Each block contains 32 entries of 128 bytes each. The directory entry table for each NetWare volume can (theoretically) contain up to 16 million entries.

The entries in the directory table contain many different types of information, including

- whether the entry represents a file or a directory,
- the file or directory name,
- the file or directory's owner, dates, and attributes,

- the name of the file or directory's parent directory,
- the location of the FAT entry representing the first block in the file,
- the location of additional name space information,
- the file or directory's trustee list.

As you might imagine, the DET performs many different functions in the NetWare file system. In fact, the DET is the repository for all of the information about files except their actual contents. As far as the directories on NetWare volumes are concerned, files exist nowhere but in the DET.

Although it may appear in the user interface as though files are stored in directories, the hierarchical arrangement of the directory tree does not correspond in any way to the physical arrangement of files on the volume. Directories are, in fact, an illusion; they are virtual structures that exist only as entries in the DET.

In order to display the contents of a directory at a workstation, the DET is scanned for all of the entries that specify that directory as their parent. These parental relationships are also used to construct the directory tree display in utilities, such as Windows Explorer.

You read in the previous section how the file allocation table is used to specify the blocks in which a particular file is stored. However, it is the DET that enables an application to locate the beginning of the FAT chain (that is, the structure with a FATValue of 0).

The directory entry table is also where the file system's security mechanisms are stored, in the form of trustee lists and file and directory attributes. You learned in Chapter 15, "Understanding Directory and File Rights," that users and groups are assigned rights to files and directories by entering them in a trustee list that is stored in the file system. Trustee information is stored in the directory table entry for each file and directory, in the form of a trustee ID list containing the unique ID numbers of the NDS objects allowed access, and a list of the trustee rights granted to each object.

Other information found in the DET includes the owner of each file and directory, as well as the three dates maintained by the file system: the creation date, the date that the file or directory was last modified, and the date that it was last accessed.

Also stored in the DET are the file and directory attributes. Attributes are single-bit flags that define the way that a file or directory is handled by the file system. You learn more about the use of file system attributes in "NetWare File Attributes" later in this chapter.

Name Spaces   The name of every file or directory on a volume is stored in the directory entry table as well. By default, NetWare uses a DOS-compatible 8.3 naming system, and this is the name that is stored in each directory entry. However, when you add additional name spaces to a volume, other names must be stored in addition to the DOS name.

NetWare supports name spaces for Macintosh, OS/2, NFS, and FTAM (File Transfer, Access, and Management) files, in addition to the long file names used by Windows 95 and Windows NT. (FTAM is an OSI-compliant standard for file transfer, including requirements for remote creation and deletion, as well as setting and reading attributes). Each name space adds different capabilities to the NetWare file system. File and directory names can be of several different lengths, and various other properties and attributes may be included as well.

All of this additional file information cannot be stored in a single standard directory table entry. Name space information is therefore stored in additional directory entries, separate from those for the files and directories themselves.

Each name space that is added to a volume requires an additional directory entry for every file and directory stored on that volume. These additional entries are stored contiguously with the primary directory entry whenever possible, so that it is only necessary to read a single DET block to access all of the entries representing a single file. However, entries may not be contiguous in every situation, so the primary entry contains a list of the locations where the related entries can be found.

Adding a single extra name space, therefore, effectively doubles the size of the directory entry table for a volume. Adding two name spaces triples its size, and so forth. This affects the file system in several ways. First, the larger directory entry table requires more storage space. The additional disk space required is usually not extensive, but if you have many small files on a volume, the effect can be noticeable. This increased storage requirement also makes it impossible to add name spaces to a volume that is completely full.

Second, and more significant, the inclusion of additional name spaces reduces the number of directory entries that can be cached in server memory. NetWare uses a most recently used (MRU) algorithm to store selected parts of the DET in memory. When you add a name space, the number of DET entries in these directory cache buffers remains the same, but only half as many files are represented. This number of files is further reduced with each additional name space. A smaller number of cached files obviously means more frequent disk accesses and slower I/O system performance.

Tuning the NetWare Directory Cache Buffers Parameters

NetWare uses two SET commands to control the number of directory cache buffers allocated in server memory. If your server requires many additional name spaces or is subject to periods of heavy usage, you may have to modify these parameters to achieve optimum file system performance.

The two commands are SET MAXIMUM DIRECTORY CACHE BUFFERS and SET MINIMUM DIRECTORY CACHE BUFFERS. The default settings for these parameters are 500 and 20, respectively. The MAXIMUM can be set to any value from 20 to 20,000, and the MINIMUM from 10 to 8,000.

These SET parameters define the upper and lower limits of how many DET blocks can be cached in server memory. When the server is started, the number of blocks specified in the MINIMUM setting is immediately allocated from available memory. Additional blocks are then allocated as usage dictates, until the maximum is achieved.

When the number of currently allocated buffers (as viewed in MONITOR's General Information screen) reaches the maximum allowable, it may be necessary to increase the MAXIMUM setting to allocate additional memory to DET buffering. It is also beneficial to note the rate at which the number of allocated buffers increases. If, when the server is restarted, the number of allocated buffers rises

continues

continued

quickly, then raising the MINIMUM setting will minimize the delays incurred as additional buffers are allocated by the operating system. The MAXIMUM setting should be set high enough so that normal server usage does not drive the number of allocated buffers to the maximum.

Of course, this practice assumes that there is a sufficient amount of memory installed in the server to support the creation of additional buffers. Memory dedicated to DET caching is permanently allocated from the file cache buffer pool. However, the memory requirements for DET buffers are modest. Adding 100 directory cache buffers requires only 400K of memory and adds 3,200 directory entries to the cache.

The impact on DET caching is the primary reason that the practice followed by some administrators of installing all of the available name spaces to every NetWare volume is strongly discouraged. In fact, name space allocation is one of the best reasons to create multiple volumes out of a single partition—installing one name space type per volume—when otherwise a single volume would suffice.

N O T E Additional name spaces can be added to a NetWare volume at any time, by loading the appropriate NAM module and executing the ADD NAME SPACE command at the server console. Name spaces can only be removed, however, by dismounting the volume and using the VREPAIR utility. Removing a name space with VREPAIR causes all additional directory entries and extended directory space associated with that name space type to be lost. In the case of MAC files, for example, this would render the files unusable to Macintosh users.

If you have various users that will be storing files using different name spaces, it is often a better idea to create smaller volumes, each with one additional name space, rather than one big volume with all of the required name spaces. This maximizes the number of directory entries that can be maintained in the cache for that volume at any one time.

Extended Directory Space   Even though a new name space provides additional directory entries, sometimes the amount of space provided is not sufficient to store all of the required information for a different file system. Just the name of an OS/2 file can be up to 255 characters, which is almost twice the size of a 128-byte directory entry, and the resource forks associated with Macintosh files can be longer. The file system, therefore, allocates an extended directory space for the storage of this additional information.

The extended directory space takes the form of a single system file that is separate from the directory entry table itself. Like the DET, it is broken up into 128-byte segments, but these extended directory entries are known as *extants*, in this case. A directory table entry can utilize as many extants as it needs to store whatever information cannot fit into a standard table entry.

The extended directory space file has a FAT chain, like any other file, with a FAT entry representing each extant. DET entries that require additional storage space contain a reference to the first extant that contains their data. Once the first extant is located, the standard FAT chain is used to locate any additional extants associated with that file or directory.

Transaction Tracking System

The NetWare file system includes a fault tolerance feature that is designed to protect database and other record-based files from corruption, when a hardware or software failure interrupts a file write. The *Transaction Tracking System* (or TTS) makes copies of certain types of database files to a special TTS backup area before any changes are applied to them. Then the modification of the original file, also called a transaction, is allowed to proceed.

If the transaction is completed normally, an additional record is written to the backup area indicating this. If the file modification process is interrupted for any reason, typically due to a server crash or a power failure, then the transaction is backed out when the server is rebooted.

During the boot sequence, the server detects the incomplete transaction by scanning the TTS records on the disk. When a transaction is found that lacks the record indicating its completion, then the backup copy of the original file is used to overwrite the one in which the transaction was interrupted. Transactions are therefore fully completed, or not applied at all.

Some database systems have their own transaction back-out capabilities built in, which should be noted in the product documentation. But for those that don't, NetWare's TTS can provide them with protection against data corruption, as long as the database application allocates record locks that the system can use to track the beginnings and ends of transactions.

Btrieve databases, for example, can be protected in this way. To implement TTS protection for specific files, you must apply the Transactional (T) attribute to the files in question, using FLAG, or another NetWare utility.

The most important database protected by the TTS, however, is that which holds the Novell Directory Services information for the entire network. It is this automatic protection that makes TTS a required element of the NetWare file system, and is the primary reason why TTS is automatically installed with NetWare.

Understanding File System Attributes

The attributes that are stored in the directory table entries for every file and directory on a NetWare volume perform many different functions, not the least of which is security. When properly applied, attributes can be used to prevent files from being viewed, modified, or deleted—either accidentally or deliberately.

Attributes, as mentioned earlier, are one-byte flags that can be switched on and off, some of them manually by users or administrators, and others automatically by NetWare system processes. You may be familiar with the basic attributes, such as Read, Write, System, and Hidden, which are like those used in DOS, but NetWare adds many others.

The effect of an attribute on a file or directory is global, that is, it affects all users regardless of their file system or NDS access rights. If the application of an attribute prevents a file from being used in a particular way, the only way to circumvent the effect is to remove the attribute. A user must have the Modify (or Supervisor) right to a file or directory in order to change its attributes. Controlling the Modify right is the way in which attributes can be used to enforce security.

In most cases, attributes are used as a fail-safe mechanism to prevent the accidental modification or deletion of files or directories, particularly by administrators with Supervisor rights to the file system. Although these users have the rights to manipulate files, a Read Only attribute adds an extra step to the process that forces them to think twice before overwriting or deleting them.

NetWare File Attributes

The NetWare file attributes corresponding to the functions that can be performed by DOS attributes are as follows:

- **Read Only** (Ro)—Allows a file to be opened and read, but prevents it from being modified or deleted (automatically includes the Rename Inhibit and Delete Inhibit attributes).
- **Read Write** (Rw)—Allows a file to be both read and written to.
- **Hidden** (H)—prevents a file from being seen in the directory listings generated by most file system utilities. Also prevents a file from being copied or deleted. Some utilities, however, such as Windows 95 Explorer, are capable of displaying hidden files. This attribute is typically set by system processes, and not by users.
- **System** (Sy)—Indicates that the file is part of the core operating system, and prevents a file from being copied, deleted, or displayed by most file system utilities. This attribute is typically set by system processes, and not by users.
- **Archive** (A)—Used to track the files that have been modified since their last backup. Typically, a backup operation will clear all of the A attributes for files as they are copied to tape. After that, any processes that cause files to be modified apply the A attribute to those files. Then, a later backup process can save time and tape by copying only the files with an A attribute.

The following attributes are those that are unique to the NetWare file system:

- **Copy Inhibit** (Ci)—Prevents Macintosh files from being copied. Has no effect on other file types. This is the only NetWare attribute dedicated to a specific file system. It is designed to support the Macintosh feature that prevents users from copying selected files.
- **Delete Inhibit** (Di)—Prevents files from being deleted or overwritten.
- **Don't Compress** (Dc)—Prevents the file from being compressed by the NetWare compression subsystem; overrides any settings applied to the volume or the directory in which the file is stored.
- **Don't Migrate** (Dm)—Prevents the file from being migrated to a secondary storage medium by the NetWare Data Migration system; overrides any settings applied to the volume or the directory in which the file is stored.
- **Don't Suballocate** (Ds)—Prevents the file from being stored using suballocated blocks to conserve disk space, whatever suballocation settings may be applied to the volume on

which the file is stored. For files that are frequently modified (such as database files), use of this attribute can save on the processing overhead incurred by repeated block suballocations.

- **Execute Only** (X)—Allows a file to be read, but prevents it from being copied or overwritten. Designed to protect program files from unauthorized copying by users, this attribute can only be applied to EXE and COM files, and cannot be removed.

> **CAUTION**
>
> Many of today's applications will not function properly with the Execute Only (X) attribute applied to them. Be sure to test applications carefully and retain a backup copy before using the X attribute in a production environment.

- **Immediate Compress** (Ic)—Causes a file to be compressed during the next daily check by the operating system, regardless of the file's date last accessed.
- **Purge** (P)—Causes a file to be purged immediately when it is deleted, overriding all other compression-related settings.
- **Rename Inhibit** (Ri)—Prevents a file from being renamed.
- **Shareable** (Sh)—Enables multiple users to access a file simultaneously.
- **Transactional** (T)—Causes a file to be protected by NetWare's Transactional Tracking System (TTS).

In addition, NetWare provides the following attributes that are intended only as indicators of a file's current status. These attributes cannot be manually applied or removed by any user. They are wholly controlled by the NetWare file system.

- **Indexed** (I)—Indicates that a file has been indexed for faster disk access.
- **Can't Compress** (Cc)—Indicates that a file cannot successfully be compressed by the NetWare compression subsystem.
- **Compressed** (Co)—Indicates that a file is currently being stored in a compressed state.
- **Migrated** (M)—Indicates that a file has been migrated to a secondary storage medium by the NetWare Data Migration system.

For more information on the attributes used to control NetWare compression, see "Setting Compression Attributes" later in this chapter. For more information on the NetWare Data Migration system, see Chapter 18, "Networking Mass Storage."

NetWare Directory Attributes

You can apply attributes to directories on NetWare volumes, as well as to files. The attributes that are applied to a directory are automatically inherited by all of the files contained in that directory.

The following attributes can be applied to directories. The functions of the attributes are the same as when they are applied to files:

- Delete Inhibit (Di)
- Don't Compress (Dc)
- Don't Migrate (Dm)
- Hidden (H)
- Immediate Compress (Ic)
- Purge (P)
- Rename Inhibit (Ri)
- System (Sy)

Using FLAG to Control NetWare Attributes

For users with any experience at all with the DOS command line, you will probably find that NetWare's FLAG program is the fastest way to modify file and directory attributes. The basic syntax of FLAG is as follows:

```
FLAG pathname [+/-] attribute(s) option(s)
```

Running FLAG with no parameters, or with only a path name, displays the attributes that are currently assigned, as follows:

```
Files                   DOS Attr NetWare Attr          Status Owner          Mode
ADDICON.EXE             [Ro----] [---ShDi--Ri------]          .NY-LIBRARY... 0
APLASER2.PDF            [Ro----] [---ShDi--Ri------] Co       .NY-LIBRARY... N/A
APPIMAGE.PDF            [Rw----] [----------------]           .NY-LIBRARY... N/A
APPLW2FG.PDF            [Ro----] [---ShDi--Ri------] Co       .NY-LIBRARY... N/A
NWAPP32.DLL             [Rw----] [----------------] Co        N/A            N/A
AUDIT3X.DLL             [Ro----] [---ShDi--Ri------] Co       .NY-LIBRARY... N/A
B5ET_AIO.OVL            [Ro----] [-----Di--Ri------] Co       .NY-LIBRARY... N/A
```

To modify the attributes of a file or directory, specify an operator (that is, a plus or a minus), and replace the *attribute* variable with one or more of the attribute abbreviations listed earlier, with spaces between multiple entries. You can also use one of the following alternatives in place of the operator and attribute:

- ALL—When applied to files, it causes the A, Ci, Di, H, Ic, P, Ri, Ro, Sh, Sy, and T attributes to be set. When applied to directories, it causes Di, H, Ic, P, Ri, and Sy to be set.
- N (Normal)—When applied to files, it causes the Rw attribute to be set and all others removed. When applied to directories, it causes all attributes to be removed.

Some of the possible options for FLAG commands are as follows:

- /D displays detailed information about the specified files or directories, as follows:
  ```
  File:  NY-LIBRARY\SYS:PUBLIC\ADDICON.EXE
  DOS Attributes:  Read-Only
  NetWare Attributes:  Shareable,Delete-Inhibit,Rename-Inhibit
  File Status: File-Compressed
  ```

```
Owner:  .NY-LIBRARY.CorpNet
Search mode:  0 - The executable file will look for instructions in the
➥NET.CFG file.
```

- ◼ /DO views or modifies the attributes of the directories in the specified path only. It ignores the files.

- ◼ /FO views or modifies the attributes of the files in the specified path only. It ignores the directories.

- ◼ /S views or modifies the attributes of the files and directories in the specified path, as well as in all subdirectories of that path.

Using attributes to protect your files is largely a matter of common sense. Application files, or the directories in which they reside, and other types of files that are not modified during normal use, are best flagged Read Only and Shareable.

Compression, migration, and block suballocation are all mechanisms that can save disk space, but do so at the expense of access time and processor utilization. If you have enabled any of these features on your volumes, you can improve the speed at which selected files are delivered to client workstations by disabling these file mechanisms with the Dc, Dm, and Ds attributes.

Attributes applied to individual files always take precedence over those applied to directories. This way, you can apply the Read Only attribute to a directory, and then flag selected files in that directory as Read Write, or the reverse, whichever is most convenient.

Controlling Attributes with Other Applications

In addition to FLAG, there are many other utilities that you can use to control NetWare attributes. When you choose Manage Files and Directories from FILER's Available options menu and then choose to View/Set Information for a file or directory, the Information screen presented displays the attributes that are currently set and enables you to change them (see Figure 16.2).

FIG. 16.2
DOS users can modify file and directory attributes using FILER.

```
Command Prompt - filer                                         _ □ X
FILER  4.25                              Monday  February  24, 1997  2:29am
Context: CORPNET
Volume object: NY-LIBRARY_SYS
Current path: NY-LIBRARY\SYS:PUBLIC
┌──────────────────── Information for file AUDITCON.EXE ────────────────────┐
│ Attributes:  [Ro────]  [──ShDi──Ri──────]   Status:  ───                   │
│ Owner: NY-LIBRARY.CORPNET                                                 │
│ Inherited rights filter: [SRWCEMFA]                                       │
│ Trustees: ↓ <empty>                                                       │
│ Current effective rights: [SRWCEMFA]                                      │
│ Owning name space: DOS                                                    │
│ File size: 604340 bytes                                                   │
│ EA size: 0 bytes                                                          │
│                                                                           │
│ Creation date: 12/22/1996                                                 │
│ Last accessed date: 2/23/1997                                             │
│ Last archived date: 2/15/1997                                             │
│ Last modified date: 7/18/1996                                             │
└───────────────────────────────────────────────────────────────────────────┘
These are the current file attributes.  Press <Enter> to modify these
attributes.
Enter=Select   Esc=Escape                                          F1=Help
```

There are also GUI attribute management alternatives to FILER. The Details dialog box for every volume, directory, and file in NetWare Administrator contains an Attributes panel like that shown in Figure 16.3. This screen enables you to set and clear attributes using check boxes, and also displays the current attributes for the file or directory, including the status-only attributes, that cannot be manually changed. In addition, attributes that do not apply to the selected file or directory (because a particular file system feature is not enabled for that volume) are grayed out.

FIG. 16.3

Windows users can view and set file and directory attributes with NetWare Administrator.

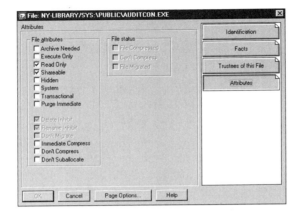

The final, and perhaps the most convenient method of setting attributes is to use Windows' own utilities. When you install one of the new IntranetWare clients to your Windows 3.1, Windows 95, and Windows NT machine, additional screens are added to the Properties dialog boxes of the File Manager, Network Neighborhood, and Explorer applications.

When you select a file or directory in any of these applications, and view its properties, you find a panel like that shown in Figure 16.4, in which you can view and modify attributes using check boxes, as with NetWare Administrator.

FIG. 16.4

The new breed of NetWare clients enable you to modify file and directory attributes through the standard operating system interface.

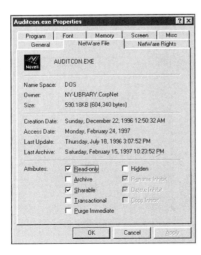

Understanding NetWare Compression

Software-based file compression programs, such as PKZIP, have been employed for many years, mostly by users of bulletin board systems and other online services. Files are manually compressed by the user before transmission over a telephone line, and must be decompressed before they can be used.

In recent years, automatic compression systems have been introduced into operating systems. They function by creating a single file on the computer's hard drive, which actually contains all of the drive's files and directories in their compressed form.

Beginning with version 4.0, NetWare has incorporated compression into its file system, but does so in a way that allows the network administrator greater control over which files are compressed, and when. This is unlike other drive compression technologies, such as Stacker and Double Space, that force you to keep all of the files on a drive compressed at all times.

By default, NetWare enables compression on all volumes as they are created. In most cases, it will not be necessary to modify the parameters that control the compression process, but you can do so using SET commands, if necessary. You can also disable the server compression process entirely, so that no additional files are ever compressed.

However, once you create a volume with compression, there is no way to completely remove it, except to delete and re-create the volume. This, of course, is because compression makes it possible to store more data than would fit on the volume uncompressed.

Understanding Server Compression

NetWare decompresses files in real time. That is, when a user requests access to a file on a NetWare volume that is currently compressed, it is immediately decompressed into memory and delivered to the user. However, NetWare does not compress files in real time. Instead, the server compression routines run at night, when file server usage is typically light.

NetWare uses the last access date that is stored with each file to determine which files should be compressed. This date represents the last time that the file was either read or written to by any user. Each night at midnight, the server begins scanning its volumes, and any file with a date last accessed that is more than fourteen days old is queued for compression.

NetWare only compresses files when a significant amount of disk space can be reclaimed as a result of the compression. Different file types compress at different rates, and some (especially those that already are compressed, such as ZIP files) are not worth the effort required to compress them again.

As each file in the compression queue is processed, the server creates a temporary file in the disk cache and determines what the size of the compressed file will be. If the compressed version of the file saves at least 20 percent of the original's disk space, then the compression process is allowed to proceed.

N O T E   Software compression algorithms always operate using a tradeoff of compression speed versus file size. Achieving the best possible compression rate takes a significantly longer period of processing time. Because NetWare performs its compression tasks during off hours and schedules them as low priority threads, it uses the maximum compression algorithm to achieve the smallest possible file size. ▨

Once the compressed version of a file is created in temporary space and checked for any errors that may have occurred during the compression process, it is carefully swapped with the original file in such a way as to maximize the safety of the operation. If the server should suffer a crash or a power outage during the swap, the original file is left in place.

Other checks are performed during the compression sequence in order to ensure the safety of the operation. One particularly important factor is the amount of free disk space on the volume. The compression procedure requires the use of temporary files, and will not proceed when there is not sufficient space to store those files.

Understanding Server Decompression

Another measure of the NetWare compression system's flexibility is the way that compressed files are treated when they are accessed by users. Unlike compression systems designed for workstation operating systems—which leave all of the files on a disk in a compressed state all of the time—NetWare's compression is designed to operate only on the files that are less frequently used. This is because decompression always introduces an additional delay to file system access, and is unnecessary when applied to files that are regularly accessed by users.

N O T E   NetWare minimizes the delay incurred by the decompression process by sending the file to the requesting client in 4K chunks as the decompression process proceeds. This method is faster than waiting for the entire file to be decompressed before it is sent to the user. ▨

When a compressed file on a NetWare volume is accessed once, it is left on the disk in its compressed state, by default. If the file is accessed a second time within the same 14-day period that determines its candidacy for compression, then the file is written to disk in its decompressed form. The 14-day clock then begins running again to determine if the file should be recompressed.

N O T E   Compressed files that have been modified during user access are always written to disk uncompressed, and are not compressed again until the specified interval of no access has elapsed. ▨

Modifying Compression Parameters

Nearly all of the actions and intervals involved in the NetWare compression subsystem described in the preceding sections can be modified by the use of SET commands at the server console prompt, or by altering the same parameters using the SERVMAN or MONITOR utility.

The following are all of the commands (along with their functions) that affect the operation of the compression subsystem:

- SET ENABLE FILE COMPRESSION

  Default: ON

  Purpose: When set to OFF, disables the compression engine, preventing any new files from being compressed. Candidates for compression are queued until this setting is re-enabled. Does not affect decompression or access to already compressed files.

- SET MINIMUM COMPRESSION PERCENTAGE GAIN

  Default: 20 percent

  Purpose: Specifies the percentage that a file's size must be reduced in order for compression to take place. Possible values are 0 to 50 percent.

- SET COMPRESSION DAILY CHECK STARTING HOUR

  Default: 0

  Purpose: Specifies the time of day that compression activities are to begin (in 24-hour military time, where 0=midnight).

- SET COMPRESSION DAILY CHECK STOP HOUR

  Default: 6

  Purpose: Specifies the time of day that compression activities are to cease. Specifying the same value as the START HOUR causes compression activities to begin at the specified time, and continue until completed.

- SET DAYS UNTOUCHED BEFORE COMPRESSION

  Default: 14

  Purpose: Specifies the number of days that a file must not be accessed before it is queued for compression. Possible values are 0 to 100,000.

- SET CONVERT COMPRESSED TO UNCOMPRESSED OPTION

  Default: 1

  Purpose: Specifies the way in which the server stores a compressed file after it is accessed. Possible values are:

  0 = Always store the file in its compressed form.

  1 = Store the file compressed after the first access; store it uncompressed after two accesses within the DAYS UNTOUCHED BEFORE COMPRESSION period.

  2 = Always store the file in its uncompressed form.

■ SET DELETED FILES COMPRESSION OPTION

Default: 1

Purpose: Specifies the way that the server should compress files that have been deleted, but not purged. Possible values are:

0 = Never compress deleted files.

1 = Compress deleted files during the next scheduled daily check period.

2 = Compress deleted files immediately.

■ SET MAXIMUM CONCURRENT COMPRESSIONS

Default: 2

Purpose: Specifies how many compression operations the server can perform at one time (on different volumes). Increasing the value of this setting causes additional processor utilization during the daily check period. Possible values are 1 to 8.

■ SET UNCOMPRESS PERCENT DISK SPACE FREE TO ALLOW COMMIT

Default: 10 percent

Purpose: The percentage of a volume's disk space that must be free in order to allow a file to be stored in its uncompressed form.

■ SET UNCOMPRESS FREE SPACE WARNING

Default: 31 min., 18.5 sec.

Purpose: Specifies the time interval between server console warnings that a volume's free disk space has fallen beneath the UNCOMPRESS PERCENT DISK SPACE FREE TO ALLOW COMMIT percentage. Possible values are 0 (which disables the warning messages entirely) to 29 days, 15 hours, 50 minutes, 3.8 seconds.

There is also another undocumented SET command that causes an additional compression screen to be displayed on the server console. Designed primarily for debugging purposes, issuing the SET COMPRESS SCREEN = ON command displays a screen that lists each file as it is compressed along with other information, such as the compressed and uncompressed file sizes, the compression ratio, and other debugging information. The layout of the display is as follows (from left to right):

■ **File Name**—The name of the file being processed. A preceding asterisk indicates that the file is being decompressed; all others are being compressed.

■ **Compression Ratio**—The percentage that the file's size is being reduced by compression.

■ **Bytes/Second In**—The rate at which data is processed into the compression engine.

■ **Bytes/Second Out**—The rate at which data is processed out of the compression engine.

■ **Compressed Size**—The size (in bytes) of the file after compression.

■ **Original Size**—The size (in bytes) of the file before compression.

■ **Debugging Flags**—Five one-byte flags used to provide information to Novell programmers regarding the compression process.

Setting Compression Attributes

Although compression activities can be globally controlled by the network administrator using the SET parameters described in the previous section, file and directory attributes can be manipulated by users or administrators to control the compression of individual files and directories. These attributes are modified using the FLAG command at the DOS command prompt, or by using any of the other utilities described in the "Understanding File System Attributes" section earlier in this chapter.

Following are file and directory attributes related to the compression process and descriptions of their uses:

- **File Compressed** (Co)—Indicates that the file or directory is currently in a compressed state. (This attribute is for informational purposes only; it cannot be altered by the user.)
- **Cannot Compress** (Cc)—Indicates that previous attempts to compress the file have failed, due either to the file having been already compressed by another system, to its small size, or to the random nature of its data. The file must be modified in order for further attempts to compress it. (This attribute is for informational purposes only; it cannot be altered by the user.)
- **Immediate Compress** (Ic)—Indicates that the file should be compressed during the next daily check period, regardless of its last accessed date. When applied to a directory, indicates that all of the files in the directory should be compressed during the next daily check period (unless the directory attribute is overridden by a conflicting file attribute, such as Dc or Cc).
- **Do Not Compress** (Dc)—Indicates that a file should never be compressed. If the file is already compressed, it will not be decompressed until the next time that it is accessed. When applied to a directory, indicates that all of the files in the directory should never be compressed (unless the directory attribute is overridden by a conflicting Ic file attribute).

Applying the Ic or Dc attribute to a directory, causes the same attribute to be applied to each of the files in that directory (unless a file already possesses a conflicting attribute). However, a directory attribute has no effect on files that are later copied into the directory.

For example, copying a file with no compression attributes into an Ic directory will not cause the file to be given the Ic attribute. However, when a file inherits a compression attribute from its parent directory, the attribute remains in place, even when the file is copied to another directory.

Copying Compressed Files   If, for example, you are copying files from one compressed NetWare volume to another, it makes no sense to decompress them just to perform the copy. If you use NetWare's NCOPY utility with the /R (retain compression) switch, files are copied to their destination fully compressed. This reduces the copy time, not only because the decompression step is avoided, but also because there is less data actually being transferred.

The NCOPY /R switch operates only when you are copying files between compressed volumes. However, you can copy compressed files to destinations that do not support compression by using NCOPY with the /RU (retain uncompressed) switch. These destinations can be NetWare volumes that do not have compression enabled, workstation hard drives, or even floppy disks or other removable media.

Uses for the retain uncompressed copy capability are relatively rare because the files must be copied to a NetWare volume with compression enabled before they can be used again, but if you must copy files from one NetWare network to another using a modem connection or floppy disks, this method can save you the trouble of compressing the files manually using a third-party utility.

Backing Up Compressed Files   Perhaps the most important situation in which direct access to compressed files is needed is when you are backing up your NetWare volumes. Backing up files in their compressed state is faster than backups of uncompressed files because you elimi-nate the decompression process from the equation, and because less data is being transferred from the hard disk drive to the tape drive (or other backup device).

Backing up compressed files does not necessarily mean that less tape will be used, though. Most backup systems already have the capability to perform some kind of data compression, realized either in the backup software, or in the tape drive hardware. Data can only be com-pressed once. Running compressed files through a second compression process will not result in any appreciable savings in size.

More important than backup speed and tape efficiency, however, is the fact that files that are backed up to tape in their decompressed state will also be restored as decompressed files. If you find yourself in a disaster recovery situation where you must restore entire volumes from tape, it is very likely that all the data will not fit in the volume in its uncompressed state.

To back up NetWare volumes in their compressed state, you must use a backup software pack-age that supports the Novell Storage Management Services (SMS) standards, and you must load the appropriate target service agent (that is, TSA411.NLM) on the server before the backup commences. For more information on Storage Management Services, see Chapter 18, "Networking Mass Storage."

Reclaiming Deleted Files

When you delete a file from a NetWare volume, it is not erased from the disk. Instead, its direc-tory entries are moved to a special area of the directory entry table that is set aside for the storage of deleted files. This area consists of standard 4K DET blocks that contain only the directory entries of deleted files, including the additional entries created by name spaces.

When the directory entries for deleted files are copied to their new location, two new fields are added, containing the date and time that files were deleted, and the names of the users who deleted them.

The reason why directory entries are moved in this manner is so that users can reclaim the files that have been deleted. In NetWare, this is known as salvaging files, after the SALVAGE utility that was included with NetWare 3.x. In NetWare 4.x, you use NetWare Administrator or the FILER utility to salvage files, instead.

The capability to salvage NetWare files is based on the amount of free disk space available on the volumes. Deleted files are retained on disk until all of the free space on a volume (except for 1/32 of the volume's size) has been filled with deleted files, and additional new data is written to the disk. As the free disk space on the volume is filled, the files with the oldest date of deletion are purged, meaning that the actual file data itself is overwritten. Once they are purged, files cannot be reclaimed.

There are several SET parameters that control the purging of deleted files in the file system. If you issue the SET IMMEDIATE PURGE OF DELETED FILES = ON command at the server console prompt, all files are purged as soon as they are deleted. This makes it impossible to salvage any deleted files.

The SET MINIMUM FILE DELETE WAIT TIME command specifies a time period, from 0 seconds to 7 days, during which deleted files cannot be automatically purged to clear disk space for the storage of new data. The default value is 65.9 seconds. Clients or services will receive a "disk full" message if no other storage space is available.

NetWare tries to keep 1/32 of a volume's space empty for the addition of new files. Normally, it will purge deleted files as needed to keep this space free. The SET FILE DELETE WAIT TIME command defines a period during which deleted files will not be purged to maintain free disk space. Files will still be purged to make room for newly added files, however. Users will not receive a "disk full" message as a consequence of this setting. Possible values are 0 seconds to 7 days, and the default setting is 5 minutes 29.6 seconds.

You can also control the capability to purge individual files through the use of the Purge attribute. When you use NetWare Administrator, FILER, or another utility to assign the Purge attribute to files, they are immediately purged when the files are deleted.

It is also possible to manually purge the deleted files in a specific directory, or on an entire volume, by running the NetWare PURGE utility from the DOS command line.

Deleted files are hidden to ordinary file system utilities, even those that can display files and directories that possess the Hidden (H) attribute. You must use NetWare Administrator or FILER to salvage deleted files.

N O T E   When salvaging and purging deleted files, you must have the same rights that you would need for any other normal file activity. You must have the Create right to any deleted file that you intend to salvage, and the Erase right to any file you intend to purge. If the file's parent directory has also been deleted, then you must have the Supervisor right in order to salvage it. ▪

Salvaging and Purging Files with NetWare Administrator

To salvage or purge files, you first browse with NetWare Administrator to the volume and directory in which the files resided when they were deleted. When you choose Tools, Salvage, you see a dialog box like that shown in Figure 16.5.

FIG. 16.5
With NetWare Administrator, you can salvage files that have been deleted from a NetWare volume.

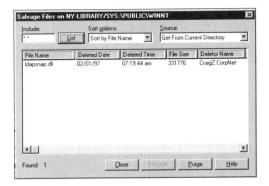

When you first see the Salvage dialog box, no files are listed, but you can salvage or purge all of the deleted files found in the selected directory simply by clicking the appropriate button. If you want to salvage or purge selected files, you must first scan the directory entry table by clicking the List button.

By default, all of the salvageable files found in the selected directory are displayed as a result of the *.* in the Include field. You can replace this entry with another file specification, in order to display only selected files.

If you want to display the deleted files that resided in directories that have also been deleted, change the Source selector to Get From Deleted Directories. You can also change the Sort Options for the display, at any time before or after you list files.

Once the list is displayed, you can select the files that you want to salvage or purge, and click the Salvage or Purge button to begin the operation. Salvaged files are returned to the directory from which they were deleted. If this directory no longer exists, the files are placed in DELETED.SAV, a hidden directory that is created at the root of every NetWare volume for this purpose.

Salvaging and Purging Files with FILER

You can also use FILER to salvage and purge files in the DOS environment. As with NetWare Administrator, you must first navigate to the directory in which the files you want to salvage or purge were contained. Then, when you select Salvage Deleted Files from the FILER Available Options menu, you are given the option to list the files in the selected directory or those from deleted directories. From these lists, you can select the files to be salvaged using the standard keystrokes of the C-worthy interface.

In the same way, selecting Purge Deleted Files from the Available Options menu allows you to enter a filespec that will be used to purge deleted files in the current directory or in the current directory plus all of its subdirectories.

Using NetWare File System Utilities

NetWare includes file management utilities that are designed to accommodate the advanced features of the NetWare file system. One of the main purposes of this chapter is to make you aware of the mechanisms that operate behind the scenes on NetWare volumes. In most cases, it is not necessary to modify the defaults used by NetWare in the creation of volumes and the storage of files, but it can be important to know that these mechanisms exist, and how they can affect the performance of everyday tasks.

Using NCOPY

NCOPY is, in many ways, similar to the DOS XCOPY utility. Some of the same command-line switches can be used to copy entire subdirectory trees to another location. NCOPY is optimized for use with NetWare and adds a measure of efficiency when copying files between NetWare volumes that XCOPY cannot. The syntax for NCOPY is as follows:

```
NCOPY source destination [options]
```

The *source* variable will consist of a filespec, with or without a path, and the *destination* will usually be a path, but may also contain a filespec as well, in order to rename the files. The standard DOS wild cards (the question mark and the asterisk) can be used in both sources and destinations.

Normally, when you copy files from one network drive to another using a workstation utility, the data must be transferred over the network from the source drive to the memory of the workstation executing the program. Then the data is copied from workstation memory to the destination drive.

NCOPY enables you to "eliminate the middleman" in this operation, as long as both the source and the destination drives are NetWare volumes. In this situation, NCOPY will cause the specified files to be copied directly from one NetWare volume to the other, with no interim stop at the workstation. This reduces the network traffic generated by the operation by one half, and eliminates processing and I/O delays imposed by the workstation.

NCOPY also includes optional switches that enable you to control the way the program treats elements that are unique to the NetWare file system, such as sparse files, compressed files, and name spaces. The NCOPY options are as follows:

- /A causes only the files with the archive attribute to be copied, with the attribute left intact.

- /M causes only the files with the archive attribute to be copied, clearing the attribute from the source files in the process.

- /C causes files to be copied in DOS mode, removing all NetWare attribute and name space information. The use of this option on certain file types (especially Macintosh files) can render them unusable on their native platform.

- /F causes sparse files to be copied (between NetWare drives) with their virtual FAT entries intact. Copying sparse files without this option will result in a file that has its empty space populated with zeroes, occupying the full amount of disk space that its size indicates.

- /I causes the user to be notified when attribute or name space information cannot be copied to the destination, either because it is not a NetWare drive or because the required name space is not present.

- /R causes compressed files to be copied to the destination in their compressed form, but only if the destination is a NetWare drive with compression enabled.

- /R/U causes compressed files to be copied to the destination in their compressed form, even when the destination drive does not support NetWare compression.

- /S causes files to be copied from all subdirectories, as well as from the specified source directory itself, re-creating the subdirectory tree at the destination.

- /S/E causes the entire specified subdirectory tree to be copied to the destination, including all files and empty, as well as populated, directories.

N O T E   NetWare 4.11 includes a new version of the NCOPY utility (version 4.14), which is the only version that should be used on NetWare 4.11 volumes. If you have servers on your network running previous versions of NetWare, you should replace their NCOPY.EXE files with the 4.14 version, found in the SYS:PUBLIC directory of your 4.11 server.

Using VREPAIR

VREPAIR is a server console utility that you use to diagnose and repair problems on NetWare volumes. It is a vital part of any NetWare administrator's toolkit, and should always be available in case of emergencies.

VREPAIR.NLM is found in the SYS:SYSTEM directory of every NetWare server, but this is obviously not the best place to store it. If you have a problem that prevents you from mounting SYS, then you cannot load VREPAIR from that directory. Therefore, the NetWare installation program always places a copy of VREPAIR on the server's DOS partition.

You can load modules from the DOS partition at the server console just as you would those on NetWare volumes. By default, the LOAD C:\NWSERVER\VREPAIR command will launch the utility. If SYS is available, you can load VREPAIR with the standard LOAD VREPAIR command, and use it to repair other volumes on the server.

NetWare volumes must be dismounted before they can be addressed by the VREPAIR utility. In fact, you can even run the program from the SYS volume, then issue the DISMOUNT SYS command and continue to use the program from memory.

Setting VREPAIR Options   There are several options that control how VREPAIR performs the volume repair process. When you choose the Set VREPAIR Options screen from the program's main menu, you see the following display of the current option settings, and the alternatives:

```
Current VRepair Configuration:
    Quit if a required VRepair name space support NLM is not loaded.
    Write only changed directory and FAT entries out to disk.
    Write changes immediately to disk.
    Retain deleted files.
Options:
    1. Remove name space support from the volume
    2. Write all directory and FAT entries out to disk
    3. Keep changes in memory for later update
    4. Purge all deleted files
    5. Return to Main Menu

    Enter your choice: 5
```

When it repairs volumes with additional name space support installed, VREPAIR attempts to auto load additional modules that support the repair of the name spaces. These modules are NLMs that are named for the name space, preceded by a "V_" (for example, V_LONG.NLM). If the required module cannot be found, the repair sequence terminates.

CAUTION

Using VREPAIR is the only way to remove a name space from a NetWare volume without deleting the volume. Any files using that name space that are still on the volume when the name space is removed will lose the additional information stored in the name space entries in the DET and in the extended directory space. Long file names will be truncated to 8.3 DOS names, and extended attributes, resource forks, and other unique file elements will be lost. This can render such files unusable by their native file systems.

You can also select whether you want VREPAIR to rewrite all of the FAT and directory entries on the volume to the disk. Normally, only the entries that are changed by the repair process are rewritten.

When VREPAIR detects errors, it corrects them in memory and then can either write the repairs immediately to the disk, or retain them in memory until the entire scan process has been completed. If there are many errors, writing the changes to disk immediately is preferable.

Finally, you can choose whether or not deleted files found on the volume should be purged during the repair process.

Repairing Volumes   When you choose Repair a Volume from VREPAIR's main menu, you first select the volume that you want to repair (when there is more than one dismounted volume available), and you are then presented with a list of additional repair options, along with their current settings. By default, VREPAIR will pause each time that it locates an error, and will not log the errors that it finds.

You can choose to change either of these settings. A volume that is severely damaged can contain hundreds or thousands of errors, making it unlikely that you will want to pause after each one is found. Fortunately, you can change this option during the repair process, if the number of errors grows too large. It is also a good idea to log the errors that are found again unless there are an enormous number of errors.

Once you have set your options and elect to continue with the volume repair, the program scans the various elements on the volume for errors, producing a display like the following:

```
Total errors: 0
Current Error Settings:
      Pause after each error.
      Do not log errors to a file.
Press <F1> to change error settings.

Start  2:50:32 pm
Checking volume VOL2:

FAT blocks>.................................................<
Counting directory blocks and checking directory FAT entries.
Mirror mismatches>.........................................<
Directories>...............................................<
Files>.....................................................<
Trustees>..................................................<
Deleted Files>.............................................<
Free blocks>...............................................<
Done checking volume.
Total Time  0:00:11
<Press any key to continue>
```

VREPAIR is the only disk repair utility that you should use on your NetWare volumes. Other disk diagnosis and repair products intended for use on DOS and Windows computers will usually not function if you try to address NetWare drives with them. If they are capable of addressing the drives, they can do great damage to your volumes unless they are specifically designed for use with NetWare.

Summary

In this chapter, you learned about the inner workings of NetWare volumes and the many features that provide added efficiency to the network file storage subsystem. Many of these processes are entirely invisible to users and are even ignored by many network administrators, but by understanding how they work, you can tailor your NetWare servers to provide the best possible performance for your network's needs. ●

CHAPTER 17

Implementing Network Printing

Sharing printers was one of the original motivations behind the networking of computers in the business environment, and Novell created a network printing architecture many years ago that has remained an efficacious solution to this day. Printer technology has advanced considerably, as have the capabilities of NetWare's print-related software modules, but the basic network printing model is the same.

A watershed has been reached, however, as Novell stands poised to release Novell Distributed Print Services as part of the IntranetWare II product in early 1998. NDPS is an entirely new concept in network printing that will have repercussions in network operating systems, network client software, and in the manufacture of printers themselves. While providing full backward compatibility, NDPS enables network administrators to remotely manage and configure print devices all over the enterprise, and takes full advantage of whatever bidirectional capabilities printers have—now and in the future. ∎

How to plan your network printing strategy

The first step in network printing is deciding where your printers will be located and how they should be connected to the network.

The building blocks of the NetWare printing architecture

Three different NDS objects must be created to allow access to a networked printer.

Creating and configuring print objects

To prepare a printer for network access, you must create new NDS objects and configure them to accommodate your architectural decisions.

Activating the printing modules

You must load the appropriate print server and port driver software modules on your servers and workstation before you can begin printing.

How Novell Distributed Print Services (NDPS) alters the NetWare print subsystem

Novell Distributed Print Services will make it easier for users to access network printers and enhance the administrator's management capabilities.

Planning a Network Printing Strategy

At its simplest, the process of networking printers is a matter of taking an application's print output and sending it through the network instead of to the workstation's printer port. From the network print queue, the print job travels to a printer, where it is processed just as though the printer was connected to the client computer.

Of course, the process is considerably more complex than that, but one of the first questions to arise concerns where the networked printers are actually located. NetWare takes care of the many complex print communication tasks for you, but this fundamental question is one that the administrator must answer before the entire process begins.

NetWare enables printers to be attached to the network in three ways:

- **Server Connection**—The printer is connected to a server PC's standard parallel or serial port.
- **Workstation Connection**—The printer is connected to a client workstation's standard parallel or serial port.
- **Direct Connection**—The printer is connected to the network medium using an interface installed in the printer itself or an external device to which the printer is connected.

The drawback to the first two methods is that the printer connection utilizes processing and I/O resources on the host computer that can detract from its other activities. A workstation with a heavily used printer connected to it can suffer from a serious degradation of performance, both because of the large amounts of incoming print job data from the network and because of the CPU time needed to process the print jobs.

Of course, you could eliminate this problem by dedicating the workstation wholly to printing tasks, but this would not be an efficient use of your hardware resources.

Connecting printers to server computers can be even more detrimental than connecting them to a workstation. Depending on whether all of the network printing modules are loaded on the same machine or not, a server's performance can degrade for want of memory, processor time, network I/O bandwidth, storage space, or any combination of these factors. In the case of a server, though, it is not a single user that suffers, but all of the users that access that server.

This is not to say that these two printer connection methods should never be used. Particularly on smaller networks, they can be the most convenient and cost-efficient ways of connecting network printers. However, the most commonly used connection method on medium- and large-size networks today is the direct connection of a printer to the network medium.

In most cases, the direct connection is accomplished by installing a special network interface adapter into the printer and plugging it into the same type of network connection used by a server or workstation. Some printers are now being manufactured with network interfaces as standard equipment, while others require the insertion of a special card.

The direct connection method provides several advantages:

■ **Location**—You can place the printer in any location where there is an available network connection. A printer can therefore be placed near enough to users for convenient centralized access, without tethering the whirring, lumbering beast to an unlucky user's desk.

■ **Traffic**—Print jobs can consist of very large amounts of data. Passing that data through a server or workstation in order to reach the printer can interfere with other traffic entering and leaving the computer. A directly connected printer uses a network interface that is wholly dedicated to the reception of print job data.

■ **Memory**—Connecting a printer to a workstation or server requires that a software component run on the computer, consuming memory that could better be used elsewhere. A directly connected printer eliminates this requirement.

Making the decisions as to where your printers will be located and how they will be connected to the network leads to the answers of other questions about how you will construct your network printing environment. However, to make these decisions intelligently, it helps to know more about the NetWare printing architecture.

Part
V

Ch
17

Introducing the NetWare Print Objects

As with many NetWare features, the elements that make up the printing subsystem are represented by objects in the Novell Directory Services database. The objects each have names that are used to uniquely identify the component. Three different types of objects are required to activate a printer for use with NetWare:

■ **Printer**—The printer object represents the physical printer itself. Its configuration data specifies the print queues that the printer will service, and the kind of interface that is used to connect the printer to the network.

■ **Print Queue**—The print queue object represents a directory on a user-selected volume of a NetWare server where print jobs are stored temporarily as they are being fed to the printer. It is the print queue that enables many different users to send jobs to the same printer.

■ **Print Server**—The print server is the arbiter that controls the process by which queued print jobs are sent to printers. A print server can be a software product, such as the PSERVER.NLM module included with NetWare, or part of a hardware device like a printer's network interface card.

Understanding the Network Print Process

A comprehension of the way in which printers, queues, and servers are used to convey print job data from the workstation to the printer will help you to make the purchasing and configuration decisions that best suit the needs of your network. The following sections describe the phases of the network printing process.

Phase One: Redirecting Print Output   As far as an application running on a client workstation is concerned, generating print output for a network printer is no different from that for a locally attached printer. An appropriate printer driver must be installed, either as part of the operating system or the application.

When the workstation is running any of the Windows operating systems, the printer driver is part of the operating system. DOS applications may have their own drivers, or they may rely on the operating system's standard output.

The primary difference in network printing is that the print output generated by the driver must be transmitted out over the network interface to a print queue, instead of the parallel port, as with a local printer. The print output from the driver is redirected in one of two ways.

Windows 95 and Windows NT have printer drivers that are capable of sending data directly to a NetWare print queue. The NetWare client enables the user to browse the NDS tree and select a queue that is serviced by the type of printer corresponding to the driver that has been installed. Some DOS applications, most notably WordPerfect, can also directly address output to NetWare queues, but this capability is rare.

N O T E   Windows 95 also includes a feature called Point and Print, which stores printer definitions and drivers on a network drive. This relieves the user from having to install the correct driver for the network printer. By dragging an icon representing a print queue object from the Explorer window to the Printer Control Panel, the correct driver is installed and the output directed to the proper queue object.

For Windows 3.1 and most DOS applications, it is not possible to address print queues directly, so it is necessary for the NetWare client to intercept the print output being generated by the application and redirect it to a queue. This is accomplished by associating a specific LPT port with a particular queue using a graphical configuration utility, such NWUSER, or the DOS-based CAPTURE program.

Phase Two: Queuing Print Jobs   When print jobs are transmitted over the network by a workstation, they are stored in a NetWare queue. A print queue must be associated with a particular NetWare server because its function is to store print jobs until they can be sent to a printer. A print queue is a directory like any other, in which print jobs are stored as files.

CAUTION

It is important that you have some idea of the amount of data that will be in your print queues at any one time. You must have enough free disk space on the queue volume to accommodate all of the temporary print files that will be created there. This is particularly important if you create print queues on the SYS volume and you have NDS partitions or replicas stored on the same server. Running out of disk space on the SYS volume can prevent NDS updates from taking place, the results of which can be very serious.

A printer can only process one job at a time, but on a network, many different users might send documents to print simultaneously. Because multiple users can write data to a NetWare volume at the same time, the use of a print queue resolves one of the biggest problems of network printing. Print queues very often speed up the printing process, as well.

Print jobs can consist of several megabytes worth of data, and printers typically do not have enough memory to store them all at once. When a PC sends a job to a local printer, delays can result when the computer must wait for the printer to finish processing data and clear its buffers. A print queue can accept as much data as a print job can generate, at the full speed of the network connection. As soon as the entire print job has left the workstation, the print process is concluded, as far as the client is concerned. The user's work can continue while the rest of the printing process is conducted elsewhere.

Print queues also insulate users from the everyday problems that can affect all printers. Print jobs can be written to a queue even when the associated printer is out of paper, offline, or malfunctioning in some other way. Files simply remain queued until the problem is resolved and printing can continue.

Utilities like NetWare Administrator and PCONSOLE enable administrators and other users to manage the queued print jobs in various ways. Specific print jobs can be paused or deleted, if necessary, or re-ordered to minimize media changes. Print jobs can also be prioritized according to importance, or scheduled to run at a later time, when print traffic is light.

Print queues need not be configured in a one-to-one relationship with printers, although they frequently are. To simplify workstation client configurations, you can have a great many users submit jobs to a single queue, and arrange for that queue to be serviced by multiple printers.

In the same way, you can create several queues, and have a single printer service them all. This is a good way to separate different types of print jobs. For example, you might have one queue for printing on letter-size paper and another for legal-size documents. One printer may be able to service both queues, but only when an operator manually changes the paper. By creating separate queues, all of the letter-size jobs can be completed before switching to legal-size paper.

Phase Three: Sending Queued Jobs to Printers   The final phase of the printing process involves taking the data from the print queue, one job at a time, and sending it to a printer. How this is done depends on the location of the printer. If the printer is physically attached to the same server where the queue is stored, then it is only a matter of reading the file from the server drive and sending it out the computer's parallel or serial port.

In other cases, the data must be again transmitted over the network, either to another server or workstation to which the printer is attached, or directly to the printer itself. It is the print server that manages the data that is to be fed to the printer.

The associations between the print-related NDS objects take the form of a domino effect. Print queues are associated with printers, and printers are in turn managed by a print server. The print server reads print jobs from the queue, and controls the rate at which data is sent to the printer. It is also responsible for implementing the additional print configuration parameters set in the NetWare client, such as banner pages and form feeds.

Part

V

Ch

17

Print servers can take several different forms. The network interface cards that you install into a printer, such as the Hewlett Packard JetDirect, function as print servers themselves. They log into the network, access the print jobs in the queue and cause them to be transmitted to the card, which feeds them to the printer.

In this scenario, each printer has its own print server, which manages only that one printer. There are also standalone hardware devices available that function as a print server for several attached printers. Basically, these are enhanced versions of the printer cards, enclosed in a separate unit that attaches to the network and has ports for multiple printers. These units are useful if you intend to place several printers in one general location, as the length of the parallel cables connecting the device to the printers is limited to approximately 10 feet.

If your printers are to be attached to servers or workstations, you will likely run the print server that is included with NetWare. NetWare's print server differs substantially from third-party products in that it consists of software only, in the form of an NLM that runs on a NetWare server. The NetWare print server is also designed to manage communication for up to 255 printers, attached to servers and workstations located anywhere on the network.

The primary module for the NetWare print server is called PSERVER.NLM. This module, apart from servicing remote printers, enables you to send jobs to printers that are attached to the server's parallel or serial ports. When printers are attached to other NetWare servers, or to workstations, those computers must run a small port driver program called NPRINTER.NLM, NPRINTER.EXE, or NPTWIN95.EXE. These utilities remain in memory on the remote system, receive the jobs from the print server, and feed them to the printer.

A print server works by periodically (every 5 seconds, by default) checking the queues that its printers have been configured to service. When a print job is found in a queue, the server reads in the data, and then contacts the NPRINTER module on the computer to which the printer is attached.

The server begins sending print data packets to the remote computer, receiving acknowledgments in return that verify the receipt of the data and indicate the status of the printer. If the printer is available for use, the server continues to send more data. If the server is informed that the printer is offline or out of paper, the outgoing data stream is stopped and a user or administrator may be informed of the problem.

Phase Four: Printing the Documents   Once print data is received by the NPRINTER program, it begins feeding it, byte by byte, to the printer. NPRINTER uses either hardware interrupts or polling to control the rate at which data is sent to the printer. These methods not only feed data at a rate that is acceptable to the printer, they also regulate the amount of CPU time that is allotted to the printing process.

Polled mode (which is the default method) causes CPU control to be passed to the NPRINTER program once every clock tick (18.2 ticks equal 1 second), allowing it to send a fixed number of bytes to the printer. Polled mode usually provides satisfactory performance for both the printer and for the other tasks running on the computer. However, as you add more printers, more processor time is taken away from the foreground applications, possibly slowing them down.

Interrupt mode uses standard hardware interrupts to allot CPU time to the printing process, and requires that each printer have an interrupt (or IRQ) dedicated to it. This can be a problem if there are to be several printers connected to one computer. Interrupt mode is generally faster than polled mode, although polled mode frequently can send data to a printer faster than the printer can process it.

Once sufficient data has arrived at the printer (a full page's worth for a laser printer, a line's worth for a dot matrix), processing begins, the output is produced, and the whole cycle repeats until the entire job is printed.

Planning Your Network Printing Strategy

As you have read, the decisions that you make concerning how you will implement network printing can affect your hardware purchases as well as your software configuration. Therefore, the first question that you should consider is what print server you are going to use.

Because the NetWare print server can manage up to 255 printers, one installation should suffice for your whole network. The exception to this would be if your network uses WAN links to a remote location. If there is one kind of traffic that you don't want clogging your WAN links, it is print traffic, so a print server at each location is strongly recommended.

Even on a local area network, print traffic can consume a lot of bandwidth. You can minimize the amount of traffic by combining the various print modules on the same system. For example, the least efficient arrangement would be to install a print server on one machine, a queue on another, and a printer on a third. A print job in this case would have to be transmitted over the network three times: from workstation to print queue, from the queue to the print server, and from the print server to the system hosting the printer.

As an alternative, you can install all three modules on one server. This reduces the trips over the network to one, but at the expense of the server's own memory and processor resources.

Perhaps the most advantageous compromise is to use individual print servers on network adapters inside the printers. This prevents the consumption of server resources, and requires only two trips over the network for each print job: from workstation to print queue, and from the queue to the printer itself. This strategy incurs the additional expense of the network adapters for the printers, but these are not expensive devices, and provide the additional advantage of a very simple installation.

Creating and Configuring Print Objects

Preparing a printer for network use is primarily a matter of creating the appropriate objects in the Novell Directory Services database and configuring them. You can create print objects with either NetWare Administrator or PCONSOLE, a DOS utility that uses the standard NetWare C-worthy interface.

Both utilities have a Quick Setup feature that enables you to create all of the objects needed to install a new printer to the network from a single dialog box (see Figure 17.1). If you have no existing print objects, Quick Setup creates a print server, print queue, and a printer object, all in the current context set in the program with simple default names. If a print server already exists in that context, it will be specified in place of a new one, by default.

FIG. 17.1

NetWare Administrator and PCONSOLE both provide a Quick Setup feature that can be used to create print server, print queue, and printer objects simultaneously.

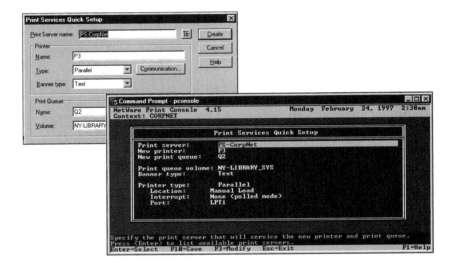

As with file servers, the best strategy is to create the required print objects in the same NDS context as the objects representing the printer's users. The print queue should also reside on a server in the same context.

This arrangement is not required, but users must browse the NDS tree when installing a new printer driver on their workstations, and the easier it is for them to locate the desired object, the fewer calls that will be made for technical support. You can also use alias objects to enable users in multiple contexts to easily access the same printer.

▶ **See** "Using Aliases," **p. 168**

Although the Quick Setup feature is convenient, especially for installing your first printer, it doesn't do anything more than consolidate several tasks into one dialog box. Apart from creating the NDS objects themselves, the dialog box contains the essential configuration settings for the objects, and automatically creates the required associations that allow the objects to work together.

If you create print objects individually, you configure many of the same parameters and you must establish the object relationships manually. Manual configuration, however, helps to give you a better idea of how you can use the objects in nonstandard ways to construct a printing strategy that better suits your needs.

The following sections describe the process of creating and configuring each of the three essential print objects. The actual creation of the print-related NDS objects is no different from that of any other object. You use the same techniques in NetWare Administrator that you learned in Chapter 7, "Creating and Managing NDS Objects." PCONSOLE operates like any of the other C-worthy utilities included with NetWare.

Creating Print Queue Objects

If you elect to create the print service objects individually (as opposed to using the Quick Setup feature), you should create the print queue object first. When you select the Print Queue object type in the New Object dialog box of NetWare Administrator, the Create Print Queue dialog box shown in Figure 17.2 is displayed. If you create the object using PCONSOLE (by selecting Print Queues and pressing Insert), you are prompted for the same information.

 TIP The PCONSOLE utility can be switched between Directory Services and Bindery Services modes by pressing the F4 key. To create a Print Queue object in the NDS tree, be sure that you are in Directory Services mode.

FIG. 17.2
To create a Print Queue object, you must specify the name of the queue and the volume where the temporary print files will be stored.

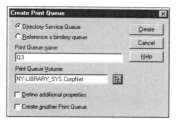

Naming the Object   In the Create Print Queue dialog box, you must first specify the name of the new object. The name of the print queue is particularly important because this is the object that users will seek when installing a new printer at a workstation. The print queue name, therefore, should represent the type of printing that is performed by the associated printers.

For example, if you have a large number of users, all of whom regularly print invoices throughout their work day, you may have several printers loaded with invoice forms, to accommodate the volume. The names that you assign to the Print Server and the Printer objects are significant to yourself and other network administrators, but it would be best to create a single Print Queue object that is serviced by all of the printers, and call it Invoices.

This makes it easy for users to select the correct print queue for their invoices without the confusion of selecting one of the many printers. This arrangement also equitably distributes the print tasks among the printers, maximizing the output volume automatically.

Selecting a Volume   When creating a queue, you must also select the server volume where the print jobs are to be stored while they are waiting to be printed. The creation of the Print Queue object causes the queue directory to be created off of the QUEUES directory of the volume you select. The requirements for the creation of a queue are that the volume have sufficient disk space to hold the temporary files, and that the location of the queue attempts to minimize the amount of network traffic generated by the printing process.

N O T E The Create Print Queue dialog box also enables you to create an NDS object for a bindery
print queue that already exists on a NetWare server. This way, you can assimilate your
legacy print architecture into the NDS tree without interrupting service to your users.

One additional factor that you should consider when calculating disk space is the possibility of
one or more printers malfunctioning. When a print server cannot send jobs to a printer because
it is out of paper or offline or for any other reason, the jobs remain in the print queue until
someone has corrected the problem. Based on the printing habits of your users, and the availability of personnel to attend to printer maintenance tasks, be sure that there is enough disk
space on the selected volume to retain the accumulated print output.

If you have three shifts of graphic artists working, for example, and the color printer goes
offline at 5:15 P.M., and there is no one to fix it until the next morning, you could build up an
enormous amount of data because color graphic print jobs can be many megabytes in size.

The volume that you select as the location for your print queues should also be based on the
location of your print server. If you are using the NetWare print server, it is recommended that
the queues be located on the same server that is running PSERVER.NLM. Although not required, this practice eliminates the additional network traffic generated by the transmission of
print job data from the queue volume to the print server.

Configuring the Object   Once the print queue has been created, you can configure the
object to control its operation and designate queue users and operators. These are the people
that will be permitted to place jobs into the queue, and those that will be able to manipulate
existing jobs.

Apart from these configuration tasks, the Print Queue does not require any further manipula-
tion. The associations between the queue and the other print services objects are established
when those objects are created. Instead, the screens in the Print Queue Details dialog box are
more often used to perform daily maintenance tasks, such as manipulating the jobs waiting in
the queue.

When you open the Details dialog box of the queue object, you find several descriptive fields
on the Identification screen in which you can enter information about the queue and its function to your users. These fields are informational only.

There are, however, three check boxes in this dialog box, all of which are enabled by default
and labeled as follows:

- Allow Users to Submit Print Jobs
- Allow Service by Current Print Servers
- Allow New Print Servers to Attach

N O T E In the PCONSOLE utility, these print options are accessed by selecting Status from the Print
Queue Information menu. All of the other queue configuration parameters are also found
on this menu.

These check boxes can be used to disable particular functions of the queue, for maintenance purposes or any other reason. If a printer is going out to be serviced, for example, it is a good idea to clear the first check box so that users cannot submit jobs to a queue that will not be serviced in the near future.

The Assignments panel is another purely informational display. It lists the printers that service the queue and the print servers that will send the jobs from the queue to the printers, but you cannot add assignments from this screen. You must do this in the Details dialog boxes for the Printer and Print Server objects.

Creating Queue Operators   The Operator panel enables you to select the users that are given the ability to manipulate the jobs waiting in the print queue. Normally, users can delete their own jobs from the queue, but an operator can delete anyone's jobs, and also adjust the order in which the queued jobs are printed.

In a large organization, it is usually a good idea to have someone in each department who knows enough about the network printing process to be designated a queue operator. A typical scenario in which this can be demonstrated is the case when a user submits a large print job that is somehow incorrect. The printer may be spurting out page after page of gibberish, or the print job may be incorrectly formatted.

Whatever the problem, the print job is only wasting paper and forcing other users to wait for their work. The user may have the rights needed to delete the job, but will often lack the knowledge. Rather than having to call a network administrator to resolve this minor problem, a qualified print queue operator can delete the job from the queue, reset the printer, and all will be well again.

To designate a print queue operator, you select an NDS object from the tree in the usual manner. Although operators are likely to be individual users, you can also select a container or group object to make all of the users in the container or group queue operators.

Creating Queue Users   The process of creating queue users is the same as that for creating operators. A person must be a queue user in order to submit jobs to the queue for printing. When you create a new print queue, the container in which the print queue object is located is added to the list of queue users. This enables everyone in the container to access the printer.

You can also add the [Root] object to the user list, enabling everyone in the enterprise to access the printer. This can provide a great convenience to users who are savvy enough to browse the NDS tree for printers located in other work areas. Rather than print a document and carry or mail it to a colleague in another department, a user can simply print the document to the colleague's nearby printer, saving time and effort.

When you are networking color printers or other devices that use more expensive consumables, you may want to restrict access to selected users. You can do this by adding individual User objects to the print queues user list. Any queue operator can add users to a queue object.

Creating Printer Objects

Every network printer must be represented by an NDS object, but unlike print queues and servers, creating the object does not establish an actual connection with the entity that it represents. You can create any number of objects to represent printers real or imaginary, and it will not be until a user attempts to actually send a job to the device that the actual existence and operational status of the hardware will be tested.

The printer object contains the configuration information that the print server needs in order to transmit print job data over the network to the port driver, including the name of the queue (or queues) that the printer is to service, and the type of connection used between the printer and its host computer.

When you create a new printer object, it is a good idea to assign it a name that will help you to identify the hardware, such as one that describes the printer type or its location. Once the object has been created, you can open its Details dialog box (see Figure 17.3) and begin the configuration process.

FIG. 17.3
The Printer object's Assignments panel is where you specify the print queues that are to be serviced by the printer.

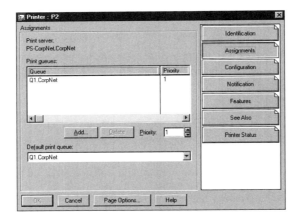

As with most NDS objects, the printer object includes parameters that you can use to identify the printer's exact location, or include any other descriptive information you desire. Users can then locate specific printers by searching the NDS database for the information stored in these parameters, which are found in the Identification, Features, and See Also screens of the Details dialog box. The following sections describe the parameters found in the other panels, which are used to configure the printer object.

Assignments   On the Assignments panel, you specify the names of the print queues from which jobs will be sent to this printer. By clicking the Add button, you can browse the NDS tree for print queue objects that have already been created.

If you have used the Print Services Quick Setup feature, the Print Server and Print Queue objects that were created at the same time as the Printer object will already be associated with the printer. If you elect to create the print services objects individually, however, you should create print queue objects before printer objects, so that you can select queues while configuring the printer.

This dialog box is also where you can select and prioritize multiple queues that are to be serviced by one printer. When you select a queue from the listing, you can use the Priority selector to modify the queue's priority in relation to the other queues. This causes the print server, when it finds jobs in more than one of a printer's queues, to select the queue with the higher priority for servicing.

You can use this feature to maximize the efficiency of your network printing, when you are using one printer for several different tasks. For example, suppose that you have a printer with a single paper tray that you use for printing both letter- and legal-size documents. If your users submit both types of print jobs to one queue, then the jobs are printed in the order that they are received. If letter-size paper is in the printer, then processing will stop as soon as a legal print job is sent to the printer.

To continue printing, someone must manually change the paper supply in the printer to legal size, and then change it back again. If, on the other hand, you create separate print queues for the two job types, then you can give letter-size jobs a higher priority than legal-size. This way, all of the letter-size jobs will be printed before the print server processes the legal-size jobs. This serves to minimize the number of paper changes needed.

Configuration   On the Configuration panel (see Figure 17.4), you provide the settings needed for the print server to communicate across the network with the printer. The most important of these settings is the Printer Type parameter, which defines how the printer is connected to the network. The possible values for the Printer Type are listed in Table 17.1.

FIG. 17.4
The Printer object's Configuration panel specifies how the printer is connected to the network.

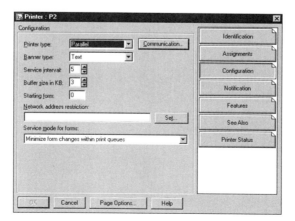

Part
V

Ch
17

Table 17.1   NetWare Printer Types

Type	Description
Other/Unknown	Indicates (in most cases) that the printer is directly connected to the network cable system, or connected to an OS/2 workstation.
Parallel	Indicates that the printer is connected to a NetWare server or workstation by means of a parallel port.
Serial	Indicates that the printer is connected to a NetWare server or workstation by means of a serial port.
XNP	Indicates that the printer uses the Extended Network Printing protocol. Follow the printer manufacturer's instructions for configuring the printer's connection.
AppleTalk	Indicates that the printer is connected to a Macintosh workstation, and that the AppleTalk protocol is to be used to communicate with the printer.
UNIX	Indicates that the printer is connected to a UNIX host.
AIO	Indicates that the printer is connected through an asynchronous communication server using the Asynchronous Input/Output protocol. Follow the communication server manufacturer's instructions for configuring the printer's connection.

After choosing a printer type, click the Communication button to display a dialog box like that shown in Figure 17.5, in which you configure the printer's communication settings. Table 17.2 list the settings for each printer type.

FIG. 17.5

Different printer types have different communication settings that must be configured.

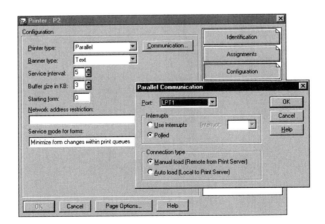

Table 17.2 Communication Settings for Network Printer Types

Setting	Options
Other/Unknown Printer Type	
Setting used for printers that are connected directly to the network. Follow the instructions of the printer or network interface manufacturer.	See manufacturer's documentation
Parallel Printer Type	
Port: the LPT address of the parallel port to which the printer is connected.	LPT1, LPT2, LPT3
Interrupts: specifies whether the printer port is activated using interrupts or polling when there is information to print.	Polled (default), Use Interrupts (specify interrupt number)
Connection Type: specifies whether the port driver is loaded automatically (by PSERVER.EXE) or manually (by one of the NPRINTER utilities).	Manual Load (remote from print server), Auto Load (local to print server)
Serial Printer Type	
Port: the COM address of the serial port to which the printer is connected.	COM1, COM2, COM3, COM4
Interrupts: specifies whether the printer port is activated using interrupts or polling when there is information to print.	Polled (default), Use Interrupts (specify interrupt number)
Connection Type: specifies whether the port driver is loaded automatically (by PSERVER.EXE) or manually (by one of the NPRINTER utilities).	Manual Load (remote from print server), Auto Load (local to print server)
Line Control: specifies the serial communication settings of the printer.	Baud Rate: 300, 600, 1200, 2400, 4800, 9600 (default), 19200, 38400 Data bits: 8(default), 7, 6, 5 Stop bits: 1 (default), 1.5, 2 Parity: none (default), odd, even Use XON/XOFF: yes, no (default)
XNP Printer Type	
No communication settings; follow printer manufacturer's directions.	See manufacturer's documentation

Part
V

Ch

17

continues

Table 17.2 Continued

Setting	Options
AppleTalk Printer Type	
Name: the name by which the printer is known on the AppleTalk network Type: the AppleTalk printer type.	LaserWriter ImageWriter, LQ, DeskWriter, PaintWriterXL, PaintJet XL300
Zone: the AppleTalk zone where the printer is located.	The actual zone name or * to designate any zone (* is the default)
Print Error Messages: PostScript printers can be configured to print error messages on a special banner page.	Print Error Messages (default), Don't Print Error Messages
Hide Printer: the parameter that prevents a printer from appearing in the Macintosh Chooser's list of available printers. If the printer doesn't appear, Macintosh users are forced to send print jobs to the printer's linked queue rather than to the printer directly.	Hide Printer, Don't Hide Printer (default)
UNIX Printer Type	
Host Name: the name of the UNIX host to which the printer is connected.	N/A
Printer Name: the UNIX name of the printer.	N/A
AIO Printer Type	
Port: specifies the port number.	Follow the manufacturer's directions
Hardware Number.	Follow the manufacturer's directions
Board Number.	Follow the manufacturer's directions
Connection Type: specifies whether the port driver is loaded automatically (by PSERVER.EXE) or manually (by one of the NPRINTER utilities).	Manual Load (remote from print server), Auto Load (local to print loaded server)
Line Control: specifies the serial communication settings of the printer.	Baud rate: 300, 600, 1200,2400, 4800, 9600 (default), 19200, 38400 Data bits: 8 (default), 7, 6, 5 Stop bits: 1 (default), 1.5, 2 Parity: none (default), odd, even Use XON/XOFF: yes, no (default)

The Banner Type option in the Configuration panel enables you to specify whether NetWare's banner pages should be printed using standard text or the Postscript page description language. If you are using a Postscript printer, you can print banner pages that are more visually appealing, but which contain the same information as standard banners, such as the user who printed the job and the file name.

The Service Interval setting dictates how often the print server should check the printer's associated queues for print jobs. The default value is 5 seconds, with possible values ranging from 1 to 255 seconds.

The Buffer Size setting specifies the maximum amount of data that can be sent to the printer at one time. The default value is 3K. Possible values are 3K to 20K.

The Default Form field indicates the number of the form that is typically loaded in the printer. You can define forms and assign them numbers in the Details dialog box of a container or User object.

Part
V
Ch
17

The Network Address Restriction field enables you to specify the network and node address of the interface that the printer uses to connect to the network. This would be the address of the network adapter in the server or workstation to which the printer is attached, or the address of an adapter installed in the printer.

The printer network address feature prevents any other printer that has been given the same name from intercepting the print jobs sent by the print server. If you intend to print confidential documents on this printer, it is a good idea to use this option to secure your printer communication channel.

The Service Mode for Forms parameter specifies how the print server will order the processing of queued jobs that specify different forms. The values are:

- **Change Forms as Needed**—No adjustments are made in the jobs' print order.
- **Minimize Form Changes Across Print Queues**—All of the jobs specifying a particular form in all of the queues associated with this printer (regardless of priority) are processed before the print server requests a form change.
- **Minimize Form Changes within Print Queues**—All of the jobs specifying a particular form in the current queue are processed before proceeding to the next job in the highest priority queue.
- **Service Only Currently Mounted Form**—All of the jobs using the currently mounted form are processed. Jobs requesting other forms are not processed until the form is changed.

Notification   The Notification panel enables you to specify the users that should receive messages indicating that the printer is offline, out of paper, or in some other way malfunctioning. You can select individual User objects or container or Group objects.

By default, the first message is generated one minute after the problem appears, and every five minutes thereafter. You can modify these times by selecting a user and modifying the Notification Settings fields. You can also specify that only the owner of a print job be notified by marking the appropriate check box.

TIP It is a good idea to limit the users that are notified of printer problems to a chosen few that have been drafted for this purpose, rather than sending notification messages to every user in the container. Few things are more annoying to a user attempting to work than repeated "Printer is out of paper" messages.

Printer Status   If you are an operator of the print server that manages the printer, and the printer is online and functioning, an additional segment appears in the Printer object's Details dialog box that enables you to view the current status of the printer, as shown in Figure 17.6.

FIG. 17.6
The Printer Status panel displays information about the job that is currently being printed.

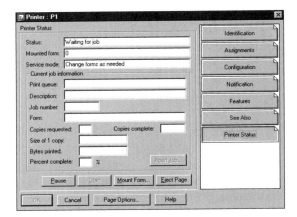

From this panel, you can also pause the printer, abort the job that is currently being processed, eject a page (that is, send a form feed command to the printer), or signal the print server that a new form has been mounted.

Creating Print Server Objects

Whether you intend to use NetWare's print server software or a third-party print server, you must still create a print server object in your NDS tree using one of the NetWare utilities. As with the Printer object, the print server software (or the hardware device that includes print server functionality) is associated with the Print Server object by the use of the name you assign during the creation of the object.

The following sections detail the configuration parameters for the Print Server object.

Identification   As with the other print services objects, the Identification panel found in the Details dialog box contains fields that are used mainly for informational purposes. In the case of a Print Server object, this panel displays the name that will be used to identify the print server when its presence is advertised to the rest of the network. This name may differ from the name that you assigned to the Print Server object, if you used characters that are not allowable in service names (that is, any characters other than A to Z, 0 to 9, hyphens, periods, and underscores).

The Identification panel also displays the type and version of print server that the object represents, and when possible, enables you to unload the server software. You can also manage the password that secures the server from access by unauthorized users.

Assignments   In the Assignments panel, you specify the names of the printers that are managed by this print server. Each printer object that you add to the list is assigned a number, from 0 to 255, that you can use to identify the printer when you load a port driver. You can change a printer's number by highlighting an object in the list and clicking the Printer Number button.

Users and Operators   Print server users can view the status of the print server. A person does not have to be a print server user in order to send documents to a printer managed by the server. A print server operator can start and stop the print server, view its status, and manage the printers that it services.

Both the Users and Operator panels contain a list to which you can add User, container, or Group objects that you select from the NDS tree.

Auditing Log   The print server is capable of logging information about each job that is printed to any of the managed printers, such as the time that each job was printed, its size, and the user who printed it, among other data. However, auditing is disabled by default.

From the Auditing Log panel, you can enable audit logging, view and delete the log, and impose a limit on the log by specifying the maximum size of the log in kilobytes, or the number of print jobs that can be written to the log file. When the existing log file reaches the specified size limit, all further logging activity stops until you delete or rename the current log file.

N O T E   If you make changes to the configuration of a Print Server object after it has already been loaded on the server, you must, in most cases, unload the print server software and reload it in order for the changes to take effect.

Print Layout   Once you have configured the Print Server object, you have completed the NDS tasks needed to implement a network printer. The Print Layout panel of the Print Server dialog box (see Figure 17.7) displays a summary of the associations that have been established between the print services objects that you have created.

Part
V

Ch
17

FIG. 17.7
The Print Layout dialog box displays a graphical representation of the queues and printers associated with the print server.

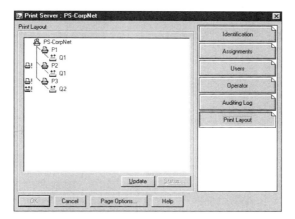

You can select any of the objects in the display and click the Status button to display its current operational status.

Activating the NetWare Print Subsystem

Once you have created and configured your print service objects, you can activate the actual elements that the objects represent. First, your printer hardware should be installed and activated, so that it can be located by the software modules. The following sections describe the process of activating your print server and port drivers.

Starting the NetWare Print Server

The PSERVER.NLM module and its accompanying files are installed to the SYS:SYSTEM directory on your NetWare server along with the rest of the operating system. When you load the PSERVER.NLM module at the server console, you specify the name of the Print Server object you created in the NDS tree, and the software reads the configuration parameters from the NDS database.

When you issue the LOAD PSERVER command at the file server console, you are prompted to enter the NDS name of the Print Server object. The default context displayed is that where the NetWare server is located. You can type the name of the Print Server object in the field provided, or press the Insert key to browse for the object using the standard C-worthy directory navigation method.

It is very likely that you will want the print server to load each time the server is restarted, so you can place the appropriate command in the server's AUTOEXEC.NCF file to automatically load PSERVER. The correct syntax is as follows:

```
LOAD PSERVER objectname
```

If the Print Server object and the NetWare server object are in the same context (which is recommended), then you can specify only the simple name of the print server on the command line. Otherwise, you must include the full context of the print server's object name.

If your printer is attached to the same server that is running PSERVER, and you have selected the Auto Load connection type in the Printer object's configuration, then loading PSERVER.NLM will cause NPRINTER.NLM to be loaded as well. If you specified the Manual Load option, then you must explicitly load NPRINTER, as detailed later in this chapter in "Using NPRINTER.NLM" and "Using NPRINTER.EXE."

Once the print server is loaded, a new screen is added at the server console. From this screen, you can check the status of any printer being managed by the print server, by displaying a screen that is the C-worthy version of the Printer Status screen found in the Printer object's Details dialog box (see Figure 17.8).

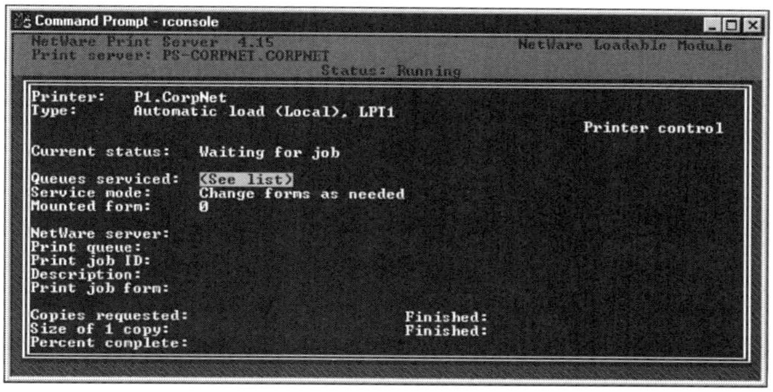

FIG. 17.8
You can view the status of each printer from the PSERVER screen on the NetWare server console.

When you select Print Server Information from the Available Options menu, you can also view the operational status of the print server. When the server is running, you can unload it from this screen in one of two ways. You can either unload the module immediately, interrupting whatever operations are currently in progress, or select Unload After Active Print Jobs, which allows the jobs in progress to be completed.

Installing a Third-Party Print Server

When you install a network adapter like the Hewlett Packard JetDirect card into a printer in order to directly connect it to the network, or if you purchase a printer with an internal network interface, it includes a print server as part of the hardware installation. After creating the print services objects in the normal manner (and selecting Other/Unknown as the printer type), you run the software included with the adapter, which enables you to select the Print Server object from the NDS tree and associate it with the attached printer.

Printer adapter devices can be used to service multiple queues with a single printer, just as you can with the NetWare print server. However, you cannot split the jobs in one queue among several printers unless you purchase an external print server device instead of an internal one. Hewlett Packard and other manufacturers also market external print servers that function in the same way as the internal models, except that they have connectors for multiple printers.

You will find that the installation and configuration of printer adapter devices is remarkably easy. However, some of the administrative functions found in the NetWare Administrator and PCONSOLE utilities are not supported, and are found instead in the software included with the product. Windows 95 even ships with a service that enables you to manage JetDirect print adapters all over your network from a single workstation.

Using NetWare Port Drivers

A NetWare port driver is necessary whenever you connect a network printer to a server or workstation computer. The port driver is a software module that reads the configuration parameters of a selected Printer object in the NDS database, communicates with the print server, receives print job data over the network, and feeds it to the printer through the selected port.

Part
V

Ch

17

All of the NetWare port drivers can be loaded up to seven times on a single machine, to address printers connected to three LPT ports and four COM ports, simultaneously. However, because of the hardware considerations involved in running seven printers from one computer, it is rare to see more than two or perhaps three printers running at once on a single server or workstation.

NetWare includes port drivers that run on NetWare servers and DOS, Windows 3.1, and Windows 95 workstations. Once your port drivers are installed and activated, your printers should be ready to process jobs from network users.

Using NPRINTER.NLM   If you connect a printer to a NetWare server other than the one that is running the NetWare print server, you have no choice other than to manually load the port driver module. The port driver is called NPRINTER.NLM, and is found in the SYS:SYSTEM directory of every NetWare server.

You load NPRINTER.NLM from the server console prompt (or from the server's AUTOEXEC.NCF file) by specifying the name of the print server and the printer number that you configured in the Print Server object on the command line, as follows:

`LOAD NPRINTER` *printserver printernumber*

When you load NPRINTER manually on a server, a printer status screen is added to the server console. This screen is not displayed when NPRINTER is automatically loaded with PSERVER.NLM.

Using NPRINTER.EXE   NPRINTER.EXE is the NetWare port driver for workstations running DOS with or without Windows 3.1. NPRINTER is a TSR program that must be loaded from the DOS command line. Each instance of NPRINTER.EXE that you load on a workstation occupies 2K of memory, plus the size of the buffer, which defaults to 3K.

Like the NLM version, you must identify the printer that is to be connected to the workstation. You can do this in two ways: interactively, by running NPRINTER at the DOS prompt and using the menus to select first a print server and then a printer from the NDS tree, or by specifying the required information on the command line, in the same way as the NLM version:

`NPRINTER` *printserver printernumber*

You can also specify the full NDS name of the printer instead of the server name and the printer number, as follows:

`NPRINTER` *printername*

There are other options that you can specify on the NPRINTER command line as well:

- ■ `/S` displays the status of all NPRINTER installations on the current computer.
- ■ `/U` unloads the most recently loaded printer.
- ■ `/T=#` modifies the timing of the NPRINTER program to slow the network printing process, thus increasing the priority of the workstation's foreground tasks. Possible values are 1 through 9; the default value is 1. Increasing the value decreases the print speed.

■ /B=# overrides the buffer size configured in the Printer object. Possible values range from 3K to 60K; the default value is 3K. The buffer is created from workstation memory. Therefore, increasing this value also increases the memory required to load NPRINTER.

Running NPRINTER.EXE from a Local Drive   NPRINTER.EXE is found in the SYS:PUBLIC directory of every NetWare 4.11 server, but to load the program from a workstation's AUTOEXEC.BAT file, which is typical, you must copy the files required to run the program to a local drive, so that they can be executed before you log in to the network.

The files required to run NPRINTER from a local drive, and the directories where they can be found, are as follows:

File	Directory
NPRINTER.EXE	SYS:PUBLIC
NPRINTER.MSG	SYS:PUBLIC\NLS\ENGLISH
NPRINTER.HEP	SYS:PUBLIC\NLS\ENGLISH
SCHEMA.XLT	SYS:PUBLIC\NLS\ENGLISH
NWDSBRWS.MSG	SYS:PUBLIC\NLS\ENGLISH
TEXTUTIL.MSG	SYS:PUBLIC\NLS\ENGLISH
TEXTUTIL.HEP	SYS:PUBLIC\NLS\ENGLISH
TEXTUTIL.IDX	SYS:PUBLIC
IBM_RUN.OVL	SYS:PUBLIC

Part
V

Ch
17

Running NPRINTER.EXE with Windows 3.1   It is possible to run NPRINTER.EXE with Windows 3.1, but you must load the program before you start Windows. If you have configured the Printer object to use Interrupt Mode, you must make the following changes to the SYSTEM.INI file on your workstation.

Under the [386Enh] heading, add the following two lines:

```
LPT1AutoAssign=0
LPT1irq=-1
```

Replace LPT1 with the appropriate port for your printer (LPT2, COM1, and so on), and replicate the two lines for each additional printer connected to the workstation. If you selected Polled Mode (the default) when you configured the Printer object, no INI file modifications are needed.

Using the NPRINTER Manager with Windows 95   NetWare also ships with a GUI port driver for Windows 95 that you can configure to automatically load printers when the program is executed. When you run NPTWIN95.EXE, found in the SYS:PUBLIC\WIN95 directory, from a Windows 95 workstation, you see the dialog box shown in Figure 17.9, which you use to select a Printer object from the NDS tree or a bindery printer.

FIG. 17.9

The NPRINTER Manager enables Windows 95 workstations running Client 32 to host network printers.

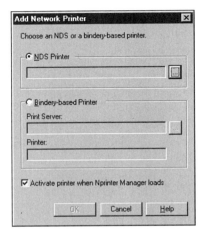

When you mark the Activate Printer When NPRINTER Manager Loads check box, you need only place the icon for the program in the Windows 95 Startup group to connect the printer whenever you start Windows 95.

It is also possible to run the NPRINTER Manager from a local drive. To do so, you must copy all of the following files from the SYS:PUBLIC\WIN95 directory:

- NPTWIN95.EXE
- NPTWIN95.DLL
- NPTWIN95.HLP
- NPTR95.NLM
- NPTDRV95.NLM
- NPTDRV95.MSG
- NRDDLL95.DLL
- NWADLG95.DLL
- NWADMR95.DLL
- NWCOMN95.DLL
- BIDS45F.DLL
- CW3215.DLL
- OWL252F.DLL

Using the Microsoft Print Services for NetWare   The NPRINTER Manager can only be used with the Novell Client 32 for Windows 95. If you are running the Microsoft Client for NetWare Networks, however, you can still despool jobs from NetWare queues using a service included with the Windows 95 operating system called the Microsoft Print Services for NetWare.

Although it ships with the operating system, the print service is not installed as part of the standard Windows 95 SETUP routine. You must install it manually by adding a new network service from the Windows 95 Control Panel, clicking the Have Disk button and specifying the \ADMIN\NETTOOLS\PRTAGENT directory on the Windows 95 CD-ROM in the Install from Disk dialog box.

Once the service has been installed (and the workstation rebooted), you can open the Properties dialog box for any printer that has been installed in Windows 95 in the usual manner and find an additional tab labeled Print Server (see Figure 17.10). In this dialog box, you enter the name of the NetWare server on which the desired queue is located, and then select the name of its associated NetWare print server. You also can set the rate at which the workstation polls the queue for the existence of new jobs from this panel.

FIG. 17.10
Installation of the Microsoft Print Services for NetWare adds an additional tab to each printer's Properties dialog box.

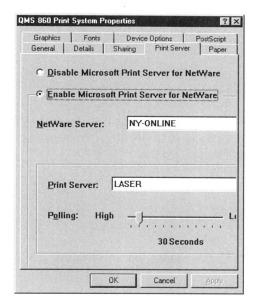

Part
V

Ch
17

After you have configured the print service, double-clicking the printer's icon in the Printers window will display the contents of the NetWare queue, instead of a local workstation queue. If you are logged in as a queue operator, you can manage the network print jobs from this interface, just as you would from PCONSOLE or NetWare Administrator.

Manipulating Queued Print Jobs

Once your print subsystem is operational, the only maintenance needed should be to manage jobs that are waiting in the print queues. You do this by accessing the properties of the Print Queue objects in the NDS tree using NetWare Administrator or PCONSOLE.

In NetWare Administrator, you can find the currently queued print jobs in the Job List screen of any Print Queue object, as shown in Figure 17.11. Selecting one of the list's column headings resorts the display. If you are a queue operator, you can also select any job in the list and pause it by clicking the Hold Job button. The job will then remain in the queue until you Resume it.

N O T E You can access the same list of currently queued jobs by selecting Print Jobs from the Print Queue Information menu in PCONSOLE. ▨

FIG. 17.11
The Job List screen for a Print Queue object contains all of the print jobs that are waiting to be processed.

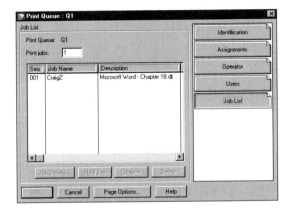

When you view the Job Details for an item in the print queue list, you see the dialog box shown in Figure 17.12. This screen displays extensive information about the job and its current status. The values for the status indicator are as follows:

■ Print job is being serviced

■ Print job has operator hold

■ Print job is ready and waiting for the print server

■ Print job is being added to the Print Queue

■ Print job will be serviced at the target date and time

FIG. 17.12
The Print Job Detail screen enables you to modify when and how the job will print.

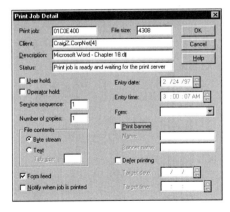

From the Print Job Detail screen in NetWare Administrator and the Print Job Information screen in PCONSOLE, you can view the settings of the following print parameters and also modify them if you have the appropriate rights:

- **User hold**—Indicates that the job's owner has placed a hold on the print job.
- **Operator hold**—Indicates that a queue operator has placed a hold on the print job.
- **Service sequence**—Indicates the selected job's place in the current queue list. The setting can be modified to move the job upwards or downwards in the list.
- **Number of copies**—Can be modified to generate multiple copies of a document without repeatedly transmitting the same data over the network.
- **File contents**—Indicates whether the current job is comprised of plain text only, or if it contains page description (such as PCL or PostScript code) or graphic data.
- **Form feed**—Indicates whether a form feed command should be appended to the current print job. In the case of a plain text print job, the final page will not eject from the printer unless it is completely filled with text. If the workstation's printer driver already sends a form feed at the end of each job, enabling this feature will cause an additional blank page to be ejected.
- **Notify when job is printed**—Indicates whether or not the job's owner should receive a message when the processing of the print job is completed.
- **Print banner**—Indicates whether or not a banner page should be printed with the job, and what text should be printed on that page.
- **Defer printing**—Enables you to specify the date and time that the print job should be processed. This enables you to schedule lengthy or complex jobs for times when printer demand is low.

Part
V

Ch
17

Summary

Because all print object configuration parameters are now located in the NDS database, the installation and management of NetWare printers has been centralized and simplified. The tasks promise to become simpler still with the advent of Novell Distributed Print Services in the near future. ●

CHAPTER 18

Networking Mass Storage

As the amount of storage needed on the average NetWare server grows, it becomes more common to see mass storage devices other than hard disk drives installed in servers. Today, the average network workstation is usually equipped with more hard disk space than a high-end server of only a few years ago. Keeping up with users' storage needs, in terms of capacity, security, and speed, requires an understanding of the new technologies available today, and how they work with your network operating system.

NetWare is capable of supporting enormous amounts of hard disk space (up to 64 volumes with 16-million directory entries each), but it is not always practical to store non-volatile or seldom-used data on a hard disk drive. Less expensive media, such as CD-ROMs, tapes, and optical disks, are a viable alternative, and NetWare includes the infrastructure needed to make use of these devices. ■

How to load and mount CD-ROM volumes on a NetWare server

NetWare's CDROM.NLM module enables you to make CD-ROM data available to all of your users by mounting CD-ROMs as volumes.

How to migrate data to less expensive media with NetWare's High Capacity Storage System

HCSS can automatically move your less frequently accessed data to optical disks and retrieve it on demand.

How to effectively back up NetWare servers and work-stations

NetWare's Storage Management Services standard enables third-party developers to create backup solutions that can accommodate all of the diverse data types found on a NetWare network.

Networking CD-ROMs

CD-ROMs have become almost ubiquitous in the software industry, all but replacing floppy disks as the default software distribution media. CD-ROMs are also an extremely convenient medium for the distribution of reference information, such as dictionaries, encyclopedias, and telephone directories. The rapidly descending cost of writable CD-ROM drives has also made it possible for permanent data archives to be saved on CDs, rather than allowing them to consume hard disk space.

Of course, CD-ROMs are an economical resource for business users only when they are shared, and passing the CD-ROM from hand to hand is hardly convenient, even if all of your workstations are equipped with CD-ROM drives. NetWare resolves this problem by making it possible to mount CD-ROMs as network volumes, from which users can read data like any other volume.

Preparing to Load CDROM.NLM

During the NetWare installation process, you may have used NetWare's CDROM.NLM module to access the operating system distribution disks. The default installation procedure begins by accessing your server's CD-ROM drive as a DOS device. Once the installation reaches the point at which the NetWare disk driver modules are loaded on the server, you may or may not have remounted the CD-ROM as a NetWare volume.

> **CAUTION**
>
> When you are preparing to mount CD-ROMs as NetWare volumes, be sure that there are no DOS drivers left over from the installation process that are addressing the CD-ROM drive. Check the CONFIG.SYS and AUTOEXEC.BAT files on the server's DOS partition, and remove or remark out any commands that are unnecessary.

If you did install NetWare from the server's local CD-ROM drive, you may have the required drivers loaded already. If you performed the installation over the network, however, the first step in networking a CD-ROM drive is to load the appropriate support drivers. These drivers vary, depending on your hardware, but generally consist of

- the NetWare Peripheral Architecture module (NWPA.NLM),
- a host adapter module (HAM),
- a custom device module (CDM) for CD-ROM drives.

If your CD-ROM drive is connected to the same host adapter as your hard drives, you should already have a HAM (host adapter module) configured to load from your server's STARTUP.NCF file. Loading the HAM causes NWPA.NLM to be *spawned* (or auto-loaded), initiating a connection with the NetWare Media Manager. You may, however, have to add a CDM for CD-ROM support, in addition to the module that is already loaded for your hard drives.

For example, an Adaptec SCSI host adapter with hard drives and CD-ROMs attached requires the following drivers:

- NWPA.NLM
- SCSI154X.HAM
- SCSIHD.CDM
- SCSICD.CDM

The three latter files must be explicitly loaded from the STARTUP.NCF (or AUTOEXEC.NCF) file. You can use the INSTALL.NLM utility to select the appropriate drivers for your hardware, or specify additional CDMs to be loaded for your existing HAMs.

NOTE   NetWare 4.11 introduces the NetWare Peripheral Architecture (NPA), a modular system of device drivers (HAMs and CDMs) that replaces the monolithic (DSK) drivers of earlier NetWare versions. Development of new DSK drivers ceased as of January 1997, and Novell will no longer provide support for monolithic drivers after January of 1998.

NetWare ships with the new style drivers for some of the most popular host adapters on the market. In other cases, you may have to obtain drivers from the hardware manufacturer or use DSK drivers until NPA drivers are available. ■

Loading CDROM.NLM

Once you have loaded the appropriate drivers, server-based applications are capable of accessing the CD-ROM hardware. CDROM.NLM is the program supplied with NetWare that enables CD-ROMs to be mounted as NetWare volumes.

NOTE   While NetWare's CDROM.NLM program works quite well, there are other third-party products that enable you to network multiple CD-ROM drives, without having to physically install the drives in your server. Some of these devices are essentially a SCSI adapter and a network adapter in a single box, to which you attach individual CD-ROM drives and your network cable. Other devices take the form of CD-ROM drive arrays, with several (or even dozens) of drives in a single housing. ■

As a storage medium, CD-ROMs are different from hard drives primarily in that they are read-only devices. The reason why such a program as CDROM.NLM is needed to mount them is so that the index and other data that would normally be written to a NetWare volume can be redirected elsewhere.

Other NetWare file system features, such as block suballocation and file compression, must also be disabled for CD-ROM volumes because these file manipulations require write access to the storage medium itself. CDROM.NLM automatically disables these features when you mount a volume, creates an index file for each CD-ROM, and stores the information on the server's SYS volume (by default).

TIP Accidentally enabling block suballocation or file compression for a CD-ROM volume (using the INSTALL.NLM program, for example) cannot damage the data on the CD-ROM itself, but it will corrupt the data in the volume index file. If this occurs, you must rebuild the index file using the CD MOUNT /R command from the server console prompt, as detailed in "Using the CD MOUNT Command" later in this chapter.

Indexing a CD-ROM can be a time-consuming process, particularly if there are many small files on the disk. Therefore, the index files created by CDROM.NLM for each CD volume that you mount are retained on the SYS volume to speed up future mounts of the same volume. The files are stored in a hidden file called CDROM$$.ROM, and are usually 8M to 9M in size each. If you mount many different CD-ROMs, these files can occupy a significant amount of disk space. To store the CD-ROM index files on a volume other than SYS, you can load the CDROM.NLM module with the /V switch, followed by the name of the desired volume, as shown:

```
LOAD CDROM /V=volume
```

You can also use the CD command with the PURGE parameter to remove the hidden index files from the selected volume.

NOTE Some CD-ROMs, particularly those distributed by Novell, include a pre-built index file on the disk itself. This saves disk space on your other NetWare volumes, and speeds up considerably the process of mounting the CD-ROM.

Be aware also that CD-ROM volumes require additional server memory to mount, just like hard drive volumes. Because the issue of writing to the disk is moot, and there is no danger of wasted space, CD-ROM volumes are always mounted using a 64K block size. This minimizes the amount of memory needed because a larger block size means that fewer blocks have to be indexed.

CD-ROM.NLM provides support for disks written in most of the popular formats, including High Sierra, ISO 9660, and those requiring the MAC or NFS name spaces. An additional module called HFSLFS.NLM is included to support disks written using the HFS (Apple) file system.

Using the *CD* Command

Once you have loaded the CDROM.NLM program, you can control the operational status of all of the CD-ROM drives installed in the server using the CD command from the server console. The CD command has a great many parameters and switches that enable you to manipulate CD-ROMs and control the access that users are granted to them. The parameters for CD are as follows:

■ CD MOUNT is used to mount a CD-ROM as a NetWare volume.

■ CD DISMOUNT is used to dismount a CD-ROM volume.

- CD DEVICE LIST is used to list all of the CD-ROM drives currently registered with the NetWare Media Manager.

- CD VOLUME LIST is used to list the volume names of all of the disks currently loaded in the registered CD-ROM drives.

- CD CHANGE is used to dismount the current CD-ROM in a selected drive, allow a media change, and then mount the new disk, all with one command.

- CD GROUP is used to grant the members of an NDS Group object rights to a CD-ROM volume.

- CD RENAME is used to rename a CD-ROM volume to prevent duplicate name conflicts.

- CD DIR is used to display the files and directories found at the root of a CD-ROM volume, in DOS format, without mounting the volume.

- CD PURGE is used to delete the hidden CD-ROM index files that have accumulated on the SYS (or other) volume.

- CD IMAGE is used to mount a CD-ROM image file stored on a NetWare volume for testing purposes before the master CD-ROM is produced.

- CD HELP is used to display detailed help information about the CD parameters and switches.

The use of the CD parameters and their switches is detailed in the following sections.

Using the *CD MOUNT* Command   The CD MOUNT command initiates the process by which a specified CD-ROM is read, indexed, and then mounted as a NetWare volume. Once mounted, the CD-ROM can be accessed by users like any other NetWare volume. To specify the CD-ROM to be mounted, you include either the volume name of the disk or a device number on the command line, as follows:

```
CD MOUNT volume¦device options
```

You can display the volume names of the disks in the registered CD-ROM drives with the CD VOLUME LIST command, and device numbers with the CD DEVICE LIST command.

N O T E   The device number that you specify on the CD MOUNT command line is a number that is designated by the NetWare Media Manager. It does not correspond to the device's SCSI ID number, or any other type of hardware setting.

You can also use the following options on the CD MOUNT command line:

- /R forces the index file to be rebuilt during the mount process, replacing the existing file. It is used primarily when remounting an existing volume with a different name space, or when the index file is damaged by the activation of block suballocation or file compression on the CD-ROM volume.

- /all mounts the disks in all of the server's registered CD-ROM drives.

- /MAC causes Macintosh name space to be added as the volume is indexed and mounted.

- /NFS causes NFS name space to be added as the volume is indexed and mounted.

Part
V

Ch
18

- /G=*number* grants a specific user group access to the volume being mounted. By default, the EVERYONE group (that is, group 0) is granted access to the volume, but with this parameter, you can limit CD-ROM access to selected users. Groups are registered and numbered using the CD GROUP command.

- /I forces the CD-ROM volume to be mounted, even when errors are discovered that prevent access to part of the disk.

- /X=*directory* is used to exclude a specified directory from the indexing process, preventing user access to that directory. You must rebuild the index file (with the /R switch) to regain access to the directory.

- /dup initiates a check for duplicate file names in the same directory while mounting the volume. When long file names on the CD-ROM are truncated to DOS 8.3 file names, duplicates can occur. This option forces each truncated file name to be unique.

- /DNVC=*megabytes* adds Direct Map caching to the volume during the indexing process, using the specified number of megabytes of disk space to create the cache. Of the three caching options, this one provides the fastest recall and the shortest cache life (that is, the time that data remains in the cache).

- /ANVC=*megabytes* adds Set Associative caching to the volume during the indexing process, using the specified number of megabytes of disk space to create the cache. Of the three caching options, this one provides intermediate performance, balancing the data recall and cache life.

- /LNVC=*megabytes* adds Associative (LRU) caching to the volume during the indexing process, using the specified number of megabytes of disk space to create the cache. Of the three caching options, this one provides the slowest recall and the longest cache life.

N O T E   The three non-volatile caching options for the CD MOUNT command (/DNVC, /ANVC, and /LNVC) enable you to use disk space to cache volume data from CD-ROMs in addition to the standard NetWare memory caching. You select the amount of disk space to be used and the type of caching that you want to perform by specifying the appropriate option on the CD MOUNT command line. The cache is stored on the volume containing the CD-ROM index. By default, no non-volatile caching is used.

Using the *CD DISMOUNT* Command   The CD DISMOUNT command removes the specified CD-ROM volume from service, allowing you to remove it from the drive. In most cases, CDROM.NLM will not allow you to eject a disk from its drive while it is mounted as a NetWare volume, even through the use of the Eject button on the hardware device itself.

You specify the same volume name or device number on the CD DISMOUNT command line that you would use with the CD MOUNT command, obtained using the CD VOLUME LIST or CD DEVICE LIST command. The syntax is as follows:

```
CD DISMOUNT volume¦device options
```

The available options for CD DISMOUNT are as follows:

- ▣ /eject causes the CD-ROM disk to be ejected from the drive once it has been dismounted.

- ▣ /purge causes the volume's index file to be deleted from the SYS (or other) volume after the CD-ROM is dismounted. (Use the CD PURGE command to delete all index files.)

Using the CD DEVICE LIST Command The CD DEVICE LIST command displays information about each of the devices registered with the NetWare Media Manager, as follows:

```
No. Act. Device Name                                    Volume Name   Mounted
 7   Y   [V020-A1-D4:0] TOSHIBA CD-ROM XM-3301TA rev:2  NOVSDKCD_10      Y
```

The information displayed is

- ▣ the device number, used in the CD MOUNT and CD DISMOUNT commands,
- ▣ whether the device is currently active,
- ▣ the identification string returned by the device in answer to a query from its host adapter,
- ▣ the volume name of the disk currently loaded in the drive,
- ▣ whether or not the volume is currently mounted.

Using the CD VOLUME LIST Command The CD VOLUME LIST command produces a display like the following, listing nearly the same information as CD DEVICE LIST:

```
No. Volume Name   Mounted Device Name
 7  NOVSDKCD_10      Y    [V020-A1-D4:0] TOSHIBA CD-ROM XM-3301TA rev:2
```

Using the CD CHANGE Command If you want to change the CD-ROM in a drive containing a disk that is currently mounted, you can issue separate CD DISMOUNT and CD MOUNT commands, or just use the CD CHANGE command, which performs both functions sequentially. The syntax for CD CHANGE is as follows:

```
CD CHANGE device/volume options
```

The volume variable should specify the name of the volume that is currently mounted. Once the volume is dismounted, you are prompted at the server console to insert the new disk. Once you strike a key, the new disk is indexed and mounted.

CAUTION

Depending on your CD-ROM hardware, it may take several seconds for a newly inserted disk to spin up to operational speed. Be sure to allow for this delay before striking a key to initiate the mounting process, or an error may occur.

You can use any of the options specified earlier in the sections on CD MOUNT and CD DISMOUNT with the CD CHANGE command.

Using the CD GROUP Command Because CD-ROM volumes are more variable than normal NetWare volumes, they are not represented in the NDS tree. As a result, you cannot limit user access to CD-ROMs by assigning trustees to the volume in the usual manner. You can,

Part

V

Ch

18

however, use the /G switch with the CD MOUNT (or CD CHANGE) command to specify the number of a Group object that already exists in the NDS tree. You use the CD GROUP command to assign numbers to Group objects, which are used in the CD MOUNT command line.

By default, access to CD-ROM volumes is granted to the EVERYONE group. To limit access to a particular CD-ROM volume, you must first create a group in the NDS tree and add the users who are to be granted access as members. Once the Group object exists, you use the CD GROUP command to assign it a number, as follows:

CD GROUP *name number*

Group numbers can be 1 to 9, with the EVERYONE group defaulting to number 0. The CD GROUP command with no switches displays the current group definitions.

Once you have assigned a number to the desired group, you then mount the volume using the /G switch and specifying that number. Only one group can be granted access to a particular volume at any one time. Specifying a new group number, therefore, replaces the access granted to the EVERYONE group.

You can also delete a group number definition using the following syntax:

CD GROUP DEL *number*

Using the *CD RENAME* Command   Volume names on a NetWare server must be unique. If you have two CD-ROMs with the same volume name that you want to mount at the same time, you must rename one of the volumes. Use the following command after dismounting the CD-ROM, specifying the device number and the new name that is to be assigned to the volume:

CD RENAME *device volume*

Using the *CD DIR* Command   Issuing the CD DIR command with a device number or volume name on the command line displays the contents of the CD-ROM volume's root directory, just as if you had run the DIR command at a DOS workstation. This command is designed to provide a quick look at the contents of a CD-ROM without mounting it as a volume. You cannot use CD DIR to view the contents of subdirectories or specify any of the DOS DIR options on the command line.

Using the *CD PURGE* Command   Use the CD PURGE command to delete all of the CD-ROM index files from the volume where they are stored. All CD-ROM volumes must be dismounted before using this command. To delete specific index files, use the /purge switch with the CD DISMOUNT command.

Understanding Data Migration

If you examine the hard drives on a typical business network, you will probably find many files that have not been accessed in a very long time. Some could surely stand to be deleted, but there are likely to be others you must keep for future reference. Depending on your business, you may even have gigabytes worth of data that you must store, on the off chance that it will be needed in the distant future.

Computer users have a tendency to fill however much disk space is allotted to them, but installing additional hard disk drives to your servers on a regular basis can be impractical if the majority of the data is not used on a regular basis. There are alternative storage media available, of course, with much lower costs per megabyte than hard disk drives.

Magnetic tape, optical disks, and CD-ROMs can easily be used in a network environment, but the problem with these media is that the task of migrating the appropriate files usually falls to the network administrator. The same holds true for the task of retrieving files when they are needed by users. Keeping track of where particular files are stored can end up being a full-time job for people who already have more than enough to do.

To address this problem, NetWare includes an automatic data migration system called the High Capacity Storage System (HCSS) that enables data to be automatically copied to an optical disk while the file name and other information remain on the hard disk drive. This way, users continue to see their files on the server volumes, even though they are actually stored elsewhere.

When a user attempts to access a migrated file, it is automatically copied back to its original location and furnished to the user. The use of optical disks or other media in this manner is sometimes called *nearline* storage because, while the data is not actually stored on a server hard drive, it is always available to users without manual intervention by an administrator.

Part

V

Ch

18

Using Alternative Media

NetWare's High Capacity Storage System is designed for use with a magneto-optical disk changer known as a jukebox. A *jukebox* is a SCSI device, consisting of one or more optical disk drives, slots for the storage of the disks themselves, and a robot mechanism that automatically inserts the disks into the drive.

The device is also equipped with sufficient intelligence to maintain an inventory of the disks in the slots so that any particular disk can be accessed on demand. Optical jukeboxes are available in various sizes and capacities, some of which can accommodate enormous amounts of data.

Jukeboxes are supported by the new NetWare Peripheral Architecture, just like CD-ROM drives. Because a jukebox is essentially two separate devices (a changer and a drive) in one case, two CDM drivers are needed. A CDM module for the jukebox changer mechanism called SCSICHGR.CDM is supplied with NetWare, which you load with your existing HAM driver, along with a module for the optical drive itself, such as SCSIMO.CDM. DSK drivers are also supplied if you are not using NPA.

Migrating Files

Once the jukebox hardware is registered with the NetWare Media Manager, you create a NetWare volume on a hard drive with the data migration feature enabled. On this volume, you create a directory structure that corresponds to the disks loaded in the jukebox, and associate the directories with specific optical disks. Only the data stored in this directory structure will be migrated.

You must create these directories using NetWare Administrator, with the plug-in modules installed that add the HCSS commands to the Tools menu. Once the directories are created, users can then store data on that volume in the usual manner, unaware of its special nature.

N O T E The HCSS plug-ins enable you to perform several different administration tasks to the optical media, such as formatting, importing, and exporting disks. You must use NetWare Administrator to perform these administrative tasks so that the system remains aware of the disks that are loaded in the jukebox.

Loading the HCSS.NLM module on the server creates a link between the jukebox and the volume, and enables the data migration process. The HCSS program enables you to establish upper- and lower-disk space thresholds that control the data migration process.

When the HCSS volume becomes filled to a certain point, the data migration engine is activated automatically. The engine scans the volume for the files with the oldest access dates and begins to copy their data to the appropriate optical disks until a specified amount of disk space on the volume has been cleared.

However, although the file data itself is copied to the optical disk, the directory entries for the files remain intact on the NetWare volume. Such information as the file name, its size, and its attributes are retained on the volume. The file system also adds the M attribute to indicate which files have been migrated.

N O T E NetWare's M attribute, which indicates that a file has been migrated, is purely informational and cannot be changed with such utilities as FLAG. However, NetWare also provides a Dm (Don't Migrate) attribute that you can add to a file or directory to prevent it from being migrated by HCSS.

Users can scan the volume with any application or utility and see a directory structure populated with files that appear to be located on the hard disk volume, but which may actually be located on an optical disk. The volume can therefore appear to users as though it holds data adding up to ten or more times its actual disk space.

Demigrating Files

When a NetWare client attempts to access a file that has been migrated to an optical disk, the application behaves no differently than when it is being used to access a file on any other NetWare volume. When the file request reaches the server, however, the HCSS engine intercepts it and copies the file data back to its original location on the volume.

The file can then be furnished to the client in the normal manner. To a user, the demigration process is invisible, except for an additional delay as the data is copied from the optical disk. There is no confusion as a result of files having been moved to different directories, and no intervention from the network administrator is required at all.

When multiple users access files that are migrated at the same time, optical disk access requests are queued, sometimes imposing additional delays. However, HCSS uses an access algorithm on the jukebox that is called *elevator queuing*. This means that disk access operations are organized to provide the most efficient access to the media. For example, if there are three requests in the queue for files located on a particular optical disk, HCSS will satisfy those three requests before inserting another disk into the drive, regardless of the order of the jobs in the queue.

Planning a Migration Strategy

Novell did not invent the concept of data migration, and NetWare's HCSS feature imposes several significant limitations on its use. You can only create a single HCSS volume and use a single jukebox on any one server. Also, device support is limited, and only the DOS name space is supported.

There are several third-party products that expand on the data migration concept, offering many additional features. Often called *hierarchical storage management* products, these systems can provide data migration services to your entire network, supporting huge arrays of optical jukeboxes as well as *tertiary* (third-stage) devices, such as tape autochangers.

A three-stage system uses multiple sets of thresholds that govern the migration of data, first to the secondary medium, and then after a continued period without user access, to the tertiary medium. With these capabilities, you can build systems that can store hundreds of gigabytes, or even terabytes of data, while still leaving that data available for use at all times.

Part
V

Ch
18

Backing Up a NetWare Network

New technologies, such as networked CD-ROMs and data migration, can expand the storage capacity of a NetWare server, but they do not replace system backups. Indeed, they further complicate an already complicated process. Backups are essential on a network of any size, and the growing heterogeneity of networks adds different file systems and ever increasing amounts of data to the job.

NetWare includes a utility with the operating system, called SBACKUP, that provides limited system backup capabilities. You can register a server tape drive with NetWare Media Manager, just like CD-ROM drives and optical jukeboxes. Then, you can run SBACKUP at the server console to back up your volumes and other data to tape.

SBACKUP is not a full-featured backup program. It lacks many of the features typically found in third-party network backup products, such as media rotation, job scheduling, and intelligent restore capabilities. Novell is well aware of this fact, however. It was clearly not its intention in creating SBACKUP to compete with the developers who specialize in backup products. Instead, it devoted its efforts to the development of an architecture that facilitates the use of other products to back up NetWare networks.

NetWare's Storage Management Services (SMS) is designed to promote extensibility and compatibility between Novell's storage management modules and those developed by other manufacturers. SMS consists of standards that define a tape format, data delivery modules, device drivers, and a central program that connects the various parts. Developers can create some or all of the modules themselves, or use those that are included with NetWare.

This modularizing allows for an open-ended system that can more easily be upgraded as new backup requirements arise. To facilitate the use of a new type of hardware device, for example, only the device driver itself has to be rewritten. All of the other backup modules can remain in operation.

Understanding the SMS Architecture

Novell's Storage Management Services consists of the following modules (which interact as shown in Figure 18.1):

- **TSA**—A Target Service Agent is a module that, during a backup operation, receives commands from the Storage Management Engine, scans a particular data source, then packages and delivers the requested data to the SME in the generic *System Independent Data Format* (SIDF) format. During restores, the TSA performs the opposite function, receiving data from the SME and writing it out to the target.

  The TSA is solely responsible for understanding the data format of the target system and converting it to SIDF, while preserving its unique attributes for possible restoration. NetWare includes TSAs for server volumes, for all of the supported client workstations, and for the Novell Directory Services database.

- **SIDF**—The System Independent Data Format is designed to enable data from many different file systems to be stored on many possible media. All data is delivered by TSAs to the Storage Management Engine using SIDF. If the SME writes the data to tape (or another medium) using this format, then any other product supporting SIDF should be able to read the data.

- **SMDR**—The Storage Management Data Requester makes it possible for SMS modules located on systems throughout the network to communicate with each other. TSAs on remote workstations, for example, use SMDR to send their data to the SME, located on a server.

- **SMSDI**—The Storage Management Services Device Interface provides a generic interface to any type of media that is used by the SME to access storage devices. The NetWare Peripheral Architecture provides the device interface used by SBACKUP.

- **SME**—The Storage Management Engine is the heart of the SMS architecture. It coordinates the activities of all of the other modules, conveying data between the TSAs and the SMSDI as needed. The SME also provides the user interface to the backup system in which the data to be backed up or restored is selected and the job configured. SBACKUP is NetWare's SME.

FIG. 18.1

Novell's Storage Management Services architecture defines several independent modules that work together to perform network backups.

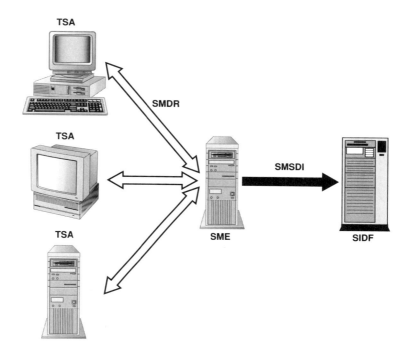

The first SMS module that is replaced by the developer of a third-party backup product is, of course, the SME. Whatever additional capabilities are built in to the system must be controlled by the central engine. Most products enable you to create complex rotation schemes that can back up both servers and workstations all over an enterprise network on a regular basis. NetWare's SMSDI is also seldom used by third-party developers. Most backup utilities include their own proprietary interface to the storage hardware in order to exercise control over the rate at which data is delivered to the device. The data transfer speed is a crucial part of writing data to tape quickly and efficiently.

Backing Up the NDS Database

Some backup products are wholly SMS-compliant, meaning that they use Novell's TSAs to back up different data types, and they write to tape using the SIDF. Other manufacturers choose to develop their own agents for backing up target services and their own tape format. However, the one task that has resulted in universal agreement among backup software manufacturers is the protection of the Novell Directory Services database.

The NDS database is, obviously, stored on a file server drive, specifically, on the SYS volume. However, it is not visible as part of the file system and cannot be backed up in the same way as the other files on the SYS volume.

There are, in fact, only two ways to back up the NDS tree to tape. One is to use the TSA included with NetWare (TSANDS.NLM) in an SMS-compliant backup product. This is the route now taken by most of the mainstream network backup solutions.

The second alternative involves a backup technique that is completely different from the standard file-based paradigm. Several new products increase the speed and efficiency of backups by avoiding file systems entirely. Instead of accessing files through the operating system and delivering them to a tape drive, the software reads the hard disk drive directly and creates a sector-by-sector image of the drive on tape. Since every bit on the drive is copied, the NDS database is necessarily included.

The concept of image backup technology has been around for some time, but until recently it suffered from the inability to perform restores of individual files. Today's products can restore single files, and can address hardware other than that from which the data was backed up.

NDS backups are a crucial selling point among backup software manufacturers, but the prospect of performing a complete restoration of the database, while preserving all of its links to the other parts of the NetWare operating system, is dubious at best. While tape backups should certainly not be omitted, the most efficient way to protect your NDS tree is to use the replication capabilities of NDS itself.

At the very minimum, a NetWare network that relies on Novell Directory Services should have two servers so that a read/write replica of the database can be stored on a different machine. Data loss is most likely to occur as a result of a hardware failure on one server, rather than a disaster, such as fire or theft, that threatens both machines.

Summary

Each of the mass storage technologies discussed in this chapter involves the capabilities provided by programs included with NetWare and the operating system's ability to accommodate the use of third-party products. Depending on the size of your network and your users' requirements, you may find NetWare's mass storage capabilities to be sufficient. Otherwise, there are many other solutions on the market that you can use to fulfill whatever needs are required. ●

Connecting Client Workstations

CHAPTER 19

Accessing Network Resources

In NetWare 4, all network resources—such as printers, file servers, and volumes—are defined as objects in NDS. For users to effectively utilize network resources, they must be able to rely on a consistent workstation environment and a certain amount of network resource stability. Even for sophisticated network users, everyday tasks are greatly simplified by the capability to assimilate network drives and printers into the workstation client configuration.

In this chapter, you learn how to perform different administrative tasks that provide the stable environment that users need and expect in order to access network resources. ■

Creating consistent drive mappings to enable users to access their data and applications

Learn how to create a drive mapping using a Windows 95 or Windows 3.1 workstation. Assigning drive letters to network paths helps ease administration and make the data stored on the network more accessible.

Capturing and troubleshooting network printing from different client platforms

Configure Windows 95, Windows 3.1, and DOS-based workstations to redirect printer output to a network queue versus local LPT ports. Learn how to troubleshoot workstation problems related to printing.

Enabling a successful turnkey environment every time a network user logs in

Review the different types of login scripts and streamline the login process. Evaluate the advantages and disadvantages for different types of login scripts.

Drive Mapping

A *drive mapping* is the NetWare term for creating a workstation drive letter that points to a specific location on a NetWare volume. The focus in this section is the mechanics of establishing drive mappings, or pointers to paths on both the local machine and on network servers. The end of this chapter demonstrates the incorporation of the MAP command into login scripts. Network and search drive MAP commands can be added to login scripts so that the drive mappings are created every time a user logs in.

Drive mappings are created using the letters of the alphabet. The first drive letter that is to be used for a network drive is specified in the client configuration on the user's workstation. The first five drive letters (A: through E:) are reserved for the local system's floppy and hard disk drives. Traditionally, F: is chosen to be the first network drive, unless the workstation contains additional hardware, such as extra hard disk or CD-ROM drives, that require drive letters beyond E:.

You can create two different types of network drive mappings on a workstation: network drives and search drives. You use *network drives* to point to a specific location on a NetWare volume, and *search drives* to make the files in a volume directory executable from any command prompt, just like the DOS PATH command.

N O T E   You have the capability to create up to 26 different drive mappings for use in both your local and network environment, 16 of which can be search drives. Although you can have 16 search drives, that number includes those created with the DOS PATH command.

Once drive mappings have been created, users can navigate their way about NetWare volumes using any of the standard client operating system tools, such as the DOS change directory (CD) command, the Windows File Manager, or the Windows Explorer. Experienced network users find that seamlessly navigating their local or network drives is an added benefit to using drive mappings.

Users that are relatively new to computers and networks often remain completely ignorant of the fact that network drive mappings can be different for different users. A good NetWare administrator creates a uniform workstation environment, mapping the same drive letters to appropriate NetWare volumes for users that require access to the same resources. This tends to prevent the confusion that can arise when one user refers to a file on the G: drive that a colleague cannot find because of different mappings.

The universal way of accessing the information on a PC's local drive is by referencing a drive letter, such as A: or C:. These drive letters are assigned by the system BIOS and are always available. NetWare volumes, however, are referenced by name: the physical name given to the volume when it was created. To access a NetWare volume or directory using a drive letter, you assign, or *map*, the NetWare volume name to the letter.

Like other NetWare resources, a volume is represented in the NDS tree by an object. The name of the object is formed by taking the volume name and adding the host server name as a prefix, separated by an underscore. For example, file server EDUC has two physical volumes, SYS: and VOL1:. The object name for each volume is EDUC_SYS and EDUC_VOL1. The volume object name is used in NetWare commands to reference the root of the volume. A complete path to a file located in a subdirectory on a volume is therefore noted as:

`EDUC_SYS:HOME\FRANK\BUDGET.WK1`

`EDUC_SYS:` represents the object name of volume SYS: located on the NetWare server EDUC. HOME\FRANK\BUDGET.WK1 is the path to the designated file located on that volume.

> **N O T E** You can still use traditional NetWare physical naming to map a drive to a volume on a particular server—for example, EDUC\SYS:HOME\FRANK. NetWare also recognizes UNC naming conventions. The UNC path for the same server, volume, and subdirectory is `\\EDUC\SYS\HOME\FRANK.`

Accessing Data with a Network Drive

When mapping drives, it is important to consider all of the subdirectories that users need to access in order to perform their jobs. All users need a network drive pointing to their own home directory, if they have one. Most network administrators utilize the same drive letter for each user's home directory to keep the mappings consistent.

For volumes or directories containing files that must be shared by users, the most efficient method is to designate the same network drive letter mapping for all users, pointing to the shared directory.

Accessing Applications with a Search Drive

Search drives are typically used to provide NetWare clients with access to networked applications. Search drives play an important role on a PC running DOS or Windows, where their function is identical to that of a directory that has been added to your DOS search path.

Every time you execute an external command, the operating system performs a search for the executable file. First, it searches the workstation's memory, in case the file is a TSR. Second, the operating system searches the current directory. If the OS does not find the command file in memory or the current directory, it begins searching the subdirectories listed in the DOS search path.

> **N O T E** When a network search drive is created, it is also added to your DOS PATH environment variable. A search drive can be inserted in any position in the path, appended to the end, or written over an existing item.

Part V

Using Directory Map Objects

One of the more powerful but less frequently used objects that you can create in the NDS tree is called a directory map. A directory map object is used to represent the path to a specified subdirectory on a NetWare volume. You can use the object as part of any path name in place of the actual volume and directory it represents. This can be a useful tool, especially when used to reference network application files that may be moved to different locations.

▶ **See** "Creating Objects," **p. 146**

Using directory map objects to point to frequently used directories helps to decrease administration time. If you move the directory represented by a directory map object or the files it contains to another location, you can simply modify the object to reflect the new location. Any path names that use the directory map object are automatically updated to reflect the new location. By the use of directory map objects, administrators can avoid the need to make changes to path names in application configurations, Windows, icons, batch files, and login scripts when reorganizing the directory structure of their NetWare volumes.

Directory map objects can also help tremendously when you need to grant access to users whose NDS objects are not located in the same container as the volume where the data is stored. Using a directory map in this way is similar to using an alias object. An alias enables you to create an object that points to the original object in a different container. A directory map holds the path to a subdirectory on a volume that is in a different container.

After creating a directory map object with NETADMIN or NetWare Administrator using the standard procedures, there are two additional steps that you must complete before a user can access the object:

1. Use NetWare Administrator to grant the user the appropriate file system rights to the directory the object points to.
2. Grant the Browse object Write and Read property rights to the Path property of the directory map object.

TIP Larger networks might have the need for an application administrator. Create an organizational role object and grant the Supervisor file system right to the network applications directories. Also, grant the organizational role object the Write property right to the ACL (access control list) property of your directory map objects. This enables the occupant of the role to administer the applications directories and the object that holds the path to these directories.

Creating Drive Mappings

All of the IntranetWare DOS and Windows clients are capable of mapping drive letters to NetWare volumes. Often, there are several different ways of mapping drives, but the resulting functionality is the same, whichever you decide to use.

Using Windows 95 or Windows NT to Access Network Resources

Windows 95 enables you to assign drive letters to server volumes and directories using the Network Neighborhood and the Windows Explorer. Both methods enable you to browse for the volume and directory that you want to map or enter the volume name and directory manually. Your drive letter assignments can be automatically reestablished every time you start the client workstation.

> **N O T E** Although this section demonstrates the drive mapping process using Windows 95, the functionality is the same in Windows NT 4.0, although some of the dialog boxes may look slightly different. ■

Displaying, Mapping, and Removing Network Drives with Network Neighborhood

You can access a list of the currently assigned drive letters on your Windows 95 workstation by double-clicking the My Computer icon on the desktop. This displays a window containing a folder for each drive letter. An alternative method is to right-click My Computer and select Explore from the pop-up menu. Windows 95 then displays an Explorer window similar to the one shown in Figure 19.1. You can also launch the Windows 95 Explorer application from the Start menu and expand the My Computer entry to view your drives.

FIG. 19.1

The Explorer window displays all of the drive letters mapped on your system, and enables you to work with the files and directories on each drive.

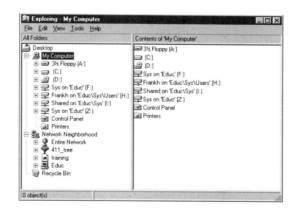

Part
VI

Ch
19

The most direct way to map a new drive letter to a NetWare volume using Explorer is to expand the Network Neighborhood entry and browse to the desired volume, then right-click it and choose Map Network Drive from the resulting context menu. The Map Network Drive dialog box appears; when you press the down arrow in the Drive box, your currently mapped network drives are shown (see Figure 19.2).

FIG. 19.2

In the Map Network Drive dialog box, select a drive letter and then supply the path to the desired NetWare volume or directory.

To add a new drive mapping, choose the drive letter you want to assign and enter the name of the NetWare volume or directory you want to access in the Path box, using UNC notation. If you want this drive mapping to be reestablished automatically every time you restart the system, check the Reconnect at Logon box in the Map Network Drive dialog box. The new drive mapping is then created, and you can access the contents of the new drive letter using any Windows 95 utility, DOS prompt, third-party file management tool, or application dialog box.

To remove a drive mapping, select Disconnect Network Drive from the Explorer's Tools menu or toolbar. You can then highlight the network drive mapping that you want to remove from the Disconnect Network Drives dialog box.

Using Windows 3.1 to Access Network Resources

Clients running Windows 3.1 rely on two tools for accessing network resources: the MAP command, which is executed from a DOS prompt, or the Windows-based NetWare User Tools program. From within Windows, you can use the NetWare User Tools program to map drives, capture printer output, send messages to other users, and perform many other functions, all of which can also be duplicated at the DOS prompt using various NetWare utilities.

Mapping a drive using the GUI tools provided by the IntranetWare clients is so easy that some people question whether it is necessary to learn how to map drives from the DOS command line. The most compelling answer is that there is no GUI interface that you can use when creating NetWare login scripts. As a NetWare administrator, you must be familiar with the syntax needed to create drive mappings from the command line because the exact same syntax is used in login scripts.

Displaying a List of Assigned Drives   The MAP command has several uses. If you type just the command MAP at the DOS prompt with no parameters, you are presented with a list of the workstation's currently assigned drive letters. The map display for user FRANK on file server EDUC follows:

```
Drives A, B, C, D, E map to a local disk.
Drive H: = EDUC/SYS:HOME\FRANK\
Drive I: = EDUC/SYS:\SHARED
-----     Search Drives     -----
SEARCH S1:= Z:. [EDUC/SYS:\PUBLIC]
SEARCH S2:= Y:. [EDUC/SYS:\PROGS\WORDPROC]
SEARCH S3:= C:\WINDOWS
SEARCH S4:= C:\DOS
```

The MAP display shows how each drive letter is being used. The first line of the display verifies that drives A: through E: are being used by the local operating system. The next section lists the drive letters (in this case, H: and I:) that have been mapped to server volumes and directories. The last section of the display lists the search drives that have been assigned to volumes and directories.

Notice that the list of search drives displays the search position number as well as the drive letter. When you create a search drive, you must designate the search position. NetWare returns the next available drive letter starting from the end of the alphabet and working backwards. These search drive letters are then added to your workstation's PATH environment variable.

Using *MAP* to Create a Network Drive Mapping   The following example demonstrates how to use MAP to create a network drive to point to a user's home directory. Notice the syntax needed for the command to execute properly; you must supply the drive letter and the appropriate path:

```
MAP H:=EDUC_SYS:HOME\FRANK
```

To confirm that the drive has been successfully mapped, NetWare responds with the following:

```
Drive H: = EDUC_SYS: \HOME\FRANK
```

If the MAP command is unable to locate the directory specified, NetWare supplies the following error message:

```
MAP-4.12-195: Directory [I:=SYS:\HOME\FRANK] cannot be located.
```

TIP Users who do not have appropriate rights to view the contents of a directory receive the `Directory cannot be located` error when trying to map a drive to that directory. This happens frequently when mapping to a directory map object. The user must have `BROWSE` object rights to the map object and the Read property right to the `Path` property. He must also have the appropriate file system rights to view the directory contents (`SCAN`).

If the volume is in a different context, you must include the volume's complete NDS name, which includes the volume object name and a list of the container objects stretching from the object to the [Root] of the tree. If, for example, your current context is .CHI.TRAINING and you need to map a network drive to the SHARED directory on a volume in the .NY.TRAINING container, you must enter the following:

```
MAP J:=.EDUC_SYS.NY.TRAINING:SHARED
```

Using *MAP* to Create a Search Drive Mapping   As mentioned in "Drive Mapping" earlier in this chapter, you can create up to 16 different search drives on a workstation. The search drives are added to your path by being inserted into a specific position, appended to the end of the drive list, or written over an existing item.

The syntax used for mapping a search drive is slightly different from that for a network drive. A network drive relies on the user to enter the desired drive letter, while a search drive is created based on the search position number. To create a search drive and place it in the first search position, you refer to it as S1:. To create a search drive and append it to the end of the path, you refer to it as S16:.

The following example demonstrates the creation of a search drive pointing to the SYS:PUBLIC directory. This is an important search drive to establish because without it, the NetWare workstation utilities located in that directory do not operate properly. The current workstation PATH environment variable is PATH=c:;c:\dos;c:\windows. The syntax for the creation of the search drive mapping to SYS:PUBLIC is as follows:

```
MAP INS S1:=EDUC_SYS:PUBLIC
```

Notice the insert option, or INS, that has been included on the command line. This ensures that the current path is preserved and that a new search drive is inserted in the first position. The NetWare confirmation and the new path are shown in the following:

```
S1:= Z:.[EDUC_SYS: \PUBLIC]
Path=Z:;C:;C:\dos;C:\windows
```

Using this same syntax, you can insert a search drive in any position in the PATH variable by using INS with the designations S1: through S16:. The following MAP command creates a search drive pointing to the WORDPROC directory in the second search position. The NetWare confirmation and the new path are as follows:

```
MAP INS S2:=EDUC_SYS:PROGS\WORDPROC
S2:= Y:.[EDUC_SYS: \PROGS\WORDPROC]
PATH=Z:;Y:;C:;C:\dos;c:\windows
```

Some network administrators prefer to append all network applications to the end of the path. This is accomplished by using the S16 option. The S16 option is interpreted as *the next available search drive:*

```
MAP S16:=EDUC_SYS:EMAIL\POSTOFF
```

Notice that with S16 there is no need to use the INS command option. NetWare confirms by responding that S5: (which is the next available position) has been mapped. In the following, X: has been appended to the end of the path:

```
Drive S5:=.[EDUC _SYS: \EMAIL\POSTOFF]
PATH=Z:;Y:;C:;C:\dos;C:\windows;X:
```

Mapping a Drive to a Directory Map Object   The directory map object holds a path name as a property. Therefore, you can simply replace the path name in a MAP command with the directory map object name. The name of the directory map object used in the following example is CHI-EMAIL.

```
MAP S16:=CHI-EMAIL
```

To map a directory map object that is not in your current context, you need to supply the fully distinguished NDS name for the object. The following example demonstrates how to map to NY-EMAIL, based on a current context of .CHI.TRAINING, where the directory map object NY-EMAIL is in the .NY.TRAINING container.

```
MAP S16:=.NY-EMAIL.NY.TRAINING
```

Choosing the Drive Letter Assigned to a Search Drive   By default, MAP assigns letters to search drives starting at the end of the alphabet and working backward. To override this default and assign a specific drive letter, you can specify the desired letter in your MAP command. To make the EDUC_SYS:PROGS\WORDPROC directory search drive S2: and assign it drive letter W:, use the following command:

```
MAP S2:=W:=EDUC_SYS:PROGS\WORDPROC
```

Notice that you supply the search drive designation (S2:) first, and then the drive letter (W:). Both the search drive and drive letter designations are followed by colons and equal signs.

N O T E   Drive letters created as a result of mapping a search drive can be used in Windows to create program icons for network applications. To do this, you use the drive letters in the Program Item Properties dialog box for the command line and working directory options. ▪

Changing Search Drives into Network Drives, and Vice Versa   You can change a drive mapping from a search drive to a network drive very easily by using the C (Change) option of the MAP command, and specifying the drive to change. To change the preceding mapped drive W: to a network drive, use the following command:

```
MAP C W:
```

Drive W: still points to the EDUC_SYS:PROGS\WORDPROC directory, but it is now a network drive and is shown at the top of the MAP display.

Deleting a Mapped Drive   Network administrators and advanced users might find the need to delete drive mappings, such as when troubleshooting network access problems. You can delete a drive mapping at a DOS prompt by typing MAP DEL followed by a mapped drive letter, as follows:

```
MAP DEL J:
MAP DEL W:
```

Mapping a Root Directory   The MAP command provides an option that you can use to make a drive mapping to a subdirectory on a server volume a "fake" root directory. In other words, you can make a drive map look as though it is pointing to the root of the volume, when in fact it is actually pointing to a subdirectory that may be several levels deep in the directory structure.

A common user requirement is a drive map to his home directory. Earlier, drive H: was mapped to the EDUC_SYS:HOME\FRANK directory. At the DOS prompt, switching to the H: drive would display the current directory as H:\HOME\FRANK. When you use the ROOT option on the MAP command line, the drive appears at the command prompt simply as H:— as though the \HOME\FRANK directory is the root of the drive. The following line demonstrates the use of MAP ROOT:

```
MAP ROOT H:=EDUC_SYS:HOME\FRANK
```

Part
VI

Ch
19

NetWare responds with the following confirmation; notice the difference in the response syntax:

```
Drive H:= EDUC_SYS:HOME\FRANK \
```

When a drive is created using the ROOT option, the backslash (\) used to indicate the root of the volume is listed at the end of the line. A drive map created without the ROOT option keeps the backslash (\) in the true root position, immediately following the volume name.

Mapping a directory as a fake root offers several advantages. The biggest benefit is that users cannot use the DOS CD (change directory) command to change to directories above the directory level that was specified as the root. Hiding elements that can be potential causes of confusion can help to decrease the time it takes to acclimate new computer users to a network environment. When the additional directory names are suppressed, they can more easily associate drive H: with their experiences using the local drive, C:.

Mapping the Next Available Drive   Another useful parameter of the MAP command is called NEXT. With the MAP NEXT feature instead of a specific drive letter, you can map a drive letter to any specified location, and NetWare automatically assigns it the next available drive letter. The following example demonstrates the use of the MAP NEXT command, including the confirmation response:

```
MAP NEXT EDUC_SYS:UPDATE\SOFTWARE
Drive L: = EDUC_SYS: \UPDATE\SOFTWARE
```

Note that you cannot use the ROOT and NEXT options on the same command line. Mapping the next available drive as a root map requires two steps. First, you assign the next available drive to the directory UPDATE\SOFTWARE. The command and the NetWare confirmation are as follows:

```
MAP NEXT EDUC_SYS:UPDATE\SOFTWARE
Drive J: = EDUC_SYS: \UPDATE\SOFTWARE
```

Then, you can use a shortcut by assigning drive J: to be a root map of J:. The command and the NetWare confirmation are as follows:

```
MAP ROOT J:=J:
Drive J:= EDUC_SYS:UPDATE\SOFTWARE \
```

Mapping a Drive Using NetWare User Tools for Client 32

NetWare User Tools provides a graphical interface with which you can map drive letters. When you launch NetWare User Tools and select the Drive icon from the toolbar, your screen displays the NetWare Drive Connections window with two selection panes. The left pane lists all of the workstation's drive letters, and the right pane displays the available network resources.

In the right pane, you can browse through the NDS tree and expand NetWare volumes to locate the desired subdirectory for the mapping. After highlighting the drive to be mapped in the left pane and the desired subdirectory in the right pane, click the Map button to associate the two (see Figure 19.3). You can also drag a volume or directory icon from the right pane and drop it on a drive letter to accomplish the same end. If you select a drive that is already in use, you are prompted to confirm the remapping of the existing drive letter.

FIG. 19.3
NetWare User Tools provides a graphical interface that you can use to map drives.

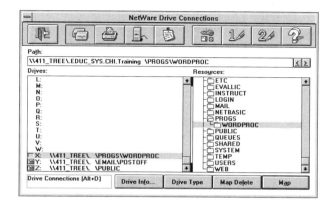

A drive mapped in NetWare User Tools is a network drive by default. Select the Drive Type button from the lower button bar to designate whether a drive is a network drive or search drive. From the Drive Type dialog box, you can also specify that the drive mapping be reestablished automatically every time you launch Windows by selecting the Permanent check box. Figure 19.4 shows a drive map to the EDUC_SYS:UPDATE\SOFTWARE directory as a permanent search drive. You can then change the search drive position, using the arrow buttons.

FIG. 19.4
Change the type of a drive pointer from Network to Search by using the Drive Type button in the NetWare User Tools Drive Settings dialog box.

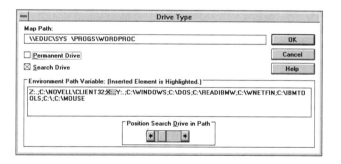

Creating a *MAP* Root in NetWare User Tools

On the NetWare User Tools Drive Connections screen, there are two arrow buttons on the far right of the directory path entry box that you can use to create fake root mappings from within NetWare User Tools. Selecting the right and left arrows moves the root and displays the current root value in the path shown in the entry box. The computer signals you with a beep when you have moved the root mapping to the true root position and when you have moved the root as far to the right as possible.

Capturing Printer Output

Sharing printers is one of the original reasons why PCs came to be networked in the first place. In order to send print jobs to network printers, users must configure their workstations using the appropriate client software. This is done in one of two ways:

■ Operating systems and applications that are network-aware can print directly to NetWare printers or print queues. This includes all versions of Windows and some DOS applications.

■ Software that is not aware of the network can print to NetWare printers by using the CAPTURE utility to redirect print output from a workstation LPT port to a NetWare print queue.

With both printing methods, the client software is responsible for adding a print header and print tail to the print job and sending it to the designated queue. The header information contains instructions on how the print job should be printed, including such options as banner pages, multiple copies, tabs, and form feeds. The instructions needed to reset the printer to its original state are contained in the print tail.

CAPTURE and NetWare 4.11

In previous versions of NetWare, you had to specify the name of a print queue in the CAPTURE command line. NetWare 4.11 enables you to use either the printer name or the print queue name. For example, you can enter the following syntax to connect LPT1 to the printer NY-LASER, which is serviced by print queue NY-QUEUE.

```
CAPTURE L=1 P=NY-LASER NFF NB TI=5
```

Using Windows 95 to Access Network Printers

In Windows 95, most network printing is accomplished by using the Add Printer Wizard in the Printer Control Panel. The only difference from setting up a local printer is the selection of a NetWare print queue object from the Browse for Printer dialog box. Once you have created a printer definition in this manner, you can select the network printer from any Windows application.

However, you may still want to print from the occasional DOS application in Windows 95, and to do this you must capture the printer port output just as you would with the CAPTURE command. Windows 95 provides GUI access to the capture function, and enables you to make the printer assignments automatic as well.

To capture printer output from a local port to a NetWare print queue, open the Windows 95 Explorer and browse the Network Neighborhood to locate the desired print queue object in the NDS tree. When you right-click the print queue object and select Capture Printer Port from the context menu (see Figure 19.5), you can select the LPT port that you want to redirect. Selecting the Reconnect at Logon check box makes the redirection permanent.

FIG. 19.5

You can redirect printer output to a NetWare print queue by accessing the appropriate device in the Network Neighborhood display.

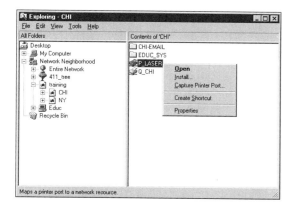

To change any of the port capture switches for the Windows 95 printer, you must access the printer's Properties dialog box in the Printer Control Panel. The capture settings are modified from the Details tab.

The capture settings are added to the printer Properties dialog box only when you install a NetWare network printer in Windows 95.

Redirecting Printer Output Using the *CAPTURE* Command

The following example demonstrates a typical CAPTURE statement performed at the DOS command line. This command instructs all print output normally sent to LPT1 to be redirected to the NetWare printer P_LASER. The command and the NetWare confirmation are as follows:

```
H:\>CAPTURE L=1 P=P_LASER NFF NB
Device LPT1 has been re-routed to printer P_Laser.
```

In the example, LPT1 is being redirected to the printer P_LASER. NFF with the option indicating that No Form Feed is to be appended to the print job. NB prevents a banner page from being printed. If you omit the printer port L= option, CAPTURE automatically defaults to LPT1.

The CAPTURE utility offers more than 20 parameters that you can use to customize the way you redirect your print output. The parameters can be specified on the command line or by selecting the options from within the desired Windows utility.

When you use CAPTURE at the DOS prompt with multiple parameters, you can separate the parameters with spaces or slashes (/). The parameters on the CAPTURE command line can be entered in any order. The following example of a CAPTURE command includes multiple parameters separated by spaces, using the full name of each parameter:

```
CAPTURE PRINTER=LASER BANNER=SUSAN TIMEOUT=60
```

You can enter the same command by using abbreviated parameters separated by slashes, as follows:

```
CAPTURE /P=LASER /B=SUSAN /TI=60
```

Part

VI

Ch

19

When you execute CAPTURE, status information appears on-screen, indicating where your output is being redirected. The following example is a typical status message from CAPTURE:

```
Device LPT1 has been re-routed to printer LASER
```

It is good practice to always designate the LPT port and either the printer or print queue object name as the first and second options on the CAPTURE command line. These are generally the most important items and sometimes are overlooked. A complete listing of CAPTURE parameters is shown in Table 19.1.

Table 19.1 *CAPTURE* **Parameters**

Parameter	Abbr.	Format	Comments
ALL	ALL	CAPTURE ENDCAP ALL CAPTURE EC ALL	Must be used with ENDCAP parameter
AUTOEND	AU	CAPTURE AUTOEND CAPTURE AU	
BANNER	B	CAPTURE BANNER=3RD_FLOOR CAPTURE B=3RD_FLOOR	
CANCEL	CA	CAPTURE ENDCAP CANCEL CAPTURE EC CA	Must be used with ENDCAP parameter
COPIES	C	CAPTURE COPIES=3 CAPTURE C=3	
CREATE	CR	CAPTURE CREATE=*path\filename.ext* CAPTURE CR=*path\filename.ext*	
DETAIL	D	CAPTURE DETAIL CAPTURE D	
ENDCAP	EC	CAPTURE ENDCAP CAPTURE EC	
FORM	F	CAPTURE FORM=1 CAPTURE F=1 CAPTURE FORM=LETTERHEAD CAPTURE F=LETTERHEAD	
FORMFEED	FF	CAPTURE FORMFEED CAPTURE FF	
HELP	H or ?	CAPTURE HELP CAPTURE H CAPTURE ?	

Parameter	Abbr.	Format	Comments
HOLD	HOLD	CAPTURE HOLD	
JOB	J	CAPTURE JOB=COMPPRINT CAPTURE J=COMPPRINT	
KEEP	K	CAPTURE KEEP CAPTURE K	
LOCAL	L	CAPTURE LOCAL=3 CAPTURE L=3	
NAME	NAM	CAPTURE NAME=SMITHFD CAPTURE NAM=SMITHFD	
NOAUTOEND	NA	CAPTURE NOAUTOEND CAPTURE NA	
NOBANNER	NB	CAPTURE NOBANNER CAPTURE NB	
NOFORMFEED	NFF	CAPTURE NOFORMFEED CAPTURE NFF	
NONOTIFY	NNOTI	CAPTURE NONOTIFY CAPTURE NNOTI	
NOTABS	NT	CAPTURE NOTABS CAPTURE NT	
NOTIFY	NOTI	CAPTURE NOTIFY CAPTURE NOTI	
PRINTER	P	CAPTURE PRINTER=ACCT-LASER CAPTURE P=ACCT-LASER	
QUEUE	Q	CAPTURE QUEUE=ACCT-LJQ CAPTURE Q=ACCT-LJQ	
SERVER	S	CAPTURE SERVER=SERV1 CAPTURE S=SERV	For use with pre-NetWare 4.x servers
SHOW	SH	CAPTURE SHOW CAPTURE SH	
TABS	T	CAPTURE TABS=5 CAPTURE T=5	
TIMEOUT	TI	CAPTURE TIMEOUT=10 CAPTURE TI=10	
VERSION	V	CAPTURE VERSION CAPTURE V	

Part

VI

Ch

19

Redirecting Printer Output from NetWare User Tools

When you select the Printer button in Client 32's NetWare User Tools, the NetWare Printer Connections window displays two selection panes. The procedure for redirecting print output to a NetWare printer or print queue is similar to mapping a drive. Use the right pane, labeled Resources, to navigate to the desired NDS object. Drag the device from the right pane and drop it onto an available LPT port in the left pane.

If you drop the selection on an LPT port that is already in use, you are prompted to confirm the change of the printer connection assignment. Alternative port capturing methods include selecting the Capture button from the lower toolbar and manually typing it in the entry box. Figure 19.6 displays the Printer Connections window from NetWare User Tools.

FIG. 19.6

You can redirect printer output from the Printer Connections window in NetWare User Tools.

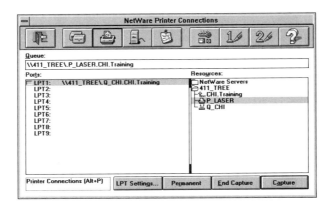

Select the Permanent button from the lower button bar to reconnect the port to the selected device every time you launch Windows. From the same button bar, select the LPT Settings button to modify the default capture settings (see Figure 19.7).

FIG. 19.7

You can modify the capture settings from within the Client 32 NetWare User Tools Printer Connections dialog box.

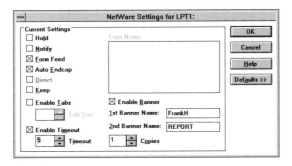

For more information about using printing utilities, see Chapter 20, "Using the IntranetWare Client 32 for DOS/Windows 3.1," and Chapter 21, "Using the IntranetWare Client 32 for Windows 95."

Login Scripts

A login script is a file that holds a series of commands that are executed every time a user logs in to the network. The commands perform tasks needed to create a consistent workstation environment by connecting the system with various network resources, such as printers, print queues, and server volumes.

Regardless of the client software used, the NetWare LOGIN utility is designed to perform three basic tasks by default:

- When used without any switches, the LOGIN program clears the workstation's network connection, if any.
- The login process authenticates the user to the network. In this step, after the user must supply a valid user name and password, NDS locates the user object and verifies its properties.
- LOGIN executes any login scripts associated with the user object.

There are several command-line switches for LOGIN.EXE that can be applied for a client running the NetWare DOS Requester client. Workstations running Client 32 have the capability to change the login parameters using the Windows client utility. The most popular options are as follows:

- Do Not Clear Current Connections
- Do Not Run Any Login Scripts
- Specify an Alternate or External Login Script
- Specify a Particular File Server or NDS Tree

Types of Login Scripts

NetWare 4.x administrators rely on a combination of four login scripts to set the workstation environment. The four script types are as follows:

- **Container login script**—A container login script is used to satisfy the general needs of the users within a container. It is the first login script to execute during the login process. The only container login script that executes for a user is the one that is associated with the container in which the user object is located.
- **Profile login script**—Profile login scripts are stored in the NDS tree in profile objects, and are used to satisfy the needs of specific groups of users who may or may not be in the same container. Profile scripts are good for department heads or other users that are located in different containers, but which require similar workstation environments. A profile script executes after the container script.
- **User login script**—An individual user login script automates a process that is unique to the associated user. The use of user login scripts can quickly become a major administrative burden. For this reason, they are frequently avoided by network managers. The user login script executes after the container and profile scripts.

- **Default login script**—The default login script provides a greeting to users and creates basic drive mappings. It is usually disabled after the appropriate container, profile, or user scripts are in place. The default login script executes last.

Table 19.2 lists the advantages and disadvantages for each of the three optional login script types.

Table 19.2   Evaluating NetWare Login Script Types

Advantages	Disadvantages
Container Login Scripts	
Commands are listed in one place. Easy to review, modify, and print.	Difficult to address needs of users that are not in the same containers.
Capability to use IF...THEN to test for group membership.	Only the user's immediate parent script executes.
Script administration can be centralized or distributed.	
Reduction of administration time. Only one script for each container of users.	
Profile Script	
Capability to address the needs of users in different containers.	Each user can have only one profile object assigned.
Small scale installations can use one profile script and assign it to all users.	Too many profile scripts can become difficult to administer.
No limit to how many can be created.	Additional objects to administer in the tree.
Can be used in conjunction with the new User_Template object.	Additional rights need to be granted to users to access the profile object and script.

Advantages	Disadvantages
User Login Script	
Use in an emergency to act as a quick fix or short-term solution to a problem.	Too many user scripts is an administration burden.
Facilitate login for traveling users.	Fosters user uniqueness versus network continuity.
Can be used to test a change in a login script before incorporating it in the appropriate container script.	Used to correct or change an action that occurs in a container or profile script versus fixing the problem.
	Increases troubleshooting time. Each user script must be edited individually.

CAUTION

When planning your login script strategy, it is important to pay attention to the order in which your scripts will execute. Commands entered in a script running last might override those previously issued. For example, if your container script maps drive K: to SYS:SHARED, and the profile script maps drive K: to VOL1:ACCTG\ PAYROLL, drive K: will be pointing to the payroll directory because the profile script executed after the container script.

Ultimately, you must decide what combination of login scripts is best for your environment. The size of your NDS tree and the network administration resources at your disposal must be considered carefully. Keep in mind that the networking industry changes rapidly and that your login scripts should be able to expand and grow with your network. Creating individual user scripts for a network with five users might be a satisfactory solution right now, but when 30 more people are hired, this method will be very unwieldy.

Part
VI

Ch
19

 TIP

After you have created the appropriate container, profile, and user scripts, it is good practice to disable the default login script by adding NO_DEFAULT to the container or profile script. If you neglect to disable the default login script, it will execute and override any directory drive mappings that have already executed.

Creating Login Scripts

Login scripts are properties of NDS user, profile, and container objects, and as with any other properties, you use the NetWare Administrator or NETADMIN utility to create and manage the scripts. Table 19.3 displays the minimum rights needed to create or modify the various login script types.

Table 19.3   Rights Required to Create Login Scripts

Script Type	Minimum Rights Required
Container	BROWSE object right to the container. READ, WRITE to the login script property.
Profile	CREATE at the container where the profile will reside. BROWSE object right to the profile object. READ, WRITE to the login script property.
User	BROWSE object right to the user object. READ, WRITE to the login script property.

Users are able to modify their own personal login scripts by default. If you do not want your users changing their own scripts, you must revoke the Write right to the login script property in their user objects.

Creating a Login Script in NetWare Administrator

User, profile, and container objects all have a Login Scripts panel in their NetWare Administrator Details dialog box. To create a script, type the commands directly into the Login Script screen, as shown in Figure 19.8. You can also create and modify login scripts using the NETADMIN utility from the DOS prompt by selecting an object and choosing Login Script from the View or Edit Properties screen.

FIG. 19.8
Use NetWare Administrator to create login scripts for user, profile, and container objects.

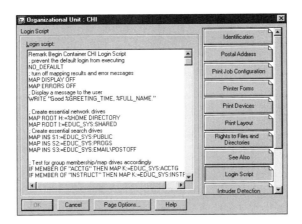

A list of the commands and variables used in NetWare login scripts is found in Appendix B, "Login Script Commands and Variables."

> **CAUTION**
>
> Always use caution when modifying existing login scripts. Use comments to mark and keep the existing lines, and add new lines for items that you would like to change. Always try to leave yourself the opportunity to return to the original script. You can create profile scripts for experimental purposes, and execute them from a container or user script with the INCLUDE command.

Example Container Login Script and Command Usage Summary

The following code demonstrates a typical container login script for the .NY.TRAINING organizational unit. As you look through this example, note the following:

- Comments have been used to help explain command and variable choices. Comment lines are preceded by the word REMARK, REM, an asterisk, or a semicolon.
- Blank lines added to a login script help improve readability and have no effect on the script's execution.
- The only items in a login script that are case-sensitive are the identifier variables.
- Each variable must be preceded with a percent sign and entered in all capital letters.
- When using IF...THEN statements, it is good practice to indent the commands inside the condition.

```
Remark Begin Container Script
; prevent the default login script from executing
NO_DEFAULT
; turn off mapping results and error messages
MAP DISPLAY OFF
MAP ERRORS OFF
; Display a message for the user
WRITE "Good %GREETING_TIME, %FULL_NAME."

; Create essential network drives
MAP H:=%HOME_DIRECTORY
MAP I:=EDUC_SYS:SHARED

; Create essential search drives
MAP INS S1:=EDUC_SYS:PUBLIC
MAP INS S2:=EDUC_SYS:PROGS
MAP INS S3:=EDUC_SYS:EMAIL\POSTOFF

; Test for group membership/map drives and capture printers accordingly
IF MEMBER OF "ACCTG" THEN
    MAP K:=EDUC_SYS:ACCTG
; map a search drive to the accounting application directory map object
    MAP INS S4:=ACCTGAPP
    #CAPTURE L=2 P=ACCTG_LASER NFF NB TI=5
END
```

Part **VI**

Ch **19**

```
IF MEMBER OF "INSTRUCT" THEN
   MAP ROOT K:=EDUC_SYS:INSTRUCT\MANUALS
; map a search drive to the instructor demo directory map object
   MAP INS S4:=EDUC_SYS:DEMOSAPP
   #CAPTURE L=2 P=CLASS_LASER NFF NB
END

MAP DISPLAY ON
MAP
; make the user's home directory the current drive
DRIVE H:
Remark End of login script
```

Mapping Drives in a Login Script   In most cases, the MAP command is used in a login script with the same syntax as at the DOS command line. The MAP statements shown in the preceding login script example are explained in detail earlier in this chapter in "Using MAP to Create a Network Drive Mapping" and "Using MAP to Create a Search Drive Mapping."

However, the syntax for the MAP NEXT function in a login script is different than that of the command line. In a login script, you must replace the word NEXT with an asterisk. The following example demonstrates the use of the MAP NEXT feature in a login script:

```
MAP *1:=EDUC_SYS:HOME\%LOGIN_NAME
```

To ensure consistency among users, most network administrators avoid the MAP NEXT feature and instead specify the desired drive letter.

Login Script Commands that Display Messages   A login script is the first interaction that your users have with the network during the login process. You can take advantage of this by adding commands that display messages on the screen. The following five login script commands can be used for this purpose: WRITE, DISPLAY, FDISPLAY, CLS, and LASTLOGINTIME.

The WRITE command is most often used to display a greeting in conjunction with the user's login name or time of day. The following lines demonstrate how to greet the user and display the time and date:

```
WRITE "Good %GREETING_TIME, %GIVEN_NAME %LAST_NAME."
WRITE "It is %DAY_OF_WEEK %MONTH_NAME  %DAY, %YEAR."
WRITE "The time is: %HOUR:%MINUTE:%SECOND"
WRITE "Have a great day!"
Pause
```

Notice the message is enclosed in quotation marks. The first WRITE statement produces a general greeting of Good Morning, Good Afternoon, or Good Evening, depending on the time of day. Each of the variables are preceded with a percent sign and are always entered in all capital letters. It is a good idea to end your message with a Pause command, which forces the login script to stop processing and wait for the user to press any key to continue.

Login Script Evolution

Originally, administrators took advantage of the login script, not only to set up a user's environment, but also to display important messages. As more and more PC users connect to the network using Client 32 instead of the NetWare DOS Requester, these messages can be construed as a nuisance. Making a Windows 95 user acknowledge what time of day it is when he logged in by clicking OK in a DOS box will probably generate a lot of complaints to the IS department.

As opposed to the WRITE command, which displays the text that is included in the login script itself, DISPLAY and FDISPLAY show the contents of an external text file. Use DISPLAY only with true ASCII text files that contain no printer or formatting codes. FDISPLAY should be used with files that do contain non-ASCII elements. FDISPLAY attempts to filter out the extraneous codes and displays only the text information from a file. Creating a true ASCII text file and using the DISPLAY command generates the most reliable results. The following demonstrates how to incorporate DISPLAY into a login script. The CLS and PAUSE commands are used to clear the screen and enable the user to read the message:

```
IF DAY_OF_WEEK = "FRIDAY" THEN
    CLS
    DISPLAY EDUC_SYS:MESSAGES\FRIDAY.TXT
    PAUSE
END
```

The LASTLOGINTIME command is used to display the last time that the user logged in. You can use the command in conjunction with a WRITE statement to generate the following output:

```
Last Login Occurred At: 01/06/97  7:53:52am
```

Commands that Control Login Script Flow   Several login script commands enable you to pause, stop, or vary the flow of command execution:

- The PAUSE command stops script processing until the user presses a key.
- BREAK controls whether the user can abort processing of the login script by using the Ctrl+Break key combination.
- The NO_DEFAULT command prevents the default login script from executing.
- IF...THEN commands are used to execute script commands based on whether a certain condition is met.
- The GOTO command can also be used with IF...THEN to conditionally execute parts of your login script.

The example login script has two IF...THEN conditionals programmed to test whether or not a user is a member of a particular group. IF...THEN statements are used with variables to test for any kind of condition, such as a certain day of the week, a user name, or group membership. To execute a series of commands within the IF...THEN conditional, list the commands on subsequent lines following the initial IF...THEN statement. Complete the series of commands by placing an END command on a line by itself. The following examples demonstrate several different types of IF...THEN conditionals:

Part
VI

Ch
19

```
IF MEMBER OF "ACCTG" THEN #CAPTURE L=2 Q=ACCTG_Q NFF NB
IF DAY_OF_WEEK="MONDAY" AND HOUR="08" THEN
   WRITE "E-mail will be out of service until 4:30pm today."
   WRITE "Sorry for the inconvenience."
   PAUSE
END
IF LOGIN_NAME="TAPEBACK" THEN MAP S16:=EDUC_SYS:TAPESOFT
```

When comparing variables to literals, you can use the following expressions:

```
EQUALS              LESS THAN

NOT EQUAL TO        GREATER THAN OR EQUAL TO

GREATER THAN        LESS THAN OR EQUAL TO
```

The following example demonstrates the use of the EQUALS option:

```
IF LOGIN_NAME IS "ADMIN"
IF LOGIN_NAME EQUALS "ADMIN"
IF LOGIN_NAME=="ADMIN"
IF LOGIN_NAME="ADMIN"
```

The following example demonstrates the use of the GREATER THAN option:

```
IF HOUR IS GREATER THAN "08"
IF HOUR > "08"
```

You can also build compound conditional statements by combining different conditions with AND and OR. The following demonstrates the use of the AND option, both with the word AND and its symbolic equivalent, a comma:

```
IF YEAR="2076" AND MONTH_NAME="JULY" AND DAY="04" THEN
   WRITE "IT IS THE USA'S TRICENTENNIAL!"
END
IF YEAR="2076", MONTH_NAME="JULY", DAY="04"
   WRITE "IT IS THE USA'S TRICENTENNIAL!"
END
```

The following demonstrates the creation of a compound IF...THEN statement using the OR option:

```
IF LOGIN_NAME="ADMIN" OR LOGIN_NAME="TAPEBACK" THEN
   MAP S16:=EDUC_SYS:TAPESOFT
END
```

Add an ELSE statement to specify an alternative command to be executed when your IF statement condition is not met. The following demonstrates the use of the ELSE option for making printer assignments:

```
IF MEMBER OF "MRKTG" THEN
   #CAPTURE L=2 P=COLOR_LASER NFF NB TI=5
ELSE
   #CAPTURE L=2 P=BW_LASER NFF NB TI=5
END
```

Notice that the word ELSE is on its own line and is followed on the next line by the statement that should be executed if the condition is not true.

You also have the capability to nest IF...THEN conditionals. One IF...THEN statement can be contained within another IF...THEN statement. The following demonstrates the nesting of an IF...THEN statement:

```
IF MEMBER OF "ACCTG" THEN
   MAP I:=EDUC_SYS:ACCTG
   IF MEMBER OF "AUDIT" THEN
       MAP J:=EDUC_SYS:ACCTG\AUDITRPT
   END
ELSE
   MAP I:=EDUC_SYS:SHARED
END
```

Notice that the IF...THEN...END commands for the nested statement (IF MEMBER OF "AUDIT") are completely contained by the first conditional statement's IF...THEN...END commands. IF...THEN commands can be nested up to 10 levels deep. Do not use a GOTO command to exit a nested IF...THEN statement because it can disrupt the logical top-to-bottom flow of your script.

You can use GOTO to send your login script's flow of execution to a different part of the script to run commands. The login script's GOTO command is almost identical to the GOTO command used in batch files and other programming and macro languages. It enables you to create a subroutine of tasks; it is most often used to create a loop that is executed a certain number of times.

Executing an External Command   The command that enables you to run external applications from a login script is named EXECUTE, but you enter it into a login script as a pound sign (#). EXECUTE runs an external application and, after this application stops running, returns control to the script. You can capture printer port output from within a login script by adding a CAPTURE command and preceding it with a pound sign. Any parameters for an external application that are normally used on the command line can be included in an EXECUTE login script command.

If the CAPTURE command is executed before you have established a search drive to the SYS:PUBLIC directory where the CAPTURE.EXE program is located, a Bad command or filename error message is generated.

For more information on the use of the CAPTURE command, see "Redirecting Printer Output Using the CAPTURE Command" earlier in this chapter.

Changing Your Context from Within a Login Script   Just as you can use the CX command to change your NDS context from the DOS command line, you can use the CONTEXT command in a login script for exactly the same purpose. If you place the following command in your login script, the user's context is changed to the LA organizational unit at login time:

```
CONTEXT .LA.TRAINING
```

Checking for an Alias Context at Login Time   You learned in Chapter 6, "Using NDS Manager," that you can rename container objects. When you rename a container object with NetWare Administrator or NETADMIN, the utilities prompt you to confirm the creation of an ALIAS container object to replace the container object in its previous location. The presence of the ALIAS object enables workstations with NAME CONTEXT statements in NET.CFG files to continue to locate the container object by its previous name. (NET.CFG is the file that contains the configuration parameters for the NetWare DOS Requester and Client 32 for DOS/Windows 3.1 client software.)

You can use login script commands to change the NAME CONTEXT statement in a workstation's NET.CFG file, if this NAME CONTEXT statement references a context that has become an ALIAS as a result of being renamed. You use the LOGIN_ALIAS_CONTEXT variable to check to see whether the workstation's context at login time is an alias.

If the context is an alias, use the EXECUTE (#) option to run a NetWare command called NCUPDATE (for *name context update*). NCUPDATE automatically sets the NAME CONTEXT setting in the workstation's NET.CFG file to match the workstation's true context (the context pointed to by the ALIAS object). After the NAME CONTEXT statement is updated, the workstation no longer tries to set the default context to the ALIAS container object. After all the workstations have been updated, you can delete the ALIAS container.

To update the context at login, place the following statements in the container login script for the ALIAS container object:

```
IF LOGIN_ALIAS_CONTEXT = "Y" THEN
     #NCUPDATE /NP
END
```

The first statement checks to see whether the workstation's context at login time is an ALIAS container object. If this is confirmed, the NCUPDATE command executes with the /NP (no prompt) parameter. This command automatically places a NAME CONTEXT statement in the workstation's NET.CFG file.

If you want the user to be able to choose whether to receive the update to the NET.CFG file, you can execute NCUPDATE without the /NP parameter. Without this parameter, NCUPDATE prompts the user to confirm that he or she wants to update the NET.CFG file before proceeding.

Exiting from a Login Script   You can use the EXIT command to halt the execution of a login script or to leave a login script and run another command. If you use EXIT without any parameter, the script stops executing at that point. You can use this feature effectively in an IF...THEN statement. If you must copy a certain group of files from one network directory to another directory every Friday, for example, you can use the following login script commands:

```
IF DAY_OF_WEEK NOT EQUAL TO "FRIDAY" THEN EXIT
WRITE "It's Friday—files are being copied to SYS:BACKCOPY"
#SERV1_SYS:PUBLIC\NCOPY SERV1_SYS:ACCTING SERV1_SYS:BACKCOPY
```

The first statement uses EXIT with IF...THEN to halt the login script if it is not Friday. On Fridays only, the last two lines execute, copying the files in SYS:ACCTG to SYS:BACKCOPY.

If you use EXIT to stop the execution of a container or profile login script, any subsequent scripts that normally run afterwards aren't executed. If your profile login script contains an EXIT statement, for example, your user login script doesn't run.

You also can use EXIT to execute a file as soon as the login script stops. If you want to run a command that starts a menu program, for example, place the following command on the last line of your login script:

```
EXIT "MENU"
```

Using the *DRIVE* Command   The DRIVE command is used to make a particular drive letter the current drive upon exiting from a login script. Be sure to place the DRIVE command after all of the map commands have been executed. This command is used most frequently in a DOS or Windows 3.1 environment. Workstations using Windows 95 execute their programs from the Windows 95 desktop; setting the current directory has no effect. The following demonstrates the use of the DRIVE command to set a user's home directory as the current drive:

```
DRIVE H:
```

Summary

This chapter focuses on establishing access to network resources in a consistent manner. Network administrators and experienced users might find themselves using MAP through NetWare User Tools or at the command line to map a drive on-the-fly. Users that are new to computers avoid these tasks at all costs. A user-friendly network provides proper connection to network resources through login scripts so that users do not have to establish the connection themselves. ●

Part
VI

Ch
19

CHAPTER 20

Using the IntranetWare Client 32 for DOS/ Windows 3.1

Even though Windows 95 has been overwhelmingly popular and seems to have taken over the world, there are still many network administrators that are supporting Windows 3.x. When correctly configured, Windows 3.1 is fully NetWare 4.11 compatible, and you can perform many NetWare tasks, such as mapping drives and connecting to shared printers, without leaving the Windows graphical desktop.

Windows 3.x provides interfaces for several NetWare-specific features within its own native utilities. SETUP, Control Panel, Print Manager, and File Manager all have features that let you manage your interface to NetWare servers. This chapter focuses on the new Client 32 for DOS/Windows installation, configuration, and use. Here you can learn to use and customize these features to meet your networking needs. Chapter 19, "Accessing Network Resources," introduces the NetWare User Tools or NWUSER.EXE program. The NetWare User Tools functionality has been enhanced due to the release of Client 32. ■

Installing Client 32 for DOS/ Windows on a PC

Existing Windows 3.1 computers can have the NetWare Client 32 installed with full Windows support. This process can be done manually or automatically.

Using NetWare User Tools, NetWare's Windows workstation utility

NWUSER is NetWare's all-in-one Windows 3.1 client utility. It performs the functions of many NetWare DOS utilities.

Using built-in Windows 3.x features to manage your network connection

Many of Windows 3.1's native dialog boxes call the NWUSER utility to manage NetWare resources.

Performing an Automatic Client Upgrade

Learn how to configure Client 32's ACU utility to keep your workstation client connection software current.

Connecting to the file server and performing a NetWare Login

Client 32 adds a new GUI interface that can be configured to fit your users experience level and needs.

What Is NetWare Client 32 for DOS/Windows?

Novell's Client 32 architecture is a new and exciting software innovation that gives users of a 16-bit operating system the capability to use NetWare services with full 32-bit functionality. Client 32 users gain increased network access speed and benefit from many new features, such as simultaneous access to multiple NDS trees and full automatic reconnection to network files and resources.

One of the traditional complaints about the NetWare DOS Requester (or VLM) client is that it requires an inordinate amount of conventional memory to run. Client 32 works in conjunction with an extended memory manager, such as HIMEM.SYS, which opens the door for all of the modules to be loaded in upper memory (above 1M), leaving only a 4K footprint in conventional memory.

There are two main components that make up Client 32. The first and most critical is the NetWare I/O Subsystem or NIOS.EXE. The NIOS component loads first; it communicates with the extended memory manager that is already loaded on the system. This union creates a window of contiguous protected memory to allow for the loading of the additional Client 32 components.

The second major component of Client 32 to load is the communication protocols and the LAN drivers. Now that the NIOS executable is in place, the NetWare client is able to use LAN drivers and client NLMs (which are traditionally associated with servers) at the workstation.

The remaining client connection software is loaded using NetWare's LOAD command from within batch files: either STARTNET.BAT or the workstation's AUTOEXEC.BAT. The files to be loaded are similar to those used in the traditional real-mode VLM client; however, they are rewritten as client NLMs to take advantage of the extended memory block that NIOS and the memory manager have reserved. The following list describes each of the communication protocol and LAN driver components that must be loaded for Client 32 to function:

- **LSLC32.NLM**—The VLM equivalent to this file is LSL.COM. LSLC32 serves as a translator between the LAN driver and the communication protocols. The ODI implementation of LSL allows one network board to service communication with multiple protocols.

- **CMSM.NLM**—This is a C-based program that offers support according to the topology used by the network, equivalent to the Media Support Module for the ODI implementation model. In addition, Client 32 uses other NLMs for media support known as *topology support modules*, or TSMs. A TSM functions on a layer between LSL and the LAN driver. All TSMs are topology specific. For example, an Ethernet network must use ETHERTSM.NLM, while a token-ring network uses TOKENTSM.NLM.

- **LAN Driver**—Client 32 supports 32-bit LAN drivers and older 16-bit ODI LAN drivers. In previous versions of the client software, the network interface adapter was loaded using a .COM driver. Client 32 now uses the same technology employed by NetWare file servers and loads the network adapter using the .LAN driver file.

- **Protocol**—Client 32 supports multiple protocols using the same network card. You can easily load support for both the IPX/SPX and TCP/IP protocols using one client.
- **Client 32 Requester**—The Requester file name for Client 32 is CLIENT32.NLM. This file replaces the NetWare DOS Requester (VLM.EXE) and the NetWare shell (NETX.EXE) from previous client versions. CLIENT32.NLM is completely backwards-compatible with the previous clients. The major difference in the architecture is that the new CLIENT32.NLM file loads all of the support modules as one file versus loading individual .VLMs, as the NetWare DOS Requester does.

Installing Client 32

There are several ways to install Client 32 from scratch or to upgrade an existing client. The different methods are described first, followed by instructions for configuring Client 32 settings.

The Client 32 for DOS/Windows 3.x software is included in the IntranetWare package. Once you have installed the NetWare 4.11 operating system, you can use the INSTALL.NLM utility's Product Options menu to create client directories on your server, or make disks for installation on new workstations.

Usually, the installation process is much faster and easier when performed from source files on a network drive. If you are installing the NetWare client on a new workstation that has no existing network connection, a boot floppy with the minimal NetWare DOS Requester or NETX client files on it can be a valuable commodity.

To install Client 32, log in to the server that stores the Client 32 installation files, or place the floppy disk labeled Disk 1—Setup into your PC's drive. The client installation program is supplied as a SETUP.EXE file for use with Windows, as well as an INSTALL.EXE file for DOS workstations. Both are located in the SYS:PUBLIC\CLIENT\DOSWIN32\IBM_6 subdirectory on your server, as the result of the INSTALL.NLM client directory creation process. The bulk of this section will describe a Windows installation of Client 32.

After you run SETUP.EXE and accept the terms of the licensing agreement, you are prompted to start the Client 32 installation. The installation screen prompts you to select a target location for the Client 32 files and enter the path to the Windows directory on your workstation. The default software location directory for Client 32 is C:\NOVELL\CLIENT32 (see Figure 20.1).

Part
VI

Ch
20

FIG. 20.1

The Client 32 installation program enables you to select a target directory for the client files on your workstation.

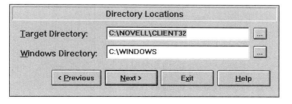

Next, you must select a LAN driver. The installation program scans to see if the workstation is already connected to a network. If the system is connected, the program selects a LAN driver for the active board. If your network adapter is not detected, select the User Supplied Driver option, which allows you to supply the driver disk that came with the network board. Choose the appropriate driver for your network card from the list that is displayed.

During the Client 32 installation process, you can configure your workstation for TCP/IP and NetWare/IP support. Figure 20.2 displays the additional options available for Client 32 installation.

FIG. 20.2

The installation program gives you the opportunity to configure additional Client 32 installation options.

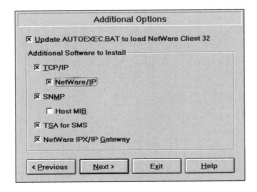

Select the appropriate check boxes to install support for TCP/IP, SNMP (the Simple Network Management Protocol) and the TSA (Target Service Agent) for Novell's SMS (Storage Management Services). To configure your workstation for TCP/IP, complete the TCP/IP configuration dialog box shown in Figure 20.3. If your workstation was previously configured for TCP/IP support and the information is contained in the current NET.CFG file, the installation program reads the settings and updates the TCP/IP dialog box automatically. Leave the configuration dialog box for TCP/IP blank if you are using DHCP or another protocol that dynamically determines the addressing information for the client. After completing the dialog box, click Next to continue the installation and configuration process.

FIG. 20.3

Configure your client connection software to use TCP/IP by completing the TCP/IP Configuration dialog box.

TCP/IP Configuration	
Client IP Address:	0.0.0.0
Default Router Address:	0.0.0.0
Subnetwork Mask:	255.255.255.0
DNS Domain Name:	
Domain Name Server Address:	

< Previous   Next >   Exit   Help

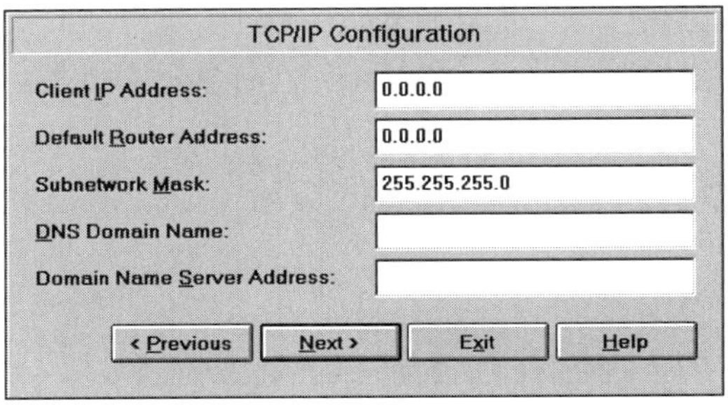

If you opted to install support for NetWare/IP, its configuration dialog box is displayed. Complete the dialog box by entering the appropriate NetWare/IP Domain Name, the Preferred DSS IP Address, and the NWIP Server address. When completed, click Next to continue installing additional components or return to the Client 32 installation.

Figure 20.4 and Figure 20.5 display the final two additional components dialog boxes for configuring SNMP and the TSA for SMS. You need the workstation name and location and the appropriate IP addresses for the TRAP to complete the SNMP configuration. To backup the workstation using SBACKUP or another SMS-compliant backup software product, you must configure the TSA on the workstation. Here you indicate the server that is running the backup NLM, the workstation name, and the target drives to be backed up.

FIG. 20.4

Configure your client software to use SNMP by completing the Client 32 SNMP Configuration dialog box.

SNMP Configuration

Workstation Name:

Workstation Location:

Contact Name:

Trap Target Addresses:

IPX Addresses:

IP Addresses (Needs TCP/IP):

Add...   Remove

< Previous   Next >   Exit   Help

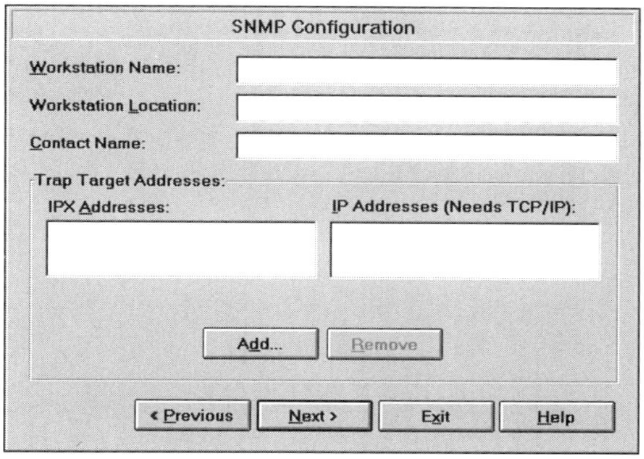

FIG. 20.5

To allow your workstation to be backed up using SMS-compliant software, you must complete the Client 32 TSA for SMS Configuration dialog box.

TSA for SMS Configuration

TSA Server Name:

Workstation Name:

Password (Optional):

Local Drives to Back Up:

Transfer Buffers [1-30]:

< Previous   Next >   Exit   Help

Part

VI

Ch

20

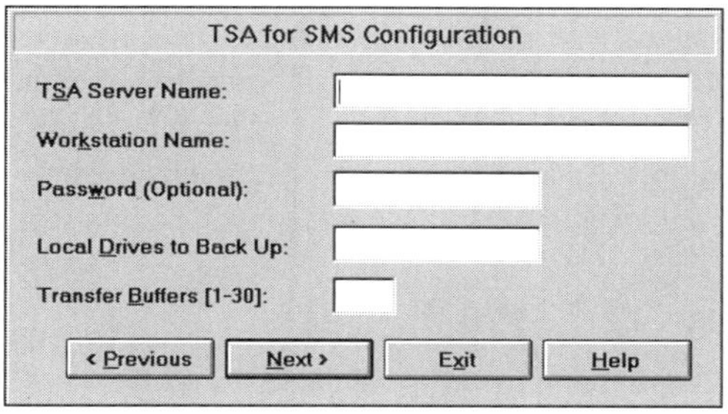

After you have entered all of the installation configuration parameters, the installation program copies the appropriate files to the destination directories. After the installation is complete, you are prompted to either reboot your PC or return to Windows to customize your installation.

Configuring Client 32 for Windows 3.x

After Client 32 is installed, configuring it to work in your environment is simple. The Client 32 installation program automatically updates your workstation's AUTOEXEC.BAT file and adds the following line:

```
@CALL \NOVELL\CLIENT32\STARTNET
```

To be sure that your workstation memory is optimized, you should load Client 32 and its components before any other device drivers. This keeps the real mode footprint at approximately 4K, increasing the memory available for additional devices and programs. However, you cannot unload the client connection software from memory without rebooting the workstation if you load additional drivers after Client 32 loads.

In a production environment, this should not be a problem. If you are still fine-tuning the workstation configuration, you might want to load the connection software last. Remember, Client 32 is a series of NLMs that are loaded (using the LOAD command) on top of the NIOS.EXE program. You can unload the connection files simply by using the standard Novell UNLOAD command. The following demonstrates how to unload Client 32:

```
UNLOAD CLIENT32
UNLOAD ETHERTSM
UNLOAD IPXODI
UNLOAD driver
UNLOAD C32LSL
```

N O T E   Some network administrators find it useful to create a batch file that unloads the client connection software. An unload batch file for the VLM client is also very handy. ■

An easy way to verify that Client 32 has been installed and loaded properly is that the Novell Client 32 splash screen appears when you launch Windows. Unlike the NetWare DOS Requester, which forced you to log in before starting Windows, Client 32 has been rewritten to support the capability of logging in through Windows, with a graphical login interface, and also ensures that any login scripts associated with the user are properly executed. The following sections describe the graphical login interface and how to customize it for your environment.

Configuring the Client 32 Login Panel

By default, the Client 32 login panel is very plain and straightforward. Initially, the only information that the user must supply is a correct user name and password. Figure 20.6 shows the default login panel. The login panel can be modified to display additional panels and prompt the user for additional information. These additional panels are examined in the following sections.

FIG. 20.6

The default Client 32 login panel offers the user an easy method to log in and access network resources.

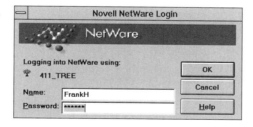

Customizing Client 32 to View Additional Panels

When all of the optional Client 32 login panels are activated, the user sees a login panel similar to the one shown in Figure 20.7. The additional panels are labeled Connection, Script, and Variables. The Connection panel enables you to select the server or tree you want to log in to and also offers additional connection method options. The Script panel is used to control login script selection, and the Variables card allows users to supply values for login script variables.

FIG. 20.7

Turn all of the Client 32 GUI Login panels on to access all of the client's features.

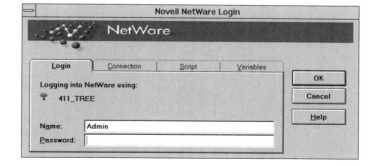

You turn on the various Login panels by accessing the NetWare Settings button from within NetWare User Tools in Windows. After you select the NetWare Settings button, the NetWare Settings dialog box opens. Click the Login tab and, by default, the check boxes are empty for the options to display the Connection page, the Script page, and the Variables page. Select those that you want to display. Figure 20.8 shows all three selected for display.

The options included in the Display Connection Page section are Login to Tree, Login to Server, Clear Current Connection and Bindery Connection. In a NetWare 4.11 environment, it is most common to log in to the NDS tree as opposed to a particular server. You might recognize this option from the NET.CFG file as Preferred Server or Preferred Tree.

The Clear Current Connections option is used to ensure that the previous user is completely logged out before a new user is authenticated and logged in. Under most circumstances, checking the clear connections box is recommended. However, a network administrator performing maintenance might find it useful to log in to several servers or trees (a new capability of Client 32) without clearing the previous connection.

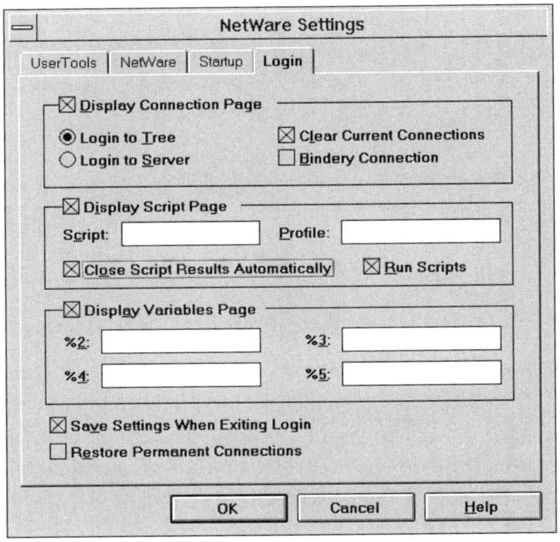

FIG. 20.8

To modify the default options, access the Client 32 Login tab settings through NetWare User Tools.

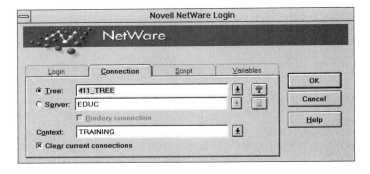

The final option on this page is Bindery Connection. There are times when you might need to establish a Bindery connection to a NetWare 4.11 server. In these cases, you must select this option prior to logging in. If you select this box, you are not connected to directory services for that session. Figure 20.9 shows the login screen GUI interface displaying the Connection page as the current panel.

FIG. 20.9

The Connection panel offers the user the capability to connect to a server other than the preferred server. You may find it helpful to leave the connection panel turned on if you have multiple users sharing the same computers.

By default, the Client 32 utility runs all of the login scripts that are associated with your user object. In other words, your parent container's login script executes (if one exists), then any profile scripts with which you are associated, and finally the user login script. You can change the scripts that naturally execute by entering a valid script file name in the Script box in the Display Script Page section.

You turn on the Script page from within the NetWare Settings dialog box, accessed through NetWare User Tools. See Figure 20.10 for an example of how to modify the Script page. The Close Script Results Automatically option causes the window containing the results of the login script commands to be closed automatically when execution of the scripts is completed.

By default, the Run Scripts check box is selected. To continue to have your login scripts execute whenever you log in, leave this box checked. As a troubleshooting technique—or to connect to another server—you might want to uncheck the box to prevent the scripts from executing and disrupting your current connection environment.

FIG. 20.10
Modify the Script panel to control how the user will attach to the file server and which login scripts will be executed.

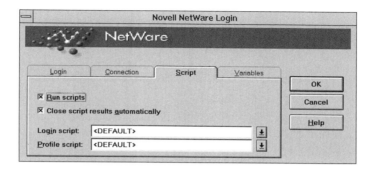

The Variables page can be turned on from within the NetWare Settings dialog box in NetWare User Tools. The Variables page and its options are probably one of the most underutilized features of Client 32. The amusing part is that the ability to log in using command-line identifier variables is not a new feature of NetWare.

The following example demonstrates the use of command-line identifier variables. In the example, the network administrator must find a way to track what floor a user is logging in from in order to determine which printer should be used. By supplying an additional parameter on the command line, the user is able to log in from any floor, on any workstation, and LPT1 is redirected to the printer on that floor.

```
LOGIN FRANKH FLOOR1
```

Excerpt from the container login script:

```
IF "%2" = "FLOOR1" THEN #CAPTURE L=1 P=1PRN NFF NB TI=5
IF "%2" = "FLOOR2" THEN #CAPTURE L=1 P=2PRN NFF NB TI=5
IF "%2" = "FLOOR3" THEN #CAPTURE L=1 P=3PRN NFF NB TI=5
```

Notice that the administrator uses "%2" in an IF...THEN statement to test for a certain condition. The variable reference uses the number two (2) because, when shown on the LOGIN command line, the LOGIN executable is %0, and the login name is variable %1.

The Variables page allows four parameters to be fed into the login script. As more and more equipment gets added to the network, you might find that you use the variables to specify that output be generated on the closest resource. For example, printers, plotters, scanners, and photo copiers are currently the most popular peripheral devices. You can control which copier or printer is assigned to a user through the variables in the login process. This can help alleviate problems that occur when users float from workstation to workstation. Figure 20.11 provides an example of the use of the Variables page.

Part
VI

Ch
20

FIG. 20.11
Supply additional variables while logging in by adding them to the Variables panel.

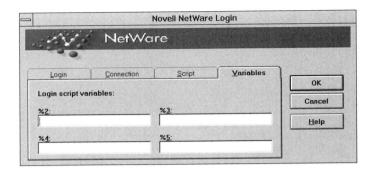

You can force all four login pages to display by using the following command syntax for launching the login utility. Modify the command line for the NetWare Login icon to reflect the following:

```
LOGINW31 /a
```

Or, select individual screens by issuing any combination of the following parameters:

```
/c     To display the Connection Page

/s     To display the Script Page

/v     To display the Variable Page
```

Limiting User Access Through the NETWARE.INI File

As your users become more advanced, they might discover the ability to turn certain login pages on and off through NetWare User Tools. After you have configured the workstation and selected the appropriate parameters, you might find it convenient to lock down the settings by making the following modifications to your NETWARE.INI file:

```
[Options]
HotKeyEnabled=1

[Restrict]
NoSettings=1
```

In the preceding example, the option HotKeyEnabled allows a user to press F12 or the appropriate function key to launch NetWare User Tools from within any Windows application. Under the restrict heading, the NoHotKey=1 option is added to disable the NetWare Settings button. This prevents users from being able to access the different settings. In the same manner, you can also disable any of the other User Tool buttons.

Table 20.1 lists the options available to restrict user access to features in the NetWare User Tools utility.

Table 20.1   Commands Available Under the NETWARE.INI *[Restrict]* Heading

INI Command	Description
[Restrict]	Heading
UserTool=0	Completely disables the NetWare User Tool utility
NoHotKey=1	Disables the HotKey access to NetWare User Tools
NoDrives=1	Disables the functionality of NetWare Drive Connections
NoLPTs=1	Disables the functionality of NetWare Printer Connections
NoConnections=1	Disables the ability to log in to other servers via NetWare Connections
NoSend=1	Disables the functionality of NetWare Send Messages
NoSettings=1	Disables the ability to access the NetWare Settings
NoUser1=1	Disables the ability to create a user-definable button
NoUser2=1	Disables the ability to create a user-definable button

Configuring Additional Settings Through NetWare User Tools

The NetWare Settings button in the NetWare User Tools utility provides access to a great many configuration parameters other than those for controlling the screens of the Login dialog box. The following sections examine these parameters, and how you can use them to customize your networking environment.

The User Tools Tab   When you click the NetWare Settings button to open the NetWare Settings dialog box, the User Tools tab displays the panel shown in Figure 20.12. From here, you can enable the HotKey feature and several other items. An important addition is the ability to control how drives are mapped. Notice that the Drive Mapping Option allows you to set whether or not the drive mappings created are Map Roots by default.

In addition, the User Tools tab contains Resource Display Options that are platform specific. For example, the Personal check box is only available for users of Personal NetWare. The Bindery option is available for NetWare 2.x through 4.x bindery users, and the DS objects are available only for users of NetWare 4.x.

By making selections here, the items are displayed as resource options from within the other screens in NetWare User Tools. You can prevent DS objects or DS containers from being displayed as available resources for your users to select by unchecking the boxes. By deselecting the DS containers option, you prevent users from being able to browse up or down the branches of the tree to view resources in other containers.

Part
VI
Ch
20

FIG. 20.12
Use the NetWare Settings User Tools tab to modify the options and defaults displayed while logging in to the network.

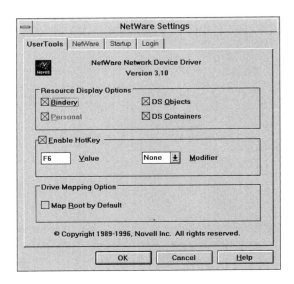

The NetWare Tab   The NetWare tab enables you to change to several settings that deal with the way that your workstation handles messages, printing issues, and DOS sessions (see Figure 20.13). The Message Reception portion of the panel has the following options: Broadcasts and Network Warnings. A *broadcast* is a message generated from the server alerting the user to a certain condition. Volume SYS almost out of disk space is a broadcast message, for example. As an administrator, you might want to selectively choose who receives these messages.

The other option is Network Warnings. This option controls the display of any warnings the user might encounter when Client 32 is loading and the network environment is being established. You may want to turn on this option for all users so they can alert you to any problems.

If you are using Windows Print Manager, there are two settings on this screen that you might want to adjust. The first option, Maximum Jobs, affects how many jobs you see in the Windows dialog box if you display the current job list. The range is from 1 to 250 print jobs; 50 is the default. Note that this does not limit the number of jobs that can be submitted to a print queue, it only limits the number you can view from within the Windows Print Manager screen. The second option, Update Seconds, controls how frequently the print queue screen is refreshed. Thirty seconds is the default. Use caution when lowering this value. If you force Windows to refresh the display more frequently, you may cause your printing to slow down.

FIG. 20.13

Modify how the client reacts to server console messages and connection information through the NetWare Settings screen's NetWare tab.

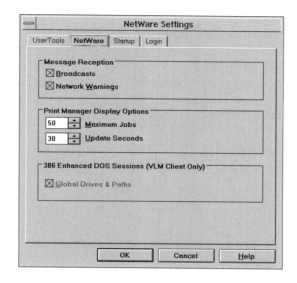

The final item on the NetWare tab is 386 Enhanced DOS Sessions. Select this option to make Windows and DOS work together when drive connections are established. Unless this option is selected, a drive mapping made through a DOS shell in Windows is only current for that session. In addition, any drives created in separate DOS Windows are independent of each other. This option allows all drive mappings, regardless of where they were created, to be available through Windows and all DOS sessions, as well as when you exit Windows and work in DOS.

The Login Tab   The functions and capabilities of the Login tab were discussed earlier in this section. You can get additional information on using the NetWare User Tools utility including the Drive and Printer Connections in Chapter 19, "Accessing Network Resources."

The Advanced Options Tab   The NetWare Settings panel offers an additional tab: Advanced Options. From within NetWare Settings Advanced Options, you have access to over 40 configurable client parameters. In previous client software, these options were configured as entries in the NET.CFG file. Table 20.2 describes the available parameters and their settings.

Part
VI

Ch
20

Table 20.2 Client 32 Advanced Settings Configurable Options

Setting	Default Option	Allowed Range	Setting
AUTO RECONNECT LEVEL	3	0–5	Yes

Purpose: Setting this option to a value higher than 0 allows your PC to automatically restore a lost server connection by reconnecting to a NetWare server that returns to service after an outage. The number that you choose determines what services are restored when the workstation reconnects:

0   No automatic reconnection

1   All server connections, drive mappings, and printer assignments are restored

2   Restores all in option 1 and reopens all read-only files previously in use

3   Restores all services in the previous options, plus reopens all previously open files, and relocks previously locked files

4   Restores all services in the previous options, plus restarts and completes all incomplete write operations in progress at the time of the disconnection

5   Restores all services in the previous options, plus additional functionality to be released in future versions of NetWare

Cache Writes	On	On or Off	Yes

Purpose: Setting this option to On causes writes to the local workstation cache buffer to be reported to your application as a completed write. Setting to Off causes a completed write to be reported only after the write request is written to the server. Leave On for best performance or Off for maximum integrity.

Checksum	1	0–3	Yes

Purpose: This option controls whether Client 32 embeds checksums in the IPX packets it sends. (A *checksum* is an error-checking code used to tell whether the packet was corrupted during transmission.) Adding checksums degrades performance slightly, and your network board might already provide sufficient error checking. Use settings 0 through 3 to cause the workstation to do the following:

0   Don't use checksums

1   Use checksums only for devices that request them

2   Use checksums only for devices that can use them

3   Require checksums for all packets from all devices

This option is ignored if you use the Ethernet_802.3 frame type, as it does not support the use of checksums.

Close Behind Ticks	0	0–65535	Yes

Purpose: Client 32 caches open server-based files in local workstation memory to maximize performance. Use this option to control how many ticks must elapse after you close a file until the file is truly closed and removed from local workstation cache (at 18.21 ticks per second). If you use an application that frequently closes and reopens the same set of files, this option can improve performance.

Setting	Default Option	Allowed Range	Setting
Delay Writes	Off	On or Off	Yes

Purpose: This option specifies whether or not an application's write request can be held in cache and delayed beyond the closing of the application. Usually, Client 32 completes all pending write requests before an application closes. If set to On, Client 32 reports to the application that all write requests are completed. The Close Behind Ticks option determines the maximum delay time before a cached write request is handled.

DOS Name	MSDOS	Any DOS name	No

Purpose: Client 32 automatically detects what version of DOS you're using. You can override this default by using this option to set the name manually.

Environment Pad	64	0–32768	No

Purpose: Set this option to cause Client 32 to add the specified number of bytes to the DOS environment when you launch a DOS application.

File Cache Level	3	0–4	Yes

Purpose: Use this option to control Client 32's local file-caching feature. You can set five levels of caching:

0   Local caching is completely disabled.

1   Client 32 uses read-ahead and write-behind caching. Read-ahead caching means that complete 4K file blocks are read into workstation memory even though the application requests a smaller amount of data. Several subsequent requests probably can be satisfied with the data contained in the 4K block already in workstation memory. When Client 32 detects that a file is being read sequentially, it caches subsequent blocks of the file in workstation memory in advance.

Write-behind caching means that file writes are cached locally until a complete 4K block is rewritten, at which point the whole block is written to the server in one operation.

2   Client 32 uses short-lived caching. With short-lived caching, file reads and writes can be cached in workstation memory until the file is closed.

3   Client 32 uses long-lived caching. Recently used blocks of a file are cached in memory, even if the file was closed. If the file is reopened and was not changed since the previous open, Client 32 reuses locally cached file blocks if they are requested.

4   Client 32 uses warehouse caching. Long-lived caching is supplemented with caching to local disk space. Use this option if local disk reads and writes are significantly faster than server reads and writes.

This option doesn't apply for write operations if the True Commit option is set to On or if Cache Writes is set to Off.

Force First Network Drive	Off	On or Off	No

Purpose: Set this option to On to specify that the sole remaining network drive when you disconnect (which is by default mapped to SYS:LOGIN) will always be the one you specify as the first network drive, using Client 32's Login settings tab. When set to Off, SYS:LOGIN is mapped to the drive letter of last active drive mapping when logout occurs.

Part
VI

Ch
20

continues

Table 20.2 Continued

Setting	Default Option	Allowed Range	Setting
Handle Net Errors	On	On or Off	Yes

Purpose: This option determines whether Client 32 handles and attempts to recover from a network error or whether the error is reported to the application.

Lock Delay	1	1–65535	Yes

Purpose: This option sets the number of ticks (there are 18.21 ticks in a second) that Client 32 waits while trying to open a file that is locked by another workstation. Increase this setting if many workstations concurrently try to open and lock the same files and get errors.

Lock Retries	5	1–65535	Yes

Purpose: This setting controls the number of times that Client 32 retries when attempting to open and lock a file.

Long Machine Type	IBM_PC	any machine	No

Purpose: Use this option to manually set the machine name stored by the requester. The name you set with this option is the same name stored in the MACHINE login script variable.

Max Cache Size	0	0–4292967295	No

Purpose: Use this option to set number of kilobytes to be available for local file caching. If set to 0 (the default), Client 32 automatically allows itself to use up to 25 percent of workstation memory that is free when Client 32 first loads. If set to a specific value, Client 32 automatically decreases the amount of memory used to 75 percent of free memory, if you specify a value higher than this amount.

Max Cur Dir Length	64	64–255	No

Purpose: This option sets the maximum character length of the current directory path name. Some programs don't operate properly if they are required to work with a directory path length greater than 64 characters.

Message Timeout	0	0–10000	No

Purpose: This option sets the number of processor ticks until a broadcast message is automatically cleared from the screen (a *tick* is approximately 1/18th second). When this option is set to 0, you must manually clear the message.

Minimum Time to Net	0	0–65535	Yes

Purpose: This option extends the allowed time (in milliseconds) before Client 32 concludes that a connection attempt failed. Increase this setting if you are attempting to connect over a low-speed link or the server to which you are connecting responds to connect requests very slowly.

NCP Max Timeout	30	30–65535	No

Purpose: This option controls amount of time (in seconds) that elapses before Client 32 retries a failed connection request. Increase this setting if you are attempting to connect over a low-speed link or if the server to which you are connecting responds to connect requests very slowly.

Setting	Default Option	Allowed Range	Setting
NetWare Protocols	NDS BIND	NDS BIND BIND NDS NDS BIND	No

Purpose: Determines which of the two NetWare protocols (Novell Directory Services and Bindery) are used and the order in which they are accessed. You should set your primary or preferred protocol first.

Network Printers	3	0–9	No

Purpose: This option sets the number of LPT ports that can be captured.

Opportunistic Locking	On	On or Off	Yes

Purpose: Setting this option to On allows Client 32 to lock and locally cache a file opened for sharing but in use by other workstations. If the file that is locked and cached by using opportunistic locking is subsequently opened by another workstation, locking and local caching stops. This setting is not supported in Client 32 for Windows 95 version 2.11.

Packet Burst Read Window Size	24	3–255	Yes

Purpose: This option sets the maximum number of packets that can be received in one read request burst. Total number of packets multiplied by the size of one packet cannot exceed 64K.

Packet Burst Write Window Size	10	3–255	Yes

Purpose: This option sets the maximum number of packets that can be transmitted in one write request burst. Total number of packets multiplied by the size of one packet cannot exceed 64K.

Print Header	64	0–1024	No

Purpose: This option sets the size of the print job header that contains the setup instructions for the printer. If you configure your print jobs to include elaborate setup strings, make sure that the print header size exceeds the size of your setup strings.

Print Tail	16	0–1024	No

Purpose: This option sets the size of the print job "tail" that contains the instructions used to reset the printer after each job. Make sure that the print tail size exceeds the size of your reset strings.

Read Only Compatibility	Off	On or Off	Yes

Purpose: This option determines whether read-only files can be opened for reading and writing. Set to On only if you must use an application that tries to open read-only files for reading and writing.

Search Dirs First	Off	On or Off	No

Purpose: Use this option to control what is displayed first when you list the contents of a directory. Setting to Off causes files to list first; setting to On causes directories to list first.

Search Mode	1	1–7	No

Purpose: This option determines how EXE or COM files that open other files will search for the other files.

    0   No search instructions

Part

VI

Ch

20

continues

Table 20.2   Continued

Setting	Default Option	Allowed Range	Setting
1	Only the directory path specified by the program is searched; if no path is specified, then the default directory and network search drives are searched.		
2	Only the default directory and the specified path (if any) are searched.		
3	Only the directory path specified by the program is searched; if no path is specified, and the program opens Read-Only data files, then the default directory and network search drives are searched.		
4	Reserved		
5	The default directory and NetWare search drives are always searched.		
6	Reserved		
7	If the program opens read-only data files, the default directory and network search drives are always searched.		

Set Station Time   On   On or Off   No
Purpose: This option determines whether workstation time is synchronized with the time on the server to which the workstation first connects when loading the requester.

Short Machine Type   IBM   Any machine   No
Purpose: Use this option to manually set the short machine name stored by Client 32. The *short machine name* determines which overlay files are used by NetWare's DOS utilities. Change the short machine name to CMPQ if you use a CGA-compatible, single-color monitor. You shouldn't change the short machine name to anything else unless you're ready to create a custom overlay file with the COLORPAL utility. The short machine name is the same information stored by the SMACHINE login script variable.

Show Dots   Off   On or Off   No
Purpose: DOS and related workstation operating systems use a period (.) to indicate the current directory and two periods (..) to indicate the parent directory. NetWare doesn't use these period entries to indicate current or parent directories, but setting this option to On causes the Requester to display period entries for the current and parent directories.

Signature Level   1   0–3   Yes
Purpose: This command controls the use of *packet signatures*, an optional identification that a server or workstation can embed in a packet to guarantee the identity of the packet sender. Packet signatures are used to defeat programs that generate and send forged packets. Your workstation packet signature setting must match signature settings on the servers to which you want to connect. Packet signatures increase server and workstation workload because each packet's signature must be read and verified. The settings 0 through 3 cause Client 32 to perform the following packet signature verifications:

0	Don't use packet signatures.
1	Use packet signatures only for devices that request them.
2	Use packet signatures only for devices that can use them.
3	Require packet signatures for all packets from all devices.

Setting	Default Option	Allowed Range	Setting
True Commit	Off	On or Off	Yes

Purpose: Usually, an application receives confirmation that a file write is completed when the information in that write operation is written to the server's memory cache, and the actual write to disk occurs a few seconds later. With this activated, the file write isn't confirmed until the information is written to the server disk. Turning it on can seriously decrease the performance of write operations but ensures maximum integrity.

When you are finished customizing the advanced Client 32 parameters, click OK to return to the NetWare User Tools menu.

Other User Tools Capabilities The NetWare User Tools utility enables users to perform many client tasks within one GUI utility. In addition to modifying the Client 32 configuration, you can also log in to other servers, send messages, and access network resources. Figure 20.14 shows the NetWare Connections page, (accessed by selecting the NetWare Connections button on the tool bar), that is used to log in to additional NetWare servers. Use the Send a Message option to send a message to other NetWare clients that are currently logged in to the network. To send a message, select the Send Message button on the tool bar. Figure 20.15 demonstrates this capability.

FIG. 20.14

Connect to additional servers by logging in to them through NetWare Connections, accessed from NetWare User Tools utility.

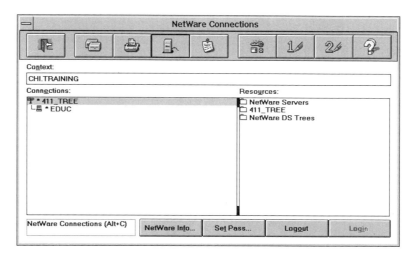

In addition to the preprogrammed toolbar button options that NetWare supplies from within NetWare User Tools, there are also two user definable buttons available. The buttons are labeled with a question mark and the numbers 1 and 2. Select the desired button to access the user definable dialog box displayed in Figure 20.16. You can enter the command line for any utility or program on the network. Most network administrators configure at least one of the user definable buttons to launch RCONSOLE. Other popular utilities are PCONSOLE and FILER. After a button is defined, you can only modify or remove the association by editing the NETWARE.INI file.

FIG. 20.15
Use the Send a Message option in NetWare User Tools to send short messages to other users that are currently logged in to the network.

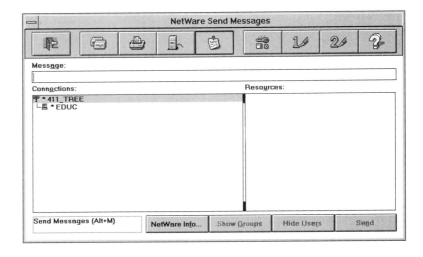

FIG. 20.16
Two user definable buttons are available to provide access to other applications, such as RCONSOLE and PCONSOLE.

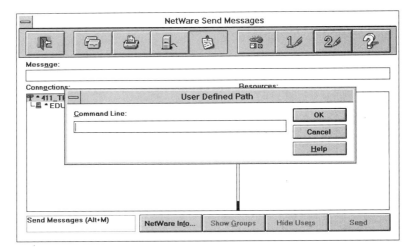

When you're finished in NetWare User Tools, select the Red Door icon from the button bar to exit the utility. You can also close or minimize the program using traditional windows keystrokes.

Using the Client 32 Automatic Client Upgrade (ACU) Feature

Client 32 includes a utility that you can use to perform automatic client upgrades to your workstations. You can use the ACU utility to upgrade previous versions of the NetWare DOS Requester (the VLM client) or the NetWare Shell (NETX.EXE). The utility can also be used to keep all of your workstations on the newest release of Client 32 by adding the ACU command line to your login scripts. The major components of the ACU process are as follows:

- **NWSTAMP.EXE**—This executable is responsible for updating and placing what is known as an Install Stamp in the NET.CFG file. The Install Stamp is used to determine the current version of the client software being used on the workstation. An example of the Install Stamp is shown in "Examining the Install Stamp in the NET.CFG File" later in this chapter.

- **NWDETECT.EXE**—The NWDETECT.EXE program starts the ACU process by examining the NET.CFG to find the Install Stamp. When it is found, NWDETECT.EXE must determine whether or not the client version on the workstation is the same as that on the server. If the Install Stamp is missing, it is assumed that the workstation client files are out-of-date.

- **NWLOG.EXE**—This component creates a log file that holds a record of all upgraded workstations. You must specify the location of the file. Pertinent information contained in the log file includes date, time, login name, cable segment, and MAC address.

The ACU process begins when a user logs in and the ACU commands are found in a login script. NWDETECT.EXE is launched to determine whether or not the client software is current, returning a value of 0 if the workstation software is current and a value of 1 if the workstation software is out-of-date.

Based on this information, ACU launches INSTALL.EXE, the DOS version of the Client 32 installation program, if necessary. The installation program reads the settings in the INSTALL.CFG file and automatically installs and upgrades the workstation client files. As a final step, the REBOOT.COM program is used to restart the workstation. The following sections highlight the individual steps of the process.

N O T E Be sure to modify the INSTALL.CFG file to include the following option under the [Setup] option.

```
[Setup]
InstallType = Auto
```

Adding ACU Commands to a Login Script   Before modifying the login script to include the appropriate ACU commands, you must determine which script to select. Remember that the only container login script that executes for a user is the script belonging to its parent container.

> **CAUTION**
>
> If you are operating with a mixed platform environment, use caution when adding the ACU to your login scripts. The process for upgrading Windows 95 clients is different from that for Windows 3.x. Be sure to include a parameter that tests the platform that the workstation is using before launching the ACU process. You can use the variables on the Login page to determine the workstation type.

There are several ways to modify the login scripts to include the ACU commands. The easiest method is to enter the commands in the scripts of the organizational units containing your users. This way, you can be sure that the server and subdirectory locations of the client files are entered properly. Another method is to create a text file containing the login script commands and use the Include statement in the container login script. This causes the text file to be executed, and the size of the actual login script is minimized. This is helpful if you want to temporarily disable the upgrade process.

The following code lines demonstrate how to include all of the ACU commands in the container login script:

```
MAP U:=EDUC\SYS:PUBLIC\CLIENT32\DOSWIN
#U:NWDETECT Novell_Client32 4.1.0
IF ERROR_LEVEL = "1" THEN
   #U:INSTALL
   IF ERROR_LEVEL = "0" THEN
      #U:NWSTAMP Novell_Client32 4.1.0
      #U:NWLOG /F U:\PUBLIC\CLIENT\DOSWIN\LOG\UPDATE.LOG
      #U:REBOOT
   END
END
MAP DEL U:
```

The preceding code breaks down into the following sequence. The first line maps a drive to the client installation files. The second line launches the NWDETECT process. This generates the first exit code value 1 if the install stamps do not match, but 0 if they do.

The test IF ERROR_LEVEL = "1" is performed to determine whether or not the client needs to be upgraded. If the ERROR_LEVEL is 0 and the workstation software does not need to be upgraded, the process ends and the U: drive is deleted. However, if the ERROR_LEVEL returns a 1, the embedded IF statement launches the Install program from the U: drive, which generates another exit code value of either 1 or 0.

If the installation process completes successfully, a value of 0 is returned and the embedded IF triggers and updates the Install Stamp in the NET.CFG file and also updates the log file. If the installation process does not complete successfully, then the embedded IF ERROR_LEVEL = "0" prevents the Install Stamp from being updated and the workstation does not reboot. The log file also is not updated. As the administrator, you can determine which upgrades complete successfully by reviewing the log file.

Examining the Install Stamp in the NET.CFG File   Following is an example of the Install Stamp generated in the NET.CFG file; it can be found under the Install Stamp section:

```
Install Stamp
        Name=Novell_Client32
        Major Version=4
        Minor Version=1
        Revision Version=0
```

These fields correspond with the NWSTAMP command entered in the login script. Novell updates the Major and Minor fields for each release. The information is always published in the README file included with the upgraded client. The revision version is a user-definable field. You can use it to force an update by increasing the Revision Version in the NWSTAMP command. However, be careful to never increase the Major and Minor version values out of sequence with Novell.

Summary

The IntranetWare Client 32 for DOS/Windows 3.1 is Novell's newest client connection software. It is very flexible and easy-to-use, offering over 40 configurable parameters in addition to the new flexibility of the NetWare User Tools utility. Unlike the DOS-based clients of the past, Client 32 provides greater flexibility while occupying only 4K of conventional memory. The new Automatic Client Upgrade feature enables network administrators to streamline the never-ending client upgrade and reconfiguration process. ●

Part

VI

Ch

20

CHAPTER 21

Using the IntranetWare Client 32 for Windows 95

Windows 95 is quickly becoming the most popular PC operating system. As a network administrator, you may be making plans or have already started to incorporate your Windows 95 PCs into your Novell Network. Once you configure the Windows 95 PC to communicate with your NetWare 4.11 network, you will be able to save files with long file name support and reap the benefits of increased network awareness from the desktop.

Windows 95 also includes a number of features that use your network to make workstations easier to manage and control. User Profiles enable different users to have personal configurations on the same Windows 95 PC. You can configure a NetWare 4.11 server to store user profiles so that Windows 95 users can access their personal profiles from any system connected to the network. A related feature called *system policies* allows you to use your network to impose restrictions on the system configuration changes that Windows 95 users are allowed to make. ■

Planning Your Windows 95 Strategy

The tactics used by network administrators for previous workstation operating systems are changing dramatically with Windows 95. Network resources and administration tools are accessed through a GUI on a Windows 95 system. In many cases, you may find that there are several ways to perform the same task with Windows 95.

One major consideration is choosing a NetWare client to use with Windows 95. There are two choices:

- **Microsoft's Client for NetWare**—This client ships with Windows 95. As the first protected mode NetWare client, it's the most time-tested and stable. The Microsoft Client for NetWare that shipped with the Windows 95 release was not NDS-aware. Microsoft then released an update, Microsoft's Service for NDS, that allows users to log in to the NDS tree.

  Recently, Microsoft merged the two clients and released the new Microsoft Client for NetWare. The Microsoft client is NDS-aware, enables support for long file names, increases file transfer speed, and provides plug-and-play networking. A noted quirk with the Microsoft Client for NetWare is that even though it includes the capability to process login scripts, not all login script command syntax works as it should.

- **Novell's IntranetWare Client 32 for Windows 95**—Novell's Client 32 is the most feature-rich Windows 95 NetWare client. It is fully NDS-compatible, allows you to simultaneously connect to multiple NDS trees, and provides a graphical login interface. It includes over 40 customizable parameters and a powerful login dialog box that lets you control precisely what happens when you connect to an NDS tree or a server.

  Client 32 supports the use of *system policies* (which enable you to use your network to control which Windows 95 options can be used and customized), and provides access to many file system features through the standard operating system utilities, such as the Windows 95 Explorer.

The following table compares the two client options:

Client Software Comparison	Novell IntranetWare Client 32	Microsoft Client for NetWare
NDS-compatible	Yes	Yes
Bindery-compatible	Yes	Yes
Ships with Windows 95	No	Yes
Best login script compatibility	Yes	No
Enables logins to multiple trees	Yes	No
Compatible with user profiles	Yes	Yes

Client Software Comparison	Novell IntranetWare Client 32	Microsoft Client for NetWare
Compatible with system policies	Individual group and default	Individual group and default
Update using ACU	Yes	No
Customizable login screen	Yes	No
Supports an extended NDS schema	Yes	No

Generally speaking, Novell's Client 32 offers more flexibility, customization, and compatibility with NetWare 4.11 than the Microsoft client, but does so at the cost of a slight decrease in speed. The bulk of this chapter covers the processes involved in installing, configuring, and using Client 32.

The Client 32 software is included in the IntranetWare package, but upgrade releases are frequent, and you can always obtain the current version from Novell's Web site at **www.novell.com**. If you purchased Windows 95 before it started shipping with the upgraded Microsoft Client for NetWare, you can download the new version from Microsoft's Web site at **www.microsoft.com**.

Using Novell's IntranetWare Client 32 for Windows 95

To log your Windows 95 workstation in to an NDS tree, you must either install Novell's Client 32 for Windows 95 or Microsoft's Client for NetWare networks. Client 32 offers far greater NetWare functionality than Microsoft's client by allowing you to log in to multiple trees simultaneously, execute all NetWare login script commands, and exercise greater control over the NetWare file system using the Explorer and other Windows 95 utilities.

Preparing the Installation Files for Client 32

The Client 32 software package is included in the IntranetWare product. Once you have installed NetWare 4.11, you can use the INSTALL.NLM utility to copy the client files to your server's SYS:PUBLIC\CLIENT\WIN95 directory, where they will always be available for new installations. However, you should also be aware that the client is always available for download, free of charge, from any of Novell's online services. Because updates to the client software are released fairly frequently, it is a good idea to keep your installation files current.

You can download Client 32 in two forms. The Network Install version is designed to be installed from a network server, and the Disk Install version is copied to floppy disks and then installed from these disks. Both versions come as self-extracting compressed files. The disk version is clearly intended for use when a Windows 95 workstation has no NetWare client installed, and cannot access the installation files on a NetWare server volume.

Part

VI

Ch

21

Floppy disk installations are time-consuming and unwieldy; however, there are several alternative methods that you can use to perform a network-based installation. These methods are as follows:

- Use a boot floppy containing a minimal NetWare DOS Requester (VLM) or NetWare Shell (NETX) client installation to gain access to the server where the Client 32 installation files are located, and copy them to the local workstation hard drive.

- Run the installation directly from the IntranetWare CD-ROM using a local workstation CD-ROM drive.

- Copy the installation files to a shared Windows network hard drive or CD-ROM, and execute the installation program using a connection provided by the Windows 95 Client for Microsoft Networks.

- Install the Microsoft Client for NetWare on the Windows 95 machine in order to gain access to the Client 32 installation files on the NetWare server. The Client 32 installation program will remove the Microsoft client before installing Client 32 in its place.

Installing Novell's Client 32

To install Client 32, you log in to the server that stores the Client 32 installation files and run SETUP.EXE from SYS:PUBLIC\CLIENT\WIN95 directory (or wherever you have stored the source files).

TIP Client 32 installation runs best when you execute the SETUP.EXE program using the Windows 95 Start menu. Avoid installing Client 32 from a directory that uses a long file name. You will also experience difficulty if you try to install from a path that includes a directory map object. For example, the installation may crash because it cannot find all of its components. Following is an example of using the directory map object titled C32_DIRMAP.

`\\411_TREE\.C32_DIRMAP.CHI.TRAINING`

When SETUP starts, you must first agree to the licensing for Client 32, after which you click Start to begin the installation process. When you do so, a completely automatic process removes your existing NetWare client (if any) and adds Client 32.

N O T E Client 32 installs itself in a directory named \NOVELL\CLIENT32 on your PC's hard drive. This is different from past client connection software. The NETX and VLM client traditionally used a directory called NWCLIENT.

During the installation, you may be prompted to confirm whether or not you want to install a 32-bit ODI driver for your network adapter. Client 32 supports both Novell's own ODI drivers and the NDIS drivers traditionally used with Windows 95. If you also use your workstation system to connect to Windows network shares, such as those found on other Windows 95 or Windows NT machines, you must retain the NDIS driver. If you will be connecting only to a

NetWare network, you can safely use the ODI driver that ships with Client 32, if one is available for your adapter.

CAUTION

The 32-bit ODI drivers included with Client 32 are not the same as the standard ODI drivers that ship with network interface adapters, which are 16-bit and intended for use with the NetWare DOS Requester. Before using an ODI driver that comes with your adapter hardware, be sure that it is a 32-bit version, intended specifically for use with Windows 95.

After the installation is complete, you are prompted to reboot your PC or return to Windows 95. At this time, you also can click the Customize button to work with Client 32's many configurable options, or you can perform these same steps after restarting the PC.

Customizing Client 32

You can customize Client 32 to tailor its login options, print capture defaults, and preferred tree and server connections. To customize Client 32, open the Windows 95 Network Control Panel, and open the Properties dialog box for the Novell NetWare Client 32 entry.

The Novell NetWare Client 32 Properties dialog box offers the following four option tabs:

■ **Client 32**—Used to control preferred server, tree, context, and network drive defaults

■ **Login**—Used to customize the behavior of Client 32's Login dialog box

■ **Default Capture**—Used to set initial printer connection assignments

■ **Advanced Settings**—Used to work with more than 40 advanced configuration settings

The following sections examine the options found on each of the tabs in the dialog box.

The Client 32 Tab   Click the Client 32 tab to customize the initial connection settings that take effect when your system starts, and loads Client 32. The Client 32 panel of the properties dialog box (see Figure 21.1) contains the following four options:

■ **Preferred Server**—Use this option to specify the name of the server to which your workstation should connect at startup when Client 32 loads. This option is most useful when you create a bindery connection to a NetWare 3.x server. If you intend to log in to an NDS tree when your system starts, specify a preferred tree instead.

■ **Preferred Tree**—This option lets you specify which directory tree your workstation should connect to at startup. Use this option if you have multiple trees on your network to choose from, or if you have a mix of NetWare 4.x and 3.x servers and want to log in to an NDS tree at startup.

■ **Name Context**—You use this setting to specify the NDS context in which your user object is stored. This becomes your current context when you log in to the network.

Part
VI

Ch
21

■ **First Network Drive**—With this option, you select the drive letter that is automatically assigned to SYS:LOGIN on a server when your system starts and Client 32 loads. Choose a drive letter by clicking the down arrow and choosing a letter. Normally, NetWare will use F: for this purpose, but you may want to reserve additional drive letters at the beginning of the alphabet for use with Windows network shares.

FIG. 21.1

To adjust the default connection options, modify the settings on the Client 32 tab. This enables your users to connect to the network by supplying only a login name and password.

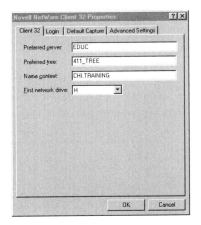

The Login Tab   Click the Login tab to customize the way that Client 32 handles the login process. The Login section of the Novell NetWare Client 32 Properties dialog box appears, as shown in Figure 21.2.

FIG. 21.2

Modify the Client 32's login options to control how a user authenticates to the network.

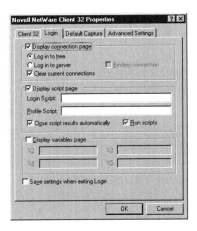

There are four main tabs in the Client 32 login dialog box that can be customized to fit your environment, as follows:

■ Login
■ Connection

- Script
- Variables

You use the Login tab of the Novell NetWare Client 32 Properties dialog box to determine which panels appear in the Login dialog box during system startup, and to provide the default values that appear in the fields of the Login dialog box's panels. Users who need simplicity, and always log in to the same tree or server can be presented with the Login tab only at boot time, while users who need the ability to log in to multiple trees or servers can be allowed to see both the Login and Connection tabs. Power users, who want to control login script execution and variables and who aren't intimidated by technical complexity, can turn on all four tabs (see Figure 21.3).

FIG. 21.3
The NetWare Client 32 Login dialog box can be customized to suit your users' level of expertise.

Displaying the various tabs in the Login dialog box allows the user to change the values for the fields configured here in the Login tab of the Client 32 Properties dialog box. At the bottom of the Login tab, the Save Settings When Exiting Login option, when activated, causes any changes made by the user at login time to be permanently saved. Clearing this check box causes the Login dialog box to revert to the settings configured in the Control Panel whenever the system is restarted.

Connection Settings   The Login panel is always available in the Client 32 Login dialog box. You can also make the Connection tab visible by filling the Display Connection Page check box. After doing so, you can set the following Connection tab defaults:

- **Tree**—Select this option to log in to an NDS tree by default.
- **Server**—Select this option to log in to a specific server by default.
- **Bindery Connection**—If you choose to log in to an individual server, you can mark this option to establish a bindery connection by default.
- **Clear Current Connections**—To clear all existing NetWare connections by default when you log in, mark this option.

Two of the preceding options have relevance only if you often use the Client 32 Login dialog box to establish connections after you start your workstation and perform your initial login. If you are already logged in to a directory tree and want to establish a manual connection to a particular NetWare 4.11 server, the Log In to Server option is useful. Similarly, if you use the Client 32 Login dialog box to add a server connection after your initial login, turn off the Clear Current Connections option (see Figure 21.4).

Part
VI
Ch
21

FIG. 21.4

Set the connection options to control how a user is connected to a server. For most users, turning on the Clear Current Connections option is recommended in order to avoid multiple connections to multiple servers.

Script Settings   The Script page enables you to control login script execution. Activating this page allows you to decide during the login process whether or not your login scripts should run. You also can specify which profile and personal login scripts are executed.

To specify that the Script page be activated, fill the Display Script Page check box. You then can configure the following four options (see Figure 21.5):

- **Login Script**—To run a personal login script from a text file rather than execute the login script associated with your user object, enter the path and file name for the script file in this box.

- **Profile Script**—To run a profile script other than your default profile script, enter the full NDS name of the profile object in this box. You must be a member of the profile that you enter.

- **Close Script Results Automatically**—When your login scripts run, the messages they generate are displayed in a text box. To have this text box close automatically, mark this option. Otherwise, the results remain on-screen until you click a button to clear them.

- **Run Scripts**—If you don't want to execute any login scripts, unmark this option.

FIG. 21.5

The script parameters enable you to specify alternative script files and control the execution of the scripts.

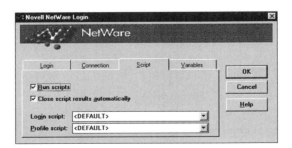

Variables Settings   If you're thoroughly familiar with NetWare's DOS-based LOGIN.EXE program, you know that you can follow the LOGIN command with parameters that trigger certain actions in your login scripts. (See Appendix B, "Login Script Commands and Variables," for more information about LOGIN command-line parameters and their use in login scripts.)

To retain full compatibility with login script syntax, Client 32 enables you to enter the command-line parameters as you log in, using the Variables panel (see Figure 21.6).

This option is seldom used, but if you need to activate it, mark the Display variables page option. You then can enter the default command-line parameters by filling in the %2, %3, %4, and %5 boxes, which correspond to the second, third, fourth, and fifth LOGIN command-line parameters.

FIG. 21.6
You can enter login script variables to vary how different users log in and connect to network resources.

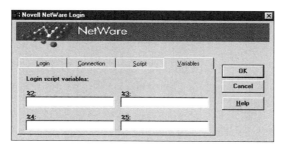

The Default Capture Tab   Click the Default Capture tab in the Novell NetWare Client 32 Properties dialog box to set the default settings that are applied when you use Windows 95 to capture a printer port. The defaults you set with this dialog box are not applied when you use the CAPTURE command from the DOS prompt or when you run CAPTURE from a login script. They are also not applied when you do not print through a captured printer port, which is the case when you configure a printer on your PC to print directly to a NetWare queue. (For details about network printing configuration options in Windows 95, see Chapter 19, "Accessing Network Resources.")

Some DOS programs require a port capture in order to print, but Windows applications print instead to a named printer. The options you set in the Default Capture section apply only for those few DOS applications that can only print to a printer port. When you click the Default Capture tab, you can set the following options (see Figure 21.7):

- **Number of Copies**—Sets the number of copies of your print job that will print.
- **Form Feed**—Determines whether or not a page-eject command is sent to the printer after each print job.
- **Enable Tabs**—Converts tabs in your print jobs to spaces.
- **Number of Spaces**—Sets the number of spaces to replace each tab.
- **Enable Banner**—Specifies that a banner page be printed as the first page of each print job.
- **1st Banner Name**—If you enable a banner, enter the information here that you want to be printed in the banner's top panel.
- **2nd Banner Name**—Enter the information here that you want to print in the banner page's lower panel.

Part
VI

Ch
21

- **Hold**—Used to specify that your print jobs be held in the print queue until you use a NetWare or Windows 95 utility to release them for printing.

- **Auto Endcap**—Use to specify that an end-of-job signal be sent as soon as the program that is sending a print job closes the DOS PRN device to signal that the job is complete.

- **Notify**—When you mark this option, you receive a notification message at your workstation as soon as your print job finishes printing.

- **Keep**—Used to instruct NetWare to print a print job that was interrupted in some way (such as by your workstation losing power suddenly). Usually NetWare discards partial print jobs.

- **Seconds Before Timeout**—This option specifies that NetWare should assume that the print job is complete if no print output is received for the number of seconds that you select.

  ▶ **See** "Redirecting Printer Output Using the CAPTURE Command," **p. 451**

FIG. 21.7

Once you have added a network printer through the Control Panel, you can modify the NetWare Client 32 Default capture settings.

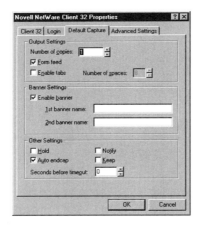

The Advanced Settings Tab   The final tab in the Novell NetWare Client 32 Properties dialog box is Advanced Settings. When you press this tab, you see the Advanced Settings panel of the dialog box, as shown in Figure 21.8.

The default settings for Client 32 are designed to work well in most situations, so it is possible that you may not have to change any of the Advanced Settings parameters. Select the Advanced Settings tab to view all of the available parameters. To display a particular category, press the down arrow in the Parameter Groups box.

Table 21.1 describes the available settings and their values. When you modify a dynamic setting, the change takes effect immediately. Changes to other settings take effect after you restart your system.

FIG. 21.8

You can control every aspect of how your workstation and client software interact with the NetWare server by modifying the parameters in Client 32's Advanced Settings panel.

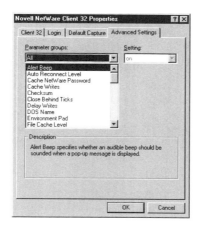

Table 21.1   Client 32's Advanced Setting Options

Setting Parameter	Default Option	Allowed Range Setting	Dynamic Parameter?
Alert Beep	On	On or Off	No

Purpose: Controls whether Client 32 beeps when an alert message box is displayed.

Auto Reconnect Level	3	0–5	Yes

Purpose: Setting this option to a setting higher than 0 allows your PC to automatically restore a lost server connection by reconnecting to a NetWare server that returns to service. The number that you choose determines what is restored when you reconnect:

    0   No automatic reconnection.

    1   All server connections, drive mappings, and printer assignments are restored.

    2   Restores all in option 1 and reopens all read-only files previously in use.

    3   Restores all in previous options, reopens all previously opened files, and relocks previously locked files.

    4   Restores all in previous options, and restarts and completes all incomplete write operations in progress at the time of the disconnection.

    5   Restores all in previous options and provides support for a future feature, DisconnectableNetWare.

Cache NetWare Password	On	On or Off	No

Purpose: Use this option to specify the Client 32 cache password you enter for automatic reuse when you connect to an additional server or tree.

Part

VI

Ch

21

continues

Table 21.1 Continued

Setting Parameter	Default Option	Allowed Range Setting	Dynamic Parameter?
Cache Writes	On	On or Off	Yes

Purpose: Setting this option to On causes writes to the local workstation cache buffer to be reported to your application as a completed write. Setting to Off causes a completed write to be reported only after the write request is written to the server. Leave On for best performance or Off for maximum integrity.

Checksum	1	0–3	Yes

Purpose: This option controls whether Client 32 embeds checksums in the IPX packets it sends. (A *checksum* is an error-checking code used to tell whether the packet was corrupted during transmission.) Adding checksums degrades performance slightly, and your network board may already do sufficient error checking. You can use settings 0 through 3 to cause the workstation to do the following:

0   Don't use checksums.

1   Use checksums only for devices that request them.

2   Use checksums only for devices that can use them.

3   Require checksums for all packets from all devices.
        (This option is ignored if you use Ethernet_802.3 frame types because these frame types do not allow checksums to be used.)

Close Behind Ticks	0	0–65535	Yes

Purpose: Client 32 caches open server-based files in local workstation memory to maximize performance. Use to control how many ticks must elapse after you close a file until the file is truly closed and removed from local workstation cache (at 18.21 ticks per second). If you use an application that frequently closes and reopens the same set of files, this option can improve performance.

Delay Writes	Off	On or Off	Yes

Purpose: This option specifies whether or not an application's write request can be held in cache and delayed beyond the closing of the application. Usually Client 32 completes all pending write requests before an application closes. If set to On, Client 32 reports to the application that all write requests are completed. The Close Behind Ticks option determines the maximum delay time before a cached write request is handled.

DOS Name	MSDOS	Any DOS Name	No

Purpose: Client 32 automatically detects the version of DOS you're using. You can override this default by using this option to set the name manually.

Environment Pad	64	0–32768	No

Purpose: Set this option to cause Client 32 to add the specified number of bytes to the DOS environment when you launch a DOS application.

Setting Parameter	Default Option	Allowed Range Setting	Dynamic Parameter?
File Cache Level	3	0–4	Yes

Purpose: Use this option to control Client 32's local file-caching feature. You can set five levels of caching:

0	Local caching is completely disabled.
1	Client 32 uses read-ahead and write-behind caching. *Read-ahead caching* means that complete 4K file blocks are read into workstation memory even though the application requests a smaller amount of data. Several subsequent requests probably can be satisfied with the data contained in the 4K block already in workstation memory. When Client 32 detects that a file is being read sequentially, it caches subsequent blocks of the file in workstation memory in advance.

Write-behind caching means that file writes are cached locally until a complete 4K block is rewritten, at which point the whole block is written to the server in one operation. |
2	Client 32 uses short-lived caching. With *short-lived caching*, file reads and writes can be cached in workstation memory until the file is closed.
3	Client 32 uses *long-lived caching*. Recently used blocks of a file are cached in memory, even if the file was closed. If the file is reopened and was not changed since the previous open, Client 32 reuses locally cached file blocks if they are requested.
4	Client 32 uses *warehouse caching*. Long-lived caching is supplemented with caching to local disk space. Use this option if local disk reads and writes are significantly faster than server reads and writes. This option doesn't apply for write operations if the True Commit option is set to on or if Cache Writes is set to Off.

Force First Network Drive	Off	On or Off	No

Purpose: Set this option to On to specify that the sole remaining network drive when you disconnect (which is by default mapped to SYS:LOGIN) will always be the one you specify as the first network drive, using Client 32's Login settings tab. When set to Off, SYS:LOGIN is mapped to the drive letter of the last active drive mapping when logout occurs.

Handle Net Errors	On	On or Off	Yes

Purpose: This option determines whether Client 32 handles and attempts to recover from a network error or whether the error is reported to the application.

Hold Files	Off	On or Off	No

Purpose: This option controls the behavior of files opened by programs using File Control Block (FCB) reads and writes. With this option set to Off, these files can be closed by the program before the program itself exits. When set to On, these files are held open until the program exits. Some applications may require that this be set to On.

Part

VI

Ch

21

continues

Table 21.1 Continued

Setting Parameter	Default Option	Allowed Range Setting	Dynamic Parameter?
Large Internet Packets	Off	On or Off	No

Purpose: Set this option to On if the routers that connect your networks can exchange packets that are the same size as those transmitted by your PC's network board. (By default, NetWare 3.x servers that act as routers limit the maximum routed packet size to 576 bytes.)

Large Internet Packet Start Size	65535	1–65535	Yes

Purpose: This option sets the beginning size that Client 32 uses when negotiating the allowed packet size that can be exchanged via a router or bridge. Use this to fine-tune the beginning packet size to reduce negotiation requests that must be exchanged if you are using a slow WAN link.

Link Support Layer Max Buffer Size	4736	100–24682	No

Purpose: This option sets the maximum allowed packet size in bytes.

Lock Delay	1	1–65535	Yes

Purpose: This option sets the number of ticks (there are 18.21 ticks in a second) that Client 32 waits while trying to open a file that is locked by another workstation. Increase this setting if many workstations concurrently try to open and lock the same files and get errors.

Lock Retries	5	1–65535	Yes

Purpose: This setting controls the number of times Client 32 retries when attempting to open and lock a file.

Log File	None	Any log file	No

Purpose: Use this option to specify the path and name of the Client 32 log file. If you supply a file name, Client 32 creates a log file to record its activity and errors.

Log File Size	65535	1–1048576	No

Purpose: This setting specifies the maximum allowed size of the log file.

Long Machine Type	IBM_PC	Any machine	No

Purpose: Use this option to manually set the machine name stored by the requester. The name you set with this option is the same name stored in the MACHINE login script variable.

Max Cache Size	0	0–4292967295	No

Purpose: Use this option to set the number of kilobytes to be available for local file caching. If set to 0 (the default), Client 32 automatically allows itself to use up to 25 percent of workstation memory that is free when Client 32 loads. If set to a specific value, Client 32 automatically decreases the amount of memory used to 75 percent of free memory if you specify a value higher than this amount.

Max Cur Dir Length	64	64–255	No

Purpose: This option sets maximum character length of the current directory path name. Some programs don't operate properly if they are required to work with a directory path length greater than 64 characters.

Setting Parameter	Default Option	Allowed Range Setting	Dynamic Parameter?
Message Timeout	0	0–10000	No

Purpose: This option sets the number of processor ticks until a broadcast message is automatically cleared from the screen (a *tick* is approximately 1/18th second). When this option is set to 0, you must manually clear the message.

Minimum Time to Net	0	0–65535	Yes

Purpose: This option extends the allowed time (in milliseconds) before Client 32 concludes that a connection attempt failed. Increase this setting if you are attempting to connect over a low-speed link or the server to which you are connecting responds to connect requests very slowly.

NCP Max Timeout	30	30–65535	No

Purpose: This option controls the amount of time (in seconds) that elapses before Client 32 retries a failed connection request. Increase this setting if you are attempting to connect over a low-speed link or if the server to which you are connecting responds to connect requests very slowly.

Net Status Busy Timeout	20	1–600	Yes

Purpose: This option sets the number of seconds that Client 32 waits for a reply before reporting that a server is not responding.

Net Status Timeout	30	1–600	Yes

Purpose: This option sets the number of seconds that Client 32 waits for a response from a network before reporting a network error.

NetWare Protocol	NDS BIND	NDS BIND BIND NDS NDS BIND	No

Purpose: Determines which of the two NetWare protocols (Novell Directory Services and Bindery) are used and the order in which they are accessed. You should set your primary or preferred protocol first.

Network Printers	3	0–9	No

Purpose: This option sets the number of LPT ports that can be captured.

Opportunistic Locking	On	On or Off	Yes

Purpose: Setting option to On allows Client 32 to lock and locally cache a file opened for sharing but in use by other workstations. If the file that is locked and cached by using opportunistic locking is subsequently opened by another workstation, locking and local caching stop.

Packet Burst	On	On or Off	No

Purpose: This option determines whether the packet burst feature is active. (*Packet burst* is the performance-enhancing capability of sending a series or "burst" of packets without waiting to receive an acknowledgment for each packet.)

Part
VI

Ch
21

continues

Table 21.1 Continued

Setting Parameter	Default Option	Allowed Range Setting	Dynamic Parameter?
Packet Burst Read Window Size	24	3–255	Yes

Purpose: This option sets the maximum number of packets that can be received in one read request burst. The total number of packets multiplied by size of one packet cannot exceed 64K.

Packet Burst Write Window Size	10	3–255	Yes

Purpose: This option sets the maximum number of packets that can be transmitted in one write request burst. The total number of packets multiplied by the size of one packet cannot exceed 64K.

Print Header	64	0–1024	No

Purpose: This option sets the size of the print job header that contains the setup instructions for the printer. If you configure your print jobs to include elaborate setup strings, make sure that the print header size exceeds the size of your setup strings.

Print Tail	16	0–1024	No

Purpose: This option sets the size of the print job "tail" that contains the instructions used to reset the printer after each job. Make sure that the print tail size exceeds the size of your reset strings.

Read Only Compatibility	Off	On or Off	Yes

Purpose: This option determines whether read-only files can be opened for reading and writing. Set to On only if you must use an application that tries to open read-only files for reading and writing.

Search Dirs First	Off	On or Off	No

Purpose: Use this option to control what is displayed first when you list the contents of a directory. Setting to Off causes files to list first; setting to On causes directories to list first.

Search Mode	1	1–7	No

Purpose: This option determines how .EXE or .COM files that open other files will search for these files.

Set Station Time	On	On or Off	No

Purpose: This option determines whether workstation time is synchronized with the time of the server to which the workstation first connects when loading the Requester.

Short Machine Type	IBM	Any machine	No

Purpose: You use this option to manually set the short machine name stored by Client 32. The *short machine name* determines which overlay files are used by NetWare's DOS utilities. Change the short machine name to CMPQ if you use a CGA-compatible, single-color monitor. You shouldn't change the short machine name to anything else, unless you're ready to create a custom overlay file with the COLORPAL utility. The short machine name is the same information stored by the SMACHINE login script variable.

Setting Parameter	Default Option	Allowed Range Setting	Dynamic Parameter?
Show Dots	Off	On or Off	No

Purpose: DOS and related workstation operating systems use a period (.) to indicate the current directory and two periods (..) to indicate the parent directory. NetWare doesn't use these period entries to indicate current or parent directories, but setting this option to On causes the Requester to display period entries for the current and parent directories.

Signature Level	1	0–3	Yes

Purpose: This command controls use of *packet signatures*, an optional identification that a server or workstation can embed in a packet to guarantee the identity of the packet sender. Packet signatures are used to defeat programs that generate and send forged packets. (For example, the program sends packets that are forged to appear as though they are from a workstation where the user is logged in with supervisory rights, enabling the program to perform supervisory tasks without authorization.) Your workstation packet signature setting must match signature settings on the servers to which you want to connect. Packet signatures increase server and workstation workload because each packet's signature must be read and verified. You can use settings 0 through 3 to cause Client 32 to do the following:

0	Don't use Packet signatures.
1	Use packet signatures only for devices that request them.
2	Use packet signatures only for devices that can use them.
3	Require packet signatures for all packets from all devices.

True Commit	Off	On or Off	Yes

Purpose: Usually, an application receives confirmation that a file write is completed when the information in that write operation is written to the server's memory cache, and the actual write to disk occurs a few seconds later. With this activated, the file write isn't confirmed until the information is written to the server disk. Turning On can seriously decrease the performance of write operations, but ensures maximum integrity.

Use Video BIOS	Off	On or Off	Yes

Purpose: This option controls how Client 32's character mode messages work with your PC's video. The Off setting causes these messages to write directly to video memory for maximum performance. If this causes problems on your workstation, switch the setting to On, which causes character mode messages to write to the screen, using video BIOS calls.

When you are finished customizing Client 32, click OK to return to the Network dialog box. Click OK again to exit the Network dialog box.

Logging In with Client 32

Client 32's Login dialog box is displayed when you start your Windows 95 system or when you request a connection to a server or directory tree (such as when you use the Network Neighborhood to browse the network). In the preceding section of this chapter, you learned how to set the defaults for Client 32's Login dialog box from the Network Control Panel, and you learned the purpose of each configurable option. Figure 21.9 shows the dialog box used to log in to the network with its four tabs, and lists the information that you supply for each option when logging in.

N O T E If you have a Windows network client installed on your Windows 95 workstation, installing Client 32 causes the Novell client to be responsible for the primary network logon. This means that the Client 32 Login dialog box will appear before the Windows network login dialog box. If, during your first connection, you specify identical user names and passwords for both logins, then only the Client 32 dialog box will appear during future logins. ▨

FIG. 21.9

Client 32 offers a user-friendly graphical dialog box that you use to log in to the network.

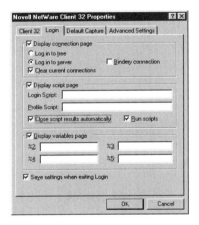

Login Scripts and Client 32

Unlike Microsoft's Client for NetWare, Client 32 is fully compatible with NetWare's login script syntax. The login script commands operate in the same manner as they do when you log in using NetWare's DOS LOGIN command. The messages generated by your login scripts are displayed in a Login Results text box (see Figure 21.10). If you marked the Close Script Results Automatically option in the Client 32 Properties dialog box, this text box closes when the login script completes execution. Otherwise, you click the Close button to close the Login Results text box.

There is one difference in the behavior of Client 32's handling of login scripts that will require special intervention. If you embed DOS commands in login scripts using the Execute (#) command (such as when you include the command #CAPTURE to connect to a printer at login time), Client 32 opens a DOS window for every DOS command that is run by the login script. These Windows do not close automatically. When you first run your login script, you can cause each DOS window to close automatically by checking the Close on Exit box in the MS-DOS Prompt Properties dialog box.

If you do this with each DOS command executed from your login scripts, the DOS windows for these commands will close automatically from this point forward. You can also replace the #

symbol with an @ symbol for a Windows 95 login script to create separate processes for each external command. This way, the login scripts do not pause while waiting for the completion of previous external commands.

FIG. 21.10
The login script results appear in a pop-up window in Windows 95.

Upgrading Novell Client 32 with Automatic Client Upgrade

Most network administrators are painfully aware that software companies constantly revise and upgrade their software products. While upgrades to NetWare clients have, in the past, been few and far between, this policy seems to have been revised with the release of Client 32. To assist you in the never-ending task of upgrading workstations, Novell has created the Automatic Client Upgrade (ACU) utility, which allows network administrators to place commands in container login scripts that verify the version of the client being used to log in. If the client software on the workstation is older than the client software stored on the NetWare server, then the ACU program automatically updates the workstation software. The following sections explain how the ACU program works and includes steps for implementing the ACU process.

The Client 32 Automatic Client Upgrade will only upgrade workstations that are currently running a copy of Novell's Client 32 or Microsoft's Client for NetWare Networks. Workstations that are currently connecting using the NetWare DOS Requester or the NetWare DOS Shell must follow a different upgrade method. (See Chapter 20, "Using the IntranetWare Client 32 for DOS/Windows 3.1," for instructions on upgrading the VLM or NETX client.)

How the Automatic Client Upgrade Works

Automatic Client Upgrades are performed by running the Client 32 SETUP.EXE utility with the /acu switch. You launch the ACU from a login script by mapping a drive to the SETUP.EXE program or using a UNC path to the file. The following examples demonstrate both alternatives, which can be entered into a container login script to launch the ACU process.

```
MAP G:=EDUC_SYS:PUBLIC\CLIENT\WIN95\IBM_ENU
@G:SETUP /ACU
     or
@\\EDUC\SYS\PUBLIC\CLIENT\WIN95\SETUP /acu
```

The SETUP program then determines whether the workstation client software is older than the source files found on the server. To do this, SETUP compares the version information contained in NWSETUP.INI to the version information stored in the Windows 95 Registry.

Part
VI

Ch
21

Following is an example of the client software version information that is stored in the NWSETUP.INI file.

```
[ClientVersion]
Version=1.1.0.0
```

The numbers on the version line represent the Major Version, Minor Version, Revision, and Level, of Client 32, respectively. Each time Novell releases an updated version of Client 32, a new NWSETUP.INI is included, indicating the new version release. The version 1.1.0.0 used in the preceding example reflects release 2.11 of Client 32 (the current client version at the time of writing). By examining the NWSETUP.INI file, SETUP determines whether an upgrade is necessary. If the workstation software is outdated, the installation process runs, installing the new version. If the versions match, SETUP terminates and processing of the login script continues.

After an upgrade is performed, the ACU process updates the Windows 95 Registry to reflect the new version installed. This prevents the ACU process from launching again until the software on the server is updated.

Preliminary Setup for Automatic Client Upgrade

The first step to automating your client software is to put a copy of the client software in an accessible place for all users. You must also copy the *.CAB files from the WIN95 directory of the Windows 95 CD-ROM into the ACU installation directory. All users that will perform the ACU must have Read and File Scan rights to the ACU installation directory. The recommended destination directory for the client software is SYS:PUBLIC\CLIENT\WIN95.

There are two optional installation screens that can be made to appear to the user during the ACU process. By default, these screens are disabled. The following code demonstrates the default options as they appear in the NWSETUP.INI file.

```
[AcuOptions]
DisplayFirstScreen=NO
DisplayLastScreen=NO
```

The first optional screen alerts users that a newer version of the client software has been detected on the server and allows them to decide whether or not to perform the upgrade (see Figure 21.11). By default, this screen is not displayed, and therefore, the upgrade process is launched automatically.

Also, by default, the workstation automatically reboots after the Client 32 upgrade is complete. The second optional user screen asks the user whether the system should be rebooted to allow new settings to take effect. You can change either of the two NWSETUP.INI options to control whether or not your users have any say in the upgrade process.

As mentioned earlier, the ACU utility is executed as a command from within a login script. You may want to test the process by modifying your own personal user login script before adding the command to your users' container scripts.

FIG. 21.11
The Automatic Client Upgrade feature includes an optional screen that allows users to choose whether an upgrade should be performed.

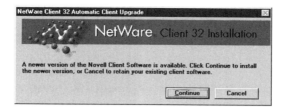

N O T E To execute a Windows program from within a login script, you must use the @ command. Be sure to use proper syntax and prefix the SETUP command line with the @ symbol to avoid Windows errors or hanging your workstation, which is a common problem when the # symbol is used.

Alternative Uses for Automatic Client Upgrade

There may be times when the Client 32 software has not changed, but you must copy a newer file or upgrade a LAN driver on all of your workstations. The Level indicator in the NWSETUP.INI file is actually a user-definable field that you can use for this purpose. You can set it to a value from 0 to 65,000. By increasing the value, you can cause the ACU program to execute even though Novell has not released an official Client 32 upgrade.

N O T E Use caution when modifying the NWSETUP.INI version field indicators. The values in the Major, Minor, and Revision fields take priority over the Level field value. If you modify a field other than the intended user-definable Level field, your client version will no longer correspond to NetWare's release version numbers. If this occurs, you will need to modify the field values for all subsequent releases of Client 32 to ensure that the ACU is operating as intended.

Removing Client 32 for Windows 95

Recently, Novell released a very handy tool for removing Client 32 for Windows 95 from a Windows 95 workstation. An executable called UNC32.EXE removes all traces of Client 32 from your Windows 95 Registry and hard drive. The program can be downloaded from Novell's online services as W95UNC.EXE.

A README file is included with the self-extracting archive file, but the instructions for the use of the utility are very simple. To uninstall Client 32 for Windows 95, just execute UNC32.EXE. You may find this utility useful for any number of reasons. The most common reason is that the client software fails to install or an upgrade did not go as planned, and now the workstation is not communicating with the network properly. You may also find the uninstall utility handy if you need to remove a workstation from the network to be used for another purpose.

Part
VI

Ch
21

Summary

Windows 95 provides the network manager with an abundance of opportunities. With a carefully chosen network client, Windows 95 PCs can take full advantage of NetWare Directory Services. Advanced Windows 95 features leverage your network and extend your capability to manage the PCs connected to it. With the right research and preparation, Windows 95 and NetWare 4.11 are a potent combination. ●

CHAPTER 22

Using Windows NT with NetWare

In the years since its initial release, Windows NT has become an important networking platform in the PC world. Although originally positioned as a competitor to the NetWare operating system, it has become, in many cases, a complement to it. A great many networks now use both systems, with Windows NT often functioning in both of the roles to which it is best suited, that is, as an application server and a high-powered workstation.

Interoperability between NetWare and Windows NT has been something of a problem throughout their history together. Questions about whether Microsoft or Novell should be responsible for the development of the client software that enables Windows NT users to access NetWare resources have caused repeated delays in the delivery of satisfactory solutions.

With the releases of Windows NT 4.0 and Novell's IntranetWare Client for Windows NT, however, the relationship between the two operating systems has never been better. Both companies have realized that the goal for many consumers is a heterogeneous network in which different computing platforms are used according to their abilities, all interrelating in such a way as to emphasize their individual strengths. ■

Choosing the appropriate Windows NT client for NetWare

Both Novell and Microsoft have released Windows NT clients for NetWare, each of which has its individual strengths.

How to install the Windows NT clients

You can perform individual installations of both clients, or automate the process for multiple installations.

Accessing NetWare resources from Windows NT

The new clients enable Windows NT to interact with NDS objects to provide seamless access to NetWare files and printers.

How to administer NetWare from the Windows NT platform

Novell provides tools designed specifically for Windows NT that enable you to manage many of NetWare's services.

Windows NT and Novell Directory Services

Both Windows NT 4.0 and the IntranetWare Client for Windows NT became available in widely distributed beta releases in the summer of 1996. Before that time, the only way to log into an NDS tree from a Windows NT system was to use the Client for Windows NT that was created by Novell, which was sadly deficient in its capabilities. This client enabled you to run a 32-bit version of NetWare Administrator, but provided virtually no other useful NDS access.

Now that both Windows NT 4.0 and IntranetWare have been released, however, you have a choice between NDS clients for the first time. The Client and Gateway Services for NetWare that are included with Windows NT 4.0 Workstation and Server products (respectively) are the first Microsoft clients that are in any way NDS-capable. They enable you to log into and browse an NDS tree, and access the standard NetWare file and print resources.

N O T E The difference between the Client Services for NetWare, which ships with the Windows NT Workstation product, and the Gateway Services for NetWare, which ships with Windows NT Server, is that the Gateway Services enable Windows network clients to access NetWare drives and printers without running a NetWare client themselves. The Windows NT server logs into a NetWare server as a client, and makes the NetWare volumes appear as Windows network shares. To other systems on the Windows network, the NetWare volumes appear to be normal Windows NT shares.

Although this is a useful feature for occasional access to NetWare resources or as a transitional measure, it is not recommended for heavy traffic. As you might imagine, the file system requests of many different users all being funneled through a single NetWare server connection results in a bottleneck that can severely affect performance.

The Microsoft clients are not suitable for administering NetWare from a Windows NT workstation, however. You cannot run any version of NetWare Administrator using this client, nor is NDS support provided in a DOS session. This prevents you from running the NETADMIN or RIGHTS utilities, as well.

For the average user, who only needs access to NetWare drives and printers, and especially for bindery or bindery emulation users, the Microsoft clients are quite adequate. They also provide a slight but perceptible advantage in file and directory access speed over the Novell clients.

Introducing the IntranetWare Client for Windows NT

The alternative to the Microsoft clients, and easily the most full-featured Windows NT client for the NetWare operating system ever to be released, is Novell's IntranetWare Client for Windows NT. This client, which was available in several public beta releases for many months before its first general release in December 1996, did not actually make it into the original IntranetWare package. You will, in fact, find no Windows NT client on the IntranetWare disks.

However, the client is readily available as a free download from Novell's Web site and other online services. The January 10, 1997 release includes not only the Windows NT client software itself, but also 32-bit versions of the NetWare GUI administration utilities, including NetWare Administrator, the NDS Manager, NetWare Application Launcher, and the NetWare Workstation Manager.

This client is referred to by different names by Novell itself, including the NetWare Client for Windows NT, and the IntranetWare Client. One rubric that has never been used for this client, however, is Client 32, and this is surprising because the appearance and the features of the software are virtually identical to those of the Client 32 releases for DOS/Windows and Windows 95.

This new Novell client is the only means of providing full support for NetWare Directory Services to the Windows NT 3.51 and 4.0 environments. You can log in to an NDS tree and manage NDS objects using either NetWare Administrator or the DOS-based utilities. You can also manage NDS partitions and replicas with the NDS Manager utility.

The IntranetWare client also integrates NetWare file system management functions into the Windows NT File Manager and Explorer utilities, enabling you to assign file system rights and attributes without launching a separate program.

In most cases, it is a good idea to select one client for use at a particular network site. Creating a standard workstation configuration and enforcing it makes it easier for network administration personnel to support their users. The Novell IntranetWare Client is clearly the more full-featured alternative for the Windows NT environment, and is recommended over the Microsoft client.

Understanding Windows NT Networking

The networking architecture of the Windows NT operating system provides support for multiple network clients. You can run a client for NetWare along with a standard Windows NT network client, or instead of it. This is because Windows NT uses network *redirectors* to control the routing of network resource requests to the appropriate protocol stack.

Network clients on a Windows NT system consist of three basic elements:

- Services
- Protocols
- Adapters

These three elements combine to form a logical conduit from an application running on the system to the network interface adapter that actually transmits data over the network. A network client can have several different services, but there is always one service installed on the system that functions as a redirector, responsible for handling all of the requests for resources on that particular network.

Windows NT clients can share a single set of protocols, or each can run its own. The adapter part of the client software is actually a driver that addresses the network interface hardware in the computer. Because there can only be one driver addressing a single network interface card, clients usually share a single adapter.

By default, Windows NT uses TCP/IP as its native transport protocols. When an application running on a Windows NT machine requests access to a resource on another Windows NT system, the Windows network redirector sends the request to the TCP/IP protocol stack and, eventually, to the network. When a NetWare client is installed, a second redirector is provided, along with a protocol stack designed to carry NetWare's native IPX/SPX protocols. When an application requests access to a NetWare resource, such as a file on a server volume, the NetWare client redirector takes over, sending the request using the IPX/SPX-compatible protocol stack, as shown in Figure 22.1.

FIG. 22.1

Clients for different network types can co-exist on a Windows NT system.

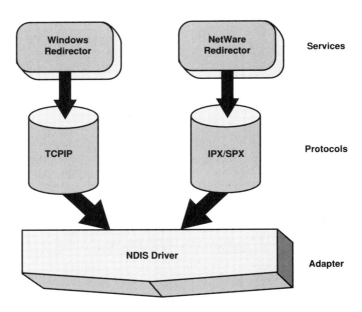

Unless there are multiple network interface adapters in the computer, both protocols end up at the same place: the adapter driver. Most of the time, the adapter driver used conforms to the NDIS specification that is the default for Windows NT. However, when only a NetWare client is running on the system, a Novell ODI adapter driver can be used.

This modular architecture makes Windows NT's networking architecture extremely flexible. You can configure the various clients in many different ways, to suit the needs of your network. You can, for example, run a Windows network client and a NetWare client using the same protocol stack, either IPX/SPX (using Microsoft's NWLink protocols) or TCP/IP (using Microsoft's TCP/IP stack and Novell's NetWare/IP service). You can also install multiple network adapters in one system, with a different client using each device, or with both clients addressing both devices.

However, these complex configurations are more properly of concern to the Windows NT network administrator. The following sections describe how to install the Microsoft and Novell clients for Windows NT, in order to establish a connection to a NetWare network.

Installing NetWare Clients on Windows NT

If, during the installation of the Windows NT 4.0 operating system, a network interface adapter is detected, the client for the Microsoft Windows network is installed by default. This consists of several different services, the TCP/IP protocols, and an NDIS adapter driver, by default.

All of Windows NT's network configuration panels are located in the Network Control Panel, as shown in Figure 22.2. Once the operating system is installed, you can add the additional modules that comprise a NetWare client.

FIG. 22.2
All of Windows NT 4.0's networking controls are located in a single tabbed dialog box.

N O T E The Network Control Panel in Windows NT versions 3.51 and earlier is substantially different in appearance from that of version 4.0, but the modules and the basic networking architecture are fundamentally the same.

The following sections describe the installation process for the Microsoft and Novell clients for Windows NT.

Installing the Microsoft Client Services for NetWare

If you are installing the Microsoft client for NetWare on a Windows NT machine that is already running the Windows network client, then you don't have to install or configure an adapter driver because the two clients will share the same NDIS driver that directly addresses the network adapter.

NDIS, the Network Driver Interface Specification, is the standard used by Windows NT to create a universal interface through which multiple protocol stacks can access the same network hardware.

On a system with no networking support installed, you must select an adapter driver and configure it to access the hardware installed in the computer. To do this, you click the Add button on the Adapters panel of the Network dialog box, and choose the name of your network interface card in the Select Network Adapter listing, shown in Figure 22.3.

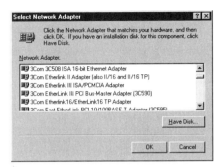

Windows NT includes drivers for most of the popular network adapters on the market today. If your adapter is not listed, you must obtain an NDIS driver from the device's manufacturer, and install it by clicking the Have Disk button on the Select Network Adapter panel.

Once Windows NT has copied the required files from your installation source (such as the Windows NT CD-ROM), you may be required to supply or confirm the hardware settings for your adapter. Although Windows NT does not have the plug-and-play capabilities of Windows 95, it is usually able to scan for the adapter and correctly identify its current settings for standard hardware parameters, such as the IRQ and the I/O address.

Once the driver has been properly configured, the adapter appears in the Network dialog box. You can then proceed to install the NetWare client service itself, whether or not you have already installed another network client.

Installing a service is very much like the adapter installation procedure detailed earlier. At the Services panel of the same Network dialog box, you can add additional clients or other network services by selecting from a list. When you click the Add button, select Client Services for NetWare to install the Microsoft client.

The network configuration interface is quite intelligent when it comes to knowing what modules are required to run a particular service. If the NWLink IPX/SPX-compatible Transport protocol is not already installed, selecting the Client Services for NetWare causes it to be installed automatically. Once again, Windows NT source files are copied, and after supplying the required login information, you can close the Network dialog box, after which you are prompted to restart the system.

When the system reboots, you need only supply your authentication information in order to access the NetWare network. For an NDS login, you must supply your User object's name, its context, and the name of the NDS tree. For a bindery login, you supply a server name and a user name. In both cases, you enter your password, and the login process begins.

TIP It is possible to modify the Windows NT installation process so that Client Services for NetWare is installed at the same time as the operating system. This is done by modifying the contents of a text file called UNATTEND.TXT found in the I386 directory of the Windows NT installation files. See the next section for more information on this process.

Part
VI

Ch

22

Installing the Novell IntranetWare Client for Windows NT

One of the advantages of the Novell client for Windows NT that is most immediately apparent is the selection of installation methods. At its simplest, the Novell client installation requires no knowledge of Windows NT's networking architecture, or of services, protocols, or adapter drivers. You can simply download the client software package, expand the self-extracting archive in an empty directory, and run the SETUPNW.EXE file from your Windows NT system. The installation program will take care of the rest, including the removal of your current NetWare client, if necessary.

NOTE The Novell IntranetWare Client for Windows NT can be installed on workstations running either Windows NT 3.51 or 4.0. ■

The Novell client includes a selection of 32-bit ODI (Open Data-Link Interface) drivers for some of the most commonly found network interface adapters, but the selection is by no means as complete as the selection of NDIS drivers included with Windows NT. The client is capable of operating with either an ODI or NDIS driver, but only one of the two can be installed for any particular adapter. In addition, if you are running the Microsoft client service for the Windows network, you must use an NDIS client.

CAUTION

Do not attempt to use the 16-bit ODI drivers that ship with virtually every network interface adapter made with Windows NT. These are intended for use with 16-bit clients, such as the NetWare DOS Requestor. The Novell IntranetWare Client for Windows NT requires a 32-bit driver: either ODI or NDIS.

As with the Microsoft client, you are prompted to install an adapter driver if one is not already present. The NWLink IPX/SPX-compatible protocol is also installed, if it is not already present. The client software includes a NetWare/IP service as well, which enables you to connect a Windows NT workstation to NetWare resources using the TCP/IP protocols instead of, or in addition to, IPX/SPX.

NOTE You must configure both your NetWare servers and workstations to use TCP/IP before you can initiate communications with NetWare/IP. See Chapter 25, "Using NetWare/IP," for more information. ■

Once the installation process is complete, the Novell Client for NetWare Networks service appears in the Services panel of the Network dialog box. You can proceed to configure the client, or restart the system and log in to your NetWare network.

Configuring an Unattended Client Installation   You can also install the Novell client using the same procedure as the Microsoft client, that is, by adding a service and browsing to the location of the client installation files. For an individual installation, there is no compelling reason to do this. But for a network administrator who is responsible for dozens or even hundreds of workstations, this conformance with the standard Windows NT installation procedure enables you to incorporate the client into a scripted installation of the operating system itself.

When you elect to use Windows NT as a workstation operating system on your network, the capability to perform multiple operating system installations with as little user interaction as possible can be an important advantage. Windows NT provides a means to do this, in the form of a text file called UNATTEND.TXT. This is a pre-configuration script file that can be customized by the network administrator to supply answers to the questions asked of the user during a typical Windows NT installation.

With a properly configured UNATTEND.TXT file, the degree of expertise required of the person performing the installation is greatly reduced. In some cases, it may even be possible for novice users to install the operating system themselves. To incorporate the installation of the Novell client into this process, a modified version of the UNATTEND.TXT file is included with the client installation files, in the I386\NLS\ENGLISH subdirectory.

This file specifies that the Novell client be installed along with the operating system, and provides the location of the client software installation files. It also includes variables for all of the Novell client configuration parameters, which you can modify as needed to pre-configure the client installation, plus all of the material from the original Windows NT version of the file. The UNATTEND.TXT file is also copiously annotated, to help you to understand the function of each setting.

The UNATTEND.TXT file can also be used to create an unattended installation of the Novell client only (without the operating system installation), by using SETUPNW.EXE with the /U switch. When you execute SETUPNW.EXE /U=UNATTEND.TXT (including a full path to the script file, when necessary), the values for the client configuration parameters found in the script file are applied to the Novell client during its installation. This enables the network administrator to control whether or not the user is prompted to supply certain pieces of information, as well as specify values for many client parameters, including

- the adapter driver to be installed,
- whether the Microsoft client for NetWare should be removed,
- whether NetWare/IP should be installed,
- the default NDS tree,
- the default NetWare server,
- the default NDS context.

In short, any parameter that you can set in the Novell client's properties dialog box (after the client is installed), can be preset in the UNATTEND.TXT file.

N O T E A certain amount of testing and debugging may be required before a pre-configuration script is suitable for use on workstations without an experienced network support person present. It may also be necessary to create several script files to suit the needs of different types of users. ▪

Using the Automatic Client Upgrade Feature   The Novell client for Windows NT also includes an automatic client upgrade (or ACU) feature that you can use to launch client installations and upgrades, and make sure that all of your workstations are running the same version of the client, with the same parameters.

To activate this feature, you execute the SETUPNW.EXE with the /ACU switch. This causes the client installation program to check the version number of the Novell client that is currently installed on the system. If the installed client is out of date, then the installation of the upgraded version proceeds. Otherwise, the program terminates.

The ACU feature is designed to be used in coordination with the /U switch and a pre-configuration script, as described in the previous section. The following command line can be executed from a login script when each user connects to the network:

```
SETUPNW.EXE /U:UNATTEND.TXT /ACU
```

When a new version of the Novell client becomes available, the administrator has only to upgrade the client source files on a network drive. Each user's workstation will be upgraded as they log in and the new installation program detects an older version of the software.

Installing the NetWare Administration Utilities for Windows NT

The IntranetWare Client for Windows NT also includes a second installation utility that you use to install the Windows NT versions of the NetWare administration utilities that ship with the client. When you run ADMSETUP.EXE from a workstation, you are given the option to install any combination of the following three programs:

- NetWare Administrator
- NetWare Application Launcher
- Workstation Manager

The NetWare Administrator option also includes a Windows NT version of the NDS Manager, and the supplementary files needed to run the utilities. These files are installed to the SYS:PUBLIC\WINNT directory on the server selected during the installation.

N O T E It is recommended that you use the Admin account (or an equivalent) when installing the administrative utilities to a NetWare server. Not only must you have the appropriate file system rights to the SYS:PUBLIC directory, you must have Supervisor object rights to the root of the NDS tree as well, in order to modify the Directory schema. ▪

NetWare Application Launcher (NAL) installation consists of three elements: the NAL client executables for all of the Windows platforms, the schema extensions that enable you to create Application objects in the NDS database, and the snap-in module that enables NetWare Administrator to display and manipulate application objects. You can learn more about installing and using NAL in Chapter 8, "Networking Applications with NDS."

N O T E   The entire NetWare Application Launcher product also ships as part of the Novell Client32 releases for DOS/Windows and Windows 95. However, the version included with the IntranetWare Client for Windows NT is the latest release, version 1.1. This release contains significant improvements over the previous releases, including different schema extensions. Be sure that you have the latest version of NAL installed before you begin to create and configure your Application objects.

Workstation Manager is the newest addition to the Windows NT client. This product enables you to store and manage Windows NT user accounts in the NDS database. For more information on this utility, see Chapter 9, "Using NDS as a Global Directory Services Solution."

Configuring the NetWare Clients

The Microsoft Client Services for NetWare offers only basic configuration capabilities. You can specify a preferred NDS tree or server, and the default context of your User object. The Novell client, however, includes an extensive array of configuration parameters that enable you to customize the degree of login control that is made available to users, and fine tune the performance of the client itself.

The default configuration that is set when the Novell client is installed is, in most cases, sufficient to enable a user to log in to a NetWare network. It is necessary to modify the client configuration only when you want to control the way that users log in, or limit their access to certain client features.

There are three ways to modify the client configuration. In "Configuring an Unattended Client Installation" earlier in this chapter, you saw how it is possible to specify values for configuration parameters during the client installation, using an UNATTEND.TXT file. You can also use Windows NT system policies to enforce certain configuration values. These methods are designed for use by network administrators to enforce global client configurations for large numbers of users without the need to travel to each workstation.

Users or administrators can also configure the NetWare client manually, using the Windows NT Control Panel, but these changes affect only the single workstation. The installation of the Novell client causes a new icon to be added to the Windows NT Control Panel. This icon provides access to the client configuration dialog box, but only in the Windows NT 3.51 environment. To configure the client in Windows NT 4.0, open the Network Control Panel, select the

Novell NetWare Client for Windows NT on the Services panel, and click the Properties button to display the Novell NetWare Client Services Configuration dialog box shown in Figure 22.4.

FIG. 22.4

You configure the Novell client from a tabbed dialog box accessed through the Windows NT Control Panel.

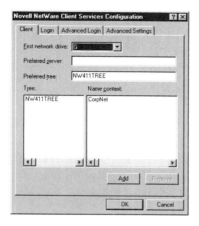

Most of the settings in this dialog box can also be defined in the login dialog box that is displayed whenever the Windows NT system is started. However, configuring them here establishes defaults for the settings, and you can control whether the defaults can be changed during a login.

The following sections describe the panels in this dialog box, and how their settings affect the NetWare client.

The Client Panel

The Client panel in the configuration dialog box is used to set the most basic parameters needed for a NetWare login. The First Network Drive selector is something of a misnomer. It refers actually to the first drive letter on the workstation that is to be used for a NetWare drive mapping. Connections to shares on the Windows network can still be mapped to any drive letter, whatever the setting of this parameter.

The value of the Preferred Server parameter is used only when there is no preferred tree specified in the client configuration. The preferred server is used when a user performs a login using bindery emulation. It is also used to determine the server from which a system policy file is read.

The Preferred Tree setting is where you specify the first NDS tree into which you will be authenticated during the login process. The IntranetWare Client for Windows NT enables you to access multiple NDS trees simultaneously, but the preferred tree is always accessed first.

On this panel, you can also create a list of NDS trees and specific contexts within them. Then, if you then use a login script to attach to multiple trees, these entries become your default context for each one.

 TIP If you have Country objects on the first level of your NDS tree below the [Root] object, you must use typeful naming when specifying your user context. For example, a context of Accounting.NewYork.US will not be processed correctly if the US container is a Country object because it will be assumed that US is an Organization. Instead, you must include object types in your context, as follows: OU=Accounting.OU=NewYork.C=US.

The Login Panel

The NetWare client login dialog box contains three panels, in addition to the main panel, on which you specify your user name and password. They are the Connection, Scripts, and Variables panels. In the Login panel of the client configuration dialog box, shown in Figure 22.5, you specify the default settings for the parameters on these three panels.

FIG. 22.5

The Login panel controls the default connection and script behavior during a NetWare login.

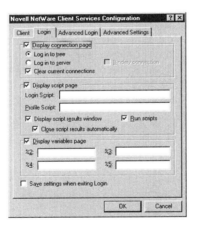

Aside from creating a configuration, you can also control whether or not the three panels even appear to the user during login. If you create a configuration, uncheck the Display Panel check boxes, and then use a system policy to restrict access to the Control Panel, then the user will be unable to change the configuration.

In the login panel, you designate whether you are going to log in to an NDS tree or to a server, using bindery emulation. You also control whether login scripts are run, and how script processing results are displayed on the workstation. You can also specify the names of an alternative login script or an alternative profile script, to be run instead of the normal scripts.

You can also specify values for up to four variables that are used in your login scripts. If you check the Save Settings When Exiting Login box, then any changes that you make in the login dialog box during the login process are saved as the new defaults. When this box is left unchecked, the you can only make changes that affect the current login.

The Advanced Login Panel

The Advanced Login panel (see Figure 22.6) enables you to specify the location of the system policy files and user profiles that are to be applied to the Windows NT workstation. You can create a policy file and access it from any location by entering a path and file name in the Policy Path field on this panel.

FIG. 22.6

Specify the locations of user profiles and system policy files in the Advanced Login panel.

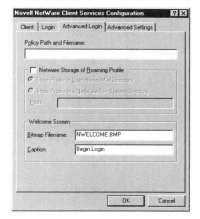

CAUTION

When specifying the path to a policy file stored on a network drive, you must use a UNC name. The standard NetWare notation of `server/volume:directory\filename` will not function, in this instance. A properly formatted UNC name is noted as follows: `\\server\volume\directory\filename`.

In addition to system policies, Windows NT provides another method of storing and applying groups of Registry settings. The Windows NT Registry consists of two files: SYSTEM.DAT and USER.DAT. The SYSTEM.DAT file stores the settings that are unique to the workstation, such as those that involve specific pieces of hardware. The USER.DAT file stores the settings that pertain to particular users, of which there can be many on a single workstation.

When you log in to a Windows NT workstation with different user names, separate user profiles are maintained, allowing each user to configure a unique environment, including desktop icons and wallpaper, Start menu entries, and other parameters. These profiles are essentially collections of alternate Registry settings that are applied to the USER.DAT file during the login process. Unlike system policies, which are shared by many users, every person has their own user profile.

By default, user profiles are stored on the Windows NT machine's local drive, but you can also store them on a network drive, to create what is known as a *roaming profile*. A roaming profile is a collection of user settings for the Registry that are stored in a central location, so that a user can log in from any Windows NT system, and always have the same desktop configuration.

When the user makes Registry changes that affect the USER.DAT file, the changes are saved not only to the currently active Registry file on the local drive, but to the copy on the network drive as well. Whenever the user logs in, the profile on the network drive is copied to the local drive for use by the active system Registry.

 T I P   You can enforce the use of a particular desktop configuration by storing a user's profile on a network drive and then using NetWare file system rights to prevent the user from changing the file. The user can then make temporary changes to the desktop configuration (by modifying the local Registry files), but those changes will not be written to the user profile, causing them to be lost at the next login.

You can choose to store user profiles on a NetWare drive by checking the NetWare Storage of Roaming Profile box on the Advanced Login panel. This activates the radio buttons that let you choose whether to store profiles in each user's SYS:MAIL subdirectory, or in another directory on a NetWare drive.

Finally, for a purely cosmetic effect, you can modify the bitmap file and caption that are displayed when the NetWare client loads, but before the user presses Ctrl+Alt+Del to begin the login sequence.

The Advanced Settings Panel

The Advanced Settings panel (see Figure 22.7) is the only part of the client configuration process that is not directly concerned with the user login process. This panel contains a listing of many different parameters that can be used to fine tune the performance of the NetWare client. Most of these are the same parameters that you can include in the NET.CFG file on a DOS/Windows client installation.

FIG. 22.7
The advanced NetWare client settings usually do not need to be changed for normal client access.

When you select a parameter from the list, an explanation of its function appears at the bottom of the panel. The Setting selector also displays the range of possible values for that parameter.

Many users get along perfectly well without ever changing any of the settings on this panel. Most of the parameters involve network communications issues of which the typical user would not even be aware. If, as the network administrator, you do have particular settings that must be changed to accommodate your network configuration, there is no better place to use system policies or an UNATTEND.TXT file to apply the required configuration changes to all client installations.

Logging In

Once you have installed the IntranetWare Client for Windows NT, the login dialog box that is presented at system startup (known as the GINA, or the *graphical identification and authentication interface*) is replaced by one of Novell's design, which is referred to as the NWGINA. In this dialog box, the user supplies the necessary login information for both the Windows NT and NetWare logins, and can configure many of the client connection and login script parameters.

You have learned that the Windows NT networking architecture enables users to connect to both Windows and NetWare networks at the same time. Even when the system is not running a Windows network client, however, it is still necessary for the user to be authenticated to the workstation itself. Therefore, two user names and passwords are always required during a login that includes a connection to a NetWare network.

Authenticating

Two separate panels in the login dialog box are used to provide credentials for the NetWare and Windows NT logins. In the NetWare panel, you enter the name and password for your NDS User object (or bindery login name), and its context in the NDS tree. In the Windows NT panel, you enter either the name of your Windows NT domain or the name of the workstation, plus an appropriate user name.

There is a check box on the Windows NT panel that enables you to perform a Windows NT login only, bypassing the establishment of a NetWare connection entirely. You use this option when you want to connect only to the Windows network, or perform a local Windows NT workstation login with no network connection at all.

Once you have supplied the required information and clicked OK, the network authentication process begins. The NetWare login always occurs first, using the information supplied on the Login panel. Once the NetWare login is completed, the Windows NT login proceeds, using the user name supplied on the Windows NT panel and the same password that you supplied for the NetWare account.

If the Windows NT login requires a different password (or if the user name you have supplied is invalid), a dialog box appears in which you supply the correct information. For this reason, it is recommended that you synchronize the passwords for your NetWare and Windows network logins, in order to simplify the login process. You need not, however, use the same user name for the two networks in order to perform a single unified login sequence.

You can easily synchronize your passwords by filling the appropriate check box when you specify your Windows NT password. When you do this, NWGINA authenticates you using the password you have supplied, and then automatically changes the Windows NT password to that which you specified for the NetWare network.

The Novell client also provides a utility with which you can change either of your network passwords. To access this feature, you must log in to the networks, press Ctrl+Alt+Del, and select Change Password from the NetWare Security dialog box. (You can also right-click the Network Neighborhood icon and select Change Password.) You can then select one or more items from the list of connections displayed, and enter a new password (after specifying the old one). Only connections that use the same password can be changed simultaneously.

N O T E   The NetWare client's Change Password utility is the only way to change both NetWare and Windows NT passwords at the same time. Other NetWare utilities with the capability to change passwords, such as SETPASS and NetWare Administrator, operate only on the NetWare password. Likewise, the Windows NT User Manager can only change Windows NT passwords.

NWGINA also detects expired passwords, and notifies the user of the number of remaining grace logins. When this occurs, the user is also given the opportunity to change the expired passwords.

Configuring the Login Parameters

Apart from the two required panels, Login and Windows NT, up to three other tabbed panels (called NetWare, Scripts, and Variables) may appear in the login dialog box. The choice of whether or not these panels are displayed, and the default values for their parameters, are controlled from the client configuration dialog box, which is accessed through the Network Control Panel. The network administrator may prevent these panels from appearing to stop users from changing the configuration, or you may want to suppress them yourself if you do not intend to use them.

If the panels do appear, you can modify the properties of your NetWare login by specifying a different preferred server, NDS tree, or context, as well as an alternate login script file name and script variables. A setting in the Control Panel determines whether or not any values you change during the login sequence are permanently saved as your client configuration defaults.

Using the *AutoAdminLogon* Feature

If you always log in to the network from your Windows NT machine using the same user names and passwords, and if the security of your workstation is not a critical issue, you can configure your system to bypass the display of the login dialog box and automatically log you in to the networks.

This is done by activating the `AutoAdminLogon` feature, which can store the user names and passwords for either your NetWare or Windows NT accounts (or both) in the Windows NT Registry, so that they are automatically accessed whenever you boot your workstation.

In most cases, this feature is used to bypass only one of the network authentication processes. You can, for example, configure an automatic logon to the Windows network, and leave the NetWare authentication process intact. This removes the Windows NT panel from the login dialog box, and prevents the user from accessing the workstation without logging in to NetWare first.

This can present a danger because it prevents a user from accessing the system if any condition (such as a down NetWare server) makes a NetWare login impossible. On the other hand, one of the advantages of `AutoAdminLogon` is that it affects only the system whose Registry has been modified. The passwords to the network accounts are still intact, secure from intrusion by users elsewhere on the network.

If your computer is protected by some other security mechanism, such as a BIOS password or even a locked office door, you can avoid the need to perform any network authentication processes on your machine by automating the login to both the Windows and NetWare networks.

To use the `AutoAdminLogon` feature, changes must be made to the Windows NT Registry, including the storage of the required user names and passwords. You can use the Windows NT Registry Editor utility (REGEDIT32.EXE) to make the changes manually, if you want. To automate the Windows NT logon, you must have the following four values in the Registry:

```
HKEY_LOCAL_MACHINE\SOFTWARE\Microsoft\Windows NT\CurrentVersion\Winlogon
            AutoAdminLogon:REG_SZ: 1
            DefaultDomainName:REG_SZ: Domain Name
            DefaultUserName:REG_SZ: NT user name
            DefaultPassword:REG_SZ: NT user password
```

If any of the values above are not present, you can add them by selecting Add Value from the Edit menu. Enter the value name, and leave the data type at its default: REG_SZ. Click OK, and you are prompted to enter the string for the value.

The `AutoAdminLogon` value of 1 indicates that the feature is turned on, and the other three values are used to store the domain name, user name, and password that are needed to perform the logon.

Part
VI

Ch

22

N O T E   There is also a utility included in the Windows NT 4.0 Server Resource Kit, called
AUTOLOG.EXE, that enables you to easily activate the AutoAdminLogon feature for the
Windows network logon only. ▩

The Registry values that must be configured to automate the NetWare login process are
as follows:

```
HKEY_LOCAL_MACHINE\SOFTWARE\Novell\NWGINA\Login Screen
                DefaultNetWareUserName:REG_SZ: user name
                DefaultNetWarePassword:REG_SZ: user password
                DefaultNDSContext:REG_SZ: NDS context
                DefaultNDSServer:REG_SZ: server name
                DefaultNDSTree:REG_SZ: tree name
                NetWareAutoAdminLogon:REG_SZ: 1
```

The default values for the first five keys, the user name, password, context, server name, and
tree name, can all be set through the Novell client configuration dialog box, in the usual manner. The final key, however, must be set in the Registry, to activate the automated login feature.

CAUTION

Manually modifying the Windows NT Registry is an inherently dangerous procedure, one in which an
improper action or a simple typing error could prevent you from gaining any further access to your system.
Before attempting this procedure, it is recommended that you first configure your Windows NT system for
remote Registry access. This way, if you are unable to log on to the workstation for any reason, you can still
access the Registry from another machine to correct the problem.

Accessing NetWare Resources

Once you have logged in to both the Windows and NetWare networks on your Windows NT
machine, you will find that there is not very much that you have to learn in order to access
NetWare resources. For the most part, NetWare drives and printers are completely integrated
into the standard Windows NT applications.

Accessing the NetWare File System

When you open the Windows NT Explorer and expand on the Network Neighborhood, you
find that the Entire Network display is broken down into two branches: the Microsoft Windows
Network and NetWare Services. Assuming that you have performed an NDS login, the
NetWare Services branch is divided further into NetWare Servers and Novell Directory Services, as shown in Figure 22.8.

These branches list all of the NetWare servers and NDS trees on your network, and you can
browse to any NetWare resource using either branch. For example, you will find all of your
NetWare volumes listed both as branches of the server that hosts them, and as objects in their
NDS tree. You can map a drive to a volume or directory in either branch, using the same procedure as when dealing with Windows NT shares.

FIG. 22.8
The Novell client for NetWare expands the functionality of the Windows NT Explorer.

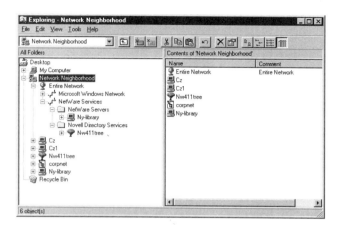

If you utilize the Map Network Drive function in the Explorer, and want to enter a path to a volume or directory manually, you can use the standard Windows NT UNC notation to define either a server or tree-based path (that is, names formatted using both \\SERVER\VOLUME\DIRECTORY and \\TREE\CONTAINER\VOLUME_OBJECT structures will function properly). You can also use NetWare's traditional notation (SERVER/ VOLUME:DIRECTORY), but a distinguished NDS name in the form VOLUME_SYS.CONTAINER will not function.

As always, you can also elect to browse to the volume or directory (see Figure 22.9), using the same expandable tree metaphor that is found in the main Explorer window. Whether you browse by server or tree, the path is inserted into the Map Network Drive window in UNC format.

FIG. 22.9
The Map Network Drive dialog box allows you great flexibility in defining the path to a volume or directory.

The IntranetWare client also modifies the context menus of the Explorer, as shown in Figure 22.10. From these menus, you can change your default NDS context, view information about your user account, and log in to and out of NDS trees.

FIG. 22.10
The IntranetWare client
adds functionality to
many of the context
menus in the Windows
NT Explorer.

Like the Client 32 releases for DOS/Windows and Windows 95, the client for Windows NT
enables users to log into multiple NDS trees simultaneously. You can select any tree in the
Explorer and access a login panel from its context menu.

This feature, and the fact that it is now being made available on all NetWare client platforms,
could have a significant effect on NDS design principles. Some administrators find it beneficial
to separate certain enterprise networking functions by creating multiple NDS trees.

For example, an NDS tree for research and development purposes that is kept separate from
the production tree can provide a tool for experimentation without jeopardizing everyday network activities. With the new NetWare clients, users can access both trees and take advantage
of all available network resources.

Accessing NetWare Printers

Accessing NetWare print queues is very much like connecting to a Windows NT network
printer. You simply add a new printer from the Control Panel in the usual manner, and browse
to the NDS object representing the print queue (as shown in Figure 22.11), instead of to a
Windows share. Of course, Windows NT always fails to locate a printer driver when you do this
(because NetWare print queues do not store drivers as Windows network printer shares do),
so you must allow the appropriate driver to be copied from your Windows NT install files.

Once the printer is installed, the IntranetWare client adds an extra NetWare Settings panel to
the printer's Properties dialog box, as shown in Figure 22.12. From this panel, you can configure the usual NetWare printer elements, including banner pages, tabs, form feeds, copies, and
user notification.

FIG. 22.11

Printing to a NetWare queue from a Windows NT system is as easy as configuring a shared Windows network printer.

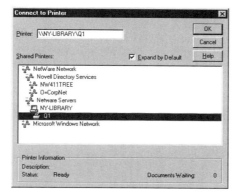

FIG. 22.12

The IntranetWare client adds an extra panel to the standard printer properties dialog box.

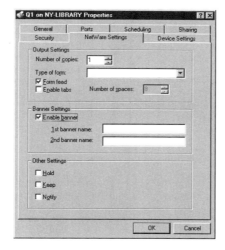

Administering NetWare

The IntranetWare Client for Windows NT ships with 32-bit versions of the NetWare GUI utilities, including NetWare Administrator that enable you to manage nearly every aspect of the NetWare environment from your Windows NT system. However, it will not be necessary for you to launch NetWare Administrator, or even open a DOS box to perform many routine NetWare file system and printer maintenance tasks.

The Novell client integrates file system rights administration capabilities into the Windows NT Explorer. You can select any NetWare volume, directory, or file and manage its trustee list and its attributes from its Properties dialog box.

Part

VI

Ch

22

Managing File System Trustees

To grant a user access to an element of the NetWare file system, you right-click a file or directory and select Properties from its context menu. When you select the NetWare Rights tab, you see the dialog box shown in Figure 22.13. Here, you see a list of the file or directory's current trustees, and the rights that have been assigned to each. To create a new trustee, you browse the NDS tree display, select an object, and click the Add button. Then you use the check boxes to assign specific rights to the new trustee.

FIG. 22.13

You can manage NetWare file system trustee rights from the properties pages of the Windows NT Explorer.

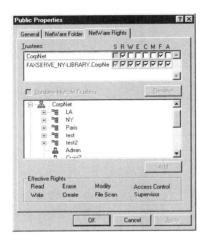

As always, to assign trustee rights, you must possess the appropriate Access Control or Supervisor rights yourself. Your effective rights to the selected file or directory are displayed at the bottom of the NetWare Rights panel.

If you select multiple files in the Explorer and access the properties dialog box, you can assign a trustee rights to all of the files at the same time. As long as a trustee assignment exists for one of the selected files, the Combine Multiple Trustees check box is activated. When you check this box, any rights that you assign that trustee are applied to all of the selected files simultaneously.

If you select the NetWare Folder or NetWare File tab in the properties dialog box, you see a display of file or directory information and check boxes that enable you to modify the file system attributes have been applied to the file or directory, as shown in Figure 22.14. Perhaps the only shortcoming of these panels is that they do not allow you to set an inherited rights filter. To do this, you must use one of the standard NetWare utilities, such as NetWare Administrator, FILER, or RIGHTS.

Managing NetWare Print Queues

When you double-click an icon representing a NetWare print queue in the Printer Control Panel, a dialog box is displayed, like that shown in Figure 22.15. This dialog box displays the print jobs that are currently awaiting service by the NetWare print server. These are not just

Part
VI
Ch
22

the print jobs generated by the local Windows NT system, however. The list displays the entire contents of the NetWare print queue, and enables you to manage print jobs without opening NetWare Administrator or PCONSOLE.

FIG. 22.14
NetWare file system attributes can also be modified from within the Windows NT Explorer.

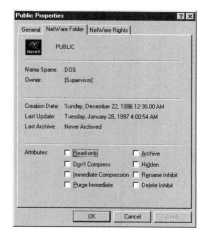

FIG. 22.15
You can manage all of the jobs in a NetWare print queue—not just the Windows NT jobs—from a Windows NT printer status window.

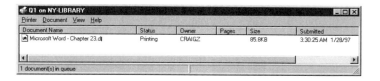

From this dialog box, you can pause individual documents or the entire queue, delete and re-order print jobs, and set the default parameters that are to be applied to the printer.

Summary

Connectivity between Windows NT and NetWare has been a problem for Novell ever since the first release of Windows NT in 1993. Only now, with the release of the IntranetWare Client for Windows NT, can the problem be considered as solved. The client places Windows NT at the same level as DOS, Windows 3.1, and Windows 95 as a NetWare workstation platform. What's more, Novell has proceeded beyond this point by releasing Workstation Services, a product that integrates Windows NT networks into Novell Directory Services, eliminating the need for Windows NT domains and separate network Directories. For more information, see Chapter 9, "Using NDS as a Global Directory Services Solution." ●

CHAPTER 23

Using NetWare with the Macintosh

NetWare provides the capability for Macintoshes and PCs to share access to NetWare file servers. A number of NetWare-compatible applications take advantage of this capability. GroupWise, the popular network e-mail program, for example, allows Macintosh and PC users on the same server—or on connected networks—to exchange e-mail messages. WordPerfect and Microsoft Word, the two best-selling word processing applications, are available in versions for PCs and Macintoshes. When a WordPerfect or Word user stores a Macintosh document on a server disk, this document can be reviewed and edited by a PC-equipped WordPerfect or Word user who's connected to the same server.

The NetWare for Macintosh module enables a NetWare server to connect Macintoshes as workstations over AppleTalk. The IntranetWare client for Macintosh OS enables a NetWare server to connect Macs as workstations over IPX or NW/IP. Both products are included on the IntranetWare CD.

You are no longer required to run AppleTalk on your network if you want Macintosh workstations to access your IntranetWare servers. The IntranetWare Client for Macintosh OS enables the Macintosh workstations to communicate with your server using IPX or NW/IP.

How a Macintosh network operates and its terminology

Macintosh networking has its own vocabulary and some unique network architecture and protocol types. You learn about these in this chapter.

The capabilities of NetWare for Macintosh

NetWare for Macintosh makes it possible to use NetWare servers to provide file and print sharing to Macintoshes.

How to install and configure IntranetWare Client for Macintosh OS

IntranetWare Client for Macintosh OS makes it possible to use NetWare servers to provide file and print sharing to Macintoshes without enabling AppleTalk on your server.

How to install and configure NetWare for Macintosh

NetWare for Macintosh makes it possible to use NetWare servers to provide file and print sharing to Macintoshes over AppleTalk.

How to install and configure NetWare's Macintosh Client software

You learn the steps to follow to set up Macintosh clients to access the NetWare server.

How do you decide whether to install NetWare for Macintosh or the IntranetWare Client for Macintosh OS? Here are a few scenarios to help you decide what is best for your network. If your company network is TCP/IP only, but you have to add some Macintosh workstations, you will want to install the IntranetWare Client for Macintosh OS. If you suddenly have to allow 100 Macintosh workstations to access your server and they need access tomorrow, you will want to install NetWare for Macintosh. In this scenario, you will not have time to install the client software on 100 Macintosh workstations. If you have two Macintosh workstations that need access to the server, you will probably want to install IntranetWare Client for Macintosh OS. You have the time to install the client on two machines, and you probably don't want to add another protocol to the server. ■

Understanding Macintosh Networks

Conceptually, networking Macintoshes is no different than networking IBM-compatible PCs. You wrestle with the same basic issues: creating a communications link between workstations and servers, sharing files, and sharing other network resources (such as printers). Macintosh experts, however, have developed some of their own obscure terms and descriptions to match the equally obscure terminology that PC networking experts use. In the following section, you learn about the common Macintosh networking elements and how they correspond to equivalent NetWare elements.

Establishing a Communication Link

Macintosh computers come equipped with a basic built-in networking capability. Every Macintosh has a built-in LocalTalk printer port that you can use to connect to a LocalTalk network. *LocalTalk* is Apple's proprietary network architecture, a low-speed network designed to connect no more than 32 Macs on a single section of cable. (LocalTalk networks transmit data at 230 Kbits per second.) When larger Macintosh networks must be built, you can use specially designed Ethernet, Token Ring, or other adapters enabling the AppleTalk protocol to run over the appropriate protocol.

The type of topology and the *communications protocol* the network operating system uses dictate the structure of a communications packet.

Macs have AppleTalk, a Macintosh communications protocol. The LocalTalk port built in to every Macintosh is designed to send and receive AppleTalk packets. An Ethernet or token-ring adapter installed in a Macintosh enables the computer to send and receive AppleTalk packets over the Ethernet or Token-Ring network.

When you activate NetWare for Macintosh on a NetWare server, you make at least one of the network adapters in that server capable of sending and receiving AppleTalk packets. The server then can "speak AppleTalk" and is ready to communicate with Macs connected to the same network. When you activate the IntranetWare Client for Macintosh OS, the server is able to communicate via IPX or NetWare/IP to the Macintosh clients.

Sharing Macintosh Files

Some fundamental differences exist between the basic structures of DOS and Macintosh files. Macintosh files have two elements: the data fork and the resource fork. The *data fork*, which is the same as a DOS file, comprises the information or data stored in the file. The *resource fork*, which is the element that makes Macintosh files different from DOS files, stores the type and creator information about the program that created the file.

If you use a Macintosh extensively, you know that you can automatically launch the program that was used to create the file in a folder by clicking the data file. The file's resource fork stores the application information. Macintosh file names can have a length of up to 32 characters and can include spaces as well as upper- and lowercase letters and special characters.

AppleTalk Filing Protocol, or *AFP*, is the translation of Macintosh file calls into network packets. These packets go out over the network to the File Server Control Program (FSCP) on the file server machine. The FSCP translates the AFP file calls from the network into a form that the server machine's native operating system can understand. AFP translation is built in to the Macintosh operating system so that an AFP server can be accessed without the need for additional software.

A NetWare server has the capability to store Macintosh files without compromising the extended capabilities provided by the AppleTalk Filing Protocol. NetWare 4.11 can work with Macintosh files easily because it is equipped to handle files created by operating systems other than DOS.

N O T E Before you start storing Macintosh files on a NetWare server, make sure that your server's backup device can back up and restore Macintosh files. Not all backup units can back up both the resource and data forks or store the complete Macintosh file name. ■

Printing

Networked Macintosh users commonly share LaserWriters and certain third-party printers. Like Macs, LaserWriters and compatible third-party printers have built-in ports that can connect directly to a LocalTalk or Ethernet network and can be connected easily to Macintosh networks.

When you add AppleShare services to a NetWare server, NetWare can control shared LaserWriters so that a print job targeted for one of these printers goes first to a NetWare queue. This arrangement provides benefits for both PC and Macintosh users. A PC user can send jobs to a LaserWriter easily by using the CAPTURE command to redirect the printed output to the appropriate NetWare queue. A Macintosh user gains access to NetWare's powerful print-queue management features. IntranetWare Client for Macintosh OS includes a utility called the NetWare Print Chooser that allows Macintosh users to print to any PostScript-compatible printer controlled by NetWare. (Macintosh machines print using the PostScript printer language natively.)

Using NetWare queues has one inherent limitation with some types of AppleTalk printers. PostScript printers can communicate directly with linked Macs to advise them of the current memory-resident fonts. When a NetWare queue acts as the intermediary between the workstation and the printer, this communication cannot occur. A PostScript printer that frequently changes its list of resident fonts isn't a good candidate for being linked to a NetWare queue.

When NetWare for Macintosh or the IntranetWare Client for Macintosh OS is up and running, Macintosh users can access LaserWriters—and compatible PostScript printers—that are controlled by the NetWare server. This procedure, however, requires much special handling and doesn't offer the dynamic font and PostScript command exchange afforded when a printer is connected to a Macintosh with AppleTalk.

Assigning print queues to AppleTalk printers is an optional feature with NetWare for Macintosh. You don't need to implement print queuing for AppleTalk printers.

Understanding NetWare's Macintosh Support Capabilities

Macintosh users who are connected to a NetWare server have many of the same capabilities that PC users connected to the same server have. Like PC users, Macintosh users can use the server disk just as they use the disks in their own workstations. Macintosh users also can use AppleTalk printers, including printers assigned to NetWare queues. Macintosh users also can access standard PC-compatible printers that aren't AppleTalk-compatible, such as PostScript printers, when these printers are assigned to NetWare queues.

Macintosh users, however, cannot use such DOS-based utilities as NWADMIN, PCONSOLE, and FILER. IntranetWare Client for Macintosh OS users can access, browse, and use drag and drop with the NetWare Directory Browser. They cannot, however, create objects with the NetWare Directory Browser.

For now, at least, full network administration and management requires a PC. If you are using the IntranetWare Client for Macintosh OS with MacIPX, you can run RCONSOLE. You can even run multiple sessions of RCONSOLE simultaneously. The following table compares the capabilities of Macintosh and PC users on a NetWare server.

Capability	Macintosh User	PC User
Store and retrieve files	Yes	Yes
Use shared printers	Yes (AppleTalk and non-AppleTalk)	Yes (including AppleTalk printers assigned to NetWare queues)
Create directory tree objects	No	Yes
Use directory tree	Yes	Yes
Manage server operations	Yes (with IPX)	Yes

Preparing to Connect Macintoshes to Your Server

A Macintosh workstation connection to a NetWare server isn't difficult to implement, but (as with most NetWare features) you have to make a few decisions before starting. You need to decide how to configure your Macintosh network and queues, which servers on your network Macintosh users will use, and whether your clients will log in to the server via AppleTalk, IPX, or NW/IP.

As a network supervisor, you generally face one of two scenarios when you want to connect Macintosh users to the network. You might need to connect a few isolated Macs to your existing network of NetWare servers and PC workstations, or you might be joining an existing AppleTalk network to your NetWare network.

If you're adding a group of isolated Macs to your network, it might be easier to use the IntranetWare NetWare Client for Macintosh OS on the Macintoshes. You need to load and configure AppleTalk on your server only if you're installing NetWare for Macintosh.

Part VI

Ch 23

> **N O T E** IntranetWare Client for Macintosh OS requires that the Mac operating system be System 7.1 or above running on a 60830-based Macintosh or above or a 601-based Power Macintosh or above. The client must have a minimum of 5M of available memory and a CD-ROM to install NetWare Client for Macintosh OS. If you do not have a CD-ROM available on a workstation but do have a modem or a connection to the Internet, you can download clt511.bin from **http://support. novell.com**. ▪

If you choose to install NetWare for Macintosh, you need to assign network numbers and zones. If you're connecting your NetWare servers to a Macintosh network using NetWare for Macintosh, you need to document the network numbers and zone names now in use. You need to use this information to activate NetWare for Macintosh.

Choosing a Network Topology

Choosing a network topology for Macs is similar to choosing a topology for a PC network. You need to consider several factors: what cable types are available, your budget, the distance and cable specifications for the network types available, and the performance level desired.

Every Macintosh has a built-in LocalTalk printer port that you can connect to a LocalTalk network. Many newer Macintoshes are Ethernet-ready. LocalTalk uses standard telephone wire, a cable type that's available in almost every environment. You cannot, however, connect more than 32 devices to a single LocalTalk network.

If you decide to use LocalTalk, you need to buy a LocalTalk PC network adapter for every NetWare server you want to place on the LocalTalk network. See your NetWare dealer for a list of currently supported LocalTalk network adapters.

You also can use Ethernet or Token Ring as your Macintosh network topology. If you already use one of these topologies to network PCs, you might want to use this topology to network Macintoshes.

Using Macintoshes and PCs on the Same Physical Network

In most cases, you can use the same cable system that you use to transmit NetWare's IPX/SPX protocol to transmit AppleTalk communications. By choosing the same topology for both PCs and Macs, you can connect both computer types to the same physical network.

 Using the IntranetWare Client for Macintosh OS, a Macintosh can be connected to the NetWare server via Ethernet, or Token Ring and LocalTalk simultaneously. The Macintosh can "speak AppleTalk" through the printer port to the LocalTalk network and either IPX or NW/IP through the network card to the server.

Connecting Multiple AppleTalk Networks

If you decide to install NetWare for Macintosh, you will create an AppleTalk network. Frequently, AppleTalk networks are divided into multiple physical networks. Because LocalTalk is a low-speed network and is limited to a maximum of 32 devices per physical network, network supervisors often must create multiple separate networks joined by routers.

Your IntranetWare 4.11 server can be used as an AppleTalk router. A server with two or more network adapters running the AppleTalk protocol links those networks, allowing Macs on one network to communicate with devices on another.

You can configure a NetWare 4.11 server as a *seed router* (the server acts as either a master router by broadcasting network number and zone information to other devices), or as a *non-seed router* (by receiving zone and network number information from other seed routers). Every AppleTalk network must have at least one seed router.

Rules for Assigning AppleTalk Network Numbers and Zone Names

AppleTalk networks are assigned network numbers and zone names. The following table lists the elements of a Macintosh network and shows the corresponding element on a NetWare network of IBM-compatible PC workstations:

Network Elements	Macintosh	IBM-Compatible
Popular topologies	LocalTalk (built-in) Ethernet Token Ring	Ethernet Token Ring
Communications protocol	AppleTalk IPX/SPX NW/IP	IPX/SPX NW/IP
File protocol	Apple Filing Protocol	DOS file structure
Physical network ID	Network number or number range Zone	Network number

After you decide how to connect the Macs, draw a network diagram showing the various physical networks. Figure 23.1 shows a sample diagram. The diagram you make can help you determine how many separate networks have Macs attached. For each network using AppleTalk, you need to assign a network number (or a range of numbers) and a zone name.

FIG. 23.1

This is a diagram of an AppleTalk network.

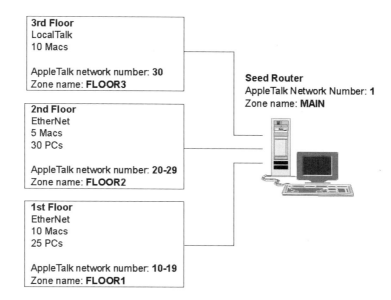

If you're connecting to your network only a few Macs that share the same physical network, you can use a single network number and zone name. The assignment of zone names and network numbers becomes more complicated if you're connecting multiple physical Macintosh networks.

You have many options for configuring interconnected physical AppleTalk networks. Two implementations of AppleTalk are now in use: AppleTalk Phase 1 and AppleTalk Phase 2. Phase 2, the most recent AppleTalk release, is designed to handle extensive networks. AppleTalk router devices handle communications between linked networks and must be Phase 2-compatible to use all the extended addressing and zone-naming capabilities of AppleTalk Phase 2. NetWare 4.11 can perform AppleTalk Phase 2 routing.

 T I P   A quick way to check which version of AppleTalk your existing workstations are running is to look at the EtherTalk icon. The EtherTalk icon is in the Network Control Panel. A double arrowhead means you are running Phase 2. A single arrowhead means you are running Phase 1.

AppleTalk Phase 1 requires that you assign only one network number per physical network. Because one network number is required for every 253 nodes you connect, you're limited to a maximum of 253 nodes per physical network under AppleTalk Phase 1.

AppleTalk Phase 2, in contrast, allows you to assign a *range* of network numbers to a physical network. To connect 500 devices to a physical network, for example, you can assign two or more network numbers. To assign five addresses, for example—where the lowest-numbered network is 1 and the highest is 5—you specify a network-number range of 1 through 5.

N O T E   An AppleTalk network number or range must be unique (no other AppleTalk network number on your AppleTalk network can be the same) and can range from 1 to 65279. Unlike NetWare's network-numbering scheme, AppleTalk network numbers are in decimal format (NetWare uses hexadecimal format).

AppleTalk also requires that you assign *zone names*. Zone names, which help users identify the location of shared devices, can be up to 32 characters long, including spaces. With AppleTalk Phase 1, you can assign only one zone name to a physical network (you can, if you want, reuse this zone name for another physical network). AppleTalk Phase 2 permits you to assign multiple zone names to a physical network. Table 23.1 summarizes the rules for assigning AppleTalk network numbers and zone names.

Table 23.1   Rules for Assigning AppleTalk Network Numbers and Zone Numbers

Rule	AppleTalk Phase 1	AppleTalk Phase 2
A range of network numbers can be assigned to a single network	No	Yes
More than one zone name can be used for a single network	No	Yes
More than 253 nodes can be connected to each network	No	Yes
Allowed network numbers	Any unique decimal number from 1 to 65279	Any unique decimal number range, including numbers 1 to 65279
Allowed zone names	Any unique 32-character name, spaces allowed	Any unique 32-character name, spaces allowed

Deciding Whether to Use NetWare Queues for Macintosh Printing

You can find complete details about NetWare print queues in Chapter 17, "Implementing Network Printing." Before you decide to use NetWare queues for AppleTalk printers, however, you need to remember that, when printing through a NetWare queue, PostScript printers cannot communicate directly with Macintosh workstations, providing updates of available printer fonts or other printer status information.

There are advantages to associating a NetWare queue with an AppleTalk printer that compensate for this shortcoming. PC users (who cannot send jobs directly to the printer because they don't use the AppleTalk protocol) can send jobs to the AppleTalk printer by placing jobs in the print queue. Macintosh users also can send jobs to non-AppleTalk PostScript printers by sending a job to a print queue associated with that printer.

When you associate an AppleTalk printer with a NetWare queue, you create a *spooler*, which serves as the intermediary between the two. Mac users can use the Chooser to select the spooler as their print output device in the same way they would select a normal AppleTalk printer.

If Macintosh users print by using spoolers and queues, a printer server must manage the interaction between the spooler, queue, and printer. NetWare for Macintosh also includes a special printer server module as part of the ATPS (for AppleTalk Print Services) NLM.

Figure 23.2 shows the options for routing print jobs between Macintoshes, PCs, and printers.

FIG. 23.2
The three possible options for handling print jobs on an AppleTalk network are shown.

AppleTalk Printer   Macintosh

1. Printing directly to an AppleTalk printer.

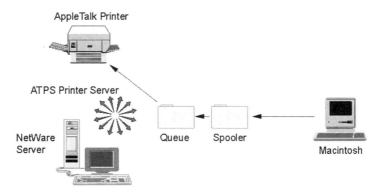

2. Printing to an AppleTalk printer through a spooler and queue managed by an ATPS printer server.

FIG. 23.2
(continued)

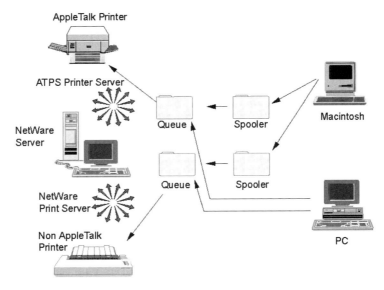

3. PCs and Macintoshes printing to AppleTalk and non-AppleTalk printers.

Preparing for Installation

NetWare's Macintosh support files are included on the IntranetWare 4.11 operating system CD-ROM. The server you're installing Macintosh support on must have a CD-ROM drive, or you must perform the installation by using RCONSOLE from a CD-ROM drive-equipped workstation.

Installing the Macintosh Name Space on Server Volumes

The Macintosh uses a file-naming scheme different than the DOS-compatible file system. The server disk volumes that you plan to use to store Macintosh files must be readied to work with the naming method required for Macintosh files. The install program will add the name space if necessary.

Behind the Menus

When the installation program adds the Macintosh name space to a volume, it invokes the following command:

```
ADD NAME SPACE MACINTOSH TO VOLUME SYS
```

(This example uses the volume named SYS.) You can type this command from the server console if you need to add the Macintosh name space to a volume and don't want to run INSTALL. This command needs to be executed only once—you don't have to execute it every time the server starts.

After the Macintosh name space is installed, a module named MAC.NAM is automatically loaded every time the server starts.

CAUTION

After you add the Macintosh name space (or any other non-DOS name space), the only way to remove that name space is to dismount the volume and run the VREPAIR NLM. If you do remove the name space, the files that used the name space might not be accessible.

Installing the IntranetWare Client for Macintosh OS Software on the Server

The IntranetWare Client for Macintosh OS uses an NLM called MACFILE, which handles the AppleTalk Filing Protocol requirements of the server instead of AFP. Basically, MACFILE is in charge of the server's Macintosh Desktop file. (See the upcoming section "Understanding the Macintosh Desktop" for further information.)

Start INSTALL by typing **LOAD INSTALL** from the server console, and perform the following steps:

1. From INSTALL's Installation Options menu, choose Product Options.
2. From the resulting menu, select Install NetWare Client for Macintosh OS. INSTALL prompts you to choose the path from which you want to install NetWare for Macintosh's files. INSTALL automatically lists the path on the server's CD-ROM drive (NW411:\ PRODUCTS\INSTALL\IBM\DOS\XXX\ENGLISH\).
3. Press F3 to specify a different local or server path, or press F4 if you're using RCONSOLE and want to specify a path on your workstation.

Avoiding Confusion

The official name of this client is IntranetWare Client for Macintosh OS. However, the install program and the online documentation refer to it as the NetWare Client for Macintosh OS.

---

4. After you enter the appropriate path, press Enter to begin installation.

INSTALL copies the files required to install IntranetWare Client for Macintosh OS to the server's SYS volume. This program displays a menu that offers two options: Easy Install and Custom Install.

Easy Install Method   The Easy Install method completes the following tasks for you:

- Adds the Macintosh Name Space to the SYS volume (if necessary)
- Installs the English language files needed to support the NetWare Client for Macintosh OS
- Loads Macintosh OS File System support

The Easy method displays a summary of what the program is going to do (see Figure 23.3). After pressing Esc, you are presented with a screen with the choices Proceed with Installation and Cancel Installation. Easy Install changes the AUTOEXEC.NCF file to automatically load MACFILE.NLM.

FIG. 23.3

The Easy Install displays a screen that lists the tasks that will be accomplished. In this example, the Mac name space will not be loaded because the SYS volume already has the name space.

```
                  Easy Installation Summary
No volumes will have the Macintosh name space added to them.

No Mac OS volume names will be changed.

These server languages will be installed:
    English

Mac OS client files will be installed in these languages:
    English

Mac OS file system support will be loaded from AUTOEXEC.NCF.
```

Custom Install Method   The Custom method completes the following tasks (see Figure 23.4):

1. Select volumes to add the Macintosh Name Space.

   With this menu prompt selected, press Enter to list the server volumes and choose those to receive the Macintosh name space. If you do not choose the SYS volume, the install program will not install the client software on the server because the Mac name space is required for the client software. The default path for the client software, if you choose to install it, is SYS:PUBLIC\CLIENT\MAC\language.

2. Edit Mac OS volume names.

   When you choose this option and press Enter, an entry box opens that lets you change the volume names. When you enter a new name and press Esc to save it, the volume's name changes only as it appears to Macintosh users, but the volume's NetWare name as it appears to PC users and as it's listed in the NetWare directory tree remains the same. The default is SERVERNAME.Volumename, for example, MACSERVER.SYS.

3. Select server languages to install.

   When you select the server language option and press Enter, a box appears that lets you choose English, French, Italian, German, Portuguese, or Spanish.

4. Select Mac OS client languages to install.

   When you select the Mac OS client option and press Enter, a box appears that lets you choose English, French, Italian, German, Portuguese, or Spanish.

5. Load Mac OS file system support.

   This option asks whether or not to Load NetWare Client for Macintosh OS File Support from AUTOEXEC.NCF. Your choices are to load MACFILE, don't add MACFILE, or do not change the AUTOEXEC.NCF.

6. Display an Installation Summary.

   This option displays a list of choices that you have made.

7. Proceed with the installation.

   This option begins the installation.

FIG. 23.4

The Custom Install Options presents you with a list of steps to accomplish.

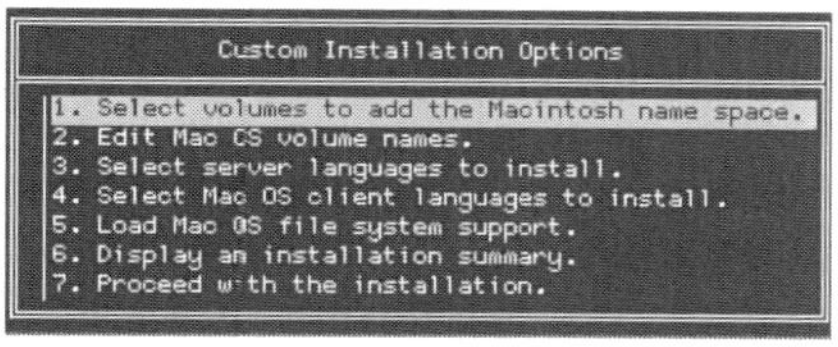

```
         Custom Installation Options
1. Select volumes to add the Macintosh name space.
2. Edit Mac OS volume names.
3. Select server languages to install.
4. Select Mac OS client languages to install.
5. Load Mac OS file system support.
6. Display an installation summary.
7. Proceed with the installation.
```

Installing NetWare for Macintosh on the Server

Part
VI

Ch
23

Now that you have read about the inner-workings of AppleTalk, you are ready to install NetWare for Macintosh. Installing and activating NetWare for Macintosh on a NetWare 4.11 server isn't difficult. The process is completely menu-driven. Use the INSTALL.NLM to copy a group of NLMs to the server and place the commands to start and configure those NLMs in the server's STARTUP.NCF and AUTOEXEC.NCF files. Specifically, the steps are as follows:

1. Install the network adapters for AppleTalk in the server. After you perform this step, load INSTALL, which prompts you to perform the next steps.
2. Transfer NetWare for Macintosh's NLMs to the \SYSTEM directory on the SYS volume.
3. Load the Macintosh file name space on each volume that will store Macintosh files.
4. Place a command in the AUTOEXEC.NCF file to load the AppleTalk protocol and configure the AppleTalk network numbers and zones.
5. Place a command in the AUTOEXEC.NCF file to load the LAN drivers for the network adapters that will run AppleTalk.
6. Place a command in the AUTOEXEC.NCF file to bind the AppleTalk protocol to the appropriate network adapters.
7. Place a command in the AUTOEXEC.NCF file to load the AFP (AppleTalk Filing Protocol) NLM.
8. If you plan to assign NetWare queues to AppleTalk printers, INSTALL places a command in the AUTOEXEC.NCF file to load the ATPS (AppleTalk Print Services) NLM.
9. Configure AppleTalk file services.
10. Configure AppleTalk print services.

Each of these steps is discussed in the following sections.

After you complete these steps, reinitialize the server's settings or restart the server so that the commands entered in STARTUP.NCF and AUTOEXEC.NCF are executed. You can then log in from a Macintosh workstation.

Installing and Configuring the Network Adapters that Run AppleTalk

You might need to install additional network adapters in the server that you're connecting to your Macintosh AppleTalk networks. Locate the LAN drivers for these adapters. LAN drivers that ship with NetWare 4.11 are located in the PRODUCTS\NW411\IBM\411\LANDRV directory on the IntranetWare NetWare 4.11 operating system CD-ROM.

Configure each network adapter according to the manufacturer's instructions. (Make sure that you choose interrupt, I/O port, DMA, and memory-buffer addresses that don't conflict with the devices currently installed in the server.) Next, down the server, power it off, and install the adapters in the server PC.

After you install the network adapters, you are ready to restart the server. Make sure that you don't issue the REMOVE DOS or SECURE CONSOLE commands from the server console after you restart the server and before you install NetWare for Macintosh. Both NetWare console commands disable access to the server PC's bootable DOS drive used during the installation process. If these commands are issued as part of the server's AUTOEXEC.NCF file, use the EDIT NLM to remove them temporarily or turn them into remarks after you restart the server. Next, down and restart the server again so that the commands aren't in effect.

Installing NetWare for Macintosh's Files with INSTALL

After you LOAD INSTALL from the server console, from the Installation Options menu, choose Product Options, Install NetWare for Macintosh.

INSTALL automatically lists the path on the server's CD-ROM drive (NW411:\PRODUCTS\ INSTALL\IBM\DOS\XXX\ENGLISH\). Press F3 to specify a different local or server path, or press F4 if you're using RCONSOLE and want to specify a path on your workstation. After you enter the appropriate path, press Enter to begin installation.

INSTALL copies the files required to install NetWare for Macintosh to the server's SYS volume, and then starts the NetWare for Macintosh installation program. This program displays a menu that offers two options: Cancel Installation and Install NW-MAC.

Choose Install NW-MAC to continue the installation process. The Final Installation Options menu appears (see Figure 23.5).

FIG. 23.5
The NetWare for Macintosh Final Installation Options screen shows you the steps required to finish the installation.

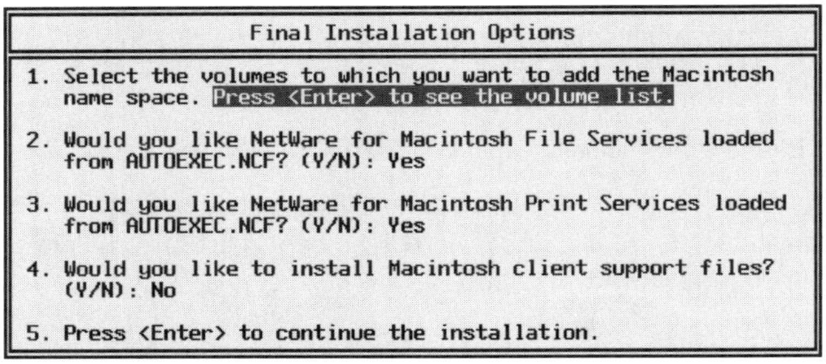

```
                  Final Installation Options
┌─────────────────────────────────────────────────────────────┐
│ 1. Select the volumes to which you want to add the Macintosh  │
│    name space. Press <Enter> to see the volume list.          │
│                                                               │
│ 2. Would you like NetWare for Macintosh File Services loaded  │
│    from AUTOEXEC.NCF? (Y/N): Yes                              │
│                                                               │
│ 3. Would you like NetWare for Macintosh Print Services loaded │
│    from AUTOEXEC.NCF? (Y/N): Yes                             │
│                                                               │
│ 4. Would you like to install Macintosh client support files?  │
│    (Y/N): No                                                  │
│                                                               │
│ 5. Press <Enter> to continue the installation.               │
└─────────────────────────────────────────────────────────────┘
```

Macintosh Name Space

If the Macintosh Name Space is not already installed on the volumes that your Macintosh users will access, refer to "Installing the Macintosh Name Space on Server Volumes" earlier in this chapter.

Choosing to Load Macintosh File and Print Services from AUTOEXEC.NCF

The NetWare for Macintosh installation program next prompts you to specify whether you want to load Macintosh file and print services automatically by including the appropriate commands in AUTOEXEC.NCF. You choose by responding to the following two prompts:

```
Would you like NetWare for Macintosh File Services loaded from AUTOEXEC.NCF? (Y/N)
Would you like NetWare for Macintosh Print Services loaded from AUTOEXEC.NCF? (Y/N)
```

Answer Yes to the first prompt to store Macintosh files on the server's disk volumes. Answer Yes to the second option to associate queues on the server with AppleTalk printers.

Behind the Menus

When you answer Yes to the prompts to load Macintosh file and print services, the NetWare for Macintosh installation program places the following two commands in the server's AUTOEXEC.NCF file:

LOAD AFP

LOAD ATPS

The first command loads the AFP NLM. The AFP NLM loads support for the AppleTalk Filing Protocol and manages the interaction between Macintosh users and the file folders they store on the NetWare server.

The ATPS (AppleTalk Print Services) NLM manages the interaction between the NetWare server and the AppleTalk printers that use the server's queues. The ATPS module broadcasts the availability of the NetWare queues so that Macintosh users can use the Chooser to select these queues. ATPS also routes print jobs waiting in queues to the appropriate AppleTalk printer via the AppleTalk network.

Choosing to Install Macintosh Client Support Files

The last option on the NetWare for Macintosh installation program's Final Installation Options menu is the following prompt:

```
Would you like to install Macintosh client support files? (Y/N)
```

If you answer Yes to this option, the NetWare for Macintosh workstation utilities install in the SYS:PUBLIC\CLIENT\MAC\ENGLISH directory (if the default language is English; otherwise, the files install in a subdirectory named after your default language, such as SYS:PUBLIC\CLIENT\MAC\ESPANOL). Macintosh users can access this directory to install NetWare's

Macintosh workstation utilities. You can install these utilities on only one server on your network, if you want.

After you respond to all the prompts on the Final Installation Options menu, select the following:

```
Press <Enter> to continue the installation.
```

The actions you select are executed.

Configuring NetWare for Macintosh

After you exit the NetWare for Macintosh installation program's Final Installation Options menu, the ATCONFIG NLM is loaded, and ATCONFIG's NetWare for Macintosh Configuration menu appears (see Figure 23.6). Use the options on this menu to configure the AppleTalk protocol on the server, the AppleTalk Filing protocol, and AppleTalk printing.

FIG. 23.6
The NetWare for Macintosh configuration screen has the next set of configuration steps.

```
NetWare for Macintosh Configuration

Configure AppleTalk Stack
Configure File Services
Configure Print Services
Configure CD-ROM Services
Install Additional Language Support
Install Macintosh Client Support
Licensing Options
Add Macintosh Name Space
Edit STARTUP.NCF
Edit SYS:\SYSTEM\AUTOEXEC.NCF
```

Configuring the AppleTalk Protocol Your first task is to activate the AppleTalk protocol on the server's network cards connected to networks that include Macintoshes. Choose the first option, Configure AppleTalk Stack, from the NetWare for Macintosh Configuration menu.

If you have never used the INETCFG NLM to manage the server's network drivers and protocol settings, you see the message shown in Figure 23.7. INETCFG provides a menu-driven way to create network driver and protocol configurations. Although you can create simple configurations by using INSTALL or manually editing the AUTOEXEC.NCF file, INETCFG makes creating more complicated configurations fairly elegant. INETCFG stores communication setting information in a series of configuration files in the server's SYS:ETC directory.

If you answer Yes to the prompt message shown in Figure 23.7, the commands that load network drivers and bind protocols to these drivers are remarked out of the server's AUTOEXEC. NCF file and transferred to a file named NETINFO.CFG in the SYS:ETC directory. The command SYS:ETC\INITSYS.NCF replaces the transferred commands. The following example shows an extract from a typical AUTOEXEC.NCF file before and after its LAN driver and protocol commands are remarked out and transferred to the configuration files managed by INETCFG.

FIG. 23.7
You will be asked to choose whether or not to transfer LAN driver and protocol commands to be managed by INETCFG.

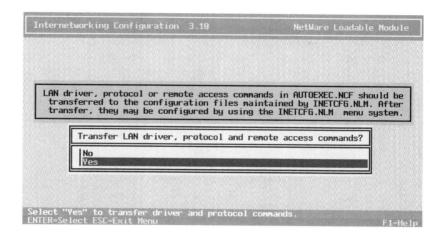

Part
VI
Ch
23

Before:

```
LOAD NE1000 INT=2 PORT=300 FRAME=Ethernet_802.2 NAME=NE1000_1_E82
BIND IPX NE1000_1_E82 NET=1
```

After:

```
; Network driver LOADs and BINDs are initiated via
; INITSYS.NCF. The actual LOAD and BIND commands
; are contained in INITSYS.NCF and NETINFO.CFG.
; These files are in SYS:ETC.
sys:etc\initsys.ncf
#LOAD NE1000 INT=2 PORT=300 FRAME=Ethernet_802.2  NAME=NE1000_1_E82
#BIND IPX NE1000_1_E82 NET=1
```

After you answer Yes to this prompt, or if you've already used INETCFG to manage the communication settings on your server, the INETCFG NLM is loaded and you see its main menu (see Figure 23.8).

FIG. 23.8
INETCFG can be used to manage AppleTalk LAN driver and protocol settings.

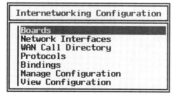

Adding Drivers for Network Boards If you added network boards to the server to handle Macintosh connections, you must install and activate the LAN driver for each board. Choose Boards from INETCFG's menu. A list of currently configured network boards appears. To add a new board, press Insert. The LAN drivers that now exist in the SYS:SYSTEM directory are listed in the available driver's box. To copy a new driver to SYS:SYSTEM, press Insert again. You're prompted to enter the path and name of the driver that you need to copy. To add the

NE2000 driver from the NetWare 4.11 CD-ROM, for example, type `NW411:\PRODUCTS\NW411\IBM\411\LANDRV \NE2000`. Notice that you type the path *and* name of the driver.

After the new driver is copied, it appears in the Available Driver box. Select this driver and press Enter. The Board Configuration box opens (see Figure 23.9). The box first prompts you to enter the board name, which is a unique 10-character name that you create to identify the board. After you enter the board name, enter the hardware settings for the board, such as the interrupt, the I/O base address, the slot number, and the memory base address. You also can enter a comment (up to 50 characters long) that describes the board in greater detail, such as `Ethernet board for 3rd floor segment`.

FIG. 23.9

INETCFG can be used to enter network board settings.

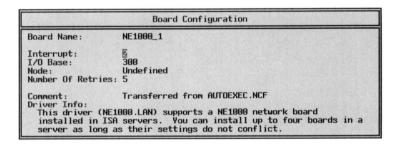

```
                        Board Configuration

 Board Name:         NE1000_1

 Interrupt:          2
 I/O Base:           300
 Node:               Undefined
 Number Of Retries:  5

 Comment:            Transferred from AUTOEXEC.NCF
 Driver Info:
   This driver (NE1000.LAN) supports a NE1000 network board
   installed in ISA servers.  You can install up to four boards in a
   server as long as their settings do not conflict.
```

After you enter the board configuration information, press Esc and save your changes, you're returned to INETCFG's menu.

Enabling and Configuring the AppleTalk Protocol   Next, you need to enable and configure the AppleTalk protocol. Choose Protocols from INETCFG's menu. A list of protocols appears. Next, select AppleTalk and press Enter. The AppleTalk Configuration box appears (see Figure 23.10).

FIG. 23.10

The AppleTalk protocol required configuration is done at this screen.

```
                      AppleTalk Configuration

 AppleTalk Status:                      Enabled
 Packet Forwarding:                     Enabled ("Router")
 Type of Packet Forwarding:             Phase 2
 DDP Checksum:                          Disabled

 Static Routes for On Demand Calls:
 Static Routes Configuration:

 Tunnel AppleTalk through IP (AURP):    Disabled
 AURP Configuration:

 Filtering Support:                     Disabled
 Internal Network:                      Enabled
 Network Number:                        100     (decimal)
 Network Zone(s) List:                  (Select to View/Configure)
 Expert Configuration Options:          (Select to View/Configure)
```

Set the following options:

- **AppleTalk Status**—Use this option to enable or disable AppleTalk on the server. Change this setting to Enabled because you're installing NetWare for Macintosh.

- **Packet Forwarding**—This setting determines whether the server routes AppleTalk communication packets between networks. If the server has more than one AppleTalk-enabled network board installed and you need AppleTalk communications from one network to another, set this option to Enabled ("Router"). If the server needs to act only as a workstation, leave this setting at Disabled ("End Node").

N O T E   If the Macintosh users will be accessing disk volumes or print queues on this server, routing should be enabled. You want the server to route AppleTalk packets between the server's internal AppleTalk network and the AppleTalk network on the wire. ▨

- **Type of Packet Forwarding**—If you decide to enable packet forwarding, use this option to specify the type of router that the server will be. In the section "Rules for Assigning AppleTalk Network Numbers and Zone Names," earlier in this chapter, you read about the difference between AppleTalk Phase 1 and Phase 2. If your AppleTalk network uses only Phase 2 routers, you can set this option to Phase 2. If your AppleTalk network includes Phase 1 and Phase 2 routers, set this option to Transition (Phase 1 and 2). (Phase 2 is the default with System 7.x.)

- **DDP Checksum**—If the routers on your AppleTalk network must transmit and receive packets that include DDP (Datagram Delivery Protocol) checksums, set this option to Enabled. (*Checksums* are used to verify the integrity of communications packets.)

- **Static Routes for On Demand Calls**—Use this option to determine whether to treat certain packet forwarding routes as pre-defined, rather than discovered as needed. This advanced option allows you to dictate the path that routed AppleTalk packets follow. Because it usually is better to allow routers to dynamically assign the best route to packets that are being forwarded, this option isn't used often.

- **Static Routes Configuration**—This option is used to specify the static routes for on-demand calls.

- **Tunnel AppleTalk through IP (AURP)**—Use this advanced option when you want to connect AppleTalk networks through an intermediate network that uses the NW/IP protocol. AppleTalk packets are encapsulated in NW/IP packets, a method known as *tunneling*. When you enable this option, you substitute the AURP (AppleTalk Update-Based Routing Protocol) for AppleTalk's normal RTMP (Routing Table Maintenance Protocol). Your server must be configured to support the NW/IP protocol to support this option.

- **AURP Configuration**—Use this option to configure the tunneling of AppleTalk packets through IP.

■ **Filtering Support**—Use this option to enable or disable AppleTalk filtering. With AppleTalk, you invoke filtering to control which types of packets are allowed to cross through routers. You create filters using the FILTCFG NLM.

You can create three kinds of AppleTalk filters:

Filter Type	Description
Device Hiding Filters	Prevents devices by certain names or types from being accessible via a router. If you want a particular printer or router to not advertise its availability on networks other than its own, you can create a device-hiding filter that filters out advertising packets for that device.
Outgoing Route Filters	Causes router to not forward packets that advertise availability of particular zones or network number ranges.
Incoming Route Filters	Causes router to block inbound packets that advertise the availability of particular zones or network number ranges.

■ **Internal Network**—Use this setting to determine whether you assign a network number and zone list to the server. If you don't enable this option, Macintosh users cannot access disk volumes or print queues on the server.

■ **Network Number**—If you enable the internal network setting, use this option to set the AppleTalk network number that you assign to the server.

■ **Network Zones List**—Use this option to specify the zones in which the server appears if you have enabled the internal network option. To add a zone name, select this option, press Enter, and then press Insert. If you enter more than one zone, the first zone that you enter is listed as the default. You can choose a different default zone by highlighting that zone and pressing Enter.

■ **Expert Configuration Options**—Use this option if you're transmitting AppleTalk packets over an X.25 link and you have a non-Novell router on the other end of the link. You use this option to specify the manufacturer of the non-Novell router.

After you enter the appropriate settings for these options, press Esc to save the changes and return to INETCFG's menu.

Binding the AppleTalk Protocol to Network Boards   After you use INETCFG to define the newly added network boards and enable and configure the AppleTalk protocol, you need to associate or *bind* AppleTalk to each network board. Choose Bindings from INETCFG's menu to perform this task. A list of the server's protocol to network board bindings appears (see Figure 23.11).

FIG. 23.11

This is a list of protocols that are bound to the network boards.

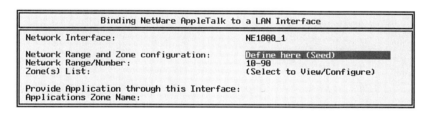

```
          Configured Protocol To Network Interface Bindings

Protocol        Interface      Status      ID String
AppleTalk        DL2000-AT      Enabled     net=200 non-extended
AppleTalk        NE1000_1       Enabled     net=10-90 extended
IPX              IPX-ATGTWY     Enabled     550
IPX              NE1000_1       Enabled     1
```

To bind AppleTalk to a network board, press Insert. The server's list of configured protocols appears. Choose AppleTalk. The server's list of network boards appears. Choose the board to which you want to bind AppleTalk and press Enter.

If you're working with a network board type that supports AppleTalk Phase 2, such as Ethernet or Token Ring, you're prompted to choose between configuring an extended or non-extended network. Choose extended if your AppleTalk network is Phase 2, or non-extended if your network is AppleTalk Phase 1. After you make this choice, the Binding NetWare AppleTalk to a LAN Interface box appears (see Figure 23.12).

FIG. 23.12

At this screen, you configure a protocol to bind to your network board.

```
          Binding NetWare AppleTalk to a LAN Interface

Network Interface:                      NE1000_1

Network Range and Zone configuration:   Define here (Seed)
Network Range/Number:                   10-90
Zone(s) List:                           (Select to View/Configure)

Provide Application through this Interface:
Applications Zone Name:
```

You're first prompted to specify the network range and zone configuration. You can choose one of two options: Define here (Seed) or Learn from network (Non-Seed).

If a network board in your server is connected to an AppleTalk network that includes a seed router, you can let this network board "learn" its network number and zone name information from that router. A *seed router* is a NetWare server (or other AppleTalk router) that broadcasts network number and zone information to devices that have what are known as *non-seed interfaces*. A non-seed interface device specifies a network number or range of 0–0 and no zone information.

If you choose to make the server a seed router, you next specify the network number range to be assigned to the network connected to the network board. Select Network Range/Number and press Enter. You're prompted to enter the starting and ending network range numbers.

You next enter the zone or list of zones assigned to the network connected to the network board. Select Zone(s) List and press Enter to work with the zone list. Press Insert to add a zone name. If you enter more than one zone, the first zone you entered is listed as the default. You can choose a different default by highlighting that zone and pressing Enter.

After you finish working with the AppleTalk to network board binding, press Esc to return to the list of protocols to network board bindings. You can press Insert to create another binding or press Esc to return to INETCFG's menu.

Part VI

Ch 23

When you finish working with INETCFG, press Esc to return to the NetWare for Macintosh Configuration menu.

Behind the Menus

The View Configuration option on INETCFG's menu gives you a look at the console commands that INETCFG generates to load network board LAN drivers and the AppleTalk protocol and to bind AppleTalk to these network boards.

If you choose View Configuration from INETCFG's menu, the View Configuration menu appears. When you choose LAN Board Commands, from this menu, you see a list of the commands used to load network board drivers. The following commands are typical and load network board drivers for an NE2000 Ethernet card and a Dayna DL2000 LocalTalk adapter:

```
LOAD NE2000 NAME=NE2000_1_E82 FRAME=ETHERNET_802.2 INT=2 PORT=300
LOAD NE2000 NAME=NE2000_1_ESP FRAME=Ethernet_SNAP INT=2 PORT=300
```

Notice that the NE2000 LAN driver is loaded twice for the same board. One driver loads with the frame type ETHERNET_802.2 (which is used for an IPX/SPX-based network) and the other with the frame type ETHERNET_SNAP (which is used for the AppleTalk protocol).

You also see the commands used to bind protocols to the network boards. The following commands bind IPX to the NE2000 board and AppleTalk to the NE2000:

```
BIND IPX NE2000_1_E82 NET=1
BIND AppleTlk NE2000_1_ESP net=10-90 zone'{"Macintosh"}
```

When you select the Protocol Commands option, you see the commands used to activate communication protocols. The commands that activate AppleTalk are as follows:

```
LOAD LLC8022
LOAD AppleTlk routing=Yes internal_net_mode=Yes net=100-100 zfile=Yes
LOAD adsp
```

INETCFG also creates a file named ATZONES.CFG, which stores the list of AppleTalk zones and their corresponding network number ranges. The following ATZONES.CFG file defines the zones ACCTING, NETZONE1, and NETZONE2:

```
net=10-90 zone={
  "ACCTING",
  "NETZONE1"
}
net=100-100 zone={
  "ACCTING"
}
net=200 zone={
  "NETZONE2"
}
```

Configuring the AppleTalk Filing Protocol File Services
The next menu option on the NetWare for Macintosh Configuration menu is Configure File Services. Use this option to configure the AppleTalk Filing Protocol on the server. You already learned that the AppleTalk Filing Protocol is activated on the server when you load the AFP NLM.

When you choose the Configure File Services option, the AFPCON NLM is loaded and displays the AFP Configuration Options menu, which offers the following options:

- Quick Configuration
- Detailed Configuration
- Maintenance and Status

Invoking Default Settings with the Quick Configuration Option   The easiest way to view and work with your server's AFP configuration is to choose Quick Configuration. The screen shown in Figure 23.13 appears and lists the default settings for AFP's configurable options. When you answer Yes to the prompt to set default AFP values, these six options are returned to their default settings, which works well in most situations.

FIG. 23.13
These are the default
settings for AFP.

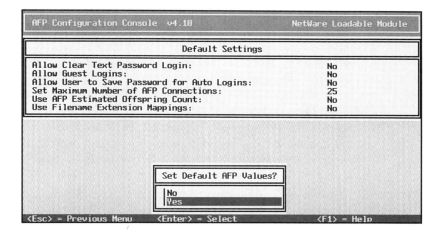

Using the Detailed Configuration Option.   To customize AppleTalk Filing Protocol options, choose Detailed Configuration from the AFP Configuration Options menu. You see the Detailed Configuration menu, which offers the following options:

- General Server Information
- User Access Information
- Performance Enhancements

When you choose General Server Information, you can perform these two tasks:

- **Modify Server Name**—Opens an entry box that lets you change the server's name on the AppleTalk network. When you enter a new name and press Esc to save it, the server's name changes only as it appears to Macintosh users, but the server's NetWare name as it appears to PC users and as it's listed in the NetWare directory tree remains the same.

■ **Modify Login Greeting**—If you want to display a message every time a Macintosh user connects to a server, move the highlight next to Modify Login Greeting and press Enter. A box opens that prompts you to enter the login greeting to display on-screen. Type the message and press Esc to save it.

 T I P The command LOAD AFPCON, which is issued at the server console, will get you quickly to this screen.

Press Esc to return to the Detailed Configuration menu after you finish working with the General Server Information options.

Choose User Access Information to work with options that control how Macintosh users log in and use passwords. When you choose this option, the Access Methods Configuration box opens and enables you to configure these options:

■ **Allow Clear Text Password Login**—This option controls whether Macintosh users must use encrypted passwords versus *clear text* passwords. Protocol analyzers or network monitors that read communications packets on a network cannot read encrypted passwords. When you activate this option, a special NetWare program known as the NetWare Client for Macintosh OS must be installed on each Macintosh and must be used to enter and change passwords.

Set this option to No if you're concerned that someone may try to discover passwords by using a device that can intercept communications packets. Set this option to Yes if password security is less important than avoiding the inconvenience caused by forcing Macintosh users to use the NetWare client to enter and manage passwords.

■ **Allow Guest Logins**—To have the server accept logins using the GUEST user name, set this option to Yes. With NetWare 4.11 and NetWare Directory Services, the GUEST ID isn't created by default (unlike previous NetWare versions), so this option is of little benefit if Macintosh users need to log in to the directory tree. If your users log in to the server in bindery emulation mode, the GUEST ID can be used, but has limited access by default.

■ **Allow Users to Save Password for Auto Logins**—Some versions of the Macintosh Chooser provide the capability to store passwords for reuse so that server logins can be automatic. Although this provides convenience for Macintosh users by relieving them of the need to enter and remember passwords every time they log in, it also compromises security because anyone with access to the Macintosh can automatically log in to the network. To permit the saving of passwords for automatic use during login, set this option to Yes. This function only works if your users are using AppleTalk and logging in via the Chooser.

Behind the Scenes of the Macintosh Workstation

If you turn on the save password option, at some point in the future you will want to stop the Macintosh from automatically mounting the volume. The Macintosh workstation stores the instructions to automount volumes in the AppleShare Prep file in the Preferences folder. Dragging this file to the trash stops a workstation from automatically mounting volumes. Don't worry, this file is automatically created again the next time AppleShare is selected in the Chooser.

Part

VI

Ch

23

After you finish setting options in the Access Methods Configuration box, press Esc to return to the Detailed Configuration menu.

Choose the Performance Enhancements menu selection to tune performance of the AppleTalk Filing Protocol on your server. The Performance Enhancements Configuration box opens and lets you work with the following five options:

■ **Set Maximum Number of AFP Connections**—Use this option to limit the maximum number of Macintosh logins allowed on the server. By default, NetWare for Macintosh can support the number of concurrent connections permitted by your NetWare license, but you can use this option to lower this number if you need to conserve connections for other purposes, such as supporting a very large number of AppleTalk printers that use NetWare queues. Enter the number of concurrent login sessions you want to allow. You might need to change the concurrent logins number if you added a license to the server and the amount of Macintosh logins doesn't increase automatically.

■ **Use Filename Extension Mappings**—If you want files on the server's volumes to be mapped by extension to the programs that were used to create them, set this option to Yes. When you do so, AFP uses an ASCII text file named EXTMAP.DAT in the SYS:SYSTEM\NW-MAC directory to cross-reference file extensions to programs. EXTMAP.DAT includes a long list of common extension cross-references, but you can use a DOS text editor to add your own extensions if you want. Some sample entries in the EXTMAP.DAT file are as follows:

```
.DOC    WDBN    MSWD
.TXT    TEXT    ttxt
.XLS    XLS4    XCEL
```

In the first column, you place the file extension preceded by a period. The second column shows the file type, and the third lists the file's creator (the program used to create the file). Each column is separated by a tab. Note that the entries in the type and creator columns are case-sensitive.

You can include comments by preceding the comments with a pound sign (#), as follows:

```
.DBF    F+DB    FOX+    # Fox Plus database file
```

■ **Use AFP Estimated Offspring Count**—The AppleTalk Filing Protocol maintains an offspring count for every directory, which, by default, is an exact count of the number of files and subdirectories beneath that directory. You can set this option to Yes to specify that the server estimate this value rather than calculate it exactly, thereby saving processing loads and time on the server. The vast majority of Macintosh programs don't use the offspring count, but if you use Macintosh software that does, you need to leave this option set to No.

■ **Use NetWare Cache Control Algorithm**—Setting this option to No delays confirming the updates to folders until the folder contents literally are written to the server disk. Usually, updates are confirmed as soon as they're received by the NetWare server's cache-buffering system. NetWare then manages writing data from its cache memory to hard disk, and this write occurs within a few seconds at most. Few situations might require you to change this and force folder updates not to be confirmed until they're written to disk, and setting this option to No can decrease performance significantly.

■ **Set Finder Accelerator Max Cache Percentage**—This option allows you to use up to 5 percent of the server's cache for NetWare for Macintosh's finder accelerator. The memory that you set aside is used to cache finder information about the most frequently accessed server folders. The default setting for this option is 0, which means that no memory is used, but you can set this from 1 to 5. The number you enter is the percentage of the server's cache memory that is used for the finder accelerator.

After you finish working with the options in the Performance Enhancements Configuration box, press Esc to return to the Detailed Configuration menu. Press Esc again to return to the AFP Configuration Options menu.

Working with Maintenance and Status Options   The Maintenance and Status menu option lets you shut down and restart the AppleTalk Filing Protocol on the server. It also lets you perform maintenance tasks and work with AFP-enabled volumes. When you choose Maintenance and Status from the AFP Configuration Options menu, you see the AFP Maintenance and Status menu, which offers the following options:

■ Shut Down AFP Server

■ Restart AFP Server

■ Volume Information

N O T E   When you load the AFP NLM on the server, your NetWare server becomes an AFP Server to the AppleTalk network.

To shut down AFP on the server, choose Shut Down AFP Server. A menu with three options appears:

■ Enter Shut Down Message

■ Set Shut Down Time

■ Cancel Shut Down

CAUTION

The Shutdown AFP Server option only shuts down the AFP part of the server, so no Macintosh users can log in. The server is still available to PC users.

To customize the shutdown message that Macintosh users receive, choose the first menu option and enter the message. This option offers an easy way to advise connected Macintosh users of the purpose and expected duration of the shutdown.

Set the time of the shutdown by selecting the Set Shut Down Time option. At the prompt, set the countdown time in hours and minutes. As soon as you enter the countdown, Macintosh users receive a warning message. If you have set a shutdown time that's an hour or more, Macintosh users receive a message at 30-minute intervals before the shutdown. At five minutes before the shutdown, the AFP server doesn't allow new Macintosh users to connect, and users receive warning messages every minute.

You can cancel a pending shutdown by choosing Cancel Shut Down. After you finish working with shutdown options, press Esc to return to the AFP Maintenance and Status options menu.

To reactivate the AFP server after it's shut down, choose Restart AFP Server. The server restarts, and Mac users can connect again.

You can use the Volume Information menu option to perform several important volume monitoring and management tasks. When you choose this option, the Volume Status box opens and lists the server's volumes and information about each one (see Figure 23.14).

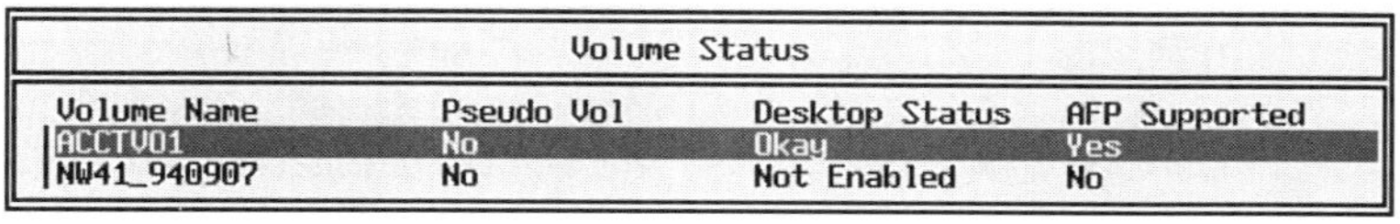

FIG. 23.14
Volume Status can be checked at this screen.

Volume Status			
Volume Name	Pseudo Vol	Desktop Status	AFP Supported
ACCTV01	No	Okay	Yes
NW41_940907	No	Not Enabled	No

The box shows the following four columns of information:

- **Volume Name**—This is the volume's name as it appears to Macintosh users.

- **Pseudo Vol**—If the volume is a CD-ROM disk, it's listed as a pseudo volume. Unlike PC workstations, when Macs access a shared CD-ROM volume, the files that are used must be migrated to a normal hard disk volume before they can be accessed. (See your NetWare documentation for information about setting up this type of file migration by using NetWare Hierarchical File System features.)

- **Desktop Status**—This column shows the status of the volume's desktop database. The desktop database cross-references icons to file types. The possible status settings are Okay, Not Okay, Rebuilding, Not Enabled, or Uninitialized. If the status is Not Okay, the desktop database needs to be rebuilt (a process you learn about in "Understanding the

Part **VI**

Ch **23**

Macintosh Desktop" later in this chapter). The Rebuilding status appears if you view volume information while the desktop database is being rebuilt. The Not An Option status indicates that the volume doesn't support the AppleTalk Filing Protocol. Uninitialized means that the desktop database was shut down.

■ **AFP Supported**—This column shows whether the volume supports AFP and is available to Macintosh users.

To work with a volume on the Volume Status list, select that volume's listing and press Enter. You see a menu that offers the following options:

Option	Description
Enable AFP Volume	Use this option to disable or enable AFP on the selected volume. To make a volume inaccessible by Macintosh users, select this option and change the setting to No. To enable a previously disabled volume, select this option and change the setting to Yes.
Modify Displayed Volume	By default, a server volume appears on a Mac desktop using a name that consists of the server name and the physical volume name. The SYS volume on a server named ACCTING is ACCTING.SYS, for example, while a volume named VOL1 on a server named MRKTING is MRKTING.VOL1. To change this name, choose this option and enter a new volume name.
Start Desktop Database	If the Desktop Status column in the Volume Status menu shows Rebuild the status Not Okay, you must rebuild the desktop database. Choose this option to rebuild and repair the database. Macintosh users can continue using the volume during the rebuild process, but they might see only generic folder icons while working with the volume.
Cancel Desktop Rebuild	Use this option to stop a desktop database rebuild operation. Canceling a desktop rebuild could corrupt your desktop.
Shut Down Desktop	To stop using the desktop database for the selected Database volume, choose this option. Do so with caution, however; the only way to reinitialize the desktop database after shutting it down is to dismount the server volume and remount it.

After you finish working with the volume status, press Esc three times to return to the AFP Configuration Options menu. Press Esc again to return to the NetWare for Macintosh Configuration menu.

Understanding the Macintosh Desktop

The Macintosh Desktop is a set of hidden files that keep track of the files on an AFP volume. These files are hidden in the DESKTOP.AFP directory if you have AFP.NLM loaded. If you have MACFILE.NLM loaded, the files are in the DESKTOP.MAC directory. The desktop tracks the resource forks and data forks. It is also responsible for linking the icons to the proper file type. After many additions and deletions of files, the desktop can become corrupted. The cure for this is to rebuild the desktop.

There are two other ways to rebuild the desktop other than the menu from Maintenance and Status of AFPCON. However, no Macintosh users can log in during this time because AFP is unloaded.

One method is to unload the AFP NLM from the server, then reload AFP with the CDT (Clear DeskTop) switch (LOAD AFP CDT). This clears the desktop files. AFP must be unloaded and reloaded to complete this process.

The other, more severe, method also begins with the unloading of the AFP NLM. Next, log in to the server with a DOS machine as supervisor. Map a drive to the root of the problem volume (SYS or Other). Execute the following commands from your DOS machine:

Command	Description
FLAG DESKTOP.AFP*.* n	Flag all the files normal
Del DESKTOP.AFP*.*	Delete all the files
FLAGDIR DESKTOP.AFP n	Flag the directory normal
RD DESKTOP.AFP	Remove the directory

Configuring Print Services

You already learned that Macintosh users can send print jobs to printers in the following three ways:

- Print jobs can go directly to AppleTalk printers by way of an AppleTalk network connection.
- Print jobs can go to a NetWare spooler, which in turn goes to a NetWare queue, and then to the printer, all managed by an ATPS print server.
- Print jobs can go directly to a PostScript printer by way of a NetWare queue, enabling both PCs and Macintoshes to share the same printers.

The ATPS (AppleTalk Print Services) NLM manages the interaction between the NetWare server and the AppleTalk printers that use the server's spoolers and queues. The ATPS module broadcasts the availability of the NetWare spoolers so that Macintosh users can use the Chooser to select these spoolers. ATPS also routes print jobs waiting in queues to the appropriate AppleTalk printer via the AppleTalk network.

After you configure your AppleTalk printing environment, you use a utility named ATPSCON to create the spoolers, queues, and print servers. *Print spoolers* are advertised as though they are printers on AppleTalk networks. Macintosh users can connect to them by using the Chooser. A printer server manages the movement of print jobs from queues to AppleTalk printers. AFP printer servers are similar to the print servers that are launched when you run the PSERVER NLM. The printer servers that route jobs from queues to AppleTalk printers operate as part of the ATPS NLM.

To set up a Macintosh-compatible shared printing environment, choose Configure Print Services from the NetWare for Macintosh Configuration menu. The ATPSCON NLM is automatically loaded, and a box labeled Directory Services Login appears and prompts you to log in to NetWare Directory Services. By default, the ADMIN login name is supplied; ATPSCON assumes that this name is located in the top organization object in the directory tree. Accept this name and enter the password, or enter a different name and the appropriate password (the login name that you use must have supervisory access to the directory context where you want to create queue objects).

ATPSCON's Configuration Options menu appears (see Figure 23.15). You can configure your AppleTalk shared printing environment in two ways. You can use the Quick Configuration option, which searches your AppleTalk network for printers, lists them, prompts you to select one, and then automatically creates a spooler, printer server, and queue for the printer you select. You also can create printer servers, queues, and spoolers separately.

FIG. 23.15

AppleTalk Print Services are configured at this menu.

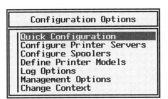

Using the Quick Configuration Option

If you want to automatically create a queue, spooler, and printer server for a particular AppleTalk printer, choose the Quick Configuration option from the ATPSCON Configuration Options menu. The Lookup Parameters box shown in Figure 23.16 appears.

Your first step is to specify the printer model. Move the highlight next to this option and press Enter. A list of printer types appears. Choose the listing that matches the printer type you're configuring.

FIG. 23.16

The Quick Configuration requires the Lookup Parameters be set.

```
┌──────────────────────────────────────────────────┐
│                 Lookup Parameters                 │
├──────────────────────────────────────────────────┤
│ Printer Model:      Generic PostScript            │
│ Printer Type:       LaserWriter                   │
│ Printer Zone:       ACCTING                       │
│ Proceed:            (Perform Lookup)              │
└──────────────────────────────────────────────────┘
```

Next, specify the printer zone where the AppleTalk printer is located. Select the Printer Zone option and press Enter. The AppleTalk zones on your network are listed. Select the zone where the printer is located.

With the right printer model and zone selected, highlight Perform Lookup and press Enter. The AppleTalk printers in the zone you selected are listed. Choose the one that you're associating the spooler and queue to and press Enter.

When you select the printer, the Quick Configuration Parameters box opens and displays the settings that you selected (see Figure 23.17). By default, ATPSCON assigns a spooler name to go with the printer you selected. It precedes the printer name with the letters NW (for NetWare). If the printer's AppleTalk name is ACCTING-LJ, for example, ATPSCON assigns the spooler the name NW ACCTING-LJ. You can change the name by backspacing over it and entering the name of your choice. After you finish, press Esc and confirm that you want to save your changes. Optionally, you can save the spooler as disabled, which means that it isn't available for Macintosh users until you enable it.

FIG. 23.17

A spooler name must be defined for the printer to work.

```
┌──────────────────────────────────────────────────┐
│             Quick Configuration Parameters        │
├──────────────────────────────────────────────────┤
│ Printer's AppleTalk Name:   ACCTING-Q             │
│ Printer's AppleTalk Type:   LaserWriter           │
│ Printer's AppleTalk Zone:   ACCTING               │
│ Spooler's AppleTalk Name:   NW ACCTING-Q          │
└──────────────────────────────────────────────────┘
```

Creating and Configuring a Printer Server

You can use the Configure Printer Servers option to manually create new printer servers or to configure printer servers that you created with the Quick Configuration option. When you select this option, the Configured Printer Servers box opens and lists the current printer servers.

Creating a Printer Server   To create a new printer server, press Insert. The Lookup Parameters box opens (refer to Figure 23.16). In "Using the Quick Configuration Option" earlier in this chapter, you learned how to use this option to create new printer servers.

Deleting a Printer Server   You also can remove a printer server while working with the printer server list. Highlight the printer server to remove and press Delete, or mark multiple printer servers with F5 and then press Delete to remove all servers.

Disabling or Enabling a Printer Server   From the list of printer servers, you can disable or enable a printer server. To disable a printer server, highlight its listing and press F3. A minus sign appears next to the printer server listing, indicating that it is disabled. If you want to enable or disable multiple printer servers in one step, mark each one with F5 and press F3. (F3 toggles the print server from disabled to enabled.)

Configuring a Printer Server   To work with a printer server's configuration options, highlight this printer server's listing and press Enter. The Printer Server Parameters list appears (see Figure 23.18).

FIG. 23.18
At the Printer Server Parameters screen, you set a number of parameters.

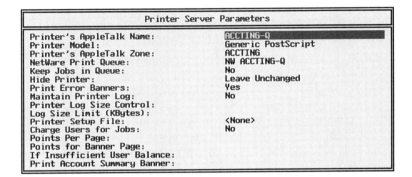

You can configure the following options:

- **Printer's AppleTalk Name**—This parameter shows the name of the printer as AppleTalk knows it. You need to edit this parameter only if the printer's name changes. Make sure that the name you enter matches the printer's AppleTalk name exactly.

- **Printer Model**—This parameter automatically reflects the printer's model as it's advertised via AppleTalk. You cannot edit this option.

- **Printer's AppleTalk Zone**—This parameter specifies the printer's zone. You shouldn't need to edit this setting unless the printer is moved to another zone.

- **NetWare Print Queue**—Use this setting to designate which queue is used to store print jobs for the AppleTalk printer. Highlight this option and press Enter to browse through the directory tree to choose a queue. To create a new queue, browse to the directory tree context where you want to place the queue and press Insert to enter the queue name.

- **Keep Jobs in Queue**—Usually, print jobs are deleted from the queue as soon as they print. To force a job to remain in the queue after it's printed, change this setting to Yes. The job remains in the queue with the User Hold setting. You can reprint the job by removing the job from User Hold.

- **Hide Printer**—When you associate an AppleTalk printer with a spooler and print queue, both the spooler and the printer appear in the Macintosh Chooser when a user browses for printers. The user can, if he wants, send jobs directly to the printer and circumvent the spooler and queue. To hide the printer, change the setting to Yes. If you don't want to hide the printer, change this setting to No. If you want to allow other AppleTalk and NetWare utilities to determine whether the printer is hidden, leave this option set to Leave Unchanged, its default.

- **Print Error Banners**—PostScript printers can be configured to print error messages on a special banner page. If you want the selected printer and spooler combination to print an error banner, set this option to Yes.

- **Maintain Printer Log**—To maintain a log of printer activity, set this option to Yes. The log, stored in the SYS:SYSTEM\ATPS directory by default, records print jobs and changes to the printer configuration. Each printer server log is given a unique number for a name.

- **Printer Log Size Control**—Use this option to limit the amount of disk space that printer log files can consume. If you activate the Printer Log Size Control option, you specify the maximum size that the log file is allowed to grow. You use this option to choose what happens when the log file reaches that limit. Set this option to Delete if Over Limit if you want to delete the log file when it reaches its allowed size limit. Use the Rename if Over Limit option to specify that the log file be renamed, using the extension .LGB. When a backup exists of the log file and the log file reaches its allowed limit, the old backup file is deleted and the log file is renamed to take its place. The log file is controlled by the ATPS print server and includes all the ATPS printers.

- **Log Size Limit**—If you opt to maintain a log file and control its size, use this option to set the maximum size in kilobytes.

- **Printer Setup File**—Use this option to send a file that consists of setup commands to the printer before each job. You need to create the file and place it in the SYS:SYSTEM\ NW-MAC\SETUP directory. When you select this option, you're prompted to choose from the files listed in the SYS:SYSTEM\NW-MAC\SETUP directory. After choosing a file, the contents of the file are displayed. Press Esc and confirm that you want to use the file that you selected.

- **Charge Users for Jobs**—If you set up the Accounting option when you installed NetWare, set this option to Yes to charge users for print jobs.

- **Points Per Page/Kilobyte**—This option specifies the amount to debit each user's account for each page or kilobyte printed (the page count is used for PostScript printers and the kilobyte count is used for other kinds of printers).

- **Points for Banner Page**—Use this option to specify how much money a user is charged per banner page. If you do not want to charge for printing banner pages, set this option to 0.

Part
VI

Ch
23

■ **If Insufficient User Balance**—This option determines what happens if a user submits a print job but has an insufficient account balance or credit limit to "pay" for the job. You can select one of four options:

Delete Job

Place Job on Operator Hold

Place Job on User Hold

Print Job Anyway

■ **Print Account Summary Banner**—This option lets you specify that a banner be printed after each job that displays the charges for printing the job and the amount remaining in the user's account.

After you finish customizing the printer server parameters, press Esc to save the changes and to return to ATPSCON's menu.

Creating and Configuring a Spooler

If you want to create a NetWare spooler and associate it with an AppleTalk printer, you create a printer server (using either the ATPSCON's Quick Configuration or Configure Printer Server option). If you need to create a spooler without a printer server, such as when you want Macintosh users to be able to print to a non-AppleTalk printer via a NetWare print queue, use ATPSCON's Configure Spoolers option. You also use the Configure Spoolers option to configure spoolers that you created by using the Quick Configuration option. When you select this option, the Configured Spoolers box opens and lists the current spoolers.

Creating a Spooler   To create a new spooler, press Insert. The Spooler Parameters box opens (see Figure 23.19). You learn how to configure the Spooler Parameters box's many options in the upcoming section "Configuring a Spooler."

FIG. 23.19

The spooler parameters are configured here.

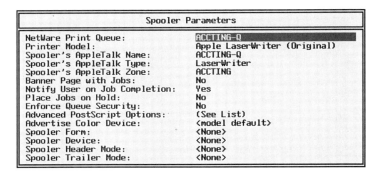

Deleting a Spooler   You also can remove a spooler while working with the spooler list. Highlight the spooler to remove and press Delete, or mark spoolers with F5 and press Delete to remove them all.

Disabling or Enabling a Spooler   From the list of spoolers, you can disable or enable a spooler. To disable a spooler, highlight its listing and press F3. A minus sign appears next to the spooler listing, indicating that it's disabled. To disable multiple spoolers in one step, mark each one with F5 and press F3.

Configuring a Spooler   To work with a spooler's configuration options, highlight this spooler's listing and press Enter. The Spooler Parameters list appears (refer to Figure 23.19). You can configure the following options:

Part

VI

Ch

23

- **NetWare Print Queue**—Use this setting to designate which queue is used to store print jobs for the spooler. Highlight this option and press Enter to browse through the directory tree to choose a queue. To create a new queue, browse to the directory tree context where you want the queue to be placed and press Insert to enter the queue name.

- **Printer Model**—Use this parameter to specify the printer model as it will be advertised via AppleTalk. When you highlight this option and press Enter, you're prompted to choose a printer model from a list.

- **Spooler's AppleTalk Name**—This parameter shows the name of the spooler as AppleTalk knows it. Enter the name that you want Macintosh users to see when they use the Chooser to browse for printers.

- **Spooler's AppleTalk Type**—This parameter automatically reflects the spooler's AppleTalk type, based on the selection you made for the Printer Model parameter. You cannot edit this option.

- **Spooler's AppleTalk Zone**—This parameter specifies the spooler's zone. Use this option to designate the zone in which the spooler is listed.

- **Banner Page with Jobs**—Use this option to specify whether a banner page is printed with each job. For more information on this, see Chapter 17, "Implementing Network Printing."

- **Notify User on Job Completion**—This option determines whether the user receives notification on completion of the print job. The user must be logged in to the server where the queue's directory resides to receive notification.

- **Place Jobs on Hold**—By default, jobs placed in the spooler's queue print as soon as a printer servicing the queue is available. With this option, you can specify instead that the job be placed on hold as soon as it enters the queue. You can choose one of three hold options:

Option	Description
Operator Hold	Only a queue operator can remove the job hold.
User Hold	A queue operator or user can remove the job hold.
User and Operator Hold	Both a user and an operator have to remove the job from hold.

■ **Enforce Queue Security**—Set this option to Yes if you want NetWare's queue security enforced. When queue security is enforced, the user must be a queue user and must be logged in to the directory tree and the server storing the queue.

■ **Advanced PostScript Options**—Highlight this option and press Enter to configure the following options:

Option	Description
Include LaserPrep	Specifies whether the PostScript Laser Prep file (a set of instructions for the printer) found in the Macintosh System Folder should precede every print job sent to the queue in Jobs. Use when a PostScript printer is a parallel or serial printer controlled by the NetWare print server, and all Macintosh users sending jobs to the printer don't use identical Laser Prep files. Using this parameter guarantees that the printer receives a user's Laser Prep file every time the user sends a job to the printer.
Query Source	Specifies what source of information the spooler used to respond to a query. When a Macintosh sends a print job to a spooler identified as a PostScript device, the Mac sends a query requesting information (font list, printer memory amount, PostScript version, and so on) about the printer. You can specify Model Default (the spooler responds with default options for the specified printer model).
	These settings are listed in files ending with the extension .PPD (PostScript Printer Description) in the SYS:SYSTEM\NW-MAC\PPDS directory. If you understand the PostScript page description language and how to customize printer description files, you can modify these files with an ASCII text editor. If you don't specify Model Default, you can optionally choose an actual AppleTalk printer to respond to the PostScript query, the best setting if spooler is associated with a real AppleTalk printer.

Option	Description
Accept Binary Data	Specifies how a spooler handles binary (non-character) data such as graphic bitmaps. PostScript binary information cannot travel over non-AppleTalk mediums such as parallel or serial printer connections. Set to Yes if the spooler is associated with an AppleTalk printer. Set to Use Binary Encoding if the printer associated with the spooler supports the Adobe Binary Communications Protocol (BCP) or the Adobe Tagged Binary Communications Protocol (TBCP). Set to No if the printer isn't an AppleTalk printer and doesn't support binary encoding.
Custom Font List	If you want the spooler to report a font list other than that specified in the printer's .PPD file, use this option to specify the name of the file containing the font list. A set of default font list files ending with .FNT are stored in the SYS:SYSTEM\NW-MAC\FONTS directory. You can customize these font list files or create a new file in this directory with an ASCII text editor.
Fast Font Response	Set to Yes if all Macintosh clients use the LaserWriter drivers version 6.x or later and use software compatible with this feature (Aldus PageMaker versions earlier than 4.2a aren't compatible, and neither are non-Macintosh applications running on PCs).
Manage Fonts	Set to Yes to have the ATPS NLM capture fonts in incoming jobs and to cache these fonts for reuse in subsequent print jobs. This option reduces network traffic because print jobs don't have to be sent with embedded fonts. Ask your font suppliers whether the fonts can legally be shared in this manner.
Custom Printer	Set to Yes to set a printer memory amount that differs from that stored in the printer's default PPD file. This memory amount is the printer memory size reported to workstations.
Free Printer	Use to specify the reported printer memory size.
Add Final EOF	Set to Yes to have the spooler append an end-of-file (Ctrl+D) character to the end of the print job.

Press Esc to return to the Spooler Parameters screen after you finish working with advanced PostScript options.

- **Advertise Color Device**—Set this option to Yes when the spooler is associated with a printer that can print black and white or color (as is the case with the ImageWriter or the Hewlett-Packard DeskWriter).

- **Spooler Form**—Use this option to specify the NetWare form to be used for all print jobs. You should use this option only if the PSERVER NLM or a compatible print server is managing the spooler's queue (see Chapter 17, "Implementing Network Printing.")

- **Spooler Device**—Use this option to specify the printer device to apply to all print jobs. The available devices are the ones you configured for the directory tree context that contains the spooler's queue. You should use this option only if the PSERVER NLM or a compatible print server is managing the spooler's queue.

- **Spooler Header Mode**—If you selected a spooler device with the preceding option, use Spooler Header Mode to specify the print mode setup commands sent before each print job.

- **Spooler Trailer Mode**—If you selected a spooler device, use this option to specify the print mode setup commands sent after each print job.

After you configure each spooler parameter, press Esc to save the settings and return to the list of print spoolers. Press Esc again to return to ATPSCON's main menu.

Using Other ATPSCON Options

ATPSCON offers several other menu options, described in the following list, that are used only when you must extensively customize your NetWare for Macintosh printing environment:

- **Define Printer Models**—Use this option to customize printer model definitions.

- **Log Options**—This option lets you set log "verbosity" or detail levels and view printer logs.

- **Management Options**—When you choose this selection, a menu appears that offers the following three options:

Option	Description
Select ATPS Directory	Lets you choose the directory where the ATPS NLM stores log files and cached fonts (if you activated these optional features). By default, these files are stored in the SYS:SYSTEM\ATPS directory. You can use this option to specify a different directory.
View Cached Fonts	Lets you view fonts stored in the font cache. You also can delete cached fonts using this option.
Set Font Cache Options	Lets you control the amount of disk space used by cached fonts.

- **Change Context**—Use this option to change to a different directory tree context.

After you finish configuring NetWare for Macintosh print services, press Esc to leave ATPSCON and return to the NetWare for Macintosh Configuration menu. Now you're finished configuring NetWare for Macintosh. You can press Esc until you return to the INSTALL menu. Press Esc again to exit.

Activating NetWare for Macintosh

After you install NetWare for Macintosh, you need to activate the configuration changes that you made. From the server console, type REINITIALIZE SYSTEM to make these changes effective.

Your best assurance that NetWare for Macintosh is properly installed and will properly activate is to down the server and restart it. The changes you made to the server's communication configuration and AUTOEXEC.NCF file are tested when you restart the server.

Understanding NetWare for Macintosh Configuration and Monitoring NLMs

In this chapter, you have learned how to install and configure NetWare for Macintosh, using NetWare 4.11's INSTALL NLM. After installing NetWare for Macintosh files, INSTALL adds the commands to load these NLMs to your server's AUTOEXEC.NCF file: APPLETLK (AppleTalk communication protocol), AFP (AppleTalk Filing Protocol), and ATPS (AppleTalk Printing Services). INSTALL then launches the ATCONFIG NLM so that you can configure NetWare for Macintosh. If you need to perform post-installation configuration tasks, you can start ATCONFIG, without running INSTALL, by typing LOAD ATCONFIG from the server console.

ATCONFIG, in turn, launches other NLMs. When you configure the AppleTalk protocol, ATCONFIG launches INETCFG. When you configure Macintosh file services, ATCONFIG launches the AFPCON NLM. When you configure printing, the ATPSCON NLM is launched.

An additional NLM named ATCON (AppleTalk Console) lets you view statistics and other useful information about your AppleTalk environment. Start this NLM by typing **load afpcon** from the server console.

Table 23.2 summarizes the NLMs used to implement, configure, and monitor your NetWare for Macintosh configuration.

Table 23.2   NetWare for Macintosh NLMs

NLM	Name	Purpose
APPLETLK	AppleTalk Communication Protocol	Loads support for the AppleTalk communication protocol
AFP	AppleTalk Filing Protocol	Loads support for the AppleTalk Filing Protocol, which is required to store Macintosh files on a server disk volume

continues

Table 23.2   Continued

NLM	Name	Purpose
ATPS	AppleTalk Print Services	Loads support for AppleTalk printing so that Mac users can send print jobs to NetWare queues and NetWare queues can be associated with AppleTalk printers
ATCONFIG	AppleTalk Configuration	Provides a master menu for NetWare for Macintosh configuration
AFPCON	AppleTalk Filing Protocol Configuration	Lets you configure the AppleTalk Filing Protocol on the server
ATPSCON	AppleTalk Print Services Configuration	Lets you configure print services
ATCON	AppleTalk Console	Lets you monitor your AppleTalk and NetWare for Macintosh environment
MAC.NAM	Macintosh Name Space	Loads support for the Macintosh name space, which is required to support storing Macintosh files

Activating Macintosh Workstations

When you have at least one NetWare server running NetWare for Macintosh and connected to an AppleTalk network, you are ready to let Macintosh users log in. In most respects, Macintosh users are treated identically to PC users. You must create and give Macintosh users login names and passwords and assign trustee rights to the folders that store the files they need to use (a folder on a Macintosh is the same as a directory on a DOS PC). If Macintosh users need to send print jobs to queues, these users must be made queue users.

After you connect a Macintosh to an AppleTalk network that's linked to a NetWare server running NetWare for Macintosh and provide the Macintosh user with a login name, no special software is required if the Macintosh is accessing the server via AppleTalk. Otherwise, you need the NetWare Client for Macintosh OS.

To log in to a NetWare server via AppleTalk and store and retrieve files, the Macintosh user can use commands and menus built in to the Macintosh operating system. Logging in to a NetWare server is just like logging in to an AppleShare server. NetWare print queues serviced by AppleTalk printers also can be used with no special software. In this section, you learn how to log in to a NetWare server and how to direct printing to a NetWare queue by using the Macintosh's built-in commands.

Configuring the Client

As a Macintosh user connected to a network with NetWare servers, you have two login methods available. You can use the simple server-based login method built in to the Macintosh System 6 or System 7 operating system. With this method, a NetWare server looks like any other AppleShare-compatible server. You can access disk volumes, folders, and print queues if you have sufficient rights. NetWare for Macintosh also includes a group of programs that allow Macintosh users to log in to the directory tree rather than to individual servers.

As with PC users, when Macintosh users log in to the directory tree, they don't have to attach to multiple servers one at a time to find the disk volumes and print queues that they need. This group of programs is known as the IntranetWare Client for Macintosh OS. The NetWare client also automatically encrypts passwords for logging in to the NetWare directory tree.

Part
VI

Ch
23

Choosing a Login Method

If you install AppleTalk on your server, the Macintosh clients can log in through the Chooser without any special software. They are logging in using Bindery Emulation. You can use NetWare for Macintosh's NDS client (NetWare Client for Macintosh OS) to log in to the network's directory tree. This option offers you the same advantages that a PC user enjoys when using the directory tree instead of bindery emulation.

N O T E If you installed the IntranetWare Client for Macintosh OS on the server, you must install NetWare Client for Macintosh OS on the client to enable the Macintosh workstation to talk to the server. ▪

Logging In to a NetWare Server Using AppleShare

Because the Macintosh has built-in AppleTalk awareness, you don't need to add software to enable a Mac workstation to log in to a NetWare server that's running NetWare for Macintosh. In fact, logging in to a NetWare server is just like connecting to any other Macintosh server.

To log in, pull down the Apple menu (which shows an Apple symbol) from the menu bar and select Chooser. The Chooser window appears (see Figure 23.20). Make sure that the Apple-Talk Active radio button is selected (in the lower-right corner) and then click the AppleShare icon. After you click the AppleShare icon, a list of servers appears in the list box on the right. In addition, if you are on a multiple-zone network, a list of zones appears in the lower-left list box. When you highlight a zone, the list of servers changes to display those servers in the selected zone.

If necessary, choose the zone where your NetWare server is located, then select the name of the server and click OK. If you have already installed the IntranetWare Client for Macintosh

FIG. 23.20

The Chooser is used to log in to a NetWare server if AppleTalk is enabled.

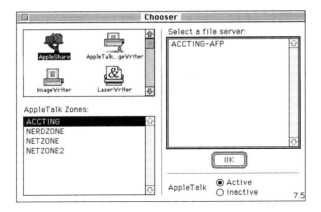

OS, a dialog box appears that asks you to select a logon method (see Figure 23.21). Your choices are Apple Standard UAMs (User Access Method) or NetWare Encryption. If you choose Apple Standard UAMs, you are logged in via Bindery Emulation. The NetWare Encryption method logs you in via NDS.

After you enter the username and password, a list of server volumes appears. Select the vol-

FIG. 23.21

If you have installed the IntranetWare Client for Macintosh OS on your Macintosh workstation, you must choose which login method to use.

umes you want to appear as file drawers on the desktop. If you click a volume to select it (an *X* appears in the check box), your Mac prompts you at startup to log in to the server so that the volume can be displayed on the desktop.

After you choose the volumes you want to have displayed on the desktop, click OK or press Enter. The NetWare server volumes you selected appear as file drawers on the desktop (see Figure 23.22). Volumes appear as file drawer icons. Close the Chooser after you finish logging in.

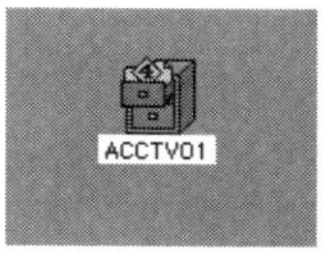

FIG. 23.22
A NetWare volume appears as a file drawer on the desktop.

Logging Out from a NetWare Server

Logging out from a NetWare server is a matter of dragging the file drawer icons for that server's volumes into the trash can. After you drag all the volume icons into the trash can, you're logged out from the server. (Don't worry—dragging the volume to the trash can doesn't delete the volume!)

Part
VI

Ch
23

Installing and Configuring the Client Piece of IntranetWare Client for Macintosh OS

NetWare comes with a special group of programs known as the IntranetWare Client for Macintosh OS. When you install this client on your workstation, you can log in to the directory tree from your Macintosh, either with the Chooser (if you have AFP.NLM running on the server) or with the NetWare Directory Browser software.

The IntranetWare Client for Macintosh OS client software consists of three client pieces: Mac IPX, NW/IP, and RCONSOLE. MacIPX enables the Macintosh client to "speak IPX" to the server. NW/IP enables the Macintosh client to "speak IP" to the server. This option requires NetWare IP on your server. The RCONSOLE piece enables you to run RCONSOLE from the Macintosh workstation if you are "speaking IPX" to the server.

If you install IntranetWare for Macintosh OS on a server, you have the option to specify that the Macintosh client support files are installed on the server. When you do so, a file named NW Client Installer is copied to the SYS:PUBLIC\CLIENT\MAC\ENGLISH directory. (If your default language isn't English, the NW Client Installer file is installed in the subdirectory under SYS:PUBLIC\CLIENT\MAC that matches your language name.)

If you installed NetWare for Macintosh, you can use a Macintosh to log in to the server. Because you're logging in to the server with AppleShare (which is similar to a PC logging in by using bindery emulation), you should use the SUPERVISOR login name or a login name that has equivalent supervisory control over the server. Mount the server's SYS volume by following the steps described in the previous section, "Logging In to a NetWare Server Using AppleShare."

After you successfully log in, the SYS volume is displayed as a file cabinet icon on the right side of your Macintosh screen. Open the file cabinet icon to display its contents; then open the folder named PUBLIC. In the PUBLIC folder, open the folder named CLIENT, open the folder named MAC, and, in the MAC folder, open the folder named ENGLISH (or the name of your default language). In the ENGLISH folder, double-click the file icon named NW Client Installer.

A dialog box opens and informs you that this product installer was created using Aladdin System's Stuffit InstallerMaker. After reading the license agreement for the software, you are prompted to start the install of the IntranetWare Client of Macintosh OS 5.11.

If you have not installed NetWare for Macintosh on your server, insert the NetWare 4.11 CD from the IntranetWare CD set in the workstation's CD drive. (If you don't have a CD-ROM on the workstation, but do have a connection to the Internet, you can download the client from **http://support.novell.com**. To start the installation, double-click the Mac OS Clients installer icon on the CD, which brings up a menu of client applications. Click Install to start the installation of NetWare Client for Macintosh OS. Select the Easy Install option if you are installing MacIPX. Select Custom Install if you are installing NW/IP. If you want to run RCONSOLE from the Macintosh, you must do a Custom Install and select the RCONSOLE Utility. (See "Using Remote Console" later in this chapter for more information on running RCONSOLE.)

FIG. 23.23
Double-clicking the Mac OS Clients Installer icon from the CD brings up this menu.

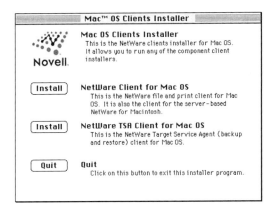

When you install the IntranetWare client for Macintosh OS using the Easy Install options, the following items are placed on your Macintosh local disk:

- The NetWare Client (in the Extensions folder).
- NetWare File Access (in the Extensions folder).
- NetWare Object Assistant (in the Extensions folder).
- NetWare Print Access (in the Extensions folder).
- NetWare Aliases (in the Extensions folder).
- The files for MacIPX, which enables your Macintosh to use the IPX protocol. This protocol is required to log in to a directory tree.
- A folder on the Macintosh hard drive called NetWare Client Utilities. Inside this folder are the Client Readme, the NetWare Directory Browser, the NetWare Print Chooser, and the NetWare Volume Mounter.

Setting NW/IP Parameters The Custom Install procedure of the IntranetWare Client for Macintosh OS software installs the files for NW/IP, which enables your Macintosh to use the NW/IP protocol. You must configure NW/IP for your environment. Use the NW/IP Control Panel to set the environment for your workstation (see Figure 23.24).

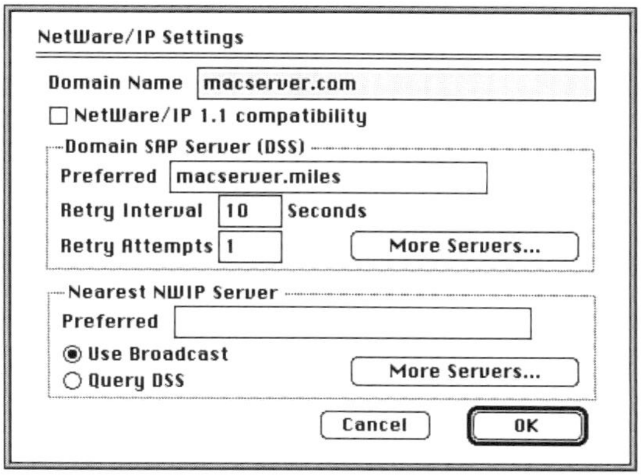

FIG. 23.24
The NW/IP Control Panel is where you define the NW/IP settings for your environment.

Setting MacIPX Parameters The Easy Installation or the Custom Installation procedure of the IntranetWare Client for Macintosh OS installs the files that enable your Macintosh to use the IPX protocol. You can change the default settings for the operation of MacIPX. You can use the MacIPX Control Panel to set the network interface that your workstation uses for MacIPX. You also can choose which MacIPX gateway your workstation uses (if your workstation is connected to a network that doesn't run IPX/SPX) and the frame type to use for your IPX link. You also can work with advanced IPX/SPX settings.

From the Apple menu, choose Control Panel and select MacIPX from the Control Panel list. If your Macintosh has more than one network interface available (such as LocalTalk and Ethernet), you can click the icon of the network interface to use for MacIPX.

After you select the network interface, you need to choose specific settings. If you're using a network interface that isn't connected to a network running IPX, you can specify which MacIPX gateway your Macintosh should use. For Ethernet or Token Ring interfaces, you can specify which frame type to use for the IPX protocol.

From the MacIPX dialog box, you can click the Advanced Options button to set advanced IPX/SPX protocol settings (see Figure 23.25). Network supervisors report that the default settings work well for directory tree logins and in virtually all other situations, but you can change the settings if a particular MacIPX-compatible application requires unique IPX/SPX settings.

Your MacIPX settings are stored in a file named MacIPX Preferences in the Preferences folder in your Macintosh's System Folder. If you want to duplicate the MacIPX settings on one workstation to other workstations, copy this file to the Preferences folder on other Macs.

FIG. 23.25
Advanced MacIPX Parameters, such as IPX Checksumming, are set in this dialog box.

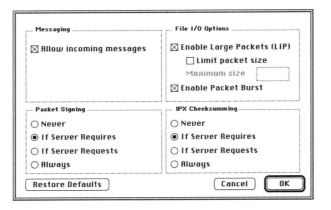

Logging In to Novell Directory Services

After you install the IntranetWare Client for Macintosh OS software on a Macintosh and restart that Macintosh, a tree icon appears on the right side of the menu bar. Before you log in to the directory tree, this tree icon is leafless. The icon grows leaves when you log in to the directory tree. Figure 23.26 shows the menu bar with the tree icon before and after you log in.

FIG. 23.26
The tree on the Macintosh menu bar has no leaves before login and has leaves after login to. Directory Services.

The tree icon is actually a pull down menu that is referred to as the Directory Services Menu, and has the following selections:

- About NetWare Client
- Login
- Configure
- Connections
- Close All Connections

To log in, click the tree icon. From the pull-down menu that appears, choose Login. Enter your name and password and click OK to log in. If you enter a valid name and password, you're logged in to the directory tree, and the tree icon grows leaves, signifying that you're logged in.

Clicking the More Options radio button displays a login box with the option to change your context and tree. Electing to change your context brings up another menu. The Tree menu shows you the last tree logged in to and an option to Find Trees.

 T I P If you're connected to a network with more than one directory tree, you can click the Change Tree button to switch to another tree before entering login information.

If you choose to change your context, you can browse the tree to find your ID, and your name is automatically filled in after you select it (see Figure 23.27). Click the Fewer Options button on this screen to go back to the name and password screen.

FIG. 23.27
The More Options Login screen enables you to specify the context for the user.

Setting Default Login Information

From the Directory Services menu, choose Configure. A Client Preferences screen is displayed (see Figure 23.28). You can set a preferred tree, add, remove, or find a tree. You can set a default context, add, remove, and browse for a context. The login name you put in this box is the default login name. (This is instead of the Macintosh Owner name.)

FIG. 23.28
NetWare Client Preferences are set in this screen.

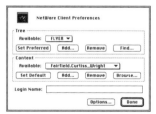

If you almost always use the same login name when you log in from your Macintosh, you can enter your directory tree name in the Directory Tree text box. After you enter the directory tree context and login name, you can click Verify Name to confirm that you entered the directory tree, context, and login name information properly. The DONE button will take you back to the screen in Figure 23.27.

If you need to change to a different directory tree, click the Change Tree button. To go back to your previous default settings, click the Revert button.

Clicking the Options button on the Client Preferences screen brings up the MacIPX Configuration screen of Figure 23.25.

Viewing Your Novell Directory Services Login Information

After you log in, you can click the tree icon and choose Connections to view your login information. You then see a dialog box, showing you the tree you are logged into, the servers, and volumes you have mounted. Clicking the Get Info radio button displays your login name, your default context, Monitored connection, and the name of the directory tree to which you're connected (see Figure 23.29).

FIG. 23.29

You can view your NDS login information here.

```
Information on NDS tree APPLETREE

Logged in as : Admin
     (Admin.MILES)
Default context : <no value set>
Monitored connection : MACSERVER
This is the preferred tree.

     [ Set Preferred ]    [ Change Context... ]    ( OK )
```

Changing Your Password

You also can click the tree icon on the menu bar to change your password. Choose Log In, then Set Password from the tree icon's pull-down menu. This should be done on initial login. If you try to change the password while you are logged in, you will be logged out of the tree and logged back in. Type your old password in the Old Password text box. Then type your new password in the New Password text box, and type it again for confirmation in the Type New Password Again text box.

Mounting a Volume

To mount a volume, open the NetWare Directory Browser and the NetWare Volume Mounter. (Both of these utilities are in the NetWare Client Utilities folder on the Macintosh hard drive). Click the volume you want to mount and drag it into the NetWare Volume Mounter window (see Figure 23.30). Your volume is automatically mounted for you. A faster way to mount a volume is to open the NetWare Directory Browser and double-click the volume you want to mount. This is especially useful if you have multiple volumes to mount. Simply select the volumes—using the shift-click key combination. After you have chosen all the volumes you want mounted, double-click a volume. All highlighted volumes are mounted.

Using the IntranetWare client for Macintosh OS, you can mount a volume on the Macintosh desktop that does not have the Macintosh file-name space added. This volume will be read-only. Note the difference in the icons in Figure 23.31.

FIG. 23.30

Dragging a volume from the NetWare Directory Browser to the NetWare Volume Mounter mounts the volume.

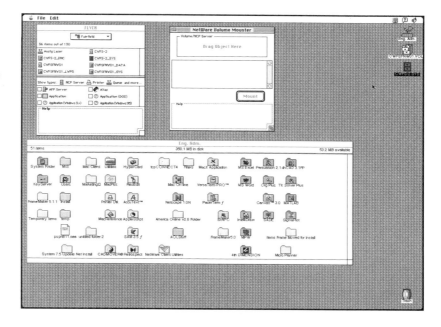

FIG. 23.31

A read-only volume mounts on the Macintosh desktop as a file cabinet with the drawers closed.

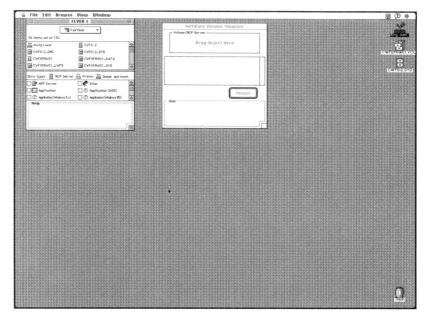

Part

VI

Ch

23

Using Aliases to Simplify Volume, Directory, and File Access

When you log in to a directory tree, you cannot specify that particular server disk volumes be automatically mounted. You have to use the Chooser or the NetWare Directory Browser to mount the volume, which is hardly convenient, especially if you have to repeat these steps every time you start your Macintosh.

You can use the System 7 alias feature (similar to the Windows 95 shortcut feature) to place on your desktop or on a local disk icons for the applications, folders, and files that you frequently access. When you click one of these icons, the volume that the file or folder resides on is automatically mounted if you're already connected to the directory tree that contains the volume. If you aren't logged in, you're prompted to do so when you click the icon for the alias.

To create an alias, highlight the appropriate file or folder, pull down the File menu, and choose Make Alias. An alias folder or file is created in the same location as the original file or folder. To place the alias on your desktop or local disk, drag it to the location where you want the alias to be displayed. This copies the alias to the right location. You then can delete the original alias.

If you create an alias for a folder or file that resides in a folder for which you don't have create rights, you're prompted to confirm that you want to create the alias on your Macintosh desktop.

Save a volume to the desktop as a shortcut to future mounting or to put in the startup folder to automatically mount when the Macintosh is started. To do this, complete the following steps:

1. Open the NetWare Directory Browser and click the volume you want to make a shortcut for (see Figure 23.32).

FIG. 23.32
The NetWare Directory Browser enables you to save objects to a folder or the desktop as a shortcut.

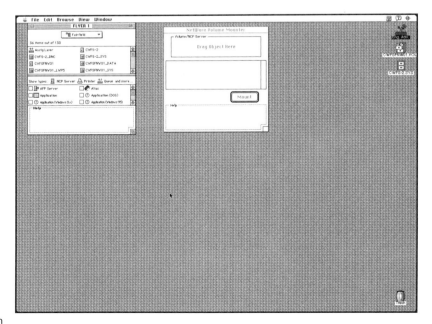

2. Choose File, then select the Save to Desktop option to save an icon of the volume to the desktop.

3. Choose File, then select Save to folder to save an icon to the folder of your choice.

Logging Out of the Directory Tree

Dragging a volume to the trash dismounts that volume, but you are still logged in to the directory tree. (Notice the Directory Services Tree icon in the upper-right is still green.)

To log out of the directory tree, click the tree icon and choose Logout Completely from the pull-down menu. A dialog box appears and prompts you to confirm that you want to log out. Click OK to log out.

Macs Connected via Networks that Run IPX/SPX and AppleTalk

If your Macintosh communicates using Token Ring or Ethernet, and the Token Ring or Ethernet segment that your Macintosh is connected to runs the AppleTalk and IPX/SPX protocols, you don't need to take special steps to log in to a NetWare directory tree. If the Token Ring or Ethernet segment isn't running IPX/SPX, you should activate it by binding IPX to the server network boards connected to the same segment or ring.

Macs Connected via AppleTalk-Only Networks

If your Macintosh is connected to the network by using its built-in LocalTalk port or is connected to another type of network that runs AppleTalk but not IPX/SPX, you need to activate an IPX to AppleTalk gateway in at least one of the servers on the network that's running the AppleTalk protocol. The IPX to AppleTalk gateway allows IPX communications to be contained or encapsulated in the AppleTalk packets that are sent via LocalTalk between the Macintosh and a server running the IPX to AppleTalk gateway.

Activating an IPX to AppleTalk Gateway

Because all incoming packets from LocalTalk-connected Macintoshes must be received and translated by IPX to AppleTalk gateways, you should install enough gateways to comfortably handle the communications load of your network's connected Macintoshes. Ideally, you should identify the NetWare servers that will receive AppleTalk packets from LocalTalk-connected Macintoshes and install an IPX to AppleTalk gateway on each of these servers.

You activate an IPX to AppleTalk gateway by using the INETCFG NLM to load a network board driver named MACIPXGW (for *Macintosh IPX Gateway*). You then bind IPX to this board driver and assign the binding a unique IPX network number.

From the console for the server where you want to activate a gateway, start the INETCFG NLM by typing **LOAD INETCFG** at the server console prompt. INETCFG's Internetworking Configuration menu appears.

Loading the MACIPXGW Driver and Creating a Board Definition The MACIPXGW isn't actually associated with a physical network board, but you configure it the same way as the network board driver for a real network board.

Choose the Boards option from INETCFG's menu. A list of the server's configured boards appears. Press Insert to load a new board driver. A list of the installed drivers appears. Choose MACIPXGW. The Board Configuration screen opens (see Figure 23.33).

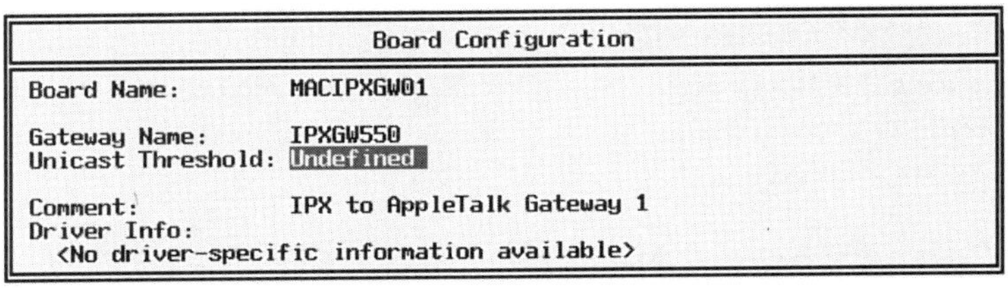

FIG. 23.33

The Board Configuration screen enables you to specify configuration options for the gateway.

```
┌──────────────────────────────────────────────────────────┐
│                     Board Configuration                  │
├──────────────────────────────────────────────────────────┤
│  Board Name:         MACIPXGW01                           │
│                                                          │
│  Gateway Name:       IPXGW550                            │
│  Unicast Threshold: Undefined                            │
│                                                          │
│  Comment:            IPX to AppleTalk Gateway 1          │
│  Driver Info:                                             │
│     <No driver-specific information available>           │
└──────────────────────────────────────────────────────────┘
```

You are first prompted to enter a board name. Enter a descriptive name that's unique from other board names. Next, enter a gateway name, which is the name Macintosh users see when they configure MacIPX on their workstations.

The Unicast Threshold option lets you determine whether the gateway broadcasts its availability via AppleTalk or sends a packet directly to each MacIPX client. With this option, you set the number of MacIPX clients that must be present before the broadcasting method is used rather than sending individual packets. If you don't want broadcasting used and you have 10 Macintosh workstations running MacIPX, for example, set the Unicast Threshold to 10 or more. If you don't want broadcasting used in this situation, set the Unicast Threshold to less than 10, or keep it at Undefined (the default threshold of 1 is used).

If you have many AppleTalk networks and Macintosh clients but only a few Macs running MacIPX, sending individual packets to these few Macs is better for your network than sending all station broadcasts to all your AppleTalk networks. If most Macs on your network use the NetWare Client for Macintosh OS, leave this option set as Undefined, which leaves the Unicast Threshold number at 1.

You also can enter a comment by selecting Comment, pressing Enter, and typing in the comment information.

After you finish configuring the MACIPXGW board driver, press Esc to save the changes and return to the list of configured boards. Press Esc again to return to INETCFG's menu.

Binding IPX to the MACIPXGW Board Definition With a board definition for MACIPXGW created and configured, you next need to bind the IPX protocol to that board definition.

Choose Bindings from INETCFG's menu. A list of your configured protocol bindings appears. Press Insert to create a new binding. A list of the protocols on your server appears. Choose IPX. Next, a list of your network interface boards appears. Choose the board definition that you created for the MACIPXGW driver. The Binding IPX to a LAN Interface screen appears (see Figure 23.34). You're prompted to enter the IPX Network Number that you want to assign to this binding. Enter a number that isn't used on any other IPX network. Press Esc to save your changes.

FIG. 23.34
Enter the unique IPX network number for the gateway (network interface) here.

```
┌────────────────────────────────────────────────┐
│          Binding IPX to a LAN Interface          │
├────────────────────────────────────────────────┤
│  Network Interface:    MACIPXGW01                │
│                                                  │
│  IPX Network Number:  [550          ]            │
│  Frame Type:                                     │
│  Expert Bind Options:                            │
└────────────────────────────────────────────────┘
```

Activating the Gateway   Press Esc to return to INETCFG's menu, and press Esc again to exit the NLM. Then activate the new settings that you created by typing REINITIALIZE SYSTEM from the console prompt and pressing Enter.

Now you're ready to log in to Novell Directory Services from your Macintosh, as covered in the next section.

Logging In to NDS Using the Chooser

If you loaded NetWare for Macintosh onto your server, you don't have to use the tree icon to log in. You can use the Chooser. You will follow steps similar to the steps you used to connect to an individual server as described in the earlier section "Logging In to a NetWare Server Using AppleShare."

1. Pull down the Apple menu and select Chooser. The Chooser window appears (refer to Figure 23.35).
2. Make sure that the AppleTalk Active radio button is selected (in the lower-right corner) and then click the AppleShare icon.

   After you click the AppleShare icon, a list of servers appears in the box on the right and, if you are on a multiple-zone network, a list of zones appears in the lower-left box. When you select a zone, the servers list changes to display the servers in the selected zone.
3. If necessary, choose the zone in which your NetWare server is located.
4. Highlight the name of the server. A dialog box prompts you to enter your name and password. If you select the Log In to Novell Directory Services check box, you can log in to the directory tree instead of the selected server. If you don't select the Directory Services check box, you are using Bindery Emulation.
5. Enter your login name in the Name text box and your password in the Password text box, then click OK.

6. A list of server volumes appears. Highlight the volumes you want to appear as file drawers on the desktop.

FIG. 23.35
The Chooser displays a list of servers communicating over AppleTalk.

NOTE   You cannot automatically mount volumes at startup as you can when you log in with AppleShare. You need to use aliases, which provide a capability similar to automatic volume mounting at startup.

7. After you choose the volumes you want displayed, click OK or press Enter.

8. Close the Chooser after you finish logging in.

If you want to connect to a server and mount a volume after you log in to the directory tree, you can use Chooser. Start Chooser and select the server as you usually do. If the server is part of the directory tree and you are using the Encrypted NetWare login method, you aren't prompted to log in to the server. Instead, you're automatically connected. You don't have to enter a separate login name and password to connect to the server and use its volumes.

Using a NetWare Print Spooler and Queue

The steps for using a NetWare print spooler are similar to steps used to log in or connect to a normal AppleTalk printer.

Pull down the Apple menu and select Chooser. Make sure that the AppleTalk setting is Active, and then click the icon for the type of printer with which the spooler is associated. If needed, from the zone list in the lower-left corner, choose the zone for the NetWare server that stores the print queue. (If you aren't on a multizone network, no zone list appears.) A list of print queues for the type of printer you selected appears on the right side of the dialog box (see Figure 23.36). Select the queue to use.

FIG. 23.36

The Chooser will display print spoolers as an available printer.

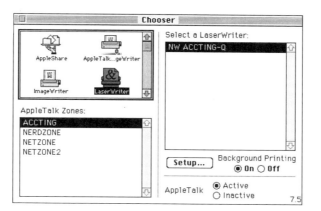

Part

VI

Ch

23

Printing via the NetWare Print Chooser

Now that the NetWare Client for Macintosh OS is up and running, Macintosh users can access LaserWriters—and compatible PostScript printers—that are controlled by the NetWare server. To print to a NetWare print queue from IPX or IP, start the NetWare Directory browser and the NetWare Print Chooser.

Drag a queue or a printer object from the NetWare Directory Browser window to the Set Current Printer To box in the NetWare Print Chooser (see Figure 23.37). The Select a Print Driver window contains a list of the printer drivers installed on your Macintosh (see Figure 23.38). A print driver might be automatically selected for you (based on the current selected Chooser driver). Click More Options to change the print driver. The list of print drivers is the same as the list in the workstation's Chooser.

FIG. 23.37

The NetWare Print Chooser Screen is blank before a queue or printer is chosen.

FIG. 23.38

The Fewer Options button of the NetWare Print Chooser is not available until a print driver is selected.

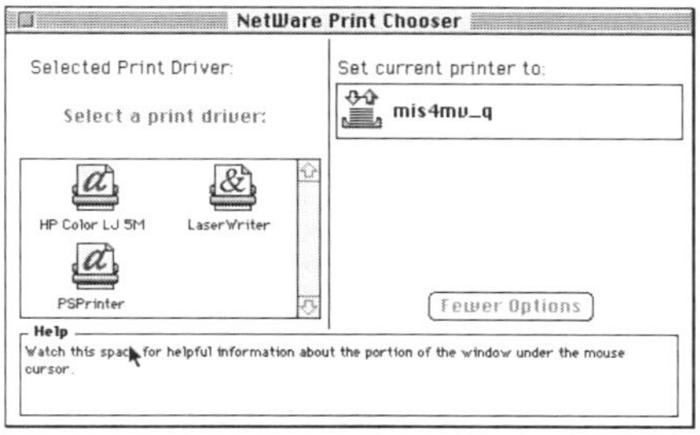

Select a print driver that matches the selected printer. Choose the LaserWriter driver if you do not have a driver for your specific printer. After you select a print driver, the setup button might or might not be visible depending on the print driver chosen (see Figure 23.41).

N O T E   After changing queues, you must re-select the print driver.   ▨

The More Options button is available after you choose a printer driver. Clicking this button brings up a screen where you can configure the NetWare Print Options (see Figure 23.39).

 T I P   To create a shortcut to the Print Chooser screen, double-click a printer or print queue from the NetWare Directory Browser. The NetWare Print Chooser screen automatically starts with your printer or queue already inserted in the Set Current Printer To: box. A printer or queue might also be saved as a Directory Services object to a folder or the desktop like a volume.

FIG. 23.39
You can enable a banner page in the NetWare Print Options screen.

The default settings for printers are Notify When Done and Assume Standard Fonts. If you drag a printer to the printer window, you cannot set any options (see Figure 23.40). Choosing a printer is the same as choosing the printer's default queue (see Figure 23.41).

FIG. 23.40
You cannot change the options if you put a printer object in the NetWare Print Chooser.

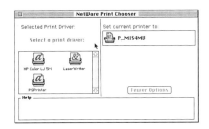

FIG. 23.41
A print driver might require setup.

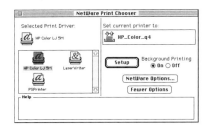

Working with Folder Rights and Attributes

You can view and work with your access privileges to folders and view attribute settings for files and folders in several ways. The File menu's Sharing command shows your access privileges to a folder. The actual folder icon shows the type of access you have, and when you open a folder, two icons show your access levels to files.

Using the File Menu's Sharing Option

If your Macintosh is running System 7, you can use the File menu's Sharing command to view your access rights to a folder or file. Highlight the folder for which you want to view your access rights, then pull down the File menu and choose Sharing. You see a dialog box similar to Figure 23.42.

FIG. 23.42

You can view your access privileges in a folder.

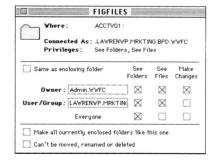

The dialog box provides the following information:

- **Where**—This shows the volume location of the selected folder.
- **Connected As**—This is your login name.
- **Privileges**—This lists your Macintosh privileges. The privileges are See Folders, See Files, and Make Changes. These privileges correspond to these NetWare directory rights:

Macintosh Privilege	NetWare Directory Right
See Folders	You have the CREATE right only, or you have no rights to the folder but have rights to a file or subfolder within the folder.
See Folders, See Files	FILE SCAN only or READ and FILE SCAN.
See Folders, See Files,	READ, WRITE, FILE SCAN, Make Changes and optionally CREATE, ERASE, and MODIFY.

- **Same As Enclosing Folder**—If marked, the folder's privilege settings are inherited from an enclosing folder.
- **Owner**—This shows the name and privilege settings of the user who is the folder owner.

- **User/Group**—This can show a single user object or group that has access privileges. If multiple users or groups have privileges, this box displays Use NetWare Utility.

- **Everyone**—This lists the privileges for the volume's container object.

- **Make All Currently Enclosed Folders Like This One**—This controls whether all subfolders inherit the same privilege settings as the current folder.

- **Can't Be Moved, Renamed or Deleted**—When this check box is selected, the DELETE INHIBIT and RENAME INHIBIT attributes are turned on for the directory.

Understanding Folder Icons

A folder icon can appear in three ways to visually convey the kind of access you have to the folder. A plain folder icon indicates that you can open the folder but you don't have rights to manage access privileges. A folder icon with a black tab indicates that you have rights to manage access privileges. A folder with a strap and arrow indicates that the folder is a "drop box." You have the CREATE right so that you can create new files in the folder, but you don't have rights to view or otherwise work with files that already exist in the folder. Figure 23.43 shows the three types of folder icons.

FIG. 23.43
The three types of folder icons are plain, black tab, and strap with an arrow.

Understanding In-Folder Icons

You also can tell what type of access you have after you open a folder. Two icons appear in the upper left of the folder if you have restricted access privileges. A lined-out pencil appears if you don't have the WRITE NetWare right to the folder. A lined-out file icon appears if you don't have the CREATE right to the folder. Figure 23.44 shows these icons.

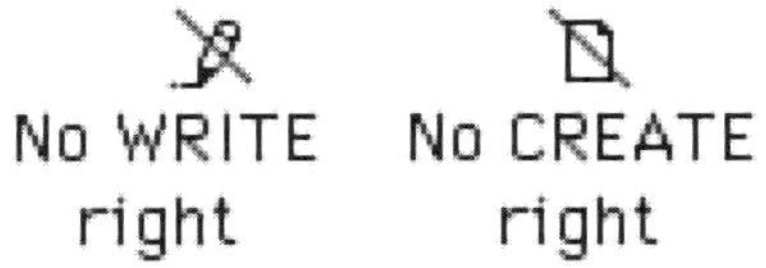

FIG. 23.44
The restricted access icons can appear in the upper-left corner after you open a folder

Turning On File Attributes

You can turn on the READ ONLY, DELETE INHIBIT, and RENAME INHIBIT attributes for a file by highlighting the file icon, pulling down the File menu, and choosing Get Info. In the dialog box that appears, select the Locked check box (make sure that an *X* appears). When you *lock* a file, you turn on the READ ONLY, DELETE INHIBIT, and RENAME INHIBIT attributes.

Removing Macintosh Support

You can use the INSTALL NLM to remove NetWare for Macintosh or NetWare Client for Macintosh OS from a server. Load INSTALL and, from INSTALL's main menu, select Product Options. From the Other Installation Actions menu that appears, choose the View, Configure, Remove Installed Products option. You see a list of currently installed NLM products. Highlight the listing for NetWare for Macintosh or NetWare Client for Macintosh OS and press Delete to remove the files from the server's SYS:SYSTEM directory. You also need to remove all statements in your AUTOEXEC.NCF and STARTUP.NCF files that pertain to Macintosh Support.

Using Remote Console

Remote Console run from the Macintosh is very similar to running RCONSOLE.EXE from a PC. Remote Console is installed using the Custom install option of the NW Client Installer application. After starting the Remote Console application, a list of available servers is displayed. Choose a server and click Connect (see Figure 23.45). You can also choose the Address button to enter an internal IPX number for a specific server. You are prompted for the remote console password. You can have Remote Console sessions open with multiple servers using this application.

FIG. 23.45
Select the server you want to start a Remote Console session with in this window.

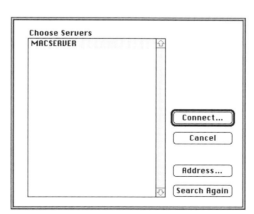

Summary

Macintosh users who are connected to NetWare networks have access to NetWare's full range of services and can store folders and files on server disks with the same ease with which they perform similar tasks on their own hard disks. Apart from learning how to log in to the directory tree, Macintosh users do not have to learn a new way of doing things when they use a NetWare server. Using a shared disk volume on a NetWare server is just like using any AppleShare server, and connecting to a NetWare print queue is just like connecting to an AppleTalk printer.

Thanks to NetWare for Macintosh and IntranetWare Client for Macintosh OS, no reason exists for not fully extending the benefits of networking to your organization's Macintosh users.

Linking PCs and Macintosh workstations on the same network with NetWare is a worthwhile objective. Macintosh and PC users can share files and useful applications, such as e-mail; PC users also can access AppleTalk printers that are linked to NetWare queues. Making this combination available requires that you install NetWare for Macintosh, so you must become familiar with the basics of the AppleTalk communications protocol and how AppleTalk networks are configured. ●

P A R T VII

Upgrading NetWare Communication

CHAPTER 24

Understanding TCP/IP

Apart from the upgraded version of NetWare, the primary selling point of IntranetWare is the collection of TCP/IP services included in the package. All Internet and intranet development efforts revolve around TCP/IP, and although NetWare does not yet use them as its native protocols, the services are well integrated with the operating system, and particularly with Novell Directory Services.

Before you can run any of IntranetWare's TCP/IP services, however, you must install and configure the protocols on your NetWare servers. It also helps to become familiar with the origins of the protocols and the basic concepts underlying their use. ■

The origins of TCP/IP

Novell NetWare has always used IPX/SPX as its native communication protocols, but the language of the Internet is TCP/IP.

The TCP/IP networking stack

TCP/IP consists of protocols that function at various levels of the traditional OSI reference model. These protocols work together to provide whatever quality of service is required for a particular networking task.

Implementing TCP/IP

Support for the TCP/IP protocols can be installed with NetWare 4.11, or you can add it later. To run TCP/IP on your network, you should understand the concepts behind configuration parameters like IP addresses, subnet masks, and default gateway addresses.

Introducing TCP/IP

TCP/IP is an abbreviation for two networking protocols: TCP (Transmission Control Protocol) and IP (Internet Protocol). However, the term has come to be used to represent a whole collection of networking protocols and applications that were developed for use on what eventually became known as the Internet.

TCP/IP began as an experiment by the Advanced Research Projects Agency (ARPA) of the U.S. Department of Defense in the 1970s. The original idea, influenced by the Cold War hysteria of the time, was to build a packet-switching network that had no central point of vulnerability that could be targeted by an enemy. This experiment grew into a nationwide network called ARPANET, which was interconnected with many regional networks, and eventually formed the basis for what we today call the Internet.

Later, the TCP/IP protocols became closely associated with the UNIX operating system, thanks in part to the University of California at Berkeley. UCB released TCP/IP as part of their general UNIX products (known by the name Berkeley Software Development, or BSD). The result was a wide acceptance of TCP/IP as a standard for computer data communications. Today, TCP/IP is the world's most widely used networking protocol suite, and is supported by almost every network operating system available.

The widespread adoption of TCP/IP is due in no small part to several important attributes that were intended as part of the protocol's design from the beginning, such as the following:

■ **Platform independence**—Often associated with UNIX, TCP/IP has been implemented to support communications on almost every type of computer system, including mainframes, minicomputer systems, UNIX host systems, and most microcomputer systems. You can find the TCP/IP protocols implemented on PCs, Apple Macintosh systems, RISC workstations, and many other peripherals and network devices like printers, bridges, routers, hubs, switches, and more.

■ **Open specifications**—Rather than being proprietary protocols that are developed, maintained, and produced by a single vendor, the TCP/IP protocol standards are public documents that have always been developed using a democratic process in which anyone's input is welcome.

■ **Universal identification and absolute addressing**—TCP/IP protocols allow data to be transferred between systems that are not directly connected to each other, often by way of intermediate networks. This requires that each system have a unique address that absolutely identifies both the system and its location. Because the TCP/IP protocols were developed for use on many different platforms, an internal addressing system was needed because no external constants could be assumed.

■ **Scalability**—TCP/IP can be used on both large and small networks. It is robust enough to support the millions of computer systems that are now connected to the Internet, far more than its designers could ever have envisaged, and yet it is simple enough to support communications on small, local area networks with just a few systems.

One of the most fascinating features of TCP/IP is that the protocols are based on a truly open set of standards. No one *owns* the TCP/IP protocols. Rather, they are based on technical specifications contained in a series of documents called Requests for Comment (RFCs).

A group called the Internet Architecture Board (IAB) is responsible for setting Internet standards, and for managing the publication of RFCs. The IAB oversees two groups, the Internet Engineering Task Force (IETF) and the Internet Research Task Force (IRTF). The IETF is responsible for the evolution and coordination of Internet protocols, while the IRTF is responsible for their development. You can access the entire collection of RFCs using a Web or FTP client on many Internet sites, including the Network Information Center (InterNIC) at the following address:

DS.INTERNIC.NET

In the RFC directory at this site, you will find a document called RFC-INDEX.TXT (see Figure 24.1), which is an index of all current RFCs (over 2,000 of them). Most RFCs are plain text documents, although there are some Postscript files in the collection.

Part
VII

Ch
24

FIG. 24.1
RFC-INDEX.TXT contains
descriptions of all of
the available RFCs that
can be viewed online
using a Web browser.

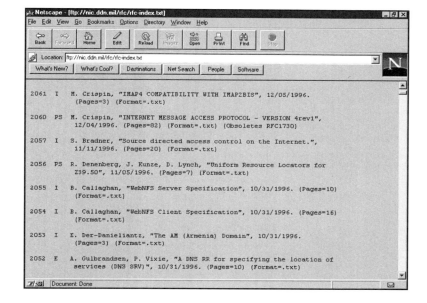

N O T E   RFCs are an extremely diverse collection of documents, ranging from the humorous to the highly technical. However, unlike many other networking standards documents, which are not even approachable by the layman, there is valuable information to be found in the RFCs for network users at any level.

Relative beginners might want to start with such documents as RFC 1118, "The Hitchhiker's Guide to the Internet." The RFC numbers of the documents associated with the various protocols are cited throughout this chapter.

In the world of TCP/IP, computer systems are often referred to as *hosts,* and are identified using a host name or an IP address. However, a host is actually the network interface found in a computer. Some systems have more than one interface, such as a PC with two network cards, and therefore have more than one host, each of which must be identified by its own IP address.

Understanding the DOD Model

It is almost impossible to work in computer networking today without being exposed to the seven-layer OSI reference model for describing communications, as discussed in Chapter 10, "Understanding NetWare Communication." However, most of the protocol stacks in commercial use today do not conform precisely to the boundaries of the seven OSI model layers. This is particularly true of the TCP/IP protocols, many of which were designed in the 1970s, long before the OSI reference model document was ratified.

The TCP/IP protocol stack is based on a four-layer communication model that is often called the Department of Defense model, owing to the historical involvement of the U. S. Department of Defense in the development of the protocols. The DOD model is much simpler than the OSI model most often used in networking today, as you can see in Figure 24.2.

FIG. 24.2

TCP/IP's four-layer DOD model differs significantly from the OSI reference model.

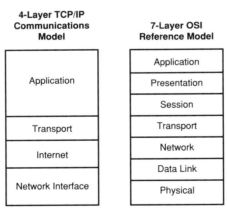

Each of the four layers shown in Figure 24.2 describes a separate part of the network communications process, and each layer interacts with the layers adjacent to it. Requests for access to network resources begin at the Application layer, which communicates directly with the programs and services running on the system. As the request travels down through the stack, each layer adds a header to the data it receives from the layer above, encapsulating the data along with the header into a new packet, and hands it off to the next layer for further processing and preparation. At the bottom of the stack, the completed data packet is sent across the physical medium (for example, the network cable) to the destination system.

The receiving system reverses the process, stripping off the header information at each successive layer and using it to direct the data to the appropriate process on the system. The following sections describe the process in more detail, and discuss the specific protocols running at the various layers.

Application Layer

Application layer protocols communicate with similar applications or services running on other host systems. Some Application layer protocols may actually provide a user interface, like FTP (File Transfer Protocol), which is often implemented as an executable client program. However, many Application layer protocols don't have a user interface, but rather are used to support other programs and provide access to network resources. A good example of this is HTTP (HyperText Transport Protocol), which is used by World Wide Web clients and servers to transfer hypertext documents across a network or the Internet.

Some of the most commonly used Application layer protocols are the following:

- **Telnet**—Provides remote terminal emulation services
- **File Transfer Protocol (FTP)** and **Trivial File Transfer Protocol (TFTP)**—Provide file transfer services
- **Network File System (NFS)**—Provides remote file system access
- **Simple Mail Transfer Protocol (SMTP)**—Provides electronic mail transfer services
- **Simple Network Management Protocol (SNMP)**—Provides network management messaging services

Of the protocols above, Telnet and FTP are often implemented as executable program applications, while the rest are most often used to support other executable programs that require access to network resources.

Application layer protocols function as either the origin or the ultimate destination of TCP/IP communications. However, the Application layer contains none of the mechanisms used to actually transmit data across the network. For these mechanisms, Application layer protocols require the services of other protocols operating at the lower layers to transmit their data to other systems.

A good analogy would be to say that the Application layer generates a properly formatted business letter. Such a letter is useless, however, unless you put it into an envelope with the correct address, and have a postal service to deliver it. The protocols operating at the lower layers provide the addressing, containment, and delivery services needed to get an application request to its destination.

Transport Layer

The Transport layer, sometimes called the Host-to-Host layer, is responsible for supporting end-to-end communications between application programs. Depending on the needs of the application, the Transport layer may provide flow control services, and verify the reliability of communications to ensure that data arrives at its destination without errors and in the proper sequence. This might require the generation of acknowledgments by receiving systems, and the re-transmission of lost packets.

The Transport layer protocol splits the transmitted data stream into small units, or packets. Before passing the data packets on to the Internet layer for transmission, the Transport layer protocol adds a code called a *port number* that identifies the application that generated the data. When receiving data packets, the Transport layer uses that port number to direct the incoming data to the correct application process.

There are two Transport layer protocols, TCP and UDP, that provide different levels of service to the Application layer protocols.

Transmission Control Protocol (TCP)   The Transmission Control Protocol (TCP), which is defined in RFC 793, is connection-based, providing reliable data transmission, sequenced delivery of data, and packet acknowledgment:

- **Connection-oriented**—TCP can be compared to making a telephone call. Before sending any data to the destination, TCP establishes a session, or *virtual circuit,* between the two computers, to ensure that the destination system is operational, and ready to receive data.

- **Packet acknowledgment**—When sending a packets to a remote system, the sending system expects to receive periodic acknowledgments indicating that data packets have been properly received. If the acknowledgments are not received on a timely basis, the sending computer assumes that the packet transmission has failed and re-transmits it.

- **Sequenced delivery**—Because applications frequently send more data than can be included in a single data packet, TCP splits the data into manageable segments before handing them off to the Internet layer. Each data packet that is sent using TCP has a sequence number included as part of its TCP header, which is used both for acknowledgment and reassembly of the received data segments into the proper sequence.

- **Reliable Transmission**—The TCP protocol includes a checksum in the header that it adds to each data packet. The checksum is used by the receiving system to verify that the packet has not been corrupted or damaged in transit.

An additional feature of the TCP protocol is known as *sliding window*, which enables the transmission of multiple data packets without waiting for acknowledgments before sending the next one. Acknowledgment is still required, but it doesn't have to be received before subsequent packets can be sent. Sliding window technology provides a big improvement in performance, especially across wide area networks and other fairly slow links.

Because Application layer protocols that use TCP for transport are session-oriented, they are usually characterized by requiring an authentication process. Some TCP-based Application layer protocols and their port numbers are as follows:

Description	Port
FTP	21
Telnet	23
SMTP	25
HTTP	80
DNS	53

The source and destination port numbers, sequence number, checksum, and other information are all added to each data packet as the TCP header and passed down to the Internet layer for further processing.

User Datagram Protocol (UDP)   The other Transport layer protocol is the User Datagram Protocol (UDP), defined in RFC 768, which is connectionless, does not provide reliable data transmission or sequenced delivery, and does not acknowledge individual packets. Applications and processes that use UDP usually provide some sort of reliability and acknowledgment at the Application layer, making it unnecessary here. In many cases, UDP is employed for message types that consist of only one packet exchange between the source and destination, while TCP is more likely to be used for the transmission of larger quantities of data, such as file transfers.

Most application layer protocols are designed to use either TCP or UDP. For example, FTP is a TCP-based file transfer protocol, while TFTP (the Trivial File Transfer Protocol) provides file transfer services using UDP. A few protocols, however, such as DNS, can use either TCP or UDP, as needed. UDP's attributes are defined as follows:

- **Connectionless**—Applications that use UDP do not establish an end-to-end virtual circuit. Instead, UDP-based applications send their data across the network without checking to see if the destination system is available or able to receive the data being sent.

- **Unreliable**—Something of a misnomer, it is more accurate to say that UDP provides no guarantee of reliability. In most cases, the protocol can be counted upon to transmit data successfully.

- **Non-sequenced**—UDP does not provide sequencing information, so it is possible for data packets to arrive at their destination out of order. It is left up to the application to verify the accuracy of the transmitted data.

- **No acknowledgment**—UDP does not provide acknowledgments itself, so receipt verification is left up to the application that uses UDP as its transport.

UDP communications take place between ports, except that the port numbers themselves are considered separately from those used by TCP. Some of the more frequently used applications and their UDP port numbers are as follows:

Port Number	Application	Description
15	NETSTAT	Network Status
53	DOMAIN	Domain Name Server
67	BOOTPS	Bootstrap Protocol Server
68	BOOTPC	Bootstrap Protocol Client
69	TFTP	Trivial File Transfer Protocol
161	SNMP	Simple Network Management Protocol

N O T E Port numbers for the standard Application layer processes are defined in RFC 1700, "Assigned Numbers," which makes several earlier versions of the document obsolete—such as RFCs 1340 and 1060. Although it is not required that an application use the port number specified in the document in order to operate, most TCP/IP software products use them by default, and require custom configuration to change them. On most computers, the port numbers used by default are defined in a text file called SERVICES. ▓

No matter whether the Application layer protocol uses TCP or UDP at the Transport layer, a header is added to each packet. The header includes the information that will be needed at the receiving system to pass the data to the proper application for processing. Figure 24.3 shows how the Transport Layer adds a header to the message sent by the Application.

FIG. 24.3
Each TCP/IP protocol adds its own header to every packet before transmission.

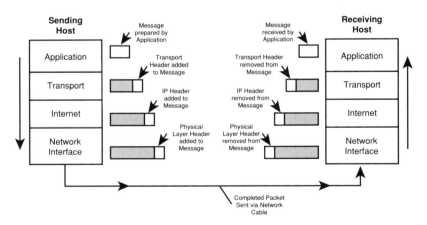

The primary difference between TCP and UDP is the amount of control traffic that is needed to implement each protocol. The TCP header, which can be up to 24 bytes in size, is much larger than that of UDP, which is only eight. TCP also requires the transmission of many more packets than are needed to carry the transmitted data. Establishing and breaking down sessions and acknowledging packets both add significantly to the overhead of a connection-oriented, reliable protocol.

TCP, therefore, is used only when its additional services are needed. One of the basic concepts that guided the design of the TCP/IP protocols is to establish a *quality of service* level for each task, and to provide a combination of protocols that meets that level, without exceeding it unnecessarily.

Internet Layer

The Internet layer is the focus of the entire TCP/IP protocol suite, because this layer implements IP, the Internet Protocol, which is responsible for many of the most crucial aspects of network data communications. IP is the protocol that is responsible for the successful transmission of data from one system to another.

In most cases, TCP/IP protocols are used to send data to systems located on other networks. This means that the packets must pass through intermediate systems on the way to their destination. In the case of Internet communications, data can pass through dozens of different routers during a transmission.

Lower-level protocols, like Ethernet and token ring, are unaware of these concepts; they are concerned only with transmitting to the next system down the line. Transport layer protocols are concerned with directing data to the correct service, once it has arrived at its destination. It is IP that bears the brunt of the responsibility for seeing that the data is routed through the intermediate systems to its ultimate destination.

The basic tool used to direct the data is the IP address, which is applied to every packet processed by the Internet layer. Every host on a TCP/IP network must have a unique 32-bit IP address that identifies both the network on which the system is located, and the specific host on that network.

N O T E The two basic TCP/IP addressing standards, the IP address and the port number, are referred to in combination as a *socket*. The specification of a socket is usually all that is needed to get a message to a specific process on a designated TCP/IP system.

IP is also responsible for packaging the data received from the Transport layer into units, called datagrams, of the appropriate size for the network type to be used. Ethernet, for example, limits its frames to about 1,500 bytes, while the maximum size of a token-ring frame may be as high as 4,200 bytes. IP is responsible for detecting the Maximum Transfer Unit (MTU), or maximum size, supported by the physical medium. Based on the MTU, the Internet layer may need to split a packet into multiple fragments before handing them over to the network interface for transmission. As the packets traverse various network segments on the way to their destination, further fragmentation may occur to accommodate the local conditions.

The Internet layer at the destination system is then responsible for reassembling the fragments into the proper order. When processing a packet for transmission, the Internet Layer adds an IP header containing the source and destination IP addresses, fragmentation control information, a protocol field that identifies which high-level protocol created the message and other information, and encapsulates the packet and IP header. The Internet layer then hands the completed packet off to the network interface for transmission.

Receiving host systems use the IP header information to decide whether the data should be processed by the local machine, or forwarded to another host system. This routing of datagrams can carry data across your local network or around the world, by passing packets from system to system.

Network Interface Layer

The TCP/IP standards do not define protocols for the actual interface of the computer and the network medium. The protocols are designed to be used with virtually any networking platform and on NetWare LANs, which means Ethernet or token ring most of the time. When used with TCP/IP, and Ethernet or token-ring protocol accepts packets from the Internet layer, adds a header containing the source and destination interface hardware addresses, prepares the packet in the proper format for the type of network being used, and transmits the completed packet as signals across the physical medium.

One of the most important aspects of TCP/IP's Network Interface layer is the way that it handles the hardware addressing that is needed to transmit data over an Ethernet or token-ring network. The software driver for the network interface adapter knows the hardware address that is coded into the adapter, which it uses for the source address when building the physical frame for transmission. In order to complete the frame, the IP address passed down from the Internet layer must be used to discover the hardware address of the destination system's interface.

IP addresses are deliberately kept separate from hardware addresses, because the TCP/IP protocols can be used on systems that employ many different hardware addressing standards. It is at the Network Interface layer, however, that a relationship between IP addresses and hardware addresses must be established. There are, therefore, a number of Network Interface protocols used to resolve IP addresses to the local hardware addressing standard.

On PC networks, the most commonly used Network Interface protocol is ARP, the Address Resolution Protocol. When a system must transmit data to a specific IP address, it first broadcasts an ARP packet containing the IP address to the local network segment. The system holding that address then responds with an ARP reply packet that contains the hardware address of the network interface. On an Ethernet or token-ring PC, this is the MAC address that is hard-coded into every network interface adapter.

This MAC address is then used to transmit the data packet over the physical medium. The MAC is also stored in an ARP cache on the transmitting system, which prevents redundant ARP broadcasts.

ARP is the most commonly known Network Interface protocol, because it is used on PC-based networks. Its purpose, however, is only to get the data to the next intermediate system. As data packets are passed from router to router, they may be transmitted over many different network types, especially on the Internet. Each network type has its own way of identifying the network interface, and therefore can use a particular protocol to transmit over the physical medium.

TCP/IP Addressing and Routing

The most important aspects of TCP/IP for the network administrator are the concepts of IP addressing and routing. These functions are provided on your NetWare servers by Novell's TCP/IP Transport module.

Every host on an internetwork must have a unique IP address. Otherwise, reliable communication is impossible. IP addresses uniquely identify the network and the individual node address of every host and network interface on an internetwork; a computer, especially a server, may have multiple interfaces that are connected to various networks or subnets. You will not be able to design and manage TCP/IP-based internetworks without first understanding IP addressing.

Understanding IP Address Structure and Notation

IP addresses are 32-bit numbers, expressed in binary notation. But because most people don't find it very easy to read, remember, or manipulate long strings of ones and zeroes, IP addresses are most often represented by splitting them into four *octets* (an octet is eight bits), expressed as decimal numbers, separated by periods. This is known as *dotted decimal* notation. Here is an example IP address, expressed as a 32-bit binary number:

```
1 0 0 0 0 0 1 0 0 0 1 1 1 0 0 1 0 1 1 0 0 1 0 1 0 0 0 0 0 0 1 0
```

Here is the same number, split into four octets of binary numbers, and converted into dotted decimal notation:

```
Binary  = 1 0 0 0 0 0 1 0 . 0 0 1 1 1 0 0 1 . 0 1 1 0 0 1 0 1 . 0 0 0 0 0 0 1 0
Decimal =      130         .       57        .      101        .       2
```

So the dotted decimal representation is 130.57.101.2.

 TIP If binary numbers are not your strong suit, you're not alone. There are several easy ways to convert binary numbers to decimals. Perhaps the easiest of all is the Calculator applet that's included with Microsoft Windows, in Scientific mode.

IP Address Classes

An IP address identifies both the network address and the unique node address of every host computer system on an internetwork. This is accomplished by splitting a host system's IP address into a network address component and a node address component, based on the TCP/IP standards outlined in the RFCs. The RFCs define several classes of IP address, three of which are of interest to network administrators. Each class splits the address into network and node components differently, as shown in Figure 24.4.

FIG. 24.4

IP addresses are assigned based on three classes defined in the TCP/IP standards.

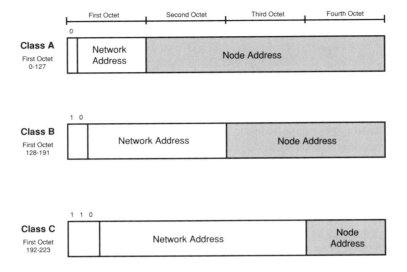

Class A Addresses   In its binary form, the first bit of a Class A IP address is always zero. The first eight bits comprise the network portion of the address, and the remaining 24 bits identify the host on that network. In decimal notation, the first octet represents the network address, which can have a value of 0 to 127, and the remaining octets represent the node address.

Class B Addresses   The first two bits of a Class B address are always one and zero. The first 16 bits make up the network portion of the address, and the remaining 16 bits define the host address. In decimal form, the first two octets represent the network address, and the remaining two octets represent the host. The decimal value of the first octet is in the range of 128 to 191 (because of the initial 01).

Class C Addresses   The first three bits of a Class C address are always one, one, and zero. The first 24 bits comprise the network portion of the address, and the remaining eight bits define the host address. In decimal form, the first three octets represent the network address, and the remaining octet represents the node address. The decimal value of the first octet can range from 192 to 223.

Class D and E Addresses   Class D and E addresses are not available for use as host addresses, although they are defined in the RFCs. Class D addresses are reserved for a special function called multicasting, while Class E addresses are reserved for future use. The values of the first four bits of a Class D address are 1110, and the decimal value of the first octet is in the range of 224 to 239. The values of the first five bits of a Class E address are 11110, and the decimal value of the first octet is in the range of 240 to 247.

Reserved Addresses   Certain IP addresses are also reserved for other special functions. The following are several specific examples:

    ■ An address consisting of all ones (binary: 11111111 11111111 11111111 11111111, or decimal: 255.255.255.255) is reserved for use as a broadcast, and cannot be assigned as a node address. The broadcast address is very important for TCP/IP protocols, such as BOOTP and DHCP, as you will see in Chapter 26, "Using the Dynamic Host Configuration Protocol (DHCP) Server."

- The node address portion of an IP address may not consist of all ones (in binary form) or use the decimal value 255 for the host address octets, as this address is reserved for use as a local network broadcast. For example, a Class C address of 200.203.192.255 cannot be assigned as a node address because the fourth octet consists of all ones (binary: 11111111).

- The node address portion of an IP address may not consist of all zeroes. Some early TCP/IP systems used addresses consisting of all zeroes for broadcast messages. For example, you should not assign the Class B address of 148.101.0.0 as a node address because the third and fourth octets are all zeroes (binary: 00000000 00000000).

- The Class A network address 127.0.0.0 is reserved for the *loopback* function, and cannot be assigned to a network. The loopback address is one that causes a system to address packets to itself.

Network Sizes On a private network, you can theoretically use any IP addresses that you want, as long as each host is unique. However, a collection of IP address have been allocated specifically for use by private networks. These addresses are as follows:

Class A	10.0.0.0 through 10.255.255.255
Class B	172.16.0.0 through 172.31.255.255
Class C	192.168.0.0 through 192.168.255.255

In order to place TCP/IP systems on the Internet, however, they must have IP addresses that have been registered with InterNIC to prevent duplication. Each network class has limits on how many networks and nodes may be defined within that class. The class of the addresses that you register depends on the number of systems in your organization (and on the availability of the addresses). The classes are as follows:

- **Class A**—A Class A network uses the first eight bits of the IP address for the network address. This leaves 24 bits for host addresses, allowing for the existence of only 126 Class A networks, each containing 16,777,314 possible hosts.

  As you may expect, all of the possible Class A IP addresses have long since been registered by large organizations. Some of these are Internet service providers (ISPs), however, that make a business of "subletting" addresses to their customers.

- **Class B**—A Class B network uses the first 16 bits of the IP address for the network address. (The first two bits are always 10, so 14 bits actually determine the network address.) That leaves the final 16 bits for use as node addresses, allowing for 16,384 possible networks of 65,534 hosts each.

  Virtually all of the possible Class B Internet addresses have been registered by large organizations as well.

- **Class C**—A Class C network uses the first 24 bits of the IP address for the network address (the first three bits are always 110, so only 21 bits actually determine the

Part
VII

Ch
24

network address). That leaves the final eight bits for use as node addresses, allowing only 254 possible hosts on each of 2,097,151 Class C networks.

Because there are virtually no Class A or B Internet addresses available any longer, the only addresses available to most organizations today are Class C. These addresses are also being used up at a phenomenal pace, raising the possibility that the Internet may run out of available addresses in the near future.

Table 24.1 shows the relationship between the number of possible networks for each class, and the number of possible hosts.

Table 24.1 IP Address Classes

Class	Subnet Mask	No. of Networks	No. of Hosts	First Octet
Class A	255.0.0.0	126	16,777,214	1–126
Class B	255.255.0.0	16,384	65,534	128–191
Class C	255.255.255.0	2,097,151	254	192–223

Direct connection to the Internet brings with it some important security issues, the most important of which is the fact that your computer systems are directly accessible to anyone around the world with a computer and an Internet connection. There are several security options open to you, each with its own unique set of costs and benefits, as described in the following sections.

Firewalls A firewall is a specialized computer software package that sits between your network and the Internet (or between any two networks where a security barrier is needed). Firewalls are the most powerful security tool available to protect your network, but can cost as much as $20,000 plus hardware and configuration.

Features vary, but firewalls generally function as a filter between the networks, blocking selected traffic based on network addresses, TCP or UDP port numbers, time of day, or other criteria. You can, for example, protect your network by allowing internal traffic to pass out to the Internet, and limiting the types of traffic that are allowed in.

Proxy Servers A proxy server enables you to connect your network to the Internet, but instead of using registered Internet addresses for your users, you create a private addressing scheme instead. The proxy server acts as a buffer between your private IP addressing scheme and the Internet. Instead of users connecting their Web browsers directly to a site on the Internet, they connect to the proxy server, which in turn communicates with the outside world. This way, the only system that can possibly be accessed from outside the local network is the proxy server itself.

IPX/IP Gateway IntranetWare includes Novell's IPX/IP Gateway product (see Chapter 27, "Using the IPX/IP Gateway"), which enables users to access TCP/IP-based services without having to load, manage, and maintain TCP/IP stacks on every workstation. Instead of the

TCP/IP protocols, workstations use IPX to communicate with a NetWare server; the server translates IPX to IP. The gateway, therefore, operates something like a proxy server, except that the internal network traffic uses the IPX protocols only. Security is enhanced because you don't have TCP/IP running throughout your network.

Understanding Subnet Masks

One of the most misunderstood parts of any TCP/IP configuration is the subnet mask, which looks like an IP address, but which actually performs another function. Very simply, the subnet mask is used to specify which part of a system's IP address identifies the network and which part identifies the host. Like an IP address, the subnet mask is also a 32-bit binary number that is usually expressed in dotted decimal notation.

The function of a subnet mask, however, is more easily understood when you consider its value in binary form. Digits with a value of one identify the corresponding digit in the IP address as belonging to the network address. Digits with a value of zero identify the corresponding digit in the IP address as belonging to the host address. For example, the 32-bit subnet mask

```
1 1 1 1 1 1 1 1    1 1 1 1 1 1 1 1    0 0 0 0 0 0 0 0    0 0 0 0 0 0 0 0
```

which can also be written as

```
255.255.0.0
```

specifies that the first two octets of the IP address represent the network, and the final two octets the host. If you apply this subnet mask to the IP address 130.57.101.2, it means that the system's network address is 130.57.0.0, and the host address is 0.0.101.2.

Default Subnet Masks   If you consider the IP address classes discussed earlier, the need for a subnet mask should become clear. How are systems to know the difference between the classes, if there is no means to identify the dividing line between the network and host addresses? The subnet masks for the standard IP address classes are as follows:

- **Class A**—The first octet of a Class A address is the network address, so the default subnet mask of a Class A Internet address is 255.0.0.0.

- **Class B**—The first two octets of a Class B Internet address are the network address, so the default subnet mask of a Class B address is 255.255.0.0.

- **Class C**—The first three octets of a Class C address are the network address, so the default subnet mask of a Class C Internet address is 255.255.255.0.

N O T E   The NetWare installation program is unusual in that it requires subnet masks to be expressed using hexadecimal values. The hexadecimal equivalent to the decimal value 255 is FF, resulting in a default Class C subnet mask of FF.FF.FF.0. ▨

Subnetting   In most circumstances, your network will have one of the default subnet masks specified in the previous section. However, sometimes you may find that a single TCP/IP network must be split into one or more smaller *subnetworks*, or *subnets*. You might do this for several reasons:

■ **Different Media**—It may not be possible to connect all nodes to a single network cable, especially if the nodes are far apart or connected to different media.

■ **Congestion**—The more nodes you have on your network, the more traffic you will have. It is often convenient to split a single large network into smaller subnetworks in order to reduce congestion and make more bandwidth available to individual nodes.

■ **Security**—In a broadcast medium like Ethernet where every node on a network has access to all data packets transmitted over that network, you may want to isolate sensitive data by creating smaller subnetworks.

If you have registered a Class B network address, the subnetting process is relatively easy. You can simply extend the subnet mask beyond the Class B network default of 16 bits (255.255.0.0), changing it to 255.255.255.0 for all nodes on the network. You can then use the third octet to identify your subnets, leaving the fourth for your host addresses. The result is that you can subdivide a Class B network into 254 subnets, each having 254 possible hosts.

In the real world, however, it is much more likely that you will have to subnet a Class C address, using a technique called *partial octet subnetting*. The previous example used the entire third octet of the IP address as the subnet address. Consider instead the case of a Class C network address that uses a default subnet mask of 255.255.255.0, which leaves only the last octet for the node address.

Using partial octet subnetting, you can use some of the bits from the fourth octet as the subnet address, effectively "robbing" them from the node address. This is most easily understood by expressing the subnet mask values using binary notation. If you apply a subnet mask of 255.255.255.192 to a Class C address, you are specifying the binary value 11000000 for the fourth octet, instead of 00000000, as shown:

```
255.255.255.192 = 11111111.11111111.11111111.11000000
```

The first two bits of the fourth octet, therefore, can be used to specify the network address of a subnet.

Compare the following addresses and see if they have the same subnet address:

```
Subnet Mask
255.255.255.192:    1 1 1 1 1 1 1 1   1 1 1 1 1 1 1 1   1 1 1 1 1 1 1 1   1 1   0 0
➥0 0 0 0
IP Addresses
200.200.200.129:    1 1 0 0 1 0 0 0   1 1 0 0 1 0 0 0   1 1 0 0 1 0 0 0   1 0   0 0
➥0 0 0 1
200.200.200.152:    1 1 0 0 1 0 0 0   1 1 0 0 1 0 0 0   1 1 0 0 1 0 0 0   1 0   0 1
➥1 0 0 0
200.200.200.68:     1 1 0 0 1 0 0 0   1 1 0 0 1 0 0 0   1 1 0 0 1 0 0 0   0 1   0 0
➥0 1 0 0
200.200.200.201:    1 1 0 0 1 0 0 0   1 1 0 0 1 0 0 0   1 1 0 0 1 0 0 0   1 1   0 0
➥1 0 0 1
```

Note that in binary form, the first two bits of the fourth octet are clearly the same in the first two addresses (200.200.200.129 and 200.200.200.152). These two hosts are on the same subnetwork. The other two addresses have different values for the same two bits, indicating that they represent hosts that are on different subnets.

The subnet mask is a critical parameter, required for proper configuration of a TCP/IP host system. Without it, or with an incorrect subnet mask, a host system may not be able to communicate reliably with other systems on the same or on remote networks. As a rule, the subnet mask should be the same for all systems within a given IP network.

Routing

You have seen that each IP address uniquely identifies both a TCP/IP host and the network on which the host is located. When a system needs to send data to a host located on another network, it must use a process called *routing*, provided by an intermediate system called a *router*. When preparing a packet for transmission, the Internet layer of the DOD model compares the network portion of the destination IP address with the network portion of its own IP address. If both systems have the same network address, they must be connected to the same physical network and can communicate directly on that network. Packets will be sent directly to the destination system's interface.

If the destination IP address is not on the same network, then the packet cannot be sent directly to the destination. It must be sent by way of a router instead. Most networks will have at least one router connected to them that provides an interface to other networks. The IP address of that router is a critical part of any TCP/IP system's configuration information, because the *default router* or *default gateway* is where a host system will send data packets when the destination address is not located on the local network.

From a hardware perspective, a router can be a dedicated device or a standard computer. Any NetWare server with two or more network interfaces, for example, functions as a router. In TCP/IP parlance, a router is often referred to as an intermediate system. When TCP/IP traffic passes through an intermediate system, it travels no higher up the protocol stack that the Internet layer. IP is responsible for reading the source and destination IP addresses and determining if the packet is to be processed by the local machine (in which case it is passed up to the Transport layer), or re-addressed and passed on to another system.

The router also determines whether a packet can be passed on directly to its destination, or must be transmitted through another intermediate system. In order to make these decisions, every router must be aware of all of the systems on the networks to which it is attached.

Routing Tables Routers build and maintain internal lists of network addresses, called *routing tables*. The entries in these routing tables usually consist of a destination network address, the IP address of the intermediate system that provides the best path to the destination (the *next hop*), and some information about how far away the destination network is (a *metric*). There are two types of routing table entries:

- **Static**—These routes are manually configured and maintained by the network administrator.
- **Dynamic**—The router learns about these routes by trading messages with other routers, using a *routing protocol*. The most commonly implemented routing protocol for most internetworks is RIP, or the Routing Information Protocol. Several other routing

protocols are widely implemented, including ICMP (the Internet Control Message Protocol), OSPF (Open Shortest Path First) and EGP (the Exterior Gateway Protocol).

ICMP is widely used on TCP/IP networks to keep dynamic routing tables up to date. When a host forwards an IP packet to a router, and that router knows of a shorter or faster route to the destination, the router will send an *ICMP redirect* packet to the host, informing it of the shorter route. Routers also use ICMP to exchange error messages.

Novell's Multiprotocol Router (MPR), which is included in the IntranetWare package, supports IP routing using the RIP, ICMP, OSPF, and EGP routing protocols (see Chapter 28, "Using the Multiprotocol Router").

Routing and the Internet   Routing data across many different network types is an essential part of Internet communications. With literally millions of computers on thousands of interconnected networks, the Internet is based on the concept of routing. Network administrators that are familiar with the constraints of Ethernet and token-ring networks may be amazed to discover that rather being limited to 3 or 4 routers between source and destination systems, Internet traffic can often pass through 20 to 30 routers before arriving at its destination.

The Internet is also the best example of the scaleability of TCP/IP. No one who worked on the protocol designs in the 1970s could possibly have imagined the explosive growth in usage that the Internet has undergone in recent years, and yet the protocols have held up remarkably well. Some of the more finite aspects of the TCP/IP standards, such as the 32-bit IP address size, will have to be modified as the Internet grows even larger, but the communications protocols themselves have continued to perform well under conditions that have come to far exceed the design limits.

Names and Name Resolution

Most people find it far easier to remember names than addresses, which explains why the TCP/IP community developed the concept of assigning host names to computer systems. In fact, host and domain names exist solely for the purpose of human convenience; the protocols themselves use IP addresses to identify other systems. When you specify a host name in a Web browser, for example, the first part of the connection process is the conversion of the name into an IP address. Then, the address is used to contact the desired system.

As a result of this practice, there must be mechanisms to translate host names into IP addresses. This process is called name resolution, and there are several tools that computer systems use to resolve the host names that people prefer into addresses that the communication protocols can use.

TCP/IP systems rely on two basic methods for resolving host names into IP addresses (which are discussed in the following sections):

- The HOSTS file
- The Domain Name Service

Using the HOSTS file   A HOSTS file is nothing more than an ASCII text file containing host names and their equivalent IP addresses that is stored on a TCP/IP system. On a NetWare server, HOSTS is stored in the SYS:ETC directory. The general format of the file is simple. Each line contains an IP address (usually entered in dotted decimal notation), followed by the host name that you want to assign that computer system, as well as any additional aliases you might want to use. The pound sign (#) indicates the beginning of a comment; anything after it is ignored when performing name resolution. Here is a sample segment of a HOSTS file:

```
# Mappings of host names and host aliases to IP addresses
127.0.0.1     loopback   lb   localhost        # normal loopback address

# Examples from Novell's network
130.57.4.2     ta    tahiti   ta.novell.com    loghost
130.57.6.40    osd-frog    frog
```

With this SYS:ETC\HOSTS file in place on your server, you can specify the host name "tahiti" in a TCP/IP application. The name resolution process would look up "tahiti" in the HOSTS file, and replace the host name you provided with the matching IP address, that is, 130.57.4.2.

The problem with HOSTS files is that they must be individually maintained on all of your computer systems, which can be extremely time-consuming.

Domain Name Service   The Domain Name Service, or DNS, consists of a database of host names and IP addresses that can be distributed among many different servers, and an Application layer protocol that allows those servers to exchange information. On the Internet, thousands of DNS servers each maintain the name and address information for their local networks. The DNS protocol allows a name resolution request that can't be satisfied by a local server to be passed up through a hierarchy of other servers until the proper DNS system is located.

IntranetWare includes a DNS server that you can use on your organization's intranet, or integrate into the DNS structure used on the Internet.

DNS is organized in an inverted tree structure, beginning with the *root* or *core* servers located at the top of the tree (see Figure 24.5). All of the domain names representing TCP/IP networks flow downwards from these servers. Domain names are written with the lowest level at the left and the highest level at the right, with each level separated by a period. A host system, for example, named "www" that resides in the "novell" subdomain of the "com" domain is fully described as **www.novell.com**.

There are six top-level domains that form the roots of the tree, each of which is designated for a different type of organization, based on the organization's primary function. These domains are as follows:

- **mil**—Reserved for use by U. S. military
- **gov**—Reserved for use by U. S. government organizations
- **edu**—For use by colleges and universities
- **com**—Commercial organizations, companies

Part VII
Ch
24

- **org**—Non-commercial and non-profit organizations
- **net**—Networks and Internet service providers

FIG. 24.5

The DNS tree flows downward from the core servers representing the top-level domains.

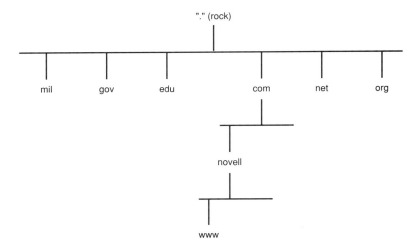

Host system "www.novell.com" in the DNS tree

Most, but not all, of the hosts using these six top-level domains are located within the U.S. Outside of the U.S., top-level domains are based on two-letter abbreviations of country names. Some examples are as follows:

- **CA**—Canada
- **DE**—Germany
- **IT**—Italy
- **UK**—England
- **US**—United States

N O T E Even more than IP addresses, effective names in the COM domain are becoming increasingly scarce. As a result, several different organizations are promoting the use of new top-level domains within the United States, such as *US.*

Beneath the top-level domains are subdomains that represent specific networks. Just as companies and other organizations register their IP addresses, they must also register their domain names. Once a company registers a domain name, the core servers representing the top-level domains are updated with the addresses of that company's DNS servers. A registered domain name can then be divided into as many subdomains as are needed.

For example, if you were to register the domain name mycorp.com, you could then create subdomains for each of your company's branch offices, such as NY.mycorp.com and LA.mycorp.com. Registering a domain name is a simple process that can be performed by filling out a form at InterNIC's Web site at **http://www.internic.net**. In most cases, the hardest part of the process is coming up with a good domain name that hasn't already been taken. If your network is not connected to the Internet, you can still use DNS internally, with no restrictions on how you use and implement host and domain names.

Individual network administrators are also responsible for assigning host names to individual systems. A host name is simply another word that is prepended to the domain name of the network on which the system is located. Although there are a few standard conventions for host names—such as *www* for Web servers and *ftp* for FTP servers—the administrators of a domain can use any host names they want.

When an Internet client program attempts to resolve a host name, it first contacts the DNS servers specified in the workstation configuration. If these servers do not know the IP address of the requested host, they pass the request up through the domain hierarchy, until it reaches one of the core servers for the top-level domain.

The core server supplies the address of the DNS servers responsible for maintaining the information about the desired domain. These are called the authoritative servers for that domain. The client can then send its request directly to the authoritative server, which responds with the correct IP address.

Thus, there is no single server anywhere on the Internet that contains the IP addresses for all available hosts. DNS is a true distributed database, in which every server must play its part to keep the system running smoothly.

Implementing TCP/IP

Before you can use any of the TCP/IP services included with IntranetWare, you must load and configure the TCP/IP protocols on your NetWare servers. You can do this in three ways:

- During the installation of NetWare
- Using LOAD and BIND commands at the server console prompt
- Using the INETCFG.NLM utility

Each of these methods has advantages and disadvantages. You may well end up using a combination of methods, depending on your needs and the complexity of your installation.

Configuring TCP/IP During the IntranetWare Installation

During an IntranetWare *Custom* installation, you are prompted to install and configure TCP/IP services during the process of selecting LAN driver protocols. However, you are able to set only a minimal number of configuration parameters at this time, as the installation process enables you to specify an IP address and a subnet mask for each interface in the server, and nothing more. This should enable your server to connect to the network using TCP/IP, but any other configuration parameters that you need for your server, such as routing parameters and additional IP addresses, will have to be configured later using another utility, such as INETCFG.NLM.

At the end of the server installation process, you will also have the option to Configure Network Protocols, which actually loads and runs the INETCFG.NLM utility. This is discussed later in this chapter in "Using INETCFG.NLM to Configure TCP/IP."

Configuring TCP/IP with *LOAD* and *BIND* Commands

For relatively simple NetWare installations, you can install and configure TCP/IP on your server with a few basic commands. After issuing the necessary LOAD and BIND commands manually from the server console, or you can automate the commands by adding them to the server's AUTOEXEC.NCF file.

The sequence of the commands is important, as TCP/IP services will not work properly if they are issued out of order. There are three general steps that you must take to load and configure TCP/IP on a NetWare server.

1. Load the TCPIP.NLM module.
2. Load the driver for your LAN adapter, using a frame type compatible with TCP/IP.
3. Bind the IP protocol to the LAN adapter driver.

Loading the TCPIP.NLM Module The first step is to load the TCPIP.NLM module on the server, using the proper parameters. It is important to know the default values so that you get the services you expect when you load the TCP/IP transport module. The two major options you should consider are support for RIP (the Routing Information Protocol), and enabling IP routing on your server. By default, RIP is enabled and IP routing is disabled when you load TCPIP.NLM with no additional parameters.

The command syntax for TCPIP.NLM is as follows:

```
LOAD TCPIP FORWARD=YES RIP=NO
```

If you plan to use your NetWare server to route IP traffic between networks, the FORWARD=YES parameter enables IP routing. The default value is FORWARD=NO. The RIP=YES parameter enables the server to exchange routing information with other servers and routers using the Routing Information Protocol. RIP=NO disables the process. The default value is RIP=YES.

Many small networks use the NetWare server's routing capabilities, but avoid the use of RIP by manually entering the routing information needed. This is called *static routing*. (For more information, see Chapter 28, "Using the Multiprotocol Router.") Larger, more complex networks may use routing protocols other than RIP. In such cases you should use RIP=NO. Unless there is a specific reason to disable the RIP routing protocol, leave this value as RIP=YES.

You can also apply the TRAP=[ip address] parameter, to specify an IP address to which the server will send SNMP trap messages. By default, traps are sent to 127.0.0.1, which delivers them to the local SNMP trap logger.

Loading the LAN Driver The second step in configuring TCP/IP is to load the driver for each LAN adapter on which you want to enable the protocols, specifying a frame type that is compatible with TCP/IP communications, as shown in Table 24.2. Be sure to note that the *standard* frame types most often used with NetWare on Ethernet networks (ETHERNET_802.2 and ETHERNET_802.3) are not compatible with TCP/IP.

Table 24.2 TCP/IP Compatible Frame Types

Protocol	Frame Types
Ethernet	ETHERNET_II, ETHERNET_SNAP
Token ring	TOKEN-RING_SNAP
FDDI	FDDI_SNAP
PCN	IBM_PCN2_SNAP
Arcnet	NOVELL_RX-NET

Part
VII
Ch
24

N O T E The Ethernet_802.2 and Ethernet_802.3 frame types cannot be used with TCP/IP because neither frame type includes an "Ethertype" field in the packet header that can be used to identify packets as carrying IP datagrams. If you intend to run both IPX/SPX and TCP/IP on your network, Ethernet_II frames are preferable, because they can support multiple network layer protocols. An Ethernet_II packet header includes an Ethertype field that identifies the Network layer protocol that generated the packet.

If you are using an Ethernet LAN adapter, such as an NE2000, your command line for loading the driver would be something like the following:

```
LOAD NE2000 [hardware parameters] FRAME=ETHERNET_II NAME=[identifier]
```

Use of the NAME= parameter will help you if you are loading the same driver with multiple frame types. If you don't use the NAME= parameter when you have multiple LOAD commands in your AUTOEXEC.NCF file, processing may pause and wait for command input. An example of a LOAD command using the NAME= parameter follows:

```
LOAD NE2000 [hardware parameters] FRAME=ETHERNET_II NAME=ETHER1
```

Binding the LAN Driver to the TCP/IP Protocol The final step needed to set up TCP/IP from the command line is to BIND the IP protocol to the LAN driver. The general format of the BIND command is as follows:

```
BIND IP TO [LAN Driver] ADDR=130.57.128.1 [MASK=255.255.0.0] [GATE={IP address}]
```

There are several other optional parameters as well:

■ [LAN Driver]—This parameter may be specified by the name of the driver itself, or by the identifier used with the NAME= parameter in the driver's LOAD command.

- `ADDR=[IP address]`—This is the IP address to be assigned to the interface, in dotted decimal notation.
- `MASK=[subnet mask]`—This is the subnet mask to be applied to this interface, in dotted decimal notation.
- `BCAST=[IP address]`—The default IP address to be used for broadcasts on this network, in dotted decimal notation. The default value is 255.255.255.255, and may never need to be changed. (Some early routers used 0.0.0.0 as the broadcast address.)
- `GATE=[IP address]`—The IP address of the default router to be used as a gateway for packets addressed to hosts on other networks. If you don't set a `GATE=` parameter, IP gets the gateway information from the RIP routing protocol.
- `DEFROUTE=[Yes or No]`—If Yes, the server will announce this interface as the default gateway for the local network via `RIP`. The default value is `No`.
- `ARP=[Yes or No]`—If Yes, `ARP` will be used to map `IP` addresses to hardware addresses. The default is `Yes`.
- `COST=[Integer from 1 to 15]`—This parameter is used in configuring routing on the network. The default value is 1.
- `POISON=[Yes or No]`—Another routing function, which enables the use of `RIP`'s `Poison Reverse` for routing updates. The default value is `No`, which enables `Split Horizon`.

Most TCP/IP network interfaces require little more than an IP address, subnet mask and default gateway address. A typical `BIND` command appears as follows:

```
BIND IP TO ETHER1 ADDR=130.57.128.1 MASK=255.255.0.0 GATE=130.57.128.2
```

A typical sequence of `LOAD` and `BIND` commands, when implemented in an AUTOEXEC.NCF file, appears as follows:

```
LOAD TCPIP FORWARD=YES RIP=YES
LOAD NE2000 INT=2 PORT=300 FRAME=ETHERNET_II NAME=ETHER1
BIND IP TO ETHER1 ADDR=130.57.128.1 MASK=255.255.0.0 GATE=130.57.128.2
```

If all the parameters are correct, you should now be able to contact another interface on the network using TCP/IP. The PING.NLM module is the standard testing tool. `PING` can be executed interactively or by way of command line parameters, as follows:

```
LOAD PING 130.57.128.2
```

PING is a standard TCP/IP program that uses the Internet Control Message Protocol to verify that one host can communicate with another. Figure 24.6 shows a PING result.

N O T E When you LOAD the TCPIP.NLM module on a NetWare server, you may notice several other modules loading at the same time. One of these is SNMP.NLM, which provides network management support by way of the Simple Network Management Protocol. The SNMP.NLM module is an *agent* that loads on the server.

When SNMP loads automatically along with TCPIP.NLM, the default values of SNMP do not enable remote management software to write configuration changes to the server. The defaults allow only remote monitoring. If you need active SNMP management, you must LOAD SNMP with appropriate command line parameters before you load the TCPIP.NLM module. ▪

FIG. 24.6
The PING.NLM program verifies your TCP/IP configuration by eliciting a response from a specified target system.

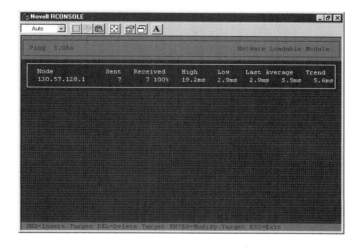

The command line approach to configuring TCP/IP is fine for small, single-interface NetWare servers. However, in a more complex environment you will probably do far better with the interactive INETCFG utility.

Using INETCFG.NLM to Configure TCP/IP

In years past, it was common to see a NetWare server with one LAN adapter and a few hundred megabytes of disk storage. Today, servers are getting more and more complex, however. It's not at all unusual to see multiple LAN adapters connecting various different network types in the same NetWare server installation. IntranetWare also includes Novell's complete Multiprotocol Router (MPR) software package, which supports a rich variety of advanced routing configuration options. With more interfaces, more protocols and many more configuration options, managing the LAN interfaces and their configurations using the server command line can get very confusing. To address this problem, Novell provides the INETCFG.NLM program, a tool that was originally developed to manage the Multiprotocol Router (MPR).

The first time you run INETCFG, you'll be asked whether the LAN driver, LAN protocol, and remote access commands should be transferred to INETCFG. Unless there is a reason not to, you should answer *Yes* to this question and allow the transfer to proceed. All LAN driver LOAD and BIND commands in the AUTOEXEC.NCF file are then remarked out and placed under the control of INETCFG. Once this is done, you should perform all future LAN drivers and communication protocols management tasks with INETCFG.

When INETCFG takes control of your network configuration, the LOAD and BIND commands are moved to two files in the server's SYS:ETC directory, SYS:ETC\INITSYS.NCF and SYS:ETC\NETINFO.CFG. Do not attempt to edit these files yourself, because INETCFG uses a checksum to verify that the files have not been altered or corrupted. Editing the files directly can cause major problems. Instead, use the View Configuration option from the INETCFG menu to see the specific command and syntax (see Figure 24.7).

FIG. 24.7
INETCFG.NLM's Internetworking Configuration menu provides access to all of the parameters needed to configure TCP/IP.

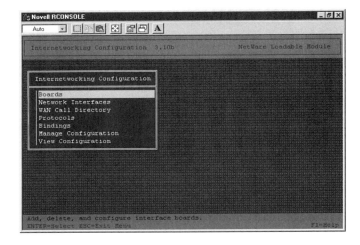

After transferring control to INETCFG, you see the opening menu shown in Figure 24.7. To configure TCP/IP on the server, you need be concerned with only three options:

- **Boards**—Load LAN drivers and set hardware parameters.
- **Protocols**—Enable and configure communication protocols like IPX and TCP/IP.
- **Bindings**—BIND protocols to LAN drivers.

These three options provide a menu-based interface to the LOAD and BIND commands discussed earlier in this chapter in "Configuring TCP/IP with LOAD and BIND Commands."

Using the Boards Menu Option   When you select the Boards option, you can load and configure drivers for your NetWare server's LAN adapters. If you have just transferred control to INETCFG, or if you selected LAN drivers for all of your adapters during the NetWare installation, you should see those drivers, already installed here.

You can add a driver for a new LAN adapter, if necessary, by pressing the Insert key. Figure 24.8 shows the screen in which you configure the hardware parameters for the new adapter, in this case, an NE2000. The Board Name parameter corresponds to the NAME= parameter you read about with the LOAD [LAN driver] command. You do not specify a frame type here; that comes later.

Using the Protocols Menu Option   When you select the Protocols option, you can configure AppleTalk, IPX, TCP/IP, and other user-specified protocols by selecting the appropriate entry in the list presented. On the TCP/IP configuration screen (see Figure 24.9), you can configure the same options found on the TCPIP.NLM LOAD command line.

FIG. 24.8
Adding a new LAN adapter using INETCFG is simply a matter of filling in an entry form.

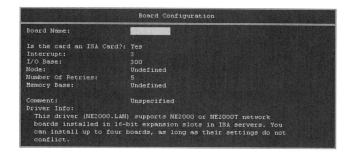

FIG. 24.9
The TCP/IP Protocol Configuration screen provides access to a wide range of communication parameters.

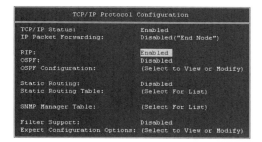

Because the aim here is only to implement basic TCP/IP service on the NetWare server, there are only three fields you should modify, which are as follows:

- **TCP/IP Status**—Setting this parameter to Enabled is the functional equivalent to loading the TCPIP.NLM module.

- **IP Packet Forwarding**—If your server is not going to be used as an IP router, leave this parameter's default setting of Disabled(End Node) intact. Setting it to Enabled(Router) is equivalent to loading TCPIP.NLM with the FORWARD=YES switch.

- **RIP**—The default value is Enabled. Setting it to "Disabled" is equivalent to loading TCPIP.NLM with the RIP=NO option.

Using the Bindings Menu Option Under Bindings, you select each protocol that you want to bind, and then match the protocol with an appropriate adapter. To bind TCP/IP to a new interface, press Insert and follow the prompts to select the desired board. You then supply the appropriate configuration information, as shown in Figure 24.10

The Local IP Address and Subnetwork Mask parameters are straightforward, as they are the equivalents to the ADDR= and MASK= switches on the BIND command line. Some of the other parameters discussed with BIND are configurable under RIP Bind options. (See "Configuring TCP/IP with LOAD and BIND Commands" earlier in this chapter.)

Once you've completed configuring the TCP/IP settings and saved the changes, you must reload the various server modules involved, in order for the changes to take effect. You can do this by downing the server and restarting it, but INETCFG provides an alternative that does not require the interruption of other server processes.

When you select REINITIALIZE SYSTEM from INETCFG's main menu, or issue the same command at the server console prompt, the LAN drivers and TCPIP.NLM are reloaded with the new parameters and rebound.

FIG. 24.10

In the Binding screen, you specify the IP address and subnet mask that will be used to identify the selected network interface.

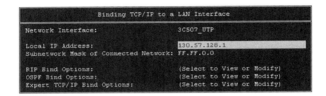

NOTE The REINITIALIZE SYSTEM command may not always be sufficient for your new TCP/IP configuration settings to take effect. Under some circumstances, it may be necessary for you to DOWN and restart your NetWare server for the new settings to take effect. ▨

Be sure to test your new TCP/IP configuration by using the PING command to verify that your server is able to communicate with other TCP/IP systems.

Summary

In this chapter, you have learned some of the basics of TCP/IP, and how to implement the protocols on your NetWare server. The installation of any of IntranetWare's TCP/IP services requires that the protocols already be installed and configured on the server. ●

CHAPTER 25

Using NetWare/IP

Novell's NetWare/IP enables you to implement your network with either a mixture of IPX and TCP/IP or strictly TCP/IP. Its primary function is to provide workstations the capability to connect to and log in to a NetWare/IntranetWare file server via a TCP/IP client. It does this by using a mix of native TCP/IP transport mechanisms along with tunneled NCP functions to communicate service requests and responses between the workstation and the server. To provide this service requires both server-side and client-side programs and configurations. It also requires that the server be configured to properly transport IPX SAP and RIP information to the workstations and other servers via Domain SAP/RIP Services (DSS).

Additionally, NetWare/IP provides UNIX connectivity services that enable your IntranetWare server to act as a Domain Name Server (DNS), provide bi-directional print services between the IntranetWare server and UNIX hosts and printers, and enables X Windows workstations RCONSOLE access to the file server. ■

Installing and configuring NetWare/IP

Learn to install the NetWare/IP services on the file server. Also, you learn how to use the configuration utilities to enable the TCP/IP transport protocol on your network.

Configuring DNS and DSS

Learn to enable Domain Name Services on your TCP/IP network to provide IP host name resolution. You also see how to configure Novell's Domain SAP/RIP Server to provide IPX SAP and RIP information across your TCP/IP network.

Installing and configuring the NetWare/IP client

Learn to install the NetWare/IP client on your workstations and how to implement the IP client for access to your IntranetWare file server via the TCP/IP protocol.

Installing NetWare/IP on the Server

NetWare/IP is installed via the INSTALL.NLM at the file server console. It is one of the native product options included with IntranetWare and as such is installed from the IntranetWare CD. During the installation process of NetWare/IP you will be asked several questions; in most cases, you can select the default option presented.

> **CAUTION**
>
> Be careful to read each option's instructions during the installation process. This is one installation process that does not maintain keystroke uniformity with other products, nor within itself. In some instances, you press Esc to continue, while in others you press Enter.

N O T E   Prior to installing NetWare/IP, you must have the TCP/IP NLM loaded on the IntranetWare server and TCP/IP bound to at least one LAN or WAN adapter. Failure to do so will cause the installation of NetWare/IP to abort.

At the end of the NetWare/IP installation process, the install program posts a message indicating that if this is the first NetWare/IP server on the network you should not continue at this point, but rather exit the NetWare/IP configuration and run the UNICON configuration process. This is a critical step and cannot be skipped or taken out of order. The UNIX Connectivity Services must be configured prior to configuring NetWare/IP. If this is your first NetWare/IP server, be sure to exit the installation and configuration at this time. When you do so, the UNICON.NLM will automatically load and present you with a login display similar to the one in Figure 25.1.

FIG. 25.1
The UNICON Server Login screen enables the system administrator access to the NetWare/IP Configuration Menu.

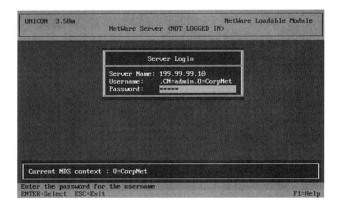

After you properly log in to the server, UNICON will finish installing the files and create the UNIX Service Handler and the UNICON Manager groups. You will then be prompted to DOWN the file server and restart it. Upon exiting the installation utility, you should do so. This will ensure that all the appropriate NLMs are loaded and the services started so that you can configure NetWare/IP.

N O T E   Be sure to add your administrator and any other users to the appropriate UNICON Manager Group, so they can manage the UNIX Services via UNICON when needed.   ▨

CAUTION

In some instances, NetWare/IP will be added to the INETCFG configuration information as an available network adapter. Prior to configuring the NetWare/IP services, you need to remove the NWIP board from INETCFG and reinitialize the system to unload the NWIP NLMs.

Using UNICON

When you have the server running again, reload UNICON and log in. You will now be presented with a menu of the following options:

- Change Current Server
- View Server Profile
- Manage Global Objects
- Start/Stop Services
- Configure Error Reporting
- Perform File Operations
- Quit

In the following sections, you learn to use each of these options to configure your NetWare/IP Server.

View Server Profile

You can view your server profile to ensure that the file server specific information is correct. This information includes the server's IP address and subnet mask, time zone information, and other general information. There are two options within this menu choice that show form-based information, NetWare Information and Installed Products. The NetWare Information option displays specific information about the version of NetWare running on the server as well as the tree and context in which the UNIX Connectivity Services are installed. The Installed Products list shows the installed UNIX Connectivity Services products. As additional products are installed, this list will grow. You cannot modify any information presented in these screens.

Manage Global Objects

The Manage Global Objects option provides you with the options to configure the specific server profile and to manage the server's local hosts table. These two files provide the information to DNS/DSS services on the file server to communicate with, and pass domain name information between hosts and clients on the network via TCP/IP.

Configure Server Profile The Configure Server Profile option is used to create and maintain the RESOLV.CFG file in the SYS:ETC directory on the file server. This file contains the information used by Domain Name System servers to identify the server's Domain and what upstream Name Servers it should contact to resolve unknown host names. Figure 25.2 shows the Server Profile Configuration display.

FIG. 25.2
The UNICON Server Profile Configuration screen is used to define DNS access information.

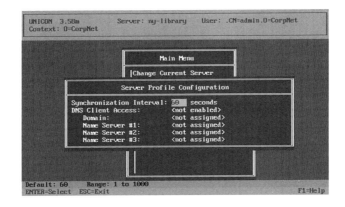

The options presented on this screen define whether, and with whom, this server will communicate to resolve domain name information.

N O T E The information entered in this form is only critical if your network has direct communication links with other TCP/IP based networks, that is, the Internet. If it does, then you must register with the InterNIC via your Internet service provider for a domain name and IP address range.

If you connect to an external network without using a properly registered domain name and/or IP address range, you could conflict with an existing network. If you do so, the group of people you conflict with and the governing body of the Internet, or the management of the external company or office you connect to, will not look kindly on you for causing significant performance and connectivity problems for their network. ▪

Server Profile Configuration Options The first option determines how often the server consults its configuration files to determine if they have changed. If it is determined that one of the UNICON configuration files has changed, the affected service is restarted automatically unless something is explicitly preventing it from doing so.

Next you have the option of enabling or disabling DNS Client Access. If this is disabled, the server will only consult its local RESOLV.CFG file and will not exchange name service information with other name servers.

Naming Your Domain   The Domain option is where you define the domain name that this server resides in. The format for this name is *second level name.top level name*. If this is a closed network environment with no external network connection you can use whatever name fits your need. For example, you can use your company name for *second level name* and the city or state this office is in for the *top level name*. If you are connecting to the Internet, or other external network service, then you should follow these general guidelines when requesting your registered domain name from the InterNIC. First, you must be sure that the name you are requesting is not already assigned. You must also use one of the approved top level domain names for your area.

> **N O T E**   You can do your own domain name search to determine whether the name you want is in use. Either connect via Telnet or connect to the Web site of the InterNIC Domain Registry Service (**internic.net**) and perform a WHOIS request on the domain name you want to check. If the name is in use, it will respond with the registration and contact information for that domain. If it is not in use, it will respond with a "No match for" message. ▪

In Table 25.1, you can see the top level domain names and the assignments generally provided for in the United States.

Table 25.1   Example of Top Level Domain Names

Top Level Domain Name	General Assignment
COM	Commercial interests
GOV	Government organizations
ORG	Non-profit organizations
EDU	Educational facilities
MIL	Military organizations
NET	Network-access providers
US	The international code for U.S. domains

Domain Name Services and Host Name Resolution   TCP/IP utilizes a numeric addressing scheme to identify the devices on the network. This addressing system, which provides the capability to globally maintain unique addresses, is not what one would call user-friendly. Utilizing just the numeric IP addresses for devices would make contacting hosts and services on a small network inconvenient, while making contacting hosts and services on a large network virtually impossible. To relieve this difficulty, there is the Domain Name System. This service provides the capability to identify hosts and other devices on the network with an easy to use, and remember, name. DNS then translates that name into the device's IP address via a distributed lookup system, transparent to the user.

The DNS server can maintain the device names and addresses in two ways, the first being through the use of static configuration files, and the second by dynamically adding information to the active host tables in the servers memory. Each DNS server on the network maintains its own local copy of the static configuration files and, as other DNS servers communicate with it, adds new device names and addresses to its own dynamic tables as they are discovered.

By utilizing this distributed name translation system, no one DNS server needs to know about every device name and address. As a request is made for an unknown host name, the first DNS server will pass the request to the next defined DNS server it knows of. If the requested host is then found, its name and address get added to the dynamic lookup tables for each DNS server all the way back to the original requesting server. The next time a request for that host name comes in, any of the DNS servers in this list will be able to provide its IP address.

Additionally, distributing the lookup service can allow local DNS servers on each segment of a large network. This provides the capability to speed access to devices on the network, as well as provide fault-tolerant name translation services to the users. This reduces the potential for failure of finding a host, as well as reducing overall network traffic when requesting a device on the network.

Enabling DNS   The next three entries identify the DNS servers that this server will "talk to" when trying to resolve an unknown host name. The order in which you define name servers will determine which one is requested first and should be based on the expected lookup speed, as follows:

- The first defined name server should be either your company's main DNS server or your Internet service provider's name server. Although this server may not know every host you might want to communicate with immediately, it will provide the fastest name resolution for locally known hosts.

- The second defined name server should be either your Internet service provider's name server or the name server at a large regional university. This will provide you with a relatively local name server that has a larger configured database of known host names. As this host will be further away from your site and generally busier than your local primary name server, its name resolution times will be a little longer.

- The third defined name server should be the InterNIC's name server. The InterNIC is the one database of all registered domain names and should be the name server of last resort for your DNS Server. The InterNIC maintains three name servers with the addresses of 198.41.0.10, 198.41.0.11 and 198.168.73.8.

Figure 25.3 shows an example of a completed Server Profile Configuration.

FIG. 25.3
The Completed Server
Profile Configuration
screen in UNICON is
showing a valid DNS
client configuration.

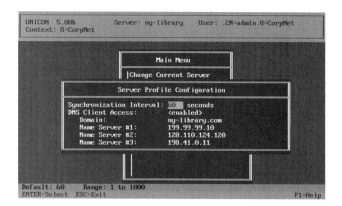

In addition to using UNICON.NLM to manage the RESOLV.CFG DNS information, you can directly edit the RESOLV.CFG file that resides in the SYS:ETC directory on the file server. This file is a standard ASCII text file and can be edited using any text editor, such as DOS EDIT or Windows Notepad. Make sure that when you save the file, if using an editor, you save it as standard ASCII text.

Manage Hosts The Manage Hosts option enables you to view and edit the server's local HOSTS file. The HOSTS file maintains a list of host names and IP addresses associated with those names so that the local machine does not have to request name resolution from an upstream DNS server. Additionally, this file is used to define the local hosts on the network common with the DNS server so you can address those machines with a host name.

Another function of the HOSTS table is to define the known aliases and alternate IP addresses of specific machines on the network. By defining these in your hosts table, you can then access a single machine by many different names. This can be handy in the case that a single server is running a name service, a Web server, and an FTP server so that you can assign multiple host names. Figure 25.4 shows an example of assigning multiple names via aliases to the server.

FIG. 25.4
The UNICON Host
Information Known
Alias list is showing
how one host can be
assigned multiple
names via aliases.

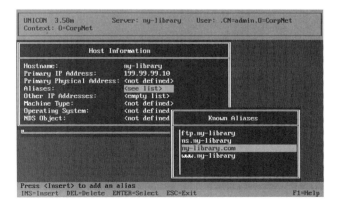

Finally, when using the UNICON utility to maintain the HOSTS table, you have the capability to maintain contact and configuration information. The available information options include the following:

- Primary Physical Address
- Machine Type
- Operating System
- NDS Object

Manage Services

The Manage Services menu option provides the capability to maintain the installed services. The available options may change as you install additional UNIX Connectivity Services modules, such as the FTP server. Initially upon installing the NetWare/IP product, you will have the capability to manage the DNS and the NetWare/IP services.

Managing DNS Services   Upon selecting the DNS option in the Manage Services menu, you will be presented with the following list of options:

- Administer DNS
- Initialize DNS Master Database
- Save DNS Master to Test Files

N O T E   Before you can administer DNS, you must first initialize the DNS master database.

When installing NetWare/IP, you must initialize the DNS Master Database before you can do any additional management or specific configuration operations on DNS. Selecting the Initialize option reads the basic information about your IntranetWare server and builds the master database records that DNS will use. Once the master database is initialized, you can then save it as a series of text files to the network or to diskette or a local workstation hard disk using the Save DNS Master to Text File Option.

Selecting the menu option to Administer DNS presents you with another list of options, as shown in Figure 25.5.

Manage Master Database   Selecting the Manage Master Database option provides you with the means to manage the host machine information in the DNS master database. Additionally it enables you to assign authority for a subzone name server to a master name server. This enables you to specify for this server which upstream DNS server will be considered the address resolution authority. Delegating subzone authority can be done either by host name or by IP address.

FIG. 25.5
The UNICON DNS
Server Administration
Menu shows the
available administration
options.

Selecting the Manage Data option displays a list of defined host names within the defined domains known to this server, as well as the host type and either the IP address or resolved name of the host.

Pressing Ins enables you to define new host information in the master database. When you press Ins, you are presented with a list of available record types the host can be defined as. Table 25.2 lists the available record types.

Table 25.2   DNS Master Database Record Types

Record Type	Type Name
a	Defines the IP address for a host name
cname	Canonical or authoritative name alias
mb	Defines a host as a mailbox
mr	Defines a host that should receive mail in place of a previous host
mx	Defines a mail server within the domain to forward mail through
ns	Defines a name server used as a DNS server on the network

After selecting the record type you want to use, you will be presented with a form in which you define the record name, the amount of time the DNS server will keep cached data, and information specific to the type of record being defined. Table 25.3 defines the specific information needed for each record type.

Table 25.3   DNS Master Database Record Types

Record Type	Specific Data Required	Function
Address	Name to Address Mapping	Defines the address to use when a host name is requested.
Canonical Name	Alias for a Host Name	Defines a secondary name by which a host can be addressed. An example is to allow a single machine to be accessed as either www.*name.name* or ftp.*name.name*.
Mail Box	Mail Box Host	Defines the address of a host used as an end node mail box.
Mail Receive	Mail Rename	Defines the address for a host that should receive mail in place of another host.
Mail Exchange	Preference	Defines the preferred upstream mail host.
	Exchange	Defines the downstream mail host to exchange mail packets with.
Name Server	Name Server	Defines known name servers within the domain.

Highlighting any record in this list enables you to edit the information about that particular host.

Manage Replica Databases   The Manage Replica Databases option enables you to define hosts on your network on which you store replicas of the DNS database. By storing replicas of the DNS database on multiple servers, you can reduce the amount of time required to resolve a particular host name, as well as reducing the amount of traffic across segments of your network.

Link to Existing DNS Hierarchy   The Link to Existing DNS Hierarchy option enables you to publish your master DNS server's address to other DNS servers on an external network. Linking to the existing DNS hierarchy is required if you want your master DNS server to receive information from other domains. When linking to the existing hierarchy, you have two options: You can link directly or link indirectly via forwarders.

Linking directly provides your DNS server's information directly to the root domain on the external network you are connecting to. Linking indirectly provides your DNS server's information only to the specific upstream DNS servers you tell it to. You can define up to three indirect forwarding DNS domains.

Query Remote Name Server   The Query Remote Name Server option provides two services to the network administrator. First it is used to determine the information that is configured on other name servers. Additionally, it can be used to determine if a specific name server is responding to name service queries. To query a name server you need to provide the host name or IP address of the DNS server you are requesting the data from, the record type you want to identify, and the domain name for which you want the information.

Disable DNS   Choosing the Disable DNS option simply enables you to enable or disable DNS services on this file server. This is helpful in trying to troubleshoot a DNS resolution conflict on a local network in that you can turn off a particular machines capability to respond to a name server query without having to change the service's configuration.

Configure the NetWare/IP Service   Selecting the option to manage the NetWare/IP service presents you with the menu options shown in Figure 25.6.

FIG. 25.6
The NetWare/IP Administration Menu shows the administration options available.

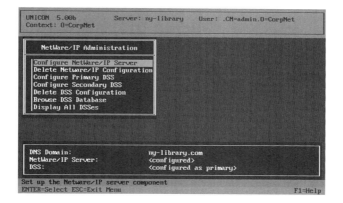

To provide an operational NetWare/IP server, you need to configure the NetWare/IP service and provide DSS information to the network. If you do not have a running DSS server on this NetWare/IP domain, you must configure a Primary DSS. If this server is joining an existing NetWare/IP domain, then you need to configure a Secondary DSS.

Configure the NetWare/IP Server   Configuring the NetWare/IP Server is a straightforward process that requires just six steps. Table 25.4 outlines these steps, but you may find that in your installation, not all of them are required.

Table 25.4   NetWare/IP Configuration Steps

Menu Option	Function
NetWare/IP Domain	Defines the local domain name used to communicate with other servers and workstations on this network. Not to be confused with the DNS domain name.
Preferred DSSes	Defines the Domain Sap/Rip Server this NetWare/IP server should contact to get RIP and SAP information from. This server also provides the virtual IPX address and UDP port number to all

continues

Table 25.4 Continued

Menu Option	Function
	devices connected to the NetWare/IP domain. You can define up to five DSSes in this list if they are available on your network.
Initial DSS Contact Retries	Defines the number of times this NetWare/IP server will attempt to contact a given DSS when a query goes unanswered.
Retry Interval	The amount of time the NetWare/IP server waits between retrying a query to a DSS.
Slow Link Customizations	This enables you to alter the communications parameters between NetWare/IP servers and DSSes across slow WAN links. This can be used to help prevent communications time outs between sites across slow links. You can define up to five such customizations per server.
Forward IPX Information To	Defines whether this server should DSS forward IPX information between IPX and IP segments.

When exiting the configuration form, you will be notified of any specific configuration concerns for this server. Follow the information provided by the configuration utility carefully.

Configure DSS   On your NetWare/IP network you are required to have one Primary Domain SAP/RIP Server and you can then have as many secondary DSSes as you want. The Primary DSS provides the network with all of the virtual IPX information, as well as all of the UDP port information. If this is the first NetWare/IP server on your network then you need to select the option to configure the primary DSS. If you already have a Primary DSS server on your network then you need to choose the Configure Secondary DSS option.

It is required that you assign the following entries for both the Primary and the Secondary DSS configurations:

- NetWare/IP Domain
- Primary DSS Host Name

The NetWare/IP Domain is the domain name defined in the NetWare/IP server configuration. The DSS Host Name is the fully qualified DNS name for this file server. Additionally, for the Primary DSS configuration there are three additional choices to select in the configuration menu: the IPX Network Number, Tunable Parameters, and DSS SAP Filters.

The IPX Network Number is the hex address NetWare/IP will use for the virtual IPX network.

Tunable DSS Parameters   The Tunable DSS Parameters option enables you to view and modify the global parameters that are downloaded by the primary DSS to the secondary DSSes, NetWare/IP servers and NetWare/IP clients as they register on the network. In most instances, these parameters do not need to be modified. Table 25.5 lists the available Tunable Parameters options.

Table 25.5 DSS Tunable Parameters

DSS Parameter	Function
UDP Port Number for NetWare/IP Service	Defines the UDP port number that is assigned to NetWare/IP. This is the first in a consecutive number pair and both numbers must be available. If either of the numbers is unavailable, a different UDP port number must be selected.
DSS-NetWare/IP Server Synchronization Interval	Defines how often the NetWare/IP servers in a common domain query DSS for updated information.
Primary-Secondary DSS Synchronization Interval	Defines how often the secondary DSS servers within a common domain query the primary DSS server for updated information.
Maximum UDP Transmissions	Defines how many times an unacknowledged packet is resent before being dropped from the network.
UDP Checksum?	Defines whether UDP packet information will be checked for errors. Setting this parameter to No provides faster transport with no error detection.
Ticks between Nodes on the Same IP Subnet	The amount of time in ticks (1/18th second) it takes for a packet to travel in one direction between any two nodes on the same subnet.
Ticks between Nodes on the same IP Net	The amount of time in ticks (1/18th second) it takes for a packet to travel in one direction between any two nodes on the same network.
Ticks between Nodes on Different IP Nets	The amount of time in ticks (1/18th second) it takes for a packet to travel in one direction between any two nodes on different networks.

Part

VII

Ch

25

Changes should be made to the tunable parameters only if you have one or more NetWare/IP Domains communicating between servers across a slow WAN link.

DSS Sap Filtering DSS Sap Filtering provides for the capability to filter outgoing SAP broadcasts. This can significantly reduce the amount of extraneous traffic across your network or can be used to shield services from users.

SAP filters are implemented by IP network or subnet address, SAP type, and file server name. This enables you to easily implement filters for entire enterprises or for specific groups of servers and clients.

As well as implementing filters, you can also set global exceptions to prevent specific SAP types from being transported regardless of the filter settings on any given network. These exceptions are always prevented from propagating to other DSSes.

Finalizing the DSS Configuration   Upon saving the settings, the configuration utility will display information specific to your server about making DSS visible as a registered service on the network. Registering DSS as an available service provides transparent access to the SAP and RIP information it is providing on the network. Leaving the DSS unregistered enables you to maintain a protected DSS host, which will only be contacted by other servers and workstations that have it explicitly defined as their primary DSS host.

N O T E In a multi-segment network, you may want to maintain all your DSSes as unregistered so that you can explicitly define which DSS-specific workstations and servers they can talk to, and in what order. This will enable you to manage traffic across the segments in a more organized fashion.

Once these options are configured, your DSS is functional and will automatically load on the file server to complete the configuration. Once that is done the service will automatically unload.

Start/Stop Services

Start/Stop Services, very simply, provides the capability to load and unload specific services without having to know all the module names associated with that service. As more services are installed on this file server, the list of available services may increase. To load a service, simply press Ins to open the list of Available Services, then select the service you want from the Available Services list and press Enter. To stop a service you simply press Del while highlighting the service in the Running Services list.

At this point, you will want to start the Domain Name Service, Domain Sap/Rip Server, and the NetWare/IP Server.

CAUTION

If the NetWare/IP server is its own preferred DSS, perform the following steps:

1. Run the UNISTOP.NCF on the server console. Verify that all NLMs unloaded successfully. If they did not, unload them manually until they are all out of memory.
2. Remove the following line from AUTOEXEC.NCF:

   `LOAD NWIP NAME=NWIP_1`
3. Load the INETCFG.NLM on the server; under Boards, delete the NWIP_1 definition.
4. Exit back to the server console prompt and issue the `REINITIALIZE SYSTEM` command.
5. Edit UNISTART.NCF. If the line `LOAD NWIP` is not there, add it right after the line `LOAD DSS`. If it is there, make sure that NWIP loads right after `LOAD DSS`.
6. At the server console run the UNISTART.NCF.

7. Load the MONITOR.NLM, and check the LAN/WAN information; verify that NWIP virtual board is listed.

If another DSS server is available, set that server as one of the Preferred DSSes in UNICON's NetWare/IP configuration options.

Configure Error Reporting

Upon selecting the Configure Error Reporting option, you will be presented with the following options:

- Display Audit Log
- Save Audit Log
- Clear Audit Log
- Clear Product Kernel Screen
- Configure Error Logging/SNMP Alert Levels

Choosing the option to Display Audit Log produces a display similar to the one shown in Figure 25.7. This screen will inform you of any operational errors during the loading or running of the UNIX Connectivity Services.

FIG. 25.7

The Display Audit Log Screen shows errors and warnings generated by the NetWare/IP Services.

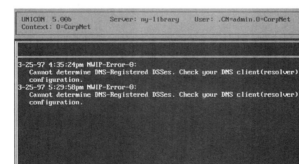

```
UNICON  5.00b          Server: ny-library    User: .CN=admin.O=CorpNet
Context: O=CorpNet

3-25-97 4:35:24pm NWIP-Error-0:
    Cannot determine DNS-Registered DSSes. Check your DNS client(resolver)
    configuration.
3-25-97 5:29:58pm NWIP-Error-0:
    Cannot determine DNS-Registered DSSes. Check your DNS client(resolver)
    configuration.




Configure the level reported to the audit log by selecting "Configure Error Log
ESC=Exit Viewing                                                     F1=Help
```

Choosing the option to Save Audit Log will prompt you for a location to save the audit file to disk. You can use any disk locally attached to the file server to save the audit file by using either the DOS path or the NetWare volume name and path.

N O T E To save the audit file to a DOS partition or diskette on file server, you must not have issued a REMOVE DOS or SECURE CONSOLE command. Issuing either of these commands removes the DOS disk handler and prevents you from accessing the DOS disks.

Choosing the option to Clear Audit Log deletes all the information from the Audit Log screen. Do this only after saving the audit log if you want to maintain the information from the system auditing functions.

Choosing the Clear Product Kernel Screen immediately blanks the server display screen showing the status of the UNIX Connectivity Services. An example of what can be displayed on this screen is shown in Figure 25.8.

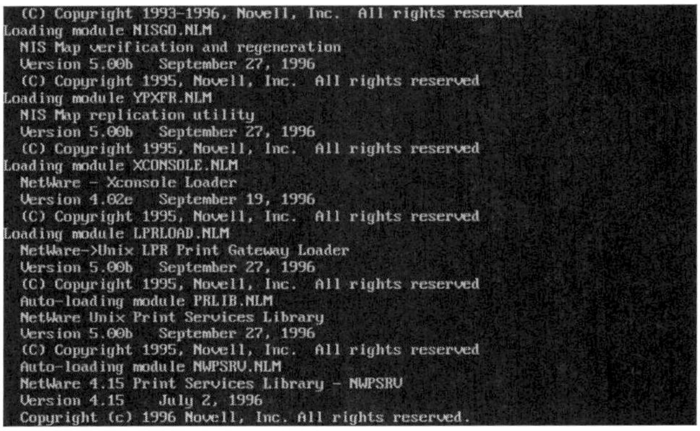

FIG. 25.8

The Product Kernel Message Display Screen shows the UNIX Connectivity Services loaded and operational messages.

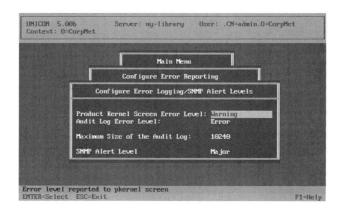

Clearing this display screen can aid in troubleshooting instances where one or more services is not starting properly by removing extraneous text.

Choosing the Configure Error Logging/SNMP Alerts Levels presents you with an input screen where you can select the error reporting options and status levels to track. Figure 25.9 shows the Configure Error Logging/SNMP Alerts Levels screen.

FIG. 25.9

The Configure Error Logging/SNMP Alert Levels configuration option shows the default settings.

Table 25.6 shows the configurable options for each of the screen selections.

Table 25.6 Configure Error Logging/SNMP Alert Levels Options

Function	Operation
Product Kernel Screen Error Level	Defines the error level information to be displayed on the Product Kernel Screen.
Audit Log Error Level	Defines the error level information to be maintained in the Audit Error Log.
Maximum Size of the Audit Log	Defines, in bytes, the maximum size the Audit Log File can become. When the maximum size is reached new messages overwrite the oldest messages in the file. The file size range is 5,120 to 262,144.
SNMP Alert Level	Defines the alert level reported to SNMP management stations on the network.

Table 25.7 shows the available alert levels for the Error Logging/SNMP Alert options. Note that each level down maintains the information of the previous level.

Table 25.7 Alert Levels for the Error Logging/SNMP Alert Options

Product Kernel Screen Error Level and Audit Log Error Level	Information Tracked by Level
None	No error level reporting.
Error	Essential notifications of critical problems.
Warning	Notifications of potential problems.
Informational	Notifications of operational information.
Debug	Detailed information about the services running; used as a diagnostic to provide information to technical support staff.

Perform File Operations

Selecting the Perform File Operations option presents you with the following choices:

- View/Set File Permissions
- Copy Files Using FTP
- Edit Files

Part
VII

Ch
25

The View/Set option is used to view or set the UNIX permissions on NetWare files and directories. To be able to utilize this option you must first load the NFS.NAM name space driver and add the NFS name space to the volume you want to work with. You can also use this option to set permissions on UNIX disks mounted on the file server as imported NFS Gateway volumes. Figure 25.10 shows the View/Set File Permissions screen.

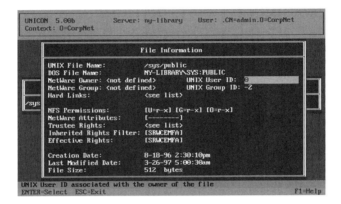

The Copy Files using FTP option invokes a server-side FTP client that enables you to copy files between the server and an FTP host. Primarily this is used to transfer configuration files between servers.

The Edit Files option invokes the same function as the EDIT.NLM. It enables you to edit any ASCII text file on the server's DOS drives or NetWare volumes. When using this file editor, there is a maximum file size of 64K.

Quit

Selecting Quit closes the UNICON utility and exits back to the server console. When you select this option, you will be prompted with a confirmation screen to determine that you really want to exit.

Using the NWIPCFG Utility

In addition to using the UNICON.NLM utility to configure the NetWare/IP server, you can use the NWIPCFG.NLM utility. Where the UNICON utility enables you to configure all of the installed UNIX Connectivity Services, NWIPCFG only provides the means to manage the functions specific to the operation and handling of NetWare/IP. Figure 25.11 shows the NWIPCFG main screen.

Each of the NWIPCFG options relates to a UNICON function, and when selected brings up the same configuration displays as seen in UNICON.

FIG. 25.11
The NetWare IP Configuration Utility Main Options screen is displayed after loading the NWIPCFG.NLM.

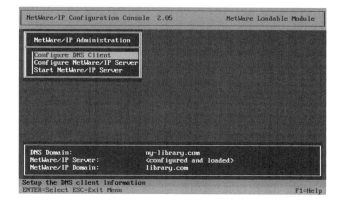

Selecting the Configure DNS Client option enables you to assign or modify the domain name assigned to this file server and the defined Name Servers this file server communicates with (refer to Figure 25.3). When using NWIPCFG, the options to set Synchronization Interval and to enable/disable DNS Client Access are not available.

Selecting the Configure NetWare/IP Server presents the same configuration screen as in the UNICON NetWare/IP Administration menu option of the same name. Refer to the "Configure the NetWare/IP Service" section under the "Using UNICON" section earlier in this chapter for more information.

The Start NetWare/IP Server option enables you to load the NetWare/IP-related NLMs after making changes to the configuration of the service.

NetWare/IP Clients

The other component needed to enable NetWare/IP on your network is the client-side pieces. As of this writing, NetWare/IP clients exist for MS DOS/Windows 3.1x, MS Windows 95, and MS Windows NT. Future clients for Apple Macintosh and IBM OS/2 operating systems are under consideration.

Configuring the NetWare/IP client for the various OS options consists of the same basic steps:

- Configure TCP/IP transport.
- Enable the NetWare/IP client.

N O T E Different TCP/IP transports can be used based on the different operating system options on the workstations. For MS DOS/Windows 3.1x workstations, you can use Novell's LAN Workplace TCP/IP stack (TCPIP.EXE), Novell's Client 32 for DOS/WIN, and FTP Software's ONNET. For Windows 95 and Windows NT, you can use and TCP/IP protocol stack written to meet Microsoft's TDI specification, including the TCP/IP stacks included with these operating systems. ▓

Configuration Considerations for the TCP/IP Protocol Stack

Regardless of the client OS or the TCP/IP transport stack used on the workstation, there are several common configuration options that need to be considered. Specific steps required for configuring the following options may vary slightly with each OS and stack option, but are generally similar in concept. As such, the next few sections focus on the Windows 95 installation, but the concepts apply for Windows NT, DOS, and Windows 3.1x as well.

When configuring the workstation for the TCP/IP protocol stack, one of the primary concerns will be whether the workstation will receive a static address or a dynamic address. A *static address* is one that is physically set in one of the configuration files, or configuration screens on the workstation explicitly. A *dynamic address* is one that is automatically assigned to the workstation when it boots. Dynamic addresses can be assigned and managed by either a BOOTP or DHCP server.

N O T E   When utilizing the NetWare/IP client on the workstation, you must use Novell's DHCP service on the file server. Novell's DHCP is currently the only product that provides the correct DSS and NetWare/IP Domain information to the NetWare/IP client on the workstation.

Assigning a static address provides for explicit control of what IP addresses are assigned to what physical nodes. In a small network environment, this can be an easy-to-manage means of providing TCP/IP addressing to the clients. In larger environments, this can become a management nightmare, especially in situations where there is a subnet mask involved or multiple network segments with different network addresses assigned.

Utilizing a BOOTP or DHCP server enables you to define the addresses you want the workstations to be assigned. Additionally, DHCP enables you to define the amount of time between assignments that a specific IP address will continue to be assigned to a specific hardware address via lease assignments. This enables the network administrator to effectively assign specific IP address to explicit workstations.

When configuring the TCP/IP protocol stack on the client workstation, or when configuring the DHCP server, you need to ensure that you have specified the proper default gateway, domain name and name server information for your network. If the client TCP/IP protocol stack has the option, you will also want to enable DNS services.

Additionally, when configuring the DHCP server for use with NetWare/IP, you need to ensure that the appropriate NetWare/IP domain name, Primary and Preferred DSS Server, and nearest NetWare/IP file server are specified. Figure 25.12 shows the DHCPCFG.NLM NetWare/IP Configuration Screen.

Enabling the NetWare/IP Client

Once the TCP/IP client protocol stack is configured and functional, you can enable the NetWare/IP client. To enable the NetWare/IP client, you need to define the NetWare/IP domain that this workstation resides in, as well as the Nearest NetWare/IP Server and Preferred DSS Server.

FIG. 25.12

The NetWare/IP Configuration screen is displayed when loading the DHCPCFG.NLM utility.

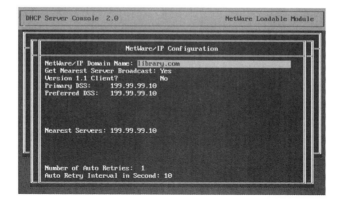

Figure 25.13 and Figure 25.14 show the Windows 95 Properties options for configuring the NetWare/IP client. Figure 25.13 shows the specific NetWare/IP Protocol Parameters that need to be configured. These include the following:

- NetWare/IP Domain Name
- Retries to DSS During Startup
- Number of Seconds Between Retries
- Broadcast SAP Nearest Server Queries to Network
- NetWare/IP 1.1 Compatibility
- Verbose

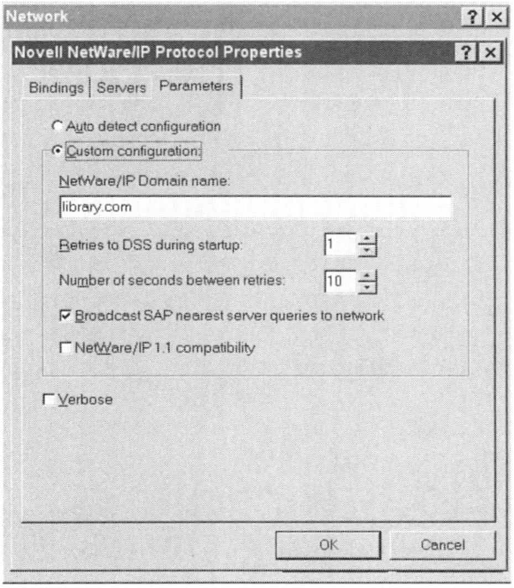

FIG. 25.13

The Windows 95 NetWare/IP Protocol Properties screen shows the Parameters options available for modification.

Part

VII

Ch

25

Of these options, only the last two are different from the NetWare/IP Server configuration options. NetWare/IP 1.1 compatibility enables this client to communicate with a NetWare 3.12 based NetWare/IP server. Verbose enables startup diagnostic messages to aid in diagnosing connectivity problems between the client and server.

Figure 25.14 shows the Protocol Properties Servers configuration where you can define the Nearest NetWare/IP server and the Preferred Domain SAP/RIP Servers.

FIG. 25.14

The Windows 95 NetWare/IP Protocol Properties screen shows the Preferred and Nearest NetWare/IP and SAP/RIP server options.

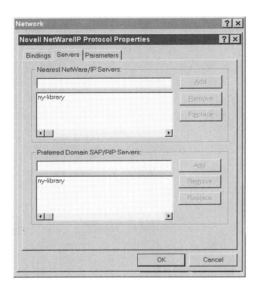

When these options are configured, your workstation is ready to communicate with the file server via TCP/IP only. If you configure all your workstations to utilize the NetWare/IP client you can remove the IPX protocol bind to the LAN card in the file server.

> **CAUTION**
>
> Before removing the IPX protocol from your file server configuration, you need to ensure that all devices attached to the LAN segment are capable of communicating via TCP/IP and NetWare/IP. This would include dedicated print servers, such as HP's JetDirect, and other such devices. If you have local devices that require IPX to communicate with the IntranetWare server, but you want to remove IPX from your primary connections, you will need to install and configure an additional LAN card in your file server to service the IPX devices.

NetWare/IP Interactivity Services

In addition to the connectivity services provided to your NetWare clients on the network, NetWare/IP provides interactivity services to UNIX stations.

XCONSOLE

The XCONSOLE.NLM utility provides the means for an X Windows workstation to connect, via a Telnet session, to the IntranetWare file server and start an RCONSOLE session to provide management functions for the server.

NetWare to UNIX Print Gateway

The NetWare to UNIX Print Gateway provides the means to enable bidirectional print services between UNIX hosts and NetWare print queues. By implementing this service, you can enable UNIX hosts to target NetWare print queues, as well as allow NetWare clients to target UNIX print services. By sharing these services the network administrator can greatly reduce the costs involved in providing high-end printers to both client bases.

Summary

As you have seen, you can configure your network to provide transport via TCP/IP only, if you so desire, or if your specific implementation requires you to do so. To do so requires that you install and configure the NetWare/IP server portion, the NetWare/IP client portion, and configure Domain SAP/RIP Services. In addition, you can configure your file server to act as a Domain Name Server to service host name resolution services to your network clients.

Along with the NetWare/IP connectivity functions, you get the services that enable you to do remote server management from an X Windows station via the XCONSOLE utility, and the NetWare to UNIX Print Gateway to allow bidirectional printing to and from NetWare to UNIX printers. ●

Part
VII

Ch
25

CHAPTER 26

Using the Dynamic Host Configuration Protocol (DHCP) Server

From the beginning, configuring TCP/IP host systems has been a tedious and time-consuming task. Almost all TCP/IP implementations for personal computers have required manual intervention to assign IP addresses, subnet masks, default gateways, and the various other parameters that are needed to connect a computer to a TCP/IP network. The job gets even harder when you consider the record keeping that is required to track your address assignments so that multiple systems are not assigned the same IP address.

Changing configuration parameters after a network upgrade can be an even bigger nightmare. Imagine having to reconfigure hundreds of workstations because of a change in your network's subnet mask, or to adjust the address of the network's default gateway router. For these reasons, network administrators have sought a way to automate the TCP/IP configuration process and make their lives easier.

The Dynamic Host Configuration Protocol (DHCP) enables you to create a pool of IP addresses that your NetWare server assigns to client workstations as needed,

The history of automated TCP/IP configuration

There have been three major methods of automating the TCP/IP configuration process, each of which builds on the foundation laid by its predecessors.

Installing the DHCP server

You install the IntranetWare DHCP server from the NetWare server console using the INSTALL.NLM utility.

Configuring the DHCP server

Configuring the DHCP server is a matter of specifying the IP addresses and other TCP/IP configuration parameters that are to be assigned to your workstations.

DHCP client configuration

To use DHCP, you must have a client or operating system that supports the protocol.

along with other TCP/IP configuration parameters. The DHCP server maintains a record of the addresses assigned to each workstation, prevents address duplication, and solves the roving user problem by renewing the IP address assignments on a regular basis. ∎

Automating TCP/IP Configuration

As the TCP/IP protocol suite has gained wider and wider acceptance, the need for an automatic TCP/IP configuration has grown with it. There have been several automated configuration methods developed over the years, each building on its predecessors and providing additional functionality. DHCP is the result of the experience gained during the development and use of the earlier technologies.

There have been three major tools used to automate the configuration of TCP/IP workstations:

- **RARP**—Reverse Address Resolution Protocol
- **BOOTP**—Bootstrap Protocol
- **DHCP**—Dynamic Host Configuration Protocol

All three of these tools are accepted standards, based on published RFCs (Requests For Comment). The following sections examine each of these three mechanisms.

▶ **See** "Introducing TCP/IP," **p. 600**

Understanding the Reverse Address Resolution Protocol (RARP)

In Chapter 24, "Understanding TCP/IP," you read about ARP, which is used by TCP/IP workstations to discover the hardware address of a remote host system by broadcasting its IP address and waiting for a reply. Without ARP, there can be no *unicast* IP transmissions on a local area network, because Ethernet and token-ring adapters require the hardware (or MAC) address of the destination system.

As you can imagine, Reverse Address Resolution Protocol works in the opposite manner. Most computer systems obtain their IP configuration information from local disk storage devices. However, at the time that RARP was developed, many systems did not have local disk storage, like printers, bridges, and even diskless workstations. During the boot process, these systems would broadcast an *RARP request* containing the hardware address of the system's network interface, as shown in Figure 26.1. An *RARP server* would then return a reply, informing the system of its IP address and allowing the boot process to proceed.

FIG. 26.1
RARP is used to provide IP addresses to clients with no local disk storage.

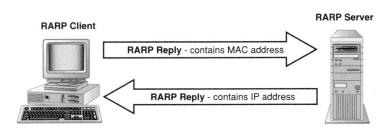

RARP Client

RARP Server

RARP Reply - contains MAC address

RARP Reply - contains IP address

The most significant advantage of RARP is that the IP address information for TCP/IP clients can be stored in a single, central location. Unfortunately, RARP suffers from some distinct disadvantages, as well. Despite the fact that IP addresses are automatically transmitted to clients, the address configurations must be manually entered on the RARP server. IP addresses are stored in a table on the server that must be manually edited whenever a new system is added or an address changed.

Also, the RARP protocol provides only IP address information and does not provide additional TCP/IP configuration to systems as they boot. For today's TCP/IP clients, this means that such parameters as the subnet mask and the default gateway must still be configured manually at each workstation. Finally, RARP relies on network broadcasts to function, which are not propagated across routers. Therefore, a separate RARP server is needed on every network segment, if service is to be provided to the whole internetwork.

Understanding the Bootstrap Protocol (BOOTP)

Because it provides only IP addresses, RARP doesn't furnish enough information to clients to be useful in automating the TCP/IP configuration process. BOOTP, or the Bootstrap Protocol, is a later development that is somewhat more useful.

A client workstation needs to have more than just an IP address to function on a TCP/IP network. Based on the client system's hardware address, BOOTP can provide the following:

- An IP address
- The IP address of the gateway router to be used by the client
- A server host name and boot file name
- The client's subnet mask

BOOTP was designed to be a mechanism used with diskless workstations that could supply not only TCP/IP configuration data, but an operating system boot file as well. During the workstation boot process, a BOOTP client broadcasts a BOOTP request message (using the destination address 255.255.255.255) to the network, as shown in Figure 26.2.

Part
VII
Ch
26

FIG. 26.2
BOOTP clients broadcast a request for TCP/IP configuration data, and receive a reply from a BOOTP server.

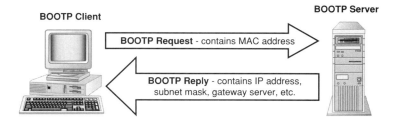

BOOTP Client

BOOTP Server

BOOTP Request - contains MAC address

BOOTP Reply - contains IP address, subnet mask, gateway server, etc.

The request message contains the hardware address of the client system's network interface. When the request is received by a BOOTP server, it checks its configuration table for an entry that corresponds to the hardware address. If an entry exists, the server returns a packet to the client containing the configuration data found in the table. When the client receives the BOOTP message, it completes the boot process using the information supplied.

Unlike RARP, BOOTP traffic can pass through routers to clients on different network segments, even though it uses broadcast messages in the process. This is possible due to a special BOOTP forwarding feature incorporated into most routers that is defined in the BOOTP RFCs. This enables a single BOOTP server to supply configuration data to clients anywhere on the enterprise network.

Although BOOTP is no longer widely used, this message-forwarding feature is critical to the operation of DHCP, which uses the same UDP port numbers as BOOTP. This design was a deliberate act on the part of DHCP's developers, who wanted DHCP traffic to be able to pass through most commercial routers without the need for another special software modification.

NOTE In most cases, routers do not forward DHCP or BOOTP messages unless you explicitly enable the BOOTP forwarding feature. This is also true with NetWare.

To enable BOOTP forwarding on a NetWare 3.x or 4.x server, you must load the BOOTPFWD.NLM module, specifying the IP address or hostname of the DHCP or BOOTP server, as follows:

```
LOAD BOOTPFWD SERVER=200.201.202.1
```

You can also load BOOTPFWD.NLM more than once to configure NetWare to forward DHCP and BOOTP messages to multiple servers, as follows:

```
LOAD BOOTPFWD SERVER=200.201.202.1
LOAD BOOTPFWD SERVER=130.57.128.2
```

BOOTP forwarding, therefore, provides some advantage over RARP, but although BOOTP enables you to furnish workstation clients with their TCP/IP configuration information from a central location, it is like RARP in that you must manually create and maintain a BOOTP database with separate entries containing the TCP/IP configuration information for every node on the network. Whenever you add a workstation to your network, you must create a new entry in the database.

Understanding the Dynamic Host Configuration Protocol (DHCP)

You've seen how both of the earlier automated IP configuration protocols require a lot of manual effort to administer and maintain, even though they can save time and effort by centralizing the administration of TCP/IP configuration information. DHCP takes the concept a step further, by introducing the concept of *dynamic* IP address allocation. Instead of manually assigning IP addresses to individual clients based on a physical layer address like BOOTP or RARP, DHCP enables you to set up a *range* of IP addresses on each subnet and dynamically *lease* those addresses to individual clients based on rules you establish.

In this way, DHCP solves several of the long-standing TCP/IP configuration problems that are frequently encountered by network administrators:

- **Manual configuration**—Because DHCP assigns IP addresses to workstations from a pool of available addresses, the administrator no longer has to travel to each workstation to manually configure the TCP/IP client.

- **IP address tracking**—Without DHCP, you must maintain a list of the IP addresses that you have assigned to clients; the result is chaos if you don't. Because DHCP assigns IP addresses dynamically, as needed, you save on the time and effort previously devoted to bookkeeping chores.

- **IP address conservation**—On networks that are connected to the Internet, IP addresses can often be at a premium. DHCP allows addresses to be allocated to systems as needed, and reclaimed when they are not used for a designated period of time.

- **Address conflicts**—One of the most frequent problems encountered by TCP/IP administrators is address conflicts. No matter how well you plan, sooner or later someone will set up a workstation client with an IP address that duplicates one already assigned to another node (usually that of your boss), causing one or both to malfunction. Some users even pick addresses and other TCP/IP configuration information out of thin air. The result is unreliable communications. DHCP makes such address conflicts virtually impossible.

- **Mobile users**—BOOTP and RARP do not address the problem of mobile users who connect portable and laptop computers to different network locations. Using DHCP, a network administrator can provide dynamic configuration of IP addresses and other configuration parameters to these mobile users no matter where they connect to the internetwork.

From the client perspective, DHCP makes the TCP/IP configuration process simple and transparent. Before a client can access network resources using TCP/IP, the client must be properly configured with an IP address, subnet mask, default gateway address, and other information. If the client system is moved to a different network, or is a *mobile user,* the TCP/IP configuration information must be changed every time the client connects to a different network segment. DHCP makes the process painless, simple, and automatic by leasing IP addresses to clients as needed.

Much of DHCP is similar to BOOTP. In fact, DHCP communication uses the same UDP port assignments that are assigned to BOOTP. The biggest difference is the lease process, which has three major steps:

- Lease Request and Offer
- Lease Selection and Acknowledgment
- Lease Renewal

IP Lease Request and Offer When a workstation configured to be a DHCP client begins its boot process, it broadcasts a request for a DHCP lease (called a DHCPDISCOVER packet) using the reserved IP broadcast address of 255.255.255.255. All DHCP servers that receive the broadcast and have an IP address available respond directly to the client with an offer (DHCPOFFER) that includes an IP address, the length of the lease offer, and other basic information, as shown in Figure 26.3.

FIG. 26.3
The DHCP lease process begins with the client broadcasting a request.

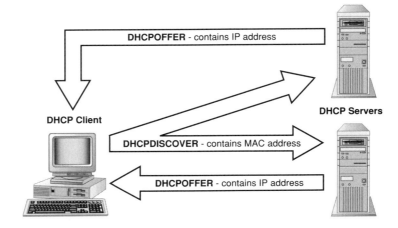

DHCPOFFER - contains IP address

DHCP Client

DHCP Servers

DHCPDISCOVER - contains MAC address

DHCPOFFER - contains IP address

The DHCP client accepts the first IP address lease offer that it receives. Meanwhile, the DHCP server reserves the offered IP address so that it can't be assigned to another DHCP client.

IP Lease Selection and Acknowledgment   After the DHCP client has received at least one lease offer, it transmits a DHCPREQUEST message announcing that it has accepted the server's offered address, as shown in Figure 26.4. The DHCPREQUEST message includes the IP address of the DHCP server whose lease offer was accepted, and is sent as a broadcast, so that all of the other DHCP servers that offered a lease can retract their offers and make those IP addresses available to other clients.

FIG. 26.4
When a DHCP client accepts a lease offer, it transmits a broadcast message that informs other servers that their offers are being rejected.

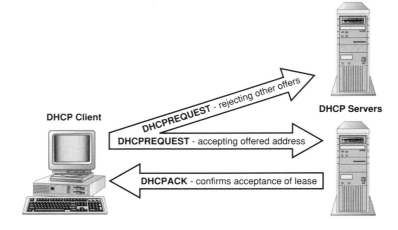

DHCP Client

DHCP Servers

DHCPREQUEST - rejecting other offers

DHCPREQUEST - accepting offered address

DHCPACK - confirms acceptance of lease

The DHCP server whose lease offer was accepted then transmits an acknowledgment (DHCPACK) directly to the client confirming the lease. Similar to a BOOTP reply, the acknowledgment may also include additional configuration information for the DHCP client, depending on the settings the administrator has applied to the DHCP server.

TIP

As defined in the RFCs and as currently implemented, DHCP does not allow multiple DHCP servers to offer leases of duplicate IP addresses. The result is that you cannot configure redundant DHCP servers; if a particular DHCP server is down or otherwise inaccessible, the IP addresses that it is configured to lease will not be available. There is a way to deal with this problem, however.

If you have a block of IP addresses that you want to configure for use by the DHCP clients on a particular network or subnet, you can configure part of that block of addresses on one DHCP server, and another part of the block of addresses on another DHCP server. In the event that one of the DHCP servers were to fail, the other one would still have at least some IP addresses available for lease.

IP Lease Renewal   The Novell DHCP Server's default lease on an IP address is three days. No matter what the term of the lease is, all DHCP clients attempt to renew their leases when 50 percent of the lease time has expired. The client sends a request for a lease renewal (DHCPREQUEST) directly to the DHCP server from which it leased the IP address. If the DHCP server is accessible, it replies with an acknowledgment of the renewed lease (DHCPACK), along with a new lease duration and any configuration parameters that may have been changed.

Whenever a DHCP client system restarts during the lease period, the client tries to lease the same IP address from the original DHCP server. If that attempt is unsuccessful, the client will continue to use the same IP address as long as the lease period lasts.

When a DHCP client lease reaches the 50 percent mark and cannot contact the DHCP server from which it leased its IP address (either because the server is down, or for any other reason), the client continues to use its current address, while repeating its lease renewal attempts. When 87.5 percent (7/8) of the lease time is expired, the DHCP client modifies its lease renewal messages, making them broadcasts that try to contact *any* DHCP server to obtain a new lease. The client is either able to renew its existing lease at this time, or it reinitializes and obtains a lease on a new IP address.

If the lease time expires without a renewal and without a lease on a new IP address, the DHCP client must stop using its current address and begin the entire leasing process again. This can occur if no DHCP servers are operating, or if all of the servers' IP addresses are in use by other systems. Finally, if the DHCP client is still unable to obtain a new IP address after the old lease expires, TCP/IP communication stops—except for DHCPDISCOVER broadcasts, which begin immediately and continue until the client can obtain a new IP address. Obviously this can result in errors in TCP/IP applications.

The DHCP protocol is defined in RFCs 2132, 1534, 2131, and 1542. Also, DHCP is largely based on the older BOOTP protocol specified in RFC 951.

Part
VII

Ch
26

Controlling DHCP Traffic   DHCP can have some impact on your network traffic. The initial DHCPDISCOVER messages are sent as broadcasts, as are the DHCPREQUEST messages used by clients to accept offered addresses. These broadcasts, however, will not be forwarded by routers to other network segments unless they support the forwarding of DHCP broadcasts as specified in RFC 1542, and you activate the forwarding feature.

If forwarding is activated, all of the DHCP servers on your internetwork that receive the initial lease request from a client will reply with a lease offer, if they have a valid configuration for the requesting client. These DHCPOFFERS are unicast transmissions, however. If you have multiple DHCP servers configured to support the same subnet, some additional traffic may be generated on your network.

In general, a successful initial lease negotiation generates four network packets (DHCPDISCOVER, DHCPOFFER, DHCPREQUEST, and DHCPACK), two of which are broadcasts. However, if the DHCP server is not on the same subnet as the DHCP client, these packets are routed across any intermediate networks between the DHCP client and the server.

A successful lease renewal generates only two network packets (DHCPREQUEST and DHCPACK), which also can be routed across any intermediate networks between the DHCP client and server.

One of the easiest ways to limit the amount of traffic generated by DHCP is to lengthen the lease interval. If you have a network that doesn't have a large number of roaming users, you can take advantage of the conveniences of DHCP's automated administration and record-keeping capabilities without the need to renew all of the leases every three days.

Installing the DHCP Server

Novell's DHCP Server is a separate product, included in the IntranetWare package that you install from the NetWare server console using the INSTALL.NLM utility. In fact, you can install the DHCP Server software on multiple file servers at the same time, without having to treat each server individually.

DHCP Server is listed on INSTALL.NLM's Product Options menu (see Figure 26.5). Once you have selected the product, you are prompted for the path from which to install the DHCP files; choose the path appropriate to your installation.

N O T E   The NetWare/IP Administrator's Guide in the IntranetWare product manuals contains the documentation for the NetWare DHCP Server. This manual specifies the path to the location of the product on IntranetWare CD-ROM disk 1 as NW411:DHCP. In fact, the installation directory for the DHCP Server on the IntranetWare release CD is as follows:

`NW411:PRODUCTS\NW411\INSTALL\IBM\DOS\XXX\ENGLISH`

FIG. 26.5
The DHCP Server installation option is incorporated into NetWare's INSTALL.NLM program.

After you specify the correct source path for the DHCP server source files, INSTALL copies the files needed for the installation, and you are prompted to select the NetWare server or servers where you want to install the DHCP service.

After you've completed the server selections, you are prompted to restart the target servers to ensure that they are using the newly installed versions of the NLM files.

N O T E During the installation process, DHCP information is stored in a file called DHCPTAB in the NetWare server's SYS:ETC directory. If you have previously installed a NetWare BOOTP server, such as the one included with the LAN WorkGroup product, the BOOTP information stored in the SYS:ETC\BOOTPTAB file is copied to the new SYS:ETC\DHCPTAB file. This is a one-time event: any future changes to the BOOTPTAB file are not copied to DHCPTAB, and would have to be performed manually. ▪

Part
VII

Ch

26

Loading the DHCP Server

After rebooting the NetWare servers on which the DHCP service has been installed, you can activate the DHCP Server by issuing the following file server console command, which you should also add to the server's AUTOEXEC.NCF file:

```
LOAD DHCPSRVR [-T x] [-A y] [-H]
```

The optional parameters on the DHCPSRVR.NLM load line are as follows:

- ▪ -T_x specifies the interval the DHCP Server will use between checks for updates to the SYS:ETC\DHCPTAB configuration file. The default value of x is 60 seconds, which is sufficient for most installations.
- ▪ -A_y specifies the interval the DHCP Server will use between checks to see if the lease time for assigned IP addresses has expired. The default value is 10 minutes.
- ▪ -H displays a help screen during the loading of the DHCP Server.

Configuring the DHCP Server

You must configure the DHCP Server with the IP addresses and other parameters that you want to assign to clients, before it can be used. You do this from the NetWare server console by running the DHCPCFG.NLM program. When you load the DHCP configuration program, you see the DHCP Configuration Menu, shown in Figure 26.6.

FIG. 26.6

DHCP Server includes a separate configuration program, called DHCPCFG.NLM.

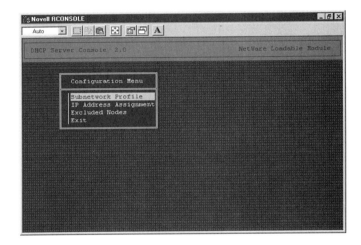

The Configuration Menu contains the following options:

- **Subnetwork Profile**—You must configure this section for each subnetwork that you plan to support with your DHCP Server. Configuration information includes the range of IP addresses that will be used as the pool for *leasing* addresses to nodes, the duration of the IP address leases, and other settings.

- **IP Address Assignment**—Even if you are using DHCP to dynamically configure most of your network clients, you will probably have a few nodes that must be assigned a permanent IP address. Printers and routers often fall into this category.

- **Excluded Nodes**—Some computer systems should not be configured automatically, and may broadcast invalid BOOTP or DHCP requests. Entering the MAC or physical layer addresses of those nodes here prevents the DHCP server from using up your available IP addresses unnecessarily.

Subnetwork Profile is the most important place to start configuring your DHCP server. Assuming you have loaded and bound TCP/IP to one or more network interfaces in your NetWare server, you'll see a *static* entry for each of those subnetworks already created, as shown in Figure 26.7. You can also configure DHCP for additional subnetworks; to create an entry for another subnet, press the Insert key.

FIG. 26.7
Subnetwork Profiles for the network adapters in the server are created during the DHCP installation.

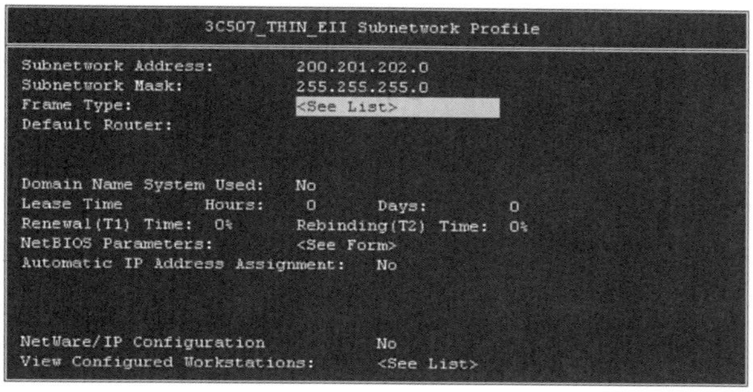

```
                    3C507_THIN_EII Subnetwork Profile

  Subnetwork Address:        200.201.202.0
  Subnetwork Mask:           255.255.255.0
  Frame Type:                <See List>
  Default Router:


  Domain Name System Used:   No
  Lease Time      Hours:     0       Days:      0
  Renewal(T1) Time:  0%      Rebinding(T2) Time:  0%
  NetBIOS Parameters:        <See Form>
  Automatic IP Address Assignment:   No



  NetWare/IP Configuration           No
  View Configured Workstations:      <See List>
```

Most of the fields in the Subnetwork Profile screen have submenus behind them. For example, when you edit the Frame Type field, you are able to select from a list of available frame types. For Ethernet networks using the TCP/IP protocol you should choose ETHERNET_II as the frame type; token-ring networks using TCP/IP should be configured for the TOKEN-RING_SNAP frame type.

N O T E DHCPCFG does not require that you enter information in every field of a subnetwork profile, because the DHCP protocol does not require that every possible piece of configuration information be provided to each client. You may want to manually configure each individual client's IP address, for example, but allow the client to obtain the rest of its configuration information from the DHCP server. ▦

Subnetwork Configuration Parameters

In this section, you learn how to configure the individual DHCP settings for each subnetwork supported by the DHCP server. Remember that not all parameters must be completed. The available parameters are as follows:

- **Subnetwork Profile Name**—When you create a new Subnetwork Profile, you are prompted for a descriptive name for the profile. This entry is used only for reference, so there is no restriction on what name you give to the profile.

- **Subnetwork Address**—This is a required field, and should contain the IP subnet address you want to configure, in dotted decimal notation. All DHCP clients on this subnet will be assigned the configuration information you supply in this profile.

N O T E The Subnet Profile Name and Subnetwork Address are created automatically for server LAN adapters that have already had TCP/IP bound to them when DHCP is installed. You need only supply values for these two fields if you create a new profile. ▦

- **Subnet Mask**—Enter the subnet mask for the subnetwork that you are configuring, in dotted decimal notation. Press Enter for a list of possible subnet mask values.

- **Frame Type**—Select the frame type used by the clients on this subnetwork. This field is required, so you must enter at least one frame type. Ethernet networks using TCP/IP work best with the ETHERNET_II frame type, while token-ring networks using TCP/IP require the TOKEN-RING_SNAP frame type.

- **Default Router**—Enter the IP address of the default gateway router that workstations on this subnet will use when communicating with host computer systems on remote networks. Normally this entry should be in dotted decimal notation, but if you have an entry for the gateway router in this server's SYS:\ETC\HOSTS file, you can use its host name instead. This field is optional because the default router address can be pre-configured on the client workstation if you want.

  If you are running a single-segment network, this field is completely optional.

- **Domain Name System Used**—This field is optional. Leave it set to No if you do not use DNS name resolution. If you change this field to Yes, a pop-up screen appears in which you can enter DNS configuration information.

- **Lease Time**—This field is optional. If you leave both Hours and Days set to 0, the NetWare DHCP server uses a default IP address lease time of 3 days. The lease time can be set as high as 10,000 days and 23 hours.

- **Renewal(T1) Time** and **Rebinding(T2) Time**—These fields are optional. If you leave them at 0.0 percent, your DHCP clients will renew their IP leases when 50 percent of the lease duration has expired, and will try to contact any DHCP server for a new IP address lease when 87 percent of the lease duration has expired.

- **NetBIOS Parameters**—Pressing the Enter key on the See Form value enables you to configure various NetBIOS settings for the DHCP clients on this subnet. These settings support WINS (Windows Internet Name Service) for Microsoft Windows network clients. Microsoft's networking features are based on NetBIOS naming; WINS is used to resolve NetBIOS names to IP addresses (a function similar to DNS name resolution).

  Configuration options include the IP addresses of up to three NetBIOS Name Servers, the Node Type (B Node, P Node, M Node, or H Node), and a NetBIOS Scope. WINS defaults to h-node, always querying the NetBIOS name server for a NetBIOS name/IP address entry before using b-node broadcasts.

- **Automatic IP Address Assignment**—This field is optional. Leave it set to No if your DHCP clients are manually configured with their own IP addresses. If you change it to Yes, the next field is activated.

- **Assign all Subnet IP Addresses**—This field is optional. If you have elected to assign IP addresses dynamically, you can also choose to make every possible IP address on the subnet available for assignment, or specify a range of available IP addresses.

 If you have one or more routers on the selected subnet, you should probably *not* allow the assignment of all Subnet IP Addresses. Instead, provide a range of addresses that does not include those assigned to your routers. It has become something of a *de facto* industry standard to assign routers and servers to fairly low-number addresses within each subnet.

- **NetWare/IP Configuration**—If you're using NetWare/IP to replace Novell's IPX/SPX protocol with TCP/IP (see Chapter 25, "Using NetWare/IP"), you should set this optional field to Yes. A screen is then displayed for the entry of the NetWare/IP configuration information for the IP addresses on this subnet, as shown in Figure 26.8. NetWare/IP configuration information can also be manually set on individual workstations.

FIG. 26.8
DHCP Server enables you to configure NetWare/IP parameters for your workstations.

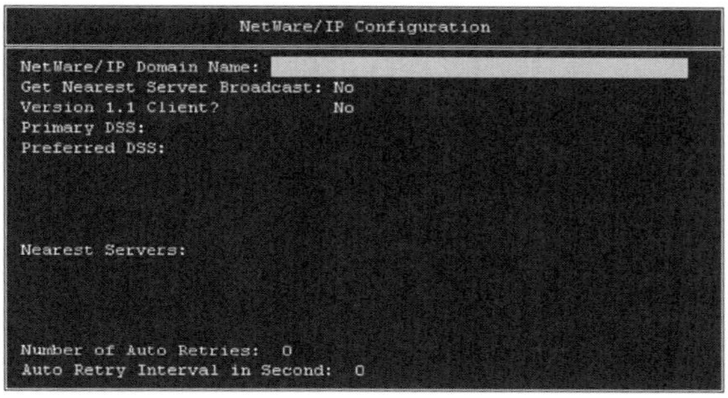

```
                    NetWare/IP Configuration

NetWare/IP Domain Name: [                                    ]
Get Nearest Server Broadcast: No
Version 1.1 Client?           No
Primary DSS:
Preferred DSS:



Nearest Servers:



Number of Auto Retries:  0
Auto Retry Interval in Second:  0
```

■ **View Configured Workstations**—Strictly speaking, this isn't a configuration parameter. Instead, you can use this field to view the list of workstations that have been configured on this subnetwork. As a network administrator you will sometimes need to be able to track down the IP configurations of your workstations, and this is a lot more efficient than visiting each workstation individually. This screen displays names, physical addresses, and IP addresses for all workstations that are configured on this subnetwork.

Assigning Static IP Addresses

Even if you configure most of your computer systems using dynamically leased addresses, you are likely to have a few nodes that must have a static, manually configured IP address. DHCP is used to its best advantage when it is allowed to manage all of the IP addresses on a network. If you do not enter the addresses of your manually configured systems here, you must keep track of them in some other way, leaving open the possibility that the DHCP server will assign the addresses to other systems.

Some systems or hosts that must have static IP addresses are the following:

■ Web servers
■ FTP servers
■ NetWare servers
■ Communication servers
■ Printers
■ Routers and bridges
■ Hubs and concentrators

Network resources like these are often accessed by IP address only, and not by host name. In order to maintain a stable network, users and clients must always be able to find certain services at the same address. Web, NetWare, FTP servers, and the like, are often accessed by

Part VII Ch 26

addresses that are obtained from HOSTS files or the DNS (Domain Name Service); both of these services use static tables to look up IP addresses based on host names. TCP/IP printing configuration almost always requires that you provide the printer's IP address. Routers, bridges, hubs, and concentrators are often managed using the Simple Network Management Protocol (SNMP), and must always be found at fixed addresses.

After selecting the IP Address Assignment option from the Configuration Menu (refer to Figure 26.6), press Insert to create a new address assignment. On the configuration screen (see Figure 26.9), you must provide the IP and physical addresses of the computer system involved. The Internet address must be a valid address on a subnet for which you have already defined a Subnetwork Profile. After you've completed the entry, DHCPCFG will fill in the Subnet Profile and lease information fields.

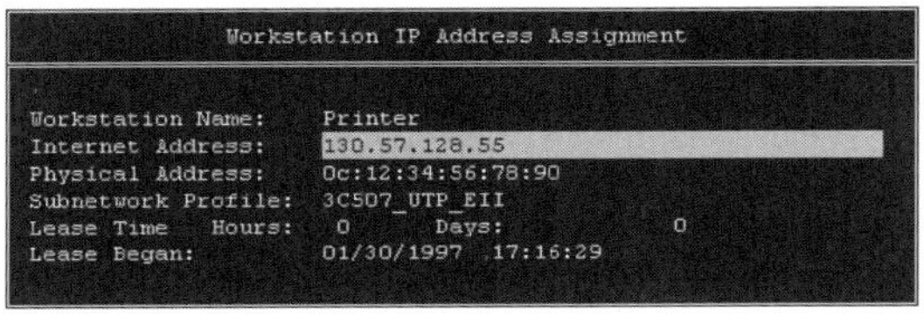

FIG. 26.9

You can create individual IP address assignments for systems that cannot be dynamically assigned configuration parameters.

```
                 Workstation IP Address Assignment

Workstation Name:     Printer
Internet Address:     130.57.128.55
Physical Address:     0c:12:34:56:78:90
Subnetwork Profile:   3C507_UTP_EII
Lease Time   Hours:   0      Days:           0
Lease Began:          01/30/1997  17:16:29
```

Excluded Nodes

Some computer systems just cannot be configured automatically by DHCP, or may be broadcasting invalid BOOTP/DHCP requests. If you enter the addresses of such systems in the Excluded Nodes screen, your DHCP server will ignore requests from these nodes and avoid using up all of your IP address assignments. You need only insert the physical addresses of such nodes, along with any identifying comments you may want.

Summary

This chapter introduces the basic concepts of automating the TCP/IP configuration process for your network clients, and describes how to install and configure Novell's DHCP Server on your NetWare servers. One of Novell's goals for IntranetWare is to minimize your cost of ownership, and the DHCP Server is one of the tools that will help you do that. The DHCP Server is also closely related to Novell's TCP/IP Transport, NetWare/IP, and DNS server, and can help you make Internet connectivity easier. ●

CHAPTER 27

Using the IPX/IP Gateway

Since its inception, NetWare has relied on a system of transport protocols that were developed by Novell specifically for use with the operating system. Proprietary systems were indicative of the networking industry at the time; customers tended to select a single network operating system and rely on it exclusively. The IPX/SPX protocols functioned well with NetWare, and could be updated as needed by Novell's developers.

Today, however, customers are more likely to select whatever operating system can best perform the task at hand, and the drive toward the use of open standards is intense. Many sites run several network operating systems over the same cable plant, and administrators have come to standardize on the TCP/IP protocols for everything except NetWare.

IntranetWare is Novell's attempt to expand the range of services provided by a NetWare network. The emergence of Internet and intranet systems as a dominant force in networking has made the capability to use TCP/IP with NetWare an essential part of a modern network. You learned in Chapter 25, "Using NetWare/IP," how to use TCP/IP for NetWare communications, enabling your clients to access intranet/Internet services in the process. However, IntranetWare includes an alternative to

The advantages and disadvantages of running TCP/IP on network workstations

TCP/IP provides network users with many additional capabilities, but it also imposes an additional support burden on network administrators.

How the IPX/IP Gateway is integrated into the IntranetWare TCP/IP services

The IPX/IP Gateway is part of the Novell Internet Access Server package, which provides a unified solution for connecting a NetWare network to the Internet.

How to install the IPX/IP Gateway on a NetWare server

Installing and configuring the IPX/IP Gateway requires the use of the INETCFG.NLM program and extensions to the NDS schema.

How to install the IPX/IP Gateway clients

The IPX/IP Gateway includes new versions of the Client 32 for DOS/Windows and for Windows 95 that provide the workstation with IP access through the gateway.

NetWare/IP, an IPX/IP gateway that provides IPX clients with access to TCP/IP services without having to install a TCP/IP stack. ■

Using TCP/IP with NetWare

Many NetWare sites are currently being faced with the need to provide Internet access to their users. In addition, new intranet development technologies are making TCP/IP services a popular alternative to groupware products like Lotus Notes. The Novell Internet Access Server (NIAS) is designed to connect a private network to an Internet service provider (ISP) using a NetWare server as a router. IntranetWare also includes the tools needed to create your own intranet applications, as well as the clients and servers needed to host them.

One of the most difficult parts of implementing these technologies, however, is equipping your workstations with the client software needed to access these TCP/IP services. You may be able to connect your network to an ISP in the course of a weekend, but installing and configuring TCP/IP stacks and browsers on dozens or hundreds of clients is another story.

IntranetWare includes tools to facilitate the addition of TCP/IP to client workstations, including a DHCP server that dynamically allocates IP addresses to clients on demand (see Chapter 26, "Using the Dynamic Host Configuration Protocol (DHCP) Server"), but the task can still be enormous.

Another vitally important issue with TCP/IP connectivity is security, both internal and external. A client workstation that can be used to access the Internet can also be accessed from the Internet, unless specific precautions are taken to prevent this. The same holds true for internal network security. There are many more tools that enable a user to access another workstation on the network using TCP/IP than there are using IPX.

Protection against intrusion is a matter that is better left in the hands of network administrators than individual users. Implementing a firewall or some other form of protection greatly complicates the tasking of rolling out TCP/IP on a network.

Carrying IP Within IPX

The Novell Internet Access Server contains a solution that addresses all of the problems inherent in providing TCP/IP access to NetWare clients. In networking, a router is a device that connects two networks running the same protocol. A *gateway* connects networks running different protocols. Novell's IPX/IP Gateway enables IPX clients to access TCP/IP services without running a TCP/IP stack themselves.

The IPX/IP Gateway is installed on a NetWare 4.1 or 4.11 server as part of the NIAS product. In addition to server modules, it consists of extensions to the NDS schema, a snap-in module that enables the NetWare Administrator to manage the NDS objects and properties provided by the extensions, and updated versions of the Client 32 for DOS/Windows and Windows 95.

CAUTION

Only NetWare client workstations running the versions of Client 32 for DOS and Windows or Client 32 for Windows 95 included with the Novell Internet Access Server can utilize the IPX/IP Gateway. Other NetWare clients, including other versions of these same two clients (such as those found on the NetWare 4.11 CD-ROM in the IntranetWare package) will not function with the gateway.

The IPX/IP Gateway clients include Winsock DLLs, just as a TCP/IP client does, but they do not actually run the IP protocol, nor do they have IP addresses. Users can run standard Web browsers, FTP, news, and mail clients, but instead of connecting directly to the target IP address specified in the application, the client connects to the gateway server using the IPX protocol. The server, which does have a TCP/IP stack, connects in turn to the target IP address and requests data from the service specified by the client.

The gateway server, therefore, functions very much like a proxy server, except that it relays TCP (Transport Control Protocol) data to and from the client using IPX instead of IP, as shown in Figure 27.1. Acting as the middleman between the NetWare client and the IP target, the gateway also functions as a security buffer. Because only the server has an IP address, outside systems cannot access the NetWare workstations using TCP/IP utilities.

NOTE The IPX/IP Gateway is capable of providing users with access to TCP-based services only. It cannot perform as a gateway for UDP (User Datagram Protocol) data. Most standard Internet applications are TCP-based, however. ▮

FIG. 27.1
An IPX/IP Gateway server accesses TCP/IP services for NetWare clients and passes them data using the IPX protocol.

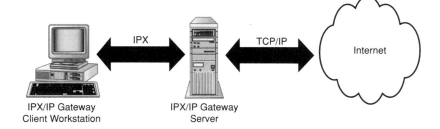

IPX/IP Gateway Client Workstation

IPX/IP Gateway Server

IPX

TCP/IP

Internet

The gateway also provides administrators with the capability to restrict user access to TCP/IP services, either by allowing access only to specific services, or by limiting the actual host IP addresses to which users can connect. You control users' access by modifying properties that are added to container, Group, and User objects in the NDS tree when you enable the gateway.

Enabling the IPX/IP Gateway

Because the IPX/IP Gateway software is installed as part of the Novell Internet Access Server, it is only necessary to enable and configure the gateway to make it operational. Before you do

Part
VII

Ch
27

this, however, you must have configured the NetWare server on which the product is installed to function as a router between your NetWare IPX LAN and a TCP/IP LAN or WAN connection.

This means that the server must have at least two network interface adapters installed in it. One adapter is connected and bound to your internal NetWare LAN like any other server. The other adapter must be bound to a TCP/IP network. This can be a local connection to your corporate intranet, or a WAN connection to a remote office or an ISP. A NetWare client should be able to connect to the server in the usual way, and you should be able to ping an address on the TCP/IP network using the PING.NLM program at the server console.

N O T E   After installing NIAS, you configure the two network connections in the server using the INETCFG.NLM utility at the server console. The installation process expands the capabilities of INETCFG, allowing control of the protocol LOAD and BIND statements to be transferred from the server's AUTOEXEC.NCF file to INETCFG's configuration files. From this point, all future LAN and WAN configuration tasks must be performed through the INETCFG utility. For more information on configuring the network connections, see Chapter 28, "Using the Multiprotocol Router." ▧

Once the server is operating as a router, you enable the IPX/IP Gateway from the TCP/IP Protocol Configuration panel in the INETCFG.NLM utility. Selecting IPX/IP Gateway Configuration displays the panel shown in Figure 27.2.

FIG. 27.2
Enable and configure the IPX/IP Gateway from the server console using the INETCFG.NLM utility.

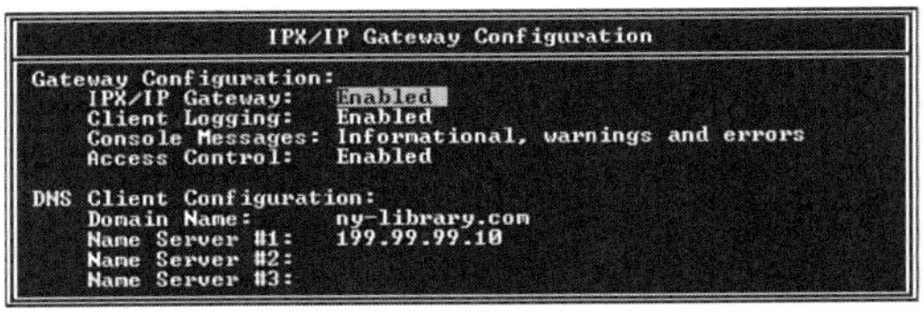

N O T E   To run the IPX/IP Gateway, your MAXIMUM PACKET RECEIVE BUFFERS setting must be at least 1000. You can modify this using the SET command from the server console prompt, or the MONITOR or SERVMAN utility. ▧

From this panel, you can configure the following gateway parameters:

- **IPX/IP Gateway**—Enabling this parameter activates the gateway by loading the IPXGW.NLM module and extending the NDS schema.
- **Client Logging**—Enabling this parameter causes all client access to TCP/IP services to be logged to a file on the root of the server's SYS volume called GW_AUDIT.LOG.
- **Console Messages**—This allows the selection of what messages should be displayed at the server console and logged into the GW_INFO.LOG file at the root of the SYS volume. Possible values are Errors Only, Warnings and Errors, and Informational, Warnings, and Errors.

■ **Access Control**—When disabled, all clients are permitted full use of the gateway. When enabled, you can use the NetWare Administrator to control access.

You also can configure the gateway's DNS client parameters from this panel, by specifying the name of the domain in which the server resides, and the addresses of up to three DNS servers. The DNS servers used by the gateway may be located on your enterprise network, at your ISP's location, or elsewhere on the Internet.

N O T E The IPX/IP Gateway can also use a DNS server running on the same computer as the gateway itself. ■

Extending the Schema

When you save your changes to the TCP/IP configuration in the INETCFG.NLM utility, you are prompted to supply the name and password for a user that has Supervisor object rights to the [Root] of the NDS tree. This provides the program with the rights needed to extend the directory schema, create an object representing the IPX/IP Gateway server, and add two new panels to the Details dialog box of every User, Organization, Organizational Unit, and Group object in the NDS tree.

N O T E Depending on the size and distribution of your tree, the modifications to the NDS database may cause noticeable delays while the changes are replicated to other servers around the enterprise. ■

The IPX/IP Gateway Server object is created in the same container as the NetWare server on which the gateway is installed. Its name is the same as that of the NetWare server object, with -GW appended to it (see Figure 27.3).

FIG. 27.3
The IPX/IP Gateway object is created in the NDS tree when you enable the gateway software.

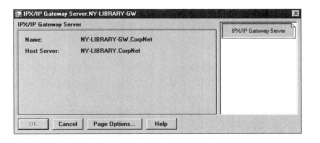

Part
VII

Ch
27

Modifying the gateway parameters with the INETCFG program manipulates the NDS database in real time, but the commands needed to load the gateway software on the server are only written to INETCFG's configuration files. They are not executed until you select Reinitialize System from INETCFG's main menu, or restart the server.

When you do this, an IPX/IP Gateway Status panel is created on the server console, and a summary of the load parameters is displayed on the main console screen, as follows:

```
Loading module IPXGW.NLM
  Novell IPX/IP Gateway [ip0100.b09]
  Version 0.22z   August 6, 1996
  (C) Copyright 1994, Novell, Inc.  All rights reserved
  Auto-loading module NETDB.NLM
  NETWORK DATABASE ACCESS NLM
  Version 3.25c   July 1, 1996
  (C) Copyright 1995, Novell, Inc.  All rights reserved

NDS Context: O=CorpNet
NetDB Library loaded successfully.
  Auto-loading module IPXF.NLM
  IPX Fragmentation Layer
  Version 3.10   January 4, 1996
  Copyright (C) 1996 Novell, Inc.  All Rights Reserved
IPX/IP Gateway Information Level is ALREADY set to 3
IPX/IP Gateway Access Control set to ON
IPX/IP Gateway Audit Log is ALREADY set to ON
```

Installing the Snap-in Module

In order to view and manage the objects and parameters created by the schema extensions applied to the NDS tree, you must use a snap-in module with the NetWare Administrator. When you install the Novell Internet Access Server, the module is copied to the SYS volume of the NetWare server as part of the new Client 32 installation directories created under SYS:PUBLIC\CLIENT.

Installing one of the Gateway-capable clients to a workstation causes the modules to be copied to the computer's local drive, in the C:\NOVELL\CLIENT32 directory, by default. There are two snap-in modules, as follows:

- **IPXGW3X.DLL**—For use with gateways installed on NetWare 4.11 servers
- **IPXGW.DLL**—For use with gateways installed on NetWare 4.10 servers

These modules are designed for use only with the 16-bit versions of the NetWare Administrator, the executables for which are found in the SYS:PUBLIC directory, as NWADMN3X.EXE (for NetWare 4.11), or NWADMIN.EXE (for NetWare 4.10). If you are planning to administer the Gateway parameters from a Windows 95 or Windows NT workstation, you must run one of these versions of the NetWare Administrator instead of the 32-bit version.

You must also manually configure the NetWare Administrator to locate the snap-in module. Running the 16-bit version of the program for the first time creates a configuration file in the workstation's WINDOWS directory, called NWADMN3X.INI. In order for the NetWare Administrator to find the snap-in module, you must have the following section in this file when you are running the gateway on a NetWare 4.11 server:

```
[Snapin Object DLLs WIN3X]
ipxgw3x.dll=ipxgw3x.dll
```

If you are running the gateway on a NetWare 4.10 server, the INI file changes must be as follows:

```
[Snapin Object DLLs]
dll=c:\novell\client32=ipxgw.dll
```

Installing Client 32 adds the C:\NOVELL\CLIENT32 directory to the computer's PATH statement in the AUTOEXEC.BAT file, so that the IPXGW3X.DLL file can be found. You can add a path identifier to the INI file if the snap-in module is located elsewhere.

The next time that you run the NetWare Administrator, you will be able to view and manage the IPX/IP Gateway Server object, as well as the IPX/IP Gateway Service Restrictions and IPX/IP Gateway Host Restrictions panels in the User, Group, and container objects.

Configuring Access Control

If you elected not to enable the Access Control feature in INETCFG's IPX/IP Gateway Configuration panel, then there is no need for you to modify the gateway parameters in the NDS database at all. If you do want to control the access that your users are granted to TCP/IP services, you must configure the NetWare Administrator to access the required snap-in module, as discussed in the previous section.

N O T E Novell recommends that if you are running more than one IPX/IP Gateway server on your network, you either enable or disable Access Control for all of your servers. ■

Then, you must assign the following rights so that the gateway server is capable of reading the access control parameters of NDS tree objects:

- Make [Public] a trustee of the IPX/IP Gateway object, with the Browse object right, and the Read and Compare rights to all properties.
- Make [Public] a trustee of the NetWare Server object on which the IPX/IP Gateway is running, with the Browse object right, and the Read and Compare rights to the Network Address property.
- Make the IPX/IP Gateway object a trustee of [Root], with the Browse object right, and the Read and Compare rights to all properties.

For more information on assigning NDS rights, see Chapter 14, "Understanding NDS Object and Property Rights."

Part
VII

Ch
27

Planning an Access Control Strategy

When you enable Access Control for the IPX/IP Gateway in INETCFG, all users still are granted full access to all TCP/IP services, until you impose restrictions using the NetWare Administrator. You can apply IPX/IP Gateway access restrictions to any Organization, Organizational Unit, Group, or User object in the NDS tree. The restrictions are inherited by users in a container and members of a group like other NDS properties, enabling you to easily apply restrictions to large numbers of users.

When you add access restrictions to a User object, then any restrictions that have been applied to the user's parent container object are ignored. If, however, a user is a member of a group, then the Group object's restrictions are combined with the User object's restrictions.

The Access Control feature does not specify which clients can communicate with the IPX/IP Gateway; all users with the appropriate client software have this capability. Rather, it controls what services users are permitted to access, and when.

You can apply access restrictions in two ways: by limiting the types of TCP/IP services that clients can access, and by limiting the actual sites they can access. You configure these controls in the IPX/IP Gateway Service Restrictions and IPX/IP Gateway Host Restrictions panels of an NDS object's Details dialog box. The following sections discuss the application of these two types of restrictions.

Applying Service Restrictions   TCP/IP client applications use various high-level protocols to communicate with the host systems on the Internet (or an intranet) that run the server component. To ensure that a data transmission reaches the appropriate process on the destination host system, each process is assigned a port number. The combination of an IP address and a port number is called a *socket*.

Most common TCP/IP services use standard port numbers that are defined in a document published by the Internet Engineering Task Force. For example, Web servers traditionally use port number 80. Although you can configure most Web servers to use a different port, this is rarely done because users must know the correct port number to connect to the server with a client.

When you apply a gateway service restriction, you are limiting the transmission of a specific protocol to a specific port. You can, for example, allow your users to send and receive Internet e-mail, but prevent them from surfing the Web. If this seems too harsh a policy, you can also impose restrictions based on the time of day, allowing Web surfing only after 5:00 p.m., for example.

The IPX/IP Gateway Service Restrictions panel (see Figure 27.4) appears in every User, Group, and Container dialog box. The panel consists of two basic parts: a series of four radio buttons used to define a general policy, and a list of exceptions to whatever policy you select.

The four general policies are as follows:

- **Inherited Default Access**—Restrictions inherited from the parent container object are applied. By default, this means full access to all services.

- **Unlimited Access to All Services**—Overrides any restrictions inherited from the parent container object.

- **No Access to Any Service**—Prevents access to any TCP/IP services.

- **Access Time**—Enables you to specify a range of hours during which access to TCP/IP services is allowed.

FIG. 27.4

The IPX/IP Gateway Services Restrictions panel enables you to control the protocols accessed through the gateway.

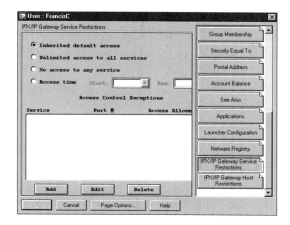

Whichever of these four policies you choose, you can create a list of specific exceptions to the rule. When you click the Add button to add an item to the list, you see a Service Restriction dialog box like that shown in Figure 27.5. Here you select a particular service, modifying the port number if necessary, and define the policy that you want enforced for that particular service, relative to the general rule you have selected. You can opt for No Access, Unlimited Access, or a specified range of Access Time.

FIG. 27.5

In the Service Restriction dialog box, you define the access control policy for an individual TCP/IP service.

You can select from the following services:

- **HTTP (HyperText Transfer Protocol)**—The standard protocol used to transmit text and graphics to World Wide Web browsers
- **FTP (File Transfer Protocol)**—Used to reliably transfer binary or ASCII files between systems using a standard interface
- **TELNET**—Used for remote terminal emulation services
- **NNTP (Network News Transfer Protocol)**—The standard protocol used by newsreader clients to access UseNet and other newsgroups
- **SMTP (Simple Mail Transfer Protocol)**—Used by a client to send outgoing Internet e-mail

Part
VII

Ch
27

- **POP3 (Post Office Protocol 3)**—Used by a client to receive incoming Internet e-mail
- **FINGER**—Used to locate information about users on a TCP/IP network
- **SNMP (Simple Network Management Protocol)**—Used to transmit network status information
- **SNMP-TRAP**—Used to transmit specialized SNMP messages, usually concerning system startups or shutdowns
- **PRINTER (lpr)**—Used to transmit print job data across the networks

When you select a service by name, its assigned port number appears with it. You can modify this port number as needed to conform to the services on network.

Applying Host Restrictions   In addition to service restrictions, you can also control users' access to specific host systems. The IPX Gateway Host Restrictions panel contains a list of IP addresses to which you either block or limit access. In the Host Restriction dialog box, shown in Figure 27.6, you specify an IP address and deny users all access, or restrict access to a particular time period.

FIG. 27.6
The Host Restrictions dialog box enables you to limit user access to particular IP host systems.

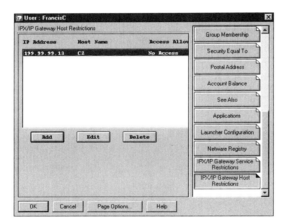

This feature is practical for intranet use, enabling you to limit users' access to certain systems. For Internet connections, however, the prospect of limiting users' access to certain sites in this way is an administrative nightmare.

Running the Gateway Clients

As mentioned earlier, users must run one of the Client 32 versions that ship with the Novell Internet Access Server in order to use the IPX/IP Gateway. The installation files for these clients are placed in the SYS:PUBLIC\CLIENT directory on the server, in the WIN31 and WIN95 subdirectories.

N O T E When installing Client 32 for DOS/Windows, you must run the SETUP.EXE program from Windows in order to use the IPX/IP Gateway. You cannot use the INSTALL.EXE from the DOS prompt. ▪

The gateway clients include Novell's own versions of the WINSOCK.DLL and WSOCK32.DLL modules that are an essential part of any TCP/IP implementation. Even though the gateway client does not actually use a TCP/IP stack, the Winsock modules are needed because TCP/IP applications look for them as a means of gaining network access. Any other TCP/IP client installed on a workstation will have a Winsock DLL, including the one that ships as part of the Windows 95 operating system.

Using the Gateway Switcher

Fortunately, the installation of a gateway client does not preclude the use of a TCP/IP client on the same system. Novell includes a utility called the Gateway Switcher with the client package that enables the user to enable and disable the gateway client at will.

This program functions by renaming the extensions of both Winsock modules, alternatively. When you disable the gateway client, its WINSOCK.DLL module is renamed to WINSOCK.N01, so that a TCP/IP application cannot use it for network access. Enabling the gateway client restores the module to its original name and renames the Microsoft Winsock to prevent its use.

When the IPX/IP Gateway client is active, the Gateway Task program runs in a minimized state. Novell provides both 16- and 32-bit versions of this program (in files called NOVGWP16.EXE and NOVGWPRC.EXE, respectively), which serves as an indicator of the client's current operational status.

Using WinPing

Perhaps the best-known TCP/IP program is PING, the command-line diagnostic utility that enables you to test your system's capability to communicate with another system by sending a message and receiving a response. PING uses the Internet Control Message Protocol (ICMP), a specialized Network-layer protocol that is carried in IP packets.

Because the standard PING program does not use TCP, it cannot function on a gateway client system. Novell, therefore, includes a TCP-based implementation of PING with its gateway clients, called WinPing. This program provides a graphical interface to the utility (see Figure 27.7), and enables users to test the functionality of the IPX/IP Gateway by sending messages to remote hosts on the TCP/IP network.

Part
VII

Ch
27

FIG. 27.7

WinPing is a GUI version of the venerable PING utility that uses TCP, instead of ICMP.

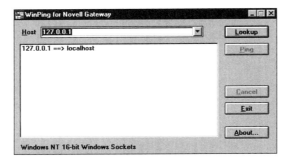

Installing the IPX/IP Gateway Protocol

When you install one of the Client 32s that ship with the Novell Internet Access Server, the IPX/IP Gateway client is not activated by default. You must manually add the IPX/IP Gateway protocol in order to install the Winsock module and the gateway utilities.

For Client 32 for DOS/Windows, you select the NetWare IPX/IP Gateway option in the Additional Options panel. When installing Client 32 for Windows 95, you add a new protocol in the Network Control Panel and select the Novell NetWare IPX/IP Gateway.

Specifying a Preferred Server   If you are running multiple gateways on your network, you can configure your clients to use a preferred gateway server in order to balance the traffic load. You specify the full distinguished name of the server, using either typeful or typeless notation, in the Properties dialog box for the IPX/IP Gateway protocol.

When a client workstation attempts to contact a gateway server, it uses the following connection priorities:

- A preferred gateway server using NDS
- Any gateway server using NDS
- A preferred gateway server using the NetWare bindery
- Any gateway server using SAP

If you have only a single gateway server on the network, it will be located in any case, regardless of the preferred server setting.

Using the NOVWS.INI File   Activating the gateway client causes a configuration file called NOVWS.INI to be created in the WINDOWS directory of both Windows 3.1 and Windows 95 systems. This file contains the parameters that specify whether the gateway client is enabled, and the name of the preferred gateway server, if any. On a Windows 95 system, the file also specifies the dummy file name extension used by the Gateway Switcher utility when it temporarily renames files.

If you are installing a complex gateway environment, you can use this INI file to enable gateway clients and set preferred servers by copying the file to your client workstations, rather than use the GUI to configure each one individually.

Summary

The IPX/IP Gateway provides network administrators with an excellent alternative to the installation of a TCP/IP stack on a fleet of client workstations. The gateway provides a measure of control over users' access to the Internet without the need for complex firewall products or an extensive IP address registration regimen. ●

CHAPTER 28

Using the Multiprotocol Router

A significant function of any network is the capability of users to communicate. IntranetWare provides the means to perform this communication among users on a local area network (LAN) or a wide area network (WAN), as well as across the Internet utilizing the components included with the Novell Internet Access Server (NIAS).

One of the pieces of NIAS is Novell's Multiprotocol Router (MPR). MPR contains components that enhance routing services across LAN segments, as well as a single port WAN Extension driver to enable communication with networks external to the LAN. By connecting LANs to a WAN, you can enhance the communication among people on your network through such services as electronic mail and file sharing. By connecting your LAN to the Internet, you will have global electronic mail service, as well as the capability to research information, download files, and publish information about yourself to a global market. ■

How to build a wide area network

Learn about the hardware needed and the means of providing the connections between sites.

How to configure link protocols

Learn how to configure PPP, frame relay, and ATM links.

How to configure network protocols to the WAN

Learn how to use IPX and TCP/IP across the WAN to connect to the IntranetWare server.

How to connect to the Internet using MPR

Learn about configuring the link to your ISP for optimum performance.

Communicating on a Wide Area Network

The primary difference between a local area network (LAN) and a wide area network is in who controls the communication media and hardware. In a LAN environment, all the communication hardware and cabling belongs to, and is the responsibility of, the owner of the network. This usually includes hubs and switches, copper and fiber optic cabling, and potentially, wireless communication devices. In a WAN the components are usually owned and managed by someone else, usually a telephone carrier service. The owner of the LAN contracts with the owner of the WAN to carry his data signal between two or more points.

As you can see, based on this definition, implementing a network via fiber optics between buildings of a campus, say at a college or university, does not constitute a WAN, although it would be a wider area than a network within a single building. If, on the other hand, the same college or university were to contract with the local telephone carrier to provide data services between campuses several miles apart, that would constitute a WAN.

WANs can be implemented over several different media, but all have specific components in common. The first is that the network signal is routed or bridged to the WAN carrier. Next, the electronic signal, as carried on the LAN, is converted to a different signaling structure via a communication device. This can be an asynchronous or synchronous, analog or digital modem, which connects to dial-up communication lines, or it can be a Data Service Unit/Channel Service Unit (DSU/CSU), which connects to dedicated digital communication lines.

In comparative terms, analog signaling is similar to AM radio with a carrier signal on which the data is piggybacked. Digital signaling is likened to FM where the DSU/CSU does not use a carrier signal to transport the data signal and therefore provides a cleaner connection that can travel at higher speeds and for longer distances.

The communication equipment you choose needs to be based upon the expected service it will be required to provide. Asynchronous analog modems can provide service for light loads up to 19.2 Kbps or 33.6 Kbps, depending on the quality of the telephone service in your area. Synchronous analog modems can provide service for light to medium loads up to 56 Kbps.

Digital modems, including ISDN and xDSL (digital subscriber line products that multiplex high-speed digital lines), can increase the level of performance for medium load networks. The speeds attained are between 56 Kbps and 1.5 Mbps, depending on the specific technology implemented by the telephone carrier and the quality of the phone lines.

For heavy network loads or for those networks that require continual connectivity with another site or concurrent connectivity to multiple sites, it is best to implement a dedicated digital carrier service. Utilizing dedicated digital circuits, you can implement network connections to speeds of 155 Mbps, depending on what your local telephone carrier provides. Dedicated digital service devices are also significantly less likely to be affected by interference generated by external electrical disturbances (electro-mechanical interference, EMI) and radio frequency generators (radio frequency interference, RFI). This means that you will transmit more data per baud cycle with less data retries leading to a much higher level of data integrity and reliability.

Connecting to a WAN

Once you have decided on the type and speed of the telephone carrier service for your network requirements, you are ready to take the next step: determining whether to bridge or route your network. Because the subject of this chapter is Novell's Multiprotocol Router, the difference between a bridge and a router is not addressed.

Generally speaking, a bridge directly connects networks of like type into a single homogenous network, passing all data to all attached segments. A router connects distinct network segments, maintaining each segment's independent integrity, passing only the data that is destined for remote destinations to the specific segment that destination address exists on.

Novell's Multiprotocol Router provides the software component needed to implement a WAN when combined with the appropriate Wide Area NIC installed in your IntranetWare server. An example of a Wide Area NIC is Novell's NW2000 adapter. This adapter provides the signaling and connection to the modem or DSU/CSU that connects to the telephone line. A list of approved Wide Area NICs can be downloaded from Novell's Yes Labs Web site (**http://labs.novell.com**) by searching on the keyword WAN. By adding the Novell WAN Extensions product to your IntranetWare package, you can increase the number of WAN ports that can be supported by a single MPR from one to a maximum of 16 ports. WAN Extensions can be purchased from your local authorized Novell reseller.

Natively, MPR supports the following protocols over a wide area network:

- IPX
- TCP/IP
- AppleTalk
- Source Route Bridge

Additionally, any protocol stack that can be loaded on the file server via an NLM can also be managed and maintained by MPR. Along with the various protocols supported, MPR natively supports the following communication medium standards for wide area networking:

- Point-to-Point Protocol (PPP)
- X.25
- Frame relay
- Asynchronous Transfer Mode (ATM)

Additional medium types may be available for specific Wide Area NICs based on their driver types and specifications. Choosing a medium type will depend on the cost of the equipment you will need, the traffic load you want to support, and the speed at which you need to move data.

Part
VII

Ch

Point-to-Point Protocol (PPP)

PPP provides the means to transmit data over serial point-to-point communication links. *Point to point* indicates that there is a single source and a single target location for this means of communication, and as such limits this protocol to connecting only two sites per link.

PPP provides a means for encapsulating datagrams over serial links, as well as a Link Control Protocol (LCP) to establish, configure, and test data-link level connections. Additionally, PPP provides Network Control Protocols (NCP) that enable the user to transport different network protocols across the serial link simultaneously. PPP works over full duplex, bit-oriented synchronous and asynchronous links supporting eight data bits and no parity. PPP was designed to provide transport capability for multiple network level protocols over the same link and is therefore a common solution for WAN connections.

PPP utilizes the High-Level Data Link Control (HDLC) Frame Check Sequence for error detection, which is supported by most WAN adapter hardware. PPP connections provide communication to speeds of over 100 Mbps. Access to PPP networks can be made via dial-up modems and dedicated link devices, such as DSU/CSUs.

X.25

The X.25 specification is an internationally agreed upon standard maintained by the CCITT (French acronym for International Consultative Committee for Telegraphy and Telephony, an organization based in Geneva). X.25 defines a packet-switched network delivered through a public data network, such as AT&T, Sprint, or MCI. In a packet switching network (PSN) datagrams are delivered through a specific path to a destination address. X.25 provides this path through the use of virtual network circuits.

A circuit is a complete connection between any two locations. A physical circuit, or true circuit, implies a direct physical link between the two sites, as with PPP. A virtual circuit is formed on an as needed basis between the sites over a variety of physical components. This can be related to the difference between an intercom and a telephone. The intercom is physically connected by wire between the two points, and when you activate one side, its only possible link is with the device at the other side of the wire. A telephone offers virtual connections to any other available telephone on the system by dialing its address (phone number). If one route to that address is busy, the system provided by the telephone carrier you use automatically reroutes the call to another wire, or circuit, to provide a link between your phone and the one you are calling.

By providing connectivity via virtual circuits, you have a greater chance of making and maintaining connections between sites. Additionally, you can connect more than one site to the virtual network infrastructure. This enables you to connect more than two isolated sites together on the same network through a single router port at each site.

X.25 networks can provide high reliability connections over a long distance, but add significantly to the packet overhead by adding the HDLC Data Link Layer Control Detection and Session Management blocks. These control blocks add to the reliability of the transmission by providing error detection and correction functions to every hop between the source and destination address, but slow the transmission down.

Access to the network is via a synchronous modem that is linked directly to the telephone line provider's switch, through a device called a packet assembler-disassembler (PAD). X.25 connections support speeds up to 56 Kbps.

Frame Relay

Frame relay is a data communication method that was developed out of the X.25 specification. Differences include that the frame relay operates on a digital circuit as opposed to an analog circuit, thus providing the means to support higher throughput with lower latency times. Frame relay is approved by the standards bodies American National Standards Institute (ANSI) and the International Telecommunications Union (ITU).

Frame relay operates with the same virtual circuit design of X.25, but each participating member of the network is assigned a specific access port number called the Data Link Connection Identifier (DLCI). A single physical port can be assigned multiple DLCI addresses and can, therefore, participate in multiple virtual networks, sometimes referred to as private networks. Because the frame relay network can dynamically make its physical link connections via any available circuit, it is often referred to as a *cloud*. As long as the frame relay system knows the source and destination DLCI address for any given frame, it will make the connection regardless of what path it needs to take through the cloud.

Because frame relay utilizes digital telephone service lines, it does not need to have as much error detection implemented in each packet, or frame. Most, if not all, of the error detection and correction is now handled by the DSU/CSU at the customer site. Therefore, more data can be sent over each frame, and more frames can be sent per second, allowing speeds in excess of 45 Mbps.

Because all of the frame relay circuits are maintained in the public cloud, most providers of the service can only guarantee a portion of the actual available line bandwidth the customer has into the cloud. This is known as the *committed information rate* (CIR) and can range from anywhere between two-thirds and one-half of the available line bandwidth. This is the line speed that the telephone service carrier is willing to commit to guarantee regardless of the load upon the physical components making up the cloud.

Because frame relay allows multiple entry points into the cloud, it can also be used to aggregate many slow links into a single high-speed link, a technique known as *multiplexing*. For example, you maintain a home office in city A with ten additional offices scattered around the area. You can maintain a link into the frame relay cloud from the main office at a speed of 512 Kbps and provide 56 Kbps links to each branch office. This will provide you with the capability to maintain all ten links to the branch offices at full available bandwidth speeds. Additionally, providing this type of service reduces the overall cost of operation by reducing hardware requirements on your network and by paying only for the bandwidth you use.

Asynchronous Transfer Mode (ATM)

Asynchronous Transfer Mode (ATM) is a broadband transport system that has been generally accepted as the transfer method of choice for Broadband Integrated Services Digital Networks (BISDN). ATM is designed in such a way that it can simultaneously handle multiple information types, including voice, data imaging, and video.

ATM provides a connection-based packet-switching network based on cell technology in which variable-length data packets are converted to a fixed-length cell of 53 bytes. By being implemented in a packet-switch environment, it offers the benefits of frame relay in that you can connect multiple concurrent sites together into a single network segment, as well as provide data aggregation services allowing multiple slower sites to be combined into a single fast main site.

ATM was designed from the ground up as a new transport method that enables multiple data stream types to be transported concurrently. As such, and based on the fixed-cell size, it can move packets at a very high data rate—up to 622 Mbps. ATM technology provides for future growth with the potential of supporting gigabit per second data transfer speeds in the relatively near future. Currently, the limitations imposed on WAN communication speeds using ATM are based on the physical media and equipment provided by the telephone service carriers.

Installing the NIAS Products

The first step in implementing MPR is to install its components, as well as the other pieces of the NIAS services, including the following:

- Multiprotocol Router
- Single Port WAN Extension
- IPX/IP Gateway

NIAS is installed through the INSTALL.NLM utility, Product Options on the file server. Because NIAS is not one of the embedded products, you need to select the option to Install a product not listed from the Other Installation Actions menu.

When you select the option to install an item that is not listed you are prompted with a screen that states the product will be installed from the default path A:\. If you want to change this path you must press the F3 key to specify the appropriate source path. To install the NIAS products you need to ensure that the NIAS CD-ROM is mounted on the server and use the path NIAS4:NIAS\INSTALL. Figure 28.1 shows the Specify a Directory Path screen with the proper path inputted to install the NIAS Services.

FIG. 28.1

Specify the correct path in the Install utility to load the NIAS services.

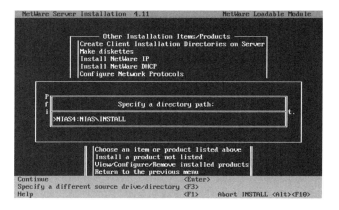

Install will then launch the product installation package included with the NIAS services, which will present you with a menu that includes the options to Install Product, Display Log File, and Exit. Selecting the option to Install Product lists the available servers to which the product can be installed. When you have all the proper servers included in the list, press Enter to install the product files. When all the files are installed, you are ready to implement MPR.

Creating Wide Area Intranetwork Connections

Implementing MPR is done through the use of the Internetworking Configuration utility (INETCFG.NLM) that is copied to the server when you install the NIAS components. When you first load INETCFG, it reads through the AUTOEXEC.NCF file stored in the SYS:SYSTEM directory on your server looking for all of the LAN and WAN driver LOAD and BIND commands, as well as all the related services and commands. When it finds them, you are asked if you want to import the network configuration information into the INETCFG configuration data-base. For MPR to function properly it must control all of the LAN and WAN adapter loading and bindings.

Once you have imported the commands from the AUTOEXEC.NCF, INETCFG comments out these commands from the AUTOEXEC.NCF and places them into the NETINFO.CFG file in the SYS:ETC directory. A sample of a modified AUTOEXEC.NCF is shown in the following listing:

```
; Network driver LOADs and BINDs are initiated via
; INITSYS.NCF. The actual LOAD and BIND commands
; are contained in INITSYS.NCF and NETINFO.CFG.
; These files are in SYS:ETC.
sys:etc\initsys.ncf
#LOAD IPXRTR ROUTING=NLSP
#LOAD 3C59X SLOT=10004 FRAME=ETHERNET_802.2 NAME=3C59X
#BIND IPX TO 3C59x NET=3
```

At this time, INETCFG presents you with the menu displayed in Figure 28.2.

FIG. 28.2
The Internetworking Configuration utility main menu shows the available options for MPR.

Part
VII

Ch
28

Boards

The Boards option defines the LAN and WAN cards, as well as specific communication ser-vices, that this server will utilize. Upon initially selecting this option you will be presented with a listing of all the currently installed and configured LAN and WAN cards and services. To install additional LAN/WAN drivers or communication services you simply press the Ins key to open the list of available drivers. This list reflects the LAN drivers currently copied to the SYS:SYSTEM directory on the server. To add a driver that is not currently listed, press Ins again and you will be asked to supply the full path and file name of the driver you want to install.

When you find or install the driver you want to use with the WAN card you are installing, highlight and select it to open the adapter configuration screen. The options you will need to configure will depend on the specific WAN adapter you are using. In general, these include a board name, as well as the IRQ, Base I/O address, and Shared RAM address the adapter uses. Additionally, information specific to the operation or configuration of the adapter may be presented in a text box on the screen.

After configuring the WAN adapter press Esc to exit the Boards option, insuring that you have saved the configuration. Exit the boards listing back to the main Internetworking Configuration menu.

Network Interfaces

The Network Interfaces selection is where you define the medium types you are going to use for your WAN connection, as well as information specific to that medium type. When you select this option you will again be presented with a list of the installed LAN and WAN drivers, as well as communication services, but in this screen you will see the services that are enabled versus those that are unconfigured. Select the WAN port you want to configure and press Enter to bring up the Select A Medium options menu. Depending on the specific WAN card you are using you may be presented with several choices.

Depending on the driver you are using, you may have more or fewer configuration choices within a particular medium option. For example, configuring a PPP connection via the AIOCOMx serial port driver you only have the option for an asynchronous modem and an RS-232 interface with a maximum data rate of 115 Kbps. Configuring the same PPP option on an NW2000 WAN card provides you with the options for a synchronous or an asynchronous modem or DSU/CSU, with transfer speeds up to 2,048 Kbps.

Frame Relay Network Interface Configuration   When configuring the frame relay option, you will be presented with the Frame Relay Network Interface Configuration options menu screen, as displayed in Figure 28.3.

From the Frame Relay Network Interface Configurations menu, you have the options to enable and disable the particular port, as well as set the physical interface port type. The option for the port physical type will depend on the type of adapter being used and the WAN driver associated with the adapter. In most cases the Interface Speed will be set to External for use on frame relay networks. This indicates that the DSU/CSU will get its clock signal from the wide area network itself.

The next configuration option enables you to set the Data Encoding to Non-Return to Zero or Non-Return to Zero Inverted. NRZ represents a binary encoding and transmission method in which ones and zeros are represented by opposite and alternating high and low voltages with no return to a reference (zero) voltage between encoded bits.

FIG. 28.3

The Frame Relay Network Interface Configuration options menu shows the available configuration options.

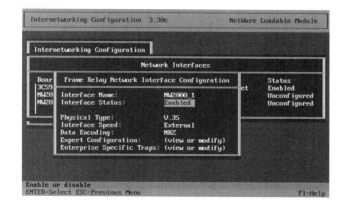

NRZI represents a binary encoding and transmission method that inverts the signal on a one and leaves the signal unchanged for a zero. In this configuration, a change in state signals a one bit, and the absence of a change signals a zero bit.

What you choose for the Data Encoding option depends entirely on the communication hardware and router at the target end of the wide area network. When setting up a frame relay network if communication cannot be established should be one of the first configuration options to check.

Frame Relay Expert Configuration   When configuring a frame relay network there are several configuration options that are considered to be reserved for the expert. Unfortunately, these configuration parameters are not necessarily optional fields. In many cases, you will find that the frame relay service provider requires specific values for these fields:

■ **User Data Size**—This is equivalent to the maximum physical receive packet size set for LAN cards. Unlike the maximum size set for LAN packets, if this value does not properly match the frame relay service providers network requirement, you will not be able to establish or maintain a reliable connection. The User Data Size value should be equal to, or smaller than what your service provider defines.

CAUTION

In addition to making sure the User Data Size value is equal to or smaller than the value defined by your frame relay service provider, the value must be equal to, or less than, the Maximum Physical Receive Packet Size set in the STARTUP.NCF on your file server. By default, the value in both cases is 4,202.

■ **Send Queue Limit**—This value defines the maximum number of outbound packets that can be queued to this port waiting for transmission. When this value is exceeded, randomly selected outbound packets are dropped from the queue and a signal is generated to resend those packets. This value is controlled locally and is dependent on the amount of RAM available to the server to buffer packets.

Part
VII

Ch

CAUTION

Setting the value for the Send Queue Limit to zero disables the limitation and allows an unlimited queue depth on the server. The only restriction at this point would be the available RAM for packet buffers. In some extreme instances in a server that is low on available RAM, you could run the server out of buffers causing a degradation in performance and potentially shutting down services.

- **Parameter Group**—This determines the communications parameters used to establish a communication link with your service provider. You are presented with four options when selecting this group:

    Annex A Parameters

    Annex D Parameters

    LMI Parameters

    Point-to-Point Test

    The options in this field are used to define the physical parameters and communication functions that are used to establish, maintain, and terminate a data link connection across the frame relay circuit. The option that you choose is based upon what the frame relay service provider has defined for use on the network. This value is controlled by the frame relay service provider.

Parameter Group Configuration Options After determining the Parameter Group that your frame relay service provider is using, you may need to change some of the default values for the Parameter Group Configuration Options, as follows:

- **Full Status Enquiry Counter**—Defines the number of status enquiries that are exchanged before issuing a full status enquiry of the frame relay circuit.

- **Error Threshold Counter**—Defines the maximum number of errors detected within the most recently monitored network event, as specified in the Monitored Event Counter field. If the number of defined errors is exceeded an SNMP alarm is generated. This field must be set to no more than the maximum value defined in the Monitored Event Counter field.

- **Monitored Event Counter**—Defines the number of consecutive network events to track at one time. This value must be greater than the value defined for the Error Threshold Counter field.

- **Status Polling Timer value**—Defines the number of seconds between consecutive status inquiries initiated by the router. When the polling timer reaches the specified time interval a request is generated for a sequence number exchange status. If the router does not receive a response within the defined polling time an error is detected and the router may reset. This value is defined by the frame relay service provider.

CAUTION

The value for the Status Polling Time must be less than the defined value provided by the frame relay service provider. For example, if the frame relay provider defines this value as 15 on the network using Annex D parameters, you should set the value for the Status Polling Time to 12. If you find that you cannot maintain a connection to the frame relay network, then you should try lowering this value if nothing else seems to work.

Enterprise Specific Traps Configuration   The final option in the Frame Relay Interface Configuration menu is the Enterprise Specific Traps Configuration options. These options relate to specific SNMP error traps and reporting on the network, as follows:

- ■ **Interface Status Change Trap**—This can be enabled to force an SNMP trap message to be sent when the frame relay interface changes state, specifically to indicate whether the interface is up or down.

- ■ **Data Link Connection Identifier (DLCI) Status Change Trap**—This can be enabled to force an SNMP trap message to be sent in the event that the DLCI status has changed. Specifically, whether the DLCI is active, inactive, or invalid.

- ■ **Physical Bandwidth Threshold Trap**—This can be enabled to force an SNMP trap to be generated if the WAN adapter hardware exceeds the upper threshold limit and then does not fall below the lower threshold limit.

N O T E   Using the Physical Bandwidth Threshold Trap can be helpful in determining whether you have enough available bandwidth for the network load you have. By knowing the committed information rate and the available burst rate provided on your frame relay circuit, you can set the upper threshold limit to 80 percent of the available burst bandwidth and the lower threshold limit to 10 percent below the committed information rate (generally 50 percent of the available burst bandwidth).

The default values are to use a 60 percent threshold for the lower limit, which you would want to change to 40 percent and 80 percent for the upper limit. For example, the maximum available burst bandwidth is 56 Kbps, and you set the values to 40 percent for the lower threshold or 22.4 Kbps, and 80 percent for the upper threshold or 44.8 Kbps. When the physical adapter reaches the 44.8 Kbps data rate, it trips an alarm that waits to see if the bandwidth then drops below the lower threshold of 22.4 Kbps. If it does not, then it continues to send alerts. ■

PPP Network Interface Configuration   When configuring the Point-to-Point Protocol option, you will be presented with the PPP Network Interface Configuration Options menu, as displayed in Figure 28.4.

The options are as follows:

- ■ **Interface Group**—Interface groups can be used to associate this interface with other interfaces in the server. This enables the router to automatically select any available interface within the group to make the connection with, when the group name is used to define the WAN call destination. This can provide for fault tolerant links by configuring multiple links to a single destination and letting the router select the available segment.

Part
VII
Ch
28

FIG. 28.4

The PPP Network
Interface Configuration
options menu shows the
available options.

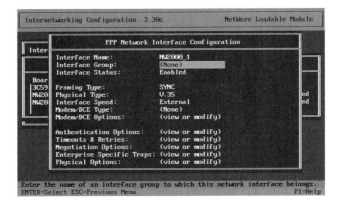

- **Interface Status**—This allows you to enable and disable the particular physical interface. By disabling the interface you make it unavailable to the system the next time it is initialized. This option is useful when using defined interface groups when you know a link will be unavailable for some time.

- **Framing Type**—This will depend on the specific interface and WAN driver used, as well as whether you are using a modem or a DSU/CSU. For example, you can use the standard COM port to configure a dial-up PPP connection to another location. The standard COM port adapter and driver will only present you with the option to set an asynchronous framing type. The NW-2000, on the other hand, is capable of supporting not only asynchronous modems, but also synchronous modems and DSU/CSU synchronous digital communication devices.

- **Physical Type field**—This defines the electrical characteristics of the port type/cable used to make the connection to the communication device (modem or DSU/CSU). Some adapters are hardware set and offer no configuration options, while others are software set and provide several options. The possible Physical Type selections include the following:

    RS-232

    RS-422

    RS-423

    V.35

    X.21

The physical type you choose will depend on the connection port on the communication device.

- **Interface Speed field**—The options available under the Interface Speed field are dependent on the physical interface adapter being used, the framing type selected, and the physical type chosen for the cable connection. In most cases, when using an adapter that supports synchronous connections, when synchronous connections are selected, the interface speed option is locked in the External option and cannot be changed.

When the asynchronous framing type is selected and the physical port type set to RS-232, you can select any baud rate between 1,200 and 115,200, depending on the adapter type and driver used. This represents the maximum connection speed allowed for the adapter, but does not necessarily represent the actual connection speed for any given connection, as most modems will automatically slow their transmission rate to maintain connectivity if there is interference on the line.

- **Modem/DCE Type and Modem/DCE Options**—These fields are used to select the modem type used, and any special initialization strings needed for asynchronous connections only. These two options relate directly to similar options in client-based modem communication packages such as ProComm Plus or Crosstalk, that is, the speed at which your modem negotiates the connection. In most cases, if your desired modem is listed in the PPP Modem/DCE Device Types list you will not need to make any changes to the Modem/DCE Options parameters.

Authentication Options   With the PPP communication option you have the capability to define session security functions to authenticate attempted inbound communication. By enabling the PPP Inbound Authentication Options functioning you can ensure that no unauthorized connection can be made to your network.

CAUTION

Unlike how it sounds, when you disable the PPP Inbound Authentication Option's Inbound Call Processing field, you do not simply turn off the security option. You disable all processing of any inbound call. If you are using an asynchronous dial up connection, the adapter is initialized with auto-answer turned off. If the connection is through a DSU/CSU or other dedicated link device, the local link protocol is set to prevent a logical connection from being established.

The options are as follows:

- **Inbound Authentication field**—Defines what type of security to implement on the connection itself. This is the option that selects whether there will be security enabled or disabled on this inbound port. There are four options available for this field, as follows:

Authentication Level	Security Level
None	No security checking is performed, and all inbound calls are processed.
Password Authentication Protocol (PAP)	Requires that the remote network send a password string across the WAN. This password is sent in clear-text format.
Challenge Handshake Authentication Protocol (CHAP)	Requires that the remote network send an encrypted challenge string based on the password defined in the authentication database.

Part

VII

Ch

28

continues

continued

Authentication Level	Security Level
Either PAP or CHAP	Allows either authentication method, and will poll all available remote system password databases for password authentication. Best used in an environment where multiple remote networks require access to a single dial-in network connection.

■ **Local System ID for the CHAP option**—Enables you to define a name to be sent to non-MPR routers that need to access the server using the CHAP authentication protocol. This name is used by the remote router to determine the correct CHAP key to respond with when challenged.

■ **Authentication Database Name**—Defines the symbolic name for the inbound caller. PPP maintains specific caller identification and password information in specific database records for each inbound network. Each interface can have a specific database, or multiple interfaces can share a common database. There is no limit on the number of records each database can maintain.

■ **Authentication Database option**—Opens the list of defined inbound network IDs. To add records to the database press the Ins key and the PPP Inbound Authentication Entry form appears, as shown in Figure 28.5.

FIG. 28.5
The PPP Inbound Authentication Entry form shows the remote system ID and password option fields.

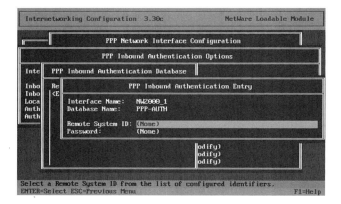

It is in this form that you define the remote network names and the passwords associated with each inbound network. You can also select the option to use different databases for different inbound networks.

Timeouts & Retries   Choosing this option presents you with the PPP Timeouts & Retries menu, as shown in Figure 28.6. The options in this menu are normally left at their default settings unless there is a specific communication fault and your PPP service provider requests that you change the timeouts to diagnose and isolate the problem.

FIG. 28.6

The PPP Timeouts & Retries options menu shows the various communication parameter options.

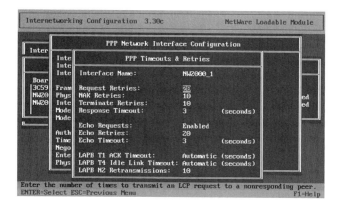

In each case, if the value in any of the Timeouts & Retries options is exceeded, the connection to the remote site is dropped. Table 28.1 details the option name and function for the Timeouts & Retries.

Table 28.1 PPP Timeouts & Retries Functions

Option Name	Value Range	Description
Request Retries	1–40	Defines the maximum number of times the router will transmit a configuration request to a non-responding remote.
NAK Retries	1–40	Defines the maximum number of times the router will transmit a negative acknowledgment to a non-responding remote.
Terminate Retries	1–40	Defines the maximum number of times the router will transmit a terminate request to a non-responding remote.
Response Timeout	1–60	Defines, in seconds, the maximum acceptable delay between sending a PPP request and receiving the response from the remote.
Echo Requests	Enabled	Defines whether local disabled generation of LCP echo requests are done on a periodic basis. This provides a means of determining the state of the network at the link layer. Responses to remote echo requests are always generated.
Echo Retries	1–40	Defines the maximum number of times the router will transmit an echo request to a non-responding remote.

Part

VII

Ch

28

continues

Table 28.1   Continued

Option Name	Value Range	Description
Reho Timeout	1–60	Defines, in seconds, the maximum acceptable delay between sending an echo request and receiving the reply from the remote.
LAPB T1 ACK Timer (Link Access Procedures Balanced)	0–999	Defines, in seconds, the maximum time the LAPB interface will wait for an acknowledgment of a previously transmitted information frame. Setting this value to zero enables Automatic operation.
LAPB T4 Idle Link Timer		0–999 Specifies, in seconds, the maximum time the LAPB interface can remain idle before the Receiver Ready (RR) or Receiver Not Ready (RNR) supervisory frame is sent to the remote. Setting this value to zero enables Automatic operation.
LAPB N2 Retransmit Count	0–999	Specifies the maximum number of times unacknowledged information frames can be retransmitted in response to the expiration of the T1 ACK Timer.

Negotiations Options   Selecting this option presents you with the PPP Negotiation Options configuration screen as shown in Figure 28.7.

FIG. 28.7
The PPP Negotiation Options Configuration screen shows the packet size and compression options.

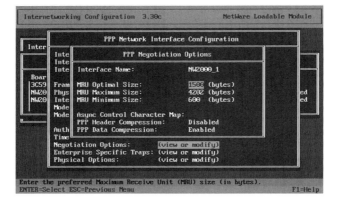

The options presented in the PPP Negotiations menu enable you to optimize the communication link between sites based on the maximum and minimum packet sizes, as well as whether packet header and data compression are enabled:

- **Maximum Receive Unit (MRU) values**—Define the minimum, maximum, and optimum frame sizes that the router will receive from the remote. The actual MRU value negotiated with the remote can be any value between the Minimum and Maximum values, with the Optimum being the preferred negotiated size.

- **PPP Header Compression field**—Defines whether the interface will attempt to enable header compression with the remote during link negotiation. Header compression affects only the Address & Control and the Protocol ID fields of the packet. Enabling PPP Header Compression does not guarantee that the header will be compressed, but rather that the router will attempt to negotiate its use with the remote during link up.

- **PPP Data Compression option**—Works in much the same way as the PPP Header Compression option, but attempts to negotiate a common data compression algorithm during link negotiation. Enabling this option does not guarantee that data will be compressed, but rather that the router will attempt to negotiate data compression during link negotiation.

  If data compression is negotiated, the compression performance is determined by the amount of available CPU cycles, type of data being processed, and the serial link speed. You can determine whether compression is active and its effectiveness by checking the LAN/WAN Driver Statistics in MONITOR.NLM or by viewing the send and receive line utilization information in the PPP Console Utility (PPPCON.NLM).

Enterprise Specific Traps   Selecting the Enterprise Specific Traps option enables you to enable or disable specific SNMP management traps and reporting information to the network. The PPP Call Failure Trap will generate an SNMP trap when a PPP connection attempt fails to connect to the remote. Specifically, it tracks whether the call fails to complete or reach an NCP open state.

The traps are as follows:

- **PPP Call Termination Trap**—Enabling the PPP Call Termination Trap generates an SNMP trap when the PPP connection terminates. This option is most useful when using a dedicated link connection that should never terminate.

- **PPP Link Up/Down Trap**—Enabling the PPP Link Up/Down Trap generates an SNMP trap whenever the Link Control Protocol experiences a transition state, either going up or down.

- **Physical Bandwidth Threshold Trap**—This can be enabled to force an SNMP trap to be generated if the WAN adapter hardware exceeds the upper threshold limit and then does not fall below the lower threshold limit. For more information, see the Note in the "Enterprise Specific Traps Configuration" section earlier in this chapter.

Physical Options   Selecting this option presents you with the PPP Physical Configuration Options menu as shown in Figure 28.8.

Part
VII
Ch
28

FIG. 28.8

The PPP Physical Configuration Options menu shows the communications options available.

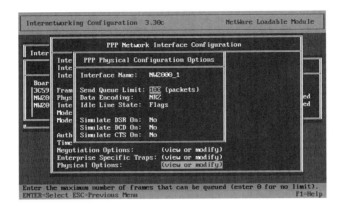

- **Send Queue Limit field**—Determines the maximum number of outbound packets that can be queued to this port waiting for transmission. When this value is exceeded randomly, selected outbound packets are dropped from the queue and a signal is generated to resend those packets. This value is dependent on the amount of RAM available to the server to buffer packets. See the Caution pertaining to the Send Queue Limit function in the "Frame Relay Expert Configuration" section earlier in this chapter

- **Data Encoding field**—Enables you to configure the router to utilize the Non-Return to Zero (NRZ) or the Non-Return to Zero Inverted (NRZI) serial data encoding methods.

  NRZ represents a binary encoding and transmission method in which ones and zeros are represented by opposite and alternating high and low voltages with no return to a reference (zero) voltage between encoded bits. NRZI represents a binary encoding and transmission method that inverts the signal on a one and leaves the signal unchanged for a zero. In this configuration a change in state signals a one bit and the absence of a change signals a zero bit.

  What you choose for this option depends entirely on the communication hardware and router at the target end of the wide area network.

- **Idle Line State option**—Defines whether you will use Flags or Marks as the serial line interframe transmission. Selecting the Flags state results in a repeated transmission of the HDLC 7E synchronization pattern. Selecting the MARKS option results in the router holding the data line in a marking state. Which you use depends on what the physical line provider expects your communications equipment to present.

The following three options provide physical Interface Signal Override in the event that the modem or other communication hardware does not provide the appropriate signal. These options should only be set to Yes if the communication device fails to operate due to its not providing the correct signal.

X.25 Host When configuring the X.25 protocol option, you will be presented with the X.25 Network Interface configuration options menu screen, as displayed in Figure 28.9.

FIG. 28.9
The X.25 Network Interface configuration options menu shows the available communications parameters.

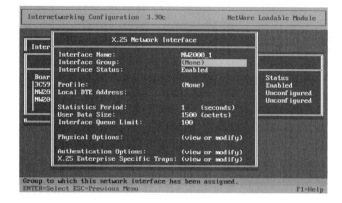

The options are as follows:

■ **Interface Group**—Much the same as it is for the PPP configuration option with the exception that you define which interface from the group should be used for a specific virtual circuit. You can define multiple virtual circuits to the same destination site to provide fault-tolerant WAN links.

■ **Interface Status**—Allows you to enable and disable the particular physical interface. By disabling the interface you make it unavailable to the system the next time it is initialized. This option is useful when using defined interface groups when you know a virtual circuit will be unavailable for some time.

■ **Profile option**—Enables you to select the X.25 configuration information from a list of pre-defined service carriers. By selecting one of the standard pre-defined configurations you can quickly set up the X.25 host communication parameters, and if necessary, only change a few options to create a specific profile for the service carrier you are using. To choose which profile to use, or to modify an existing profile, you need to contact your X.25 service carrier for the specific profile parameters they require.

■ **Local DTE (Data Terminal Equipment) Address field**—Defines the X.121 address allocated to your interface by the X.25 service carrier. This field is similar to the DLCI address assigned to a port under frame relay with the exception that only one address can be assigned to an interface.

■ **Statistics Period**—Defines, in seconds, the rate at which statistical information is collected from the interface adapter and reported to MONITOR, LAN/WAN Statistics for updating purposes. Unless you're looking for specific information to diagnose a problem, this is best left at its default.

Part
VII

Ch
28

■ **User Data Size field**—Defines the largest allowable packet size that can be received or transmitted across the interface adapter.

■ **Interface Queue Limit**—Defines the maximum number of packets that can be queued for each port on the interface adapter. This serves the same function as the Send Queue Limit for the frame relay and PPP protocols and has the same limitations.

Physical Options   Selecting the Physical Options function presents you with the X.25 Physical Configuration Options menu where you can set the specific physical port options for your interface adapter. These options are similar to those in the PPP configuration, as follows:

■ **Physical Type field**—Defines the port electronics and cable type and includes the following options:

   RS-232

   RS-422

   RS-423

   V.35

   X.21

The option you choose will depend on the type of modem or DSU/CSU you are using to connect to the X.25 service carrier.

■ **Port Connection field**—Defines whether you have a dedicated, hard-wired link to the X.25 pad, or are using a DTR Dialed link via a modem. Again, this option is dependent on the modem or DSU/CSU type you are using.

■ **Interface Speed field**—Defines where your router gets its clock timing signal from and at what speed. Normally the X.25 circuit provides the clock signal and you would select the External option. Some WAN adapters provide the capability to override this and let you set a fixed speed between 1,200 and 2,048,000 baud.

The following three options provide physical Interface Signal Override in the event that the modem or other communication hardware does not provide the appropriate signal. These options should only be set to Yes if the communication device fails to operate due to its not providing the correct signal.

Authentication Options   Because X.25 provides the capability to create virtual circuits on a public data network, you have the same authentication options you do for PPP connections, as follows:

■ **Inbound Authentication option**—When enabled, your router will only accept calls from a remote that is defined in the authentication database. If the remote is not in the database the connection will be terminated.

■ **Authentication Database Name**—This field is where the administrator defines the name to be used for this database. You can have as many databases on your system as you want, and there can be as many remote records defined as you want.

- **Authentication Database option**—Opens the list of defined inbound network IDs. To add records to the database press the Ins key and the X.25 Inbound Authentication Entry form appears. To define the remote to allow access to this system you must input the Remote System ID as well as the Remote DTE Address as defined by the X.25 service carrier.

X.25 Enterprise Specific Traps This option provides much the same as does the frame relay and PPP options with some information specific to X.25 virtual circuits, as follows:

- **Physical Bandwidth Threshold Trap**—When enabled, forces an SNMP trap to be generated if the WAN adapter hardware exceeds the upper threshold limit and then does not fall below the lower threshold limit.

- **Link State Trap**—When enabled, generates an SNMP trap when the link layer initialization is completed or when a link failure is detected.

- **Packet Layer Restart Trap**—When enabled, generates an SNMP trap when a Restart Indication or Request packet is sent or received at the packet layer.

- **Packet Layer Reset Trap**—When enabled, generates an SNMP trap when a Reset Indication or Request packet is sent or received at the packet layer.

- **Call Failure Setup Trap**—When enabled, generates an SNMP trap when an X.25 connection terminates or the virtual circuit drops.

- **Virtual Circuit Cleared Trap**—When enabled, generates an SNMP trap when an X.25 connection terminates or the virtual circuit drops.

WAN Call Directory

When you have selected the Network Interface type that you will be utilizing to make your wide area connection you then have to define the destinations that you want to communicate with and by which network type you will make the connection.

Each of the network types defined in the previous section provide different WAN call parameters specific to the type of connection made. In this section, the specific configuration requirements to make the logical connection to the destination network are addressed.

When you choose the WAN Call Directory option from the Internetworking Configuration menu you will be presented with a list of currently Configured WAN Call Destinations. To add a new destination to the list press Ins. You will be prompted for a New Call Destination Name. This is the name by which your router will know what connection is being made; this is a symbolic name and is not tied to the remote network's configuration.

After entering the Call Destination Name, you will be presented with the available Wide Area Medium options based on the Network Interface type you defined previously. The version of MPR included with IntranetWare supports only a single WAN port and so you should only be presented with a single Supported Wide Area Medium option. By adding Novell's WAN Extensions to your IntranetWare server you can increase the available number of WAN ports to 16. The options you will be presented with will depend on the Wide Area Medium selected.

Part

VII

Ch

28

Frame Relay   When you select the Frame Relay wide area medium type you will be presented with the Frame Relay Call Destination Configuration screen as shown in Figure 28.10.

FIG. 28.10
The Frame Relay Call Destination Configuration screen enables you to define the interface name and create the circuit definition.

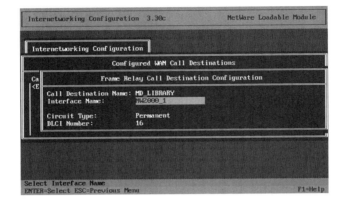

Using this configuration menu, you can define the information for the following options:

■ **Interface Name field**—Enables you to select the specific WAN interface adapter and port you want to use for this network connection. By pressing Enter in this field you will be presented with a list of available adapters and ports to select from.

■ **Circuit type**—Defines whether this will be a permanent or a switched connection. Novell's MPR only supports a permanent connection type over a frame relay circuit. A permanent connection provides for a dedicated, full-time connection to the frame relay network.

■ **DLCI number**—Defines the frame relay virtual circuit information for this port. A single frame relay connection can support multiple virtual circuits, and it is the DLCI number that defines which virtual circuit connects to which remote. The DLCI number for each location and each virtual circuit is determined by the frame relay service carrier. To define multiple virtual circuits, add additional WAN Call Destinations to the interface adapter using different DLCI numbers and Call Destination Names.

PPP   When you select the PPP Wide Area Medium type you will be presented with the PPP Call Destination Configuration screen, as shown in Figure 28.11.

FIG. 28.11

The PPP Call Destination Configuration screen enables the administrator to define the call parameters.

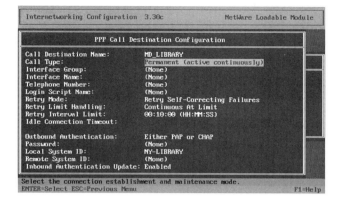

```
Internetworking Configuration  3.30c                NetWare Loadable Module

                    PPP Call Destination Configuration
      Call Destination Name:    MD_LIBRARY
      Call Type:                Permanent (active continuously)
      Interface Group:          (None)
      Interface Name:           (None)
      Telephone Number:         (None)
      Login Script Name:        (None)
      Retry Mode:               Retry Self-Correcting Failures
      Retry Limit Handling:     Continuous At Limit
      Retry Interval Limit:     00:10:00 (HH:MM:SS)
      Idle Connection Timeout:

      Outbound Authentication:  Either PAP or CHAP
      Password:                 (None)
      Local System ID:          NY-LIBRARY
      Remote System ID:         (None)
      Inbound Authentication Update: Enabled

    Select the connection establishment and maintenance mode.
    ENTER=Select ESC=Previous Menu                         F1=Help
```

Using this configuration menu, you can define the information for the following options:

- **Call Type field**—Enables you to choose whether this will be a Permanent connection to the remote network, or a dial On Demand connection. If On Demand is selected the connection will be initiated by data with a destination address belonging to a remote network. If Permanent is selected the connection will remain active continuously if there are no outside interruptions in service.

- **Interface Group Name**—Enables you to select from an Interface Group that was defined previously. This allows you to select a group of interface adapters or ports that are configured similarly to make the WAN call with. When a network connection is required the router determines the first available interface and port within the group to make the connection with. Use of this option is best suited to On Demand dial-up links to other networks.

- **Interface Name field**—Enables you to select the specific interface adapter and port you want to use for this connection. By pressing Enter you will be presented with the list of available interface adapters and ports that can be used for this connection.

- **Telephone Number field**—Defines the telephone number your router should call for this connection if you are using a modem that utilizes the AT commands or V.25bis functions as defined previously for the Dialing Mode in the Network Interface options.

- **Login Script Name field**—Defines the script that will be run to connect to and log into the remote network. The default of None should be used unless the remote network specifically requires a login sequence be initiated.

- **Retry Mode field**—Defines how the router should handle a failed connection attempt. The available options are:

  Never Retry

  Retry All Failures

  Retry Self-Correcting Failures

Part
VII

Ch
28

All connection failures are tracked and reported to the system console. Additionally, you can monitor call activity in the Call Manager utility (CALLMGR.NLM). Self correcting errors include things like a detected busy signal, as opposed to errors that require user intervention, such as a call authentication fault.

- **Retry Limit Handling field**—Defines what the router will do when the connection retry interval exceeds the configured limit. Retry attempts can be made indefinitely or the retries can be terminated and the call connection marked as failed. Selecting the Continuous At Limit option provides continuous retries and should be used for permanent connection types or where a router is unattended and needs to be able to reconnect independent of user intervention. The Stop At Limit option should be used for dial On Demand connections where the network administrator can monitor the operation of the router.

- **Retry Interval Limit**—Defines the maximum time interval between attempts to establish a connection. Initially the delay is about eight seconds and increases with each failed attempt to connect until the maximum Retry Interval Limit is reached or a connection made.

- **Idle Connection Timeout field**—Defines the countdown time that an On Demand connection uses before terminating a connection when there is no activity on the line.

- **Outbound Authentication field**—Defines the type of password authentication used to connect to the remote network. This option should be set to match the Incoming Authentication type chosen at the remote network, or set to either PAP or CHAP to provide for the remote site using any of the available options.

- **Password field**—Defines the password used to authenticate to the remote network and should be set to match the defined password on the remote network.

- **Local System ID**—Defines the name by which this network will be identified to the remote network. The Remote System ID is the name by which this network knows the remote network. Usually this is the server name.

- **Inbound Authentication Update field**—Defines whether the inbound authentication database for the interface associated with this WAN call destination should be updated to reflect the connection information entered in this form. If a group name is selected, then all interfaces within the group will be updated.

X.25   When you select the X.25 Wide Area Medium type, you will be presented with the X.25 Call Destination Configuration screen shown in Figure 28.12.

FIG. 28.12

The X.25 Call Destination Configuration screen enables the administrator to define the call options.

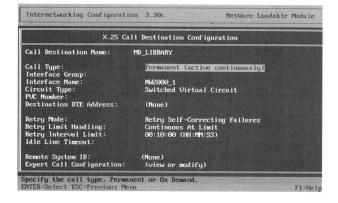

```
 Internetworking Configuration  3.30c          NetWare Loadable Module

                    X.25 Call Destination Configuration

 Call Destination Name:    MD_LIBRARY

 Call Type:                Permanent (active continuously)
 Interface Group:
 Interface Name:           NW2000_1
 Circuit Type:             Switched Virtual Circuit
 PVC Number:
 Destination DTE Address:  (None)

 Retry Mode:               Retry Self-Correcting Failures
 Retry Limit Handling:     Continuous At Limit
 Retry Interval Limit:     00:10:00 (HH:MM:SS)
 Idle Line Timeout:

 Remote System ID:         (None)
 Expert Call Configuration:  (view or modify)

 Specify the call type, Permanent or On Demand.
 ENTER=Select ESC=Previous Menu                          F1=Help
```

Using this configuration menu, you can define the information for the following options:

- **Call Type field**—Enables you to choose whether this will be a Permanent connection to the remote network, or an On Demand connection. If On Demand is selected the connection will be initiated by data with a destination address belonging to a remote network. If Permanent is selected the connection will remain active continuously if there are no outside interruptions in service.

- **Interface Group option**—Enables you to select from an Interface Group that was defined previously. This allows you to select a group of interface adapters or ports that are configured similarly to make the WAN call with.

- **Interface Name field**—Enables you to select the specific interface adapter and port you want to use for this connection. By pressing Enter you will be presented with the list of available interface adapters and ports that can be used for this connection.

- **Circuit Type field**—Enables you to define whether this connection will be made using a Switched Virtual Circuit (SVC) or a Permanent Virtual Circuit (PVC). Permanent Virtual Circuits are always available while the interface is active. Switched Virtual Circuits require a call initiation generated by the interface or by an incoming call and are terminated after use. Switched Virtual Circuits are used most often in areas where the cost of permanent connections cannot be cost justified.

- **PVC Number field**—Defines the Permanent Virtual Circuit Logical Channel Number (LCN) assigned by the X.25 service carrier. This option is only available when the circuit type is set to Permanent Virtual Circuit.

- **Destination DTE Address field**—Defines the destination X.121 address as assigned by the X.25 service carrier and is used to establish the logical switched virtual circuit to the destination network. This option is only available when the circuit type is set to Switched Virtual Circuit.

Part
VII

Ch

28

- **Retry Mode field**—Defines how the router should handle a failed connection attempt. The available options are:

  Never Retry

  Retry All Failures

  Retry Self-Correcting Failures

  All connection failures are tracked and reported to the system console. Additionally, you can monitor call activity in the Call Manager utility (CALLMGR.NLM). Self correcting errors include things like a detected busy signal, as opposed to errors that require user intervention, such as a call authentication fault.

- **Retry Limit Handling field**—Defines what the router will do when the connection retry interval exceeds the configured limit. Retry attempts can be made indefinitely or the retries can be terminated and the call connection marked as failed. Selecting the Continuous At Limit option provides continuous retries and should be used for permanent connection types or where a router is unattended and needs to be able to reconnect independent of user intervention. The Stop At Limit option should be used for dial On Demand connections where the network administrator can monitor the operation of the router.

- **Retry Interval Limit**—Defines the maximum time interval between attempts to establish a connection. Initially the delay is about eight seconds and increases with each failed attempt to connect until the maximum Retry Interval Limit is reached or a connection made.

- **Idle Connection Timeout field**—Defines the countdown time that an On Demand connection uses before terminating a connection when there is no activity on the line.

- **Remote System ID field**—Used to define the host name for the remote system and is usually set to the file server name. This field is used to identify the proper WAN Call Destination needed to restore a part-time connection to a remote network and is not required for a permanent connection.

Expert Call Configuration   When you select the Expert Call Configuration option you will be presented with the X.25 Expert Call Configuration screen as shown in Figure 28.13.

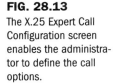

FIG. 28.13
The X.25 Expert Call Configuration screen enables the administrator to define the call options.

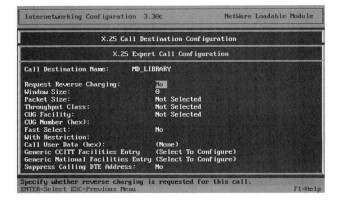

Using this configuration menu, you can define the information for the following options:

- **Request Reverse Charging field**—Used to define whether reverse charging is requested for outgoing calls. Used to reduce costs on collect calls for dial-up links.

- **Window Size field**—Used to define the size of the protocol window during call negotiation for a specific call. The value in this field overrides the Packet Negotiation value. Setting the Window Size value to 0 disables window size negotiation, and the default window size is used.

- **Packet Size field**—Defines the maximum packet size that can be negotiated for this specific call. If this value is set it overrides the Packet Negotiation value.

- **Throughput Class field**—Defines the baud rate to be negotiated during this specific call. This option is only valid for dial-up links.

- **CUG Facility field**—Defines how remote sites sharing a common X.25 carrier service will interoperate. The Closed User Group defines a set of DTEs that belong to a single communication group, thus allowing the configuration of a smaller private network within the larger public network. The sites within that group can communicate with each other, but not with any other DTE remote site. The following are the options for this field:

CUG Option	Communication Option
Not Selected	No communication restrictions imposed. Closed User Groups do not exist on this network.
Incoming	Restricts access so this host can only receive calls from the group.
Outgoing	Restricts access so that this host can only make outgoing calls to the group.
Bilateral	Bilateral defines a relationship that is limited to a single pair of DTEs. Access between this pair is unrestricted. However, access to or from any other DTE is not possible.

- **CUG Number field**—Defines the Closed User Group number specific to the defined group this host belongs to. This option is only available if the CUG Facility field is set to an option other than Not Selected.

- **Fast Select field**—An optional setting that enables the network administrator to use up to 128 bytes of user data in call request packets, making the data field more useful for short-duration, low-volume, transaction-oriented applications.

- **With Restrictions field**—Defines restrictions to be placed upon the Fast Select field option. This value defines whether the host will be allowed to accept a call with the Fast Select option set. This option is only available if the Fast Select Option is enabled.

- **Call User Data field**—Defines the actual user data information that is sent in the Call Request Packet User Data field. The length of the data sent is dependent on whether you have enabled Fast Select or not. The following are the available options:

Packet Type	Data Length with Fast Select	Data Length without Fast Select
IPX	122	10
AppleTalk	122	10
CLNS	124	12
IP	124	12

■ **Generic CCITT Facilities Entry field**—Enables you to define and add new facilities codes to the current configuration. This allows you to extend the facilities available to your router. CCITT facilities are specified in hexadecimal format per the X.25 recommendations.

■ **Generic National Facilities Entry field**—Enables you to define entries for national or proprietary facilities for use in the Call Request Facilities field. This is useful when connecting to a proprietary service provider or when communicating across an X.75 gateway.

■ **Suppress Calling DTE Address field**—Defines whether the calling DTE address will be included in the outgoing Call Request packets. When this option is enabled the calling DTE address will not be included in the Call Request Packet.

Inbound Authentication Update   The final option in the X.25 Call Destination Configuration screen is the Inbound Authentication Update field. This option defines whether an inbound authentication database should be updated to reflect the connection information defined in this call configuration screen. If this value is set to Enable then inbound authentication entries will be made consisting of the remote system ID and password entered for this call destination. If an Interface Group was selected, all interface databases in that group will be updated.

Protocol Configuration

The next step in establishing the wide area network is to define and configure the protocols that will be used to make the connection and transport data. Configuring the protocols you want to use for the WAN are the same as configuring them for use on the LAN. General guidelines to follow are that you want to enable routing services for the specific protocols you are using. If routing is disabled and the server set to end node operation mode the file server will not pass packets from the WAN adapter to the workstations on the LAN and visa versa.

The WAN adapter appears the same as a LAN adapter to the file server. Any protocol that can be bound to the local LAN adapter within the file server can generally be bound to the WAN adapter. Once you have selected and configured the protocols you want to use on the file server you will need to check and make sure that any specific parameters required for WAN operation are set. This usually consists of checking the values for protocol timeouts and setting them to the values recommended by your telephone service provider. These values will be dependent upon the speed and latency of the telephone service.

Bindings

Selecting the Bindings option enables you to specify what protocols will be bound to what interfaces and the network addresses assigned to them. Binding protocols to the WAN adapter may be slightly different from the procedures for binding to a LAN adapter. This may be due to the WAN card supporting multiple concurrent network connections via a frame relay or X.25 connection, for example. It is best if you select the defaults for these fields and to document the addresses and assignments you make carefully.

Binding IPX to a WAN Adapter Selecting the Bindings option from the Internetworking Configuration menu presents you with the Protocol To Interface/Group Bindings screen. This is a list of the defined protocols and adapters that have been configured for use on this server. This list shows the configured protocol, the interface or group name that it has been assigned to, the operational status of that interface or group, and the address assigned to that segment. Pressing Enter on a configured adapter/protocol brings up the Binding *protocol* to a LAN or WAN Interface configuration screen.

If you are presented with an empty configuration screen when opening the Protocol To Interface/Group Bindings screen, it means that no adapters or protocols have been configured for use in this server. To add an adapter to this list press Ins. This will provide you with a selection list of the available protocols that have been configured for use on this server. To configure the protocol to adapter select the protocol you want to configure, in this case IPX.

After selecting IPX as the protocol you want to configure, you will be asked whether this protocol will be bound to a single interface or to the Interface Group you may have defined earlier.

After selecting either the Interface Group or the specific interface adapter, you will be presented with a list of available configured LAN and WAN adapters or Interface Group Names to select from to bind IPX to. Selecting the WAN adapter presents you with the Binding IPX to a WAN Interface screen where you can select the WAN Call Destination you defined previously.

Upon selecting a call destination from the available list of destinations defined previously you will be presented with the WAN Call Destination Entry configuration screen as shown in Figure 28.14.

FIG. 28.14
The WAN Call Destination Entry configuration screen showing the call configuration options.

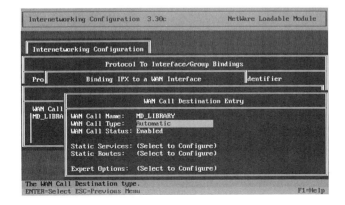

The options are as follows:

- **WAN Call Name**—The destination name you previously selected.

- **WAN Call Type**—Defines how the connection is initiated and maintained. A call defined to use the On Demand call type is activated by traffic that is directed to or through the remote network. If set to Routed On Demand then routing information will be passed through the link. If set to Static On Demand then routing information is not passed and the link requires static routing to be defined to find the destination address.

  Automatic defines a permanent connection in which the router attempts to make the WAN link immediately upon initialization of the WAN adapter for use with permanent calls. Manual defines a connection that requires user intervention for outgoing calls, or an incoming call to initiate the link.

N O T E   When using a PPP connection between two sites, one site should be designated as using the automatic WAN call type, and the other site defined as using the manual WAN call type. The automatic site will initiate the call and connect to the remote site. The manual site will not attempt to initiate the connection between the two sites, but rather, will wait for the incoming call. If both sites are in automatic mode, they will both attempt to initiate the call, and neither will make a link with the other.

- **WAN Call Status field**—Defines whether this link should be enabled or disabled upon initialization of the WAN adapter.

Static Services   The Static Services option opens the list of defined static services. Static services are used to define the specific target information needed to connect to a remote network by an On Demand link. Table 28.2 shows the list of services available in the Static Service Configuration screen.

Table 28.2   Static Service Configuration Options

Static Service	Function
Service Name	Defines the name of the service to be accessed across the network link. Adds this name to the local service and routing tables without the need to receive periodic routing broadcast information from the remote network.
Service Type	Defines the IPX SAP service type for the remote service.
Service Address	The IPX network number for the remote service. If the remote service is a NetWare file server or MPR use the internal network number of that server.
Service Address Node	The IPX node address assigned to the remote service. If the remote service is a NetWare 3 or NetWare 4 file server or MPR this value is 1. If the remote service is a NetWare 2 server this value is the IPX address assigned to the LAN A adapter in the server.

Static Service	Function
Service Address Socket	Defines the IPX socket address used by the remote service. If the remote service is a NetWare file server or MPR the value is 0451.
Hops To Service	Defines the maximum number of routers that need to be crossed to reach the service.
Ticks To Service	Defines the time a packet is allowed to remain active on the network in ticks. Setting this value too high will result in connections never timing out. Setting this value too low results in frequent connection faults across the WAN link.

Static Routes   Static routes are used to define specific target network addresses. This allows the router to establish connections only when the specific networks in the list are accessed. When you select this option a list of defined static routes is opened. To add a static route press the Ins key and the Static Route Configuration screen will open.

To define the static route you need to supply the Network Number defined for the remote service in the previous step. You can also, optionally, configure the Hops To Network and Ticks To Network values for this specific route.

Expert Bind Options   Selecting this option in the Binding IPX to a WAN Interface form opens the Expert WAN Bind Options screen. The options on this screen enable you to set overrides for the Delay, Throughput, and MTU values defined for the physical adapter. Normally, IPX uses the default values provided by the hardware configuration. In some instances you may need to force a fixed rate for the protocol to isolate faults on the network.

Additionally, you can configure IPX packet spoofing for On Demand network connections so that users appear to see the remote network, even if the physical connection has been terminated. Spoofing will also maintain some information from the remote network cached for local access.

The Header Compression and Compression Slots Overrides determine whether to use the default header compression option defined for the hardware itself or to configure specific compression options for this specific call.

The RIP, SAP, and NLSP Option functions allow the network administrator to override the default values defined for the IPX protocol for this specific call. These values will normally be configured to use the default values unless a specific fault needs to be isolated or you are experiencing WAN link throughput problems and need to adjust the timeout values so as not to drop the connection.

Binding IP to a WAN Adapter   To configure the TCP/IP protocol for a WAN adapter start by pressing Ins while viewing the list of defined bindings in the Protocol To Interface/Group Bindings list. This will present you with the same options you were presented with previously when selecting the IPX option. When selecting the option to bind TCP/IP you will be presented with the Binding TCP/IP to a WAN Interface or Group screen, as shown in Figure 28.15.

Part

VII

Ch

28

FIG. 28.15

The Binding TCP/IP to a WAN Interface screen shows the TCP/IP WAN communications options.

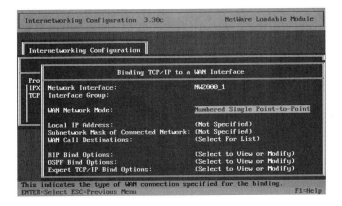

The WAN Network Mode field defines the specific addressing option to be used when connecting to the remote site. The options are defined in Table 28.3.

Table 28.3   WAN Network Mode Options

Operational Mode	Function
Multi-access	Allows the router to connect to the remote site through multiple destinations that are all part of the same IP network. Allows redundant links in a frame relay or x.25 network where multiple routers at each site are available for the initiating router to connect to.
Numbered Single Point-to-Point	Allows the router to connect only to another single destination point and requires that a TCP/IP address be assigned to each site on the link.
Unnumbered Single Point-to-Point	Allows a router to connect to one or more remote destinations that do not use an IP address. This option provides for the facility to maintain unnumbered serial links between networks to reduce the need for distinct IP network segments.

The BIND options for the TCP/IP Protocol Suite enables the administrator to configure the following options:

- **Local IP Address field**—Defines the TCP/IP address assigned to this interface adapter and port. This field is not available when using the Unnumbered Point-to-Point network mode.

- **Subnetwork Mask of Connected Network field**—Defines the subnet mask used for this network connection. This field is unavailable when using the Unnumbered point-to-point Network mode.

- **WAN Call Destinations option**—Brings up the list of Configured WAN Call Destinations and shows their connection Type and IP Address. To add destinations to the list press Ins and you will be presented with the WAN Call Destination To IP Address Mapping Configuration menu.

WAN Call to IP Address Mapping   The first field in the WAN Call Destination To IP Address Mapping Configuration screen is the WAN Call Destination. Pressing Enter presents you with the list of available destinations defined previously. Selecting the destination you want this call to be connected to sets several of the following fields to their default values for the connection type:

- **Type field**—Defines the WAN Call Destination Type. This can be Routed On Demand, Static On Demand, Automatic, or Manual. The functions of these call types is the same as discussed previously in the "Binding IPX to a WAN Adapter" section.
- **Remote IP Address field**—Defines the TCP/IP address of the remote site. This field is only available for numbered point-to-point links and multi-access links.
- **Verify Remote Address field**—Defines whether the router should check to see if the remote network it has connected to has the appropriate address. If this is enabled and the remote site is not using the defined network address the connection is terminated.
- **Header Compression field**—Defines whether the TCP and IP headers will be compressed over serial link point-to-point connections.
- **Static Routing Table field**—Enables you to insert specific static routes for this call connection. This option allows you to only define routes to other networks or to specific hosts, you cannot define a default route using this option. To add a static route press Ins from the Static Routes For This WAN Call list of defined routes.

Routing Information Protocol (RIP) Bind Options   Selecting this option presents the RIP Bind Options screen. This form enables you to select the RIP version used for this specific network call, as well as set specific RIP time operations. The options presented to the administrator are as follows:

- **Status field**—Allows you to enable or disable RIP for this connection. When RIP is enabled the router will pass routing table information with other attached hosts on the network. If disabled, this router will only receive RIP information but will not exchange RIP information with other hosts.
- **Cost of Interface option**—Enables the network administrator to manually override the network hops count this router reports to other routers to discourage the use of this router to a common destination. For example, you have both a T1 dedicated link router and a 33.6 dial On Demand router to the same destination network. You could add an additional cost to the dial-up router port so that the dedicated T1 will always be the preferred route to the destination, and the dial-up will only be used if the preferred route is unavailable.
- **Originate Default Route field**—Defines whether RIP will only advertise the local router as the default router for the network. If this option is enabled the router will only advertise as the default route and will not advertise any other routes.

Part
VII

Ch
28

- **Poison Reverse option**—Defines the manner in which the router sends out route information it received from this interface. When this option is enabled it causes RIP to advertise a route back through the same path from which it learned the route, but with a hop count of 16. This makes the route unreachable from external sources. Although enabling poison reverse will prevent routing loops, the unreachable routes carried in each RIP packet increase the bandwidth consumed by RIP traffic. This increase becomes significant in large networks.

- **Split Horizon field**—Defines how the router will propagate route information on the same interface port that it received it from. When this option is enabled the router will not propagate route information received by RIP over the same interface port that it received the information from.

- **Update Time field**—Defines the time, in seconds, that the router uses to initiate a send update message to the other routers on the network. If a router does not respond within six attempts, the route is considered invalid.

- **Expire Time field**—Defines the amount of time, in seconds, that the router expects to receive an update from the network. If a route update is not received in this time frame the route is considered invalid.

- **Garbage Time field**—Defines the amount of time, in seconds, that a route that is reported as down will remain valid. When this time is reached for a downed route the route is considered invalid.

- **RIP Version field**—Enables you to choose RIP I or RIP II or both. RIP I is the standard RIP operation used in most nodes and routers. RIP II is an enhancement of RIP that includes subnet mask information in the routing information exchanged with other routers. If you use a lot of subnets of varying sizes, using RIP II can greatly improve performance.

- **RIP Mode field**—Defines what operation mode RIP is working in. Normal defines that both RIP I and RIP II information is sent and received by the router. Send Only defines that the router will only send RIP I packets to other hosts. Receive Only defines that the router will only receive RIP I packets from other hosts.

- **RIP II Options field**—Enables you to define authentication rules to prevent RIP information from being exchanged with routers you do not want to be included in the RIP operations. Enabling the Authentication option forces other routers and hosts to provide a password to gain access to the RIP II information from this router.

Open Shortest Path First (OSPF) Bind Options   Selecting the OSPF Bind Options choice opens the OSPF Bind Options screen, which enables you to define the specific Open Shortest Path First (OSPF) configuration options to be used by the WAN connection. OSPF is a link state protocol for TCP/IP, which allows the network to maintain multiple connections between sites, and to dynamically find the shortest route between those sites. OSPF routers are also capable of dynamically rerouting packets in the event that the preferred route fails.

Configurable options available to the administrator are as follows:

- **Status field**—Defines whether OSPF should be used on this interface.
- **Cost of Interface field**—Defines the route cost that OSPF associates with sending a packet on this network. A higher cost will prevent the router from using this interface if another route exists to the same destination.
- **Area ID field**—Defines the address assigned to the unique OSPF identifier for this specific area. Backbone areas are identified as address 0.0.0.0. This address is required if areas are defined.
- **Priority field**—Defines which router takes precedence when more than one router exists to a single destination.
- **Authentication Password**—Defines the key used to access a defined area when authentication is enabled. If authentication is desired, it must be enabled on all routers in the same area.
- **Hello Interval field**—Defines the time, in seconds, that the router waits between sending Hello packets on the network or virtual link. This value must be the same for all routers on the same network or virtual link.
- **Router Dead Interval**—Defines the time, in seconds, that a router will wait before declaring its neighbor dead after sending a Hello packet.
- **Neighbor List field**—Enables you to add known neighbors to the OSPF routing table. An OSPF router normally discovers its neighbors through the exchange of Hello packets. In broadcast networks, such as an Ethernet local network, the OSPF router multicasts a Hello packet. In nonbroadcast networks, such as X.25, the location of the OSPF neighbors are configured manually. The router sends Hello packets to its configured neighbors to indicate it is alive.

Expert TCP/IP Bind Options   Selecting the Expert TCP/IP Bind Options choice opens the Expert TCP/IP WAN Options screen. This screen enables you to modify the advanced TCP/IP functions, as follows:

- **Router Discovery Options field**—Allows you to enable the Internet Control Message Protocol (ICMP) Router Discovery Protocol. ICMP enables hosts to discover routers on their network and determine, automatically, which router to use as their default. When ICMP is configured on a router, that router advertises itself with periodic ICMP router advertisement messages, which the host listens to in order to determine whether to use that particular router as its default.
- **Broadcast Address option**—Defines the explicit address the routers on this network use for broadcast packets. All routers on the network must use the same broadcast address.
- **Multicast Override IP Address**—Defines an IP address that is used to replace the standard TCP/IP Multicast handler address. By setting this value you can either direct TCP/IP to have the Broadcast address handle all multicast requests or you can direct all multicast packets to a single node on the network that is designated to handle all multicast traffic.

Part

VII

Ch

28

■ **Header Compression option**—Allows you to enable or disable TCP and IP Packet Header compression across a serial point-to-point link.

■ **IPCP Address Assignment Range**—Used to define the start and end IP addresses to be used by IP to assign an address to a remote node when that node requests the address from IPCP (Internet Protocol Control Protocol).

Finalizing the Network Configuration

After selecting the WAN interface adapter type, the communication type, and the protocols to use, you must initialize the adapter and protocols. You can do this in one of three ways: reboot the server, select the Reinitialize System option from the Internetworking Configuration menu, or issue the Reinitialize System command at the file server console.

N O T E   For the Reinitialize System option to function, the MPR functions must have been loaded on the server. If this is the first time installation of the MPR products, you must reboot the server to initialize all LAN and WAN adapters properly. ■

After the router has initialized the WAN adapter and established a physical link with the network you can test router to router or router to host communication by using the IPXPING.NLM for IPX and the PING or TPING NLMs for TCP/IP.

Using IPXPING

The IPXPING utility allows an MPR router to test the IPX communication link integrity with any NetWare workstation or server, or any MPR router on the network. This can be used to help determine whether a route is available to a specific server or workstation, or whether a static route was properly defined.

To use the IPXPING utility you issue the LOAD IPXPING command at the MPR server console prompt. Upon loading the utility you will be presented with the IPXPING New Target definition screen shown in Figure 28.16.

FIG. 28.16
The IPXPING New Target definition screen enables you to specify the network address of the target IPX network or server to ping.

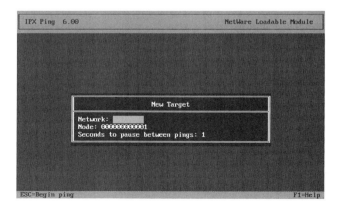

N O T E To run IPXPING on an IntranetWare file server or MPR router, it must be running the IPXRTR.NLM. The functions necessary to ping across an IPX link do not exist without the enhanced routing information provided by this NLM set. ▨

The following fields define what IPX network or server to Ping:

- **Network field**—Defines the IPX network segment address for the server or workstation you want to ping. When pinging a workstation you would use the LAN segment address assigned to the LAN adapter in the file server attached to the segment the workstation is on. When pinging a file server or another MPR router you would use the IPX Internal address assigned to the server in the AUTOEXEC.NCF.

- **Node field**—Defines the address the workstation or server uses. If you are pinging a workstation then you would use the physical node address assigned to the LAN adapter in the workstation. If you are pinging a file server or another MPR router you would use a node address of 1.

- **Seconds to Pause Between Pings field**—Defines the delay between PING packets on the network. You would change the delay time for connections over slow links or saturated network segments.

Once you have input the required address information, press the Esc key to start the ping operation. You can add additional file servers, MPR routers, and nodes to the target list by pressing Ins and defining the appropriate network and node addresses. IPXPING will continue to operate and ping the defined nodes until you exit the utility. Figure 28.17 shows an active IPXPING session that is pinging an MPR router/IntranetWare file server and a workstation on the Ethernet network.

FIG. 28.17
This example of the IPXPING display screen shows both a server and a workstation on the network.

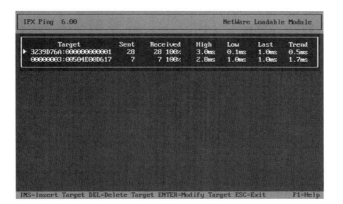

Using PING and TPING

The PING and TPING utilities enable the MPR router to test the existence of and integrity of a TCP/IP connection. These utilities can be used to ping any TCP/IP host or service on the network, as long as the address is not filtered in some way.

Part
VII

Ch
28

Functionally, PING operates in the same manner as IPXPING in that you supply the appropriate TCP/IP address you want to check for and press Esc to start the test. If the host has been defined in the routers HOST table in the SYS:ETC directory you can address the target by its canonical name. Additionally, with PING you can define the packet size used during the PING test. Figure 28.18 shows the PING utilities New Target definition screen.

FIG. 28.18

The PING Utility New Target definition screen enables you to define the target host by name or IP address and configure PING parameters.

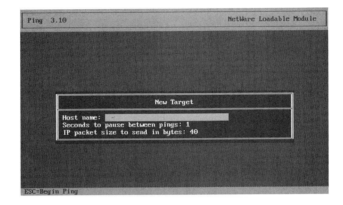

As with the IPXPING utility, you can define multiple concurrent addresses to ping by pressing Ins. The PING screen looks similar to the IPXPING display shown in Figure 28.17 with the only difference being that the first column is names Node rather than Target.

The TPING utility, on the other hand, is something completely new with IntranetWare. It is a simple, one shot utility designed strictly to test to see if the defined host is alive or not. To use TPING simply issue the LOAD TPING *host address/name* at the MPR server console. Figure 28.19 shows the TPING message for both an active and an inactive address.

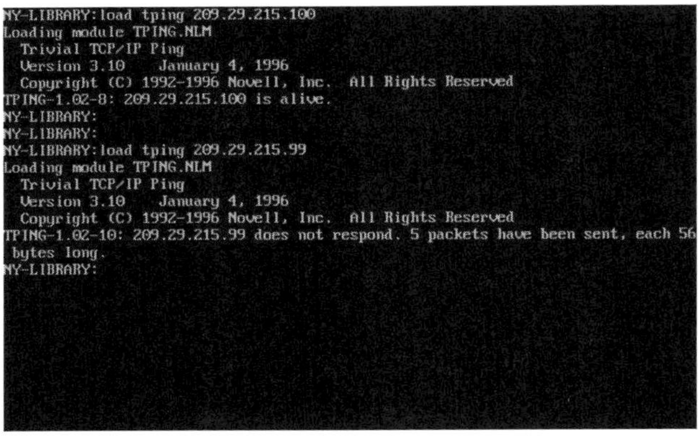

FIG. 28.19

TPING response messages to both an active and inactive host address is displayed on the server monitor.

Managing the WAN Communication

Once you have determined that the physical links have been established and the protocol links are functional you are ready to use your WAN. To ensure that it is operating at optimum performance Novell has included several management console products. These include both network protocol consoles for IPX (IPXCON.NLM), TCP/IP (TCPCON.NLM), and AppleTalk (ATCON.NLM) and all run at the file server or MPR server console. Figure 28.20 shows the TCP/IP Console screen.

FIG. 28.20
The TCP/IP Management Console main information screen shows the TCP/IP network management options.

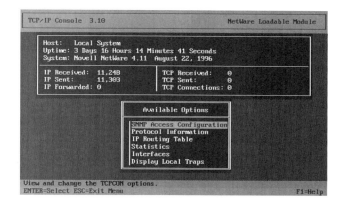

In addition to the network protocol management consoles, there are also management facilities included to track the WAN call configurations. The management consoles available for this are for AIO asynchronous links (AIOCON.NLM), ATM links (ATMCON.NLM), PPP links (PPPCON.NLM), Frame relay links (FRCON.NLM), and X.25 links (X25CON.NLM). Figure 28.21 shows the console screen X25CON.

FIG. 28.21
The X.25 Management Console main information screen shows the X.25 network management options.

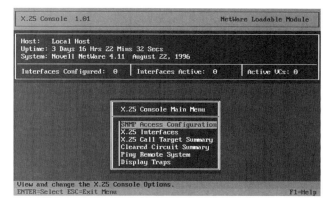

Part
VII

Ch
28

Additionally, hardware specific information can be garnered from the MONITOR.NLM utility under the LAN/WAN Information menu selection. This will inform you of specific hardware and driver level events that occur on the WAN adapter itself.

Connecting to the Internet via MPR

As has been defined throughout this chapter, you can configure Novell's Multiprotocol Router to act as a high performance wide area network routing device that is capable of transporting many different protocols. One of the available protocols is the TCP/IP protocol suite. This is the protocol utilized to communicate across the Internet, and therefore by definition, Novell's MPR is capable of connecting your network to the Internet.

The specifics on how you physically connect to the Internet will be dependent on the services your Internet service provider (ISP) offers, as well as the telephone service your local carrier can provide. Generally, the following are the most common means of routing to the Internet:

- PPP asynchronous dial-up service via modem
- PPP synchronous digital dedicated link service via leased line
- PPP ISDN switched access or dial-up service
- Frame relay service via leased line

N O T E When configuring the WAN hardware, keep the following configuration points in mind:

- When selecting an asynchronous modem on a serial port, use the driver WHSMAIO.
- When using a CAPI-compliant ISDN board, use the WHSMCAPI driver.
- All other WAN adapters will have board-specific drivers provided by the adapters' manufacturers.

MPR does not currently support ISDN modems or terminal adapters. Check with the manufacturer to see if they provide their own ISDN scripts and LAN/WAN drivers for use with MPR/IntranetWare.

Asynchronous Connections to the Internet

Asynchronous connections to the Internet are likely to be the most troublesome and most costly in the long term due to their lack of reliability and service line costs. When configuring an asynchronous connection to the Internet you need to ensure that your ISP can provide a static address to your router, and that your router is calling another router and not a terminal server.

Most ISPs that provide dial-up access to a network do so through an IP gateway service connecting to their terminal servers. These gateways are generally Windows 95 or Windows NT workstations that can be assigned a dynamic address by the ISP upon connecting to the terminal server. This gateway then connects to your network via a LAN card installed in the machine. These gateways do not route TCP/IP packets, but rather pass the data from one TCP/IP network to another via gateway services.

Additionally, you will need to ask your ISP if it is your responsibility to provide the asynchronous communication devices (the modem and router) on their side of the connection. In many cases, because an asynchronous router requires a dedicated port with a static address be available, you may find that your ISP expects you to cover the additional hardware costs at their end. Along with this, you may find that the ISP expects you to cover the cost of the telephone line coming into this router port at their end. What this means is that beyond the cost of the local phone line and hardware required at your site, you may have to cover the cost of the hardware and phone line at your ISP's site as well.

PPP Digital Connections to the Internet

PPP digital connections to the Internet can be accomplished in one of two ways. The first is through the use of dedicated leased lines and DSU/CSUs to maintain constant open links to your ISP. The second is through the use of an Integrated Services Digital Network (ISDN) dial-up device. Because ISDN provides an On Demand connection to the Internet, and because it generally operates at lower speeds than a dedicated T1 line, it can be significantly more cost effective for use in a low to medium utilization network environment.

As with asynchronous PPP connections, Digital PPP connections require dedicated hardware at both ends of the link and your ISP may require that you purchase the equipment at their site and pay for the line into their site as part of their service fees.

Frame Relay Digital Connections to the Internet

Frame relay connections to the Internet can provide the highest cost/benefit ratio available. This is in part due to the capability for multiple customers of your ISP to share access into a single port in a router at their site. In general, this means that the only hardware costs and telephone service fees you will need to be responsible for are the ones at your site. Your ISP then amortizes the costs for equipment and telephone lines to all their customers who use the shared access ports.

Additionally, frame relay provides an easy-to-upgrade bandwidth path. If you start your connection out with a fractional T1 link to your ISP, you can easily upgrade the service to any speed available between 128 Kbps and 1.5 Mbps simply by reprogramming the DSU/CSU and scheduling a service change with your frame relay service carrier and your ISP.

Addressing Your Network

When connecting to the Internet you have to be in control of the TCP/IP addresses you use on your network. Getting a TCP/IP address registered is something you can get as part of the service your ISP provides. Additionally, your ISP can perform a domain name search and assist you in registering your Internet domain name with the InterNIC, the organization in charge of administrating domain names. For information on registering a domain name you can request information directly from the InterNIC on the Internet at **http://rs.internic.net.**

Because the TCP/IP addresses on your network will be directly connected to the Internet via your router you need to ensure that the addresses you use on your workstations are valid for your site. Using addresses that are not properly registered can cause performance and reliability problems for your network, as well as cause routing problems for the network that is rightfully assigned the address you are using. Another problem with directly attaching your network to the Internet is that someone on the outside can see devices on the inside of your network.

To resolve both of these potential routing and security problems you can either implement a firewall between your router and your network or you can utilize Novell's IPX/IP Gateway (see Chapter 27, "Using the IPX/IP Gateway").

Utilizing the IPX/IP Gateway enables you to connect to the Internet by only assigning a single TCP/IP address, as provided by your ISP to the WAN adapter in your IntranetWare/MPR server. Because TCP/IP is not bound to the LAN card in the server, TCP/IP requests from external sources cannot pass through to your network. The drawback to this is that some Internet sites require the capability to perform reverse resolution of the workstation address and these requests will not pass the gateway. In these instances the connection to the Internet site will be terminated. Also, some services you may want to implement on your network require the capability to communicate directly with a next upstream service host, one such example could be the use of an SMTP mail gateway.

To resolve the limitations of using IPX/IP gateways you can bind TCP/IP to both the WAN and the LAN ports in your IntranetWare/MPR server and implement an Internet firewall. A firewall is a software program, or software and hardware package that analyzes all packets coming from and going to a remote network to determine whether the packet is from a valid host or network, or is requesting a valid service from the local network. For example, you can define your firewall to allow all packets from the network at address 199.99.98.0 regardless of what their service request is. Or, you could configure your firewall to allow all FTP service requests regardless of what network they originate from.

Another service that a firewall can provide is to proxy the outbound addresses seen by the remote networks. In this case, the proxy service receives an outbound service request from a station using one assigned IP address, for example, 199.99.99.150 and converts it to another. The proxy server receives the packet, determines that it is for an external network resource and translates the assigned IP address to an address within a range assigned by your ISP.

For more information on firewalls and proxy services contact the National Computer Security Association (NCSA) on the Internet at **http://www.ncsa.com**. A list of NCSA certified firewall products is maintained at **http://www.ncsa.com/fpfs/fwindex.html**.

Summary

In this chapter, you learned what Novell's Multiprotocol Router product is and how it can help provide seamless communication over a wide area intranetwork. We reviewed the commonly available WAN hardware options, including ATM, ISDN, synchronous digital devices, and asynchronous analog devices. By way of these discussions, you have reviewed how to determine the option that best suits the needs of your network based on required throughput and data load, as well as some cost information.

We discussed the available link options including point-to-point, frame relay and X.25 services, and how to determine which service option is best suited to your needs. As part of the discussion on service types available we also discussed the differences between On Demand network connections and Permanent network connections and some of the benefits and drawbacks of each.

We also discussed the network transport protocol options available, including IPX and TCP/IP. In these discussions we reviewed the basic configuration requirements for each protocol, as well as defining the advanced functions that may need tuning in your particular environment.

And finally we discussed the use of IntranetWare and the MPR functionality to connect your network to the Internet. As part of this discussion we defined some of the specific issues with each of the commonly available connection types, including asynchronous dial-up, point-to-point digital service, including dedicated links via leased lines and ISDN dial-up links, and finally frame relay services. As part of the Internet connectivity discussion we discussed the TCP/IP addressing issues and domain name registration. We also discussed the use of IPX to IP gateways and firewall services as a means of implementing network security on your IntranetWare network. ●

CHAPTER 29

Migrating to NetWare Link Services Protocol (NLSP)

What NLSP is

Learn the differences between standard IPX and the enhanced IPX functions of NLSP.

How to configure NLSP

Find out how to configure SAP and RIP information exchange.

How to configure load-balanced and redundant networks

Learn about using IPX across the WAN to connect sites.

NetWare networks have traditionally used the IPX protocol to communicate among the file servers and workstations. When networks were small and contained within workgroups, this protocol was fast and efficient. As workgroups expanded into departments, and departments expanded into campuses, and campuses expanded into multi-server, multi-location enterprises, the original IPX protocol capabilities were stretched to their limits trying to maintain efficient communication among workstations and servers.

To alleviate the limitations in the IPX protocol, Novell developed the NetWare Link Services Protocol (NLSP) as an extension of IPX. NLSP provides a link-state routing protocol that eliminates the need for servers to generate SAP packets to maintain route information, thereby reducing bandwidth overhead and providing a means for the network to automatically recover a connection to a service if the original route drops.

Additionally, NLSP provides a means to automatically load-balance network traffic among servers, as well as provide fault-tolerant links to critical services.

When utilizing NLSP, each server maintains its own record of every known communication link on the network and determines the best route available to any other server. When a change occurs on the network, each server broadcasts its information table about itself and its immediate neighbors out to all servers on the network. Each receiving server can then use that information to build new tables on the best route to any other server on the network. ■

How NLSP Works versus IPX

Some of the limitations of the original IPX protocol are its inability to provide for duplicate routes to a single destination server, its inability to recover from a lost connection, and its inability to dynamically load-balance or provide fault-tolerant links on the network. Many of these limitations are due to IPX's basic design as a distance-vector routing protocol.

To maintain the router information tables among servers, IPX uses Service Advertisement Packets (SAP) broadcast every 60 seconds to carry server information across the network. In a network with more than a few file, print, and communication servers, this can lead to a large amount of SAP packet traffic on the network, reducing the total available bandwidth for data. When using SAP to determine a route from workstation to server, once the route is established, the only way to change the route is to reboot the workstation.

In contrast, NLSP provides its functionality through the use of four packet types and three databases to maintain information about the network map. The four packets that are used to determine the information to be placed in the databases are as follows:

- **Hello packet**—Used to identify the server's nearest neighbor
- **Link State packet**—Used to identify routes and services on the network
- **Complete Sequence Number packets**—Used to determine how often the server should look for changes on the network
- **Partial Sequence Number packets**—Used to determine the information needed to update the route and services tables

The following are the three databases that NLSP uses:

- **Adjacency database**—Tracks the server's immediate neighbors
- **Link State database**—Tracks the available routes and services on the network
- **Forwarding database**—Maintains the information on the fastest or least costly route to any destination on the network

As services are brought up on the network, they broadcast their information to their neighbors. The neighbors add the new information to their databases, rebuilding route and services tables in the three databases so that each server now has a better detail of the network map, and then the neighbor broadcasts its updated database to its neighbors. In this way, updated network information is always cascading down the network to every service device available. The following list breaks down the steps NLSP goes through to build and maintain its routing information tables:

1. NLSP uses Hello packets to talk with all of a server's neighbors.

2. Using the responses to the Hello packets, each server creates a list of its immediate neighbors.

3. Each server determines which of the neighboring routers will serve as the *designated router* (DR). The DR controls the updates to each of the servers within its network segment.

4. Link State packets are passed among each of the servers and its neighbors so that each server can determine its own network map.

5. From this network map, NLSP builds the forwarding database, which tells the server the cheapest route for various destinations.

6. The DR uses Complete Sequence Number packets to broadcast its Link State database to all other servers on its network segment.

7. The other servers respond using Partial Sequence Number packets to request missing information.

Determining the Cost

When routing packets from one network segment to another, each delay point adds a cost factor, in time, to getting the packet to its destination. When using IPX, cost was determined simply by how many hops (routers) a packet had to pass through to get to the destination, and which route responded first. Using the IPX network in Figure 29.1 as an example, it is possible for the workstation to connect to server A directly on LAN segment 1. It is also possible for the workstation to connect through server B on LAN segment 1 and route back to server A on LAN segment 2 if server A was too busy to respond directly to the station's Get Nearest Server request.

FIG. 29.1
A Multi-server IPX network is showing duplicate routes between servers.

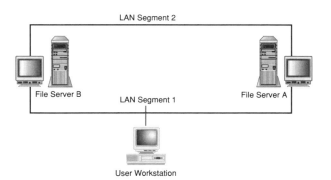

By implementing NLSP, each connection would determine the cost using a more involved algorithm, which would include the speed of the link among the servers as well as hop count. Thus, for the first time in an IPX environment, you can create a network link among servers on a LAN or a WAN and predetermine which route the packets will use to get to the destination server.

For LAN adapters, the cost factor is based on its throughput. For WAN connections, the cost factor is based on the actual measured data throughput of the link itself. The cost factor can be any whole number between 1 and 63—the higher the number the slower the link. Table 29.1 shows some of the common link costs imposed by various link types.

Table 29.1   Link Cost Associated with Link Type

Network Link Media Type	Default Cost	Throughput Range
FDDI/Fast Ethernet/TCNS	14	64–128 Mbps
16 Mbps token ring / 20 Mbps ARCnet	19	16–32 Mbps
Ethernet	20	10–16 Mbps
4 Mbps token ring/ Corvus Omninet/	25 4	4–8 Mbps
E1 WAN/ARCnet	26	2–4 Mbps
T1 WAN/Omninet / IBM Baseband/Broadband	27	1–2 Mbps
ISDN/56k	45	48–128 Kbps
Asynchronous modem	61	0–48 Kbps

By utilizing NLSP in the network from Figure 29.1, you can virtually guarantee that the workstation will communicate with server A on LAN segment 1 based on the routing cost factors server B would use to determine the best route back to server A.

It is also possible to manually override the cost factors for any given LAN or WAN adapter installed in the file server. For example, you want to provide a fault-tolerant link among servers, but you don't want the second segment to be used unless something causes the first segment to fail. You can assign a higher cost factor to the LAN card servicing the second segment in each server thus preventing that segment from being used unless the first were to go down.

Another reason you may want to manually override the cost factor for a LAN or WAN card is to force load balancing across unlike networks. For example, you have both an Ethernet and a 16 Mbps token-ring LAN connection among servers on your network. By default, NLSP will always find the token ring to be your preferred route because it has a lower cost factor. You can either increase the token-ring adapter's cost factor to match the Ethernet, or lower the

Ethernet to match the token ring's cost and force the NLSP routers to utilize both segments equally to balance the network load. NLSP can support up to eight concurrent load balanced paths among servers.

N O T E Although NLSP will discard duplicate path information for routes with a higher cost from the forwarding database, that information is always retained in the link state database. This enables NLSP to rebuild route information in the event of a segment failure. By being able to transparently rebuild routing information, a workstation may never lose connection to a server that is supported by fault-tolerant links.

Implementing NLSP on Your Network

NLSP services are provided by a series of NLMs loaded on the file server. The main NLM is IPXRTR.NLM, which is included as part of the IntranetWare package. NLSP functionality is configured and maintained through the Internetworking Configuration Utility (INETCFG.NLM) run at the file server console. If this represents the first time you are loading the INETCFG utility it will prompt you to import all the LAN and WAN configuration information from the AUTOEXEC.NCF into its databases. When INETCFG does so, it will also set up and configure the basic configuration options you had established in the AUTOEXEC.NCF.

When INETCFG has finished importing the information from the AUTOEXEC.NCF you will be presented with the Internetworking Configuration menu, as shown in Figure 29.2.

FIG. 29.2
The Internetworking Configuration menu lists the available options.

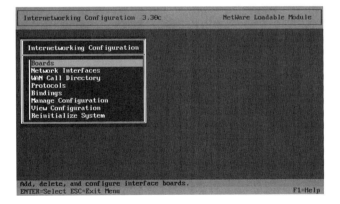

Select the Boards option and confirm that the LAN and/or WAN adapters that were loading are listed in the Configured Boards list. If they are not, then press Ins to add the appropriate LAN and WAN adapters to the list of configured boards. If you are configuring WAN connections, refer to Chapter 28, "Using the Multiprotocol Router," for specific information about setting up the Network Interfaces and WAN Call Directory information.

When you have ensured that all the appropriate LAN and WAN adapters are installed and configured, it's time to set up and configure NLSP.

NLSP is an extension of the IPX protocol. As such, its functionality only applies to the IPX protocol stack and does not impact the operation of TCP/IP, AppleTalk, or any other protocol stack you may load on your file server. Configuring NLSP, therefore, is a function of the Protocol and Bindings operations provided in the Internetworking Configuration utility.

Protocols

Selecting the Protocols option from the Internetworking Configuration utility presents you with the default list of available protocols. To configure your server to utilize NLSP functionality select the IPX protocol. When you select the IPX protocol option, you are presented with the IPX Protocol Configuration screen, as shown in Figure 29.3.

FIG. 29.3
The IPX Protocol Configuration screen lists the available configuration options.

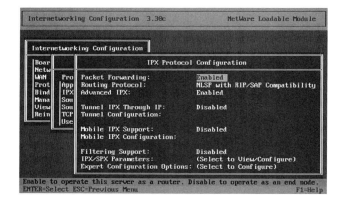

By default, if NLSP options were not specified in the AUTOEXEC.NCF during importation by INETCFG, NLSP with RIP/SAP Compatibility is enabled under the Routing Protocol option. If it is not, then parse to the Routing Protocol option and select NLSP with RIP/SAP Compatibility. This option enables the NLSP driver (IPXRTR.NLM) to be loaded on the file server.

N O T E As NLSP is an evolving protocol enhancement to the IPX protocol stack, Novell regularly releases updates for it. These updates can be found in the IntranetWare Patch Kit on Novell's FTP server at either of the following addresses:

> **ftp://ftp.novell.com/pub/updates/nwos/inw411**
>
> **ftp://ftp.novell.de/pub/updates/nwos/inw411**

NLSP functions are maintained from the Expert Configuration options within the IPX Protocol Configuration. Selecting this option presents you with the screen shown in Figure 29.4. The NLSP specific functions within this screen are the following:

- Maximum Number of Path Splits
- Load Balance NCP Packets to Local Clients
- LSP Size
- NLSP Local Area Addresses
- Override NLSP System ID
- NLSP System Identification (only available if Override NLSP System ID is enabled)
- NLSP Convergence Rate
- NLSP Convergence Rate Configuration

FIG. 29.4

The IPX Expert Configuration screen shows the expert configuration options available.

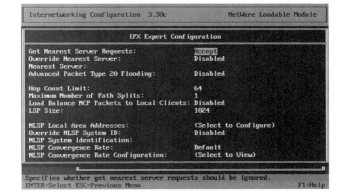

Maximum Number of Path Splits   The Maximum Number of Path Splits defines the number of equal cost paths that NLSP will use to forward packets. This is the value that determines the number of segments common to a destination server that NLSP will use for load balancing. The available values are 1 through 8.

N O T E   If you configure equal cost routes on two or more interfaces, you must ensure that the associated media throughputs are within or near the same range. For example, you can use the cost override to define a load-balanced route between a 10 Mbps Ethernet and a 16 Mbps token ring. You should not configure a load-balanced route between a 16 Mbps token ring and a 4 Mbps token ring. Trying to load-balance on disparaging network media types will lead to operational problems for IPX applications on the network. Effectively, packets could reach their destination out of sequence.

Load Balance NCP Packets to Local Clients   The Load Balance NCP Packets To Local Clients enables NLSP to provide a load-balanced network segment, as opposed to a fault-tolerant network segment. When this option is disabled, only one LAN adapter in the server will be maintained in the forwarding database for NLSP at a time. When enabled, NCP service requests are automatically load-balanced across the LAN cards bound to the same network segment, up to the maximum number defined for path splits. This option provides the same functionality as the loading of the SET LOAD BALANCE LOCAL LAN=ON command at the server console.

LSP Size   The LSP Size field defines the size, in bytes, that the Link State Packet can be. The LSP size must be smaller than the minimum size of the largest frame supported by your network minus the size of the packet header (30 bytes).

For example, if your largest frame size supported on your network is 4,202 bytes, then the LSP Size must be no larger than 4,172. Under certain circumstances, such as implementing an NLSP-based server in an older NetWare 2 or NetWare 3 environment, you may want to reduce the LSP Size to maintain SAP/RIP compatibility.

NLSP Local Area Addresses   The NLSP Local Area Addresses field enables you to specify up to three IPX network numbers and masks to allow for filtering of RIP routes. RIP information that does not match the address/mask pairs defined will be dropped.

Override NLSP System ID   The Override NLSP System ID field defines whether to allow the default ID specified by NLSP to be overridden. Each NLSP router requires a unique ID number, therefore, it is critical that all NLSP devices be properly identified. It is recommended that you not change the system ID unless you manually control all the IDs on your network, both local and wide area.

NLSP System Identification   The NLSP System Identification field enables you to define the NLSP System ID if the Override System ID option has been enabled. It is recommended that some unique addressing option be implemented if you are going to override the default. One such unique address would be the MAC address of one of the network adapters installed in the server.

NLSP Convergence Rate   The NLSP Convergence Rate field defines the rate at which NLSP routers are expected to obtain the current state of the network. The faster your network converges, the more traffic can flow across your network. If your network does not converge fast enough, the more likely your network will experience network traffic and communication problems.

NLSP Convergence Rate Configuration   The NLSP Convergence Rate Configuration option provides a READ ONLY view of the Convergence Rate parameters, unless the NLSP Convergence Rate field previously discussed is set to MANUAL mode. It is recommended that these parameters be left to their default values unless there is a specific cause or reason to change them. Improperly setting these values could cause your server to stop communicating with other servers on the network.

Bindings

The next step in implementing NLSP is to bind the IPX protocol to an adapter, or multiple adapters in your server. Selecting the Bindings option from the Internetworking Configuration menu will present you with the list of configured LAN cards and the protocols that are currently bound to them in the Protocol To Interface/Group Bindings screen.

If the interface you want to implement NLSP on is listed, select that interface. If it is not listed, you can add it by pressing the Ins key, selecting IPX and the board to which you want to bind the protocol.

Once you have selected the adapter for which you want NLSP configured, you will be presented with the Binding IPX to a LAN Interface screen. This screen enables you to input the IPX network address to be associated with this LAN adapter and the frame type used.

> **CAUTION**
>
> If you are going to implement load-balancing or fault-tolerant links for a particular network segment, you must ensure that the network adapters sharing the same physical segment have been assigned the same IPX Network Number.

N O T E When implementing load balancing on a network segment, it is possible to do so in several different ways. The network adapters in the file server could share ports in a common hub or MAU, or they could be connected to the same physical cable bus as in the case of a thin Ethernet segment. But, you will get the highest level of performance by connecting the LAN cards directly to dedicated ports in a high-speed-multi-port switch.

Utilizing a switch can provide additional benefits in that broadcast and multicast traffic can be filtered out, as well as enabling the network adapters in the server to operate in full duplex mode—effectively doubling their available bandwidth.

Additionally, the Expert Bind Options selection is available. Selecting the Expert Bind Options enables you to configure several operating parameters for IPX networks, but this section focuses on the NLSP Bind Options function. Selecting the NLSP Bind Options from the Expert Bind Options menu presents you with the screen shown in Figure 29.5.

FIG. 29.5
The NLSP Bind Options screen shows the available tunable parameters.

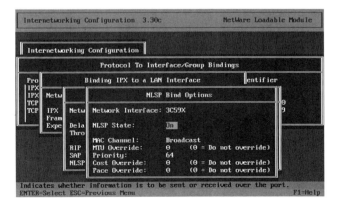

The configurable NLSP options available to the network administrator are as follows:

- **NLSP State field**—Defines whether NLSP functionality will be enabled for this network adapter. This enables you to disable NLSP for troubleshooting purposes without having to reconfigure the network adapters.

- **MAC Channel field**—Defines whether to use the Broadcast or Multicast channel as the default information packet transport channel. All servers on the network must be set to the same value to communicate. If one server on the network is using broadcast, all other servers will use broadcast.

- **MTU Override field**—Defines the maximum packet size for this network adapter. Setting this value overrides the default value for the adapter. Use this option only to set a smaller than default packet size to maintain compatibility with non-NLSP bridges or routers.

- **Priority field**—Defines the priority this server has for becoming the Designated Router. You would want to change this value on servers that are not available to the system often so that they do not become the DR. Set this value to a high number on a server you want to force to become the DR, such as a high-performance, lightly loaded server on the network.

- **Cost Override field**—Defines the additional cost to be added to this network adapter. You would want to override the default cost when you want to utilize load balancing across different network types or when you want to force a particular LAN segment to be the fault-tolerant backup segment. All servers connected to the segment with the Cost Override should use the same value for that particular network adapter. Setting this value to 0 disables the override function.

- **Pace Override field**—Defines the maximum number of routing packets per second that can be sent over this interface. Changing this value overrides the default. Setting this value to 0 disables the override function.

NLSP Over the Wide Area

The benefits of NLSP are not limited to only the LAN adapters in your servers. NLSP can also benefit the wide area adapters installed in your servers. By implementing NLSP across a PPP WAN link you can provide both load balancing over multiple serial lines, as well as fault tolerance via redundant links among sites. Figure 29.6 shows two sites connected via a load balanced T1 WAN link connection.

In this network, IPX packets are transported over both network segments simultaneously, providing the equivalent of 3 Mbps throughput among the sites. This also provides some level of fault tolerance if the T1 service is provided by different carriers over different lines in that if one T1 link fails the other will maintain the network connection.

Figure 29.7 shows a multi-site, wide area network connecting each site to the others. This network configuration, when utilizing NLSP on the router at each site, can provide a fault-tolerant network that will transparently maintain connections to all sites even if one of the links were to fail.

FIG. 29.6
A load-balanced WAN
link connection is
showing two active links
between sites.

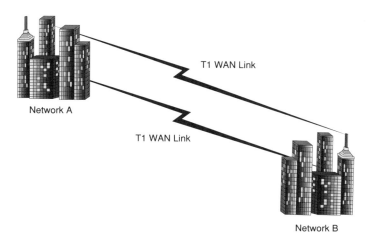

FIG. 29.7
A fault-tolerant multi-
site WAN link connec-
tion is demonstrating
redundant link
capability.

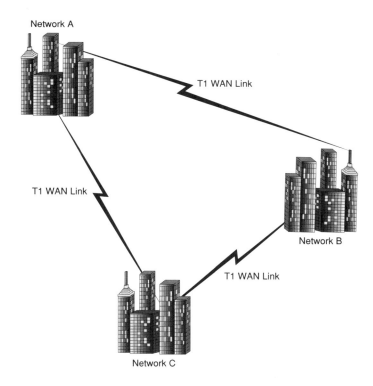

In this example, if the link between networks B and C were to fail, the NLSP routers would re-
negotiate the least-cost route to all three networks and would begin routing data to the appropriate destination server through the remaining WAN links. Thus, a user on network B who is
accessing data on a server on network C may never be aware that the physical link between B
and C went away, as the data is now being routed through network A between B and C.

Summary

This chapter addressed implementing NLSP on your IntranetWare servers and routers to reduce the amount of packet overhead that your network experiences by removing SAP traffic between routers. This also improves overall network performance by providing a higher amount of network bandwidth to the data.

You further learned how NLSP can allow for load balancing on both local and wide area networks. This provides a higher level of network performance among servers, or from a workstation to a particular server. Similarly, NLSP can allow for fault tolerant links between servers and routers, thereby increasing the overall network reliability and serviceability. ●

Implementing the IntranetWare Services

CHAPTER 30

Using the NetWare Web Server

As the name implies, IntranetWare is designed to combine the networking abilities of NetWare with the tools needed to create an intranet. You've read elsewhere in this book about the systems and services needed to implement the TCP/IP protocols on your network, but the most vital part of an intranet is the Web server that actually sends documents to client browsers. Novell's Web Server product is an NLM-based service that supports all of the standard features found in the typical Web servers that run on UNIX and Windows NT systems.

Although Novell may have placed its primary emphasis on intranet development, the Web Server can be considered to be "Internetware" as well. By connecting your NetWare network to a service provider using the Multiprotocol Router included in the IntranetWare package, you can serve Web pages to Internet clients just as easily as you would to internal users.

IntranetWare ships with version 2.51 of the Web Server product, which is registered in the Product Options menu of the INSTALL.NLM utility. However, as of this writing, version 3.0 is available as a free download from Novell's Web site, and provides a wealth of improvements over the earlier version. This chapter covers the 3.0 version of the software. ■

How to upgrade an existing Novell Web Server installation

Web Server 3.0 provides significant improvements in speed and efficiency over the 2.x versions, as well as many new features that you can use to provide additional services to intranet and Internet users.

How to configure Novell Web Server

You can begin to publish documents immediately after Web Server installation simply by placing HTML files in the correct directory, but you can also customize the server configuration to suit the specific needs of your intranet.

How to control access to Web services

Novell Web Server uses NDS to authenticate users, enabling you to create Web sites that are restricted to specific users without the need to create new accounts.

How Novell Web Server supports the development of intranet applications

Web Server 3.0 supports many of the industry standard tools for building Web-based applications, and also provides a script interpreter for its own NetBasic programming language.

Upgrading to Web Server 3.0

The 3.0 release of Novell Web Server is a significant upgrade to the version included in the IntranetWare package. In addition to palpable improvements in speed, the new version includes several important new features, such as the following:

- **Multihoming**—A single Web Server installation can host multiple Web sites, each with its own IP address, host name, documents, logs, and server configuration.
- **Virtual directories**—Documents that are to be published as Web pages can now be located on any NetWare server, not just the one running the NWS software.
- **QuickFinder**—Novell Web Server now includes a built-in search engine that automatically indexes your Web sites and enables users to locate specific documents through Web-based forms.
- **Secure Socket Layer 3.0**—SSL 3.0 is the newest version of a standard defining a protocol for encrypted communications over a TCP/IP network. When combined with NDS authentication, you can create Web sites that are secure from unauthorized access.
- **Perl 5**—NWS now supports version 5 of the Practical Extraction and Report Language (Perl), one of the most popular interpreted scripting languages used in Web development today.
- **Database connectivity**—Through the NetBasic scripting language, NWS can be used to create applications that access Oracle databases, enabling users to access corporate information through a Web browser.

If you have installed a previous version of Novell Web Server, you can upgrade the software by installing the new version using the NetWare INSTALL.NLM utility and specifying the same target directories that you used originally. All of your configuration data and Web documents are left intact.

As with any Web server product, you must have TCP/IP installed and configured on your server. However, NWS 3.0 requires that your server also be upgraded to the newest versions of several key NetWare modules. Before running the new Web server, you must install the IntranetWare Support Pack 2, available as IWSP2.EXE from Novell's online services. This is a collection of all of the patches needed to bring your IntranetWare server up to date.

Web Server also requires version 4 of the TCPIP.NLM module, also available for download as TCPN03.EXE. Without this module, the primary Web server program, HTTP.NLM, fails to load, displaying only a brief message on the server console. If you attempt to start the Web server and do not see a Novell Web Server statistics panel on the console, then check the version of the TCPIP.NLM file that is currently in memory and the CONSOLE.LOG file (in the SYS:ETC directory) for any pertinent error messages.

N O T E   Novell Web Server 3.0 is available for download from Novell's Web site at **http:// www.novell.com/intranetware/products/novell_web_server/**. The IntranetWare Support Pack 2 is available as a self-extracting archive called IWSP2.EXE at **http://support.novell.com/**

cgi-bin/search/download?/pub/updates/nwos/nwebs30/iwsp2.exe&sr. The URL for the TCPN03.EXE upgrade file is **http://support.novell.com/cgi-bin/search/download?/pub/updates/ unixconn/lwg5/tcpn03.exe&sr**. ▦

Configuring Novell Web Server

As mentioned earlier, the Novell Web Server requires no initial configuration at all to be usable. The installation program, by default, creates a single Web site that is accessible to all users. If you have accepted the default directory names suggested by the program, you can simply place your Web pages in the SYS:WEB\DOCS directory, and your site is ready for user access.

> **N O T E** The installation process creates two NCF files in your server's SYS:SYSTEM directory, called WEBSTART.NCF and WEBSTOP.NCF. These batch files are used to load and unload all of the modules required for the operation of the Web server. The installation program also adds the WEBSTART command to the end of the server's AUTOEXEC.NCF file, so that the Web server is started whenever NetWare boots. ▦

The Novell Web Server software, however, is very configurable. Depending on the needs of your network, you can

- create virtual servers and hosts that function as independent Web sites for different departments or types of users,
- secure your site against unauthorized access,
- modify the default server configuration parameters,
- provide user access to NDS information,
- publish documents located on different servers,

as well as perform many other development, administration, and maintenance tasks.

Understanding Web Server Architecture

The Novell Web Server product is comprised of four basic elements. The server modules provide the basic functionality of the program. Web Manager is a Windows application that you use to configure and monitor server activities. Snap-in modules are provided that extend the NDS schema to add Web-related parameters to User and Group objects, and finally, the documents, images, and scripts that make up the online documentation and a sample Web site.

Installing Web Server places all of these elements onto the SYS volume of the chosen server, and creates the directory structures in which the various elements of your Web sites are stored. Because NWS is capable of hosting multiple sites on a single server, there are two directory structures created by default. The INW_WEB directory contains the files that are shared by all of the Web sites hosted on the server, including the online documentation, sample scripts, the script language interpreters that the server uses to execute Perl and

NetBasic programs, and templates used to create the server configuration files. If you create your own Web applications and want to use them on multiple sites, you would store them in these directories.

The shared directory structure is shown in Figure 30.1.

FIG. 30.1

The INW_WEB directory houses the shared files that are used by all of the server's Web sites.

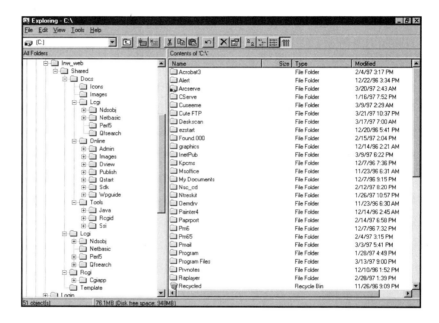

The WEB directory houses the files for the one virtual server that is created during the installation process. Here, you place the actual HTML, graphic, and script files that make up this particular site. The Web server also keeps the log and configuration files for this site in the WEB directory structure. If you create other virtual servers, each one is stored in a separate directory structure, with its own logs, configuration files, and Web pages.

The WEB directory structure is shown in Figure 30.2.

FIG. 30.2

Every virtual server host by NWS has its own directory structure, where its configuration, log, and document files are maintained.

Web Server Console Statistics

When Web Server is running, the status screen on the server console (see Figure 30.3) displays the following information:

- **Uptime**—Indicates the length of time (in days, hours, minutes, and seconds) since Web Server was last started. Reloading the server at the console or restarting HTTP from the Web Manager program resets the clock.

- **Total Requests**—Specifies the number of file requests processed by the Web server since it was last restarted.

- **Current Requests**—Specifies the number of requests that have been received by the Web server, but not yet fulfilled.

- **Errors Logged**—Indicates the number of times that a request could not be satisfied. Large numbers of errors can indicate the existence of a server malfunction, or attempts by an intruder to access protected files.

- **Bytes Transmitted**—Indicates the total number of bytes served to Web clients since the Web server was last restarted.

- **Peak Requests**—The first figure indicates the maximum number of threads (that is, requests) that the server has processed at one time since it was last restarted. The second figure specifies the maximum number of threads that the server is configured to handle at one time. If the value of the first figure nears or equals the value of the second, consider increasing the maximum allowable threads (by modifying the MaxThreads parameter in the WEB.CFG file), assuming that your server hardware is capable of handling the additional burden.

- **Virtual Servers**—Specifies the number of virtual servers currently operating.

- **Virtual Hosts**—Specifies the total number of virtual hosts (in all virtual servers) currently operating.

- **File Server Context**—Specifies the name of the container in the NDS tree in which the server object is located.

FIG. 30.3

The Novell Web Server panel on the console displays statistics concerning the current state of Web Server's activities.

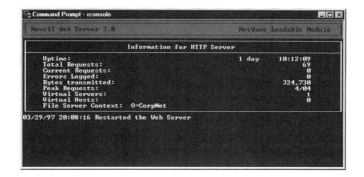

Running Web Manager

The Web Manager utility runs on any of the Windows operating systems and lets you create and manage your Web server's virtual servers and virtual hosts. You can also view and configure the Web server logs through this interface. The program itself is called WEBMGR.EXE and is located in the SYS:PUBLIC directory.

When you create a shortcut to Web Manager, you discover that no icon is found in the executable file. To display the Web Manager icon, you must change the shortcut's icon file parameter to point to the SYS:PUBLIC\NLS\ENGLISH\WEBMGDLL.DLL file.

Modifying the Web Server Configuration Files

Novell Web Server's configuration parameters are stored in several different files, all with CFG extensions. These files are located in different directories, depending on how they are used. The WEB.CFG file, for example, contains general parameters that are applied to the main Web server program. The file is therefore located in the SYS:ETC file.

Other files, such as SRM.CFG and HTTPD.CFG, contain settings that are applied only to one virtual server. These files are stored in a CONFIG directory off of the root for that virtual server (for example, SYS:WEB\CONFIG\SRM.CFG). Each time you create a new virtual server, a new set of configuration files is created from templates stored in the SYS:INW_WEB\SHARED\TEMPLATE directory.

CFG files can contain both directives that are set using Web Manager, and those that you must configure by manually editing the CFG file. The former are located in a section with the heading *#Computer generated,* while the latter are found in the *#Computer preserved directives* section. The HTTPD.CFG file contains only computer generated directives, while the SRM.CFG and WEB.CFG files contain both types. Although you could conceivably reconfigure the server by modifying the computer generated directives, be aware that they are designed to be managed by the Web Manager utility, which can cause your manual changes to be overwritten without warning.

N O T E   You must restart the Web server before any changes that you have made to the configuration files can take effect.

Modifying the WEB.CFG File   Located in the SYS:ETC directory, the WEB.CFG file contains the most basic configuration parameters for the Web server, including its name, the administrator password (in encrypted form), and the location of the main program directory (SYS:INW_WEB, by default). There are also individual sections for each of the virtual servers managed by the NWS installation.

All of these directives are configured using Web Manager. There is, in fact, only one parameter that you should modify manually in the WEB.CFG file. The MaxThreads directive specifies how many HTTP requests can be handled by the Web server at any one time. Possible values are 1 to 256, and the default is 16. You should raise this value if the Maximum Requests figure in the Web Server console panel regularly approaches the Maximum Threads value.

The value of the `MaxThreads` parameter is also dependent on the capabilities of the computer running the Web server. Each thread requires 30K of memory. This may not seem like a lot, but the default value of 16 threads (or 480K of memory) is suitable only for a lightly trafficked intranet server. If you have a large number of users, or especially if you intend to run a high-volume Internet Web server, a much higher value will be required.

Modifying the Server Resource Map   There is a server resource map file (SRM.CFG) for every virtual server, stored in the CONFIG directory off of the server root. The file for the Web server created by the NWS installation is therefore found in the SYS:WEB\CONFIG directory.

Like WEB.CFG, the SRM.CFG file also contains certain computer generated parameters, but there are also many more manually configurable directives than in WEB.CFG. The parameters in an SRM.CFG file affect only the virtual server in whose root directory it is located. The location of the configuration files for each virtual server is automatically added to the HTTPD.CFG file when you create a new virtual server.

The directives in the SRM.CFG file provide a great deal of flexibility in the basic configuration parameters of a virtual server. You may never have a reason to change many of these settings, but they are available if needed. The following sections examine the function and use of the most useful SRM.CFG directives.

N O T E   Whenever the Web Manager program makes changes to the SRM.CFG file (or to any CFG file in a virtual server's CONFIG directory), a backup of the unmodified file is saved with a BAK extension. It is possible for changes that you have made manually to be overwritten when Web Manager writes its parameters to the SRM.CFG file. In this case, you can find your modified settings in the backup file and copy them to the live version. ▪

AltDocRoot   There are two directives needed to specify an alternative root directory for the shared document files used by a virtual server. The `AltDocRoot` directive specifies the full path name of the directory to be used, as follows:

`AltDocRoot path`

The default shared document root directory for all virtual servers is SYS:INW_WEB\SHARED\DOCS. During Web Server installation, you can specify an alternative to the INW_WEB directory, but this is applied to all virtual servers. The `AltDocRoot` directive enables you to modify the setting for a single virtual server.

The Web server searches the alternative document root directory whenever a requested file cannot be located in the virtual server's primary document root (for example, SYS:WEB\DOCS). In order for NWS to locate files in the alternative document root directory, the directory structure beneath the root must be the same as that of the primary document root, and the `AltDocEnable` directive must have the value `on`, as follows:

`AltDocEnable on`

Setting `AltDocEnable` to `off` prevents the directory specified in `AltDocRoot` from being searched.

N O T E The `AltDocRoot` and `AltDocEnable` parameters comprise one of three methods that you can use to publish Web documents located outside the virtual server's document root directory. The other two methods are the `Alias` and `Redirect` parameters, as discussed in the following sections. ■

Alias   The `Alias` directive is another way of publishing documents that are located outside of a virtual server's document root directory. An alias is a logical directory that clients can access using a standard URL, but its documents can be located on any NetWare server on the network. An `Alias` directive takes the following form in the SRM.CFG file:

```
Alias directory path
```

where `directory` is the name of the logical directory that clients use in URLs, and `path` specifies the actual location of the directory on the network. For example, adding the following command to the SRM.CFG file

```
Alias \sales ny-sales/vol1:web
```

enables a client to specify an URL, such as http://www.website.com/sales, in a Web browser. Even though no SALES directory exists under the www.website.com root directory, the Web server accepts the URL and accesses the INDEX.HTM file in the VOL1:WEB directory on the NY-SALES server instead.

N O T E If the path name specified in an `Alias` command is located on a NetWare 3.x server, there must be a Guest account with no password in order for NWS to access the files. ■

Redirect   The `Redirect` parameter performs essentially the same function as `Alias`, except that the logical directory represents an URL instead of a network path name. Thus, `Redirect` enables you to publish the contents of another Web site on your site. The redirected site can be located on the same Web server, on another local network server, or on any Internet Web server. The syntax for `Redirect` is as follows:

```
Redirect directory URL
```

An SRM.CFG entry of `Redirect \sales http://www.sales.com` would therefore enable clients to access the www.sales.com site using the local URL http://www.website.com/sales.

DirectoryIndex   The `DirectoryIndex` directive indicates the names of the default home pages that the Web server sends to clients when a specific file name is not specified in the URL. By default, the value for this directive is INDEX.HTM. You can, however, add other file name extensions to the entry. For example, if you were to modify the entry to appear as

```
DirectoryIndex Index.htm Index.html
```

then the Web server, when it receives an URL specifying only a directory, will first search for a file called INDEX.HTM in the chosen directory. If that file is not found, then the directory is searched for a file called INDEX.HTML.

The `DirectoryIndex` entry can include any number of file names, up to a 255-character limit for the entire entry. However, the file names can only differ in their extensions. All must begin with INDEX.

DefaultType The `DefaultType` directive indicates the MIME (Multipurpose Internet Multimedia Extensions) type that the Web server will specify to clients for a file that does not conform to any of the explicitly configured MIME types. NWS uses a configuration file called MIME.TYP to equate file name extensions with particular MIME file types. A MIME type consists of a type and a subtype, which are separated by a slash. The value of the `DefaultType` directive in SRM.CFG, therefore, takes the form:

```
DefaultType type/subtype
```

The type specifies a general category of files, and the subtype a more specific file format. The possible values for the type are as follows:

- `application`
- `audio`
- `image`
- `message`
- `multipart`
- `text`
- `video`

For example, the MIME type `image/jpeg` is equated with the extensions jpeg, jpg, and jpe by the following entry in MIME.TYP:

```
image/jpeg                     jpeg jpg jpe
```

Whenever an URL refers to a file with one of these extensions, the server instructs the browser to treat that file as a jpeg image.

If an URL points to a file with an extension that is not listed in the MIME.TYP table, the server uses the MIME type specified by the `DefaultType` directive when communicating with the browser. The default value for the directive is `text/plain`, which causes the browser to display the file as unformatted ASCII text.

In most cases, it is not necessary to change the `DefaultType` setting. A more common scenario would be to add entries or additional extensions to the MIME.TYP file. You can, for example, use any file name extension that you want for your jpeg graphics, as long as that extension is registered in MIME.TYP as specifying the `image/jpeg` type.

MIME types have no effect on the actual capabilities of a browser, however. Creating a MIME type for a new file format does not make the browser capable of displaying that format. MIME types only instruct the browser to use certain existing routines to display files with a particular extension.

Understanding Virtual Servers and Virtual Hosts

Novell Web Server is capable of hosting many different Web sites on a single machine. There are several reasons why you might want to do this, and two distinct mechanisms that you can use to create and configure the sites.

A virtual server is a completely separate Web site with its own IP address and port number, configuration files, documents, and logs. NWS creates a single virtual server, called WEB, during the installation process. Each virtual server can contain multiple virtual hosts. A virtual host has its own documents and logs, but it uses the configuration files of the virtual server with which it is associated.

Like a virtual server, a virtual host can have its own IP address, but it can also use a unique host name, which resolves to the same IP address as the virtual server's other hosts. The virtual server then sees to it that the requests for specific host names are sent to the appropriate virtual host, even if the IP address is the same.

The configuration settings for virtual hosts and virtual servers are stored in the HTTPD.CFG and WEB.CFG files, but you do not modify them manually, as you do the general server settings discussed earlier in this chapter. Instead, you use the Web Manager utility to create and manage virtual hosts and servers. This utility writes out the settings to the configuration files using the proper syntax.

Separating Your Sites

Virtual servers are most useful when there is no connection between the Web sites hosted on a machine. The best example is the case of an Internet Web hosting business that maintains sites for many different clients. Customers of this type of business usually pay a premium for a Web site that can be configured to their precise specifications, using their own registered domain names and IP addresses.

Each virtual server has its own root directory, which you can place anywhere on any server volume. Aside from subdirectories for documents and logs, a CONFIG directory is added, and a new set of configuration files are created from default templates stored in SYS:INW_WEB\SHARED\TEMPLATE.

The independent structure of a virtual server's root directory makes it easier to control access to the files for your different Web sites. In the case of a Web hosting business, it would be typical for customers each to have access to their own site's files for maintenance and upgrade purposes using FTP. Virtual servers and their separate directory structures make it a simple matter to create a user account for each site, with the root directory specified as the user's home directory. This gives customers full access to their files while keeping administrative overhead to a minimum.

If you want to create separate sites on your intranet for the sake of convenience or security, you usually do not need to create additional virtual servers because the server configuration settings for all of the sites will probably be the same.

In the case of a corporate intranet, for example, virtual hosts are recommended because you can easily create individual sites for different departments, such as www.sales.com and www.marketing.com. When you are operating on an internal network, you are free to create any IP addresses and host names that you want, so there is no need to be concerned about registering names and addresses.

When you create a virtual host, NWS creates subdirectories for its documents and logs under the server root directory. Creating a virtual host called WEB2 in the default virtual server WEB, for example, results in a directory structure for the host at SYS:WEB\WEB2.

Adding IP Addresses

In order to create virtual servers or hosts that are accessible by different IP addresses, you must first configure the TCPIP.NLM module to recognize those addresses. A virtual server can conceivably use the same IP address as another virtual server, as long as you specify a different port number for the network interface. The combination of an IP address and a port number is called a *socket*, which is expressed in an URL by appending the port number to the IP address after a colon (for example, 199.99.99.10:80).

The default port number used by Web servers is 80. Web browsers assume this value for the port number when no other value is specified. You can create a virtual server without adding an additional IP address by specifying a port number of 85, for example. This results in URLs for that site that must always include the port number, as in HTTP://199.99.99.10:85.

> **CAUTION**
>
> Many different TCP/IP services have default port numbers that are specified in a file called SERVICES, located in the NetWare server's SYS:ETC directory. When assigning port numbers to virtual servers, be sure not to duplicate a number that is already being used for another purpose.

Because many Web users are unaware of the significance of the port number in an URL, it is usually simpler to create virtual servers that use the same port number (80), and different IP addresses. When your NetWare server is started, its IP address is specified either in the AUTOEXEC.NCF file, or in the configuration file used by the INITSYS.NCF during the boot sequence (if you have installed the NetWare Internet Access server product).

You can specify as many additional IP addresses for the server as you want by adding the following command to the AUTOEXEC.BAT file after the last BIND command or the call to INITSYS.NCF:

```
add secondary IPaddress IPaddress
```

Repeat the command for every additional IP address needed. It is possible to create virtual servers and configure them to use nonexistent IP addresses, but the sites will not be accessible until the addresses are recognized by TCPIP.NLM. If you create your additional IP address assignments first, you can select an address from a pull-down list during the virtual server's creation process.

T I P Placing the ADD SECONDARY IPADDRESS commands in the AUTOEXEC.NCF file is recommended, so that the addresses are registered whenever the NetWare server is rebooted. You can also issue the commands from the server console prompt, however, which causes the new IP addresses to be activated immediately.

The virtual hosts contained in a virtual server can be differentiated using different IP addresses or different host names that resolve to the same IP address. You cannot use the same IP address with different port numbers to distinguish virtual hosts, however, as you can with virtual servers. You must add the IP addresses used by virtual hosts to the NetWare server configuration before the sites are accessible, using the same procedure detailed earlier.

Creating a Virtual Server

When you create a virtual server using the Web Manager utility (by selecting Create Server from the Server menu), first specify a name for the server, and the path where you want its root directory to be created, in the Create Virtual Server dialog box shown in Figure 30.4. By default, the name of the root directory is the same as that of the server.

FIG. 30.4

The Create Virtual Server dialog box enables you to create the server's root directory on any server volume.

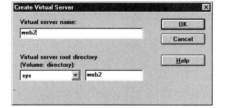

Once the virtual server is created, the Server dialog box is displayed, in which you can configure the operational parameters that are stored in the WEB.CFG file, in a section named for the virtual server. The default values specified in this dialog box should be acceptable, in most instances. The following sections cover the various panels of the dialog box and the parameters found there, except for the Virtual Host, User Access, and System Access panels, which are addressed later in this chapter.

After a virtual server is created and configured, you must activate it by checking the Web Manager's File menu to see that the server is selected (as indicated by a check mark) and then selecting Enable from the Server menu. As always, you must the restart the Web server before your changes take effect.

Using the Server Panel   All of the parameters found in the Server panel of a virtual server's dialog box (see Figure 30.5) are configured with defaults that are acceptable in most cases. You can change any of the supplied values as needed, but the server will function without any modifications.

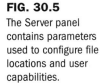

FIG. 30.5

The Server panel contains parameters used to configure file locations and user capabilities.

The Enable NDS Browsing check box specifies whether or not you want users of this server to be able to browse the NDS tree using a Web client. NWS includes snap-in modules for the NetWare Administrator program that enable users to store pictures of themselves in their user objects and configure personal Web sites. If this feature is enabled, the tree hierarchy is reproduced on the site in HTML format, allowing clients to browse to other users' objects and Web pages. The NDS browsing capabilities provided by NWS are discussed in greater detail in the "Browsing the NDS Tree" section later in this chapter.

The Enable Document Indexing and Search check box specifies whether the virtual server should be automatically indexed so that clients can use the QuickFinder feature to locate documents. Enabled by default, this option creates an additional panel on the server console, called QuickFinder Search, that enables you to monitor the server's indexing activities.

The next two fields in the Server panel indicate the locations of the directories that will hold the server's document and log files. The Directory Containing HTML Documents field specifies the virtual server's document root. This means that the INDEX.HTM file found in the specified directory is delivered to a client when a request containing an URL that specifies only the server's host name or IP address is received.

When a virtual server is created, directories called DOCS and LOGS are created off of the server root directory. These directories become the default values for these two fields. You can specify the paths to different directories for these fields, located anywhere on your network.

N O T E   The sections on the AltDocRoot, Alias, and Redirect parameters of the SRM.CFG file—found in "Modifying the Server Resource Map" earlier in this chapter—define three different ways to publish Web documents located on a server other than that running NWS. You can, therefore, use the default DOCS directory as your document root, and still publish documents located on other servers on the Web site. ▪

The Enable User Documents check box indicates whether or not you want NDS users to be able to publish Web documents stored in their home directories. The User Subdirectory field specifies the name of the subdirectory beneath a user's home directory in which they should place their HTML documents.

With this feature, intranet users can publish their own personal home pages using the virtual server. Because the document files are located in their home directory structures, the users have complete access to the files and can maintain them without the need for intervention by a network administrator. The creation of personal home pages is usually coupled with the Enable NDS Browsing feature, as this allows the use of the NDS tree to locate pages.

Using the Directories Panel   In the Directories panel (see Figure 30.6), you set options that define the type of documents stored in directories off of the server root. Other options indicate whether certain Web server features are enabled for a particular directory. Creating a virtual server adds four entries to the Existing Directories list. The DOCS directory, for example, is defined as containing documents, and has indexing enabled.

FIG. 30.6

On the Directories panel, you specify the types of documents stored in specific directories and the options that should be applied to them.

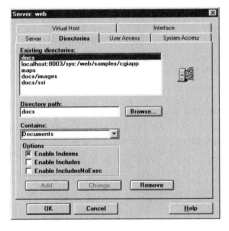

You can freely create subdirectories off of DOCS using standard file management tools. You only have to add the subdirectory to this list if you want to specify different values for the directory parameters. Otherwise, the values are inherited from the parent directory.

When you create a new virtual host, its document root directory is automatically added to the Existing Directories list, with the default options enabled.

When you add a directory to the list, you must specify the type of files stored there by making a selection from the pull-down list in the Contains field. The possible values are as follows:

- **Documents**—Indicates that the directory contains document files that can be displayed by a client browser with no special treatment from the server. Documents can be HTML or text files, graphic images, or multimedia files.

■ **Scripts**—Indicates that the directory contains script files that must be interpreted by the server before data is transmitted to a client. Scripts can use NetBasic, Perl, or any other interpreter that you have installed on the server.

■ **Image Maps**—Indicates that the directory contains image map files that define the links that are to be assigned to specific areas of a graphic image. Image map files contain pixel coordinates that divide the graphic image into discrete segments, each of which can be linked to a different URL.

In addition to the document type, there are three options that you can enable or disable for each directory in the list. The options are as follows:

■ **Enable indexes**—This option causes the specified directory to be indexed so that a listing of the files contained there can be displayed in a browser. If a client browses to an URL that specifies only a directory name, and there is no file called INDEX.HTM (or any alternatives that you may have added using the `DirectoryIndex` feature) in that directory, then the indexing feature displays a list of links to each of the files in the directory, from which the user can choose. The list includes all of the files in the directory, not just those that would typically be accessible through hyperlinks. Indexing of all document root directories is enabled by default.

■ **Enable Includes**—Novell Web Server's SSI (server-side includes) feature lets you insert special commands into an HTML file that cause the server to modify the data sent to the client based on current conditions or computed results. The `#echo var="DATE_LOCAL"` command, for example, causes the server to insert the current date and time into the document at the place where the command appears. Disabling this feature causes all such commands to be ignored. All server-side includes are disabled for document root directories, by default.

■ **Enable IncludesNoExec**—Server-side includes, such as the `DATE_LOCAL` command, are relatively innocuous. They simply read the contents of a server variable and insert it into the document. Other SSI commands are much more powerful, and dangerous. The `#EXEC_CGI` command, for example, is used to execute NLM programs on the NetWare server hosting the Web site. A user that is permitted to run untested NLMs on your server can do a great deal of inadvertent or deliberate damage. Enabling this option allows for the use of most SSI commands, but prevents any programs from being executed through the common gateway interface.

Using the Interface Panel   The Interface panel (see Figure 30.7) contains the only settings that you must specify when creating a new virtual server. You must specify the port number and IP address that clients will use to access this server. If you are running only a single virtual server on this computer, the simplest course of action is to specify the standard HTTP port number of 80, and an asterisk in the IP Address field. The asterisk functions as a wild card, allowing the use of any valid IP address configured for use by TCPIP.NLM. See "Adding IP Addresses" earlier in this chapter, for more information on configuring TCPIP.NLM.

FIG. 30.7
On the Interface panel, you specify the IP addresses and port number that will be used to connect to this virtual server.

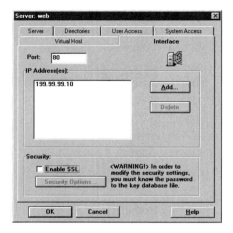

You would use a port number other than 80 for two basic reasons: Either you want to run two or more virtual servers using a single IP address, or you want the virtual server to remain hidden from the casual user. When an HTTP service is running on a port number other than 80, clients must specify that port number in their URLs.

 Although it is not a *bona fide* security measure, running a Web site on a nonstandard port can be a good way of hiding its existence from unwanted users. One of the best ways to keep potential intruders from trying to pick a lock is to hide the door.

When you are running two or more virtual servers, you must specify IP addresses in the Interface panel, instead of using a wild card. The Web Manager utility will warn you of a conflict if you specify duplicate sockets in two or more virtual servers. (A socket is the combination of an IP address and a port number.) For example, if you specify port 80 in two virtual servers, along with an IP address in one and an asterisk in the other, a warning message is displayed, and you will be unable to save your changes.

 If you intend to create virtual hosts on this server that are differentiated by IP addresses, you should add all of the addresses you will need in the Interface panel before creating the hosts. When you do this, you can select the desired IP address from a pull-down list when you create each virtual host.

Web Manager does, however, let you add IP addresses that do not exist. If you specify an IP address as a virtual server interface and fail to add the address to the TCPIP.NLM configuration, the Web server will not restart. Instead, the following errors appear on the server console:

```
3-28-97  11:48:57 am:     HTTP-3.08r-80009A  [Http]  Informational
    TCP failed to bind to IP Address 199.99.99.7 Port 80
 3-28-97  11:48:57 am:     HTTP-3.08r-800053  [Http]  Informational
    The NetWare Web Server could not get TCP socket.
```

When this occurs, the HTTP.NLM module fails to load on the server. As a result, the Web Manager program can no longer communicate with the Web server, and cannot restart the service, even after you remedy the problem by removing the offending IP address from the Interface panel or adding it to the TCPIP.NLM configuration. You must, in this case, restart NWS from the server console prompt using the WEBSTOP and WEBSTART commands.

The final option in the Interface panel lets you enable the SSL (secure sockets layer) protocol for the virtual server, providing encrypted communications between server and clients. See "Securing Your Web Sites" later in this chapter, for more information on using the SSL option.

Part
VIII

Ch
30

Creating a Virtual Host

In the Virtual Host panel of a virtual server's dialog box (accessed by selecting the virtual server from Web Manager's File menu), you can create additional hosts for the server, each of which is accessed as a separate Web site. You configure each host using the Create Virtual Host dialog box, shown in Figure 30.8. If you plan to run only a single Web site, then you do not have to create any virtual hosts. A single host (or Web site) is implied for each virtual server.

FIG. 30.8
You create virtual hosts by specifying the IP address or host name that the server will use to uniquely identify this Web site.

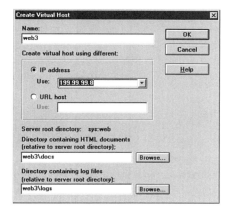

The primary purpose of virtual hosts is to provide easy access to different Web sites on an intranet. The whole idea of an intranet is to simplify the process of accessing corporate information over the network. Many computer users are unaware of the basic concepts involved in NetWare networking. Rather than attempt to explain how files are stored using directories, volumes, and servers, it is much easier to provide hyperlinks to the desired files on a Web page. The simpler the design of the Web site, the better users will like it.

One way of using virtual hosts effectively would be to create a main company Web page using a host name that points to the virtual server's document root, such as www.mycorp.com. This main page could provide access to general company information, and include links to individual Web sites created and maintained by the company's individual departments. You would then create virtual hosts for each of these departmental sites, with host names like www.sales.com, www.marketing.com, and so on.

Depending on the size of the company, you may end up with dozens or even hundreds of sites, representing branch offices, divisions, departments, or workgroups. Without virtual hosts, this process could result in very long URLs, such as www.mycorp.com/US/NY/sales/customerservice, as all of the sites must be maintained within a single directory structure.

This makes the process of accessing a particular site inconvenient for the users that need it most: the customer service people in the NY sales office. By creating virtual hosts, users can access their local sites with a simple, intuitive host name, rather than an extended path.

When you create a virtual host, you must specify either an IP address or a host name that uniquely identifies the site. If you elect to use an IP address, you must activate the address in both the TCPIP.NLM module and the virtual server interface. The addresses configured in the virtual server's Interface panel are carried over to the IP Address pull-down list in the Virtual Host panel.

If you specify host names for your virtual hosts, you do not have to create additional IP addresses. You configure your DNS to resolve all of the virtual host names to the same IP address, and the virtual server forwards the client requests to the appropriate host.

Every virtual host has its own root directory, beneath which subdirectories for its documents and logs are located. By default, the root is named for the virtual host created as a subdirectory of the virtual server's root. Thus, a virtual host called WEB2, created on NWS' default virtual server (WEB), would have SYS:WEB\WEB2 as its root directory. You can, however, create the virtual host's root directory anywhere within the directory structure of the server root by changing the relative path names in the Create Virtual Host dialog box.

Securing Your Web Sites

Security is a major issue on any network, and as you develop your intranet or Internet services, you are likely to encounter situations in which you want to restrict access to certain documents. Novell Web Server provides several means by which you can implement authenticated user access control for any document directory on your server.

User authentication is the most basic form of Web site security. When accessing files in a particular directory on the Web server, the client browser pops up a dialog box that requires the user to enter a login name and password before access to the directory is granted. Novell Web Server provides the capability to use NDS user and group accounts to authenticate users, as well as encrypted password files, should NDS not be available or practical.

Apart from user authentication, NWS also provides the capability to limit site access to particular systems, identified either by host name or IP address. You use the Web Manager program to implement global access control parameters, which are stored in a file called ACCESS.CFG, found in the CONFIG directory off of each virtual server root.

It is also possible to implement user access control on a per-directory basis that overrides the global settings. You do this by creating a file called ACCESS.WWW in the directory that you want to protect. ACCESS.WWW uses the same format as ACCESS.CFG, except that you must create and configure it manually, using any standard text editor.

Controlling Global Access with NDS

NDS surely provides the most convenient method of authenticating Web clients. Web Manager enables you to browse the NDS tree and select the users and groups that are to be allowed access to a directory.

> **N O T E** The default user access configuration, in which there are no objects in the authorized users list, allows unlimited and unauthenticated access to the Web sites controlled by the virtual server. Adding a single authorized user for a directory effectively blocks all other users from accessing that directory (by adding a Deny From All directive to the ACCESS.CFG file) unless they too are added to the list. ▪

In a virtual server's User Access panel (see Figure 30.9), the Directory pull-down list contains all of the directories that have been configured in the Directories panel. After choosing a directory, you specify an NDS context and select user or group objects in order to add them to the authorized users list. Clicking the All Valid Users check box allows all of the users in the specified context to access the directory.

FIG. 30.9

The User Access panel enables you to select the NDS users and groups that will be permitted access to a selected document directory.

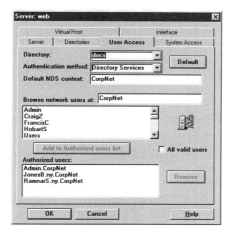

After selecting the desired users in the specified context, you can change the context and select users anywhere else in the NDS tree. As with NetWare access control, a user's permission to access a directory is passed down to all of the subdirectories it contains.

> **N O T E** Granting NDS users access to a Web site directory does not affect their NetWare rights to that same directory. Novell Web Server uses NDS on a read-only basis to verify passwords. Users that are properly authenticated through a Web browser will have access to the specified directory whether or not they can access that directory with a NetWare client. ▪

Controlling System Access

In the same way that you can limit document directory access to specific NDS users and groups, you can impose restrictions based on the system running the client browser. Also stored in the ACCESS.CFG file, system access restrictions can exist independently of user and group access restrictions, or alongside them. You can therefore specify that access to a particular directory is limited to a specified group of users, and only when those users are authenticated from a particular system, subnet, or domain.

You use the System Access panel in the Web Manager program (see Figure 30.10) to specify the IP addresses or host names that are to be allowed access to Web document directories. The list of directories is the same as that in the User Access panel. After selecting a directory, you enter the IP addresses or host names of the systems that you want to be able to access that directory.

FIG. 30.10

The System Access panel enables you to specify the IP addresses or domain names of the systems that are to be allowed access to a Web document directory.

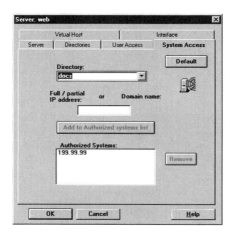

Neither the IP addresses nor the host names that you add to the authorized systems list have to be complete. You can use part of an IP address in order to specify the network on which a system must be located. A value of 123.45.67, for example, would allow all systems with IP addresses ranging from 123.45.67.0 to 123.45.67.255 to access the specified directory. In the same way, you can add a domain name to the list, such as mycorp.com, rather than a fully qualified host name, in order to provide access to all systems in the domain.

> **CAUTION**
>
> System access specifications are far from being a secure method of access control. If an intruder is able to determine the address of a system that is permitted access to a site, it is a small matter to reconfigure a client to use that address.

Configuring Per-Directory Access Control

NWS also recognizes a second form of user access control that overrides the global permissions set by Web Manager and stored in the ACCESS.CFG file. By creating a text file called ACCESS.WWW that contains the proper access control commands and placing it in a document directory, only the users, groups, and systems specified in the file are permitted access.

The primary difference between the global and per-directory access control methods is that the latter is not configured using the Web Manager program. You must create the ACCESS.WWW file manually, and store it in the correct directory. The other difference is that you are not limited to the use of NDS for user authentication services. Instead, you can create an encrypted file containing user names and passwords, and have the Web server refer to that file when authenticating users.

Creating an ACCESS.WWW File   ACCESS.WWW files contain two basic sections: one that contains commands specifying the type of authorization to be used, and a second LIMIT section that contains the instructions regarding the specific users to be permitted access. A typical ACCESS.WWW file using NDS to authenticate users and groups appears as follows:

```
AuthType Basic
AuthName NDS
AuthUserMethod nds .CorpNet
AuthGroupMethod nds .CorpNet
<LIMIT GET>
require user Admin
order deny, allow
allow 199.99.99.12
deny from all
</LIMIT>
```

This file specifies that NDS is to be used for authentication, and that the Web server should search the context CorpNet for the users and groups specified in the file. The LIMIT section specifies that the NDS user Admin be allowed access, and that all systems except the one with the IP address 199.99.99.12 should be denied access.

Placing the file in any document directory on a Web site causes the restrictions it contains to be activated when a client attempts to access any file in that directory, or any of its subdirectories.

As you can see in the example, the authentication commands appear first in the file, and the LIMIT commands are contained within the delimiters <LIMIT GET> and </LIMIT>.

N O T E   The GET parameter included in the <LIMIT> delimiter is required, as it is currently the only option limitation available for the ACCESS.WWW file. Future versions of NWS may implement other commands and authentication techniques. ▨

The commands allowed in the authentication section of an ACCESS.WWW file are as follows:

■ AuthType (required)—Specifies the type of authentication that should be used. The only value permitted at this time is BASIC, which specifies that the server should use basic HTTP password encryption when communicating with a client.

■ `AuthName` (required)—Specifies a text string that is sent to clients during the authentication process to identify the source of the login name and password that they should use. The value NDS, for example, informs users that they should use their NDS name and password.

■ `AuthUserMethod` (optional)—Specifies the user authentication mechanism to be used. NDS is the only value that is currently supported, and must be followed by a valid NDS context.

■ `AuthGroupMethod` (optional)—Specifies the group authentication mechanism to be used. This command uses the same syntax as `AuthUserMethod`, and should not be used in a file that doesn't contain the `AuthUserMethod` command also. Both entries should specify the same NDS context.

■ `AuthUserFile` (optional)—Used instead of `AuthUserMethod`, specifies the name of a file (with a path relative to the server root) containing the names and passwords to be used for authentication.

■ `AuthGroupFile` (optional)—Used instead of `AuthGroupMethod`, specifies the name of a file (with a path relative to the server root) containing the names of groups and their members to be used for authentication. This command should not be used in a file that doesn't contain the `AuthUserFile` command.

N O T E The user and group files used for non-NDS authentication must be encrypted using the PWGEN.EXE utility. See the "Creating User and Group Database Files" section later in this chapter for more information. ■

The commands in the `LIMIT` section of the ACCESS.WWW specify the actual users, groups, or systems that are to be granted or denied access. The permitted commands are discussed in the following sections.

REQUIRE   The `REQUIRE` command is used to specify a user or group that is to be permitted access to the directory. The syntax for the command is as follows:

```
REQUIRE USER name1 name2
REQUIRE GROUP name1 name2
```

Each `REQUIRE` command can list multiple user or group names, up to 255 characters. An ACCESS.WWW file can have up to 50 `REQUIRE` commands in the `LIMIT` section.

You can also use the command

```
REQUIRE VALID-USER
```

to grant access to any valid user account in the authentication database.

ALLOW   The `ALLOW` command is used to specify the systems that are to be permitted access to the directory. The syntax is as follows:

```
ALLOW FROM hostname/IPaddress
```

As in the Web Manager's System Access panel, you can use full or partial host names or IP addresses with the ALLOW command to provide access to specific users or members of a particular domain or subnet. You can also use the following command to grant access to all users:

```
ALLOW FROM ALL
```

DENY   The DENY command performs the function opposite of ALLOW. You use it to deny access to hosts or IP addresses with the same syntax as ALLOW, including the ALL option.

Per-directory access control is unlike the global method, in which granting a user access to a directory automatically denies all other users access. If you want to grant access to only a selected few users, groups, or systems, then you must explicitly deny access to everyone else. This is the primary reason for the existence of the DENY command.

ORDER   ORDER is the only one of the LIMIT commands that is not used to grant or deny access rights to the directory, and yet it can be the most important factor in your access control strategy. ORDER is used to specify which command in the ACCESS.WWW file should be processed first: ALLOW or DENY.

The syntax for the ORDER command can take only two possible forms:

```
ORDER ALLOW,DENY
ORDER DENY,ALLOW
```

Because of the ORDER command, you do not have be concerned about the arrangement of the commands in the ACCESS.WWW file. ORDER can force the DENY commands to be executed before the ALLOW commands, even when they appear in the opposite order in the file.

The order in which the Web server executes the ALLOW and DENY commands can be critical. If you have an ALLOW FROM 123.45.67.89 command, followed by a DENY FROM ALL command, then the effect of the ALLOW is negated by the DENY. To prevent this, place the following command in the LIMIT section of ACCESS.WWW:

```
ORDER DENY,ALLOW
```

This way, access is first denied to all users, and then an exception is noted, and access is granted to the system at the specified IP address. For a more complete example of this technique, see the sample at the beginning of "Creating an ACCESS.WWW File" earlier in this chapter.

N O T E   ORDER has no effect on the processing of REQUIRE commands in ACCESS.WWW. Considered separately from the other three commands, REQUIRE only instructs the server to request authentication before granting a user access to the directory. Even if the user is properly authenticated, files from the directory will not be served to a system whose host name or IP address has been denied access. ▨

Creating User and Group Database Files   In order to use database files for user and group authentication, you must first create ASCII text files containing the required information and then encrypt them. A user database file is simply a list of user names and their passwords in the following format:

Part
VIII
Ch
30

```
userA:passwordA
userB:passwordB
```

Each entry must be on a separate line, with no spaces. A group database file contains group names and their members, in the following format:

```
groupA:user1 user2 user3
```

A group entry can wrap over several lines, to accommodate multiple user names.

In each case, save the file and encrypt it using the PWGEN.EXE found in the SYS:PUBLIC directory. This is a DOS command-line utility that you use by specifying the name of the text file you created, followed by the name that should be used for the new encrypted database file, as follows:

```
PWGEN textfile databasefile
```

Finally, copy the database file to the root directory of the virtual server where you intend to use it. You then specify the names of the databases in the `AuthUserFile` and `AuthGroupFile` commands of your ACCESS.WWW files. A typical ACCESS.WWW file that employs user database authentication would appear as follows:

```
AuthType Basic
AuthName Administrators
AuthUserFile adminpw.www
<LIMIT GET>
Require user john paul george richard
allow from 123.45.67
deny from all
order deny,allow
</LIMIT>
```

Using the Secure Sockets Layer

Sometimes, from a security standpoint, password-protecting Web sites and restricting system access is not enough. Network communication itself is subject to unauthorized access from intruders, and NWS includes support for the Secure Sockets Layer protocol (SSL) to provide encrypted communication for any of your virtual servers. SSL guarantees secure communication between HTTP servers and clients by the use of encryption keys, a message hashing algorithm, and certificates that identify the source of a transmission.

SSL is designed for use on Web servers that must transmit highly sensitive data, such as credit card numbers or other financial information. The protocol provides three separate services that combine to provide a highly secure communication solution for intranet or Internet use. The three services are as follows:

- **Data encryption**—Private and public encryption keys are used for all communication between the server and the browser to ensure that no data is transmitted in clear text during an SSL session.

- **Server authentication**—To ensure that a client is actually communicating with the server that it expects, SSL sends a digital certificate to the browser that guarantees the server's identity.
- **Message hashing**—To guarantee that the data received is exactly the same as the data transmitted, a message digest is computed at the source and transmitted with the message. On receipt, the destination system computes again the digest using the same algorithm and compares the results with the transmitted version.

Once configured at the server, all three of these services are entirely transparent to users. Web browsers that support the SSL standard (such as those made by Netscape and Microsoft) automatically negotiate with the Web server before a secure channel is established and communication begins.

Activating SSL is simply a matter of clicking a check box on the Interface panel of a virtual server's dialog box. You can choose whether or not to use SSL on each of your virtual servers, making it possible to run both secure and open servers on the same machine.

However, before you activate the protocol, you must obtain a digital certificate that identifies your server and verifies that it actually belongs to your company. The certificate must be sent to client browsers by the Web server before a secure communications channel can be established. This protects the client from the possibility of transmitting confidential data to a server that is masquerading as belonging to another company. Each Web server (or virtual server) running SSL requires its own certificate.

Digital certificates are issued by a third-party firm called a certification authority (or CA) upon receipt of a request and a fee. Novell Web Server includes a server console utility called KEYMGR.NLM that enables you to create a key file on your server and generate a properly formatted certificate request, which you then submit to a CA, such as VeriSign. VeriSign is the default CA specified by the KEYMGR program, but you can use any CA that you want. VeriSign allows you to submit your request through their Web site, and returns the certificate via e-mail after verifying your company's identity.

The digital certificate that you receive back from the CA contains information that identifies your company and the specific server for which it is intended. It also contains the public key that client browsers require in order to read the encrypted communication received from your server. (SSL uses a combination of public and private keys, maintained by both the server and the browser, to ensure the security of its encrypted transmissions.)

Once you have received the certificate, install it to the key file, again using KEYMGR.NLM. You can only have one key file on your server, but the file can contain multiple certificates. Once you have installed the certificate in your key file, return to Web Manager and specify the file's location by selecting Set Key Database File from the Options menu. Only then can you activate SSL in the virtual server's Interface panel.

The default port number for a Web server running SSL is 443, and this value is set for you automatically when you enable SSL, although you can change it. Once enabled, you can click the Security Options button on the Interface panel to configure SSL by selecting the certificate and the versions of the SSL protocol that you want to use. You can also choose to require a client certificate, which forces the client browser and the Web server both to authenticate themselves before the secure channel can be established.

Using QuickFinder

QuickFinder is a search engine that is included and installed with the Novell Web Server package. It is implemented as a server-based program called QFSRCH30.NLM, which is launched through the *local common gateway interface* (LCGI). When NWS is loaded, the program scans the document directories of your Web sites and creates a full-text index of all of the documents it finds there. The index includes not only HTML files, but 20 other file formats as well, including popular word processor and spreadsheet files in several languages.

Thus, your Web site index can contain information on the files that you provide to users for download, but which cannot be directly displayed in the Web browser. When a client searches for a word or phrase using an HTML form, the server scans the index and presents the results in the form of a dynamic HTML page with links to the documents found by the search.

QuickFinder is fully functional the first time that you start the Web server, but there are many parameters that you can configure to customize its operation. These parameters are stored in a file called QFSRCH30.CFG, found in the SYS:INW_WEB\SHARED\LCGI\QFSEARCH directory. This is a fully annotated text file that demonstrates how to make changes, such as the following:

- **Schedule re-indexing**—QuickFinder rebuilds its index at regular intervals to accommodate documents that have been added or modified. You can schedule the re-indexing to occur at specified intervals and at certain times of day.

- **Control logging**—You can specify whether user queries and indexing activities should be logged, as well as how large the logs should be allowed to grow before the oldest entries are purged. The logs are called QUERY.LOG and INDEX.LOG and are located in the SYS:INW_WEB\SHARED\LCGI\QFSEARCH directory.

- **Configure results list**—QuickFinder dynamically creates an HTML page to display the results of a client's query. You can customize the appearance of the results list by specifying HTML files to be used as the list's header and footer, how many hits should be displayed on each page, how the results list should be formatted, and precisely what information should be displayed for each hit.

NWS also includes Web pages containing the QuickFinder search form (see Figure 30.11), and detailed help on using the search engine's query language. You can modify the appearance of these pages to integrate them into your Web sites. The main search form is called QFSEARCH.HTM and is located in the SYS:INW_WEB\SHARED\DOCS\LCGI\QFSEARCH directory.

FIG. 30.11
The NWS QuickFinder feature enables Web clients to search the contents of 21 different document types.

N O T E The QuickFinder search pages and the QFSRCH30.NLM program itself are located in the shared directory structure that your Web sites access through the AltDocRoot feature. To be able to access these pages, you must leave the AltDocEnable and AltDocRoot directives configured to their default values in the SRM.CFG files for your virtual servers. QuickFinder also requires that the LoadableModule and EventNotify directives in the SRM.CFG file be left intact. ■

Browsing the NDS Tree

Novell Web Server includes another LCGI program that lets clients browse the NDS tree using a Web browser. The program creates dynamic HTML pages for users and other objects that can contain links to personal home pages. Although it is not an administrative tool because it can only read from the NDS database, the NDS browser can provide users with valuable information about the network.

The HTML page for a printer, for example, can be used to supply information on the printer's location, its technical specifications, and who to contact for technical support, as well as links to the printer drivers needed for various operating systems. User pages can display a photograph and links to a personal home page created and maintained by the user.

The NDS browser module (NDSOBJ.NLM) is automatically installed with the Novell Web Server. To activate it, you need only fill the Enable NDS Browsing check box in the Server panel of your virtual server's dialog box. Once activated, users can browse the tree by specifying an URL of http://*servername*/nds in a browser. This displays a page containing links to the trees found on the network. You can then navigate your way down the tree hierarchy by clicking container object icons (see Figure 30.12).

URLs of specific container objects can be constructed by specifying their contexts, beginning from the top of the tree. For example, an object in a tree called NW411TREE with the context Accounting.NY.CorpNet would have an URL that lists the containers in the reverse order: http://*servername*/nds/NW411TREE/CorpNet/NY/Accounting.

FIG. 30.12
The NDS browser enables users to navigate through a graphical representation of the NDS tree in a Web browser.

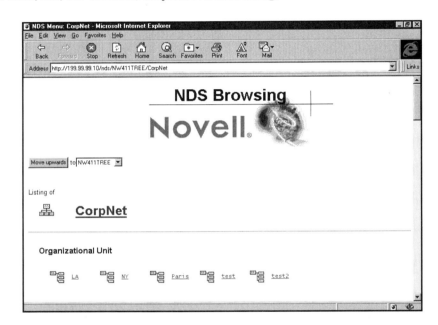

Modifying NDS Browser Properties

The NDS Browser also includes the capability to extend the schema of the NDS database in order to add new properties to the tree's leaf objects. These properties are used to configure the way that object pages are displayed when browsing NDS. A Home Page and Photo button is added to the Details dialog box of every leaf object. A second button, labeled Web Publishing, is added to every user object's dialog box.

Before you can manage these properties with the NetWare Administrator program, you must install the snap-in modules included with NWS for your workstation operating system. For Windows 3.1, you must edit the NWADMN3x.INI file in your workstation's WINDOWS directory and add the following line to the [Snapin Object DLLs WIN3X] section:

```
WEBSNP3X.DLL=WEBSNP3X.DLL
```

For Windows 95 and Windows NT workstations, you must launch the registry editor and import a registry file called SYS:PUBLIC\WIN95\WEBREGED.REG or SYS:PUBLIC\WINNT\WEBREGNT.REG.

The Home Page and Photo panel found in every leaf object's NetWare Administrator Details dialog box (see Figure 30.13) enables you to specify a graphic file and an URL that will be displayed in the selected object's page in the NDS browser. The graphic, which should be a GIF or JPG file, is read into the NDS database, and the URL is displayed on the user's object page as a hyperlink (see Figure 30.14).

FIG. 30.13
In the Home Page and Photo panel, you can specify a graphic and an URL that will be displayed in an object's NDS Browser page.

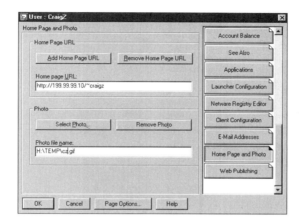

N O T E Because the graphic file specified in the Home Page and Photo panel is stored in the NDS database during the configuration process, you cannot change the graphic simply by replacing the file in the source directory with a different file of the same name. Instead, you must re-select the file in the NetWare Administrator to import the new graphic into the database. ▨

FIG. 30.14
Leaf objects are displayed in the NDS Browser with a graphic and an URL that can be used for any purpose.

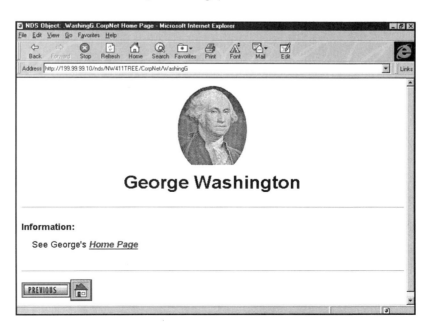

Limiting Tree Access

By default, enabling the NDS Browser feature allows users access to all of the NDS trees on the network. You can, however, limit the trees that can be browsed by editing the NDSOBJ.CFG file, located in the SYS:INW_WEB\SHARED\LCGI\NDSOBJ directory.

This text file contains two sections that demonstrate the use of the `BrowseTree` and `DenyTree` commands. You can use either of these commands to specify which trees users should be able to access, simply by specifying the tree name on the command line as follows:

```
BrowseTree NW411TREE
DenyTree TESTTREE
```

These commands can only be used to limit access to trees, not containers, objects, or attributes. To do this, you must modify the tree browsing rights that have been assigned to the [Public] object in the NetWare Administrator or NetAdmin utility. By default, [Public] is granted the Browse right for the entire tree. If you modify this policy, then you limit users' tree browsing rights in all NetWare utilities, not just the NDS Browser.

Using Virtual Directories

The second panel added by the NWS snap-in modules is one that allows users to publish their own Web pages, which are stored in their home directories. These pages are accessed using *virtual directories* that make them appear as though they are part of the Web server's directory structure. Because users have full file system rights to their own home directories, they also have full maintenance access to the files that comprise their home pages. This technique also provides the Web administrator with another method of publishing files that are not located in the Web server's root directory structure.

N O T E   There are three other ways to publish Web pages located outside the server root. All three involve the manual editing of the virtual server's SRM.CFG to add an `Alias`, `Redirect`, or `AltDocRoot` directive. For more information on these techniques, see the "Modifying the Server Resource Map" section earlier in this chapter.

To create a virtual directory for a user or a group of users, you must first check the Enable User Documents check box in the server panel of User Manager's virtual server dialog box, and specify a directory name (PUBLIC.WWW, by default). Then, in NetWare Administrator, make sure that the user or group NDS object has a home directory assignment specified in its Environment panel.

The Web Publishing panel created by the NWS snap-in module lets you enable the Web publishing feature for a selected user or group (see Figure 30.15). When you save the changes, the subdirectory shown as the Web directory is created in each user's home directory.

FIG. 30.15
The Web Publishing panel is used to give users the right to create and maintain their own home pages.

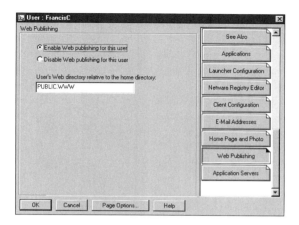

> **CAUTION**
>
> Do not create the PUBLIC.WWW directory manually in the user's home directory before enabling the Web publishing feature. NetWare Administrator generates an error when it cannot create the directory itself because it already exists.

The users can then place Web pages in their newly created PUBLIC.WWW directories, and modify them at will. To access a user's page from a Web browser, a client specifies the user's object name in an URL, preceded by the tilde (~), just as though it were a subdirectory of the Web server root. For example:

```
http://www.mycorp.com/~smithj
```

To combine the functionality of virtual directories with the NDS Browser, you can specify URLs that are shown in the example in your users' Home Page and Photo panels.

Summary

Novell Web Server provides an effective and comprehensive Web development and publishing environment that is equally effective for intranet and Internet use. The addition of the NDS authentication services makes NWS the Web server of choice for intranets that are committed to the use of Novell Directory Services. ●

CHAPTER 31

Using the NetWare FTP Server

Unlike the Novell Web Server, which is a relatively recent addition to the Novell product line, a NetWare-based FTP service has been available for some time, as part of NetWare NFS Services. Originally intended as a means for UNIX workstations to transfer files to and from NetWare servers, the FTP service has taken on new significance as a result of the increased emphasis on TCP/IP services in IntranetWare.

As a companion to the Novell Web Server, the FTP service enables intranet or Internet users to access files on NetWare servers using a standard Web browser or an FTP client. Novell's FTP service, however, goes beyond those of other network operating systems in its capabilities. For NDS users, the service can function as a gateway to the other NetWare servers on the network, even those that are not running TCP/IP. ▪

How to configure the FTP service

Installed as part of NetWare NFS Services, you configure the FTP service at the server console with the UNICON program.

How to control access to the FTP service

User authentication services for FTP are provided by NDS. You can specify the names of users allowed access to the FTP service, or grant anonymous access.

How to access NetWare servers using FTP

FTP users can change NDS contexts and access remote NetWare servers using command structures that are unique to the NetWare FTP service.

Introducing NetWare NFS Services

NetWare's FTP server software can only be installed as part of the NetWare NFS Services 2.11 product. Shipping on Disk 4 of the IntranetWare package, the NFS services are separate from the core NetWare 4.11 product. You install them, using NetWare's INSTALL.NLM utility, to an existing server that has already had the TCP/IP protocols loaded and bound to a network adapter driver.

Originally designed to support the needs of UNIX workstations on a NetWare network, the NFS Services product includes a collection of different services, all of which are installed to the target server at one time. You do not have to run all of the services, however. Also included in the product is UNICODE.NLM, a server-based utility that you use to start, stop, and configure the various components.

The version of NFS Services included in the IntranetWare package lacks the NFS Server module, which enables UNIX workstations to access the NetWare file system, and the NFS Gateway, with which NetWare clients can access UNIX drives. These modules are available as a separate product, for an additional fee.

The NetWare NFS Services package that ships with IntranetWare includes the following:

- **Name services**—DNS (Domain Name Service) and NIS (Network Information Service) modules are required by the other components, but they need not run on the same server as the FTP server. You can also use any other non-NetWare NIS and DNS services installed on your network.
- **Print services**—The UNIX-to-NetWare and NetWare-to-UNIX print services let UNIX users print to NetWare printers, and vice versa.
- **File transfer services**—The FTP (File Transfer Protocol) Server provides authenticated TCP-based file transfer capabilities to any client running the TCP/IP protocols. The TFTP (Trivial File Transfer Protocol) Server provides UDP-based file transfers with no authentication.
- **RARP service**—The Reverse Address Resolution Protocol uses a mapping table to reply to queries specifying a network adapter hardware address with the equivalent IP address. It can also be used to automatically supply an IP address to a workstation as it is booted.
- **SNMP service**—The Simple Network Management Protocol is used to notify a central network management station of errors or problems with the other NFS services.
- **Management utilities**—UNICON is a NetWare server-based utility that you use to control and configure the NFS services. The XCONSOLE utility provides access to the NetWare server console from any X Windows system, using the Telnet protocol.

Introducing FTP

FTP was created to provide file transfer services to UNIX clients from a standardized command-line interface. Although its use was originally confined largely to the UNIX world,

FTP has now become a staple for Internet users. There are now many FTP client software packages available that add a graphical interface to the venerable service, making it much more intuitive.

However, the primary drawback of FTP for the casual Internet user is that you must know what you are looking for and where it is located. Some FTP servers maintain enormous directory structures with thousands of cryptically named files. This is a familiar environment to the typical UNIX addict, but far too sophisticated for today's average Internet user.

The use of FTP has skyrocketed with the rest of the Internet, though, even though it is largely invisible to most of its users. Web browsers provide user-friendly access to FTP file transfers using hyperlinks that can refer to files stored on the same computer as the Web site, or on a system thousands of miles away. The same collection of files can, therefore, be furnished both to standard FTP clients and to Web users from the same server.

The principle of using Web links to FTP sites is equally valid on a corporate intranet. It may seem odd to have users download files stored on an internal server with FTP when they could also access them directly through the NetWare file system. However, combining the FTP service with intranet Web sites enables administrators to create well-documented pages that are much more readily comprehensible to the non-technical user than a directory display. Any administrator who has struggled through an explanation of NetWare servers, volumes, and drive mappings to a user who simply wants access to a file (without a tour of the MIS department), can recognize the need for simple, unified access to network file resources.

Using the Novell Web Server with FTP

If you elect to run the Novell Web Server in order to host Web sites for Internet or intranet clients, you may want to run the FTP service as well. However, FTP is not required in order to download files using a Web browser. A normal hyperlink to a file other than an HTML, script, or graphic file in a Web page causes the file to be transferred to the client using HTTP, the standard Web protocol. This is a perfectly effective means of transferring files from server to client. For more information on hosting Web sits using NetWare, see Chapter 30, "Using the NetWare Web Server."

If the file transfer links on your Web pages point to files on the same machine as the Web server, the additional system resources required by the FTP service may not be justified. Unless you require the other features that FTP provides, such as user authentication and access via clients other than Web browsers, HTTP links may be sufficient.

Modifying your file transfer hyperlinks to use FTP instead of HTTP can be advantageous, however, under certain circumstances. Your FTP service need not run on the same system as your Web server. An FTP hyperlink in a Web page can point to any FTP server on your network, or on the Internet. FTP links, therefore, enable you to balance the traffic load and the system resource requirements incurred by your TCP/IP services among several machines (see Figure 31.1).

FIG. 31.1

An FTP server separates file transfer from Web page traffic, and allows users to access files using various types of client programs.

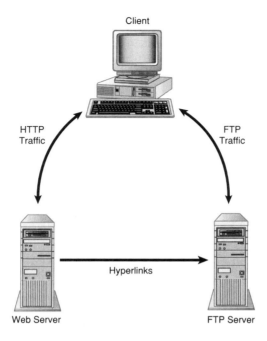

Client

HTTP
Traffic

FTP
Traffic

Hyperlinks

Web Server

FTP Server

Managing the FTP Service

The only prerequisite for installing NetWare NFS Services on a 4.11 server (apart from suffi-cient memory and disk space resources) is the installation and configuration of the TCP/IP protocols. Your clients must also be running TCP/IP, using NetWare/IP, the IPX/IP Gateway, or another protocol stack.

▶ **See** "Implementing TCP/IP," **p. 619**

The FTP server also requires three name services: NDS, NIS, and DNS. NDS, of course, should already be running on your network. You can run the NIS and DNS modules that are included with the NFS Services product on the same server as the FTP service, or on another NetWare server. If you already have NIS or DNS services running on another operating sys-tem, such as UNIX or Windows NT, you can use those instead of the NetWare versions. In any case, you only need one instance of each name service on your network.

Using UNICON

When you install NetWare NFS Services, the UNICON utility is installed on the target server. UNICON is the primary configuration and management interface to all of the NFS services, including the FTP server. The NFS Services installation routine automatically installs all of the modules listed in "Introducing NetWare NFS Services" earlier in this chapter, but in UNICON, you select which services you actually want to run on the server.

When you load the UNICON program at the server console, you must first log in to the NDS tree by specifying a user name and password. By default, the Admin user is specified. Using Admin or an equivalent is recommended because some of UNICON's functions make changes to the NDS database. In the case of the FTP service, UNICON adds the Anonymous user object to the NDS tree in the same context as the FTP server.

After the NFS Services installation sequence, you must manually start the FTP service by adding it to the Running Services list, which you access from the Start/Stop Services menu item in UNICON (see Figure 31.2). Once you have started the service, it is available whenever you reboot the server, until you explicitly stop it.

FIG. 31.2
You must start the FTP service with the UNICON utility before it can be used by clients.

The FTP service's primary module is called FTPSERV.NLM. However, starting the FTP Service with UNICON does not immediately load this program. Instead, the service remains idle until it is needed. When an FTP client attempts to connect to the server, FTPSERV is automatically loaded on the server, and the connection request is processed. Once the user closes the connection, FTPSERV remains in memory for a specified period of time (30 minutes, by default), after which it unloads itself again. This automatic loading feature conserves system resources when the FTP service is not being used.

In addition to starting and stopping the FTP service, you also use UNICON to perform the following management tasks (as discussed in the following sections):

- View the currently active FTP sessions
- Set FTP service parameters
- View and clear FTP log files
- Restrict FTP user access

Monitoring FTP Sessions

When you select the FTP Server from the Manage Services menu, the FTP Administration screen displays the number of current active FTP sessions at all times. When you view the current FTP sessions, a list of the NDS names and IP addresses of the currently connected

users is shown. Selecting a user from the list displays a Detailed Session Statistics screen like
that shown in Figure 31.3, which identifies the user and summarizes the file transfer activity for
the session.

FIG. 31.3

From the server
console, you can
monitor the activities of
connected FTP clients in
real time.

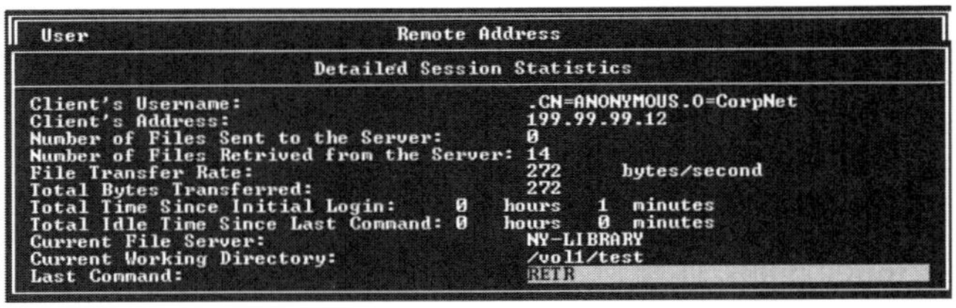

You can also disconnect a user from the FTP server instantaneously by deleting an entry from
the session list.

Configuring FTP Service Parameters

The FTP Server Parameters screen—accessed by selecting Manage Services from UNICON's
Main Menu and choosing FTP Server/Set Parameters—enables the network administrator to
control the amount of user traffic allowed by the server and other basic operational properties
(see Figure 31.4).

FIG. 31.4

You set the configura-
tion parameters for the
FTP service using the
UNICON.NLM utility at
the server console.

The following list describes these parameters:

- Maximum Number of Sessions—Specifies the number of FTP clients that can be
  connected to the server at the same time. The default is 9; adjust this figure based on the
  hardware capabilities of your server and your network.

- Maximum Session Length—Specifies the amount of time (in minutes) that a client can
  remain connected to the FTP server. The default value is 400.

- Idle Time Before FTP Server Unloads—Specifies the amount of time (in minutes) that
  the FTPSERV.NLM module remains loaded in memory when there are no active
  connections. The default value is 30 minutes.

- Anonymous User Access—Used to indicate whether or not the server should permit the
  use of the login name "anonymous" during connections. The default value is NO,
  meaning that users must specify a valid NDS user name and password to be permitted
  access.

- ■ Default User's Home Directory—When a client connects to the FTP server using an NDS user name, the user's home directory, as specified in the NDS User object, becomes the root in the FTP client interface. If no home directory is specified in the NDS object, then the user's home directory on the server running the FTP service becomes the root. Only if home directories are not specified in either place is the value of the default home directory field used as the root.

- ■ Anonymous User's Home Directory—Specifies the root directory for FTP clients that log in with the user name "anonymous." By default, the home directory is the root of the FTP server's SYS volume.

- ■ Default Name Space—Specifies the format (DOS or NFS) used to display files and directories on the FTP server. The default value is DOS. Selecting NFS displays a UNIX-style listing, as follows:

```
-rw-rw----  1       ftpuser      -2     14848 Oct 27 00:34 Outline.back.doc
drw-rw----  1       ftpuser      -2     41984 Dec 11 03:06 Chapter2
-rw-rw----  1       ftpuser      -2 13110125 Mar 19 23:25 ntenu41n(3).exe
```

Part VIII

Ch

31

The NFS listing displays, in order, a code indicating whether the entry is a file (-) or a directory (d), the NFS rights granted to the file or directory, the number of links to the file or directory, its owner, its group ID number, its size, its date and time of creation, and its name.

Selecting DOS truncates the file and directory names to the 8.3 format, and adds the owner's name, as shown:

```
- [RWCEAFMS] craigz                    14848 Oct 27 00:34 intranet.doc
- [RWCEAFMS] craigz                    41984 Dec 11 03:06 chapter2.doc
- [RWCEAFMS] craigz                 13110125 Mar 19 23:25 ntenu41n.exe
```

- ■ Intruder Detection—Indicates whether the FTP server will maintain a log of the users' attempts to log in to the service unsuccessfully, for intruder detection purposes. The default value is ON.

- ■ Number of Unsuccessful Login Attempts—Specifies the number of unsuccessful logins that must occur within the specified time period before intruder logging begins. The default value is 6.

- ■ Detection Reset Interval—Specifies the time interval (in minutes) within which the number of unsuccessful login attempts must occur before intruder logging begins. The default value is 3,000 minutes.

- ■ Log Level—Specifies the amount of information to be captured in the FTP service log. Possible values are as follows:

> NONE—No information is recorded

> LOGINS—Only login information is recorded

> STATISTICS—The number of files copied to and from the FTP server is recorded, along with login information

> FILE—All FTP transactions are recorded, including login and statistics information

You can modify the FTP service parameters at any time, without restarting the service.

If you intend to provide anonymous FTP access to Internet users, it is recommended that you specify the use of the NFS name space in the FTP Server Parameters screen. The NFS format more closely resembles that of the UNIX-based servers that are used to host the majority of FTP sites, and allows for the use of file and directory names up to 255 characters long, while the DOS name space is restricted to 8.3 names.

Displaying Message Files   In addition to the parameters listed, you can optionally configure the FTP service to display a message when users log in to the service and when they change to a specific directory. If you create an ASCII text file containing your greeting message called BANNER.FTP, and place it in the SYS:ETC directory of the FTP server, the contents of the file will be displayed to all users at login.

 An authenticated user can bypass the display of the BANNER.FTP file by adding a hyphen (-) as the first character of the account password.

In addition, any ASCII file called MESSAGE.TXT that is stored in a directory accessible to FTP clients will be displayed when a user switches to that directory. You can use this feature to provide users with instructions for the use of the FTP site, or descriptions of the files contained in each directory.

Using Web Browsers with FTP   The NetWare NFS Services product was originally developed before Web browsers came into popular use as FTP clients. You must take the following steps to ensure that anonymous FTP access is properly granted using a Web browser client:

- Make sure that anonymous user access is enabled in the FTP Server Parameters screen and that the anonymous user's home directory is set.

- Make sure that NFS name space support is added to the volume on which the anonymous user's home directory is located.

- In UNICON, select Manage Global Objects/Manage Users/All Entries and make sure that the NetWare user "anonymous" is mapped to the UNIX user "anonymous." The User Information screen should show a UID of 32,000 and a GID of –2, by default.

- Make sure that the "anonymous" user is the owner of the home directory specified in the Set Parameters screen for the FTP service. To change the owner with UNICON, select Perform File Operations/View-Set File Permissions from the Main Menu and browse to the home directory using the standard C-worthy interface keystrokes. The File Information screen for that directory should show "anonymous" as the NetWare owner. If it does not, you can specify a new owner by changing the UNIX User ID field to the UID number shown in the User Information screen (usually 32,000).

- The anonymous user should also have the appropriate trustee rights to the home directory, depending on the functions to be performed. You can, for example, prevent users from uploading files to the FTP server by withholding the WRITE and CREATE rights, just as you would with a NetWare user.

Viewing the FTP Log File

The FTP log is an ASCII file stored in the SYS:ETC directory as FTPSERV.LOG. The information found there depends on the value if the Log Level setting in the FTP service Set Parameters screen. You can view the log from the FTP Administration screen in UNICON, or use any other text viewer or editor. Typical log entries appear as follows:

```
-----------------------------------------------------------------
Sat Mar 22 13:35:48 1997 FTP Session Starts from 199.99.99.12.
Sat Mar 22 13:35:54 1997 .CN=ftpuser.O=CorpNet login from 199.99.99.12.
Sat Mar 22 13:36:10 1997 0 files copied from server.
0 files copied to server.
Sat Mar 22 13:36:10 1997 FTP Session Ends from 199.99.99.12.
-----------------------------------------------------------------
Sat Mar 22 13:36:06 1997 FTP Session Starts from 199.99.99.12.
-----------------------------------------------------------------
Sat Mar 22 13:36:06 1997 Guest login '' from 199.99.99.12.
Sat Mar 22 13:36:09 1997 .CN=ANONYMOUS.O=CorpNet login from 199.99.99.12 without
➥password.
-----------------------------------------------------------------
Sat Mar 22 13:36:09 1997 Retrieved file /vol1/test/message.txt.
Sat Mar 22 14:56:10 1997 1 files copied from server.
0 files copied to server.
Sat Mar 22 14:56:10 1997 FTP Session Ends from 199.99.99.12.
-----------------------------------------------------------------
```

N O T E FTP log entries are not posted to the FTPSERV.LOG file until the user connection is closed. This can affect the order of the entries in such a way as to place the entry of a user that connected at 1:00 P.M. (for example) after the entry for a user who logged in at 2:00 P.M., as long as the second user logged off first. ▨

Viewing the Intruder Log File

The FTP service's intruder detection system does not lock accounts in the same way as NetWare's security mechanism. When users exceed the number of failed logins specified in the FTP service parameters, their activities are logged in a separate file called INTRUDER.FTP, stored in the SYS:SYSTEM directory.

The log includes the login name and password used in each failed attempt, the time of day, and the IP address of the system where the attempt was made, as shown:

```
Intruder Alert. Address 199.99.99.13 has exceeded the limit
Time 3-22-97 5:24:55pm  User .CN=admin.O=CorpNet used password ftp.
Time 3-22-97 5:24:34pm  User .CN=admin.O=CorpNet used password netuser.
Time 3-22-97 5:23:51pm  User .CN=admin.O=CorpNet used password user.
4 unsuccessful logins from address 199.99.99.13
Time 3-22-97 5:25:27pm  User .CN=admin.O=CorpNet used password gopher.
5 unsuccessful logins from address 199.99.99.13
Time 3-22-97 5:26:24pm  User .CN=admin.O=CorpNet used password retro.
Successful Login from address 199.99.99.13 after reaching the intruder limit.
3-22-97 5:26:59pm  User .CN=admin.O=CorpNet.
```

Part
VIII

Ch
31

For a more immediate reaction to FTP intrusions, NFS Services can also send SNMP alerts to a network management console. To do this, you identify the target for the SNMP alerts in the TCP/IP Protocol Configuration screen of the INETCFG utility, and set the SNMP Alert Level by selecting Configure Error Reporting from UNICON's Main Menu.

N O T E You can erase either the FTP or intruder log file by selecting Clear Log Files from the FTP Administration menu and selecting the appropriate log. A new log file is created when the FTP service is next started.

Restricting FTP Access

Although user access to the FTP service is controlled by NDS, you do not grant users rights to the service using the standard NDS utilities, such as the NetWare Administrator and NETADMIN. Instead, you must modify a text file called RESTRICT.FTP, located in the SYS:ETC directory. You can do this by selecting Restrict FTP Access from the FTP Administration menu, or you can modify the file directly using any ASCII text editor.

FTP and File System Rights   It is important to understand that RESTRICT.FTP is used only to specify what users are permitted access to the FTP service itself. It is a mechanism that is entirely separate from the file system access rights that a user needs to transfer files to and from network servers. The file and directory trustee rights needed by FTP clients are exactly the same as those granted to local NetWare users.

In many cases, you do not have to manually assign additional rights to users for FTP access. Users logging in to the FTP service are automatically placed in the home directory specified in their NDS user object properties. Because NDS automatically grants users all file system rights (except Supervisor) to their home directories, no modifications are needed.

This is true for the anonymous user as well as existing NetWare users. When you specify a home directory for the anonymous user in UNICON's FTP Server Parameters screen, that directory is added to the Anonymous user object in the NDS tree, granting it the rights needed to access files.

However, when a NetWare user object does not have a home directory defined, then when logging in to the FTP service, the user is placed in the directory specified in the Default User's Home Directory field in the FTP Server Parameters screen. If the user does not have file system rights to that directory, the FTP login will be successful, but the directory will not be found, resulting in an error message and no useful access.

Modifying the RESTRICT.FTP File   The RESTRICT.FTP file is annotated with instructions for its use and sample entries. By default, the file contains only a single live entry, an asterisk that functions as a wild card, allowing all users access to the service. Removing this entry or deleting the entire file prevents all users from accessing the FTP service. You can create additional entries by specifying the NDS names of users whose access you want to grant, limit, or deny. The syntax for an entry is as follows:

```
username [ACCESS=GUEST¦READONLY¦NOREMOTE, DENY, NORMAL] [ADDRESS=hostname,
➥IPaddress]
```

N O T E By default, the NFS Services installation program creates RESTRICT.FTP as a read-only file. Editing a read-only file in the UNICON program fails to save any changes made without notifying the user. Be sure to flag the file as read/write before you make modifications.

You specify user names in RESTRICT.FTP using any of the accepted NDS notation conventions. You can use a simple name (for example, SmithJ), as long as the user object is located in the default context, which is the container object in which the FTP server is located. You can also use distinguished NDS names using either typeless or typeful notation (for example, SmithJ.NY.CorpNet or CN=SmithJ.OU=NY.O=CorpNet).

▶ **See** "Understanding NDS Object Naming," **p. 89**

You can also use an asterisk as a wild card character in a distinguished NDS name. For example, an entry specifying *.NY.CorpNet represents all of the user objects in the NY container.

Part
VIII
Ch
31

The additional parameters that you can include in a RESTRICT.FTP entry let you specify access restrictions for the designated user. With the ACCESS= parameter, you can limit a user's access to the FTP server, or deny access entirely. This way, you can approach the creation of the RESTRICT.FTP file in two ways. You can allow all users access (using the * wild card) and create entries for the exceptional users whose access is to be limited or denied, or you can take the opposite approach and deny all access, creating specific entries for the users who are to be allowed to use the service.

The possible values for the ACCESS= parameter are as follows:

- NORMAL—The default setting; imposes no additional restrictions on the user's access
- GUEST—Permits the user access only to the files in the home directory and its subdirectories
- READONLY—Prevents the user from uploading files to the network through the FTP service
- NOREMOTE—Permits the user access only to the files and directories on the FTP server itself; access to all other servers on the network is denied
- DENY—Revokes all access to the FTP service granted by previous entries

The GUEST, READONLY, and NOREMOTE values can be combined in a single entry by specifying two values, separated by a pipe character (¦), as in ACCESS=GUEST¦READONLY.

N O T E If you elect to remove the wild card entry from the RESTRICT.FTP file that permits FTP access to all users, remember that you must explicitly grant access rights to the Anonymous user if you want it to be used. The Anonymous user is automatically given the equivalent of the ACCESS=GUEST parameter, no matter what status you grant it in RESTRICT.FTP.

The ADDRESS= parameter lets you specify the host name or IP address of the system from which the designated user must access the FTP service. This can function as an added security measure to prevent an account with special access (such as Admin, for example) from being used by outsiders.

CAUTION

The use of Novell Directory Services for FTP authentication raises a security issue that all network administrators should bear in mind. Unlike a NetWare workstation client, FTP clients transmit passwords over the network in an unencrypted form. It is therefore possible for a network monitor or protocol analyzer product to capture TCP/IP packets and read the passwords of NDS users. For this reason, you should use accounts with extraordinary access (like Admin) sparingly, if at all, over an FTP connection.

Changes made to the RESTRICT.FTP file do not take effect until the next time that the FTPSERV.NLM is loaded on the server. You can either wait for the module to be automatically unloaded when the client inactivity period expires, or unload it manually at the server console. The next time that a user logs in, the modified file is read into memory and the changes are applied.

Using the NetWare FTP Service

The NetWare FTP service depends on the NDS database for user authentication. If you plan to provide anonymous FTP service to Internet clients, the use of NDS can remain transparent to these users. Anonymous users can only access files and directories that are stored in the home directory on the server used to host the FTP service. This prevents clients outside the local network from accessing the other files on the server.

FTP clients that log in using a user name other than anonymous, however, can have a great deal more access. Authenticated NDS users can, in fact, access any files on the NetWare network to which they have been granted the required file system rights. This includes files on NetWare servers that are not running the FTP service, and even servers that are not running the TCP/IP protocols.

The FTP server acts as a gateway, receiving FTP requests from clients and sending its own NCP (NetWare Core Protocol) requests to other NetWare servers in turn, as shown in Figure 31.5. The remote server supplies the requested file to the FTP server, which passes it in to the FTP client.

These capabilities take NetWare's FTP service well beyond those of most other operating systems. For example, in many cases, users that want to work at home do not require a full-featured remote access solution. They only need access to their files. By connecting a NetWare FTP server to the Internet, users can be provided with full, authenticated access to all of the same files they use in the office, without the need to create new accounts or install modems for dedicated remote access.

To use these capabilities, users must be aware of additional client procedures that are not a part of standard FTP implementations. The NetWare FTP server recognizes several commands and syntax structures that would be rejected by other FTP servers, and which are not recognized by FTP clients either.

FIG. 31.5

The NetWare FTP server enables users to access files on any NetWare server through an intranet or Internet connection.

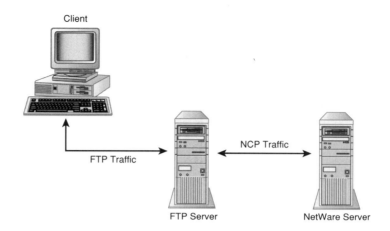

Accessing Remote Servers

When a user accesses a typical FTP site, the home directory specified by the FTP server becomes the root directory in the client interface. Represented by a single slash (/), the root is at the top of the directory structure available to the anonymous user, no matter where the home directory actually is located on the server drive.

The NetWare FTP server functions in exactly this way when hosting anonymous users. However, any other authenticated NDS user logging in to the NetWare FTP server will see the name of the home directory in relation to the directory structure of the volume on which it is located. For example, an anonymous FTP user that logs in and issues the pw command is informed that / is the current directory, no matter what the anonymous user's home directory is. However, a user logging in under a standard NDS name is informed by the pw command that the current directory is /vol1/users/smithj, that is, the user's actual home directory.

This enables users to access any other files or directories on the server to which they have been granted access by the network administrator, even if those files and directories are located higher up in the directory tree than the home directory.

Users can therefore issue the standard CD command that is common to all FTP clients, in order to change to any directory on the server. The client must use UNIX-style directory notation, however. Volume, directory, and file names are all separated by a single forward slash. The standard NetWare notation, in which a volume name is followed by a colon, is not acceptable in this case.

As with other FTP servers, clients can use the standard asterisk (*) and question mark (?) wild cards to specify multiple files in a single command. Also allowed are two periods (..) to represent the parent directory (as in CD ..) and the tilde (~) to represent the user's home directory. The single slash (as in CD /) represents a theoretical root directory of the FTP server, from which all of the server's volumes can be accessed as subdirectories.

Clients use the same directory notation to specify path names of files and directories on other volumes or even other servers. To download a file stored on a NetWare server other than the FTP server, a user must issue a GET command with a path name noted using the following syntax:

```
//server/volume/directory/file
```

The double slash indicates that the file or directory is located on another NetWare server. The FTP service automatically handles the communications tasks needed to access the remote server, including whether it must use a TCP or NCP connection.

Remote server access through an FTP connection is subject to a few limitations, however. They are as follows:

- Remote server connections are limited to the use of the DOS name space.
- The tilde (˜), which represents the user's home directory, is invalid on a remote server.
- The single slash (/) always represents the *root* of the FTP server, even when the user is working in a directory on a remote server.

TIP Another useful method of accessing files on other servers through FTP is with directory map objects. By creating directory map objects in the same NDS context as the FTP server, users can access remote directories without having to know exactly where they are located.

Understanding the *SITE* and *STAT* Commands

NetWare's FTP service supports two commands called SITE and STAT, which provide functions that support the unique capabilities of this FTP server. It should be noted that although SITE and STAT are part of the IETF (Internet Engineering Task Force) standard on which FTP services are based (RFC959), their functions are unique to the NetWare FTP service.

STAT is a valid FTP command that is used in most FTP services to return a report to the client regarding the status of an ongoing procedure, or of the server's operational status. SITE is mentioned in the standard as a provision for the implementation of system-specific services that do not warrant inclusion in a universal standards document.

What this means is that the NetWare FTP server responds to these two commands differently than do other FTP servers. STAT is recognized as a valid command by FTP clients, but elicits a different response than the NetWare-specific STAT command. SITE is not considered by FTP clients to be a valid command; it is rejected by the client software before it is even transmitted to the server.

Therefore, to send these commands to the NetWare FTP server from a client, you must precede them with the QUOTE command. QUOTE instructs an FTP client to send whatever text follows on the command line to the server without comment or intervention.

Using *SITE*   The primary function of the SITE command is to support the NetWare FTP service's remote server access functions. With SITE, you can get information about the network resources that are available to FTP clients, and change context and name space settings to facilitate access to those resources.

You use SITE by specifying the command along with one of several parameters on the FTP command line (preceded by QUOTE, as shown in the previous section). For example, to display a list of all of the NetWare servers available on the network, you use the QUOTE SITE SLIST command.

The parameters that you can use with the SITE command are as follows:

- SLIST—Displays a listing of all of the NetWare servers found on the network, including non-TCP/IP and bindery-based servers
- SERVER—Displays a listing of all of the NetWare 4.x servers found in the current context
- PATH—Displays a list of the directory maps found in the current context
- OU—Displays a listing of the container objects found in the current context
- CX—With no further parameters, displays the user's current NDS context. CX is also used to change the current context, by specifying the relative or absolute path to any container object (in the form OU=*objectname*), or by adding two periods (..) to represent the parent context, or by adding SERVER to change to the context in which the correct server object is found. Examples:

```
QUOTE SITE CX
QUOTE SITE CX OU=NY
QUOTE SITE CX OU=NY.O=CorpNet
QUOTE SITE ..
QUOTE SITE SERVER
```

- DOS—Enables the user to switch the FTP server's file and directory displays to the DOS format, for that user and that session only
- NFS—Enables the user to switch the FTP server's file and directory displays to the NFS format, for that user and that session only (available only on the server running the FTP service)

N O T E The SITE SERVER, SITE SLIST, and SITE PATH commands also can include a partial name with a wild card to limit the size of the listing. For example, the command QUOTE SITE SLIST NY* displays a list of all the NetWare servers on the network with names that begin with NY.

An FTP user's default context has the same significance as that of a normal NetWare user. Logging in to the FTP service sets a user's context to be the same as that in which the FTP server object is located. Switching to a directory on another server, however, causes the context to be changed to that of the remote server.

For convenience when browsing other servers, clients can use the SITE CX command to avoid typing the distinguished names of objects, just as a NetWare client can use the CX command at the DOS prompt. Other SITE parameters, such as SERVER, OU, and PATH, list only the objects found in the current context, making it necessary for users to move about in the NDS tree in order to browse effectively using the FTP interface.

Using STAT   The STAT command displays a list of statistics concerning the client connection to the FTP server and its current data transfer parameters, as follows:

```
211-Status on ny-library
        Client node:           199.99.99.13
        Client name:           .CN=ftpuser.O=CorpNet
        UNIX User Name:        ftpuser
        UNIX UID:              32001
        Directory:             /vol1/ftptest
        Type:                  Ascii Non-Print
        Structure:             File
        Mode:                  Stream
        Namespace:             NFS
        NDS Context:           O=CorpNet
211 End of Status.
```

Summary

NetWare's FTP service provides all of the functionality of those running on other operating systems—and a good deal more. As a companion to the Novell Web Server, the FTP service provides standard Internet and intranet data transfer capabilities. Its use of NDS authentication, however, allows internal network users an alternative means of accessing server-based files, from either the local network or via the Internet. ●

PART IX

Appendixes

NetWare *SET* Commands

In most cases, a properly installed NetWare server will run efficiently without any special configuration changes. However, there are a great many parameters that you can use to adjust and fine-tune the performance of your server. All of the parameters in this appendix can be modified from the server console prompt, using the SET command or by using the menu-driven interfaces found in the MONITOR and SERVMAN utilities.

The only restriction on your use of these parameters is that you should fully understand the ramifications of any changes that you make. It is also a good idea to keep a record of all of your default settings before making any adjustments so that you can reset them if necessary. You can use either the MONITOR or SERVMAN program to save your current settings to a file.

Table A.1 Commands that Control Communications

Command with Default	Allowed Range	Used in AUTOEXEC.NCF and from Keyboard?	Used in STARTUP.NCF?
SET ALLOW IP ADDRESS DUPLICATES=OFF	Off/On	Yes	Yes

Purpose: Normally, TCPIP.NLM does not allow an IP address to be bound to a server LAN driver if the address is already being used on the network. Turning this option on allows the binding to take place, despite the address conflict. IP address conflicts can prevent both systems from operating properly.

SET MAXIMUM PACKET RECEIVE BUFFERS=100	50 to 2000	Yes	Yes

Purpose: This command specifies the maximum number of packet receive buffers the server can allocate. These buffers are used to hold communication packets while they're waiting to be serviced. The default setting of 100 often is too low on a busy server, where temporary bursts of activity can require more buffers for incoming communication packets. Watch this setting closely; the MONITOR NLM lets you view the actual number of packet receive buffers that are used.

SET MINIMUM PACKET RECEIVE BUFFERS=50	10 to 1000	No	Yes

Purpose: This option sets the minimum number of packet receive buffers allocated by the server, which is the amount allocated by the file server when it starts. Set to the level the server usually uses, based on what you observe by using the MONITOR NLM.

SET MAXIMUM PHYSICAL RECEIVE PACKET SIZE=4202	618 to 24682	No	Yes

Purpose: This option specifies the size of the largest packet the file server can receive through a software driver that controls a network adapter. Set to exceed the largest packet size used by any network adapter on your network. Default setting is correct for the largest packet sizes now in use for ARCnet, Ethernet, Token Ring, and FDDI.

SET IPX NETBIOS REPLICATION OPTION=2	0 to 2	Yes	No

Purpose: This option controls how the IPX router deals with NetBIOS-replicated broadcasts. Default setting 2 prevents duplicate broadcasts from being replicated when redundant routes exist. A 0 setting means that the router doesn't replicate NetBIOS broadcasts; a 1 setting causes duplicate NetBIOS broadcasts to be replicated exactly as they are.

SET MAXIMUM INTERRUPT EVENTS=10	1 to 1000000	Yes	No

Purpose: This option controls the maximum number of high-priority tasks allowed when a *thread switch* occurs. NetWare schedules server-based operations by using *threads*. When a task has a thread, it's allowed to run but must surrender the thread periodically to other tasks that need to run. Between thread switches, *interrupt events*—tasks that can't wait (such as routing a packet to another network)—are handled. This setting controls how many of these tasks can occur during thread switches.

Command with Default	Allowed Range	Used in AUTOEXEC.NCF and from Keyboard?	Used in STARTUP.NCF?
SET REPLY TO GET NEAREST SERVER=ON	On or Off	Yes	Yes

Purpose: This option determines whether server responds to workstations that just loaded the NetWare Requester and are seeking a server to connect to. A fast server near its licensed connection limit can use up its remaining available connections by responding to workstations loading the NetWare Requester. If this becomes a problem on a particular server, change the setting for this option from On to Off.

SET NUMBER OF WATCHDOG PACKETS=10	5 to 100	Yes	No

Purpose: This option controls the number of times the file server asks a previously connected workstation whether it's still connected. If the workstation doesn't respond before the required number of packets has been sent, the workstation's connection is released. *Watchdog packets* are used to check for workstations that are no longer connected to the server because the workstation was turned off, has connected to another server, or has lost its network link to the server.

SET DELAY BETWEEN WATCHDOG PACKETS=59.3	9.9 sec to 10 min 26.2 sec	Yes	No

Purpose: This parameter sets the time interval between watchdog packets. Use to control how rapidly the server sends the required number of watchdog packets to check for an inactive workstation.

SET DELAY BEFORE FIRST WATCHDOG PACKET =4 MIN 56.6 SEC	15.7 sec to 14 days	Yes	No

Purpose: A server sends watchdog packets to a workstation only after it receives no requests from that workstation for a certain period of time. This option sets the length of time the server waits before sending the first watchdog packet.

SET NEW PACKET RECEIVE BUFFER WAIT TIME=0.1 SECONDS	0.1 sec to 20 sec	Yes	No

Purpose: This option sets the minimum time to wait before allocating a new packet receive buffer. Leaving this setting at its minimum ensures that the server responds immediately when a new packet receive buffer is needed. Raising the setting can deter the server from allocating packet receive buffers under spurious circumstances, such as when communication errors are on the network.

SET USE OLD WATCHDOG PACKET TYPE=OFF	On or Off	Yes	No

Purpose: This command causes NetWare to transmit type 0 watchdog packets between clients and servers instead of the standard type 4. Some older model routers filter out type 4 packets, causing client connections to be dropped.

continues

Table A.1   Continued

Command with Default	Allowed Range	Used in AUTOEXEC.NCF and from Keyboard?	Used in STARTUP.NCF?
SET CONSOLE DISPLAY WATCHDOG LOGOUTS=OFF	On or Off	Yes	No

Purpose: Set this option to On to have the server display an alert on the console when a workstation is disconnected because it didn't respond to its watchdog packets.

Table A.2   Commands that Control Memory Usage

Command with Default	Allowed Range	Used in AUTOEXEC.NCF and from Keyboard?	Used in STARTUP.NCF?
SET ALLOW INVALID POINTERS=OFF	On or Off	Yes	Yes

Purpose: This command allows NLMs to create an invalid pointer that maps to a 4K page in memory that doesn't exist. A notification is issued to the server console and server error log the first time the NLM creates an invalid pointer, but not thereafter.

SET READ FAULT NOTIFICATION=ON	On or Off	Yes	Yes

Purpose: This option determines whether notification is issued to the server console and error log if an NLM tries to read from a nonexistent memory *page* (a *page* is a 4K range of memory).

SET READ FAULT EMULATION=OFF	On or Off	Yes	Yes

Purpose: This command determines whether NetWare *emulates* a successful read from memory when an NLM tries to read from a page of memory that doesn't exist.

SET WRITE FAULT NOTIFICATION=ON	On or Off	Yes	Yes

Purpose: This command determines whether a notification is issued to the server console and error log if an NLM tries to write to a nonexistent memory page.

SET WRITE FAULT EMULATION=OFF	On or Off	Yes	Yes

Purpose: This command determines whether NetWare *emulates* a successful write to memory when an NLM tries to write to a page of memory that doesn't exist.

SET GARBAGE COLLECTION INTERVAL=15 MIN	1 min to 1 hour	Yes	Yes

Purpose: *Garbage collection* is a process the server runs periodically to recycle memory that previously was allocated to an NLM or other server task but no longer is in use.

Command with Default	Allowed Range	Used in AUTOEXEC.NCF and from Keyboard?	Used in STARTUP.NCF?

Periodic garbage collection ensures that server memory is reclaimed and reused with maximum efficiency. The garbage collection process runs during low-usage times of the server processor, but is used to specify the maximum amount of time the server waits before running garbage collection under any circumstances.

| SET NUMBER OF FREES FOR GARBAGE COLLECTION=5000 | 100 to 100000 | Yes | Yes |

Purpose: This command specifies the number of memory areas that must be available to be reclaimed for the garbage collection task to run.

| SET MINIMUM FREE MEMORY FOR GARBAGE COLLECTION =8000 | 1000 to 1000000 | Yes | Yes |

Purpose: This option determines the minimum amount of memory in bytes that must be available for reclaiming before the garbage collection task can run.

| SET ALLOC MEMORY CHECK FLAG=OFF | On or Off | Yes | Yes |

Purpose: This option checks for corruption in the allocated memory nodes.

| SET AUTO REGISTER MEMORY ABOVE 16 MEGABYTES=ON | On or Off | No | Yes |

Purpose: This command determines whether NetWare 4.1 should automatically use memory above 16M in EISA bus servers. It's technically possible to put in an EISA server an ISA card that cannot address memory above 16M. Disk controllers that use DMA (Direct Memory Access) are the most common examples. If you must use such a card, use this command to change the setting to OFF.

| SET RESERVED BUFFERS BELOW 16 MEG=16 | 8 to 300 | No | Yes |

Purpose: This command sets the number of cache buffers that device drivers that cannot access memory above 16M can use. Some older disk drivers make use of this set parameter.

Table A.3 Commands that Control File Caching

Command with Default	Allowed Range	Used in AUTOEXEC.NCF and from Keyboard?	Used in STARTUP.NCF?
SET READ AHEAD ENABLED=ON	On or Off	Yes	No

Purpose: *Read-ahead file caching* means that NetWare is intelligently placing blocks of a file into its memory cache before this block is requested by a workstation. When NetWare

continues

Table A.3   Continued

Command with Default	Allowed Range	Used in AUTOEXEC.NCF and from Keyboard?	Used in STARTUP.NCF?

senses that a file is being read sequentially—the file is being read from beginning to end—NetWare automatically *reads ahead* by placing blocks of the file in memory in anticipation that they will be read. Use to enable or disable this feature.

Command with Default	Allowed Range	Used in AUTOEXEC.NCF and from Keyboard?	Used in STARTUP.NCF?
SET READ AHEAD LRU SITTING TIME THRESHOLD=10 SEC	0 sec to 1 hour	Yes	No

Purpose: The LRU sitting time (LRU stands for *least recently used*) is a measure of how rapidly the server's file cache is filling up because of new read and write requests. If the LRU cached file block sits in memory for less time than specified by this command, the read-ahead caching activated by the preceding command doesn't occur.

SET MINIMUM FILE CACHE BUFFERS=20	20 to 1000	Yes	No

Purpose: This option sets the minimum number of file cache buffers the server will maintain. NetWare uses memory not needed by other processes and NLMs for file caching. This command determines the minimum amount of memory that must be left for file caching. A cache buffer is 4K.

SET MAXIMUM CONCURRENT DISK CACHE WRITES=50	10 to 4000	Yes	No

Purpose: This command controls the maximum number of concurrent writes of dirty cache buffers that the server can queue for writing to disk in one disk seek operation. (A *dirty cache buffer* contains information that was changed in memory and must be written to disk; a *disk seek* is a movement of the disk's read/write heads to seek the area of the disk platter that needs to be written to.)

SET DIRTY DISK CACHE DELAY TIME=3.3 SEC	0.1 sec to 10 sec	Yes	No

Purpose: This option determines and sets the minimum allowed time the server must wait before writing to disk a cache block that was partially changed. A completely rewritten cache block is scheduled to be written to disk as soon as possible, but a disk write for a partially changed block can be postponed in anticipation that other changes may be written to cache block.

SET MINIMUM FILE CACHE REPORT THRESHOLD=20	0 to 1000	Yes	No

Purpose: This command sets the point at which a warning is issued about a low file cache block count. The number you set is added to the minimum number of cache blocks you reserved with the SET MINIMUM FILE CACHE BUFFERS command. For example, if your minimum cache buffer count is 20 and your report threshold count is 30, a warning is issued when 50 (20+30) buffers remain.

Table A.4   Commands that Control Directory Caching

Command with Default	Allowed Range	Used in AUTOEXEC.NCF and from Keyboard?	Used in STARTUP.NCF?
SET DIRTY DIRECTORY CACHE DELAY TIME=0.5 SEC	0 sec to 10 sec	Yes	No

Purpose: This sets the minimum time delay before writing a dirty directory cache buffer to disk. A *directory cache buffer* is a memory buffer used to store the list of files on server disks. Having portions of the directory cached in memory speeds directory searches that programs perform before they open and use files. (A *dirty directory cache buffer* is a directory cache buffer that a change has been written to. Until this change is written to disk, the buffer is "dirty.")

SET MAXIMUM CONCURRENT DIRECTORY CACHE WRITES=10	5 to 50	Yes	No

Purpose: This command controls the maximum number of concurrent writes of dirty directory cache buffers that the server can queue for writing to disk in one disk seek operation. (A *disk seek* is a movement of the disk's read/write heads to seek the area of the disk platter that needs to be written to.)

SET DIRECTORY CACHE ALLOCATION WAIT TIME=2.2 SEC	0.5 sec to 2 min	Yes	No

Purpose: This option determines how long the server waits before allocating a new directory cache buffer. The memory used to create directory cache buffers is taken from the pool of file cache buffer memory.

SET DIRECTORY CACHE BUFFER NONREFERENCED DELAY=5.5 SEC	1 sec to 5 min	Yes	No

Purpose: This option sets the amount of time a directory cache buffer must remain unread and unused before it can be rewritten with another portion of the directory.

SET MAXIMUM DIRECTORY CACHE BUFFERS=500	20 to 4000	Yes	No

Purpose: This command sets the maximum number of directory cache buffers that the server can allocate.

SET MINIMUM DIRECTORY CACHE BUFFERS=20	10 to 2000	Yes	No

Purpose: This option sets the minimum number of directory cache buffers the server will maintain. This is the number of buffers allocated when the server starts.

continues

Table A.4 Continued

Command with Default	Allowed Range	Used in AUTOEXEC.NCF and from Keyboard?	Used in STARTUP.NCF?
SET MAXIMUM NUMBER OF INTERNAL DIRECTORY HANDLES=100	40 to 1000	Yes	Yes

Purpose: Use this option to set maximum number of directory handles available to NLMs. Directory handles are used by NLMs to access the file system and check NetWare trustee rights assignments for a directory.

SET MAXIMUM NUMBER OF DIRECTORY HANDLES=100	20 to 1000	Yes	Yes

Purpose: Use this option to set the maximum number of directory handles available to each user connection. Directory handles are used by NLMs to access the file system and check NetWare trustee rights assignments for a directory.

Table A.5 Commands that Control the NetWare 4.1 File System

Command with Default	Allowed Range	Used in AUTOEXEC.NCF and from Keyboard?	Used in STARTUP.NCF?
SET MINIMUM FILE DELETE WAIT TIME=1 MIN 5.9 SEC	0 sec to 7 days	Yes	No

Purpose: This command sets the minimum wait time after a file is deleted before NetWare can purge the file so that space occupied by the file can be reused.

SET FILE DELETE WAIT TIME=5 MIN 29.6 SEC	0 sec to 7 days	Yes	No

Purpose: This command sets the standard wait time after a file is deleted before NetWare can purge the file so that space occupied by the file can be reused.

SET ALLOW DELETION OF ACTIVE DIRECTORIES=ON	On or Off	Yes	No

Purpose: This setting controls whether the server allows a user to delete a directory when another user has a drive mapped to it.

SET MAXIMUM PERCENT OF VOLUME SPACE ALLOWED FOR EXTENDED ATTRIBUTES=10	5 to 50	Yes	No

Purpose: This option controls how much of the volume can be used to store extended attribute information (*extended attributes* refers to the non-DOS file name and attribute information that NetWare stores on volumes that have name spaces installed in addition to

Command with Default	Allowed Range	Used in AUTOEXEC.NCF and from Keyboard?	Used in STARTUP.NCF?

the DOS name space). This setting is checked when the volume is mounted. To activate a new setting on a volume, you must dismount and remount the volume.

Command with Default	Allowed Range	Used in AUTOEXEC.NCF and from Keyboard?	Used in STARTUP.NCF?
SET MAXIMUM EXTENDED ATTRIBUTES PER FILE OR PATH=16	4 to 512	Yes	No

Purpose: This command sets the maximum number of extended attribute entries allowed for a file or directory.

SET FAST VOLUME MOUNTS=ON	On or Off	Yes	Yes

Purpose: This command relaxes the checking that is performed during volume mounts to increase their speed.

SET MAXIMUM PERCENT OF VOLUME USED BY DIRECTORY=13	5 to 50	Yes	No

Purpose: This option sets the maximum percentage of each volume that can be allocated to store the file directory.

SET IMMEDIATE PURGE OF DELETED FILES=OFF	On or Off	Yes	No

Purpose: Setting this option to On causes all deleted files on the server to be purged immediately on deletion.

SET MAXIMUM SUBDIRECTORY TREE DEPTH=25	10 to 100	No	Yes

Purpose: This command sets the maximum depth (or levels of subdirectories) allowed in directory trees on the server.

SET VOLUME LOW WARN ALL USERS=ON	On or Off	Yes	No

Purpose: Use this option to control whether a warning is issued to all server users when a volume is low on disk space.

SET VOLUME LOW WARNING RESET THRESHOLD=256	0 to 100000 blocks	Yes	No

Purpose: This option sets the level above the low-volume warning level to which a volume's free disk space must rise before the current low-volume warning condition is canceled. The setting for this command is in units of disk blocks, the size of which is set when you install a volume. The default disk block size is 8K.

SET VOLUME LOW WARNING THRESHOLD=256	0 to 100000 blocks	Yes	No

Purpose: This command sets the point at which a low disk space warning is issued for a server volume. Enter the low warning threshold in disk blocks.

continues

Table A.5   Continued

Command with Default	Allowed Range	Used in AUTOEXEC.NCF and from Keyboard?	Used in STARTUP.NCF?
SET TURBO FAT RE-USE WAIT TIME=5 MIN 29.6 SEC	0.03 sec to 1 hour 5 min 54.6 sec	Yes	No

Purpose: A *turbo FAT* is a list of disk blocks that comprise a very large file. The list is indexed so that particular blocks of the file can be accessed quickly. When a large file is opened, a memory buffer is used to store the file's indexed FAT entries. This command specifies how long this index remains in memory after the file is closed.

SET COMPRESSION DAILY CHECK STOP HOUR=6	0 to 23	Yes	Yes

Purpose: This command sets the hour when NetWare stops scanning compression-enabled volumes for files ready to be compressed. Setting the start and the stop hour to the same setting causes compression to run continuously. A setting of 0 is equivalent to midnight; a setting of 23 is equivalent to 11 p.m.

SET COMPRESSION DAILY CHECK STARTING HOUR=0	0 to 23	Yes	Yes

Purpose: This command sets the hour when NetWare begins scanning compression-enabled volumes for files eligible to be compressed. A 0 setting is equivalent to midnight; a 23 setting is equivalent to 11 p.m.

SET MINIMUM COMPRESSION PERCENTAGE GAIN=2	0 to 50	Yes	Yes

Purpose: This command specifies the minimum percentage of disk space that must be gained by compressing a file for the file to be compressed.

SET ENABLE FILE COMPRESSION=ON	On or Off	Yes	Yes

Purpose: This command enables or suspends file compression on compression-enabled volumes.

SET MAXIMUM CONCURRENT COMPRESSIONS=2	1 to 8	Yes	Yes

Purpose: This command specifies how many concurrent compression operations can occur. For best compression performance, set to equal the number of server volumes that are compression-enabled. You can't have more than one compression operation at a time for a single server volume.

Command with Default	Allowed Range	Used in AUTOEXEC.NCF and from Keyboard?	Used in STARTUP.NCF?
SET CONVERT COMPRESSED TO UNCOMPRESSED OPTION=1	0, 1, or 2	Yes	Yes

Purpose: This command controls how NetWare 4.1 decides to allow a compressed file to be replaced by its decompressed counterpart. Setting to 0 causes the compressed file never to be left uncompressed until the file is changed. Setting to 1 leaves the file compressed if it's read only once within the number of days specified in the SET DAYS UNTOUCHED BEFORE COMPRESSION command. Setting to 2 means that the file is left uncompressed after the first time it's retrieved and decompressed.

| SET DECOMPRESS PERCENT DISK SPACE FREE TO ALLOW COMMIT=10 | 0 to 75 | Yes | Yes |

Purpose: This option establishes the percentage of free disk space that must be available on a compression-enabled volume before compressed files can be replaced by their decompressed counterparts.

| SET DECOMPRESS FREE SPACE WARNING INTERVAL =31 MIN 18.5 SEC | 0 sec to 29 days 15 hours 50 min 3.8 sec | Yes | Yes |

Purpose: This command specifies the interval between warnings issued when a compression-enabled disk no longer can leave files decompressed because free disk space has fallen below the percentage specified in the preceding SET command.

| SET DELETED FILES COMPRESSION OPTION=1 | 0, 1, or 2 | Yes | Yes |

Purpose: This command determines whether deleted files are compressed and how soon they're compressed after deletion. A 0 setting means that deleted files are not compressed. A 1 setting means that deleted files are compressed the next day. A 2 setting means that deleted files are compressed immediately.

| SET DAYS UNTOUCHED BEFORE COMPRESSION=7 | 0 to 100000 | Yes | Yes |

Purpose: This command sets the number of days that a file must be unused before NetWare tries to compress it. To compress a file without waiting, turn on the IMMEDIATE COMPRESS attribute for the file or its directory.

| SET ALLOW UNOWNED FILES TO BE EXTENDED=ON | On or Off | Yes | Yes |

Purpose: This command controls whether a file without an owner can increase in size. If this option is set to Off, a file created by a user whose object was deleted cannot increase in size.

Table A.6   Commands that Control File and Record Locks

Command with Default	Allowed Range	Used in AUTOEXEC.NCF and from Keyboard?	Used in STARTUP.NCF?
SET MAXIMUM RECORD LOCKS PER CONNECTION=500	10 to 100000	Yes	No
Purpose: This option controls the maximum number of simultaneous record locks allowed per user. A record lock can be a physical or logical record lock or a semaphore.			
SET MAXIMUM FILE LOCKS PER CONNECTION=250	10 to 1000	Yes	No
Purpose: This option controls the maximum number of simultaneous file locks allowed per user.			
SET MAXIMUM RECORD LOCKS=20000	100 to 400000	Yes	No
Purpose: This command sets the maximum number of record locks allowed at one time on the server.			
SET MAXIMUM FILE LOCKS=10000	100 to 100000	Yes	No
Purpose: This command sets the maximum number of concurrent open files and file locks allowed on the server.			

Table A.7   Commands that Control the Transaction Tracking System (TTS)

Command with Default	Allowed Range	Used in AUTOEXEC.NCF and from Keyboard?	Used in STARTUP.NCF?
SET AUTO TTS BACKOUT FLAG=ON	On or Off	No	Yes
Purpose: This command determines whether backouts of incomplete TTS transactions are done by default on restarting the server. An incomplete transaction is an update to a file that isn't complete, perhaps because of an abrupt crash or loss of power to the server. NetWare 4.1's Transaction Tracking System (TTS) backs out of an incomplete transaction by returning file to its pre-transaction state.			
SET TTS ABORT DUMP FLAG=OFF	On or Off	Yes	No
Purpose: This command determines whether the server writes the data backed out from an incomplete transaction to the TTS$LOG.ERR file in the root directory on the SYS volume.			

Command with Default	Allowed Range	Used in AUTOEXEC.NCF and from Keyboard?	Used in STARTUP.NCF?
SET MAXIMUM TRANSACTIONS =10000	100 to 10000	Yes	No

Purpose: This command sets the maximum number of concurrent transactions for the server.

| SET TTS UNWRITTEN CACHE WAIT TIME=1 MIN 5.9 SEC | 11 sec to 10 min 59.1 sec | Yes | No |

Purpose: This command sets the maximum time a cache buffer write can be delayed by TTS.

| SET TTS BACKOUT FILE TRUNCATION WAIT TIME=59 MIN 19.2 SEC | 1 min 5.9 sec to 1 day 2 hours 21 min 51.3 sec | Yes | No |

Purpose: This option sets the minimum time to wait before truncating the TTS backout file. When the TTS backout file is larger than required to store current number of active transactions, its size can be decreased (and disk space freed) by truncating the file.

Table A.8 Commands that Manage Server Disks

Command with Default	Allowed Range	Used in AUTOEXEC.NCF and from Keyboard?	Used in STARTUP.NCF?
SET ENABLE DISK READ AFTER WRITE VERIFY=ON	On or Off	Yes	Yes

Purpose: This option enables NetWare-based read-after-write verification. When set to On, NetWare activates its *hot fix* feature, which rereads all data written to disk and verifies correctness. When set to Off, the verification process is left to the hard disk and controller. Most modern hard disks have hardware-based read-after-write verification.

| SET REMIRROR BLOCK SIZE=1 | 1 to 8 | Yes | No |

Purpose: This command specifies the remirror block size in 4K units (1=4K, 2=8K, 3=12K, 4=16K, 5=20K, 6=24K, 7=28K, and 8=32K). The *remirror block size* is the unit of information transferred from the source partition to the destination partition during a remirroring operation.

| SET CONCURRENT REMIRROR REQUESTS=4 | 2 to 32 | Yes | No |

Purpose: This command sets the number of simultaneous remirror operations that can occur at once for a mirrored volume. A volume can consist of multiple physical partitions, several of which might need to be remirrored at the same time in the event of a major disk failure or replacement.

continues

http://www.quecorp.com

Table A.8 Continued

Command with Default	Allowed Range	Used in AUTOEXEC.NCF and from Keyboard?	Used in STARTUP.NCF?
SET MIRRORED DEVICES ARE OUT OF SYNC MESSAGE FREQUENCY=30	5 to 9999	Yes	Yes

Purpose: This command sets the frequency in minutes with which NetWare checks and confirms that mirrored devices are synchronized.

Command with Default	Allowed Range	Used in AUTOEXEC.NCF and from Keyboard?	Used in STARTUP.NCF?
SET SEQUENTIAL ELEVATOR DEPTH=8	0 to 4294967295	Yes	Yes

Purpose: NetWare's Media Manager sends no more than the specified number of requests to a single device. If the device is mirrored, then requests are sent to the other devices in the mirror set when the maximum number of requests has been reached in the primary device.

Command with Default	Allowed Range	Used in AUTOEXEC.NCF and from Keyboard?	Used in STARTUP.NCF?
SET IGNORE DISK GEOMETRY=OFF	On or Off	Yes	Yes

Purpose: This setting causes a disk drive's internal geometry to be ignored during disk reads and writes. This allows you to create nonstandard partitions on the disk, but can affect the performance of non-NetWare file systems.

Command with Default	Allowed Range	Used in AUTOEXEC.NCF and from Keyboard?	Used in STARTUP.NCF?
SET ENABLE IO HANDICAP ATTRIBUTE=OFF	On or Off	Yes	Yes

Purpose: This command allows drivers or applications to set an attribute that handicaps or inhibits the read requests sent to a storage device. It should only be turned on at the explicit instruction of the device's manufacturer.

Table A.9 Commands that Control Network Time Synchronization

Command with Default	Allowed Range	Used in AUTOEXEC.NCF and from Keyboard?	Used in STARTUP.NCF?
SET TIMESYNC ADD TIME SOURCE=*fileservername*	Any server name (use server's common name, not its full directory services name; maximum name length is 48 characters)	Yes	No

Command with Default	Allowed Range	Used in AUTOEXEC.NCF and from Keyboard?	Used in STARTUP.NCF?

Purpose: This command adds the name of a server to the list of servers that can be contacted as a time source. With NetWare 4.1 time synchronization, servers are classified as primary or secondary time servers. A secondary server contacts a specified list of primary servers to learn the correct network time and adjusts its own time accordingly. A secondary server can maintain a list of primary servers to contact and normally contacts only the first server on this list. If the first server is unavailable, subsequent primary servers are checked until one responds. This command is used to add a server to the list of primary servers that a secondary server can contact to learn the network time.

SET TIMESYNC CONFIGURATION FILE =SYS:SYSTEM\TIMESYNC.CFG	Any path and file name on the server; maximum path/file name length is 255 characters	Yes	No

Purpose: This command specifies that a new path and file name be used to store time synchronization configuration information.

SET TIMESYNC CONFIGURED SOURCES=OFF	On or Off	Yes	No

Purpose: This command controls whether the server responds only to its configured list of primary time servers or to any server that advertises itself as a time source. When On, the server synchronizes its time only with its configured list of primary time servers.

SET TIMESYNC DIRECTORY TREE MODE=ON	On or Off	Yes	No

Purpose: This command determines whether the server responds to time sources outside its own NetWare directory tree. Set to Off if your network has more than one directory tree, but you still need all servers synchronized to a common time. Set to On to have each directory tree maintain its own unique time.

SET TIMESYNC HARDWARE CLOCK=ON	On or Off	Yes	No

Purpose: This command controls how the server's hardware clock is involved in time synchronization. If server is a primary or secondary time server, server's hardware clock is set to match the network time whenever a new time setting is received. If server is a reference server, the server's hardware clock is used as the source of the time that's broadcast to other servers. (You set up a reference server every time a server has a reliable hardware source of time, such as an atomic clock or a link to a time broadcasting service.)

continues

Table A.9   Continued

Command with Default	Allowed Range	Used in AUTOEXEC.NCF and from Keyboard?	Used in STARTUP.NCF?
SET TIMESYNC POLLING COUNT=3	1 to 1000 packets	Yes	No

Purpose: This command controls the number of packets sent in a single time-polling operation.

SET TIMESYNC POLLING INTERVAL=600	10 to 2678400 seconds	Yes	No

Purpose: This command specifies the frequency with which time synchronization polling occurs. To ensure all servers are synchronized with the same frequency, all servers in your time synchronization configuration should have the same setting for this command.

SET TIMESYNC REMOVE TIME SOURCE=*fileservername*	Server name (use server's common name)	Yes	No

Purpose: This command removes a primary server from the list of servers that a secondary server may contact to learn the network time. This command returns no confirmation that the server is removed, but you can use the SET TIMESYNC TIME SOURCE= command (without a file server parameter) to view the current list of time sources.

SET TIMESYNC RESET=OFF	On or Off	Yes	No

Purpose: When set to On, this command resets all time synchronization settings to NetWare 4.1's default settings. Every option is set to its default value, and the list of primary servers that can be contacted are emptied.

SET TIMESYNC RESTART FLAG=OFF	On or Off	Yes	No

Purpose: When set to On, this command automatically causes the TIMESYNC NLM to restart. The settings in the time-synchronization configuration file (SYS:SYSTEM\ TIMESYNC.CFG) are reread. After using this command with the On option, the setting automatically reverts to Off.

SET TIMESYNC SERVICE ADVERTISING=ON	On or Off	Yes	No

Purpose: When set to On, the server broadcasts its time to the network if the server is configured as a primary time server. (Secondary time source file servers never broadcast their times.)

SET TIMESYNC SYNCHRONIZATION RADIUS=2000	0 to 2147483647 milliseconds	Yes	No

Purpose: This command sets the number of milliseconds the server can be off from the network time and still be considered synchronized. Allows you to set acceptable range of time variance permitted among servers. It's easy to assume that you should set this option

Command with Default	Allowed Range	Used in AUTOEXEC.NCF and from Keyboard?	Used in STARTUP.NCF?

to 0 so that you have a perfectly synchronized network. It's better, however, to allow for variance to account for the synchronization differences resulting from network communication times and the slight vagaries of server internal software clocks. Otherwise, you create the additional overhead that results from servers constantly re-synchronizing times because they never stay precisely synchronized.

Command with Default	Allowed Range	Used in AUTOEXEC.NCF and from Keyboard?	Used in STARTUP.NCF?
SET TIMESYNC TIME ADJUSTMENT=*none_scheduled*	+*hh*:*mm*:*ss* −*hh*:*mm*:*ss* +|−*hh*:*mm*:*ss* AT *date time* CANCEL	Yes	No

Purpose: This command allows you to schedule time adjustment, which is a network-wide time change scheduled to occur at a particular time. You issue a time adjustment only from a primary time server. You specify two parameters—the number of hours, minutes, and seconds to advance or reverse the current time setting and (optionally) the date and time at which the adjustment will occur. To advance the network time by 1 hour, 30 minutes, and 15 seconds at 10 p.m. on January 1, 1995, type SET TIMESYNC TIME ADJUSTMENT= +01:30:15 AT 01/01/95 10:00pm and press Enter. If you omit the date and time parameter, the time automatically adjusts 6 polling cycles or 1 hour (whichever is larger) from the time you issue the command. To roll back the network time setting by 3 minutes and 30 seconds and to make the adjustment occur 1 hour from now, type SET TIMESYNC ADJUSTMENT= -00:03:30 and press Enter. If you schedule a time adjustment and then want to cancel it, use the parameter CANCEL with the command; type SET TIMESYNC TIME ADJUSTMENT=CANCEL and press Enter.

Command with Default	Allowed Range	Used in AUTOEXEC.NCF and from Keyboard?	Used in STARTUP.NCF?
SET TIMESYNC TIME SOURCE =*fileservername*	Server (use server's common name)	Yes	No

Purpose: This command adds the name of a server to the list of servers that can be contacted as a time source. If you use this command with no parameters, the current list of time sources is displayed.

Command with Default	Allowed Range	Used in AUTOEXEC.NCF and from Keyboard?	Used in STARTUP.NCF?
SET TIMESYNC TYPE=SINGLE	PRIMARY SECONDARY REFERENCE SINGLE	Yes	No

Purpose: This command specifies what type of time source the server is. PRIMARY servers collectively establish the network time based on averaging their individual times, and then adjust their individual times to be the same as this average. SECONDARY servers contact primary servers to learn the network time. A REFERENCE server is a special type of primary server that doesn't adjust its time after the primary servers collectively establish the average time. A SINGLE (single reference) server is considered the sole source for time on the network, and all other primary servers derive their times from the single reference

continues

Table A.9   Continued

Command with Default	Allowed Range	Used in AUTOEXEC.NCF and from Keyboard?	Used in STARTUP.NCF?

server. Reference and single reference classifications usually are reserved for servers that are connected to some highly accurate external time source.

| SET TIMESYNC WRITE PARAMETERS=OFF | On or Off | Yes | No |

Purpose: This command determines whether changes that you make to the server's time synchronization configuration are written to the current configuration file. When you issue this command with the ON parameter, some or all changes that you make are written to the configuration file. Use the SET TIMESYNC WRITE VALUE command to specify which types of configuration options are written.

| SET TIMESYNC WRITE VALUE=3 | 1, 2, or 3 | Yes | No |

Purpose: This command determines which types of time synchronization parameters are written to the configuration file. Using a setting of 1 causes time-synchronization operating parameters (such as polling intervals, hardware clock options, and the synchronization radius) to be recorded. A setting of 2 causes only time source changes to be recorded. A setting of 3 causes all changes to be recorded.

| SET TIME ZONE =<<NO TIME ZONE>> | Time zone abbreviation | Yes | Yes |

Purpose: This command specifies the abbreviation for the server's time zone, the number of time zones offset from universal time coordinated (UTC), and the abbreviation for the time zone name to be used for daylight saving time.

| SET DEFAULT TIME SERVER TYPE=SECONDARY | SINGLE REFERENCE PRIMARY SECONDARY | Yes | Yes |

Purpose: This command establishes the server's default time server type. This setting can be overridden temporarily by the SET TIMESYNC TYPE command.

| SET START OF DAYLIGHT SAVINGS TIME=(APRIL SUNDAY FIRST 2:00:00 AM) | (*month day week# time*) or *date time* | Yes | No |

Purpose: With this command, specify the date or a rule that determines when the change to daylight saving time will occur. Simply specify a date by entering SET START OF DAYLIGHT SAVINGS TIME=APRIL 3 1994 2:00:00AM, which obligates you to enter a new date every year. A better method is to write a rule (enclosed in parentheses) that automatically determines the date of the switch year after year. To specify that the switch to daylight saving time falls on the first Sunday in April, for example, you use the following command: SET START OF DAYLIGHT SAVINGS TIME=(APRIL SUNDAY FIRST 2:00:00AM). You must set the starting and ending dates for daylight saving time before either are scheduled.

Command with Default	Allowed Range	Used in AUTOEXEC.NCF and from Keyboard?	Used in STARTUP.NCF?
SET END OF DAYLIGHT SAVINGS TIME=(OCTOBER SUNDAY LAST 2:00:00 AM)	(*month day week# time*) or *date time*	Yes	No

Purpose: Use this command to specify date or a rule that determines when the change from daylight saving time to standard time occurs. The requirements for specifying a date or a rule are the same as those described for the preceding command.

| SET DAYLIGHT SAVINGS TIME OFFSET=+1:00:00 | Any time offset | Yes | Yes |

Purpose: Use this command to specify the time advance or reversal required when daylight saving time goes into effect. The default setting is +1:00:00, which specifies an advance of 1 hour.

| SET DAYLIGHT SAVINGS TIME STATUS=ON | On or Off | Yes | Yes |

Purpose: This command specifies whether current server time reflects that daylight saving time is (On) or is not (Off) in effect. Information returned by this command automatically changes from Off to On when daylight saving time goes into effect. Setting this command to On doesn't cause server time to recalculate to include the offset specified for daylight saving time—it just specifies that the existing server time already reflects the adjustment required for daylight saving time.

| SET NEW TIME WITH DAYLIGHT SAVINGS TIME STATUS=ON | On or Off | Yes | No |

Purpose: This command specifies whether daylight saving time is (On) or is not (Off) in effect. Also causes server time to recalculate, using the offset specified for daylight saving time, unlike the preceding command.

Table A.10 Commands that Control NetWare Core Protocol Options

Command with Default	Allowed Range	Used in AUTOEXEC.NCF and from Keyboard?	Used in STARTUP.NCF?
SET NCP FILE COMMIT=ON	On or Off	Yes	No

Purpose: This option allows NetWare-aware programs to force file writes to be confirmed after they're written to disk. Usually, an application receives confirmation that a file write is completed when the information in this write operation is written to the server's memory cache, and the actual write to disk occurs a few seconds later. With this option active, an application can request that the file write not be confirmed until information is actually written to disk.

continues

Table A.10   Continued

Command with Default	Allowed Range	Used in AUTOEXEC.NCF and from Keyboard?	Used in STARTUP.NCF?
SET DISPLAY NCP BAD COMPONENT WARNINGS=OFF	On or Off	Yes	Yes

Purpose: This option controls whether an alert message is displayed when an NCP call to the server includes incorrect parameters or options. Such an alert occurs when someone is using a program or NLM with improperly designed NetWare calls.

SET REJECT NCP PACKETS WITH BAD COMPONENTS=OFF	On or Off	Yes	Yes

Purpose: This option tells the server whether or not to reject NCP packets that are improperly structured.

SET DISPLAY NCP BAD LENGTH WARNINGS=ON	On or Off	Yes	Yes

Purpose: This option tells the server to display an alert message when an NCP packet is received with an incorrect size.

SET REJECT NCP PACKETS WITH BAD LENGTHS=OFF	On or Off	Yes	Yes

Purpose: This command causes the server to reject NCP packets that don't pass a size check.

SET MAXIMUM OUTSTANDING NCP SEARCHES=51	10 to 1000	Yes	No

Purpose: This command sets the maximum number of concurrent NCP searches per connection.

SET NCP PACKET SIGNATURE OPTION=1	0 to 3	Yes	Yes

Purpose: This command controls the use of packet signatures. A *packet signature* is an optional identification that a server or workstation can embed in a packet to guarantee the identity of the packet sender. You use packet signatures to defeat programs that generate and send forged packets—the program sends packets forged to appear as though they're from a workstation where the user is logged in with supervisory rights, enabling the program to perform supervisory tasks without authorization. Packet signatures increase the server and workstation workload because each packet's signature must be read and verified. You can use settings 0 through 3 to cause the server to do the following:

0	Don't use packet signatures.
1	Use packet signatures only for workstations that request them.
2	Use packet signatures only for workstations that can use them.
3	Require packet signatures for all packets from all workstations.

SET ENABLE IPX CHECKSUMS=1	0 to 2	Yes	Yes

Purpose: This command controls the use of checksums in IPX packets. A *checksum* is a number placed in each packet by the sender and that can be used by the receiver to verify

Command with Default	Allowed Range	Used in AUTOEXEC.NCF and from Keyboard?	Used in STARTUP.NCF?

that the packet wasn't corrupted during transmission. Use settings 0 through 2 to achieve the following results:

0	Don't use checksums.
1	Use checksums only for workstations that can use them.
2	Require checksums for all IPX packets from all workstations.

| SET ALLOW CHANGE TO CLIENT RIGHTS=ON | On or Off | Yes | Yes |

Purpose: This command allows a process, such as a print server or fax server that receives jobs from users, to operate with the same rights as the user who submits the job.

| SET ALLOW LIP=ON | On or Off | Yes | Yes |

Purpose: This option determines whether the server can send large Internet packets (LIPs). When set to Off, the server uses the smallest supported packet size (512 bytes) when sending packets through a router to a device on another network. When set to On, the server sends packets using its normal packet size. Set to On if all networks in your internetwork use the same packet size as your server.

Table A.11 Commands that Control Miscellaneous Options

Command with Default	Allowed Range	Used in AUTOEXEC.NCF and from Keyboard?	Used in STARTUP.NCF?
SET COMMAND LINE PROMPT DEFAULT CHOICE=ON	On or Off	Yes	Yes

Purpose: This command sets the default response that is furnished to the ? console command when no response is received from the keyboard. On is equivalent to Y and Off to N.

| SET COMMAND LINE PROMPT TIME OUT=10 | 0 to 4294967295 | Yes | Yes |

Purpose: This command specifies the amount of time (in seconds) that must pass before the COMMAND LINE PROMPT DEFAULT CHOICE is applied in response to the ? console command.

| SET SOUND BELL FOR ALERTS=ON | On or Off | Yes | No |

Purpose: Setting this option to On causes the server to beep when an alert message appears on the server console.

continues

Table A.11 Continued

Command with Default	Allowed Range	Used in AUTOEXEC.NCF and from Keyboard?	Used in STARTUP.NCF?
SET REPLACE CONSOLE PROMPT WITH SERVER NAME =ON	On or Off	Yes	Yes

Purpose: Use this option to include the server name in the console prompt. Setting to Off changes the prompt to a colon (:).

Command with Default	Allowed Range	Used in AUTOEXEC.NCF and from Keyboard?	Used in STARTUP.NCF?
SET ALERT MESSAGE NODES=20	10 to 256	Yes	Yes

Purpose: This command sets the number of external devices that can receive alert messages from the server. Use when the server participates in network-management systems that must receive error alerts from the server.

Command with Default	Allowed Range	Used in AUTOEXEC.NCF and from Keyboard?	Used in STARTUP.NCF?
SET WORKER THREAD EXECUTE IN A ROW COUNT=10	1 to 20	Yes	No

Purpose: NetWare 4.1 prioritizes the tasks the server must perform. The highest-priority (first-level) tasks are known as *interrupt events*, the second-level tasks are known as *work threads*, and the third-level tasks are known as *threads*. Determines how many second-level work threads are allowed to execute before third-level threads are allowed to run.

Command with Default	Allowed Range	Used in AUTOEXEC.NCF and from Keyboard?	Used in STARTUP.NCF?
SET HALT SYSTEM ON INVALID PARAMETERS=OFF	On or Off	Yes	Yes

Purpose: This option controls whether the server halts when an invalid parameter or other inconsistency is encountered.

Command with Default	Allowed Range	Used in AUTOEXEC.NCF and from Keyboard?	Used in STARTUP.NCF?
SET UPGRADE LOW PRIORITY THREADS=OFF	On or Off	Yes	No

Purpose: The lowest-priority task on a NetWare 4.1 server is known as a low-priority thread, and the most common example of this type of task is file compression. Some NLMs, including NetWare 4.1's remote console, cause low-priority threads to stop executing. If you run one of these types of NLMs continuously, set this command to On to cause low-priority threads to receive the same priority as regular thread tasks.

Command with Default	Allowed Range	Used in AUTOEXEC.NCF and from Keyboard?	Used in STARTUP.NCF?
SET DISPLAY RELINQUISH CONTROL ALERTS=OFF	On or Off	Yes	Yes

Purpose: This command controls whether alert messages are displayed when a poorly behaved NLM doesn't relinquish control to other tasks on a frequent basis.

Command with Default	Allowed Range	Used in AUTOEXEC.NCF and from Keyboard?	Used in STARTUP.NCF?
SET DISPLAY INCOMPLETE IPX PACKET ALERTS=ON	On or Off	Yes	Yes

Purpose: This option determines whether the server displays alert messages when incomplete IPX packets are received. An incomplete packet can be an indicator of a failed network adapter or a problem with the network communication system.

Command with Default	Allowed Range	Used in AUTOEXEC.NCF and from Keyboard?	Used in STARTUP.NCF?
SET DISPLAY OLD API NAMES=OFF	On or Off	Yes	Yes

Purpose: This command controls whether the server displays the list of outdated NetWare program calls that an NLM, disk driver, or network driver is using. If set to On, these API (Application Program Interface) routine names are displayed when the module is loaded.

SET CPU HOG TIMEOUT AMOUNT=60	0 to 3600	Yes	Yes

Purpose: The setting specifies the amount of time (in seconds) that must pass before a NetWare server terminates a process that has not relinquished control of the server CPU. Setting the value to 0 disables the timeout feature.

SET DEVELOPER OPTION=OFF	On or Off	Yes	Yes

Purpose: This option activates the features useful to software developers (for example, extended debugging messages).

SET DISPLAY SPURIOUS INTERRUPT ALERTS=ON	On or Off	Yes	Yes

Purpose: This command controls the display of alert messages generated by *spurious hardware interrupts*. NetWare 4.1 defines a spurious hardware interrupt as a request received by a device for an interrupt that was allocated for another device. If you see an error message on the server console that refers to a spurious interrupt, it usually indicates an incorrectly written driver for a network adapter, disk controller, or other card in the server. You often can identify the responsible device or driver by unloading the drivers for each device one at a time until the message stops. You then should contact the manufacturer of the offending device to report the problem.

SET DISPLAY LOST INTERRUPT ALERTS=ON	On or Off	Yes	Yes

Purpose: NetWare 4.1 defines a *lost interrupt* as an interrupt request made by a device or driver that's suspended before NetWare 4.1 can respond to the request. You often can identify the offending device or driver by unloading the drivers for each device one at a time until the alerts stop. Contact manufacturer of the offending device to report the problem.

SET PSEUDO PREEMPTION COUNT=10	1 to 4294967295	Yes	No

Purpose: This option controls the number of times in a row a thread can issue file read or write requests before NetWare 4.1 forces the thread to relinquish control to other tasks. This option applies only when the setting for the next command is On.

SET GLOBAL PSEUDO PREEMPTION=OFF	On or Off	Yes	No

Purpose: This option determines whether NetWare 4.1 forces all threads to relinquish control to other tasks after a certain number of file reads and writes (number of reads and writes is specified in the preceding command).

continues

Table A.11   Continued

Command with Default	Allowed Range	Used in AUTOEXEC.NCF and from Keyboard?	Used in STARTUP.NCF?
SET MAXIMUM SERVICE PROCESSES=40	5 to 100	Yes	No

Purpose: A service process stores and processes the server's incoming requests. The server automatically allocates the number of service processes needed, up to the maximum you specify with this command. The number of service processes the server allocates is a gauge of how many concurrent requests the server has had to handle.

SET NEW SERVICE PROCESS WAIT TIME=2.2 SEC	0.3 sec to 20 sec	Yes	No

Purpose: This command establishes the amount of time the server waits before allocating a new service process. All previously allocated service processes must be in use for the entire time specified by this command before a new process is allocated.

SET AUTOMATICALLY REPAIR BAD VOLUMES=ON	On or Off	Yes	Yes

Purpose: When this option is set to ON, NetWare 4.1 automatically loads and runs the VREPAIR NLM to try to repair a disk volume that fails to mount. The most frequent cause of disk volumes that don't mount is the abrupt shutdown of a server due to a power failure. Files in use during the shutdown weren't properly closed and might have inconsistent size and disk block information.

SET ENABLE SECURE.NCF=OFF	On or Off	Yes	Yes

Purpose: This command causes the SECURE.NCF file to be executed during the server boot process. This is typically used to implement the NetWare Enhanced Security Server standard.

SET ALLOW AUDIT PASSWORDS=OFF	On or Off	Yes	Yes

Purpose: The command enables the use of audit password requests.

SET ALLOW UNENCRYPTED PASSWORDS=OFF	On or Off	Yes	No

Purpose: This command determines whether users can use unencrypted passwords. With versions of the NetWare workstation shell that accompany NetWare 3.x or 2.x, the LOGIN command transmits the user's password to the server in encrypted form so that a protocol analyzer or other device that can intercept network packets can't be used to learn a user's password. Very old versions of NetWare workstation shell don't support encrypted passwords. This command can be used to accommodate workstations with old NetWare workstation shells.

Table A.12 Commands that Control Error Handling

Part
IX

App
A

Command with Default	Allowed Range	Used in AUTOEXEC.NCF and from Keyboard?	Used in STARTUP.NCF?
SET SERVER LOG FILE STATE=1	0, 1, or 2	Yes	Yes

Purpose: This command tells the server what to do if the SYS:SYSTEM\SYS$LOG.ERR file grows larger than allowed size limit (which you set with the SET SERVER LOG FILE OVERFLOW SIZE command). A 0 setting results in no action, a 1 setting causes the log file to be deleted, and a 2 setting causes the log file to be renamed.

SET VOLUME LOG FILE STATE=1	0, 1, or 2	Yes	Yes

Purpose: This command is like the preceding command, except this one controls the VOL$LOG.ERR file in the root directory of each server volume.

SET TTS LOG FILE STATE=1	0, 1, or 2	Yes	Yes

Purpose: This command is like the preceding two commands, except this one controls the TTS$LOG.ERR file in the root directory of each server volume.

SET SERVER LOG FILE OVERFLOW SIZE=4194304	65536 to 4294967295	Yes	Yes

Purpose: This command sets the size point of SYS:SYSTEM\SYS$LOG.ERR file at which the server takes the action you specified with the SET SERVER LOG FILE STATE command.

SET VOLUME LOG FILE OVERFLOW SIZE=4194304	65536 to 4294967295	Yes	Yes

Purpose: This command is like the preceding command, except this one is for the VOL$LOG.ERR file in the root directory of each server volume.

SET VOLUME TTS LOG FILE OVERFLOW SIZE=4194304	65536 to 4294967295	Yes	Yes

Purpose: This command is like the preceding two commands, except this one is for the TTS$LOG.ERR file in the root directory of each server volume.

SET ENABLE DEADLOCK DETECTION=OFF	On or Off	Yes	Yes

Purpose: This command activates a deadlock detection mechanism in NetWare's SMP code that should only be used when debugging an NLM.

SET AUTO RESTART AFTER ABEND DELAY TIME=2	2 to 60	Yes	Yes

Purpose: This command is used to specify the amount of time (in minutes) that a NetWare server waits before restarting itself after an abend occurs.

SET AUTO RESTART AFTER ABEND=1	1 or 0	Yes	Yes

Purpose: This command is used to enable (1) or disable (0) the NetWare auto restart feature.

Table A.13   Commands that Control Novell Directory Services

Command with Default	Allowed Range	Used in AUTOEXEC.NCF and from Keyboard?	Used in STARTUP.NCF?
SET NDS TRACE TO SCREEN=OFF	On or Off	Yes	No

Purpose: This command enables or disables an NDS trace screen that shows replication activity.

SET NDS TRACE TO FILE=OFF	On or Off	Yes	No

Purpose: This command is like the preceding command, except the trace goes into the NDS trace file. When this file grows to approximately 500K, it begins overwriting the oldest information at the beginning of the file.

SET NDS TRACE FILENAME =SYSTEM\DSTRACE.DBG	Any file name (max. length 255 characters)	Yes	No

Purpose: This command sets the name and the path of the NDS trace file on the SYS volume.

SET NDS CLIENT NCP RETRIES=3	1 to 20	Yes	No

Purpose: This command specifies the number of NCP retries before a non-responding client logged in to the directory loses his or her connection.

SET NDS EXTERNAL REFERENCE LIFE SPAN=192	1 to 384	Yes	No

Purpose: An *external reference* is an ID assigned by a server to a user logged in via the directory tree. This command sets the length of time, in hours, that unused external references are allowed to exist before being removed.

SET NDS INACTIVITY SYNCHRONIZATION INTERVAL=30	2 to 1440	Yes	No

Purpose: This command sets the maximum elapsed time, in minutes, between exhaustive synchronization checks when a period occurred of no updates to the directory tree. When you issue this command, an exhaustive synchronization is performed immediately.

SET NDS SYNCHRONIZATION RESTRICTIONS=OFF	Off or On, *version*, *version*	Yes	No

Purpose: This command controls the versions of Novell Directory Services with which the server can synchronize. The Off setting allows synchronization with any version. When you set this option to On, you must follow On with the versions of directory services that you will allow synchronization with (for example: ON, 420, 421).

Command with Default	Allowed Range	Used in AUTOEXEC.NCF and from Keyboard?	Used in STARTUP.NCF?
`SET NDS SERVERS STATUS=UP/DOWN`	Up or Down	Yes	No

Purpose: This command marks the status of all server objects in the local directory database as Up or Down. Use to fix an incorrect status setting for a server. Set all servers as Up, for example, to correct for a server that's improperly listed as Down. Server status settings are corrected individually as NDS rechecks them.

Command with Default	Allowed Range	Used in AUTOEXEC.NCF and from Keyboard?	Used in STARTUP.NCF?
`SET NDS JANITOR INTERVAL=60`	1 to 10080	Yes	No

Purpose: This command sets the interval, in minutes, at which the NDS *janitor process* is executed. The janitor process purges directory tree database records marked for deletion and reclaims all unused disk space in the directory tree database.

Command with Default	Allowed Range	Used in AUTOEXEC.NCF and from Keyboard?	Used in STARTUP.NCF?
`SET NDS BACKLINK INTERVAL=780`	2 to 10080	Yes	No

Purpose: This command sets the interval, in minutes, at which NDS backlink consistency checking is performed. A *backlink* is an object ID maintained by a server that has no replica that contains these objects. These backlinks enable directory tree objects to use the server.

Command with Default	Allowed Range	Used in AUTOEXEC.NCF and from Keyboard?	Used in STARTUP.NCF?
`SET NDS TRACE FILE LENGTH TO ZERO=OFF`	On or Off	Yes	No

Purpose: This command empties the NDS trace file. After issuing this command, it resets itself back to Off. The `SET NDS TRACE TO FILE` command must be set to On to use this command.

Command with Default	Allowed Range	Used in AUTOEXEC.NCF and from Keyboard?	Used in STARTUP.NCF?
`SET NDS DO NOT SYNCHRONIZE WITH=ON,290,291,296,332, 463,477`	On or Off	Yes	No

Purpose: This command is used to specify version numbers of the DS.NLM module that you want to prevent NDS from addressing during synchronization processes. A value of Off allows synchronization with all versions. The On value should be followed by the version numbers to be excluded from synchronization.

Command with Default	Allowed Range	Used in AUTOEXEC.NCF and from Keyboard?	Used in STARTUP.NCF?
`SET BINDERY CONTEXT =org unit.org; org unit.org`	Up to 16 allowed contexts	Yes	Yes

Purpose: Use this command to set the parts of the directory tree that can be employed by users logging in to the server using bindery emulation. The default is where the server's SYS volume was installed.

Login Script
Commands and
Variables

This appendix is designed to give you a point of reference for the commands and identifier variables that you can use in NetWare login scripts. For examples of using the commands or incorporating them into your network, refer to Chapter 19, "Accessing Network Resources." ■

Table B.1   Login Script Commands

Category	Command(s)
Control drive letters	MAP DRIVE
Show information	WRITE DISPLAY FDISPLAY CLS LASTLOGINTIME
Control login script's flow of execution	NO_DEFAULT BREAK IF...THEN...ELSE PAUSE WAIT GOTO PROFILE
Execute external programs	# EXIT
Control LOGIN command swapping	SWAP NOSWAP
Change directory tree context	CONTEXT
Synchronize workstation time to network time	SET_TIME
Control workstation DOS environment	BREAK SET DOS SET DOS VERIFY COMSPEC
Specify information about workstation	MACHINE NAME PCCOMPATIBLE
Tell login script to look to an external file to run login script commands	INCLUDE
Comment in login script	REMARK ; *
Make noise	FIRE PHASERS
Shift position of command-line variables	SHIFT
Attach user to another server	ATTACH

Table B.2 Login Script Command Alphabetical Summary

Command	Function	Example(s)
#	Executes an external executable command (.EXE or .COM file)	#command
ATTACH	Attaches user to pre-NetWare 4 server	ATTACH server /user_name;passwrd (server, user name, and password can be omitted; user is prompted for information not entered)
BREAK	Enables or disables the use of Ctrl+Break to halt a login script	BREAK ON BREAK OFF
CLS	Clears the screen	CLS
COMSPEC	Sets the DOS COMSPEC environment variable to designate an alternative command processor	COMSPEC d:file (replace d: with drive specification and replace file with file name)
CONTEXT	Changes the directory tree context	CONTEXT context
DISPLAY	Displays the contents of an ASCII file	DISPLAY path\file
DOS BREAK	Turns DOS BREAK status on or off	DOS BREAK ON DOS BREAK OFF
DOS SET	Lets you place variables in the DOS environment	DOS SET varname="Varinfo"
DOS VERIFY	Turns DOS read-after-write verification on or off	DOS VERIFY ON DOS VERIFY OFF
DRIVE	Establishes drive letter that's the default after the login script is executed	DRIVE d: (replace d: with a drive identifier)
EXIT	Halts execution of login script and (optionally) executes a command on exiting	EXIT "command"
FDISPLAY	Displays the contents of	FDISPLAY path\file

continues

Part IX

App B

Table B.2   Continued

Command	Function	Example(s)
	a text file and filters out format characters	
FIRE PHASERS	Makes a phaser-like sound	FIRE PHASERS *n* TIMES (replace *n* with a number from 1 to 9)
GOTO	Moves login script processing to the specified label	GOTO *label*

IF...THEN...ELSE	Executes a command or series of commands based on a condition or series of conditions	IF *condition* THEN *command*
		 IF *cond1, cond2* THEN...
		 IF *cond1* and *cond2* THEN...
		
		 IF *condition(s)* THEN
		     command 1
		     command 2
		 END
		
		 IF *condition*
		 THEN *command*
		 ELSE *command*

INCLUDE	Executes login script commands stored in an external ASCII file	INCLUDE *path\file*
LASTLOGINTIME	Displays the time and date of the most recent login	LASTLOGINTIME
MACHINE	Sets the MACHINE NAME to a new setting	MACHINE="*name*"
MAP	Creates a drive letter	MAP *d:=server/volume:directory* MAP *d:=directory object name*
	Displays currently mapped drives	MAP
	Turns screen messages resulting from MAP commands on or off	MAP DISPLAY ON MAP DISPLAY OFF

Command	Function	Example(s)
	Turns screen messages resulting from MAP errors on or off	MAP ERRORS ON MAP ERRORS OFF
NO_DEFAULT	Causes default personal login scripts not to execute	NO_DEFAULT
NOSWAP	Causes LOGIN command not to be swapped out of memory	NOSWAP
PAUSE	Halts login script execution until the user presses a key	PAUSE
PCCOMPATIBLE	Allows workstations with a customized long machine name to use the EXIT login script command	PCCOMPATIBLE
PROFILE	Forces script assigned to profile object to be executed instead of user's normal profile script	PROFILE *profile name*
REMARK	Allows comments and non-command information to be inserted in scripts	REMARK *comment text* REM *comment text* * *comment text* ; *comment text*
SET	Lets you place variables in the DOS environment	SET *varname*="*Varinfo*"
SET_TIME	Controls whether workstation time is synchronized to network time	SET_TIME ON SET_TIME OFF
SHIFT	Shifts the position of the login command-line parameters	SHIFT *n* (replace *n* with a number)
SWAP	Causes LOGIN command to swap out of memory to specified drive and directory	SWAP *drive\directory*

Part
IX

App
B

continues

Table B.2   Continued

Command	Function	Example(s)
WAIT	Halts login script execution until the user presses a key	WAIT
WRITE	Displays text on-screen	WRITE "*message*"

Table B.3   Login Script Variables by Category

Category	Variables
Time variables	AM_PM GREETING_TIME HOUR HOUR24 MINUTE SECOND
Date variables	DAY DAY_OF_WEEK MONTH MONTH_NAME NDAY_OF_WEEK SHORT_YEAR YEAR
User information	CN FULL_NAME LAST_NAME LOGIN_ALIAS_CONTEXT LOGIN_CONTEXT LOGIN_NAME MEMBER or MEMBER OF NOT MEMBER or NOT MEMBER OF PASSWORD_EXPIRES *property name* REQUESTER_CONTEXT USER_ID
Workstation information	MACHINE or MACHINE NAME NETWARE_REQUESTER OS OS_VERSION P_STATION SHELL_TYPE SMACHINE STATION

Category	Variables
DOS environment variable	< >
Network information	ACCESS_SERVER FILE_SERVER NETWORK_ADDRESS
Results of executed commands	ERROR_LEVEL
Login command-line parameters	%0, %1, %2, and so on

Part
IX
App
B

Table B.4 Login Script Variable Summary

Variable	Information Returned	Source of Variable Data

ACCESS_SERVER	Provides checking for availability of access server.
	Sample usage:
	`IF NOT ACCESS_SERVER`
	`THEN WRITE`
	`"Comm server's down."`
		Access server

AM_PM	Returns am or pm based on the current time.
	Sample usage:
	`WRITE`
	`"It's %HOUR:%MINUTE%AM_PM"`
	Displays: `It's 06:30 am`
		Workstation time

CN	Returns the user's object name. *Sample usage:* `WRITE: "Hello, %CN."` *Displays:* `Hello, SMITHFD`	User's object name

DAY	Returns a number from 0 to 31 based on the current day.
	Sample usage:
	`WRITE`
	`"It's %MONTH-%DAY-%YEAR"`
	Displays: `It's 04-12-90`
		Workstation date

DAY_OF_WEEK	Returns the current day (Monday, Tuesday, Wednesday, and so on).
	Sample usage:
	`WRITE`
	`"Today is %DAY_OF_WEEK"`
	Displays: `Today is WEDNESDAY`
		Workstation date

continues

Table B.4   Continued

Variable	Information Returned	Source of Variable Data
ERROR_LEVEL	Returns the error level (as set by the last error level command executed with EXECUTE #). *Sample usage:* `#SERV1_SYS:PUBLIC\CAPTURE` `IF ERROR_LEVEL != "0" THEN` `   WRITE` `"CAPTURE COMMAND FAILED!"` `   WRITE` `"ERROR LEVEL IS %ERROR_LEVEL"` `END`	Workstation operating system
FILE_SERVER	Returns the server name. *Sample usage:* `WRITE "You are connected` `to %FILE_SERVER"` *Displays:* `You are` `connected to SERV386`	NetWare server
FULL_NAME	Returns user's full name. *Sample usage:* `WRITE "Hello, %FULL_NAME"` *Displays:* `Hello,` `FRANK SMITH`	User's name information from directory database
GREETING_ TIME	Returns morning, afternoon, or evening. *Sample usage:* `WRITE "Good %GREETING_TIME!"` *Displays:* `Good afternoon!`	Workstation time
HOME DIRECTORY	Returns the user's assigned Home directory and volume location. Sample usage: `MAP H:%HOME DIRECTORY` (Do not use an underscore if this variable is two words.)	Very useful for mapping home directories to users that are within the same container but do not have their home directories on the same volume
HOUR	Returns a number from 1 to 12 based on the current hour. *Sample usage:* `WRITE` `"It is %HOUR:%MINUTE%AM_PM"` *Displays:* `It is 10:20 pm`	Workstation time

Variable	Information Returned	Source of Variable Data
HOUR24	Returns a number from 00 to 23 based on the current hour. *Sample usage:* `WRITE "It is %HOUR24:%MINUTE"` *Displays:* It is 22:20	Workstation time
LAST_NAME	Returns value in user's LAST NAME property. *Sample usage:* `WRITE "Greetings, Mr. or Ms. %LAST_NAME."` *Displays:* Greetings, Mr. or Ms. Smith.	Value in LAST NAME property
LOGIN_ALIAS_CONTEXT	Provides checking to see whether REQUESTER_CONTEXT is an alias. *Sample usage:* `IF LOGIN_ALIAS_CONTEXT = "Y" THEN #NCUPDATE /NP`	Context at login time
LOGIN_CONTEXT	Returns name of context where user's object is stored. *Sample usage:* `WRITE "Your object context is %LOGIN_CONTEXT"` *Displays:* Your object context is MRKTING.BPD.WWFC	User object context
LOGIN_NAME	Returns the user's login name (truncated to eight characters). *Sample usage:* `MAP F:=SERV1_SYS:USERS\ %LOGIN_NAME` *Result:* Assigns F: to SERV1_SYS:USERS\SMITHFD	User's login name
MACHINE	Returns the long machine name stored by the NetWare workstation shell (IBM_PC or a customized name). *Sample usage:* `IF MACHINE != "IBM_PC" THEN PCCOMPATIBLE`	NetWare workstation shell
MEMBER or MEMBER OF	Provides checking for membership in a group. *Sample usage:*	Group membership in NDS database

continues

Part
IX
App
B

Table B.4   Continued

Variable	Information Returned	Source of Variable Data
	IF MEMBER OF "ACCT" THEN MAP I:=SERV1_SYS:ACCT	
MINUTE	Returns a number from 00 to 59 based on the current time. *Sample usage:* WRITE "It's %HOUR:%MINUTE%AM_PM" *Displays:* It's 06:30 am	Workstation time
MONTH	Returns a number from 01 to 12 based on the current month. *Sample usage:* WRITE "It's %MONTH- %DAY-%SHORT_YEAR" *Displays:* It's 04-12-90	Workstation date
MONTH_NAME	Returns the current month (January, February, March, and so on). *Sample usage:* WRITE "It is %MONTH_NAME %DAY, %YEAR" *Displays:* It is May 12, 1990	Workstation date
NDAY_OF _WEEK	Returns the number of the current day of the week from 1 to 7 (1=Monday, 2=Tuesday, and so on). *Sample usage:* WRITE "It's day %NDAY_OF_WEEK of a long week!" *Displays:* It's day 2 of a long week!	Workstation date
NETWARE_ REQUESTER	Returns version of NetWare DOS Requester. *Sample usage:* WRITE "Your requester version is %NETWARE_REQUESTER." *Displays:* Your requester version is 1.20.	NetWare DOS Requester
NETWORK_ ADDRESS	Returns IPX number of workstations connected to physical network.	IPX number of work-stations connected to physical network

Variable	Information Returned	Source of Variable Data
	Sample usage: WRITE "Your network address is %NETWORK_ADDRESS" *Displays:* Your network address is 0000010A	
NOT MEMBER OF	Checks for non-membership in group. *Sample usage:* IF NOT MEMBER OF "STUDENTS" THEN MAP I:=SERV1_SYS:STAFF	Test to verify if user is not a member *of a particular group.*
OS	Returns the operating system used to boot the user's workstation. *Sample usage:* MAP INSERT S2:=SERV1_SYS:%OS *Result:* Assigns the second search drive to SERV1_SYS:MSDOS	Workstation operating system
OS_VERSION	Returns the version number of the operating system used to boot the user's workstation (such as V5.0 or V6.0). *Sample usage:* MAP INSERT S2:=SERV1_SYS: %OS\%OS_VERSION Result: Assigns the second search drive to MSDOS\V5.00.	Workstation operating system
PASSWORD_ EXPIRES	Returns the number of days left before the user's password expires. *Sample usage:* WRITE "Your password expires in %PASSWORD_EXPIRES days." *Displays:* Your password expires in 37 days.	NetWare security
property	Returns value for specified property. *Sample usage:for a user object.* WRITE"Welcome aboard, %TITLE.î	Ability to address any of the properties

Part
IX

App
B

continues

Table B.4   Continued

Variable	Information Returned	Source of Variable Data
	Displays: `Welcome aboard, Admiral.`	

P_STATION	Returns as a hexadecimal number the node number of the network board inside the workstation.
	 Sample usage:
	 `WRITE "You are`
	 `logging in from node`
	 `%P_STATION"`
	 Displays:
	 `You are logging in from node`
	 `00000000002B`
		Workstation network adapter

REQUESTER_ CONTEXT	Returns your current directory tree context.
	 Sample usage:
	 `WRITE "You logged in from`
	 `%REQUESTER_CONTEXT."`
	 Displays: `You logged in from`
	 `MRKTING.wwfc.`
		NetWare DOS Requester

SECOND	Returns a number from 00 to 59 based on the current time.
	 Sample usage:
	 `WRITE "It is exactly %HOUR24:`
	 `%MINUTE:%SECOND"`
	 Displays: `It is exactly 12:31:17`
		Workstation time

SHELL_TYPE	Returns the shell version number.
	 Sample usage:
	 `IF SHELL_TYPE != "V4.01C" THEN`
	 `  WRITE`
	 `"Your shell type is incorrect!"`
	 `  WRITE`
	 `"Please see the administrator`
	 `  for upgrade."`
	 `END`
		NetWare workstation shell

SHORT_YEAR	Returns a number from 00 to 99, based on current year.
	 Sample usage:
	 `WRITE "It is %MONTH-%DAY-`
	 `%SHORT_YEAR"`
	 Displays: `It is 04-12-92`
		Workstation date

Variable	Information Returned	Source of Variable Data
SMACHINE	Returns the four-character short machine name stored by the NetWare workstation shell (IBM or a customized name). *Sample usage:* WRITE "Your machine type is %SMACHINE" *Displays:* Your machine type is IBM	NetWare workstation shell
STATION	Returns a decimal number that is the user's connection number. *Sample usage:* WRITE "Your connection number is %STATION" *Displays:* Your connection number is 213	NetWare server
USER_ID	Returns the number assigned to the user by NetWare. *Sample usage:* WRITE "Your user id number is %USER_ID" *Displays:* Your user id number is 1007A	NetWare Directory Database
YEAR	Returns the year (1990, 2001, and so on). *Sample usage:* WRITE "It is %MONTH_NAME %DAY, %YEAR" *Displays:* It is May 12,1993	Workstation date
< >	Returns the contents of a DOS environment variable. *Sample usage:* WRITE "Your temporary directory is %<TEMP>." *Displays:* Your temporary directory is directory is C:\WINDOWS\TEMP.	DOS environment
%0, %1, %2, and so on	Returns the command-line parameter that corresponds to the number	Command used to enter parameters on the LOGIN command line

Part

IX

App

B

continues

Table B.4   Continued

Variable	Information Returned	Source of Variable Data
	(%0 parameter returns the command name itself). You can enter and display up to 40 parameters. *Sample usage:* WRITE "You typed %1, %2 and %3 after LOGIN" *Displays:* You typed SMITHFD, HI and HELLO after LOGIN	

Index

Symbols

A

X-Y-Z

Complete and Return this Card
for a *FREE* Computer Book Catalog

Thank you for purchasing this book! You have purchased a superior computer book written expressly for your needs. To continue to provide the kind of up-to-date, pertinent coverage you've come to expect from us, we need to hear from you. Please take a minute to complete and return this self-addressed, postage-paid form. In return, we'll send you a free catalog of all our computer books on topics ranging from word processing to programming and the internet.

Mr. ☐   Mrs. ☐   Ms. ☐   Dr. ☐

Name (first) ☐☐☐☐☐☐☐☐☐☐☐☐☐ (M.I.) ☐   (last) ☐☐☐☐☐☐☐☐☐☐☐☐☐☐

Address ☐☐☐☐☐☐☐☐☐☐☐☐☐☐☐☐☐☐☐☐☐☐☐☐☐☐☐

Address ☐☐☐☐☐☐☐☐☐☐☐☐☐☐☐☐☐☐☐☐☐☐☐☐☐☐☐

City ☐☐☐☐☐☐☐☐☐☐☐☐   State ☐☐   Zip ☐☐☐☐☐ ☐☐☐☐

Phone ☐☐☐ ☐☐☐ ☐☐☐☐   Fax ☐☐☐ ☐☐☐☐☐☐☐

Company Name ☐☐☐☐☐☐☐☐☐☐☐☐☐☐☐☐☐☐☐☐☐☐☐☐

E-mail address ☐☐☐☐☐☐☐☐☐☐☐☐☐☐☐☐☐☐☐☐☐☐☐☐

1. Please check at least (3) influencing factors for purchasing this book.

Front or back cover information on book .... ☐
Special approach to the content .... ☐
Completeness of content .... ☐
Author's reputation .... ☐
Publisher's reputation .... ☐
Book cover design or layout .... ☐
Index or table of contents of book .... ☐
Price of book .... ☐
Special effects, graphics, illustrations .... ☐
Other (Please specify): _____ ☐

2. How did you first learn about this book?

Saw in Macmillan Computer Publishing catalog .... ☐
Recommended by store personnel .... ☐
Saw the book on bookshelf at store .... ☐
Recommended by a friend .... ☐
Received advertisement in the mail .... ☐
Saw an advertisement in: _____ ☐
Read book review in: _____ ☐
Other (Please specify): _____ ☐

3. How many computer books have you purchased in the last six months?

This book only .... ☐   3 to 5 books .... ☐
2 books .... ☐   More than 5 .... ☐

4. Where did you purchase this book?

Bookstore .... ☐
Computer Store .... ☐
Consumer Electronics Store .... ☐
Department Store .... ☐
Office Club .... ☐
Warehouse Club .... ☐
Mail Order .... ☐
Direct from Publisher .... ☐
Internet site .... ☐
Other (Please specify): _____ ☐

5. How long have you been using a computer?

☐ Less than 6 months   ☐ 6 months to a year
☐ 1 to 3 years   ☐ More than 3 years

6. What is your level of experience with personal computers and with the subject of this book?

	With PCs	With subject of book
New	☐	☐
Casual	☐	☐
Accomplished	☐	☐
Expert	☐	☐

Source Code ISBN: 0-7897-1156-7

7. Which of the following best describes your job title?

Administrative Assistant .... ☐
Coordinator .... ☐
Manager/Supervisor .... ☐
Director .... ☐
Vice President .... ☐
President/CEO/COO .... ☐
Lawyer/Doctor/Medical Professional .... ☐
Teacher/Educator/Trainer .... ☐
Engineer/Technician .... ☐
Consultant .... ☐
Not employed/Student/Retired .... ☐
Other (Please specify): _____ ☐

8. Which of the following best describes the area of the company your job title falls under?

Accounting .... ☐
Engineering .... ☐
Manufacturing .... ☐
Operations .... ☐
Marketing .... ☐
Sales .... ☐
Other (Please specify): _____ ☐

9. What is your age?

Under 20 .... ☐
21-29 .... ☐
30-39 .... ☐
40-49 .... ☐
50-59 .... ☐
60-over .... ☐

10. Are you:

Male .... ☐
Female .... ☐

11. Which computer publications do you read regularly? (Please list)

_____
_____
_____
_____
_____
_____
_____
_____
_____
_____

Comments: _____
_____
_____

Fold here and scotch-tape to mail

II'I'I'I''I''I'''II'I'I'I'I''I'''III'''II'''II'I'I.I.I

Check out Que® Books on the World Wide Web
http://www.quecorp.com

As the biggest software release in computer history, Windows 95 continues to redefine the computer industry. Click here for the latest info on our Windows 95 books

Make computing quick and easy with these products designed exclusively for new and casual users

Examine the latest releases in word processing, spreadsheets, operating systems, and suites

The Internet, The World Wide Web, CompuServe®, America Online®, Prodigy® —it's a world of ever-changing information. Don't get left behind!

Find out about new additions to our site, new bestsellers and hot topics

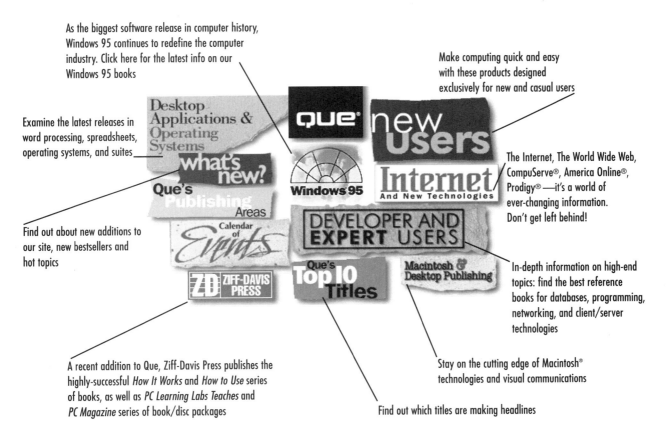

In-depth information on high-end topics: find the best reference books for databases, programming, networking, and client/server technologies

A recent addition to Que, Ziff-Davis Press publishes the highly-successful *How It Works* and *How to Use* series of books, as well as *PC Learning Labs Teaches* and *PC Magazine* series of book/disc packages

Stay on the cutting edge of Macintosh® technologies and visual communications

Find out which titles are making headlines

With 6 separate publishing groups, Que develops products for many specific market segments and areas of computer technology. Explore our Web Site and you'll find information on best-selling titles, newly published titles, upcoming products, authors, and much more.

- Stay informed on the latest industry trends and products available
- Visit our online bookstore for the latest information and editions
- Download software from Que's library of the best shareware and freeware